The

GREEK DIALECTS

The
GREEK DIALECTS

Grammar
Selected Inscriptions
Glossary

By
Carl Darling Buck

WIPF & STOCK · Eugene, Oregon

Wipf and Stock Publishers
199 W 8th Ave, Suite 3
Eugene, OR 97401

The Greek Dialects, Third Revised Edition
Grammar, Selected Inscriptions, Glossary
By Buck, Carl Darling
Softcover ISBN-13: 978-1-6667-3183-5
Hardcover ISBN-13: 978-1-6667-2479-0
eBook ISBN-13: 978-1-6667-2480-6
Publication date 6/25/2021
Previously published by University of Chicago Press, 1955

This edition is a scanned facsimile of the original edition published in 1955

PREFACE

The changes from the previous editions of the *Introduction to the Study of the Greek Dialects* have been so great that the old plates could not be used, and this is virtually a new book.

I have changed the title to *The Greek Dialects*, as both simpler and in a measure also appropriate. For it is fair to claim that the book is, for the time being, the most up-to-date treatment of the subject. Bechtel's monumental work (3 vols; 1,781 pp.) is a storehouse containing many items of detail not noticed here. But there is a deal of repetition incident to the arrangement adopted, and, more important, much new material has become available since its date.

The new material furnishes significant additions to our knowledge of several dialects, as Thessalian, Boeotian, and notably that of Cyrene. But I have hoped in vain for the greatest desiderata—early inscriptions of some extent from Lesbos and from East Locris.

I am more than ever convinced that the arrangement adopted here is not only more economical of space, but also more illuminating, than the separate treatment of the several dialects followed in other works.

I am indebted to the University of Chicago Press, to which the copyright has been transferred from the previous publishers, for undertaking the new publication and for the competent services in its execution; and to Dr. D. Georgacas for painstaking proofreading and other assistance.

CONTENTS

PART II: SELECTED INSCRIPTIONS

APPENDIX

PART I

GRAMMAR OF THE DIALECTS

ABBREVIATIONS

The following abbreviations are employed for languages, dialects, and local sources of the forms quoted.

Acarn. = Acarnanian
Ach. = Achaean
Aegin. = Aeginetan
Aetol. = Aetolian
Agrig. = of Agrigentum
Amorg. = of Amorgos
Amphiss. = Amphissan
And. = of Andania
Arc. = Arcadian
Arc.-Cypr. = Arcado-Cyprian
Arg. = Argive (of Argos)
Argol. = Argolic (of Argolis, outside of or including Argos; but mostly marked Epid., Troez., etc.)
Astyp. = of Astypalaea
Att. = Attic
Att.-Ion. = Attic-Ionic
Avest. = Avestan
Boeot. = Boeotian
Calymn. = of Calymna
Carpath. = of Carpathos
Chalced. = of Chalcedon
Chalcid. = Chalcidian
Cleon. = of Cleonae
Cnid. = Cnidian
Corinth. = Corinthian
Corcyr. = Corcyraean
Cret. = Cretan
Cypr. = Cyprian
Cyren. = Cyrenaean
Delph. = Delphian
Dodon. = of Dodona
Dor. = Doric
El. = Elean
Eng. = English
Ephes. = Ephesian
Epid. = Epidaurian
Epir. = Epirotan
Eretr. = Eretrian

Eub. = Euboean
Germ. = German
Gortyn. = Gortynian
Heracl. = Heraclean
Herm. = of Hermione
IE = Indo-European
Ion. = Ionic
Lac. = Laconian
Lat. = Latin
Lesb. = Lesbian
Locr. = Locrian
Mant. = Mantinean
Meg. = Megarian
Mel. = of Melos
Mess. = Messenian
Mil. = of Miletus
Mycen. = of Mycenæ
Nisyr. = of Nisyros
N.W.Grk. = Northwest Greek
Olynth. = of Olynthus
Orop. = of Oropus
Pamph. = Pamphylian
Phlias. = Phliasian (of Phlius)
Phoc. = Phocian
Rheg. = of Rhegium
Rhod. = Rhodian
Selin. = of Selinus
Sicil. = Sicilian
Sicyon. = Sicyonian
Skt. = Sanskrit
Stir. = of Stiris
Styr. = of Styra
Sybar. = of Sybaris
Syrac. = Syracusan
Teg. = Tegean
Thas. = of Thasos
Ther. = Theran
Thess. = Thessalian
Troez. = of Troezen

For abbreviations of modern works of reference see pp. 337 ff. Those used for the names of Greek authors are familiar. Likewise those used for grammatical terms, as adj., adv., sb. (= substantive, noun), vb., cpd., sg., pl., masc., fem., gen., dat., act., mid., pass., subj., opt., infin., imv., pple., etc. Note also gram. = grammarians or grammatical (with reference to forms quoted from the ancient grammarians), and lit. = literary (with reference to forms quoted from the literary dialects without mention of the individual authors).

INTRODUCTION

CLASSIFICATION AND INTERRELATION OF THE DIALECTS

1. When the ancient grammarians spoke of the four dialects of Greece—Attic, Ionic, Aeolic, and Doric, to which some added the κοινή as a fifth—they had in mind solely the literary dialects, which furnished the occasion and object of their study. But these literary dialects represent only a few of the many forms of speech current in Greece, most of which play no part whatever in literature, and, apart from some scattered glosses, would be entirely unknown to us were it not for the wealth of inscriptions which the soil of Greece has yielded in modern times.

The existence of Ionic, Aeolic, and Doric elements in the people and speech of Greece is an undoubted fact of Greek history, and one of the first importance to an understanding of the dialect relations. But there is no warrant, either in the earlier Greek tradition or in the linguistic evidence, for making this an all-inclusive classification. These three elements were precipitated, as it were, on the coast of Asia Minor, where their juxtaposition gave rise to the historical recognition of the distinction. And as the Ionians, Aeolians, and Dorians of Asia Minor were colonists from Greece proper, it was a natural and proper inference of the historians that they reflected ethnic divisions which also existed, or had once existed, in the mother country.

As to who were the Dorians of Greece proper there was of course no mystery. They formed a well-defined group throughout the historical period, and the tradition that they came originally from the Northwest is completely borne out by the close relationship of the Doric and Northwest Greek dialects (see below).

That the Ionians were akin to the inhabitants of Attica was an accepted fact in Greek history, and the Athenians are called Ionic both in Herodotus (e.g., 1.56) and Thucydides (6.82, 7.57). The linguistic evidence is equally unmistakable. The only un-

3

certainty here is as to the extent of territory which was once
Ionic. There are various accounts according to which Ionians
once occupied the southern shore of the Corinthian gulf, the later
Achaea (e.g., Hdt. 1.145-46, 7.94), Megara (e.g., Strabo 9.392),
Epidaurus (e.g., Paus. 2.26.2), and Cynuria (Hdt. 8.73). If these
accounts in themselves are of questionable value, yet we cannot
doubt that the Ionians before the migration were not confined
to Attica. The close relations of Epidaurus and Troezen with
Athens, in cult and legend, are significant for the Argolic Acte,
and it is reasonable to assume that at least the entire shore of
the Saronic gulf was once Ionic. Indeed it is now a widely favored
view, uncertain yet not unlikely, that the ancestors of the Ionians
(the name of course is later) constituted the first wave of Greek
migration and once occupied much of the territory which, with
the next waves of migration, was held by speakers of Aeolic
and the dialect which later survived as Arcado-Cyprian.

The affinities of the Aeolians were more obscure, for theirs
was the earliest migration to Asia Minor, the most remote from
the historical period. But Thessaly was the scene of their favorite
legends, the home of Achilles, as also of their eponymous hero
Aeolus, and many of their place-names had their counterpart
in Thessaly. In Herodotus we find the tradition that the Thessalians of the historical period were invaders from the west who
occupied what had hitherto been an Aeolic land [1], and with
this the linguistic evidence is in perfect accord. For Thessalian
is of all dialects the most closely related to Lesbian, and at the
same time shares in some of the characteristics of the West
Greek dialects, this admixture of West Greek elements being
somewhat stronger in Thessaliotis than in Pelasgiotis. See **201,
202, 210,** and Charts I, II. The Boeotians also are called Aeolians
by Thucydides, [2] and the Boeotian dialect is, next to Thessalian,
the most closely related to Lesbian. These three have several
notable characteristics in common (see **201** and Charts I, II),

---

[1] Hdt. 7.176: ἐπεὶ Θεσσαλοὶ ἦλθον ἐκ Θεσπρωτῶν οἰκήσοντες γῆν τὴν
Αἰολίδα, τήν περ νῦν ἐκτέαται.
[2] Thuc. 7.57: οὗτοι δὲ Αἰολῆς Αἰολεῦσι τοῖς κτίσασι Βοιωτοῖς τοῖς μετὰ
Συρακοσίων κατ᾽ ἀνάγκην ἐμάχοντο, i.e., the Aeolians of Methymna, Tenedos,
etc., were compelled to fight against the Aeolians who founded these
cities, namely, the Boeotians; id. 3.2: Βοιωτῶν ξυγγενῶν ὄντων (of the
Lesbians)

and are known as the Aeolic dialects. But in Boeotian there is an even stronger admixture of West Greek elements than in Thessalian (see **217** and Charts I, II), the historical explanation of which must be the same. If we credit the statement of Thucydides that the Boeotian invaders were from Arne, whence they had been driven by the Thessalians, [3] we should recognize in these Boeotians not a part of the old Aeolic population of Thessaly, but a tribe of West Greek invaders from Epirus (cf. Mt. Boeon), like the Thessalians who forced them onward. The Aeolic element is to be ascribed rather to the tribes, or some of them, comprising the early stratum, as, for example, the Minyans of Orchomenos. However obscure such details may be, the evidence is perfectly clear that both Boeotia and Thessaly were once Aeolic, but were overrun by West Greek tribes which adopted the speech of the earlier inhabitants in greater or less degree.

It is a natural presumption, of which there are some specific indications, that not only Thessaly and Boeotia but the intermediate lands of Phocis and Locris, and even southern Aetolia—in fact, all that portion of Greece north of Attica which plays a role in the legends of early Greece—was once Aeolic. Phocaea in Asia Minor, which, though later Ionic, surely belonged originally to the strip of Aeolic colonies, was believed to be a colony of Phocis and in the dialect of Phocis there are actually some relics of Aeolic speech as the dative plural of consonant stems in -εσσι, which is also found in Locris (**107**.3). As for southern Aetolia, the region of Calydon and Pleuron was once called Aeolis according to Thucydides, [4] and the probability is that the Aetolians of the Homeric period were Aeolic, though their name was taken by the later, West Greek, invaders. The Aetolian occupation of Elis was an accepted tradition, and the existence of an Aeolic element in the dialect of Elis, like the dative plural in -εσσι, may be brought into connection with this if we assume that while the invaders were Aetolians in the later sense, that is, West Greek, as Elean is distinctly a West Greek dialect, they

---

[3] Thuc. 1.12: Βοιωτοί τε γὰρ οἱ νῦν ἑξηκοστῷ ἔτει μετὰ Ἰλίου ἅλωσιν ἐξ Ἄρνης ἀναστάντες ὑπὸ Θεσσαλῶν τὴν νῦν Βοιωτίαν, πρότερον δὲ Καδμηίδα γῆν καλουμένην ᾤκησαν.

[4] Thuc. 3.102: ἐς τὴν Αἰολίδα τὴν νῦν καλουμένην Καλυδῶνα καὶ Πλευρῶνα.

had nevertheless adopted certain characteristics of the earlier
Aeolic Aetolian and brought them to Elis. Corinth was also once
occupied by Aeolians according to Thucydides, [5] and it is a
noteworthy fact that the dative plural in -εσσι, which is unknown in other Doric dialects, is found in various Corinthian
colonies (107.3).

But we have passed beyond the limits within which the term
Aeolic, or in general the division into Ionic, Doric, and Aeolic,
can with any propriety be applied to the peoples and dialects
of the historical period. It is only in Strabo that these three
groups are made into an all-inclusive system of classification,
by means of an unwarranted extension of Aeolic to include
everything that is not Ionic or Doric. And yet it is, unfortunately,
this statement of Strabo's, [6] the error of which has long since
been recognized, that has often been taken as representative
of ancient tradition and still colors, in the literal sense, our
maps of ancient Greece. The historical Phocians, Locrians,
Aetolians, etc., were not, as Strabo's statement implies, called
Aeolic. Neither in Herodotus, Thucydides, nor any early writer
are they ever brought under any one of the three groups. Their
dialects, with that of Elis, which Strabo also calls Aeolic, all of
which may be conveniently designated the Northwest Greek
dialects are, in spite of some few traces of Aeolic as mentioned
above, most closely related to the Doric dialects. There is scarcely
one of the general characteristics common to the Doric dialects
in which they do not share, though they also have certain peculiarities of their own (see 223, 226, and Charts I, II). If we
were to classify them under any one of the three groups, it is
unquestionably Doric to which they have the best claim, and if
Strabo and our maps so classed them there would be no very

[5] Thuc. 4.42: ὑπὲρ οὗ ὁ Σολύγειος λόφος ἐστίν, ἐφ' ὃν Δωριῆς τὸ πάλαι
ἱδρυθέντες τοῖς ἐν τῇ πόλει Κορινθίοις ἐπολέμουν, οὖσιν Αἰολεῦσι.
[6] Strabo 8.333: πάντες γὰρ οἱ ἐκτὸς Ἰσθμοῦ πλὴν Ἀθηναίων καὶ Μεγαρέων
καὶ τῶν περὶ τὸν Παρνασσὸν Δωριέων καὶ νῦν ἔτι Αἰολεῖς καλοῦνται ... καὶ οἱ
ἐντὸς (sc. Ἰσθμοῦ) Αἰολεῖς πρότερον ἦσαν, εἶτ' ἐμίχθησαν, Ἰώνων μὲν ἐκ τῆς
Ἀττικῆς τὸν Αἰγιαλὸν κατασχόντων, τῶν δ' Ἡρακλειδῶν τοὺς Δωριέας καταγα-
γόντων ... οἱ μὲν οὖν Ἴωνες ἐξέπεσον πάλιν ταχέως ὑπὸ Ἀχαιῶν, Αἰολικοῦ
ἔθνους· ἐλείφθη δ' ἐν τῇ Πελοποννήσῳ τὰ δύο ἔθνη, τό τε Αἰολικὸν καὶ τὸ Δωρικόν.
ὅσοι μὲν οὖν ἧττον τοῖς Δωριεῦσιν ἐπεπλέκοντο, καθάπερ συνέβη τοῖς τε Ἀρκάσι
καὶ τοῖς Ἠλείοις, ..., οὗτοι αἰολιστὶ διελέχθησαν, οἱ δ' ἄλλοι μικτῇ τινι ἐχρή-
σαντο ἐξ ἀμφοῖν, οἱ μὲν μᾶλλον οἱ δ' ἧττον αἰολίζοντες.

serious objection. Indeed, modern scholars do often class them under "Doric in the wider sense," calling them specifically "North Doric". But on the whole it seems preferable to retain the term Doric in its historical application and employ West Greek as the comprehensive term to include the Northwest Greek dialects and the Doric proper. As to the Arcadians too, calling them Aeolic is without warrant in earlier usage. For example, Thucydides in describing the forces engaged at Syracuse (7.57) makes the most of the distinction between Ionic, Doric, and Aeolic elements, but does not class the Arcadians with any of these.

The most fundamental division of the Greek dialects is that into the West Greek and the East Greek dialects, the terms referring to their location prior to the great migrations. The East Greek are the "Old Hellenic" dialects, that is, those employed by the peoples who held the stage almost exclusively in the period represented by the Homeric poems, when the West Greek peoples remained in obscurity in the northwest. To the East Greek division belong the Ionic and Aeolic groups, though, of the latter, Thessalian and Boeotian, as explained above, are mixed dialects belonging in part also in the West Greek division. And to East Greek belongs also the Arcado-Cyprian.

No two dialects, not even Attic and Ionic, belong together more obviously than do those of Arcadia and the distant Cyprus. They share in a number of notable peculiarities which are unknown elsewhere. See **189** and Chart I. This is to be accounted for by the fact that Cyprus was colonized, not necessarily or probably from Arcadia itself, as tradition states, but from the Peloponnesian coast, at a time when its speech was like that which in Arcadia survived the Doric migration. This group represents, beyond question, the pre-Doric speech of most of the Peloponnesus, whatever we choose to call it. The term Arcado-Cyprian, while describing accurately what is left of the group in historical times, is strikingly infelicitous when applied to the prehistoric period. But it is difficult to find a substitute which is not arbitrary or ambiguous. [7]

[7] Both, in the case of "Achaean," a term used in this sense by some and so in the previous editions of this book, but now discarded. Its

This group is by several scholars combined with the Aeolic under the head of "Achaean" ("North Achaean" = Aeolic, "South Achaean" = Arcado-Cyprian) or "Central Greek." There are in fact notable points of agreement between Arcado-Cyprian and Aeolic (see **190**.3-6 and Chart I), which cannot be accidental. On the other hand, many of the common Aeolic characteristics are lacking, and there are certain points of agreement with Attic-Ionic (see **190, 193**.1, 2), as well as many quite special features (see **189**). It is probable that the connections with Aeolic reflect a remote period of geographical contiguity with Aeolic peoples in northern Greece or even before the migration into Greece, with a subsequent quite independent development. If, then, we classify the dialects, not according to supposed prehistoric relations, but as we actually know them, it is only proper to class Arcado-Cyprian as a distinct group coordinate with others of the East Greek division. [8]

Just as in the Northwest Greek dialects some traces of the former Aeolic speech have survived, as noted above, so there are also some traces of pre-Doric speech (either Aeolic or of the Arcado-Cyprian type) in the Doric dialects. Thus Lac. Ποhοιδάν and Ποhοίδαια unmistakably represent (with Lac. h from σ) a form of the name which is attested in Arc. Ποσοιδᾶν, and is in contrast to the genuine Dor. Ποτειδάϝων, Ποτειδάν. And the Ποσειδάν which also occurs in inscriptions of many Doric lands may represent another pre-Doric form. But see **61**.4. The ἰν = ἐν, regular in Arcado-Cyprian and Pamphylian, occurs also in two Cretan towns and the Achaean colony of Metapontum (see **10**a). The occurrence of the Aeolic dat. pl. -εσσι in consonant stems

specific application to this group does not conform to any of the accepted uses of 'Αχαιοί, namely, (1) those of Achaea Phthiotis, (2) those of the Peloponnesian Achaea, (3) in Homer a generic term for the Greeks before Troy by no means restricted to the southern group; and furthermore stands in rivalry with various other modern and partly visionary applications of the same term.

[8] The partial decipherment of the tablets in Cretan script (Linear B) from Pylos, Mycenae, and Cnossus, dating from about 1400-1200 B.C. (Pylos) and earlier, has revealed an early Greek dialect, one that must be a precursor of Arcado-Cyprian. In view of the incomplete state of decipherment, it would be premature to attempt a detailed description of this dialect. But a notable feature is the preservation of the old labiovelar voiceless stop with a value like that of Lat. qu, as in quetro- = Att. Τετρα- (for ro cf. Thess. πετρο-, etc., 6). This lines up with the fact that in Arcado-Cyprian labiovelars show a special development different from that in other dialects (see **68**.3).

in Corinthian colonies, as well as in the Northwest Greek dialects, has already been noted.

The peculiar development of secondary νσ as seen in Lesb. παῖσα from πάνσα, etc. is now fully attested for Cyrene, with traces in Thera (see **77**.3). The agreement is such a striking innovation that it is surely not accidental. True, any direct connection with the Asiatic Aeolians is unlikely. For the missing link we must assume that a continental mother dialect of the Asiatic Aeolic, one containing forms like παῖσα though such are unknown in the actual Thessalian and Boeotian dialects, once existed in a part of this once Aeolic territory before the West Greek overlay. We may then credit the accounts of Minyan participation in the colonization of Thera (e.g., Hdt. 4.145 ff.) with reflecting some genuine tradition.

There are some other alleged, and possible, but more dubious, examples of pre-Doric survival. The question of survival versus accidental agreement or historical borrowing is often difficult.

The classification of the dialects is then, in outline, as follows:

WEST GREEK	EAST GREEK
NORTHWEST GREEK	ATTIC-IONIC
Phocian	Attic
Locrian	Ionic
Elean	AEOLIC
Northwest Greek	Lesbian
κοινή	
	Thessalian
	Boeotian
DORIC	ARCADO-CYPRIAN
Laconian	Arcadian
Heraclean	Cyprian
Megarian	
Argolic	
Rhodian	
Coan	
Theran, Cyrenaean	
Cretan, etc.	
	Pamphylian

2. The Greek dialects, classified in accordance with the preceding scheme, and with their important subdivisions noted, are the following. For summaries of the characteristics of each, see **180-273**.

EAST GREEK

I. THE ATTIC-IONIC GROUP

    1. **Attic.**

    2. **Ionic.**

    A. **East Ionic,** or Ionic of Asia Minor. The Ionic cities of the coast of Asia Minor and the adjacent islands, Samos, Chios, etc., together with their colonies, mostly on the Hellespont, Propontis, and Euxine. There are some local varieties, of which the most marked is Chian, containing some Lesbian features.

    B. **Central Ionic,** or Ionic of the Cyclades. The Ionic Cyclades, Naxos, Amorgos, Paros with its colony Thasos, Delos, Tenos, Andros, Ceos, etc.

    C. **West Ionic,** or **Euboean.** Chalcis (with its colonies in Italy, Sicily, and the Chalcidian peninsula) and the other cities of Euboea. A local dialect with marked characteristics is the Eretrian, seen in the inscriptions of Eretria and Oropus.

II. THE ARCADO-CYPRIAN GROUP

    1. **Arcadian.** The material is now considerable, owing to the increasing number of newly found inscriptions.

    2. **Cyprian.** There are numerous short inscriptions, and one of considerable length, the bronze of Idalium. All are in the Cyprian syllabary. Inscriptions in the Greek Alphabet, beginning in the Macedonian period, are all in the κοινή.

    3. **Pamphylian.** The only inscription of any extent (Schwyzer 686), though the interpretation is in many parts doubtful, contains plenty of clearly identifiable words. The dialect shows many notable characteristics of this group, combined with others which are West Greek or reminders of Cretan. See **200**. The earliest colonists were doubtless pre-Doric Peloponnesians, as in Cyprus, followed by Dorians. The mixture is then somewhat similar to that of Aeolic and West Greek in Thessaly and Boeotia.

III. THE AEOLIC GROUP

1. **Lesbian**, or Asiatic Aeolic. [9] The inscriptional material is fairly extensive, but late. There is nothing approaching the time of the poems of Alcaeus and Sappho, and very little that is older than the Macedonian period. Most of the inscriptions are from the cities of Lesbos, but a few are from other islands and towns of the Aeolic mainland.

2. **Thessalian**. [10] Two subdivisions with marked differences are formed by the dialect of Pelasgiotis and that of Thessaliotis. For these and for other parts of Thessaly, see **214**.

3. **Boeotian**. [10] The material is very extensive, and representative of all the important Boeotian towns, but is meager for the early period.

WEST GREEK

IV. THE NORTHWEST GREEK GROUP

1. **Phocian**. A large part of the material, including nearly all that is of an early date, is from Delphi, and is quoted specifically as **Delphian**.

2. **Locrian**. The two early inscriptions long known, to which a third is now added, are from Western Locris, but one of these is presumably based on an East Locrian draft. Most of the other material is much later and with more or less mixture. See **236**.

3. **Elean**. Numerous very early inscriptions from Olympia, with a few later ones that are still in dialect with some mixture. See **241**.

4. The **Northwest Greek** κοινή. Employed in Aetolia and other regions under the domination of the Aetolian league. See **279**.

NOTE. Only Phocian, Locrian, and Elean are known to us as distinct dialects of this group. Of others which presumably belong here we have almost no material from a time when they retained their individuality. In Aetolia, except for a few very short inscriptions, the material is from the time of the Aetolian league, and in the mixed Northwest Greek κοινή.

[9] Sometimes simply called Aeolic. But, to avoid confusion with Aeolic in its wider sense, the designation Lesbian is to be preferred in spite of the formal impropriety of applying it to a dialect not restricted to Lesbos. Most of the material is actually from Lesbos.

[10] That Thessalian and Boeotian are only in part Aeolic, in part West Greek, has been explained above.

Of the speech of Aeniania and Malis previous to the Aetolian domination we have no remains. It is natural to suppose that Northwest Greek dialects were once spoken also in Acarnania and Epirus. But here the influence of the Corinthian colonies was strong from an early period, as shown by the use of the Corinthian alphabet in the few early inscriptions; and in later times, from which nearly all the material dates, the language employed is not the Northwest Greek κοινή, but the Doric κοινή, like that of the contemporaneous inscriptions of Corcyra. See **279**. Hence the actual material from Acarnania and Epirus is more properly classified with Corinthian. From Cephallenia and Ithaca we have decrees in the Northwest Greek κοινή from the Aetolian period (see **279**), but from earlier times not enough to show whether the dialect was Northwest Greek or Doric. From Zacynthus there is almost nothing. The dialect of Achaea (i.e., Peloponnesian Achaea in the historical period) is generally believed to belong to this group. This is probable on general grounds, but there is as yet no adequate linguistic evidence of it. For, apart from the inscriptions of Achaean colonies in Magna Graecia, which, on account of both their meagerness and the mixed elements in the colonization, are indecisive, nearly all the material is from the time of the Achaean league, and this is not in the Northwest Greek κοινή, but in the same Doric κοινή that was used in Corinth and Sicyon.

V. THE DORIC GROUP

1. **Laconian** and **Heraclean**. Laconia and its colonies Tarentum and Heraclea. Heraclean, well known from the Heraclean Tables, has peculiarities of its own, and is treated as a distinct dialect.

2. **Messenian**. Most of the material is late and with considerable κοινή mixture, as the famous cult inscription of Andania (nearly 200 lines).

3. **Megarian**. Megara, and its colonies in Sicily (especially Selinus) and on the Propontis and Bosporus (as Byzantium, Chalcedon, etc.). Except from Selinus the material is late.

4. **Corinthian**. Corinth, Sicyon, Cleonae, Phlius, and the Corinthian colonies Corcyra (with its own colonies Apollonia and Dyrrhachium), Leucas, Anactorium, Ambracia, etc. For Syracusan, etc., see below, 10. Material from places other than Corinth, though coming under the general head of Corinthian, is generally quoted specifically as Sicyonian, Corcyraean, etc.

5. **Argolic**. Argos, Mycenae, etc., and the cities of the Acte, as Hermione, Troezen, and Epidaurus, together with Aegina.

Argolic (Argol.) is used as the general term, while Argive (Arg.) refers more specifically to the material from Argos (with the Argive Heraeum), as Epidaurian to that from Epidaurus. From Aegina there is not much material from the period before the Athenian occupation, but enough to show that the dialect was Argolic.

Argos (or in some sources one of the other Argolic cities) was the reputed mother city of Crete, Rhodes, Cos, etc., and in historical times Argos was often chosen as arbitrator in their local disputes (cf., e.g., nos. 85, 86). There are in fact some, but not too impressive, points of agreement (besides the general Doric) in the dialects.

6. **Rhodian**. Rhodes with the adjacent small islands and the mainland settlements (the Rhodian Peraea), Phaselis in Pamphylia, Cnidus, Syme, Telos, Nisyros, Carpathos, Casos, the Sicilian colonies of Gela and Agrigentum. An inscription of Rhegium, though not a Rhodian colony, is in the same dialect and there are other signs of the spread of Rhodian influence, notably the infin. -μειν (**154**.5). The material is extensive, but little of it early. The inclusion of Cnidus and some of the islands named, in which examples of distinctive features like the infin. -μειν are lacking, is at least convenient and probably justified (cf. now IG XII. Suppl., p. 1).

7. **Coan**. Cos and Calymna. The material is considerable, but not early.

8. **Theran** and **Cyrenaean**. Thera, with Melos, Cimolos, Pholegandros, Sicinos, probably Anaphe, and perhaps Astypalaea.—Cyrene. There are archaic inscriptions in the same type of alphabet from Thera, Melos, Sicinos, and Anaphe. Those of Sicinos (IG XII. Suppl. pp. 178, 180), which was formerly classed among the Ionic islands, indicate that it was, at least in the early period, Doric. For, though metrical to be sure, they show regular Doric forms like σᾶμα and μνᾶμα and the loss of Ϝ as in the earliest Theran.

The dialect of Cyrene, a colony of Thera, is now by far the best known, owing to the discoveries of the last decades.

9. **Cretan**. This is now the best known of all the Doric dialects, owing to the very extensive early material, especially from

Gortyn. The dialect of Gortyn and other cities of the great central portion of the island is also known more specifically as Central Cretan, to exclude the divergent type seen in the inscriptions, mostly late, from the eastern and western extremities of the island. See **273**. But the term Cretan alone is to be understood as referring to this Central Cretan, unless otherwise stated.

10. **Sicilian Doric**. Owing to the mixture of population it is the exception that the dialect of Sicilian cities can be clearly grouped with that of their mother cities. That of Selinus and Megara Hybla may be classed as Megarian, and that of Gela and Agrigentum as Rhodian. But in Syracuse Gelon's wholesale transplantation of population from Gela and other cities must have left the old Corinthian element in a minority. There are (at least, as yet) no inscriptions written in the Corinthian alphabet or with the typical early OV for secondary ō (**25d**), and there is nothing distinctively Corinthian in the dialect of either the inscriptions or the works of the Syracusan writers. With but few exceptions, the inscriptions of Syracuse and the other cities are late. The longest, those of Halaesa and Tauromenium, are in a mixture of Doric and Attic κοινή, with some local features in vocabulary. A noteworthy spread of Rhodian influence is seen in the typical infin. -μειν used by Epicharmus and occurring in several places in Sicily and Magna Graecia (**154**.5).

The Dialects in Literature

3. Of the numerous dialects of Greece a few attained the rank of literary dialects, though for the most part in a mixed and artificial form not corresponding to anything actually spoken at a given time and place. Moreover, in the course of literary development these dialects came to be characteristic of certain classes of literature, and, their role once established, the choice of one or the other usually depended upon this factor rather than upon the native dialect of the author.

The literary development of epic songs began with the Aeolians of Asia Minor, whence it passed into the hands of the neighboring Ionians, and the language of Homer, which became the norm of all epic poetry and strongly affected subsequent poetry of all

classes, is a mixture of Aeolic and Ionic—in the main Old Ionic
but with the retention of many Aeolic forms, such as ἄμμες beside ἡμεῖς, genitive singular in -αο beside -εω, etc. The language
of Hesiod is substantially the same, but with some Aeolic forms
not used in Homer, also some Boeotian and Doric peculiarities.
The elegiac and iambic poets also use the epic dialect with some
modifications, not only Ionians like Archilochus, but the Athenian Solon, the Spartan Tyrtaeus, the Megarian Theognis, etc.

Of the melic poets, Alcaeus and Sappho followed very closely
their native Lesbian dialect, though not entirely unaffected by
epic influence. The language of these and other Lesbian poets
was directly imitated by some later writers, notably by Theocritus
in three of his idyls, and contributed an important element to
the language of many more, e.g., Anacreon of Teos, who in the
main employed his native Ionic (New Ionic), and, in general,
to the choral lyric, which was mainly Doric.

The choral lyric was developed among Doric peoples, though
under the impulse of Lesbian poets, who we know were welcomed
in Sparta, for example, in the seventh century. Its language is
Doric, with an admixture of Lesbian and epic forms, no matter
whether the poet is a Dorian, or a Boeotian like Pindar, or an
Ionian like Simonides and Bacchylides. This Doric, however,
is not identical with any specific Doric dialect, but is an artificial
composite, showing many of the general Doric characteristics,
but with the elimination of local peculiarities. An exception
is to be made in the case of Alcman, whose Doric is of a severer
type and evidently based upon the Laconian, though also mixed
with Lesbian and epic forms.

The earliest prose writers were the Ionic philosophers and
historians of the sixth century, and in the fifth century not only
Herodotus, but Hippocrates of Cos, a Dorian, wrote in Ionic.
In the meantime, with the political and intellectual supremacy
of Athens, Attic had become the recognized language of the
drama, and before the end of the fifth century was employed
in prose also, though the earlier prose writers as Thucydides,
like the tragedians, avoided certain Attic peculiarities which
were still felt as provincialisms (e.g., ττ = σσ, ρρ = ρσ). Henceforth Attic was the language of literary prose.

The dialects mentioned are the only literary dialects known and cultivated throughout the Greek world. But some few others were employed locally. Epicharmus and Sophron wrote in their native Syracusan Doric, as did later, but in a more mixed form, Archimedes and Theocritus. A form of Doric prose was developed among the Pythagoreans of Magna Graecia, seen in some fragments of Archytas of Tarentum, Philolaus of Croton, and others, though the greater part of the writings of this class are spurious. The comic poet Rhinthon, from whom the grammarians sometimes quote, used the Doric of Tarentum. The fragments of Corinna of Tanagra, whose fame was scarcely more than local, are in Boeotian, and the Boeotian dialect, as well as Megarian and Laconian, are caricatured by Aristophanes. But the great majority of the dialects play no role whatever in literature.

Even for those dialects which are represented, the literary remains must for the most part be regarded as secondary sources, not only because of their artificial character but also because of the corruptions which they have suffered in transmission. Exceptional importance, however, attaches to the language of Homer because of its antiquity, and to the Lesbian of Alcaeus and Sappho because it is relatively pure and much older than the inscriptional material.

NOTE. In the following exposition, dialectal forms from literary and grammatical sources are not infrequently quoted, especially where the inscriptional evidence is slight, as it is, for example, quite naturally, for the personal pronouns. Such forms are sometimes quoted with their specific sources, sometimes simply as literary Doric (lit. Dor.), literary Lesbian (lit. Lesb.), literary Ionic (lit. Ion.), or grammatical (gram.). But a detailed treatment of the dialectal peculiarities observed in our literary texts is so bound up with questions of literary tradition and textual criticism that it is best left to the critical editions of the various authors. It would be impracticable in a work of the present scope, and would, moreover, tend to obscure that more trustworthy picture of the dialects which is gained from inscriptions, and which is so important as a basis for the critical study of the mixed literary forms. However, see the Appendix, pp. 342 ff.

PHONOLOGY

THE ALPHABET

4. The numerous differences in the local alphabets, so far as they consist merely in variations of the forms of the letters, need not be discussed here, important as they are to the epigraphist in deciding the age and source of inscriptions. But certain points in the use of the alphabet and its development as a means of expressing the Greek sounds should be noted.

1. In the most primitive type of the Greek alphabet, as it is seen in the earliest inscriptions of Crete, Thera, and Melos, the non Phoenician signs Φ, X, ᛉ have not yet been introduced, and the Ⰶ is not in use. The sounds of φ, χ are represented by πh, χh (or Ϙh), or, as in Crete, where Ⱨ (H) when used is η not h, are not distinguished from π, κ; those of ψ, ξ by πσ, κσ.

2. In the next stage of development, after the introduction of Φ, X, ᛉ, the alphabets fall into two classes, according to the values attached to these signs. The eastern division, to which Ionic belongs, employs them as φ, χ, ψ, and also uses the Ⰶ as ξ, though a subdivision of this group, represented mainly by the Attic alphabet, uses only the first two and expresses ψ, ξ by φσ, χσ. The western division, [1] to which belong the majority of the alphabets of Greece proper as well as that of Euboea, and which became the source of the Latin alphabet, employs Φ, X, ᛉ as φ, ξ, χ, not using Ⰶ at all, and generally expressing ψ by πσ or, oftener, φσ (but a special sign for ψ in Locris and Mantinea, another rarely in Elis and Laconia).

3. In the earliest inscriptions nearly all the alphabets have the

---

[1] This distinction of Eastern and Western alphabets, the distribution of which is clearly shown in the map in Kirchhoff's Studien zur Geschichte des griechischen Alphabets (which, however, now needs some corrections; see Appendix), has no connection with that of East and West Greek dialects and is anything but coincident with it. From the coloring of Kirchhoff's map the convenient short terms, "red", "blue," and "green" alphabets, have come into use.

Ϝ (vau or digamma); and many the Ϙ (koppa), which is used before ο or υ, and that too even if a liquid intervenes, e.g., Ϙορινθόθεν, hόρϘος, ΛοϘρός, ἐϘρότε͂, ΠάτροϘλος, λέϘυθος, Ϙλύτος (in other positions it is very rare).

4. The four Phoenician signs for sibilants were taken over, but with varying distribution or values. Both the ϟ or ϟ (sigma) an Ϻ (san) were used for σ, but, with few exceptions (e.g., once Ϻ beside ϟ in the Locrian no. 59), only one or the other at the same place and time. A sign ᴎ, a simplified form of Ϻ is used in an Arcadian inscription for a sibilant of special origin, as ᴎις = τίς, Cypr. σις (no. 17; see **68**.3). T, occurring also in the Carian alphabet and perhaps ultimately another modification of the san, is used for usual σσ = Att. ττ at Halicarnassus (ʼΑλικαρναΤέ(ω)ν beside ʼΑλικαρνασσέων), Teos (θαλάΤης beside θάλασσαν), Ephesus (τέΤαρες, etc.) and elsewhere (see p. 348). This is the source of the numeral sign for 900, namely ⅄, known by the late name "sampi" (σὰν πῖ 'like πῖ', from its form).

Ξ and I were adopted, but for a time without full stabilization in value. Ξ = ξ in the Ionic, Corinthian, and (ᴴ) Argive alphabets, but lacking in the majority of alphabets (not only where X = ξ, but also in Attic where φσ = ξ, and occurring = I in Theran Ξεύς, Ξηύς, Corinth. ΞΒΥΜ = Ζεύς. Conversely I for Ξ in Epid. ἌναΙις. I in earliest Cretan, precise phonetic value uncertain, = later ττ; Att. σ, as ὅΙος, etc. (**82**).

5. In Boeotian ᚼ, a compromise between E and I, is sometimes used for the close ε, later ι (**9**.4). At Corinth with Corcyra, Sicyon, Cleonae, and Megara there were two characters for the *e*-sounds, namely, Corinth. ʙ, Sicyon, Ꙅ = ε or η, but ʙ or (Corcyr.) ʙꙅ = original ει or secondary ε̄ (but ʙ in an archaic Meg. inscription = ε only, not η, and at Cleonae = η only. Cf. nos. 91-97.

6. In most of the alphabets the ʜ (early ᴮ) is the sign of the spiritus asper, and neither η and ω nor the secondary ε̄ and ō (**25**) are distinguished from the short ε and ο. But in East Ionic, where the sound of the spiritus asper was lost at a very early period, the ʜ, which was thus left free, was turned to account as a vowel sign, not so much to show a difference in quantity (in the case of ᾱ, ῑ, ῡ no such need was felt) as one of quality. It was probably used first only for the extremely open *e̦* coming

from ᾱ, that is, for the specifically Attic-Ionic η (**8**), which for a time was more open than the sound of the inherited *ē*, though this was also open as compared with the short ε, and both soon became identical and were denoted in the same way. To be sure, no such distinction is to be observed in East Ionic inscriptions, but it is seen in some of the Cyclades, to which the use of the н has passed from East Ionic, e.g., from Naxos (no. 6) Νικάνδρη, ϙόρη, etc. but ἀνέθεκεν (with E in the penult). Similar examples from Andros and Ceos (nos. 7, 8), also Amorgos.

The use of ɐ = η extended not only to the Ionic but also to the Doric islands, Rhodes, Thera, Melos, and Crete, where it is found in the earliest inscriptions, though in Crete it went out of use for a time, not appearing, for example, in the Law Code. In Central Ionic, where the sound of the spiritus asper still survived, as also in Rhodes, Thera, and Melos, the sign was used both as η and as *h*. It occurs also with syllabic value = *hε* or *hē*, as ɐκηβόλōι (Naxos, no. 6), Hσπέρης (Oropus, no. 14.46), Hλλεν (Paros), Ther. Hρμοχρέ(ōν), Arg. (no. 85) Hραι beside HEραι, Boeot. (no. 39) Hνδεκα, Hξ, Hμιττα, even late Aetol. Hτέων (= hετέων, cf. ἔτος **58**c).

The Ionic alphabet is also characterized by its distinction of the o-vowels through differentiated forms of O, usually Ω = ω, which became universal, but in archaic inscriptions of Delos, Paros, Thasos, and Siphnos Ω = o and O or ☉ = ω; of Thera O = o, ☉ = ω; of Melos and Cnidus ᴄ = o, O = ω.

7. In 403 B.C. the Ionic alphabet was officially introduced at Athens, and not much later replaced the native or "epichoric" alphabets in other parts of Greece. Inscriptions of the end of the fifth or the beginning of the fourth century often show a transitional form of the alphabet, partly epichoric, partly Ionic. Even with the full Ionic alphabet, ϝ was generally retained where it was still sounded, and sometimes a form of н was used for the spiritus asper, as ⊦ in the Heraclean Tables and occasionally elsewhere (Elis, Cumae, Sicyon, Epidaurus). The Delphian Labyadae inscription (no. 52) has ɐ = *h*, н = η; likewise an Argive inscription.

For the Cyprian syllabary, see p. 210.

Vowels

α

5. ο for α before or after liquids. Examples are most numerous in Lesbian, mainly from literary and grammatical sources, as στρότος = στρατός, βροχέως = βραχέως, χόλαισι = χαλῶσι; etc. (see p. 342). So ἀμβρ[ό]την (no. 25) = ἁμαρτεῖν, like Hom. ἤμβροτον = ἥμαρτον (μβρ from μρ, as regularly). Both στρόταγος and στράταγος occur in inscriptions; likewise in Boeotian στροτός in numerous proper names, στροτιώτας, ἐστροτεύαθη, but also στρατός in proper names, στραταγίοντος. The στρατ-forms, which are the only ones so far attested for Thessalian, are to be attributed to κοινή influence. Boeot., Thess. ἐροτός = ἐρατός, βροχύς = βραχύς, attested by proper names, Boeot., Lesb. πόρνοψ = πάρνοψ, whence Lesb. Πορνοπία, Thess. πετρο- = τετρα-.

In Arcado-Cyprian also we find Arc. ἐφθορκώς = ἐφθαρκώς, πανάγορσις belonging with West Ion. ἄγαρρις (**49**.2) τέτορτος, Βρόχυς, στορπάος = ἀστραπαῖος (also Arc. στορπά, Cypr. στροπά in Hesych.), Cypr. κορζία (Hesych.) = καρδία, κατέϜοργον = *κατε-Ϝαργον aorist of *κατ-εϜέργω (κατείργω) with the weak grade of the root as in ἔδρακον from δέρκομαι (**49**.2).

Here perhaps also, as an Aeolic survival, Aetol. Λόφριον beside usual epithets Λάφριος, Λάφρια. But for the widespread γροφεύς, etc. see **49**.2.

6. ο for α in other cases. ὀν = ἀνά in Lesbian, Thessalian (Pelasgiotis), and Arcado-Cyprian (also ὐν-, see **22**). Cf. also Thess. ὀστροφά, from *ὀνστροφά=ἀναστροφή. Lesb., Arc. δέκοτος = δέκατος, also Arc. δέκο = δέκα, ἑκοτόν = ἑκατόν, and Lesb. ἔνοτος = ἔνατος. Thess. ἐξόμεινvον = ἐξάμηνον. Delph. ἐντοφήια 'burial rites,' Cyren. ἐντόφιον 'burial gift,' Heracl. τοφιών 'burial place' (cf. τάφος). κοθαρός = καθαρός in Heraclea, Sybaris, Locris (Περ-Ϟοθαριᾶν), Lesbos, Elean κόθαρσις.

a. The explanation is uncertain, and not necessarily the same for all the forms cited here. For example, it is possible that the ο of δέκοτος, etc. is to be viewed in the some light as that of εἴκοσι = West Greek Ϝίκατι. See **116***a*. But the preference for ο appears to be, here as in 5, an Aeolic-Arc.-Cypr. characteristic.

7. ε for α. For forms with ε beside α which fall within the regular system of vowel-gradation, see **49**.2-4.

An actual change of final α to ε is seen in Thess. διέ = διά. Cf. Thess. -ει=-αι (27).

ᾱ

8. Attic-Ionic η from ᾱ. Original ᾱ, which remains unchanged in all other dialects, becomes η in Attic-Ionic. Thus τιμή, φημί, ἴστημι, but in other dialects τιμά (ᾱ-stem), φᾱμί (Lat. *fārī*), ἴστᾱμι (Lat. *stāre*). For the contrast between this η and that which represents an inherited *ē*-sound and is common to the other dialects also, note Att.-Ion. μήτηρ, elsewhere μάτηρ (Lat. *māter*).

But Attic differs from Ionic, in that it has ᾱ, not η, after ε, ι, and ρ, as γενεά, οἰκίᾱ, χώρᾱ = Ion. γενεή, οἰκίη, χώρη.

a. In some Central Ionic inscriptions, as noted in **4.**6, only this η from ᾱ was written ⴱ, ⵀ, vs. E for η = original *ē*. This distinction was probably once general Attic-Ionic, the sound resulting from ᾱ being still somewhat more open than that representing original *ē*.

b. It is a widely held, but also disputed, view that the change of ᾱ to η, or rather to the sound close to but not quite identical with η = original *ē* (above, *a*) was general Attic-Ionic and that the ᾱ of Att. γενεά, etc., was a reversion rather than an uninterrupted retention of ᾱ in such cases. The evidence is complicated and open to more than one interpretation. As the problem is a purely Attic one, it need not concern us further.

c. In Att. κόρη, δέρη the η after ρ is explained by the fact that it was originally preceded by ϝ (**54**). But Att. εἰρήνη, κρήνη vs. Dor. ἰρᾱνᾱ, κρᾱνᾱ are anomalous and variously explained.

d. The ᾱ arising from lengthening of α in connection with original intervocalic, νσ, σν, etc., undergoes the same change, e.g., Att.-Ion. ἔφηνα from ἔφᾱνα, original *ἔφανσα. See **76, 77**.1. But in τάς from τάνς and πᾶσα from πάνσα, original *πάντι̯α, the ᾱ was of later origin and was unaffected. See **77**.3, **78**.

ε

9. ι from ε before (mostly α- and ο-) vowels.

1. Even in Attic an ε before another vowel had a closer sound than in other positions, and was frequently written ει, as θειός = θεός, νειώς = νεώς. So, sometimes, in Ionic, as εἴως = ἕως, δειόμενος (Oropus) = δεόμενος.

In several dialects the ε progressed so far in the direction of ι that it was frequently, or even regularly, written ι. Thus:

2. Lesbian. Spelling ε in θεός, ἐών, etc. But χρύσιος, χάλκιος,

συκία, κυνία, ὅστιον, etc., show the same phonetic tendency as in other dialects, although the uniform spelling here may be due to the favoring influence of parallel suffixes. So also τίωι, τίοισι (cf. Hom. τέω, ὁτέοισιν) in which the ι may have been reinforced by that of τίς.

3. **Thessalian.** Frequently ι, as θιός, λίθιος, Λίοντα, etc., but also ε in hυλōρέοντος, παρέοντος, τοίνεος, etc.

4. **Boeotian.** The spelling is usually ι, but sometimes ε, ει, or ⊦ (see **4**.5), as θιός, θειός = θεός, ἀνέθιαν, ἀνέθειαν, beside ἀνέθεαν, Πολυκλⱶἐς = Πολυκλέης, ἰόντος = ἐόντος, ῥίοντος = ῥέοντος.

a. Boeotian ε in general had a relatively close sound, and the spelling ει occurs occasionally even before a consonant, as Ξενκρείτω = Ξεναρέτου, Θιόφειστος = *Θεόθεστος (68.2), πεποιόντεισσι = -εσσι. In ἐν Θεισπιῆς, Θεισπιεύς, etc., the spelling ει is so constant that perhaps it stands for original η (16), which in other dialects was shortened as if the name of the town were connected with θέσπις, etc.

5. **Arcadian.** Regularly ε before a back vowel, as θεός, Ϝέτεα, ἐόντος, etc. But ι before a front vowel in ἀπυδίει = ἀποδέει, Αὐκλίεια = Εὐκλέεια (?); so also -εϊ to -ιϊ, whence -ῑ in dat. sg. πλήθι, ἔτι, ἱερῖ, etc. A somewhat different, but related, case is ἀπυλιῶναι (no. 22.20), from an elsewhere attested ἀπολειόω (162.10).

6. **Cyprian.** At Idalium the spelling is regularly ι, as θιός, ἰό(ν)τα = ἐόντα, Ϝέπιjα = ἔπεα. So Pamph. Ϝέτιια, ἀνδριῶνα.

7. **Cretan.** We find ι regularly, except where the ε was once followed by Ϝ. That is, the change was prior to the loss of inter-vocalic Ϝ; and the ε which later, with the loss of Ϝ, came to stand before another vowel, was unaffected. Thus ἰόντος = ἐόντος, καλίων = καλέων, πλίες = Hom. πλέες,—but υἱέος, Ϝοικέος, δρομέōν.

8. **Laconian.** We find ι, with the same restriction as in Cretan, in early inscription (also in Alcman and Ar. Lysist.), e.g. θιός, ἀνιοχίōν = ἡνιοχέων. In later inscriptions the spelling is usually ε.

9. **Heraclean.** Verbal forms show ι, with the same restriction as in Cretan, e.g., ἀδικίων, ἐμετρίωμες, ἀναγγελίοντι, but ῥέοντα, δεόμενα. In other words, Τιμοκράτιος, τοφιών, but usually ε, as Ϝέτεος, owing to κοινή influence.

10. **Argolic.** Frequently θιός, Θίων, etc., in Argos and Epidaurus, but otherwise usually ε.

11. Corinthian. Usually ε, but θιαρός in two late decrees of Corcyra and Epidamnus.

10. ι from ε before ν in Arcado-Cyprian. Here ἰν = ἐν is the regular form (cf. also Pamph. ἰ πόλιι and ἰς from *ἰνς = ἐνς, εἰς), also in compounds as Arc. ἰνάγω, ἰμφαίνω, ἰνφορβίω, ἰγκεχηρήκοι, ἴνδικος, ἴνπασις, ἰνπολά, ἴγγυος, ἰνμενφής and ἴνμονφος 'blameworthy' (opp. to ἀμεμφής, ἄμομφος), Cypr. ἰναλίνω (ἰναλαλισμένα). Cf. also Arc. μίνονσαι = μένουσαι, Ἐρχομίνιοι = Ὀρχομένιοι, ἀπεχομίνος, ἀπυσεδομίνος, διαβωλευσαμίνος = -μένους, etc., but in such forms the later inscriptions have εν. There are a few examples in other positions, as Arc. Τιλείας, Cypr. Μιγαλαθέō, indicating that in general ε had a relatively close sound (as also in Boeotian, 9.4a). The foreign names appearing as Ἐδάλιον, Κέτιον in the Cyprian texts were usually rendered Ἰδάλιον, Κίτιον.

a. ἰν = ἐν is found also, probably a pre-Doric survival, in some inscriptions of the Cretan towns of Eleutherna and Vaxus, and the Achaean colony of Metapontum.

11. ι beside ε in other cases. The interchange is occasionally seen among dialectal forms of the same word, as in Hom. πίσυρες = πέσσυρες, τέσσερες. Att. ἑστία appears with ι in all other dialects, so far as quotable, e.g., Ion. ἱστίη, Lesb. ἱστία, Thess. Ἱστιαίειος, Boet. Ἱστιήω, Delph. Ἱστιώ (but homέστιος), Locr. ἱστία, Heracl. Ἱστίειος, Syrac. Ἱστία, Rhod. ἱστιατόριον, Coan ἱστία, Cret. Ἱστία, Arc. Ϝιστίαν. Here the ι may be due to the influence of ἵστημι.

12. α from ε before ρ in Northwest Greek. Locr. φάρειν, πατάρα, ἀμάρα, ἀνφόταρος, Ϝεσπάριος (but μέρος no. 57, περί, ἐνφέροι, Ϝερρέτō no. 59). Here also ϝαρέσται (no. 57; but ϝελέσται no. 58) = ἑλέσθαι, with ρ for λ after the analogy of the present αἱρέω (as, conversely, Cret. αἰλέω = αἱρέω, with λ from the aorist). El. φάρεν, Ϝάργον, Ϝάρρεν, πάρ (= περί), ὁπόταρος, ἐλεύθαρος, ὕσταριν, but the spelling αρ is not quite uniform even in the early inscriptions, and later gives way to ερ (see 241). Delph. φάρεν, ματάρα, Ϝαργάναι, δάρματα, πενταμαριτεύων, but in the later inscriptions the spelling is ερ (φέρεν even in no. 52) Cf. also Ach. Ζεὺς Ἀμάριος, Pamph. ὕπαρ = ὕπερ, Thess. Κιάριον = Κιέριον.

a. Elean has α also after ρ, as λατραι[όμενον] beside λατρειόμενον, μαστράαι from *μαστρεία (31), κατιαραίων, κατιαραύσειε in contrast to φυγαδείην, φυγαδεύαντι (see 161.1); also before final ν, as μάν = μέν, γνῶμαν = γνῶμεν, 3 pl. opt. ἀποτίνοιαν, ἐπιθεῖαν, συνέαν, etc.; occasionally elsewhere, as εὐσαβέοι = εὐσεβέοι, σκευᾶον = -έων, showing that Elean ε in general had a very open sound. Cf. El. ᾱ = η (15).

b. A similar change before λ in Delphian appears in Δαλφοῖς of an inscription and in Δα, Δαλ, Δαλφικόν of the earliest coins.

c. Epid. κραμάσαι = κρεμάσαι and μάντοι = μέντοι, though more isolated, and open to other possible explanations (μάντοι blend with μάν = μήν, κραμάσαι weak grade or assimilation), are perhaps to be viewed in the same light as the Elean forms under α.

13. West Greek α = East Greek ε. Besides the examples of dialectal interchange of α and ε cited under the head of vowel gradation (49.2-4), in which the distribution of the α and ε forms is various (e.g., ἄρσην, ἔρσην,—βάλλω, δέλλω), there is a group of parallel forms in which the preference for the α forms is a marked West Greek characteristic.

1. ἱαρός (or ἰαρός) is the regular form in early inscriptions of all West Greek dialects, Pamphylian (hιαρύ), and Boeotian, ἱερός occurring only later and plainly due to κοινή influence. The situation is probably the same in Thessalian, though the occurrences of both forms are late. ἱερός (or ἰερός) is Attic-Ionic and Arcado-Cyprian, while a third form is seen in Lesb. ἶρος, (likewise ἶρευς, ἶρεια, ἰρητεύω, late κατείρων with ει = ῑ), Ion. ἱρός, ἰρός beside ἱερός, ἰερός. There are many other words with variation between -ερός and -αρός, as μιερός, μιαρός (likewise πύελος, πύαλος, etc.), but with widely different dialectal distribution.

2. Ἄρταμις, so far as the name is quotable from early inscriptions, is the form of all West Greek dialects except Cretan, and of Boeotian. In later Doric and Delphian inscriptions this is usually replaced by Ἄρτεμις. Thessalian has both forms.

3. κα = κε (ἄν) is the form of all West Greek dialects and Boeotian, while Thessalian has κε, like Lesbian and Cyprian. See **134.2**. West Greek and Boeotian ὅκα, etc. = Att.-Ion., Arc.-Cypr. ὅτε, etc. (but Lesb. ὅτα, etc.). See **132.11**. -γα = -γε is likewise West Greek and Boeotian. Adverbs in -(σ)θα = -(σ)θεν, -(σ)θε are usual in West Greek (προσθα- also Arc.). See **133.1**.

a. ἅτερος = ἕτερος is not confined to West Greek dialects, but is also quotable from Arcadian, Boeotian, and Lesbian, and even for Attic is implied by ἄτερος with crasis. So far as we know, ἕτερος belongs to Attic-Ionic only, all examples in other dialects being late.

η

14. Original η, that is, η representing original ē, remains unchanged in nearly all dialects. Contrast the special Attic-Ionic η from ā (**8**), both being seen in Attic-Ionic μήτηρ = μάτηρ of other dialects. On the introduction of the character н, see **4.6**.

15. ā from η in Elean. The sound of η was so open in Elean that it approximated that of ā, and was frequently, though by no means consistently, denoted by α. Thus μά (but also μέ, μή) = μή, Ϝράτρα = ῥήτρα, βασιλᾶες = ἦες, ἔα (but also εἴε) = εἴη, δαμοσιοία = -οίη πλαθύοντα beside πλεθύοντι, 3 sg. subj. ἐκπέμπᾱ (**149**). Cf. α for ε (**12a**).

    a. An isolated case outside of Elis is ποίασε on a vase from Ithaca.

16. ει from η in Thessalian and Boeotian. In these dialects the sound was so close that with the introduction of the Ionic alphabet it was uniformly denoted not by η but by ει, which at that time represented a close ē. Thess., Boeot. μεί = μή, ἀνέθεικε = ἀνέθηκε, μεινός = μηνός, Thess. βασιλεῖος, Boeot. γραμματεῖος = -ῆος, Thess., Boeot. στατεῖρας, Boeot. μάτειρ, πατείρ = -τηρ.

    a. The spelling ι also occurs in Cypr. ἴ = ἤ 'or' (no.23.24), perhaps ὅπι (no. 23.29) = ὅπη (**132.**7), in Pamph. Μάνιτους beside Μάνειτυς (gen. sg. = -ητος), and some late Boeot. forms, as παρῖς beside παρεῖς (εἰς = ἦς, Att. ἤν. **163.**3).

17. Lesb. αἰμισέων (no. 25), αἰμιθέων (Alc.), αἰμιόνοις (Sappho), all = ἡμι-. The explanation is difficult, since in all other cases η remains unchanged in Lesbian. Perhaps η was more open initially than in other positions, and this, in connection with an epenthetic vowel (but see **47**), led to αι.

ι

18. ε from ι after ρ in the Aeolic dialects. An open pronunciation of ι after ρ is indicated by occasional spellings such as Lesb. Δαμοκρέτω = Δημοκρίτου (but κρίννω, κρίτων), Thess. κρεννέμεν (Lesb. κρίννω), Ὑβρέστας beside Ὑβρίστας, ἀπελευθερεσθένσα from ἀπελευθερίζω, Boeot. Διοκρένες = -κρίνης, τρέπεδδα, τρεπεδδίτας (Hesych. τρίπεζαν· τὴν τράπεζαν. Βοιωτοί).

a. Cf. also Lesb. ερ = ρι (probably through the medium of a syllabic ρ) in τέρτος (in glosses and proper names) = τρίτος, and in forms cited in 19.2; also Lesb. ερ = ιρ in κέρναν = κιρνάναι (influence of ἐκέρασα, etc. ?).

b. There are scattered examples of ε for ι elsewhere, as El. πόλερ beside πόλιρ = πόλις, βενέοι = *βινέοι (Att. βῑνέω), Ach. ἐρανεσταί = ἐρανισταί, Sicil. Dor. περιωρεσία = *περιωρισία.

19. Consonantal ι (ι̯) from antevocalic ι in Lesbian and Thessalian. The consonantal pronunciation of antevocalic ι might occur anywhere in rapid speech, but was especially characteristic of Aeolic, as indicated by the following related phenomena in Lesbian and Thessalian.

1. Lesb. ζ from δι in ζά, κάρζα, Ζόννυσος, from glosses or late inscriptions, the usual inscriptional spelling being διά, etc. Cf. also Ζιονύ(σιος) on an early coin of Phocaea, Cypr. κορζία · καρδία (Hesych.). Compounds with ζα- = δια- are frequent in the Lesbian poets, as ζάβαις, ζάδηλος, etc., and occur elsewhere, as Hom. ζάθεος (Boeot. δάθιος Corinna), etc.

2. Lesb. μετέρρος, ἀλλότερρος, Πέρραμος, Πέραμος = μέτριος, ἀλλότριος, Πρίαμος, the development being ρι, ρι̯, ερι̯, ερρ.

3. Thessalian doubling of consonants before ι, which may then be retained or omitted in the spelling, as ἰδδίαν, ἰτδίαν, πόλλιος, προξεννιοῦν, ἐξακάττιοι, ἐκκλησσία, κῦρρον beside κύριον, ἀργύρροι gen. sg. = ἀργυρίου beside Μνασσᾶ = Μνασία. Cf. Att. βορρᾶς from βορέας.

4. Omission of ι, as Lesb. ἄργυρα = ἀργύρια, Thess. τρακάδι = τριακάδι, etc. (see also under 3.)

20. Interchange of ι and υ. Assimilation of ι to υ of the following syllable is seen in ἥμυσυ = ἥμισυ, which appears in an Ionic inscription of the fifth century B.C. (τώμυσυ), also in Attic and elsewhere; the opposite assimilation in βιβλίον beside βυβλίον. Influence of the preceding ευ, or of the suffix -σύνη, in Lac. Ἐλευhύνια = Ἐλευσίνια (also Olynth. Ἐλευσύνιος, name of a month). Other by-forms, the relation of which is uncertain, are Ἀμφικτίονες and Ἀμφικτύονες, Meg. αἰσιμνάτας, αἰσιμνάω = Ion. αἰσυμνήτης, αἰσυμνάω, μόλυβδος beside μόλιβος, βόλιμος, etc. (**88**).

a. A secondary ι before σ + consonant appears in sporadic spellings, as Boeot. αἴστεα = ἄστεα, Lesb. παλαίστα = Att. παλαστή (but also παλαιστή Aristot., papyri), Argol. Αἰσκλαπιός (cf. also Corinth. Αἰσχλαβίος and Lat. *Aesculapius* from a similar source) = usual Ἀσκλαπιός, Τροιζάνιος

(in a fourth-century inscription of Hermione, otherwise only late) = usual Τροζάνιος, beside Τροζάν, the usual spelling until Roman times.
But for Lesb. εἴχοστος, etc., commonly cited in this connection, the uniform spelling (seven occurrences) favors a different and more special explanation, for which see **77**.2, **116**a. For Thess. πρεισβεία, etc., see **86**.3.

ι

21. ῑ remains unchanged everywhere. But in late inscriptions it is sometimes denoted by ει, which had come to have the sound ῑ, as τειμά or τειμή = τῑμή.

ο

22. υ from ο, especially in Arcado-Cyprian. In both Arcadian and Cyprian, final ο nearly always appears as υ. Gen. sg. -ᾱυ = -ᾱο, as Arc. Καλλίαυ, Cypr. Ὀνασιγόραυ. Middle endings -τυ, -ντυ = -το, -ντο, as Arc. διωρθώσατυ, ἐγάμαντυ (but also -το, from Attic), Cypr. γένοιτυ, ἐϜρετάσατυ. Arc., Cypr. (also Lesb., Thess.) ἀπύ = ἀπό, Arc. ὀπύ = ὑπό, also κατύ by analogy, ἄλλυ = ἄλλο. Cf. also ὺν for ὸν = ἀνά (6) in Cypr. ὑνέθεχε (once) beside ὀνέθεχε, and Arc. ὑνέθυσε, ὑνιερόσει beside ὄνδιχα (later ἀν- due to Attic influence).

a. In Pamphylian, υ for ο not only when final, but also in final syllables ending in a consonant and once medially in composition, e.g., gen. sg. Πυλώραυ, 3 sg. mid. ἐβόλάσετυ, nom. sg. ὺ βόλέμενυς (= ὁ βουλόμενος), gen. sg. Μάνετυς, cpd. νοικυπολίς (= *Ϝοικοπολίς).

b. In Lesbian there are several examples (beside ἀπύ = ο, especially before μ, as ὑμοίως, ὑμολογία, and (lit.) ὔμοι, ὑπίσσω, ὔσδων. Also Arc. ὑμοίοις, στυμέον.

c. ὄνυμα = ὄνομα is common to nearly all, perhaps all, dialects except Attic-Ionic. Cf. the compounds ἀνώνυμος etc., which are universal.

d. In Chalcid. hυπύ = ὑπό, and ϙύϙνυς, the second υ is due to assimilation to the first.

ω

23. ου from ω in Thessalian. Long ō in Thessalian, whether original or secondary (**25**), became a close ō, then ū, and, after the introduction of the Ionic alphabet, was regularly denoted by ου. χούρα = χώρα, φιλάνθρουπα = φιλάνθρωπα, τοῦν ταγοῦν πάντουν = τῶν ταγῶν πάντων. Cf. ει from η (**16**).

υ and ῡ

24. Instead of becoming a sound like German *ü*, French *u*, as it did in Attic at an early period, the original *u*-sound (English *oo* in *food*) was retained in several, perhaps the majority of, dialects. This is most obvious where, the Attic values of the letters being taken as a basis, the spelling υ was replaced by ου.

In Boeotian, ου begins to appear in the early fourth century B.C. (no. 39), and is frequent after 300 B.C., though υ is not uncommon until the last quarter of the century. Thus ούπέρ, χούριος, ἀργούριον, τούχα, ὄνουμα, (**22c**), etc. In the third century the spelling ιου (pronounced like English *u* in *cube*?) is also employed, though never consistently, after τ, δ, θ, ν, and λ, as τιούχα, διού = δύο, ᾽Ιθιούδικος, ὄνιουμα, Διωνιούσιος, Λιουκίσκω, etc.; also once after σ (Σιούνεσις) and once initially (ἰουιῶ = υἱοῦ). Another spelling is ο, as Boeot. ὁπέρ=ὑπέρ, θοσίης=θυσίαις, also (no. 39) δοώδεκα, σκόφος, and perhaps κόρτον, κότος, Arc. ὁπύ, ὁπέρ.

a. Except in Boeotian, the spelling υ is generally retained in inscriptions. So in Laconian, for which the retention of the *u*-sound is amply attested by the numerous glosses spelled with ου in accordance with Attic values, and by the pronunciation of the modern Tsakonian. In various other dialects, as Arcadian, Cyprian, Thessalian, Lesbian, Cretan, Euboean, there are indications, of one kind or another, of the same pronunciation, such as the occasional spelling ου or ο for υ, or υ for ο (**22a**), use of ϙ before υ (Chalcid. ϙύϙνυς, λήϙυθος, etc.) and occasional F for υ (**52c**).

Secondary ē and ō. „Spurious Diphthongs"

25. In many dialects, as in Attic, ε and ο differed in quality from η and ω, being close vowels (*ẹ, ọ*). Consequently the long vowels which came from them by contraction or compensative lengthening, since they retained the same quality, were not identical with η and ω, but were ẹ̄ and ọ̄, the latter becoming *ū*, and eventually came to be designated by ει and ου after these original diphthongs had become monophthongs in pronunciation (**28, 34**). But in other dialects they became identical with η and ω, and were so written. Hence such dialectal variations as τρεῖς—τρῆς from *τρέ̣ες (**42**.3), (ἐ)κεῖνος—κῆνος (-ε-ενος), εἰμί—ἠμί from *ἐσμί (**76**), φθείρω—φθήρω from *φθέρι̯ω (**74**), ξεῖνος—

ξῆνος from ξένϝος (54), χείλιοι—χήλιοι from *χέσλιοι (76), χείρ—
χήρ from *χεσρ (76), βουλή—βωλά (75), κούρη—κώρᾱ from κόρϝᾱ
(54), gen. sg. -ου——ω from -οιο (106.1), acc. pl. -ους—ως
from -ονς (78).

The dialects which regularly have η and ω in such forms are
Arcadian (and presumably Cyprian, though the spelling of course
is indeterminate), Lesbian, Elean, Laconian, Heraclean, and
Cretan. Boeotian and Thessalian properly belong to this group,
since Boeotian has ω, and ει is the same as for original η (16),
and Thess. ει, ου are the same as for original η, ω (16, 23).

In several dialects there is some evidence of a qualitative
difference between the vowels resulting from lengthening and
those resulting from contraction.

a. Cretan. The earliest Cretan inscriptions which have the letter Ɓ
show this for the vowel resulting from the early lengthenings (before
original σμ, etc. as ƁμEν), but E for that before original νϝ, as κσEνιος =
later ξήνιος, and usually for the result of contraction, as ἀναιρEσθαι,
μōλEν (= later μωλῆν, κοσμEν, ἀποδόμEν, ƁμEν, etc. (rarely -μƁν; ἀπο-
στάμƁν, and ƁμEν and ƁμƁν in the same inscription, no. 116). After the
introduction of ω there are a few cases of O for the contracted vowel,
as gen. sg. κόσμO. In later times regularly η, ω for both lengthened and
contracted vowels.

b. Theran and Cyrenaean. Regularly η, ω for the lengthened vowels,
as δήλομαι, ἦμεν, βωλά (in proper names), Cyren. χήλιοι. Before original
νϝ, etc., Cyren. ἤνατος but Ther. οὖροι. For contraction archaic Theran E
(vs. Ɓ) in ἐποίE, etc., later ει, rarely η as τρῆς. Cyren. 3 sg. mid. Dor.
future δησῆται and παισεῖται in the same inscriptions. Ther. gen. sg.
archaic -O (vs. Ꙩ == ω); similarly in Melos gen. sg. -Ϲ (vs. Ꙩ = ω), later
-ου. Cyren. gen. sg. -O in a fifth-century inscription which has ω, later
always -ω; also ω from οε in λωσάμενος.

Somewhat similar situation in Rhodes, Cos, etc. Rhod. ἤμειν, Rhod.,
Coan δήλομαι, βωλά (in proper names), κῆνος, but more commonly ει, ου.

c. Argolic. By lengthening, ἠμί, χηρός, χῆρα, ἤνατος, βωλά, ὦρος, etc.,
but frequently, and especially later, ει, ου. By contraction η in augmented
forms, ἦρπε, ἦχον, ἤλετο (beside εἴλετο), but in forms of verbs in -εω usually
ει and at Argos even ι in τελῖτο, ἀφαιρῖσθαι (no. 85, about 450 B.C.) and
later καλῖσθαι. Also, strangely, ι for genuine ει in the thrice recurring hῑ,
ῑ = εῖ (132.2). By contraction ω in λωτήριον gen. sg. and acc. pl. of
σ-stems, -ω,-ως at Hermione, but usually -ου and -ονς, -ος.

d. It is to be remembered that in the inscriptions of most dialects
before the introduction of the Ionic alphabet, and except for the early
vowel use of Ɓ, H in Crete, Rhodes, etc., or the use of different signs for

o and ω in some of the islands, the spelling was simply E, O, which we transcribe ē̆,ō̆, whether the later spelling is ει, ου or η, ω.

In Corinthian the identity of secondary ē̆, ō̆ and original ει, ου belongs to the earliest period, owing to the very early monophthongization of the diphthongs (28, 34). The spelling is E at Corinth and Sicyon (vs. Corinth. Ꙅ, Sicyon Ⴟ = ε, η), � at Corcyra, and OV in all three places. It is possible that the situation was similar in Megarian, where there is some indication of early monophthongization of ει (28).

In early Locrian, no. 58, 59 have only E, O, while no. 57 has EI (φάρEIν, etc.) and OV in the acc. pl. (τOVς) but O in the gen. sg. (δάμO). Later regularly ει, ου.

In Attic-Ionic, E, O are common until after 400 b.c. and occasionally much later, while EI, OV in general begin to appear in the fifth century b.c. But remarkable is the exceptionally early appearance of EI in EIμί, of which there is one example from the eighth (Hesperia 5.33) and several from the sixth century b.c. in Attic (e.g., no. 1 in the Attic, vs. Εμί in the Ionic version), Eretrian, etc. Conversely, there are a few very early examples of E = original ει, as 3 sg. άρχE, etc.

e. An early change of ē̆ to ῑ occurs in Att. χίλιοι vs. Ion. χείλιοι, etc. (76), and ἱμάτιον vs. εἱμάτιον in other dialects, like εἷμα.

f. The lengthening of o before σ + nasal (76), gives Att.-Ion. ω not ου, as in ὦμος (cf. Goth. *ams*, Skt. *aṅsa-*, Lat. *umerus*, and Lesb. ἐπομμαδίαις), ὠνή (cf. Skt. *vasna-* 'price,' Lat. *vēnum* 'sale,' and Lesb. ὄννα), Hom. Διώνυσος. The relation of Att. οὖν to ὦν of other dialects is obscure; likewise the history of Att.-Ion. δοῦλος vs. Dor. (Cret., Lac., etc.) δῶλος.

Diphthongs

αι

26. η from αι in Boeotian. The diphthong is retained in the earliest inscriptions, sometimes as αι, sometimes as αε, especially at Tanagra, e.g., Ἀεσχόνδας, Ὀκίβαε. But it came to be pronounced as a monophthong, an open ē̄, and with the introduction of the Ionic alphabet was regularly denoted by η, e.g., κή = καί; ἠ = αἰ; Θειβῆος = Θηβαῖος; dat. sg. and nom. pl. -η = -αι; dat. pl. -ης = -αις; infin. -ση, -σθη = -σαι, -σθαι. In very late inscriptions even ει is found, as Θειβεῖος.

a. An alleged Cret. κή = καί in an early inscription (SEG 2.509, Inscr. Cret. 1, p. 90) is at variance with all other evidence and is surely to be rejected. The first occurrence has already been eliminated by a corrected reading. Namely, αἱ δέ κα κή ρίς ροοσει is to be read αἱ δέ κα κηρί (= χηρί) τρόοσει. The second occurrence, which still stands in the latest edition, namely, αἱ δέ κή ρινὸς αἷμα ρυῆι, may be read αἱ δέ κ' with elision (and so corresponding to αἱ δέ κα of the previous clause), followed by ἡ ῥινὸς αἷμα from ἐς (=ἐκ) ῥινός with the development as in medial σρ (**76**).

27. ει from αι in Thessalian. In general αι remains, but at Larissa we find ει for final αι; e.g., ἐψάφιστει = ἐψήφισται, βέλλειτει = βούληται, γινύειτει = γίγνηται; and with added ν (**139**.2, **156**) πεπεῖστειν = πεπεῖσθαι, ὀνγράψειν = ἀναγράψαι, ἐφάνγρενθειν = ἐφαιροῦνται, βέλλουνθειν = βούλωνται. Also Εἰμούνειος (Αἵμων).

ει

28. Sooner or later ει became everywhere a monophthong, a close ẽ (ē), though the spelling was retained and in certain dialects extended to the secondary ē (**25**). In Corinthian this had taken place at the time of the earliest inscriptions, and, while at Corcyra the spelling was ßₓ (**25**d), at Corinth the sound was nearly always denoted by a single sign, though generally differentiated from ε or η, e.g., ΔϜΕνία = Δεινίου, ΠοτΕδάν (rarely with Εε or βε), but ἀνвθвκв = ἀνέθηκε. From Megara there are a few examples of Ε = ει, as names in -κλΕδας.

a. At a late period the ē progressed still further to an ī, usually with retention of the old spelling ει, which then came to be used also for original ῑ (**21**), but sometimes with phonetic spelling ι. In some words this late spelling with ι became fixed in our texts, e.g., τίσω, ἔτισα, ἔκτισις, of which the proper spelling, as shown by inscriptions and papyri, is τείσω, ἔτεισα, ἔκτεισις.

b. But before vowels it remained ē for some time after it had become ῑ elsewhere, and to distinguish it from ει = ῑ, was often written η, e.g., πολιτήαν, ἱερῆα, etc., especially in the Augustan period.

c. For Elean αι from ει after ρ, see **12**a.

29. ι from ει in Boeotian. The change in pronunciation which took place everywhere at a late period (**28**a) occurred very early in Boeotian, and here showed itself in the spelling, which in the fifth century varies between ει, Ⱶ (**4**.5), and ι, but later is regularly ι, e.g., Τⱶσιμένες = Τεισιμένης, ἐπί = ἐπεί, ἐπιδεί = ἐπειδή (cf. also **16**), ἔχι = ἔχει, χιμένας = κειμένας. For Arg. hῑ = εῑ, see **25**c.

οι

30. υ from οι in Boeotian. The diphthong οι was retained much longer than αι (**26**) or ει (**29**), appearing as οι, but also, in some of the earliest inscriptions especially of Tanagra, as οε, e.g. Χοερίλος, Ϝηεκαδάμοε. But in the third century it became a monophthong, probably similar to the German *ö*, to denote which, approximately, the υ, with its Attic value of *ü* as a basis, was employed with increasing frequency from about 250 B.C. on, though not uniformly until the end of the century, e.g., Ϝυκία = οἰκία, datᵉ sg. and nom. pl. -υ = -οι, dat. pl. -υς = -οις. Where οι is followed by a vowel, it is usually retained (in contrast to αι, **26**), as Βοιωτῦς, though Βυωτῶν occurs once.

In some late inscriptions of Lebadea and Chaeronea the spelling ει is also found, indicating the further progress of the sound to ῑ (see **28a**), e.g., αὐτεῖς = αὐτοῖς.

a. Late Cret. Ποίτιος (no. 120.24) = Πύτιος illustrates the confusion of οι and υ which later prevailed in the κοινή (hence, with still later change in sound to ι, their identity in Modern Greek).

αι, ει, οι before Vowels

31. In the case of αι, ει, οι, also υι, before vowels the omission of ι, consequent upon its consonantal pronunciation with the following vowel, is to be observed in various dialects, though the spelling is anything but constant, and it is impossible to make any general statement as to the conditions of the loss. Thus, as in Attic Ἀθηναία, later Ἀθηνάα, Ἀθηνᾶ, δωρεά beside earlier δωρειά, εὔνοα beside εὔνοια, ὑός beside υἱός, υἱύς, so, e.g., Ion. ἀτελέη beside ἀτελείη, ποιήσεαν = ποιήσειαν, Lesb. δικάως = δικαίως, εὔνοαν = εὔνοιαν, Thess. Γενναίοι = Γενναίου, Arc. στορπάος = ἀστραπαῖος, El. ἔα beside εἴε̄ = εἴη, μαστράα = *μαστρεία (**12a**), Cret. ἀγελάοι = ἀγελαῖοι, Delph. φαωτός = *φαιωτός (φαιός). So especially in forms of ποιέω, as Att. ποεῖ, ποέσω (but ποιῶν), Lesb. πόησαι, etc., Boeot. ἐπόεισε, Arc. ποέντω, El. ἐπιποέντων, Coan ναποᾶν beside ναποιάς. Contraction, as in Ἀθηνᾶ, in Lesb. Φώκαι = Φωκαίαι.

a. Owing to the variation in forms like the above, the diphthongal spelling sometimes appears in words where it has no etymological justification, as late ὀγδοίης, ὀγδοιήκοντα, βοιηθέω.

αυ, ευ, ου

32. In αυ, ευ,ου, the υ remained an *u*-sound, not becoming *ü* as it did in Attic when not part of a diphthong. This is shown not only by Ionic αο, εο (**33**), but by occasional varieties of spelling such as Corinth. 'Αχιλλεούς, Corcyr. ἀϜυτάν, Att. ἀϜυτάρ, Ion. ἀϜυτο͂, Cret. ἀμεϜύσασθαι, where Ϝ indicates the natural glide before the *u*-sound, and Locr. ΝαϜπακτίο͂ν, Cret. σποϜδδάν, etc.

33. αο, εο from αυ, ευ appear in East Ionic inscriptions (εο also in Amphipolis and Thasos) of the fourth century and later, e.g., αὸτός, ταὸτα, εὸνοια, εὸεργέτης, φεόγειν. This spelling is frequent even in κοινή inscriptions of this region.

a. Cretan inscriptions show several examples of ου beside usual ευ, as early 'Ελτυνιοῦσι, τιτοϜτός, τιτουϜέσθο͂ (from *τιτεύομαι 'impose a fine'), later ἐλούθερος, ἐπιτάδουμα, etc. For El. αυ from ευ after ρ, see **12a**. Sporadic cases of αυ = ευ elsewhere, as late Delph. ἐλαύθερος, ἱεραύς, βουλαυόντων, Arc. Αὐκλίεια (= Εὐκλέεια?), Ther. αὐνοίας, αὐεργέταν, Αὐήμερος, Pholeg. ψαυδῆ, late πέταυρον v.l. of πέτευρον (hence *petaurum* in Lucil., etc.).

34. ου became, in most dialects, a monophthong (first ǭ, later *ü*), though the spelling ου was generally retained and eventually extended in certain dialects to the secondary ō. In Corinthian this had taken place at the time of the earliest inscriptions. See **25d**.

a. Occasionally words which contain genuine ου are found with the spelling O in early inscriptions when O for secondary ō was usual, e.g., ὸκ = οὐκ, βο͂ν = βοῦν (or = βῶν? See **37**.1). In forms of οὗτος, which in general have genuine ου (e.g., Cret. τούτο͂ etc.), this spelling is so frequent in early Attic, e.g., το͂το, τόττόν (το͂το also in Thasos; cf. also Orop. ἐντο͂θα, i.e. ἐντοῦθη = ἐνταῦθα), as to point to some special cause. Possibly, as has been suggested, there existed beside the usual forms with genuine ου (e.g. τοῦτο from *το-υ-το), a gen. sg. τόττο͂ (τούτου,), formed by doubling of το͂ (τοῦ), which then influenced the other forms.

35. Certain words show a υ diphthong only, or mainly, in Lesbian. So αὔως = Dor. ἀϜώς (Arg. ποτ' ἀϜώ, Lac. ἀβώρ Hesych.), ἄως, Hom. ἠώς, Att. ἕως, from *αὐσώς (cf. Lat. *aurōra* from *ausōs-ā*); παραύα = Dor. παραά (implied by εὐπάρᾱος), Ion. παρηή (implied by καλλιπάρηος, παρήιον), Att. παρεά, from *παρ-αυσ-ᾱ (cf. Lat. *auris*); ναῦος = Dor. etc., νᾱ(Ϝ)ός (cf. Lac. ναϜόν),

Hom. νηός, Att. νεώς, probably from *νασϜός (54d); δεύω (also Thess., no. 33.27 and Hom.), from *δεύσω (?); αὐάδης (Sappho) = Att. ἀηδής, from *ἀ-σϜαδής. Cf. also Hom. εὖαδε from *ἔσϜαδε, and αὐερύω from *ἀϜϜερύω, *ἀν-Ϝερύω.

a. In such forms υ comes from a combination containing υ or Ϝ, not from simple intervocalic Ϝ, which in Lesbian, as elsewhere, regularly drops out without affecting the preceding vowel. Forms like αὐάτα (Alcaeus, Pindar) = ἀϜάτα (cf. 53), ε[ὔ]ιδε (Balbilla), etc. (several forms in glosses, presumably from the Lesbian poets; some also in Homer) are poetical only, and represent an artificial doubling or shift in syllabification, perhaps in imitation of cases like the above, coming from a combination. The consonant-doubling in hypocoristic proper names (89.5) accounts for the diphthong in Thess. Κλεύας, from *ΚλέϜας, Calymn. Κλεύαντος, Cret. Φαῦος, Νεύαντος.

36. In words with regular antevocalic ευ the natural glide between υ and the following vowel is often expressed by Ϝ, as Boeot. ΒακεύϜαι, Cypr. κατεσκεύϜασε, Lac. Εὐβάλκης (β = Ϝ, 51), Locr. ΕὔϜανδρος.

In late inscriptions υ is sometimes omitted, especially in derivatives of σκεῦος, as Att. παρεσκεασμένων, Lesb. ἐπισκεάσαντα, Corcyr. ἐπισκεάζειν, σκεοθήκας, Delph. κατασκεώσηται.

Long Diphthongs

37. 1. The original long diphthongs āi, āu, ēi, ēu, ōi, ōu, except when final, were regularly shortened in prehistoric times to ai, au, ei, eu, oi, ou, or, in some cases, lost the second element. Hence such by-forms as βοῦς from *βῶυς (cf. Skt. gāus), acc. βοῦν, but Arg., Epid., Cret., Syrac. βῶς, βῶν (cf. Lat. bōs, Skt. acc. sg. gām), Ζεύς from *Ζηύς (cf. Skt. dyāus) but acc. Ζῆν (cf. Lat. diēs), whence, with transfer to consonant declension, Ζῆνα, Ζηνός, etc., Cret. Δῆνα, Τῆνα (84).

2. The Greek long diphthongs may be original when final, but otherwise are of secondary origin. Most of the latter arose by loss of an intervening consonant, as κλᾶις, κληις, from *κλᾶϜίς (cf. Lat. clāvis), and in the earlier period these were not diphthongs but were pronounced in two syllables. So κληίς, χρηίζω, πολεμήιος, πατρώιος, etc., regularly in Homer, and often in the later Ionic poets. This pronunciation is also indicated by occasional

spellings such as Τήιοι, θωιήν, ίερήιια, χρηιίζω, in inscriptions.
On the other hand the change of ηι to ει (**39**) or the loss of the ι
(**38**) presupposes the diphthongal pronunciation; and where we
find, e.g., χρήζω, ίερῆον, and χρηιίζω, ίερηιον, side by side, the latter
must be understood as χρήιίζω, ίερῆιον. But in general it is impossible to determine just when the change from dissyllabic
to diphthongal pronunciation took place, and hence it is often
uncertain whether we should accent, e.g., κληίς (κληίς) or κλήις
(κλῆς), χρηίζω or χρήιζω, οίκήιος, οίκηίου or οίκῆιος, οίκήιου, and
editors of the same texts differ in their practice. We employ
the accentuation which goes with the earlier pronunciation,
though without the mark of diaeresis, for the early Ionic inscriptions; and likewise in general, simply as a matter of convention,
in citing forms of this kind in the grammar.

38. ᾱ, η, ω from ᾱι, ηι, ωι. In Attic the ι ceased to be pronounced in the second century B.C., and the spelling without ι (the
iota subscript is a medieval device; in inscriptions ι is written
like other letters or omitted entirely) became more and more
frequent, and may be found in late inscriptions from all parts
of Greece. But in some dialects this dates from an earlier period.

East Ionic has occasional examples of dat. sg. -η = -ηι from
the sixth century B.C. on, though -ηι is the usual spelling.

Lesbian has τō̄ Νικιαίōι in a fifth-century inscription (no. 24),
the earliest loss of ι in the article. No. 25 (first half fourth century) and no. 26 (324 B.C.) have uniformly dat. sg. -ᾱι, -ωι
(3 sg. subj. -ηι in no. 25, -η in no. 26), while no. 27 (319/7) has
3 sg. subj. -η, dat. sg. -ω, but -ᾱι, a difference observed in some
other texts (also, though anachronistic, in some texts of the
Lesbian poets; see pp. 342 f.). After the fourth century the forms
in ·ᾱ, -ω, -η predominate.

Thessalian has from the fifth century dat. sg. τᾰφροδίται τᾶ,
and ταγᾶ beside άταγίαι (in no. 35), and in inscriptions in the
Ionic alphabet we find regularly dat. sg. -ᾱ, -ου (=ω, **23**), 3 sg.
subj. -ει (= η, **16**).

Cyprian has dat. sg. -ᾱ, -ō̄, beside -ᾱι, -ōι, but in the Idalium
bronze (no. 23) only in the case of the article when followed
by ι, as τᾶ ι(ν).

a. The loss of ι probably began in the article, which was proclitic.

b. The fluctuation between the historical and the phonetic spelling in late inscriptions introduced confusion in the spelling of forms with original η, ω; hence such spellings as nom. sg. βουλῆι, gen. sg. τῶι δάμωι, imv. ἐχέτωι. Such imperative forms in -τωι and -σθωι, where this spelling was favored by the subj. in -ηι, are especially frequent.

39. ει from ηι. The history of ηι differs in some dialects from that of ᾱι, ωι,—especially in Attic, where it became ει (i.e., $\bar{e}$) some two centuries before ᾱι, ωι became ᾱ, ω.

In the case of ηι of secondary origin (**37.**2) the spelling ει is frequent in the fourth century and from about 300 B.C. is almost universal, e.g., κλείς from κληίς, λειστής from ληιστής, λειτουργέω from ληιτουργέω.

In inflectional endings ει is also frequent in the fourth century and predominates in the third and second, e.g., dat. sg. βουλεῖ, 3 sg. subj. εἴπει. But here, owing to the analogy of other forms with η of the same system, as βουλῆς, βουλήν, εἴπητε, ηι was never given up and eventually was fully restored, so that the normal spelling in imperial times was ηι or η (**38**).

The spelling ει beside ηι, partly at least due to Attic influence, is also frequent in third- and second-century inscriptions of other dialects, or even earlier as in the Heraclean Tables, where we find 3 sg. subj. νέμει, φέρει, etc. (so usually, but twice -ηι, once -η).

a. The change of ηι to ει is also Euboean, where it was accompanied by a change of ωι to οι. In Eretrian this was effected about 400 B.C. Somewhat later ει occurs beside ηι at Amphipolis, and οι beside ωι at Olynthus. Dat. sg. ει is found also in an inscription from Naples.

Non-Diphthongal Combinations of Vowels
(Contraction, Etc.)

40. Owing to the proethnic loss of intervocalic ι and σ, a large number of new vowel combinations arose, and these were subsequently augmented by the dialectal loss of intervocalic F (**53**). An exhaustive treatment of their history in the several dialects would require not merely that each of the numerous combinations should be considered by itself, but that further distinctions should be made according to the character of the consonant which was lost, that of the sound which preceded the combination, the accent, the number of syllables in the word, etc. See **45**. Only some of the most important facts can be stated here.

α or ᾱ + Vowel

41. 1. α + ε, ē (secondary ē), or η. Att.-Ionic ᾱ, but η in West Greek and Boeotian. Similarly ᾱι or ηι from α + ει, ηι. Examples are forms of verbs in -αω, as Att.-Ion. νικᾶι(αει), νικᾶτε (αε), νικᾶν (αε̣), etc., but η in West Greek and Boeotian, e.g., Cret., Arg. νικῆν, Lac. ἐνίκē, Rhod. θοινῆται, Meg. φοιτήτω, Corcyr. τιμῆν, Locr. συλε̄ν, Delph. συλῆν, Boeot. φυσῆτε (Ar.), etc.

a. For Lesbian, Thessalian, and Arcado-Cyprian direct evidence is lacking but η is probable in view of the η in crasis (**94**.6). Lesb. τίμαι, βόαι (gram.; βόα text of Sappho), Thess. ἐρουτᾶι, probably belong to the -ᾱω type (**159**)?

2. α + ο or ω. When contracted, the result is ω in all dialects. So regularly in forms of verbs in -αω, as Att. τιμῶ, τιμῶμεν, Meg. (Selinus) νικο̄μες, νικο̄ντι, Locr. συλο̄ντα, Boeot. σουλῶντες, Lac. hεβο̄ντι (subj.), ἐνhεβόhαις (ἠβώσαις from ἠβαώσαις), but also, rarely, uncontracted as Boeot. ἰαόντυς. Cf. also Heracl. τέτρωρον 'group of four boundary-stones' from *τετρα-ορον, παμῶχος (παμωχέω) from *παμα-οχος. αο from αϝο is uncontracted in Boeotian (as in Homer), but in most dialects yields ω, as φῶς from φάος (*φαϝος, cf. Hesych. φαυοφόρος), Boeot. Καλλιφάων, etc., 'Αγλω- from ἀγλαο- (*ἀγλαϝο-), Boeot. 'Αγλαόδωρος, etc. ('Αγλαο- also Thess., Coan, etc.), σῶς, σω-, Σω-, from σάϝος (cf. Cypr. Σαϝοκλέϝēς). Boeot. περίσαος, Σαυκράτεις, Σαυγένεις, etc. Arc., Σακρέτης, Σάδαμος, Σακλῆς (beside Σαοκλῆς), Σάανδρος, Boeot. Σαχράτης, etc., are to be read Σᾰ-, this from Σαο-, or parallel to Meg. Θέδωρος, etc. (**42**.5*f*)?

3. ᾱ + ε. Attic-Ionic η, elsewhere ᾱ. Att.-Ion. ἥλιος (Hom. ἠέλιος) from ᾱϝέλιος (Cret. gloss ἀβέλιος), ἀέλιος (Pind., etc., Arc.), Dor. ἅλιος, Lesb. ἄλιος.

4. ᾱ + ο or ω. Attic-Ionic εω or ω, elsewhere ᾱ or uncontracted. In Attic-Ionic first ηο, ηω (cf. **8**), often preserved in Homer, whence εω (with shortening of the first vowel, and, in the case of ηο, lengthening of the second; cf. **43**), which may be further contracted to ω (in Ionic mostly after vowels, cf. **45**.2;

in Attic not so restricted, but the conditions are complicated and not wholly clear). In the other dialects the uncontracted forms are most general in Boeotian.

Gen. sg. masc. ā-stems, Ion. -εω, -ω (also -ηο in no. 6), from -āο as in Homer (here Aeolic, beside Ion. -εω) and Boeotian (rare in Thessalian), Arc.-Cypr. -āυ (**22**), Lesb., Thess., West Greek -ā. Att.-Ion. ἕως (Hom. εἶος, i.e. ἦος) from *ἆϜος (Skt. *yāvat*), Lesb. ἆς, Boeot., West Greek ἆς (late Boeot. also hybrid ἇως).

Att.-Ion. λεώς, νεώς, ἕως (Hom. νηός, ἠώς), ληός (in Eub. 'Αγα-σιλέϜō) from λᾱϜός (seen in personal names of several dialects), νᾱϜός, ἆϜώς (but see **35**, **54***d*), in most dialects λᾱός, νᾱός, ἀώς but λᾱ-, νᾱ-, in compounds as Λᾱκρίνης, νᾱκόρος νᾱποῖαι, also -λᾱς frequent for -λᾱος, etc., in personal names, as the widespread 'Αρκεσίλας (Cyrene sixth century, etc.) beside the rare 'Αρκεσί-λαϜος (on an Apulian vase).

Gen. pl. ā-stems, Ion. -έων, -ῶν (also -ηōν in no. 6), Att. -ῶν, from -āων (*-*āsōm*, Skt. *-āsām*) as in Homer (Aeolic), Boeotian (but always τᾶν, see **45**.4), Thessalian (τᾶν κοινάουν, etc. at Crannon, but otherwise -ᾶν), Lesb. -ᾶν, Arc., West Greek -ᾶν. Att.-Ion. θεωρός, Lesb. θέᾱρος, West Greek θεᾱρός, beside uncontracted Arc. θεᾱορός, from *θεᾱ-Ϝορός (or-horós, cf. φρουρός from *προ-horós; both from -hϜορος). Boeot. θιαωρία could be from a parallel form with ω-grade in the second part, but more likely is a hybrid, influenced by Att. θεωρία.

Att. κοινών, ξυνών, Ion. ξυνεών (Hes. ξυνήονας) from *-āϜων, *-āϜονος, ξυνᾱονες Pindar, Arc., West Greek κοινᾶν. So Epid. κυκᾶν = κυκεών.

Att. Ποσειδῶν, Ion. Ποσειδέων, Hom. Ποσειδάων (-άωνος), Co-rinth. ΠοτΕδάϜονι, ΠοτΕδᾶνι, ΠοτΕδάν, Boeot. Ποτειδάονι, Cret., Rhod., Delph. Ποτειδάν (-ᾶνος), Lesb. Ποσείδᾱν, Arc. Ποσοιδᾶνος, Lac. Ποhοιδάν (-ᾶνι).

Arc. Πάονι beside Πᾶνός, Πᾶνί. Here the native Arcadian form was adopted in Attic-Ionic.

a. In Ionic, beside usual εω, there are some examples of εο or ευ (cf. **33**), as θεορός, θευρός (Paros, Thasos), gen. sg. -ευ (Erythrae, etc.).

b. In Ionic some of the older forms with unshortened η, as in Homer, are employed also by later writers, as νηός, etc. So ἠώς in Herodotus and in an inscription of Oropus (gen. sg. ἠ̄ος).

c. Homer has the non-Ion. λᾱός, which also displaced λεώς in the κοινή and Modern Greek. Similarly νᾱός instead of νεώς in the κοινή and Modern Greek.

d. In Thessalian there are some examples of ō, ου (from ω, **23**), where we expect ᾱ, as gen. pl. προξεννιοῦν, Γομφιτοῦν, θεουρός, Ποτείδουνι, hυλōρέοντος (cf. ὑληωρός, ὑλωρός). But the first four are probably κοινή forms with dialectal coloring (for such hybrids, see **280**), and hυλōρέοντος is from ὑλο- beside ὑλᾱ- (see **167**).

ε + Vowel

42.1. ε + α. Uncontracted εα in most dialects, contracted η in some. Acc. pl. neut. of σ-stems, Arc., Locr., Lac. Ϝέτεα, Boeot. Ϝέτια, Pamph. Ϝέτεια, Ion., Delph. ἔτεα, Cret. μέρεα, Lesb. μέλεα—Heracl. Ϝέτη (but δένδρεα), Att., Argol., Rhod. ἔτη, Coan μέρη, θύη, etc., also Ion. θύη (no. 8), σκέλη, etc. beside ἔτεα, etc. Acc. sg. masc. σ-stems, mostly εα, but η in Attic, also Rhod. λειόλη (no. 100, sixth century B.C.), Lac. Θιοκλε͞ (sixth century B.C.), Κλεογένε͞, Ion. ἐξώλη (but earlier ἀφανέα, no. 4.11), Troez. ἐπιαλε͞, Delph. ἐνδογενῆ, 'Αγαθοκλῆ, etc. Acc. pl. masc. fem. -εας, but Cyren. τριήρης. Cf. also Coan ἡὐτῶν = ἑαυτῶν. Att.-Ion. ἔαρ, gen. ἦρος, but ἦρ in Alcman, Delph. ἠρινός.

Even εα from εϝα, which is uncontracted in Attic, sometimes becomes η in West Greek, as Delph., Rhod., Coan, Cyren. ἐννῆ = ἐννέα, Ther. ἡμίση = ἡμίσεα, Κληγόρας = Κλεαγόρας, Rhod. 'Αγῆναξ = 'Αγεαναξ, Dor. κρῆς (Theocr., etc.) = κρέας, Sicil. (Acrae) φρήτιον = φρεάτιον (cf. φρητί Callim.). Dor. βλῆρ (Alcman) = Att. δέλεαρ (cf. dat. sg. δέλητι Hesych., δελήτιον Sophron).

2. ε + ᾱ. Personal names in -εας, as Τιμέας, Δημέας, usually remain uncontracted in Attic ('Ερμῆς is the Ionic form) and most dialects, though in late times partly replaced by -ᾱς, as Δημᾱς, Δαμᾱς. But -ῆς regularly in Ionic (from -έης), as Δημῆς, Απελλῆς, and sometimes elsewhere, as Rhod. 'Αριστῆς, Ther. Κυδρῆς, Θαρῆς (archaic). Cf. Rhod. Χαλκῆ from Χαλκέᾱ.

3. ε + ε. Regularly contracted to ε͞ (ει) or η (see **25**), as Att. τρεῖς, Ther. τρῆς, from *τρέϳες (Skt. *trayas*). But uncontracted forms also occur, as Cret. τρέες, δρομέες, Arg. γροφέες, Boeot. ϝικατιϝέτιες. See **45.**5.

4. ε + ει, ηι, or η. Regularly contracted to ει, ηι, η, as φιλεῖ, φιλῆι, φιλῆται. Uncontracted forms, like Locr. δοκέει, ἀνχōρέει,

λιποτελέει (but read -έει by some, as belonging to type -ηω, 159), Delph. ἀδικέη, ποιέη, Lesb. ἔη, Boeot. ἴει, δοκίει (9, 16), are rare. See 45.5. But forms like δέηι, δέηται (from εϝη, see 45.1) are usually uncontracted. Names in -κλέης occur in some dialects, though most have only -κλῆς. See 108.1a.

5. ε + o. The contraction to secondary ō (ου), as in γένους from *γενεσος,φιλοῦμεν from *φιλέιομεν (but πλέομεν, ἡδέος, etc., see 45.1), is Attic only. Most dialects have εο or ιο (9), as γένεος (-ιος), φιλέομεν (-ιομεν).

In Ionic εο often has the value of one syllable in poetry, and this diphthongal pronunciation came to be represented by ευ (cf. εο = original ευ, 33). This spelling, though found in our texts of earlier authors (sometimes even in Homer, as μευ, φιλεῦντας), does not appear in Ionic inscriptions until the fourth century B.C. But it occurs also in Rhodes, Cos, Thera, Cyrene, Megara, Delphi, Corcyra, etc., mostly late but an exceptionally early example is Corinth. Θευγένες of the sixth century B.C.

Also from ε + secondary ō (Att. ου) spelling εο or ευ, Coan κυεōσα, κυεῦσα, τελεῦσα, παρεῦσα.

a. Boeotian has some examples of ιυ, ιου, beside ιο (both original and from εο), but mostly after dentals, where it was supported by the prevalence of the spelling ιου = υ (24). Thus Νιουμείνιος and Νιυμείνιος, νιουμεινίη, Θιουτίμυ, Διουκλεῖς, but once also Βιούτη.

b. Change to εω in Cyren. ἐπαρεώμενοι, παρβεῶντας (with transfer from -αω to -εω type, 161.2), and (with ι from ε, 9.8, 9) Lac. ὁμιώμεθα, Heracl. ἐμετρίωμες, μετριώμεναι (before single consonant, vs. ιο in ἀναγγελίοντι, etc.). Cf. also Tarentine pron. gen. sg. (gram.) ἐμίω(ς), τίω(ς) = ἐμεο(ς), τεο(ς).

c. Contraction to ω in some towns of East and West Crete, mostly in open syllables, as ἐπαινῶμεν, εὐχαριστῶμες, ὠνωμένος, etc., but also παρακαλῶντι, διατηρῶντες. Likewise ἐξαιρῶντες in an inscription of Phaselis.

d. Change to o before ντ or final ν. East Cret. (especially Hierapytna; but some examples also in the west) κοσμόντες, κρατόντες, ἐπιορκόντι, ἐπεστάτον, etc., Arg. διατελόντι, κοινανόντι, ἐμφανιξόντας, δαμιοργόντōν, ἐπῶλον, (here also probably Heracl. fut. κοψοντι, etc., but disputed; see 141b), Delph. θεαρόντōν, ποιόντων (beside ποιέοντα in the same inscription), Heracl. ποιόντασσι, ἐξεποίον, Mess. ποιόντι, Chian ποιόντος. In these last examples, from ποιέω, the fact that a vowel preceded the original εο is a special factor, and the similar loss of ε is seen in other forms of the same verb, as Delph. ποιῶντι, ποιοῖ, El. ἐνποιōν, ἐνποιον (beside ἐξαγρέōν, ἐξαγρέοι in the same inscription), Troez. ποιōν.

e. Change to ε before ντ in Cyren. ἐκτιμασέντι (3 pl. Dor. fut.), δαμιερ-γέντων, Λέντιχος, τελεσφορέντες, etc. (thus showing that the old view of τελεσφορέντες as an unthematic form was mistaken).

f. Personal names compounded of θεός show forms in Θε- and Θο-. Though found elsewhere, these are most common in Megarian and nearly always with θε- before a simple consonant, Θο- before two, as Θέδωρος, Θέτιμος, but Θοκρίνης, Θοκλείδας. Cf. also Ion. Θόκλος, Κλόδεινος, ὁρτή = ἑορτή, νοσσιή, late Att. νοσσιά, νοσσίον, etc. for earlier νεοττία, etc.

g. More isolated is Arc. πλός from *πλέος = πλέον (**113**.2).

6. ε + ω or οι. In Attic regularly contracted, as φιλῶ, φιλοῖ, but πλέω, ἡδέων, etc., see **45**.1). In other dialects regularly uncontracted εω, εοι, or ιω, ιοι (**9**), but sometimes ω, οι, mostly after a vowel (see **45**.2). Ion. εἰδέωσιν but ποιῶσιν, ἀνωθεοίη but ποιοῖ, Lesb. ἀνατεθέωσι, Delph. ἐνκαλέοι, εὐδοκέωντι but ποιῶντι, Locr. ἔοντι, προξενέοι. El. ἐξαγρέον, δοκέοι but ποιόν, ἐνποιοῖ, ποιοῖτο (also ποιέοι), Heracl. ἀδικίων, ἐγϜηληθίωντι, but ποιῶν, ποιῶντι, Cret. ἐνθίωμεν, πόνιοι(φωνέοι), Arg. (early) δαμιοργοῖ, ἀφικνοῖτο.

η + Vowel

43. In the declension of nouns in -ευς the η of the stem is retained, as in Homer, in the Aeolic dialects, Arcado-Cyprian, and Elean, but shortened in most West Greek dialects and Attic-Ionic; in Attic this is accompanied by lengthening of the second vowel, if ο or α (βασιλέως, βασιλέᾱ). See **111**. This "quantitative metathesis" seen in Attic is in many other words Ionic also (as usually from ηο = ᾱο, **41**.4), e.g., ἵλεως (Herodas—Hdt. ἵλεως or ἵλεος?) from ἵληος (**49**.5), πόλεως (**109**.2), Mil. ἱερέως (**111**.5), also τέλεως (Herodas, and, borrowed from Ionic, in Coan) = Cret. τέληος, though the usual Ionic form is τέλειος, τέλεος.

Cret., Arc. χρῆος (Hom. χρεῖος), Att. χρέως and χρέος; χρέος in most dialects (for verbal forms, see **162**.13).

Cf. also the subjunctives with η retained in Hom. θήομεν (θείομεν), Boeot. κουρουθείει, etc., but shortened in most dialects, as Ion. θέωμεν (Att. θῶμεν), Cret. ἐνθίωμεν, etc. See **151**.2.

Contraction of ηα to η (but probably through εα, cf. **42**.1) is seen in Eub. 3 pl. εἰρῆται from *εἰρήαται (cf. Hom. βεβλήαται), εἰρέαται (Hdt.), and in βασιλῆ, etc. of Delphian and most Doric dialects (**111**.3).

o + Vowel

44. 1. o + α. When contracted, the result is ω in all dialects (cf. ω from α + o, **41**.2), e.g., Att. ἡδίω, Heracl. μείω from -ο(σ)α, Τιμῶναξ, Ἱππῶναξ, etc. in West as well as East Greek dialects, from -ο-(ϝ)αναξ (for Rhod. Τιμᾶναξ, see **167**). Cf. also ω in crasis, as Corinth. τώγαθόν = τὸ ἀγαθόν, etc. (**94**).

a. The older view that o + α gives Dor. ᾱ rests on a false derivation of Dor. πρᾶτος (see **114**.1a).

2. o + ᾱ.· Usually uncontracted (Att. οη), but in Ionic regularly ω, in other dialects sometimes ᾱ, e.g., Rhod. βοᾱθέω, Cret. βοᾱθίω, Aetol. βοᾱθοέω, Att. βοηθέω, but Ion. βωθέω, Lesb. βᾱθοέω, Att. βοηδρομιών, but Coan, Rhod. Βᾱδρόμιος, Att. dat. sg. ὀγδόηι, Coan, Rhod. ὀγδᾶι. For Ionic ω from οη, no matter whether η is from ᾱ or original η, cf. also ὀγδῶι (once) = ὀγδόηι, and ὀγδώκοντα from ὀγδοήκοντα (with original η), and Hdt. βῶσαι, νῶσαι, ἀλλογνώσας.

3. o + o. Regularly contracted ·to secondary ọ(ου) or ω (see **25**), as gen. sg. -ου or -ω from -οιο (**106**.1).

4. o + ε. When contracted, the result is the same as from o + o (3), e.g., Att. ἐλάττους (nom. pl., from -ο(σ)ες), but Lac. ἐλάσσως, Att. λουτρόν (Hom. λοετρόν), Arg., Heracl. λωτήριον, Cyren. λωσάμενος. So Heracl. πρώγγυος from *προέγγυος. Cf. also the crasis in Att. τοῦτος, Lesb. ὠνίαυτος, etc. (**94**.2). But we also find uncontracted οε, mainly from οϝε, and, before two consonants, sometimes o, e.g., Lesb. ὁμονόεντες, λοεσσάμενος, Μαλόεντι, Arc. Σινόεντι, Locr. Ὀπόεντι and in the same inscription Ὀποντίους, Meg. Σελινόεντι but Σελινόντιοι, Cret. Βολόεντα, Βολοεντίων, later Ὀλόντι, Ὀλοντίοις, all from -ο-ϝεντ- (**164**.2). For δαμιοργός, δαμιεργός, etc., see **167**.

45. Notes to **41-44**. Besides the so-called "hyphaeresis" in ε or o from εο (**42**.5d, e, f, g), o from οε (**44**.4), and ε from εε as in the widespread gen. sg. -κλέος in proper names, there are also scattered examples of o from οο. So late Cret. βοᾱθός, Att.-Ion. βοηθός (Hdt., Thuc.) beside -θοος (Hom.), as in several dialects βοᾱθέω instead of βοᾱθοέω. Arc. βουσός 'cattle-run' from *βουσόος like μᾱλοσόᾱ, μηλοσόη 'sheep-run' (Hesych.). Here apparently gen. sg. Cyren. λεχός, etc. (**111**.5a) from -οος. Some of the factors which help to account for divergence in the development of the same combination of vowels are the following.

1. A combination which arises by the loss of Ϝ, being of later origin than that arising from the loss of ι or σ, may remain uncontracted, or be contracted only later. So Att. πλέομεν, ἡδέος, ἡδέα, ἡδέων, in contrast to φιλοῦμεν, γένους, γένη, γενῶν, Locr. Ὀπόεντι, later Ὀποῦντι.

2. A combination which is otherwise uncontracted may be contracted after a vowel, Att. βασιλέως but ἁλιῶς, Ion. Μεγαβάτεω but Παναμύω (-ω sometimes after consonants also, but not usually), ἀνωθεοίη but ποιοῖ, El. δοκέοι but ποιοῖτο, etc. (see 42.6).

3. A combination which is otherwise contracted may remain uncontracted in dissyllabic words. Att. πέος, θεός, ζέω, and likewise, though belonging also under 1, Att. νέος and νεώς, λεώς, Dor. νᾱός, λᾱός. Such words may be contracted in compounds, as Att. Θούτιμος, νουμηνία, Dor. νᾱκόρος, Λᾱκρίνης, Ἀρκεσίλᾱς. Cf. also Meg. Θέδωρος, Θοκρίνης (42.5ƒ).

4. The article, as proclitic, is often the first form to show contraction. Cf. Boet. τᾶν μωσᾱ́ων, Thess. τᾶν κοινᾱ́ουν (Crannon; elsewhere -ᾶν in nouns also), Eub. τῶν δραχμέων.

5. The analogical influence of grammatically related forms in which the vowel, either of stem or ending, is not subject to contraction often counteracts the normal phonetic development. So Cret. τρέες, etc., with -ες after forms like πόδες, Ion. βασιλέος, etc. (not -εως), after ποδός etc., Locr. δοκέει, etc., after δοκέομεν etc.

6. A late contraction of ιο to ι is indicated by the frequent spelling ι or ει in Hellenistic times, e.g., in proper names Διονύσις, etc. = -ιος, nom.- acc. sg. neut. ἀργύριν, παιδείν, etc. = -ιον (hence modern παιδί, etc.). So late Lac. κασσηρατόριν beside -τοριον, likewise (for ιο from εο) Σίδαμος = Θεόδαμος, acc. sg. θίν = θεόν, gen. sg. Καλλικράτις, Ἀριστοτέληρ.

Assimilation and Dissimilation of Vowels

46. 1. The assimilation of vowels is comparatively rare in Greek, and not characteristic of any particular dialect. Here may be mentioned Ὀρχομενός from Ἐρχομενός, the regular native form of the name of both the Boeotian and the Arcadian town, Τροφώνιος from Τρεφώνιος, name of the Boeotian local hero, Chian 'Ερμώνοσσα = -ασσα, Thess. Ϝεκέδαμος = Boeot. Ϝhεκάδαμος, Delph. Φανατεύς beside Φανοτεύς. Cyren. βάβᾱλος = usual Dor. βέβᾱλος, Att. βέβηλος, late Cret. θαραπεύσαντες, 'Απταραῖος, etc. For examples of ι and υ, see **20**. For Boeot. τρέπεδδα, see **18**. For Ποσοιδάν, 'Απόλλων, ὀβολός, in which assimilation is a possible but not necessary assumption, see **49**.1, 3.

2. Prehistoric dissimilation of Ϝευ- to Ϝει- in εἶπον, ἔϝειπον (cf. Cret. Ϝεῖπαι) from *εϝευπον (= Skt. *avocam*) and probably (though disputed) in ἀ(Ϝ)είδω. Dissimilation of -αια to -εια is generally assumed for Mess. αὐλεία = αὐλαία, Heracl. προτερεία = Att. προτεραία (ἡμέρα), Att. 'Ρήνεια beside 'Ρηναιεύς, Thess. Μελίτεια beside Μελιταιεύς, Arc. Αὐκλίεια (if = *Εὐκλέεια). But possibly these are cases of suffix-interchange rather than phonetic change.

Epenthetic Vowels

47. Lesb. γέλαιμι, etc. quoted by grammarians, are of doubtful authenticity. (3 sg. φαῖσι, Sappho, may be due to 3 pl. φαῖσι, **77**.3). For epenthesis in the case of original νι, ρι, λι, see **74**a, b.

Anaptyctic Vowels

48. ἕβδομος and ἔβδεμος (**114**.7) from *ἔβδμο-, *ἔπτμο-. Other examples are of only exceptional occurrence, as Att. 'Ερεμῆς = 'Ερμῆς, El. Σαλαμόνᾱ = Σαλμώνη, Thess. 'Ασκαλαπιός = 'Ασκλαπιός, Delph. Τολοφώνιος = Τολφώνιος. The widely attested πέλεθρον = πλέθρον (Cret., Delph., Thess., etc., as in Homer) is perhaps an inherited by-form.

Vowel-Gradation

49. In the system of inherited vowel-gradation (or "ablaut," to use the widely adopted German term) the dialects generally agree in the grade shown by corresponding forms, e.g., λείπω, λέλοιπα, ἔλιπον, in all dialects alike. But there are some examples of dialectal differences, of which the following may be mentioned.[2]

---

[2] Some cases where the variation is quite possibly not inherited, but which fall into the same system, are included for convenience.

1. Series, ει, οι, ι (λείπω, λέλοιπα, ἔλιπον). Cret. δίκνυμι (προδίκνυτι) = Att. δείκνυμι (cf. δίκη, etc.). Ion. δέκνυμι is perhaps due to a blend of δεικ- and δικ-. Lesb. ὀείγω (*ὀϜειγ-) = Att. οἴγω (*ὀϜιγ-). ἤνεικα and ἤνικα in various dialects (144a). Ποσειδῶν, Ποτειδάν, etc. (41.4) with ει (Ποτιδάν very rare), but usually ι in derivatives, as Att. Ποσίδειος, Ion. Ποσιδήιος, Carpath. Ποτίδαιον (but the famous Potidaea was Ποτείδαια), also οι (assimilation?) in Arc. Ποσοιδᾶν, Lac. Ποhοιδάν, Ποhοίδαια, and Π]οτοιδᾶνι of uncertain dialect (Schwyzer 642).

2. Series ερ, ορ, αρ or ρα (δέρκομαι, δέδορκα, ἔδρακον). τέσσερες, τέτορες, τέτταρες, etc. (114.4). Ion. (Hdt.), Lesb., Cret., Mess., Epid., Coan, Cyren., El. ἔρσην, but Ion. (Miletus, Thasos) ἄρσην (also in the κοινή and hence in late Arcadian, Theran), Lac. ἄρσης, Att. ἄρρην, Arc. ἀρρέντερος, etc. (80). θέρσος = θάρσος in Aeolic (gram.; Lesb. θέρσεισ' in Theocritus), and in proper names most frequently in Lesbian, Thessalian, Boeotian, and Arcadian, as Lesb. Θέρσιππος, Thess. Θερσίτας, Θέρσουν, Boeot. Θερσάνδριχος, Arc. Θερσίας, etc. κρέτος = κράτος in Lesbian (poet.), and in proper names also frequent in Arcado-Cyprian, as Τιμοκρέτης, Σωκρέτης, etc. Ion. κρέσσων (in κρείσσων, κρείττων, the ει is not original), but Cret. κάρτων (cf. καρτερός, κρατερός), Cret. τράπω = τρέπω, as sometimes in Herodotus, Cret., Meg. τράφω = τρέφω, as in Pindar, etc., Delph. ἀποστράψαι = ἀποστρέψαι. East Ionic ἄγερσις 'assembly' (ἀγείρω, ἀγορά), West Ion. ἄγαρρις (Naples), Arc. πανάγορσις (see 5) = πανήγυρις (with obscure υ). Beside usual γράφω, etc., also (like -τροφος beside τρέφω, τράφω) Mel. γρόπhōν, γρόφων 'carving,' Arg., Mycen., Epid., Sicyon., Cyren., El. γροφεύς, in Argolis also γροφά, γροφίς, γροφεύω, ἀγγροφά, ἐγγροφά, σύγγροφος (the last also Delph.), Heracl. ἀνεπίγροφος, Cret. ἀντίγροφον, ἔγγροφος. Here probably Delph. σταρέστω, from aor. of στέρομαι (rather than pres. with α from ε).

a. The weak grade varies between αρ and ρα, as in Hom. κράτος and κάρτος, κρατερός and καρτερός, etc. So Cret. κάρτος, καρταῖπος, καρτερός, κάρτων, likewise σταρτός = στρατός, Arc., Cypr., Boeot., Corcyr., El. δαρχμά, Cret. δαρκνά = δραχμή, Epid. φάρχμα, φάρξις = φράγμα, *φράξις, Boeot. πέτρατος (Hom. τέτρατος) = τέταρτος, Lesb. ἀμβρ[ό]τμην (5) = ἁμαρτεῖν. This variation is in part due to transposition, and clearly so in Cretan, which has αρ uniformly, as it also has πορτί = προτί. See **70.1.**

3. Series ελ, ολ, αλ or λα (στέλλω, στόλος, ἐστάλην), Arc. δέλλω = βάλλω (cf. βέλος, etc.). West Greek and Arc. ὀδελός, Boeot. ὀβελός (rarely early Attic), Thess. ὀβελλός (89.4)=ὀβολός (assimilation ?). West Greek δείλομαι, δήλομαι, Boeot. βείλομαι, Thess. βέλλομαι, all from a grade in ελ, = βούλομαι (see 75). Cypr. δάλτος = δέλτος (but this is a Semitic loanword). Coan ἔτελον, Lesb. ἔταλον 'yearling' (cf. Lat. vitulus). Cret., Lac., Mess., Corinth., Pamph. 'Απέλλων, Cypr. 'Απείλōν (cf. 74b) = Att.-Ion., Delph., Locr., Cyren., 'Απόλλων (also Lac., Corinth. beside 'Απέλλων), Thess. "Απλουν (with weak grade πλ). Coan, Calymn. Δολφοί = Δελφοί (cf. δολφός = δελφύς Hesych.). Epid., Cret. καταλοβεύς 'support' = *καταλαβεύς. Cret. ἀβλοπής (Hesych.), ἀβλοπία = ἀβλαβής, etc.

4. Series εν (εμ), ον (ομ), α or αν (αμ) (τείνω from *τενϳω, τόνος, τατός), Ion., Dor. τάμνω = Att. τέμνω (εμ from ἔτεμον). For Ϝίκατι = εἴκοσι, etc., see 116a. For participles with ατ beside εντ and οντ, as ἔασσα, ἴαττα = οὖσα, and ἔντες = ὄντες, see 163.8.

5. Series η, ω, α (ῥήγνυμι, ἔρρωγα, ἐρράγην), ἵηος (Lac. hίλεϜος), whence Att.-Ion. ἵλεως, Cret. ἵλεος, but Arc. ἵλαος like Hom. ἵλαος, Ion. γλάσσα = γλῶσσα. For Heracl. ἐρρηγεῖα = ἐρρωγυῖα, Dor. ἔωκα = εἶκα, see 146.3.

CONSONANTS

Ϝ

50. In Attic-Ionic the Ϝ was lost at a very early period. In East Ionic there is no trace of it even in the earliest inscriptions; it is very rare in Central and West Ionic; and in Attic the only evidence of its existence is its occasional use to express the glide sound before υ, as ἀϜυτάρ (32). In Thera, too, it is absent from the earliest inscriptions; likewise at Rhodes, Cos, etc., though here early material is scanty. In Lesbian it was already on the wane in the time of Alcaeus and Sappho, and is not found in inscriptions, of which, however, none of any extent is earlier than the fourth century.

But in most dialects it is of frequent occurrence initially, where it survives till the fourth century, and in some much later (especially as β; see 51). Between vowels it occurs in the earliest inscriptions of many dialects, after consonants in several, and before consonants in a very few.

a. In some cases the disappearance of Ϝ from inscriptions is due to κοινή influence rather than to an organic loss of the sound within the dialect. So evidently in Laconian, as shown not only by its reappearance in the spelling β (**51**), but by its survival in some words in Tsakonian, the modern representative of Laconian, e.g., βάννε (*vanne*) 'lamb' (Ϝαρν-).

b. Even where there is no reason to doubt the actual loss of the sound, the spelling, as is natural in such cases, only gradually adapted itself to the pronunciation, and often there is an interval of considerable length in which the older spelling with Ϝ and the later spelling without Ϝ occur promiscuously, even in the same inscription. In the Heraclean Tables the presence or omission of initial Ϝ is constant for certain words, e.g., always Ϝ in Ϝέξ, Ϝίκατι and derivatives, also Ϝέτος, Ϝίδιος, ἐγϜηληθίωντι, but οἶκος, ἐργάζομαι, ἕκαστος, ἴσος and ἥσος, etc.

51. β for Ϝ. Ϝ is represented by β, which we must understand in its later value of a spirant (Eng. *v*), in numerous glosses and in the later inscriptions of several dialects. So frequently in Laconian from the fourth century B.C. to the second century A.D., e.g. βίδεοι, βίδυοι, title of officials (Ϝιδ-), Βωρθέα, Βωρσέα beside Ϝωρθέα (cf. nos. 75-78) = ᾿Ορθία, προβειπάhας = προϜειπάσας, διαβέτης = διαϜέτης, ὠβά from *ὠϜά (cf. Hesych. ὥας· τὰς κώμας, ὠγή· κώμη, and οὐαί· φυλαί), etc.; and in Cretan, e.g. Βόρθιος, Βολόεντα, βέρδηι, βεκάτεροι, διαβειπάμενος, ὑπόβοικοι, etc. Cf. also Arg. Βορθαγόρας, Πυρβαλίων = older ΠυρϜαλίōν, Corcyr. ὄρβος = earlier ὄρϜος, El. βοικίαρ = Ϝοικίας (no. 66, in the stereotyped phrase γᾶρ καὶ βοικίαρ, otherwise Ϝ lost). For initial βρ = Ϝρ, see **55**.

a. Conversely, Ϝ is used in place of β in ἀμοιϜά = ἀμοιβά of an early Corinthian inscription. The name of the Cretan town Ϝάξος was sometimes represented by Ὄαξος, as Lat. *Nerva* by Νέροα. Cf. κοάξ of the quacking of frogs. Ϝ is also represented by υ in Cret. ὑέργων once = Ϝέργων, as conversely Ϝ for υ (**52c**). In the lexicographers Ϝ is represented by β, or from graphic confusion by γ (likeness of Γ and Ϝ), and other letters.

b. Pamphylian has Ϝ in some words (Ϝέτια, etc.), but in others a sign Ͱ (e.g. Ͱοικυπολίς = *οἰκοπολίς), which is used also for β (e.g., ἐφιεͰόται), and for υ in the αυ, ευ diphthongs (e.g., ἀͰταῖσι) and the glide (e.g., Σελύͱιυς). A similar sign occurs in the Cretan towns of Eleutherna and Vaxus with the value of Ϝ, and at Selinus and Melos for β. It presumably represented a fricative pronunciation like that of English *v* and so is best transcribed as *v* (*w* in German publications). Also once φίκατι = Ϝίκατι.

52. Ϝ initially before a vowel. Examples are numerous in inscriptions of most dialects, e.g., Ϝέτος (cf. Lat. *vetus*), Ϝοῖκος (cf. Lat. *vīcus*), Fίχατι (cf. Lat. *vīgintī*), Fάναξ, Fαρήν, Fαστός, Fέπος, Fειπ-, Fέργον, Fέρρω, Fίδιος, Fίσος, Fοῖνος, and many others, especially in proper names.

a. In several dialects which otherwise preserve F it is lost before o and ω (but not before οι), as in Homer, e.g., in Gortynian forms of ὠνή, ὠθέω, etc., without F beside Fίχατι, Fέκαστος, Fοικεύς, etc. (Fόν, Fōν by analogy of Fά, Fίν, etc.). But the precise dialectal scope of this phenomenon is not yet determined, and Fo is by no means unknown, e.g., Arc. Fōφλεκόσι (no. 17, fifth century; in no. 18, fourth century, ὀφλέν beside Fαστόν, Fέκαστον, etc.), Fορθασία, Cret. Βόρθιος, Lac. Βωρθέα, etc. (see 51).

b. Initial σF yields hF, occasionally written Fh (cf. Eng. *which*) but usually simply F, which, however, was pronounced as hF (or a voiceless F), as shown by the fact that after the loss of F such words have the spiritus asper. Thus Pamph. Fhέ = ἕ (cf. Cypr. Fοι, etc.), Boeot. Fhεκα-δάμοε, Thess. Fεκέ-δαμος, Cret., Locr. Delph., El., Arc. Fέκαστος, later ἕκαστος, Arg. Fhεδιέστας = ἰδιώτης (cf. Arg. hίδιος = ἴδιος). In some dialects this F was lost earlier than F in general, e.g., in Boeotian, where ἕξ (from Fέξ, i.e., Fhέξ, from *sweks) and ἕκαστος are frequent in inscriptions which otherwise have initial F, as Fιχαστῆ κὴ ἕκτη (no. 43.8).

c. The unique Fhιός = υἱός (no. 97) represents a dissyllabic pronunciation tion of the word, with Fh = hF as usual (above) and F for consonantal *u*, as in Arg. Faκίνθια = Ὑακίνθια (no. 85.17) and Cret. Faκίνθιος name of a month.

d. There are also some words with initial F and ' in their later forms for which there is no trace of an initial s in cognates (a hypothetical initial "laryngeal" is now assumed by some), e.g., Att. ἴστωρ, ἱστορία (cf. Boeot. Fίστωρ, from Fιδ-, Lat. *vid*-), ἕννυμι, εἶμα (cf. Cret. Fῆμα, Lat. *ves-tis*), ἕσπερος (cf. Locr. Fεσπάριος, Lat. *vesper*), ἑκών (cf. Locr. FεϞόντας, Skt. *vac*-), ἁλίσκομαι (cf. Thess. Fαλίσκεται, Goth. *wilwan*).

53. Intervocalic F. This was lost sooner than initial F, hence is found in fewer dialects, and in most of these only in the earliest inscriptions. Often we find forms with and without F from the same period or the same inscription, showing that it was either weakly sounded or wholly lost in pronunciation and retained only in the spelling. This inconstancy is much greater than in the case of initial F. The spelling with F often persists in proper names, and sometimes in certain conventional or solemn expressions, longer than elsewhere.

Examples are most frequent in Cyprian, where it appears almost uniformly except in some later inscriptions, e.g., αἰFεί, οἶFος, ῥόFος, δοFέναι, βασιλέFος, etc. (but always παῖς, παιδός, with loss of F). Eub. ἈγασιλέFō with F in the proper name

beside ἐποίεσεν (no. 9). Thess. ΔάϜον, but otherwise lost, as in
ἔσοσε (no. 35). Boeot. ΠτōιἔϜι, ἐποίϜεσε, χαρίϜετταν, ΚαρυκεϜίō,
γαϜεργείσει, also late διϜύκισις, τραγαϜυδία, τραγαϜυδός, κωμαϜυδός,
etc. (these last probably archaistic). Phoc. κλέϜος, αἰϜεί, Delph.
ΛαϜόσοϜος, Ach. ʼΑρχεσίλαϜος. Locr. καταιϜεί (also ἐπίϜοικος,
μεταϜοικέοι, ϜεϜαδἔκότα, but see a) beside παῖς, ʼΟπόεντι, δαμιορ-
γούς. El. [πο]ιϜέοι once (also ἀποϜἔλέοι, but see a), but usually
ποιέοι, even in the same inscription, βασιλᾶες, etc. Lac. hιλέϜōι,
ναϜόν, ΓαιαϜόχō (cf. Cypr., Pamph. Ϝέχω, Lat. *vehō*), ἀϜάταται
(cf. Lesb. αὐάτα, El. ἀνάατορ, elsewhere contracted as in Att.-Ion.
ἄτη, Cret. ἄτα, ἄπατος, etc.), late ὠβά (**51**). Arg. ΔιϜός, ὄϜινς,
ποιϜέματα, ἐϜεργάσατο. Corinth. ΠοτΕδάϜονι beside ΠοτΕδᾶνι,
ΑἴϜας, ΛαϜοπτόλεμος, etc. Corcyr. ϸhοϜαῖσι, στονόϜεσαν, etc.
There are no examples of intervocalic Ϝ in even the earliest
Cretan (cf. αἰεί, ναός, Ϝοικέος, etc.) except for the gloss ἀβέλιος
(Cret. in Hesych.) and in compounds or augmented forms (*a*);
nor in Arcadian (cf. ἐποίες, ἵλαος, Παδόεσσα vs. init. Ϝ, ρϜ, Ϝρ),
except ἄ]Ϝεθλα(?) in an archaic inscription.

a. Even where intervocalic Ϝ is regularly lost, it may appear in compounds or in augmented or reduplicated forms, owing to the influence of
the simplex or of the forms without augment or reduplication, where Ϝ
has survived as initial, e.g., Cret. προϜειπάτō, ἔραδε, and late διαβειπάμενος.
Hence such forms are not necessarily evidence of the survival of true
intervocalic Ϝ.

b. Ϝ is often used to indicate the natural glide before or after υ. So
before or after the υ of diphthongs, as already noted (**32, 36**), and Chalcid.
δύϜο, Eretr., Aetol. δύϜε, Sicyon. ΣεϟυϜόνιιος, Pamphyl. Σελύνιιυς.

54. Postconsonantal Ϝ. The combinations νϜ, ρϜ, λϜ, and
(secondary) σϜ are preserved in the earliest inscriptions of some
dialects. The loss of Ϝ was accompanied by lengthening of the
preceding vowel in East Ionic, Central Ionic (in part; see *a*),
Doric of Argolis, Crete, Thera, Cos, Rhodes and colonies, while
in other dialects, as in Attic, the vowel was not affected.

Corinth. ΞένϜον, Corcyr.	Ion. ξεῖνος, Cret. πρό-	Att., etc. ξένος,
πρόξενϜος, El. Ξεν-	ξηνος, Cyren. Φιλό-	πρόξενος
Ϝάρεορ	ξηνος, Rhod. Ξην-,	
	Ξειν-	

*ἐνϜατος	Ion. εἴνατος, Arg., Cyren., Cret. ἤνατος	ἔνατος
*ἐνϜεχα, *μόνϜος	Ion. εἴνεχα, μοῦνος	ἔνεχα, μόνος
Arc., Corinth. κόρϜα	Ion. κούρη, Cret. κώρα	κόρα (κόρη)
Corcyr. ὅρϜος, Arc. εὐθυορϜία	Ion. οὖρος, Arg., Cret. ὦρος, Ther. οὖρος	ὅρος
Arc. κάταρϜος	Ion. ἀρή	ἀρά
Boeot. καλϜός	Ion. κᾱλός	καλός
*ὅλϜος	Ion. οὖλος	ὅλος
Boeot., Arc., Cret., Sicyon. ϜίσϜος	Ion. ἴσος	ἴσος
Arc. δέρϜα	Ion. δειρή	δέρα (δέρη)
*ὀδϜός	Ion. οὐδός, Cyren. ὠδός	ὀδός

a. To the lengthening in East Ionic there are possibly some local exceptions, but, in general, forms like ξένος, and especially πρόξενος, are due to Attic influence. Similarly in Rhodian, etc., where ξεῖνος has survived only in proper names, and in late Cretan where πρόξενος is far more common than πρόξηνος. In Central Ionic the lengthening is attested for Paros and Thasos, but it is uncertain how far west this extended. From many of the islands, both Ionic and Doric, decisive material is lacking.

b. Lesb. ξέννος, ἔννεχα, in grammarians and late inscriptions (ἔννεχα also codd. Alcaeus, Theocr.), are probably hyper-Aeolic, due to the frequency of νν from νι, σν, etc. (74, 76, 77.1). Cf. also ἰσσοθέοισι in an inscription of A.D. 2-14. For Thess. προξεννιοῦν see 19.3.

c. In Arcadian there is fluctuation in the same inscription, e.g., no. 18 κάταρϜος but ξένος, no. 20 δέρϜα, εὐθυορϜία, but ὅριον, ὥρισαν, δίωρος (this last with ω by composition lengthening, 167a).

d. In Cretan the Ϝ of σϜ survives longer than that of νϜ, etc. So in the Law-Code ϜίσϜόμοιρον beside κσενίō and καλōς. This is a secondary σϜ (ϜίσϜος probably from *ϜιτσϜος cognate with εἶδος 'form'). The development of original σϜ, somewhat similar to that of σλ, etc. (76), is seen in Lesb. ναῦος, Dor. νᾱ(Ϝ)ός, Ion. νηός, probably from *νασϜός, also ἰός 'arrow' from *ισϜός (cf. Skt. iṣu- 'arrow').

e. Different from ὅρϜος, etc., is Corinth. ΠύρϜος (cf. Argol. ΠυρϜίας, ΠυρϜαλίōν), probably for *ΠύρρϜος (from *ΠυρσϜος with assimilation of ρσ before Ϝ), whence the Πύρρος of most dialects.

f. Preservation of Ϝ after a stop is rare. There are a few examples of δϜ in archaic inscriptions, as Corinth. ΔϜενίᾱ = Δεινίου (cf. the indirect evidence of Hom. ἔδδεισεν, etc.), Aetol. ΧελιδϜόν (IG IX².i.86.1). But τϜ was changed in prehistoric times, becoming σσ or ττ (see 81). Likewise κϜ (IE k̂w), becoming ππ, as in ἵππος (Skt. açvas).

55. Ϝ before consonants. Corresponding to Att. ῥήτρα, ἐρρήθην,

etc. (from Ϝρη- beside Ϝερ- in ἐρέω, cf. Lat. *verbum*), we have
El. Ϝράτρα (15), Cypr. Ϝρέτα (70.3) with its denominative Ϝρētάω
(ἐϜρētάσατυ, also spelled εὐϜρētάσατυ, indicating an anticipation of the Ϝ. Cf. *a* and 35. So also χενευϜόν from χενεϜόν),
Arg. ϜεϜρēμένα, ἀϜρέτευε, later ἀρήτευε 'was spokesman,
presided,' Arc. Ϝρῆσις. El. ἀϜλανέος 'wholly' (cf. Hesych. ἀλανέως·
ὁλοσχερῶς, also ἀλλανής· ἀσφαλής and ἀλανές· ἀληθές), is from
ἀ-Ϝλα-, and related to ἀελλής (ἀ-Ϝελ-), ἀολλής (ἀ-Ϝαλ- with
Aeolic ο, cf. 5), ἅλής, Dor., Delph. ἁλία 'assembly,' Ion. (Hdt.)
ἁλίη (also from ἀϜαλ-, with Ion. ᾱ from αϜα as in ἄτη, ἀναλίσκω),
Cleon. Ϝρέξαντα (= Att. ρέξαντα, ἔρξαντα, cf. Cret. Ϝέρχσαι,
etc.).

Ϝρ appears as βρ, indicating a pronunciation *vr*, in Lesbian
words quoted by grammarians and in our texts of the Lesbian
poets (βρήτωρ, βρόδον, etc.), though this has become simply ρ
at the time of our earliest inscriptions. Cf. also Boeot. Βρανίδας
beside Ϝάρνων.

In most dialects Ϝ was lost before the time of our earliest
inscriptions, and we find, as in Attic, ῥ, medial ρρ or ρ. See *a*.

a. In the case of medial Ϝρ, the Ϝ unites with the preceding vowel to
form a diphthong in Lesb. εὐράγη, αὕρηκτος (Herodian) from *ἐ-Ϝράγη,
*α-Ϝρηκτος (Att. ἐρράγη, ἄρρηκτος), Hom. ταλαύρινος, καλαῦροψ, ἀπούρας,
from *ταλά-Ϝρινος, etc. But generally the syllabification of the simplex
(or form without augment or reduplication) was retained (i.e., Ϝρ with the
following vowel), and later this Ϝρ became ρρ or sometimes ρ, e.g., Arg.
ϜεϜρέμένα, ἀϜρέτευε, later ἀρήτευε. In Attic and most dialects augmented
and reduplicated forms have ρρ, as Att. ἐρρήθην (εἴρηκα is formed after the
analogy of forms like εἴληφα, 76), ἐρράγην, ἔρρωγα, Heracl. ἔρρηγα, while
compounds also usually have ρρ but sometimes ρ under the continued
influence of the simplex, as Att. ἀναρρηθείς but also ἀναρηθείς, Delph.
hεμιρρήνιον (from *ἡμί-Ϝρην, like ἡμί-ονος, cf. Hom. πολύ-ρρην). Cf. ρρ
and ρ from σρ, 76. For medial Ϝλ, cf. El. ἀϜλανέος (above), but diphthongization in αὔλαξ (from *ἀϜλακ- beside *ἀϜολκ-, *ἀϜλοκ- in Hom. ὦλξ,
Att. ἄλοξ), Dor. αὔληρα (Epich.; ἄβληρα Hesych.).

b. The much discussed Arg. ἀϜρέτευε, ἀρήτευε is best taken as from a
compound of ἀν- = ἀνα- (perhaps first in an agent noun *αν-Ϝρέτας)
with assimilation of νϜ and further simplification, as in Arc. συϜοικία =
συνοικία (see 96.5). Cf. also Hom. αὐερύω from *αϜϜερύω, *αν-Ϝερύω.
The view that α stands for the augment (no present forms occur) cannot
be made plausible by reference to the cases of αυ = ευ, which are all
only sporadic spellings and none of them Argive (33α), whereas in this

word the α is constant (examples, including the abbreviations ἀρ, α,
very numerous) vs. the regular ἑ in ἐϜεργάσατο, etc.

Consonantal ι (ι̯)

56. Original consonantal ι (IE *y* with the value of *y* in Eng.
yet; for Greek we use the symbol ι̯) almost wholly disappeared
from Greek in prehistoric times, giving ʻ or, rarely, ζ initially,
as in ὅς (Skt. *yas*), ἧπαρ (Lat. *iecur*), ζυγόν (Skt. *yugam*), etc.,
yielding various results in combinations with a preceding consonant (**74, 81, 82, 84**), and being dropped between vowels,
as in τρεῖς from *τρέι̯ες (Skt. *trayas*), etc. But between ι and a
following vowel, as in ἵππιος, it always existed as a natural
glide in pronunciation, and in a few dialects this is expressed
in the spelling. So, by the repetition of ι, in Pamphylian, as διά,
ηιαροῖσι, etc., frequently in early Argive as Πολιιάδι, Σικελίιας,
θιιοῖν, δαμιιοργοῖ, and occasionally elsewhere, as Ion. (Priene)
Διιοφάνης, Sicyon. ΣεϘυϜόνιιος. Cf. also Ion. Τήιιοι, etc. (**37**.2),
Arg. ʼΑθαναίιας, Καρνείιας, ʼΕράτυιιος. In Cyprian a special
character, which we transcribe *j*, is generally employed, though
not uniformly, as in the Idalium bronze (no. 23) regularly before α,
but not before ε or ο, e.g. ἰjατῆραν but ἱερεϜίjαν, Ϝέπιjα but θιόν.

The Spiritus Asper. Psilosis

57. The spiritus asper generally represents an IE initial *s*
(**59**) or *y* (**56**), but in some words is of secondary, and sometimes
obscure, origin, e.g., ἵππος (cf. Lat. *equus*; ἵππος regularly as the
second part of compounds, ῎Αλκιππος, ῎Αντιππος, etc., rarely
῎Ανθιππος), ἡμεῖς, ἁμές (cf. Skt. *asmān*) with ʻ after the analogy
of ὑμεῖς (with ʻ from *y*). The sound was denoted by н (earlier в)
until the introduction of the Ionic η = η, after which it was
generally left undesignated. [3] But see **4**.7.

---

[3] In quoting forms from inscriptions, wherever the sign for the spiritus
asper appears in the original it is transcribed *h*, to be distinguished from ʻ,
which is supplied as a purely diacritical sign, like accent marks, and the
employment of which is, in many special cases, of doubtful propriety.
That is, the evidence is often insufficient to determine whether the omission of the sign of the asper is merely graphic, in which case we should
transcribe the form with ʻ, or due to an actual loss of the sound, in which
case we should transcribe with ʼ. As a working rule we employ the lenis

Psilosis, or the loss of the spiritus asper, is characteristic of East Ionic (whence the sign was left free for use as η; see **4**.6), Lesbian, Elean, Cyprian, and Cretan.

a. Psilosis is shown, not only by the absence of Η = *h*, but by the presence of phrases and compounds in which a preceding stop is not changed to the aspirate, e.g., East Ion. ἀπ' ἑκάστου, ἀπ' οὗ, κατάπερ, El. κατιστάιε̄, Cret. κατιστάμεν But psilosis is no bar to the retention of aspirated stops in phrases and compounds which were formed prior to the loss of the asper. For they would be affected, if at all, only by the analogical influence of the simplex, as Cret. κατιστάμεν by ἱστάμεν. Hence East. Ion. κάθοδος, El. ποθελόμενος, etc. Cf. Mod. Grk. καθίσταμαι (of the written puristic language), ἀφοῦ, etc., in spite of the loss of the spiritus asper.

b. The denial, by some, of Cretan psilosis is unwarranted, certainly for Central Cretan. In the early inscriptions the letter Β, Η is used only for a vowel, never also = *h* as was the case at Rhodes, Thera, and Melos. Examples of aspiration, as χιρήνα, ἀφ' ἅς are late and may be due to external influence, which is evident in other matters. The late inscriptions of Hierapytna and Drerus (as nos. 119, 120) are generally edited with supplied (οἱ, ὅτι, etc.).

c. Even in Central and West Ionic, where Β, Β for the spiritus asper is frequent in archaic inscriptions, it ceased to be so used at an early period. So in no. 7 (Andros) only once (*h*ελέσθō) vs. 26 cases of omission in no. 8 (Ceos) not at all, in no. 14 (Oropus) only once Η = *h*ε vs. over 30 cases of omission. Even the archaic Βύβων inscription at Olympia (Ditt. Syll. 1071), which the combined evidence of forms and script shows to be based on a West-Ionic dialect (cf. also Eub. names Βύβα, Βύσαλκος), has psilosis, and in the case of τε̇τέρει with the attendant crasis it is impossible to attribute this to an Elean engraver.

58. Even in those dialects which generally preserve the spiritus asper, and which, in distinction from those with psilosis, we may call the *h*-dialects, there are many irregularities, partly in special words, where by-forms evidently existed, partly due to the weak pronunciation of the sound in general (cf. the variations in Latin spelling).

a. In several dialects the forms of the article, ὁ, ἁ etc., appear regularly or frequently without *h*, showing that in these proclitic forms it was either wholly lost or more weakly sounded than elsewhere. So in Locrian (nos. 57-59) always ὁ, never ho (cf. also κ' ὁ), also ὅδε, fem. twice ἁ, once *h*α; in Delphian (no. 52) ὁ as article (A 30, 38, C 19), but demonstrative *h*ο (B 53); Thess. κοί = καὶ οἱ; ὁ likewise in some early inscriptions of

in quoting forms without *h* from inscriptions which have the character or are of a period when it was certainly in common use.

Boeotia, Pamphylia, Syracuse, Metapontum, and Sybaris. Cf. also Boeot. ὅς = ὥς (no. 38.5) and Delph. ἆς (ho. 52 A 28) beside usual hō, hόστις, etc.

b. Other forms which regularly have the spiritus asper, but for which by-forms with the lenis are to be recognized, are: ἡμέρα, but even in Attic inscriptions frequently ἐμέρα, and Argol., Lac., Mess., Ther. ἀμέρα, Delph., Locr. ἀμάρα. ἱερός (hιερός, hιαρός, in numerous dialects), but with lenis in Rhodian and Argolic, as Rhod. ἐπ᾿ ἱερέως, Arg. ἱαρομνάμονες (nos. 81, 82, with ho, etc.), Epid. ἱαρομμνάμονες (no. 89, with hομονάοις, etc.), Aegin. ἱαρέος (beside hοῖκος = ὁ οἶκος, χō = καὶ ὁ). So ἐπ᾿ ἱαρεῦς in the Megarian inscription no. 99, in contrast to hιαρόν at Selinus, is probably due to the Epidaurian engraver. ἡμεῖς (see 57), in Doric dialects ἁμές (Lac. ποθ᾿ ἁμέ, Heracl. hαμές), but also ἁμές (Coan μετ᾿ ἁμῶν, etc.), Att. ἕστηκα, but also Thess. ἐπεστάκοντα, Mess. κατεσταμένοι.

c. Conversely, several words which regularly have the lenis show secondary forms with the asper in various dialects. Thus ἔτος (from Ƒέτος), but Heracl. πεντα-hετηρίδα (beside Ƒέτος), Aetol. Ητέων = hετέων, Epid. πενθ᾿ ἔτη, and frequently καθ᾿ ἔτος,, etc., in the κοινή (cf. Mod. Grk. ἐφέτος). ἴσος (from Ƒίσƒος), but Heracl. hίσος beside ἴσος, and ἐφ᾿ ἴσης in the κοινή. Locr. ἔντε (cf. ἔστε), but Delph. hέντε. Heracl. hοκτώ, hοκτακάτιοι, hεννέα, Delph. Ther. hένατος, all after ἑπτά. Ther. hικάδι = εἰκάδι. ἄκρος, but Corcyr. καθ᾿ ἄκρον, Heracl. hακροσκιρίας. Boeot. Ηιράνα, late Cret. χἰρήνα vs. usual ἰράνα, εἰρήνα. Epid. ἐγκαθιδών with θ from present καθοράω. Delph., Locr. ἐφιορκέω, occurring also in κοινή inscriptions, with φ by anticipation of the asper in ὅρκος, like φρουρός from *προ-hορός (or blend of ἐπιορκέω and *ἐφορκέω?). In Att. ὅρος (hόρος very frequent) the asper is probably secondary vs. Corcyr. ὅρƑος (so, not hόρƑος; see IG IX.ii.695), Heracl. ὅρος, Arg. ὅροι (no. 85.26), ὧρος. In Delph. ἐφακείσθων, Arg. ἀφακεσάσθō vs. Att. ἄκος, ἀκέομαι the asper is, by a probable etymology, original. So also in Arg. hίδιος (from *swidios; cf. Arg. Ƒhεδιέστας = ἰδιώτης), Thess. καθ᾿ ἰδδίαν (similar forms in late inscriptions of several dialects, even Attic) vs. usual Ƒίδιος, ἴδιος. In Thess. ἀνγρέω (ἐφανγρένθειν) = Lesb. ἀγρέω, etc. (162.2) the asper, as well as the ν, is probably due to a blend with some other word.

d. Besides such special cases as have been noted above, there are in some dialects irregularities which seem to be due to confusion in spelling consequent upon the asper being weakly sounded or on the verge of disappearance. This is especially noticeable in Arcadian and Locrian, to some extent in Heraclean and Argolic.—In Arcadian the early no. 16 has no h, and no. 17 only once (and this unetymological if Ηέσχλαρος = *Ἐκκλήρος), but ἱεροῖ, ὀσέοι, ἴλαον. The somewhat later no. 18 has h uniformly in hιερά, hιερέν, etc., hεβδόμαι, hέκοτον, hίκοντα, παρhεταξαμένος, but ἔμισυ three times without h vs. once hέμισυ, ὑστέρας, ὅτι, ἄν = ἄν = ἀ ἄν, and conversely hάν = ἄν.—The early Locrian inscriptions nos. 57-59 have usually νότι, hόστις, hοίτινες, hόπō, hόπōς, (but in no. 59 ὅιτινι beside hότι, hόστις), hυπό, Ηυποκναμίδιος, (but in no. 59 ὑπαπροσθίδιος),

hόρχον, hορχōμότας, but πεντορχίαν, hιαρός, ιαρός (both in no. 58), hεχατόν
(no. 57) but χέχατόν (no. 59); further without h (beside ἀ, ὅδε, ἀμάρα, for
which see above, a, b) ἕμισον (no. 59), ὑδρία (vs. hυπό), ιστίαι, χατιϠόμενον;
unetymological h in hάγεν, εϕάγεσθαι (vs. ὀπάγōν), Hοποντίōν vs. usual
'Οποντίους, etc.—The Heraclean Tables have more examples of h than any
other single inscription, and most of them correct. But (besides the cases
mentioned above, c) unetymological h in hοισόντι, hάρνησις.—Argolic has
h regularly in ho, hα, hᾱι, hῖ, hοιζ(=οῖς), hόπαι, hόπυι, hίδιος, hέμισα, hέπεσθαι
(all these in no. 85), etc., but also (besides ιαρομνάμονες, above, b) ιχέτας
(no. 80), ἄτερον (no. 89, four times beside words with h), ἔλοιεν beside
hέλōμες (no. 85), and conversely unetymological h in hέ = ἤ 'or' and
Hαισχλαπιεῖ.

σ. Loss of Intervocalic σ

59. Original initial s became the spiritus asper in proethnic
Greek, as in ἕδος (Lat. *sedeō*, Skt. *sad-*), ἕπομαι (Lat. *sequor*,
Skt. *sac-*), etc. At the same time intervocalic s was changed in
the same way and then lost, as in γένεος (Skt. *janasas*, Lat.
generis), etc. Nevertheless there are many Greek words with
intervocalic σ, either retained by analogy as in the aorist, or of
secondary origin as σ from τ (**61**).

This Greek intervocalic σ was subjected to a similar process,
namely, became h and was later lost, in Laconian, Argolic,
Elean, and Cyprian.

1. Laconian. Early ἐποίēhε, νιχάhας, ἐνhēβόhαις, Ποhοιδᾶνι,
Λύhιππον, 'Ελευhύνια, etc.; later Παhιϕᾶι, προβειπάhας, πᾶhιν,
νιχάας, 'Οναιτέλης ('Ονασι-), Πειχλείδα (Πεισι-), βαιλέος (βασιλέος),
etc. Cf. also **97**.5a. In Aristophanes' Lysistrata occur similar forms
with omission of σ (μῶα, πᾶα, etc.), also γερωχία representing
γερωhία, which, though not as yet quotable, is the correct
native form for which the Attic writers substitute γερουσία or
γεροντία (Xen.). This was a characteristic of Laconian speech
from the earliest known period, and is faithfully represented in
the spelling of most of the early inscriptions. But it was felt as
a provincialism and ignored in the spelling of some of the early
and the majority of the later inscriptions.

2. Argolic. Mycen. Φραhιαρίδας, Arg. ἐποίēhε, 'Αρχεhίλας,
etc. Later, mostly in Arg. inscriptions of the third century B.C.,
numerous examples of total loss (sometimes with σ- forms in

the same inscription), e.g., θηαυρός (= θησαυρός), χρῆις (= χρῆ-σις), ἔμπαις (= ἔμπασις), ἐμέτρηε (= -ησε), στεφανῶαι (=-ῶσαι), etc. But several early Arg. inscriptions (as nos. 81, 83, 84, 85, 86) show only σ-forms, as θēσαυρός, etc., and so many of the later ones.

a. The explanation of the fluctuation is the same as that given for Laconian. See above, 1 and 275. Significant of this is the contemporaneous appearance of Κνόσιος and Κνōhίαν in different drafts of the same document (see no. 85 with note).

On present evidence this change of intervocalic σ seems to belong only to Argos and the vicinity, in contrast to the towns of the Acte, where we find only σ from the earliest times (ποιϝέσανς Methana, sixth century b.c.). The only apparent exceptions, Νικαhαρίστα and Κτēhίλας in dedications found at Epidaurus, may be names of Argives, like the 'Αρκεhίλας 'Αργεῖος of the same source (IG IV².i.137, 138, 140).

3. Elean. In no. 65 (middle of fourth century) ἀδεαλτώhαιε, φυγαδεύαντι (aor. subj.), beside δαμοσιῶμεν, δαμοσιοία. In no. 66 ποιήασσαι (ποιήσασθαι), ποιήαται (aor. subj.), beside ἀναθέσιορ, etc. In all the earlier inscriptions intervocalic σ is unchanged.

4. Cyprian. φρονέōι (φρονέωσι), ποεχόμενον (ποσ-εχόμενον), also in sentence combination (cf. 97a), as κὰ ἀ(ν)τί (κὰς ἀντί), τᾶ ὐχέρōν (τᾶς ὐχήρων). But generally σ is written in the inscriptions. Several glosses in Hesychius show loss of intervocalic (and also initial) σ.

a. In Arcadian the unique πόεστι (no. 22.12) for πόσεστι is probably a special case of dissimilatory loss of the first σ.

Rhotacism

60. Rhotacism, or change of σ to ρ, is found in Elean, late Laconian, and Eretrian, rarely elsewhere.

1. Elean. Final ς appears uniformly as ρ in the later inscriptions, nos. 65, 66, e.g. τιρ, αἵματορ, ὅπωρ, πόλιορ. Most of the earlier inscriptions show -ς and -ρ side by side without any apparent system. Rhotacism of intervocalic σ is unknown (cf. 59.3).

a. In the earlier inscriptions ρ is relatively most frequent in forms of the article and the indefinite or the relative pronoun, e.g., τοίρ, τιρ, ὅρ, and possibly the rhotacism began in such enclitic and proclitic forms. But even here there is great fluctuation in the spelling.

2. Laconian. Rhotacism of final ς is seen in very late inscriptions, e.g., νικάαρ, βουαγόρ, etc. (nos. 75-78), confirmed by numerous glosses, and in the spurious Timotheus decree.

3. Eretrian. Rhotacism of intervocalic σ is frequent in inscriptions of Eretria and Oropus, e.g., Eretr. ἔχουριν, θύωριν, ἐπιδημέωριν, συνελευθερώραντι, παιρίν, σίτηριν, Ἀρτεμίρια, Orop. δημορίων. But there are many exceptions, and the use of ρ is gradually given up under Attic influence. Although Plato, Cratylus 434 C, remarks that the Eretrians say σκληρότηρ for σκληρότης, there is no inscriptional example of ρ for final ς except once ὅπωρ ἄν, for which see **97a**.

4. Rhotacism of σ before a voiced consonant is seen in Eretr. Μίργος = Μίσγος, late Cretan (Gortyn) κόρμοι = κόσμοι, Thess. Θεορδότειος, Lac. Θιοκορμίδας. In most dialects σ in this position was pronounced as a voiced sound (z), and in late times often indicated by ζ, as ψήφιζμα.

Change of τ to σ

61. τ is changed to σ very frequently before ι, and sometimes before υ. The more precise conditions are uncertain, and the change is in part independent of dialectal variation, τ being retained in some words in all dialects, e.g., ἀντί, and in some words becoming σ in all dialects, e.g., most words like βάσις (Skt. ga-ti-s), στάσις, etc.

But in a considerable class of words there is a distinct dialectal distribution of the τ- and σ-forms, the retention of τ being a notable characteristic of the West Greek dialects, in which Boeotian, Thessalian, and Pamphylian also share.

1. Verb forms with the endings -τι, -ντι, as δίδωτι, φέροντι = δίδωσι, φέρουσι (Arc. φέρονσι, Lesb. φέροισι). Examples are plentiful in all the West Greek dialects and Boeotian (-τι, -νθι), and for Thessalian and Pamphylian (in which no 3 sg. μι-forms are yet quotable) the third plural forms are attested. See **138**.2, 4.

2. The numerals for 20 and the hundreds, (ϝ)ίκατι = εἴκοσι, -κάτιοι = -κόσιοι (Arc. -κάσιοι). See **116**, **117**.2.

3. Some nouns and adjectives in -τις, -τιος, etc. Att.-Ion. -σις,

etc. Boeot. Εὔτρητις (shown by Εὐτρειτιδεῖες and Εὐτρετίφαντος; see no. 38.5), the native name of the town vs. Εὔτρησις in Homer. Delph., Coan ἐνιαύτιος = ἐνιαύσιος. Arg. ῥύτιον (no. 86.41; cf. Troez. ῥυτιάζω), Boeot. πλατίος, lit. Dor. (Epich.), Epid. πλατίον = πλησίος, πλησίον. 'Αρταμίτιος, 'Αφροδίτιος in many West Greek dialects. Rhod., Thess. ἐναράτιον = ἐνηρόσιον.

4. Corinth. ΠοτΕδάϝōνι, ΠοτΕδᾶνι Ποτειδᾶν with similar τ-forms in Cretan, Rhodian, Coan, Delphian, Boeotian, and Thessalian, also Ποτοιδᾶνι of uncertain dialect (Schwyzer 642), all = Hom. Ποσειδάων, Ion. Ποσειδέων, Att. Ποσειδῶν, Lesb. Ποσείδᾶν, Arc. Ποσοιδᾶν (49.1). Lac. Ποhοιδᾶν (cf. also Ποhοίδαια) is plainly from the pre-Doric form represented by Arc. Ποσοιδᾶν. So perhaps from another pre-Doric σ-form the Ποσειδᾶν occurring in Argolic (Argos, no. 86.15; later at Mycenae, Calauria, Epidaurus) and in later inscriptions of various dialects, as Arcadian (no. 22.57), Cretan, Rhodian, etc. But one suspects that in some of the late occurrences it may be merely a hybrid, influenced by the familiar Ποσειδῶν, as conversely Thess. Ποτειδοῦνι with native τ but -ουνι from Att. -ῶνι.

a. The distribution of West Greek προτί, ποτί vs. Att.-Ion., Lesb. πρός, Arc.-Cypr. πός is like that in 1-4 above, except that Homer has πρότι, πότι beside πρός. But here there are no forms in -σι, and it is a question whether the -ς of πρός, πός comes from -σι by elision and apocope or is a different ending, original -ς.

5. Lit. Dor. τύ, Boeot. τού = Att.-Ion., Lesb. σύ. Cret. ἥμιτυς (in ἡμιτυέκτō; cf. also Epid. hēμίτεια) = Att.-Ion., Arc. ἥμισυς, Lesb. αἴμισυς, with suffix -τυ- beside -τϝο- in ἥμισσον, etc. (81).

β, δ, γ

62. In general β, δ, γ remained simple mediae, but in some dialects there are indications of their pronunciation as spirants, which eventually prevailed even in Attic (cf. Mod. Grk. β = Eng. *v*, δ = Eng. *th* in *then*, γ guttural spirant). Such are:

1. The use of β for ϝ in later Laconian, etc. **51.**

2. The occasional representation of δ by ζ, as in three of the very earliest Elean inscriptions, e.g., ζέ, ζέκα, ζίκαια, ζίφυιον, ζαμιοργία, ϝειζός, also early Rhod. τόζ' = τόδε (no. 100), early Arg. ϝισζείē (for σζ see 89.1) = εἰδείη, and Phlias. ζέκα =

δέκα (SEG 11.275).—Cret. ρ from ρδ (**86**.6). Cret. ἀντρήιον (= usual ἀνδρήιον) with τ indicating retention of stop after a nasal (as in Mod. Grk. ἄντρας pronounced *andras*), perhaps Cret. σποϜδδάν (**89**.4).

3. The occasional omission of γ or substitution of ι, as in Boeot. ἰώ, ἰών (Ar., Corinna) = ἐγώ, Paniph. μhειάλαν, μhειάλε̄τι, etc. (μεγάλος), Arc. ἐπιθιάνε̄ (ἐπιθιγγάνῃ) ,Mess., Arc. Φιάλεια beside Φιγάλεια, and ὀλίος (ὀλίγος) in late inscriptions of various places. The occasional representation of γ by ζ in Cyprian, as ζᾶ (γᾶ), ἀζαθός (ἀγαθός).

φ, θ, χ

63. In general, φ, θ, χ remained true aspirated stops, and in the earliest type of the alphabet, which had a sign for θ but none for φ or χ, these two were represented by πh and κh, as at Thera, or, where a sign for *h* was not in use, simply by π and κ, as in the Gortyn Law Code (e.g., κρόνος = χρόνος, πυλά = φυλή). Spellings like γέγραπφα, δεδόκχθαι are mostly late, an exceptionally early example being Delph. λεχοῖ (no. 52 D 13; dat. sg. of λεχώ).

But the pronunciation as spirants (Eng. *f*, *th* in *thin*, Germ. *ch*), which eventually prevailed even in Attic, existed at a much earlier period in some dialects. Such a pronunciation of θ is certainly presupposed by Lac. σ = θ (**64**), probably by El. σσ = σθ (**85**.2), late Cret. θθ = σσ (Ϝέτεθθι), Thess. φεῶν, φύοντες (**68**.5), and possibly by some other spellings which, however, may be variously interpreted.

64. Laconian σ = θ. The use of σ by Aristophanes in the Lysistrata to indicate the sound of the Laconian θ (and there is no good reason to doubt that this belongs to the original text) shows that it had become a spirant which would strike the Athenian ear as σ, even if not yet fully identical with it. The Laconians themselves retained the spelling θ in all the earlier inscriptions, but ἀνέσηκε (ἀνέθηκε) and σιῶ (θεοῦ) occur in a fourth century inscription, and in very late inscriptions ἀνέσηκε, Βωρσέα (Ϝορθία), κασσηρατόριν beside καθθηρατόριον, etc.

Interchange of Voiceless and Voiced Stops and Aspirates

65. Dissimilation and assimilation of aspirates, or transposi-

tion of the aspiration. The dissimilation seen in τίθημι from
*θίθημι, τρέχω from *θρέχω (cf. θρέξομαι), etc., belongs to the
proethnic period. But there are some examples of later, dialectal
assimilation. So Cret. θιθέμενος = τιθέμενος, θύκα (i.e., θύχα) =
τύχη, West Ion. (Cumae) θυφλός = τυφλός, Arc. (also early Att.
inscr.) φαρθένος = παρθένος, Thess. Φερσεφόνα = Περσεφόνη, Boeot.
φεφύλαχσο = πεφύλαξο, Lac., Epid., Thess. θεθμός, Locr. θέθμιον
= τεθμός, τέθμιον, Att. θεσμός, θέσμιον (164.4), Att. (inscr.)
ἐνθαῦθα = usual Att. ἐνταῦθα. Ion. ἐνθαῦτα is the more original
form (from ἔνθα), whence Att. ἐνταῦθα through transposition
of the aspiration and influence of ταῦτα. Cf. also Eub. ἐντοῦθα
like τοῦτα (124), El. ἐνταῦτα, Argol. ἐντάδε = ἐνθάδε, influenced
by ταῦτα, τάδε (but cf. also 66). Regular dissimilation in Arc.
μεσακόθεν vs. Att. πανταχόθεν, etc., and in Arc. ἐσκεθῆν, Lesb.
ὑποσκέθην vs. Hom. σχεθέειν, etc. For transposition cf. also Ion.
ἄχαντος = ἄκανθος, Cret. καυχός = χαλκός, Thess. Πετθαλός
from Φετταλός (68.2).

66. There are scattered examples of variation between stop
and aspirate and between voiceless and voiced stops, especially
before a nasal. Locr. τέκνα = τέχνη, Cret. τνατός, τετνακός =
θνητός, τεθνηκός (also ἄντρθπος, Pamph. ἄτρθπος), Heracl.
διαχνόντων beside διαγνόντων, Eretr. ἀποδείγνυσθαι, Ther. ἐνδειγνύμενος to δείκνυμι, Aetol. ἀχνηκότας beside ἀγνηκώς (ἀγνέω
= ἄγω). Ion. πρῆχμα = πρῆγμα, μέλιχμα = μείλιγμα, Epid. φάρχμα = φράγμα, πάρδειχμα = παράδειγμα, Arg. ῥηχμός = ῥηγμός
(-σμα, -σμος). Cf. τέχνη from *τέκσνᾱ. (So perhaps Delph., Locr.,
Arg. ἐχθός from *ἐχτός, this from *ἐκσ-τός. Cf. early Att. ἔδοχσε,
etc.)

In Pamphylian ντ became regularly νδ (influenced by languages
of Asia Minor in which the change of nt to nd is widely attested),
with ν not written (69.2), as πέδε = πέντε, ἐξάγοδι = ἐξάγωντι.
Cret. ἀβλοπία, καταβλάπεθαι = ἀβλαβία, etc., Mess. κεκλεβώς
(κλέπτω), Arg. γεγράβανται = γεγράφαται, are examples of analogical interchange in roots ending in a labial, owing to common
forms in ψ. So also Coan στέπτω = στέφω. Locr. φρίν = πρίν and
Arc., Cret., Pamph. Πύτιος = Πύθιος, are obscure.

El. πάσκω = πάσχω is probably due to the influence of other
verbs in -σκω (but possibly like στ = σθ, cf. 85.1). For Att.-Ion.

δέχομαι other dialects (and Ionic in part) have the original δέκομαι (cf. Att. δωροδόκος), οὐδείς, μηδείς are replaced by οὐθείς, μηθείς, with θ from δ + the spiritus asper of εἷς, in later Attic and elsewhere.

a. Very late inscriptions show numerous examples of confusion, not confined to any special conditions, as ἀδελπός = ἀδελφός, φρεσβύτερος = πρεσβύτερος, Lesb. ὑπάρκοισαν = ὑπάρχουσαν, Delph. βρυτανεῖον (also Cretan), βρυτανεύω = πρυτανεῖον, etc., and Βαλλάντιον = Παλλάντιον. Some such forms as these last, reflecting occasional colloquial pronunciation, presumably underlie the too sweeping statement of Plutarch (Mor. 292E) that the Delphians used β in place of π.

Interchange of π and πτ

67. Of the Homeric by-forms of πόλις and πόλεμος, πτόλις is found also in Cyprian, and in Thess. οἱ ττολίαρχοι, ἀρχιττολιαρχέντος (ττ from πτ, **86**.2) and Arc. Πτόλις (place name), Cret. Πτολίοικος; πτόλεμος is found in Cyprian (gloss) and in proper names like the Maced. Πτολεμαῖος and others from various places.

Interchange of Labials, Dentals, and Gutturals

68. 1. Those sounds of the parent speech which are called labiovelars and are here designated as *kʷ, gʷ, gʷh*, appear in Greek regularly as (1) labials before the back vowels α, ο, ω and before consonants, (2) dentals before the front vowels ι, ε, η, (3) gutturals before and after υ. Thus ποῦ, πόθεν (Lat. *quod*, cf. Osc. *pod*), ὁποῖος, but τίς (Lat. *quis*), τε (Lat. *que*), Cret. ὀτεῖος,— πεμπάς πέμπτος, but πέντε (Lat. *quinque*),—λύκος (Eng. *wolf*), γυνή (Eng. *queen*) beside Boeot. βανά. But before ι usually β, φ, e.g. βίος (Lat. *vīvus*), with δ only in Heracl. ἐνδεδιωκότα = ἐμβεβιωκότα. Many exceptions are due to leveling between related forms, e.g., βέλος after βάλλω, etc. Instead of πρέσβυς, with analogical β, several dialects have forms with γ, which is regular before υ, e.g., Cret. πρεῖγυς, Boeot. πρισγεῖες, etc. (see **86**.3). Examples of the normal relation are Arc. δέλλω = βάλλω, West Greek δήλομαι, δείλομαι (**75**) = βούλομαι, West Greek and Arc. ὀδελός = ὀβολός (but if from the rare early Att. ὀβελός, β is analogical, as in ὀβελίσκος. Boeot. ὀβελός, Thess. ὀβελλός may belong under 2, below), Dor. βλῆρ = δέλεαρ.

2. But it is a notable characteristic of the Aeolic dialects that they very frequently show a labial even before a front vowel, where the dental is regular elsewhere. Thus Lesb., Thess. πέμπε = πέντε. Lesb. πέσσυρες (Hesych., cf. Hom. πίσυρες), Boeot. πέτταρες, πέτρατος, πετραμείννιον, Thess. πετροετηρίς = τέτταρες, etc. Thess. πεῖσαι, ἀππεισάτου, Boeot. ποταποπισάτω = τεῖσαι, etc., Lesb. πήλυι (Sappho), Boeot. Πειλε-στροτίδας to τῆλε. Thess. βέλλομαι, Boeot. βείλομαι = West Greek δήλομαι, δείλομαι. Lesb. Βέλφοι (gloss), Boeot. Βελφοί = Δελφοί, Thess. Βέλφαιον = *Δέλφαιον. Boeot. βέφυρα = Cret. δέφυρα, Att. γέφυρα (for γ see 88), Lesb. φήρ (gloss), Thess. πεφειράκοντες = θήρ, τεθηρακότες (though this is a case of original ĝhw not gʷh). Boeot. Φετταλός, whence Thess. Πετθαλός with transposition of the aspiration (65) = Att. Θετταλός, Ion. Θεσσαλός. Yet some words always have the dental, e.g., τε, τις, τιμά, the reason for this being obscure.

a. An apparently similar case is Lesb. σπέλλω = στέλλω (fut. κασπολέω Sappho 42 Diehl; Hesych. κασπέλη· στορνύει, σπελλάμεναι· στελλάμεναι, σπολεῖσα· σταλεῖσα), with Thess. σπόλος 'stake.' But στέλλω is almost certainly from a root *stel- with original dental (seen also in Lesb. στάλλα), and we have to do with two parallel roots στελ- and σπελ-.

b. Cypr. πείσει = τείσει is in striking agreement with the Aeolic forms quoted above. But if it is the result of the same phonetic change (and not with π by analogy of ποινά, etc.), and so to be reckoned as an Aeolic element in Arcado-Cyprian, it is quite isolated in this development in contrast to that seen in Arc. ἀπυτεισάτω, δέλλω, Cypr. Τελεφάνō and in Arc. σις, Cypr. σίς, etc. (below, 3).

3. In Arcado-Cyprian there is evidence of a sibilant pronunciation before a front vowel. Cypr. σις = τις (no. 23), σί = τί (Hesych.). Arc. ὄζις = ὄτις (no. 16), and in no. 17 (written with a special letter, 4.4) σις = τις, εἴσε = εἴτε, ὁσέοι = ὅτεῳ. Further, τζετρακάτιαι = τετρακάτιαι in no. 70, due to the Arcadian engraver. Cf. also the gloss ζέλλω (Hesych.) beside inscriptional δέλλω = βάλλω, and ζέρεθρον (Strabo) = δέρεθρον, βάραθρον.

a. The σ occurs also for an original dental in ἀπυσεδομένος = ἀποδεδομένος. But this is probably a special case of dissimilation like that in Ἀρκασίδης = Ἀρκαδίδης. Otherwise the dentals appear without change in the same inscription, e.g., δέ, τότε, etc. The sibilant development is definitely linked with labiovelar origin, and this goes well with the preservation of the old labiovelar voiceless stop in the pre-Arcado-Cyprian of Cretan script (p. 8, footnote). The fact that in Arcadian the sibilant appears only in early inscriptions is like the case of El. ϝ = δ only in the earliest inscriptions, then replaced by the usual (see 275).

4. There are some pronominal forms with κ in place of the usual π or τ. Thus Ion. κῶς = πῶς, κότερος, etc. (in texts of Ionic authors; in inscriptions only once ὁκοῖα, otherwise π), Thess. κίς, διὲ κί, πὸκ κί = τίς, etc.

a. Thess., Cypr. δαύχνα in συνδαυχναφόροι, Δαυχναφόριος (cf. δαυχμός in Nicand., Hesych.) is from *δαυκσνᾱ (cf. 66) belonging with δαῦκος, δαῦκον, a plant much like the δάφνη (cf. δαῦκον δαφνοειδές, Theophr.). The form δαύχνα then served as the equivalent of the similar though unrelated δάφνη.

5. A change of θ to φ, that is, doubtless, of spirant *th* to *f*, is seen in φεῶν, φύοντες = θεῶν, θύοντες, of an inscription found at Dodona.

Nasals and Liquids

69. Nasal before consonant. The nasal was always assimilated to the character of the following consonant, but was less distinctly sounded than in the intervocalic position. With this are connected the following facts.

1. The letter ν is freely used for the guttural and the labial nasal, as well as for the dental, e.g., Ὀλύνπιος, ἀνφί, λανχάνω.

2. The nasal is omitted in the spelling, occasionally in all dialects, and regularly in Cyprian and Pamphylian, as Cypr. ἀτί = ἀντί, Pamph. πέδε = πέντε.

3. Complete assimilation to a following stop, though not regular in any dialect, sometimes occurred in careless pronunciation, as shown by occasional, and mostly late, spellings, e.g., Att. ξυββάλλεσθαι, Boeot. Ὀλυππίχην (late κοινή inscription), Delph. Ἄθαββος, σύββολον, λαββάνοντες. From Crete, where in general consonant assimilation is most extensive (86), there are several examples, as ποππάν = πομπάν, ἀφφάνω = ἀμφάνω, and the assimilated form was usual in the name of the town Lappa, whose coins show Λαππαίων. In some cases the dissimilative influence of a preceding or following nasal was probably a factor, e.g., Delph.

ἀνεκκλήτως = ἀνεγκλήτως, ἐπάνακκον (papyr.) = ἐπάναγκον, Locr. ἔκκλημα = ἔγκλημα, ἀνακκάζηι = ἀναγκάζῃ, Thess. ἐξξανακάδεν = ἐξαναγκάζειν.

4. A special case is Boeot. ἔππασις (uniformly so spelled) = ἔμπασις. This is from *ἔμ-ππᾶσις as also Boeot. ἀππασάμενος (Corinna) from *ἀν-ππᾶ-. So also Boeot. τὰ ππάματα. See 162.12.

a. Assimilation of a nasal to the character of the preceding stop is perhaps to be seen in Coan Ἀρίσταιχνος = Ἀρίσταιχμος, and, Cret. δαρκνά = δαρχμά, δραχμή. Cf. Mod. Grk. Πάτνος from Πάτμος, λαχνός from λαχμός.

70. Transposition of a liquid, or loss by dissimilation.

1. Transposition within the same syllable. Cret. πορτί = προτί, Ἀφορδίτα = Ἀφροδίτη, also κάρτος, σταρτός, etc., for which see **49.2a.** Pamph. περτ', Ἀφορδίσιυς, Πρείας = Περγαίας, Ther. Καρτι-, Σταρτο-.

2. Transposition between different syllables. Heracl. τράφος, Amorg. τράφη = τάφρος, τάφρη, Syrac. δρίφος = δίφρος (Hesych.).

3. Loss by dissimilation. Cypr. Ϝρέτα = ῥήτρα, El. Ϝράτρα, Epid. ῥόπτον = ῥόπτρον, φατρία or φάτρα in various dialects = φρατρία, Hom. φρήτρη, conversely φρήταρχος at Naples.

71. Cretan υ from λ. In Cretan the λ was a deep guttural *l* closely resembling *u* (cf. French *autre* from Lat. *alter*, etc.), and the spelling υ is fairly common. So ἀδευπιαί = ἀδελφεαί (once in Law-Code beside usual ἀδελπιός, etc.), Ϝευμένας = Ϝελμένας, καυχός = καλχός, αὐφίτων = ἀλφίτων, ἐπευθών, πορτῆυθον = ἐπελθών, προσῆλθον (further examples in Hesychius).

a. Cret., Epid. μαίτυρες (hence nom. Cret. μαίτυρς, μαῖτυς) = μάρτυρες, with Sicil. μαιτυρήσηι (SEG 4.31, with p. 141) are apparently to be explained as due to dissimilation of the two ρ's with palatalization of the first.

b. A palatalized λ is indicated by the spelling λε, which is frequent in Cos, and occurs also in Melos, Thasos, and Cnidus. Thus Coan ξύλεα, ξύλεων=ξύλα, ξύλων, κοτύλεαι. = κοτύλαι, Παμφύλεων beside Πάμφυλοι. Φιλεωνίδας, etc., Thas. Φιλεωνίδεος, Mel. Φίλεων, etc.

c. The change of λ to ρ before a consonant, regular in popular Mod. Grk. (ἀδερφός = ἀδελφός, etc.) appears in occasional forms from the second century A.D. on, e.g., Delph. Δερφοί, Att. ἀδερφοί.

72. ντ, νθ from λτ, λθ. Several examples occur in West Greek and Arcadian. Φίντων (Φίλτων) or Φιντίας in many West Greek dialects and Arcadian. Arg. Μίντων (Μίλτων), κέντο (κέλτο) in Alcman, φίντατος (φίλτατος) in Epicharmus, βέντιστος (βέλτιστος) in Theocritus. Cyren. τένται from *τέλται = τέλεται = ἔσεται. ἐνθεῖν (ἐλθεῖν) is most widespread, occurring in Doric wiiters and in Corcyrean, Cyrenaean, Arcadian, late Delphian, late Cretan. Meg. ἐνπίδες = ἐλπίδες stands alone.

Double Liquids and Nasals in Lesbian and Thessalian

73. The combinations discussed in **74-76**, also **77**.1, **79**, have in part a common history, since they all become double liquids and nasals in Lesbian and Thessalian, but in other dialects a single liquid or nasal accompanied by lengthening of the preceding vowel.

a. This doubling is observed regularly only in Lesbian and Thessalian, and is one of the most distinctive Aeolic characteristics, one that is familiar in Lesbian poetry and in some Homeric forms (ἄμμε, ἔμμεν, etc.). But there are scattered examples elsewhere, which are relics of an Aeolic element. Thus from the once Aeolic Chian region (cf. **184**) Πελινναῖον, Ἄργεννον, Φαννόθεμις, Lac. Φάβεννος, Φαβέννα, Arc. (Orchomenos) ὀφέλλω (vs. ὀφήλω Tegea), ἔκριννα; Ther. ἐλλύτα = Boeot. εἰλύτα 'a kind of cake' (from εἰλύω 'roll').

74. ρ, ν, + ι, when preceded by any other vowel than α or ο. From *φθέρι̯ω, Lesb. φθέρρω (gram.), Att. etc. φθείρω, Arc. φθήρω. From *κρίνι̯ω, Lesb. κρίννω (gram.), Thess. κρέννω (**18**), Att., etc., κρίνω. From *κτένι̯ω, Lesb. κτέννω (gram.), Att., etc. κτείνω.

a. But if α or ο precedes, epenthesis takes place, the result being the same in all dialects, e.g., χαίρω from *χαρι̯ω, μοῖρα from *μόρι̯α, βαίνω from *βάνι̯ω.

b. λι̯ gives λλ in nearly all dialects, e.g., ἄλλος (Lat. *alius*), στέλλω from *στέλι̯ω. But Cyprian has αἶλος (beside ἀλ(λ)ά) and Ἀπείλōν = Ἀπόλλων, and Elean once αἰλότρια (beside ἄλλα, στέλλω).

75. λν or/and λσ. Lesb., Thess. στάλλα, Dor. στάλα, Att.-Ion. στήλη, Lesb. βόλλομαι, βόλλα, Thess. βέλλομαι, Att.-Ion. βουλή, βούλομαι, Boeot. βωλά, βείλομαι, West-Grk. βωλά, βουλά, δήλομαι, δείλομαι, Lesb. ἀπέλλω (gloss), Ion. εἴλω, εἰλέω, Delph. εἰλέσθω, El. ἀποϜελέοι, -έοιαν, Heracl. ἐγϜηληθίωντι (in these forms the meaning is 'shut out' or 'prevent'; cf. also Att. δίκη ἐξούλης 'action of ejectment.' Cret. Ϝευμένας = Ϝελμένας and καταϜελμένōν are perf. pass. participles, like Hom. ἐελμένος but meaning 'assembled' (cf. ἀολλής, etc. 55), Lesb., Hom. ὀφέλλω 'owe' (also Arc., 73a), Att. ὀφείλω, Arg., Cret., Arc. ὀφήλω.

a. The dialectal relations are clear, but whether the original consonant group was λν or λσ has been a matter of dispute. From the point of view of word formation a ν-suffix is distinctly the most probable in most cases, e.g., στάλλᾱ, etc., from *σταλ-νᾱ, εἴλω from *Ϝέλ-νω. The conflicting λλ of Att. ὄλλῡμι may be explained as a later treatment of a restored *ὄλνῡμι, parallel to that in Att. ἔννῡμι vs. Ion. εἴνῡμι with the normal development of σν. (Some other cases of λλ, apparently from λν, are not so easy.) But the group βούλομαι, etc. (also Hom., Eretr., Arc.-Cypr. βόλομαι without suffix), is now generally believed to be based on an λσ (perhaps an aor. subj.) form, with the same development as in Lesb. ἔστελλα, Att. ἔστειλα, etc. (79).

76. 1. Medial σ + liquid or nasal. From *χέσλιοι (cf. Skt. sahasra-), Lesb., Thess. χέλλιοι, Ion. etc., χείλιοι, Lac. χήλιοι (Att. χῑ́λιοι, see 25e). From *χεσρ- (cf. Hitt. kessar and kessras 'hand'), Lesb. χέρρας (Alc., Theocr.), elsewhere χείρ or χήρ. From *ἐσμι (Skt. asmi), Lesb. ἔμμι, Thess. ἐμμί, elsewhere εἰμί or ἠμί (25). From *ἀσμε (cf. Skt. asmān), Lesb. ἄμμε, Thess. ἀμμέ, elsewhere ἀμέ, Att.-Ion. ἡμέας. From *σελάσνᾱ (σέλας), Lesb. σελάννᾱ, elsewhere σελᾱ́νᾱ, Att.-Ion. σελήνη.

a. Initial σλ, etc., became hλ, etc., later simple λ, etc. The earlier stage is represented by occasional early spellings with λh, etc. (cf. Ϝh, 51b, c), e.g., Aegin. λhαβών (cf. εἴληφα, Hom. ἔλλαβε,, below), Corcyr. ρhοϜαῖσι (cf. Skt. srava = Eng. stream). But also where there is no trace of an initial s in cognates (some assume an initial "laryngeal"), Corcyr. Μhείξιος, Meg. Μhεγαρεύς, Pamph. μhειάλαν, Att. μhεγάλō in an early inscription.

2. Compounds and augmented or reduplicated forms of such words only rarely show the development proper to intervocalic σλ, etc., as Att. εἴληφα from *σέσλᾱφα. Usually this was checked by the analogical influence of the simplex, and the subsequent development was to λλ, etc., later (under the continued influence of the simplex and of words with original initial λ, etc.) simply λ, etc., e.g., Hom. ἔ-λλαβε, ἄ-λληκτος, ἔ-ρρεον, ἔ-ννεον, φιλο-μμει-δής, later ἔλαβε, etc. Locr., Delph., Cret. ἀμφιλλέγω, Arc. ἀμφίλλο-γος, from ἀμφισ-λ-, whence Meg. ἀμφέλλεγον as if from ἀμφι-λλέγω. But ρρ usually remained, e.g., Att. ἐρρύην beside ἔλαβε, Dor. -ερρύᾱ, though here there is considerable variation, especial-

ly in compounds (Att. παραρύματα and παραρρύματα, etc.). Cf.
ρρ from Ϝρ, 55a.

νς

77. 1. Original intervocalic νσ. From *μηνσός (cf. Lat. *mēnsis*),
Lesb. μῆννος (also μῆνος), Thess. μειννός (also μεινός), Att. etc.
μηνός (in this word the vowel was already long). From *ἔκρινσα,
Lesb. ἔκριννα, Att., etc., ἔκρῖνα. From *ἔμενσα, Thess. ἔμεννα,
Att., etc. ἔμεινα. From *ἔφανσα, Dor., etc., ἔφᾱνα, Att.-Ion. ἔφηνα.
Similarly μσ, as, from *ἔνεμσα, Lesb. ἔνεμμα (gram.), Att., etc.,
ἔνειμα.

a. The dat. pl. of ν-stems, as ποιμέσι, δαίμοσι, is not formed from -ενσι,
-ονσι, but from -ασι (cf. φρασί Pindar) with substitution of the vowel of
the other cases. But in Arc. ἱερομνάμονσι the ν also is introduced from the
other cases, and this secondary νσ is retained (cf. 3).

2. νσ + consonant lost its ν in proethnic Greek without effect
on the preceding vowel, e.g., κεστός from *κενστός (cf. κεντέω),
συσκευάζω, etc., from συν-. So also later in Thess. ὀστροφά from
*ὀνστροφά = ἀναστροφή. But ν might be restored by analogy,
with resulting treatment of νσ as in 3. Att. ἔσπεισται from
*ἔσπενσται, Lesb. εἴκοιστος, etc. (116 with a), Arg. ποιγραψάνσθω,
etc. (140.3b).

3. Secondary intervocalic νσ, in which σ comes from τι, dental
+ σ, or τ before ι, had an entirely different history from that of
original νσ, which was changed before the new νσ came into
existence. This νσ is retained in Cretan (i.e., Central Cretan, cf.
273), Argolic (mainly Argive, cf. 251), Thessalian, and Arcadian,
while in other dialects it loses the ν with lengthening, in Lesbian
and Cyrenaean with diphthongization, of the preceding vowel.
Thus from *πάντια, Cret., Arg., Thess., Arc. πάνσα, Att., etc., πᾶσα,
Lesb., Ther., Cyren. παῖσα. From *μόντια, *μόνσα (not yet
quotable), Lesb. μοῖσα, elsewhere μοῦσα or μῶσα. From nom.
sg. fem. pres. part. -ντ-ια, Cret. ἔχονσα, ἄγονσα, ἐβίονσα, etc.
(but ὑπάρχωνσα, etc., in East and West Cretan), Thess. ἔνσα,
λειτορεύσανσα, ἀπελευθερεσθένσα, Arc. μίνονσα, etc., Arg. ἀντι-
τύχονσα, etc., Lesb. ἔχοισα, ἁρμόζοισα, δάμεισα, etc., Cyren. ἐχοῖσα,
καθάραισα, etc., elsewhere -ουσα or -ωσα, -ᾱσα, -εισα. From dat.
pl. of the ντ-stems, Cret. ἐπιβάλλονσι, ἑλόνσι, νικάσανσι, etc., Arg.

θύονσι, ἄπανσι, Arc. πάνσι, πολιτεύονσι, Cyren. ἐμμένοισι, πλέοισι, etc., elsewhere -ουσι, -ωσι, -ᾶσι, etc. From aor. *ἔσπενδσα, Cret. ἔσπενσα, Att., etc. ἔσπεισα. From 3 pl. -ντι (West Greek φέροντι, etc.), Arc. κρίνωνσι, ποίενσι, etc., Lesb. ἔχοισι, γράφωισι, τίθεισι, etc. (so also Chian λάβωισιν, πρήξοισιν, cf. **184**), Att., etc., φέρουσι. Observe that 3 pl. -νσι is exclusively Arcadian, since this is the only dialect which belongs both to the νσ and the σι from τι (**61**) groups.

a. In derivatives in -σις from verbs in -νω, νσ is kept in all dialects, e.g., not only Cret. ἄνπανσις = ἀνάφανσις, Epid. ἄλινσις, but Att. πρόφανσις, ὕφανσις, etc., owing to the influence of the verbs.

78. Final νς. Since νσ + consonant lost its ν in proethnic Greek (**77.**2), the same would be true of final νς in close combination with a following word beginning with a consonant. Hence there arose doublets such as (1) before vowel τόνς, τάνς, (2) before consonants τός, τάς. Such doublets are found in Cretan, the Gortyn Law-Code still adhering very closely to the original distribution in the case of the article, e.g., τὸνς ἐλευθέρονς, but τὸς καδεστάνς. But elsewhere the use of one or the other set of forms has ceased to depend at all upon the initial of the following word.

Accusatives in -ος, -ας are the regular forms in Thessalian, Arcadian (so probably Cyprian -ος not -ōς), Theran, Cyrenaean, Coan, and are occasionally found in other Doric dialects and in literary Doric (e.g., frequent in Theocritus). Other dialects have -ονς, -ανς, or forms coming therefrom by the same development as that seen in the case of secondary intervocalic νσ (πάνσα, etc., **77.**3), e.g., Argol. -ονς, -ανς, -ινς (less commonly -ος), Lesb. -οίς, -αίς, in most dialects -ούς or -ώς (**25**), -ᾱς. Only Elean, though medially it has πᾶσα not παῖσα, has here a development similar to the Lesbian, namely, -αις (and presumably -οις, but no o-stem acc. pl. forms occur in the inscriptions which have -αις), and later -αιρ, -οιρ. But there are also early forms in -Aς, -Oς, later -Oρ, of which the proper transcription and relation to the preceding are uncertain (short-vowel forms parallel to Cret. -ος beside -ονς?).

Similarly the preposition ἐνς, whence ἐς or εἰς. Cret., Argol. ἐνς and ἐς. ἐς in most Doric dialects (Lac., Heracl., Rhod., Coan,

Ther., Cyren., but also εἰς in some, mostly from the κοινή). Ion., Att.-Ion. ἐς and εἰς (both in Homer; Ion. mostly ἐς, Att. mostly εἰς), Lesb. εἰς (but here with genuine diphthong like τοῖς). Cf. also the treatment of final νς from -ντ-ς, e.g., nom. sg. part. Cret. νικάσανς, καταθένς, Argol. ποιϝέσανς, Heracl. καταλυμακωθής, Att., etc., τιθείς, Lesb. στοίχεις, Thess. εὐεργετές, Arc. hιεροθυτές, Ther. αἱρεθές, Cyren. κοιμαθές, πωληθές.

λσ, ϱσ

79. From *ἔστελσα, Lesb., Thess. ἔστελλα, Att., etc., ἔστειλα, Cret. ἔστηλα. Cf. also Lesb. βόλλομαι, Att. βούλομαι (**75** with *a*). From *ἔφθερσα, Att., etc., ἔφθειρα.

80. But in another set of words λσ and ρσ did not have this development, but remained unchanged in most dialects, while in several this ρσ was assimilated to ρρ. Cf. Hom. κέλσαι, ἔκερσεν, ὦρσε, ἄρσην, θάρσος, the widespread ἔρσην (**49**.2), and θάρσος or θέρσος in most dialects (partly in proper names only).

The assimilation to ρρ is Attic as ἄρρην, θάρρος, etc. (so in the earliest inscriptions; ρσ in early Attic writers is Ionic), West Ionic as ἀρρενικός (Cumae), ἄγαρρις (Naples), Θαρριπίδης, etc., Arcadian as φθέραι (for φθέρραι corresponding to φθέρσαι, like φθέρσαντες in Lycophron, not to φθεῖραι, which would be φθῆραι in Arcadian), ἀρρέντερος, Elean as θάρρος, θαρρέν (ερσ in later ἐρσεναίτερος is due to κοινή influence), Theran as ([ἄ]ρενα dubious), Θαρῆς, Θhαρύμαϙhος, etc. (all archaic; in later ἄρσην, Θάρσων, ρσ is due to κοινή influence). Proper names with ρρ = ρσ occur also in several other dialects, e.g., Delph. Θαρρίκων, Θάρρανδρος, Amphiss. Θάρρυς, Boeot. Θάροψ, Meg. Χερρίας, Ὅρριππος, Corinth. Δαμοθέρρης. Cf. also κάρρων from *κάρσων (Cret. κάρτων, **81**), in Alcman, Epicharmus, Sophron, Plut. Lyc., etc.

a. Even in dialects which regularly have ρρ, ρσ may be retained by analogy, e.g., Att. θηρσί after other datives in -σι, κάθαρσις etc. after other nouns in -σις. So Arc. πανάγορσις. But even in these words there is sometimes assimilation, as Att. δέρρις, West Ion. ἄγαρρις.

σσ, ττ

81. Att. ττ = Ion. σσ comes from κι, χι, and in the following categories also from τι or θι (but see **82***a*). So in presents like

φυλάττω, φυλάσσω (κι), κορύττω, κορύσσω (θι), in feminines like
γλῶττα, γλῶσσα (χι), μέλιττα, μέλισσα (τι), and in comparatives
like ἥττων, ἥσσων (κι), κρείττων, κρέσσων (τι). τϜ gives the
same result. So τέτταρες, τέσσερες (cf. Lat. *quattuor*, Skt.
catvāras; see **114.**4), and ἥμισσον (also ἥμισον, **89.**6) in many
dialects (Arc., Locr., Delph., Arg., Meg., etc.), Boeot. ἥέμιττα,
εἵμιττον (nos. 39 and 42), from *ἥμι-τϜο- beside ἥμι-τυ- in a Cret.
compound and Att.-Ion. ἥμισυς (**61.**5). Inscriptions show that
Attic had ττ from the earliest times, the σσ of earlier writers
being due to Ionic influence. But in the later κοινή, σσ is more
common than ττ. Most of the dialects agree with Ionic, but
ττ, as in Attic, is also Boeotian (φυλάττω, θάλαττα, πέτταρες,
ἥέμιττα), Cretan (ἴαττα = Arg. ἔασσα, κάρτων from *κάρττων),
and Euboean, at least in Styra, Eretria, Oropus (ἐλάττων, πρήττω,
Κιττιής).

a. Late Cret. σσ in πράσσω, θάλασσα, ἥμισσον, also in ὅσσος, δασσάσθωσαν
belonging under **82**, is due to (Attic-Ionic or Doric) κοινή.

b. Late Cret. θθ in words of this class, as θάλαθθα, ἴαθθα, also in ὑθθάκιν,
Ἀρκάθθι belonging under **82**, and even for original σσ in Ϝέτεθθι. For
σθ it is earlier and more frequent (**83**).

c. Although the Thessalian inscriptions usually have σσ, there is some
evidence that the dialect had ττ originally, or at least in certain localities.
Aside from θάλαττα, πίττα, which are quoted as Thessalian, cf. the proper
names Κόττυφος, Φαύττιος, etc., and especially Πετθαλός from Φετταλός
(**65**).

σ, σσ, ττ

82. τι and θι give Att. σ not ττ, and Ion. σ (early σσ often in
poetry, but never in inscriptions) in ὅσος, ὁπόσος (τι), μέσος
(*μέθιος, cf. Skt. *madhyas*). A dental + σ gives precisely the
same result, e.g., ἐκόμισα, ἐδίκασα, etc. In all such cases most
dialects have σσ (but σ, as Att.-Ion., in Arcadian, as μέσος, ὅσος,
ἐδικάσαμεν, δάσασθαι, elsewhere late), e.g., ὅσσος, τόσσος, Lesb.
μέσσος, ἐδίκασσαν, Heracl. μέσσος, ἐδασσάμεθα, Arg. ἠργάσσαντο,
ἐδίκασσαν, ἡίσσατο, ἐσσάμενοι, Cyren. ἴσσαντα, ἰσσάμενος. But
Boeotian and Cretan have ττ, e.g., Boeot. μέττος, ὁπόττος, ἐψαφί-
τατο, ἀπολογίτταστη, Cret. μέττος, ὅττος, ὁπόττος, δάτταθθαι.
In some very early Cretan inscriptions we find ζ, as ὅζος, ἀν-
δάζαθαι.

a. This is to be recognized as the normal development of τι̯ and θι̯. The different result seen in the classes of words mentioned in **81** is due to the influence of the forms containing gutturals. After a consonant τι̯ gives σ in all dialects; e.g., πάνσα, πᾶσα, from *πάντι̯α.

b. Forms of Dor. ἴσαμι (**162**.9) regularly show single σ. Only late Cret. ἴθθαντες, ἴθθᾶντι seem to point to σσ (unless Hom. ἴσᾶσι beside ἴσᾱσι stands for ἴσσᾶσι), and these are not to be taken too seriously.

Original σσ

83. Original σσ, which becomes σ in Attic (ἐτέλεσα, γένεσι), is retained, as in Homer, etc., in most dialects (cf. ὅσσος, etc., **82**), e.g., Lesb. ἔσσονται, Thess. ἔσσεσθειν, Heracl. ἐσσῆται, Ther. ἐσσεῖται, dat. pl. -εσσι in numerous dialects, Heracl. -ασσι (**107**.3). For late Cret. Fέτεθθι see **81***b*.

ζ, δδ

84. Attic-Ionic ζ, the early pronunciation of which was *zd* and which comes from *zd* (ὅζος, cf. Germ. *Ast*,; ᾿Αθήναζε from -α(ν)ς-δε) or, more often, from γι̯ (μείζων, μέζων) or δι̯ (πεζός)), is also ζ in the majority of other dialects. Lesb. σδ, found in our literary texts and in a few late inscriptions, is only another spelling of the same sound, adopted perhaps because ζ was used with the value of *z* in ζά = διά, etc. (**19**.1).

But assimilation to δδ, initial δ, is Boeotian, Thessalian, Elean, Cretan, Laconian, and Megarian (?). Boeot. γραμματίδδω, ψαφίδδω, δοκιμάδδω, ἱαρειάδδω, τρέπεδδα, δώω (ζώω), Δεύς, δύγαστρον, μέδδονος (= μέζονος), Thess. ἐξξανακάδεν (no. **35**; the only example, so possibly δδ only in Thessaliotis, but there is no evidence against its being general Thessalian). El. δικάδω, χραίδω, Cret. δικάδδω, ψαφίδδω, ἐργάδδομαι, φροντίδδω, δώω, δωός, δυγόν, Δῆνα (Ζῆνα), Lac. γυμνάδδομαι, etc. in Ar. Lys., μιχκιχιδδόμενος, ὀπιδό[μενος], Δεύς in inscriptions. Δεύς occurs also on a vase from Rhodes, and is perhaps genuine Rhodian. Cf. the occasional assimilation of σδ in external combination in Rhodian (**97**.4). Meg. δδ is doubtful (Ar. Ach. μᾶδδα, χρήδδω, but only ζ in inscriptions).

In Cretan and Elean the spelling ττ is also found, as Cret. φροντίττω, ἐσπρεμμίττω (ἐκπρεμνίζω), ἀπολογίττω (but see also below, *a*), Ττῆνα, Τῆνα (Ζῆνα), El. νοστίττω (νοστίζω), ἀττάμιος (ἀζήμιος).

a. There is some interchange between presents in -σσω or -ττω and those in -ζω or -δδω, owing to the identity of their future and aorist forms. Thus Att. σφάττω = Ion. σφάζω, Boeot. σφάδδω, Boeot. φράττω (Corinna) = Att. φράζω, Thess. ἐμφανίσσω = Att. ἐμφανίζω, and, conversely, Cret. πράδδω, συνεσσάδδω = Att. πράττω, -σάττω, Cret. ἀλλάδδω, Locr. ἀλάζω (regular from γχ, cf. ἀλλαγή) = Att. ἀλλάττω, Ion. ἀλλάσσω.

σθ

85. I. στ = σθ. The use of στ for σθ is mainly characteristic of Northwest Greek. It is the regular spelling in Locrian, as hελέσται, hαρέσται, and early Elean, as χρεῖεσται, λυσάστō, and occurs with some frequency in Phocian, as Delph. πρόστα, hιλαξάστō, later γινέστω, etc., Stir. θέστων, ἀποπολιτεύσασται. It occurs also in Boeotian, in late inscriptions of Orchomenus (ἀπολογίτταστη, etc.), where it is perhaps due to Aetolian influence, and rarely in Thessalian (πεπεῖστειν, ἐλέστειν, πρόστεν). But there are some early examples in other dialects, as Cret. μιστός, Lac. ἀποστρυθεῖεσται, χρῆσται, Arc. (probably) [ἀφάε]σται, and in late times it is found in many parts of Greece, even at Athens.

2. σσ = σθ. This is found in late Elean, as ἀποδόσσαι (no. 65), ποιήασσαι (no. 66).

3. θθ = σθ. This is regular in Central Crete, e.g., πρόθθα, ἀποϜειπάθθō, πράδεθθαι, δατεῖθθαι, etc. (numerous examples in Law-Code, always θθ or θ), also rarely τθ as δέκετθαι, χρῆτθαι (no. 118), ἀπολογιττέτθω. But σθ occurs in some of the earliest inscriptions, and also (here probably from the κοινή) in the late inscriptions from other parts of Crete.

Assimilation, Dissimilation, and Transposition of Consonants

86. Assimilation in consonant groups. Many of the changes belonging under this head have been given already, e.g., under **55a, 69**.3, **74-76, 77**.1, **80, 84, 85**.2, 3. See also under external combination **96-100**. No notice is taken of assimilation which is common to all dialects and presumably proethnic, as δλ to λλ, etc.; nor of the partial assimilation involved in the familiar shift of voiced to voiceless before voiceless or conversely (but ζμ, ζβ, ζγ, ζδ, for σμ, etc., though widespread, are mostly late). This class of phenomena is one in which the difference between colloquial and careful speech is most noticeable, as may readily be observed in English. While some assimilations are so uniformly effected that the unassimilated form is completely displaced and forgotten, others remain colloquial only, the unassimilated form being still preferred in careful speech and writing. This accounts for much of the lack of uniformity in the evidence as regards some of the changes mentioned in this and the other sections. In some cases the spelling varies greatly even in the dialects where the change is best attested. Sometimes the assimilation is uniform in certain dialects, but evidently existed colloquially in others also and only sporadically made its appearance in the spelling. Assimilation is most extensive in Cretan.

1. κτ > ττ in Cretan. νυττί = νυκτί, ἐσπράτται = ἐκπράκται, Λύττος = Λύκτος.

2. πτ > ττ in Cretan and Thessalian. Cret. ἔγρατται = γέγραπται, ἐττά = ἐπτά, πέντος (also Amorg., but here special case) = πέμπτος, Thess. Λεττίναιος (Λεπτίναιος), οἱ ττολίαρχοι, ἀρχιττολιαρχέντος (πτόλις, 67), also ἀτ τᾶς, etc. in external combination (99.2). Cf. also Thess. Ἀτθόνειτος = Ἀφθόνητος.

3. σγ > γγ or γ (with graphic or actual simplification). Cret. πρείγōν, πρείγιστος (both in Law Code), πρεῖγυς, πρειγήια, πρειγευτάς, πρειγευσάντων, Locr. πρείγα (no. 59.10), all from πρεισγ-seen in Boeot. (ι from ει, 29) πρισγῆες, πρισγεῖες (no. 40), πρισγού-τερος (Ἀρχ. Δελτ. 14, πίναξ 4a, l. 48), beside πρεισ-β- in Thess. πρεισβεία and πρεσ-γ-, πρεσ-β- in Arg. πρεσγέα (no. 85.39), later πρεσβήα (hybrid form), Att.-Ion. πρέσβυς, etc.

a. The form πρεισ- is not from πρεσ-, but an independent parallel form (cf. Lat. *preiscus, priscus,* and *pris-* in Lat. *primus,* Pael. *prismu*). For the interchange of γ and β, see 68.1. Late Cret. πρεισγευτάς and πρεγγευτάς in inscriptions of Teos are hybrid forms. In late Cret. πρήγιστος and late Coan πρηγιστεύω the η is due to the late confusion of ει and η.

b. A parallel change of σκ to κκ is attested for late Laconian by glosses like ἀκκόρ · ἀσκός. Λάκωνες (Hesych.), in this case confirmed by the modern Tsakonian form.

4. στ > ττ. Examples in several dialects, beside usual spelling στ. Cret. μεττ' ἐς beside μέστα, Lac. βεττόν 'dress' (Etym. M.)

= *Ϝεστόν, Boeot. ἔττε = ἔστε, ἴττω (Ar., Plato) = ἴστω.

5. ρν > νν. Cret. ἀννίοιτο = ἀρνέοιτο, ὄννιθα = ὄρνιθα, ᾽Ελευθενναῖος = ᾽Ελευθερναῖος.

6. ρδ (through ρρ) > ρ with lengthening of the preceding vowel. Cret. Ϝέροντι, Ϝηρόντων (Gortyn) beside Ϝέρδηι (Lato), πῆριξ · πέρδιξ Hesych.

7. μν > μμ. Cret. ἐσπρεμμίττω = ἐκπρεμνίζω.

8. νμ > μμ. Att. (inscriptions) ὕφαμμα, Cyren. ποτιπίαμμα, Troez. πεπεμμένος (from πένομαι). But usually replaced by analogical σμ, as ὕφασμα, etc.

9. γμ > μμ. Cret. ψάφιμμα = ψάφιγμα (142a).

10. γν > ν. γίγνομαι appears as γίνομαι in most dialects except Attic (here also, but late), or as γίνυμαι (Thess., Boeot.). γινώσκω = γιγνώσκω occurs in Lesbian and in Ionic prose writers (Att. γεινώσκω very late), and in some late Doric inscriptions. This is not really assimilation, but loss of γ by dissimilation from the initial γ, supported, in the case of γίνομαι, by the γεν of other tenses.

87. Transposition in consonant groups. As τίκτω from *τίτκω, so probably δάκτυλος from *δάτκυλος, to which points Boeot. δακκύλιος (κκ from τκ as in Thess. πὸκ κί from πὸτ κί, whereas κκ from κτ would be contrary to all analogy, cf. **86**.1). But most examples are of colloquial and transitory character, more or less frequently repeated slips of the tongue, or sometimes, without doubt, only graphic. Thus from Attic inscriptions σχυναρχόντων = χσυν- (ξυν-), εὐσχάμενος = εὐχσάμενος, σφυχή = ψυχή, ἔγρασφεν (often on vases) = usual ἔγραφσεν, μεσόμνη = μεσόδμη (δμ first to νμ by assimilation); Arg. ξύλλεσθαι = σκύλλεσθαι; Syrac., Cret. ψέ, ψίν (Cret. ψὲ αὐτόν, ψσὶν αὐτοῖς) = σφέ, σφίν.

88. Assimilation, dissimilation, and transposition, between non-contiguous consonants. Except for the regular dissimilation of aspirates in proethnic Greek (**65**), these phenomena are of the same occasional character as the preceding (**87**). They are most frequently observable in the case of aspirates, or of liquids, for which see **65, 70**. A nasal may interchange with an oral stop of its own class, by assimilation or dissimilation with another nasal, e.g., Cret. νύναμαι = δύναμαι (cf. Mod. Grk. Μεντέλη beside Πεντέλη, name of Mt. Pentelicus), or, conversely, Att.

τέρβινθος beside τέρμινθος, Att. κυβερνάω from *κυμερνάω beside Cypr. κυμερênαι and βάρναμαι = μάρναμαι, which occurs in certain inscriptions in epic style from Athens, Corcyra, etc. (nos. 94, 95). But Arg. σπάδιον = στάδιον is perhaps the earlier form, the Att. στ due to influence of στάδιος. Dissimilatory loss of the labial element in the labiovelars (**68**), as in ἀρτοκόπος from -πόπος, Att. γέφυρα (**68**.2), Dor. γλέπω, γλέφαρον = βλέπω, βλέφαρον, Ion. γλήχων, Dor., Boeot. γλάχων = Att. βλήχων. Transposition, e.g., Ion. ἀμιθρέω = ἀριθμέω, Arg. φάλυρον = λάφυρον, Delph., Epid. βόλιμος = μόλιβος (Att. usually μόλυβδος, βόλυβδος), also with assimilation Rhod. βόλιβος in περιβολιβῶσαι, Cret. νεμονηία, Νεμονήιος = νεομηνία, Νεομήνιος.

a. Among the examples of haplology or syllabic loss by dissimilation (Att. ἀμφορεύς vs. Hom. ἀμφιφορεύς) some are dialectal. Epid. hεμίδιμμνον from ἡμι(μέ)διμνον, as Att. ἡμέδιμνον from ἡ(μι)μέδιμνον. Cret. νεότας 'body of young men,' gen. νεότας from νεότα(το)ς, acc. νεότα from νεότατα, Lac. ΣαϜάναξ from Σα(Ϝο)Ϝάναξ.

b. There are other cases of syllabic loss which do not come under the head of haplology. Many Thess. proper names in 'Αστο- = 'Αριστο-, as 'Αστοκράτεις, 'Αστόδαμος, etc., Thess. Λασαίοις (no. 32.19), Λασχίοι (gen. sg.), also Λάσαν· τὴν Λάρισσαν Hesych., beside usual Λαρισαῖος, etc. (or later σσ).

Doubling of Consonants, Simplification of Double Consonants, and Other Losses of Consonants

89. A single consonant is often written double, this indicating a syllabic division by which it was heard at the end of one syllable and the beginning of the next. But not all the examples below can be understood in this way.

1. σστ, σσχ, σζ, ξσ, ξξ, etc. Such spellings as 'Αρισστο-, ὅσστις, 'Ασσκλαπιός, κόσσμος, γράσσμα are frequent and not confined to particular dialects. Similarly σζ (= zzd) in Arg. δικάσζω (no. 84, early), Delph. δουλίσζω, etc.; ξσ (= κσσ) in Corinth. Ϙόραξς, Rhod. κύλιξς, Πραξσιόδō (no. 101), Ion. ἔξς (no. 4.5), Boeot. ἀργυροτόξσοι, Naxian Ναξσίō, Φηράξσō, ἔξσοχος (probably; see no. 6); ξξ in Thess. ἔξξοι, ἐξξανακάδεν, Locr. ψάφιξξιν, δόξξαι, ἐξξόλλειαν, ἀξξιομάχōς, Arc. Πολυξξένα, etc. Cf. also Locr. ἐκκπρᾶξαι, Lesb. ἐκκτός, Ion. (Ephesus) ἔκττη, ὀκττώ, ἡμίεκττα (also ἐκ ττῶν, etc.).

2. μμν, ττρ. Epid. μέδιμμνον, hεμίδιμμνον, ἰαρομμνάμονες (no.
89), Arg. γυμμνικός, πέττρινον, Cret. ἀλλόττριος.
3. Doubling before consonantal ι in Thessalian. See **19**.3.
4. Doubling between vowels (besides ξξ, for which see above,
1), mainly of nasals or liquids. Thess. μναμμεῖον, Δαμμάτρειος,
ὀβελλός, δούρραντα, Lesb. πραγρηημμένω, φίλημμι, δίννηντες,
διννάεις, ἀρότρωμμεν, etc., Rhod. εἴμμειν, Dodon. ἄμμεινον,
Boeot. θάλλατταν, Delph. ἐλλευθερία. Likewise in external combination (**101**.1). But also El. ἀνταποδιδῶσσα, Cret. σποϝδδάν
(spirant δ?).

a. The frequency of such forms in Lesbian and Thessalian was promoted
by the numerous cases of regular μμ, etc., from combinations (**74-76**).
b. Single σ is the correct early spelling of Cret. Κνωσός (single σ also
confirmed by Arg. Κνόhιοι = Κνόσιοι), and the Thessalian and Argive
Λάρισα. The forms with σσ are late.

5. Doubling in hypocoristic proper names, where it originates
in the vocative and is due to the emphatic utterance in calling.
Examples, though found elsewhere, are by far most frequent
in Boeotian, e.g., ᾿Αγαθθώ, Βίοττος, Μέννει, etc.

a. Similar to this "expressive" doubling in hypocoristic names is that
in nursery words like πάππα, ἄττα, etc., and in some colloquial words like
γύννις (from γυνή), Lat. *gibbus, lippus,* etc. Here lies the probable explanation of the widespread μικκός (Dor., Boeot., etc.; proper names Μίκκος,
Μικκιάδης) formed from the μικ- of μικρός. Hence also with diminutive
suffixes μικκύλος and Lac. *μικκιχός implied by μι(κ)κιχιδδόμενος (cf.
nos. 75-78, note).

6. The simplification of double consonants is in part only
graphic. For the writing of single for double consonants is common
in early inscriptions, with varying degrees of frequency. Thus in
the earliest Attic inscriptions it is the usual practice. In the
Gortyn Law-Code, in case of the infinitives from -σθαι the pro-
portion of -θαι to -θθαι is roughly 3 : 1, while in external combination the double consonants resulting from assimilation are
so written in the majority of cases (**97**.3, 4, 5; **98**). Graphic
simplification is of course to be assumed in all cases of θάλασα =
θάλασσα, feminine adjectives in εσα = -εσσα (for στονόϝεσαν,
no. 94, there is the added metrical evidence), and many others.
So for early examples of ἥμισον = usual ἥμισσον (e.g., Locr. no.

59.17, Arg. no. 85.7), in spite of the frequency in later times of ἥμισον, which was probably influenced by Att. ἥμισυς.

7. But actual simplification occurs in Att.-Ion., Arc. σ from σσ in forms like μέσος, aor. ἐδίκασα, dat. pl. γένεσι, etc. (**82, 83**), more exceptionally in Arc. φθέραι, Boeot. Θάροψ, etc. (**80**). It is also probable in external combination and composition in the numerous cases like κὰ τόν, πὸ τόν from κὰτ τόν, πὸτ τόν, El. καδαλέοιτο, καθυτάς, Arc. κακρίνε̄, κακριθέε̄, κακειμέναυ, ἰνηάταν, ἰμέσουν, ἰμέσος, (= ιν- ιμ-), τὰ Ϝάδω (= τὰν Ϝάδω), συϜοικία, κὰ Ϝοικίας τὰ δέ, (**96.**5, **97.**2), Lac. τᾶ σιῶ (= τᾶς σιῶ), Locr. ἐ τᾶς, ἐ δάμο̄, ἐ λιμένος, etc., from assimilated ἐκ (**100**), Locr. also αἴ τι, ἀνάτο̄, ἀδίκο̄ = αἴ τις, ἀνάτος, ἀδίκος, all before συλο̄ι, etc.

a. In many editions of texts it is the practice to expand the spellings, e.g., θάλα(σ)σα, πὸ(τ) τόν, etc. But in this book, with occasional exceptions to save comment, the simple consonants are left as in the original.

8. The loss ot a consonant in groups of three is mainly pre-historic and general Greek, as in γεγράφθαι from *γεγράφσθαι. But there are some cases of loss in a secondary group of special dialectal forms. Att.-Ion., Delph., Epid. παστάς from *παρστάς, παραστάς, Thess. πεστάντες from *περστάντες (= περι-), Arc. θύσθεν from *θυρσθεν (**133.**1), Lesb. ἔσλος, Ion. (Chios), lit. Dor. (Pindar) ἐσλός, also ηεσλός (Olympia, dialect uncertain) = ἐσθλός, Lesb. μάσλης = μάσθλης.

9. The loss of final ν, frequent in inscriptions and papyri of Hellenistic times, is also seen in Pamph. πόλι beside πόλιν, ἰ = ἰν. Some alleged early anticipations of this tendency are of uncertain significance, in part perhaps only graphic errors, e.g., Arg. τελαμό̄ (no. 82) = τελαμών, and Arg. gen. dual τοῖ Ϝανάκοι (the τοῖ could be from τοιν by assimilation and simplification, like that in Arc. τὰ Ϝάδω, συϜοικία, **96.**5).

CHANGES IN EXTERNAL COMBINATION [4]

90. The phenomena of external combination, or sentence phonetics, such as elision, crasis, consonant assimilation, etc., are found in all dialects. But in Greek, as in most other languages,

---

[4] Some matters which strictly belong under this head have been discussed elsewhere, as the rhotacism of final ς, treatment of final νς, etc.

there is a tendency to limit more and more the scope of such changes, and to prefer, in formal speech and its written form, the uncombined forms. The inscriptions, Attic as well as those of other dialects, differ greatly in this respect according to their time and character. The following general observations may be made.

1. The changes occur mainly between words standing in close logical relation. Thus oftenest in prepositional phrases, or between the article, adjective, or particle and the noun with which it agrees; frequently between particles like καί, δέ, μέν, etc., and the preceding or following word; less often between the subject or object and the following verb; and very rarely in looser combinations.

2. While the less radical changes, such as the elision of a short vowel or the simpler forms of consonant assimilation, are least restricted in scope and survive the longest, the more violent forms of crasis and of consonant assimilation are the most infrequent and the soonest given up. Thus, in the matter of consonant assimilation, the partial assimilation of a nasal to a following stop, especially a labial, as in τὰμ πόλιν, is very common in all dialects down to a late period and sometimes observed even in loose combinations (cf. 96.1), but examples like τὸλ λόγον, τοὺν νόμους, etc., are comparatively infrequent and practically restricted to early inscriptions.

3. Although the dialects differ in the extent to which they exhibit these phenomena and in some details (e.g., Cretan shows the most extensive and radical series of consonant assimilations), the differences depend more upon the time and character of the inscription, the degree to which the language has been formalized.

4. There is no consistency in the spelling, even as regards the milder changes, combined and uncombined forms often standing side by side in the same inscription.

Elision

91. Elision is common to all dialects, but, as in Attic, subject to great inconsistency as regards the written form, which even in metrical inscriptions is very often not in accord with the

demands of the meter. In general, elision is most frequent in the conjunctions and particles such as δέ (ὅδε, οὐδέ, etc.), τε, κα, ἀλλά, etc., the prepositions, and, among case-forms, in stereotyped phrases like πόλλ' ἀγαθά, etc. The elision of a diphthong, e.g., Locr. δείλετ' ἀνχōρεῖν, is comparatively rare. For elision in place of usual crasis, see **94**.

a. Elision in περί (Attic only before ι), as in Doric poetry, in Cypr. περ' 'Εδάλιον, and in compounds Delph., Lesb., Boeot. (also in Pindar) πέροδος, Locr. Περόχθεος, Boeot. περαγείς (Corinna). Cf. πέρ by apocope (**95**).

Aphaeresis

92. Examples of aphaeresis occur in various dialects. Ion. ἢ 'ς, μὴ 'λάσσονες (Chios, no. 4), Locr. ἒ 'δελφιόν, ἒ 'χεπάμōν, μὲ 'ποστᾶμεν, ἒ 'ν πόλι, ἒ 'ν ἀποκλēσίαι, El. μὲ 'νπōι, μὲ 'πιποεόντōν, μὲ 'πιθεῖαν, Lesb. σ[τάλλ]α 'πι, Cret. ἢ 'ν, ἢ 'πί.

Shortening of a Final Long Vowel

93. The shortening of a final long vowel before an initial vowel, so well known in poetry, may occasionally show itself in the spelling of inscriptions, e.g., Cret. μὲ ἔκηι (μὴ ἔχῃ), μὲ ἔνδικον, etc., Meg. ἐπειδὲ 'Ικέσιος.

Crasis

94. Crasis, mostly of καί or forms of the article with the following word, is found in the early inscriptions of all dialects, though the uncombined forms are more frequent. As between the "phonetic principle", where the result of crasis is in accordance with the regular laws of contraction, and the "etymological principle," with lengthening of the vowel as in Att. ἀνήρ = ὁ ἀνήρ, the former is almost, if not wholly, predominant outside of Attic.

1. ο, secondary ō (ου), ω, + α (cf. **44**.1). Ion. ὠνήρ, τώγῶνος (τοῦ ἀγῶνος), with the regular contraction to ω, where Attic has ἀνήρ, τἀγῶνος. Similarly Lesb. (lit.) ὤνηρ, Arc. κὰ τὸρρέντερον (κατὰ τὸ ἀρρέντερον), Delph. τὠπελλαίου (τοῦ 'Απελλαίου), τὠπόλλωνι (τῶι 'Απόλλωνι), Boeot. τὸπόλλōνι (τοῖ 'Απόλλωνι), Corinth. τὸπέλōνι (τῶι 'Απέλλωνι), τὠγαθόν (τὸ ἀγαθόν), Meg. ὀρχέδαμε (ὤ

'Αρχέδαμε), and so regularly in literary Doric. Elision, rather than crasis, according to the "etymological principle", is probably to be assumed in Arc. τἀπόλλωνι [5] (τοῖ 'Απ-), Corinth. τἀριστερόν (τὸ ἀριστερόν), Arg. τἀργεῖοι (τοὶ 'Αργεῖοι), τἀργείō (τοῦ 'Αργείου), Locr. τἀπόλογοι (τοὶ ἀπόλογοι).

2. ο + ο, ε or η (cf. **44**.2, 3, 4). Att.-Ion. τοὔνομα, Lesb. ὠνίαυτος (ὁ ἐνίαυτος), Locr. ὁπάγōν (ὁ ἐπάγων). Ion. τὤμισυ (τὸ ἤμισυ).

3. α + ο (cf. **41**.2). Att., Dor. χώ (καὶ ὁ), Ion., Cret. κώ (καὶ ὁ), Lesb. (lit.) κὤττι (καὶ ὅττι), El. κὀπόταροι (καὶ ὁπόταροι). Cf. Aegin. χὀλέφας (καὶ ὁ ἐλέφας) with double crasis, like χὼκ (καὶ ὁ ἐκ) in Theocritus.

4. ᾱ + ο (cf. **41**.4). Meg. ἀλυνπιάς (ἁ 'Ολυνπιάς).

5. ᾱ + ε (cf. **41**.3). Locr. hαπιϜοικία (ἁ ἐπιϜοικία).

6. α + ε (cf. **41**.1). Att.-Ion. κἀγώ (καὶ ἐγώ), κἀπί (καὶ ἐπί), τἀν (τὰ ἐν), etc., West Greek κήν, κήκ, κήπί (καὶ ἐν, καὶ ἐκ, καὶ ἐπί), Boeot. κἠπιχά̄ριτται (Ar.), etc. So also in Thessalian (no. 35) κ̄εν and τ̄ες (τὰ ἐς). Lesbian has κ̄εμέ (καὶ ἐμέ) in an early inscription, while the texts of the Aeolic poets vary between α and η (see p. 343); and Arcadian has κ̄επί. Elision before ε plus two consonants, Cret. κέρσενος, Epid. κένκαύσιος, etc.

7. With words beginning with a diphthong. Delph. κηὔκλεια (καὶ Εὔκλεια), κ]ωὔτε (καὶ οὔτε), Rhod. ōὐδάμō (ὁ Εὐδάμου), Ion. ὠισυμνήτης (ὁ αἰσυμνήτης), like lit. ωὐτός (ὁ αὐτος) in Homer, etc., κωὐδέν (καὶ οὐδέν) in Epicharmus, ὡπόλος (ὁ αἰπόλος), τωὐβούλοιο (τῶ Εὐβ-) in Theocritus. But also with diphthong unchanged, that is, with what is really elision, as commonly in lit. Attic and Ionic (κοὐ, κοὔτε, χοί= καὶ οἱ, κεὐ- = καὶ εὐ-), Thess. κοί (καὶ οἱ), Ion. τοἰκόπεδον (τὸ οἰκό-), κοἰνοπίδης (καὶ Οἰνο-), Arc. κεὐορ-κέντι (καὶ εὐ-). The proper transcription of forms in the pre-Ionic alphabet is sometimes uncertain, but, in general, crasis is most common in early inscriptions, and it is probable that we should transcribe Thess. κ̄εὐϜεργέταν (no. 35), Boeot. τεὐτρετι-φάντō (no. 38.5), and Aegin. hōικος (ὁ οἶκος).

---

[5] We continue, as a matter of convention, to transcribe in the form of crasis when the combination belongs to those which commonly suffer crasis, even in cases where we believe the phenomenon is elision. For it is impossible to draw the line between crasis and elision with certainty. See also here under 7, 8, 9.

8. With words beginning with ι or υ. Cret. κυίέες (καὶ υἱέες), El. κύπαδυκίοι (καὶ ὑπα-), Delph. κίδιῶται (καὶ ἰδιῶται). In such cases there is of course no evidence as to whether the υ or ι was lengthened, as usually in Attic-Ionic, but probably we have here simply elision.

9. In Elean in the forms of the article the final vowel or diphthong disappears, sometimes even the vowel with final consonant. Thus τἰαρόν (τὸ ἰαρόν), τἰαρō (τῶ ἰαρῶ), τἰαροῖ (τοῖ ἰαροῖ), τἐπιάροι (τοῖ ἐπιάροι), and even τὸρ ἰαρομάορ τόλυνπίαι (τὸρ 'Ολυνπίαι). This is clearly not crasis proper, but an extension of the principle of elision. Cf. θυίῶι (τῶι υἱῶι) in an Attic inscription and Locr. (Halae) τὸαροί = τοὶ ἰαροί.

Apocope

95. Apocope of prepositions, while very rare in Attic-Ionic prose, is common in other dialects, with differences in frequency, chronology, and especially in the range of prepositions affected. Most widespread are ἄν (or ὀν-, ὐν-, **6, 22**) and πάρ. — κάτ and (in the ποτί-dialects) πότ are common, in the West Greek dialects mostly before a dental (in Heraclean only so), and frequently with simplification of the double consonants (**89.**6), κὰ τόν, πὸ τόν, etc. But also before other consonants (like Hom. κὰκ κεφαλῆς, κὰγ γόνυ, κὰν νόμον, etc.), as Boeot. κὰγ γᾶν, πὸκ κατόπτας, Thess. κὰπ παντός, πὸκ κί, Lac. καββαλικός, Καβάτα, Lesb. κάλλιπεν, etc. Regularly κά, κα- in the early Arcadian and Elean inscriptions, as Arc. κὰ μῆνα, κακρίνē, El. καδαλέοιτο, καθυτάς, etc.—Arc. also πέ from πεδά in πὲ τοῖς Ϝοικιάταις.— πέρ from περί occurs in Delphian, Elean (πάρ), Thessalian, lit. Lesbian, and in proper names in Locrian (ΠερϞοθαριᾶν), Laconian, Messenian and Cretan. —ἄπ, ἔπ, ὐπ are (except for a few cases in compounds before a labial, as Hom. ἀππέμψει, ὑββάλλειν, Lesb. ἀπ πατέρων (Alcaeus) only Thessalian, which in general has more extensive apocope than any other dialect, namely ἄν, πάρ, πέρ, κάτ, πότ, ἄπ (ἀτ τᾶς), ἔπ (ἐτ τᾶ, ἐτ τοῖ), ὑπ- (ὑππρό). Cf. also Thess. gen. sg. -οι from -οιο, doubtless first in the proclitic article.

a. There is an unimportant difference of practice in regard to the apocopated forms beginning with a vowel. In some editions of literary texts and inscriptions they are given without accent, on the analogy of ἐκ, ἐν, etc., e.g., Lesb. ἀπ πατέρων, Thess. ἀτ τᾶς. But consistently with the prevailing reading of Hom. ἄμ πεδίον, etc., we read ἀτ τᾶς, etc.

Consonant Assimilation

(in part with further simplification of· the double consonants. 89.6)

96. Assimilation of final ν.

1. To the class of a following labial or guttural. Cases like τὴμ πόλιν, τὸγ κήρυκα, νῦμ μέν, are frequent in Attic inscriptions, and likewise in the other dialects. So also between object and verb as Delph. τόκιομ φερέτω, Arc. πόσοδομ ποέντω, and in looser combinations as Att. ἐστὶμ περί, Arc. ἰν ἐπίκρισιγ κατάπερ, Arg. ποιοῖεγ κατά.

2. To σ. Att. ἐς Σάμωι, ἐᾶ Σαλαμίνι (= ἐᾶν Σ-), Ion. τῶς συμπάντων, Epid. τὸς σακόν. Cf. Ion. πασσυδίηι beside πανσυδίηι, and Lesb. πασσυδιάσαντος.

Before σ + consonant. Att. ἐσ στήληι but oftener ἐ στήληι, also τὲ στέλεν. So Rhod., Cret. ἐ στάλαι, El. τὰ στάλαν. These do not arise by assimilation but by regular loss of ν. See **77**.2, **78**.

3. To λ. Att. ἐλ λίμναις, τὸλ λόγον, Ion. ἐλ Λαρυσσῶι, Delph. τῶλ Λαβυαδᾶν, Lac. ἐλ Λακεδαίμονι, Epid. τὸλ λίθον, τῶλ λίθων. Cf. συλλέγω, ἀλλύω = ἀναλύω, etc.

4. To ρ. Att. ἐρ ῾Ρόδωι, τὸρ ῾Ρόδιον. Cf. συρρίπτω, etc.

5. To Ϝ. Arc. συϜοικία, τὰ Ϝάδω = τὰν Ϝάδω.

a. In Cyprian, where ν before a consonant is always omitted in the interior of a word, it is also frequently omitted in sentence combination as τὰ(ν) πτόλιν.

97. Assimilation of final ς.

1. To ν. Delph. τοὺν νόμους. Cf. Πελοπόννησος (Πέλοπος νῆσος), Arc. ταῖννυ, ταιννί (ταῖς-νυ, -νί), ταννί (τασ-νί, acc. pl.), τανί (gen. sg.).

2. To μ and Ϝ. Cypr. Ϝέπο μέγα = Ϝέπος μέγα, τᾶ Ϝανάσας = τᾶς Ϝανάσσας. In the same way arose κά = κάς (καί) in Cypr. κὰ μέν, Arc. κὰ Ϝοικίας.

3. To λ. Att. τὸλ λίθ͡ος, Cret. τοῖλ λείονσι, τὶλ λε͡ι, Lac. ἐλ Λακεδαίμονα (ἐλ = ἐς), τοῖ Λακεδαιμονίοις, Cyren. ἐλ Λιβύαν, Arg. κὲλ Λευκόπορον (καὶ ἐλ Λ-).

4. To δ. So regularly in Cretan, e.g., τᾶδ δαίσιος, τᾶδ δέ, ἐδ δικαστέριον, πατρὸδ δόντος τᾶ δίκας, τὸδ δ' ὀδελόνς. Rarely else-

where, but cf. Rhod. Ζεὺ δέ (no. 100), ματρὸ δέ, τὰ δευτέρας, Arc. τὰ δέ = τὰς δέ. Assimilation in the opposite direction is seen in Arg. βωλᾶς σευτέρας (no. 86). Partial assimilation in early Arg. τοῖζ δε. Cf. late Arg. πρεζβευτῶν, etc.

5. To θ. Cretan only, as τὰθ θυγατέρας. Cf. Cret. θθ = σθ medially (85.3).

a. Before a word beginning with a vowel final ς may be treated as intervocalic, e.g., Lac. Διοηικέτα, Διōλευθερίō = Διὸς ἱκέτου, Διὸς ἐλευθερίου (cf. 59.1), Cypr. κὰ ἀ(ν)τί, τᾶ ὑχέρον (59.4), Eretr. ὅπωρ ἄν (60.3).

98. Assimilation of final ρ to δ. So regularly in Cretan, e.g., ἀνὲδ δõι, πατὲδ δόει, and πατὲ δόει. Cf. Cnid. πὰ Δάματρα = παρὰ Δ-.

99. Assimilation of a final stop.

1. Final τ. The apocopated forms of κατά and ποτί, so far as they occur otherwise than before τ (cf. 95), are generally assimilated (sometimes with further simplification; see 89.7), e.g., Thess. κὰπ παντός, πὸκ κί (πὸτ κί = πρὸς τί), Boeot. πὸδ Δάφνη, πὸκ κατόπτας, Lesb. κὰκ κεφάλας (Alcaeus), κὰμ μέν (Sappho), etc. So in compounds, e.g., El. καδαλέοιτο, καθυτάς, Lesb. κάββαλλε (Alcaeus), καλλύοντος, Arc. κακειμέναυ, κακρίνε͞, Lac. Καβάτα (Καταβάτου), καβαίνων (Alcman), etc. But -τ θ- is often unassimilated.

2. Final π. Thess. ἄπ, ἔπ = ἀπό, ἐπί are assimilated in ᾶτ τᾶς, ἔτ τοῖ. Cf. 86.2.

3. Final κ. See 100.

100. ἐξ. In most dialects, as in Attic, ἐξ becomes ἐκ before a consonant, thus appearing often as ἐχ before an aspirate, and ἐγ before voiced stops and λ, μ, ν, Ϝ, until late times, when ἐκ is usual before all consonants. The general rule is, then, ἐξ before vowels, and ἐκ (ἐχ, ἐγ) before consonants. But the antevocalic form ἐξ occasionally appears before consonants in various dialects (so regularly in Cyprian, as ἐξ τõι, etc.).

In Locrian it is fully assimilated to all consonants, whence, with the simplification of double consonants, it appears simply as ἐ, e.g., ἐ τᾶς, ἐ δάμō, ἐ Ϙοινάνōν, ἐ θαλάσας, ἐ λιμένος, ἐ Ναυπάκτō. Cf. also Mess. ἐ Φιαλείας.

In Thessalian, Boeotian, Arcadian, and Cretan the regular form before consonants is ἐς, e.g., Thess. ἐς τᾶν, ἐσδόμεν, Boeot. ἐς τῶν, ἐσλιήνω (cf. also ἐσκηδεκάτη from ἐξ), Arc. ἐς τοῖ, ἐσδέλλοντες, ἐσπερᾶσαι, Cret. ἐς τόν, ἐσκλησία, Thess., Boeot., Cret. ἔσγονος = ἔκγονος. All these dialects have ἐξ before vowels except Boeotian, where ἐχς appears in an early inscription, but usually ἐς, as ἐς ἐφείβων, ἔσσειμεν. This is probably a transfer or the ante-consonantal form in an intermediate stage of its development (ἐξ, ἐς, ἐς).

a. There are some traces of ἐς in other dialects which generally have ἐκ or ἐξ, e.g. Cypr. ἐς πόθ' ἔρπες · πόθεν ἥκεις (Hesych.), Arg. ἐ Σικελίας, ἐς πόλιος, Rheg. ἔσκλητος (no. 107, note), Delph. ἐς τοῦ δρόμου (no. 50), ἔσγονος (no. 52 C 45).

Consonant Doubling

101. 1. Before vowels. Cret. τὰνν ἐμίναν, συνν-ἔι, Boeot., Co-rinth. ἀνν-έθηκε, Att. ξυνν-όντι, lit. Lesb. ὀνν-ώρινε, ἀσύννετος, Delph. ἐλεύθεροννν εἶμεν.

2. With ὅσστις etc. (**89.1**), compare Att. εἰς τήν, Epid. ἐς τό, etc., or Epid. τὸ σσκέλος, Coan τοῦ σστεφάνου. Ion. ἐξς (no. 4) like ψάφιξξις, Ion. ἐκ ττῶν like ὀκττώ (**89.1**), ἐκκ τοῦ in Attic inscriptions, etc.

ν Movable

102. The ν movable in the dative plural in -σι(ν) and in the verb forms in -σι(ν) and ε(ν) is a marked characteristic of Attic-Ionic, where it appears from the earliest inscriptions on with increasing frequency and before both vowels and consonants. (In Attic its use becomes gradually more and more uniform before vowels, and it is also somewhat more common before a pause in the sense than elsewhere.) In verb forms it is wholly unknown in the older inscriptions of other dialects, and where found is a sure sign of κοινή influence. But in the dative plural (where the ν is due to the analogy of pronominal datives like Att. ἡμῖν, Dor. ἁμίν, Lesb. ἄμμιν beside ἄμμι in which the ν is inherited) it appears outside of Attic-Ionic at an early period. Thus Thess. χρέμασιν (no. 35), Locr. ἀνδράσιν, γονεῦσιν, παμάτε-σιν (no. 59), Sicyon. φέρουσιν, Ϝοικέουσιν (no. 96); and so the later Lac. πᾶhιν, Heracl. ἔντασσιν, etc., Arc. χρήμασιν, ἀναλώμασιν, need not necessarily be charged to the κοινή.

ACCENT

103. Of the dialects outside of Attic-Ionic, Lesbian is the only one of whose accentual peculiarities we have any adequate knowledge. This was characterized by the recessive accent, e.g., πόταμος, σόφος, βασίλευς, λεῦκος,

The Doric accent is said by the grammarians to be processive in certain classes of forms, e.g., ἐλάβον, στάσαι, αἶγες = Att. ἐλαβον, στῆσαι, αἶγες. But the statements are too meager to admit of generalization as to the system as a whole, nor is it known whether all Doric dialects had these peculiarities. Hence the practice now frequently adopted, and followed in this book, of giving Doric forms with the ordinary Attic accent, except in a few well-established forms like Ποτιδάν. In general our accentuation of dialect forms can be little more than a matter of convenience. [6]

a. A question of detail, touching which there is considerable difference of practice among editors of dialect texts, is whether, in the case of inflectional forms which differ in their quantitative relations from the corresponding Attic forms, to adopt the actual accent of the Attic forms or to change the accent to accord with the Attic system, e.g., infin. κρίνεν like κρίνειν, or κρῖνεν, acc. pl. φερομένος like φερομένους, or φερόμενος, Cret. κάρτονανς, στατῆρανς like κρείττονας, στατῆρας, or καρτόνανς, στατήρανς. The question of the true accentuation is a complicated one, differing in each class of forms, and impossible of any certain answer. But practical convenience favors the use of the Attic accent in some cases, as in the accusative plural to distinguish it from the nominative, and we adopt this alternative in all the cases mentioned.

b. The pronominal adverbs in -ει, -αι, and -ω we accent as perispomena, following here what the grammarians laid down as the Doric accent, since this affords a convenient working rule, and serves to distinguish, e.g., τουτῶ from gen. τούτω. But it is far from certain that the accent was uniform, and that we should write, e.g., ἀλλεῖ, ἀλλᾶι, παντᾶι, as we do, and not, with some, ἄλλει like Att. οἴκει, and ἄλλαι, πάνται like Att. ἄλλη, πάντη. And as between ὀπεῖ and ὀπει, etc., about which the grammarians were in doubt, we definitely prefer ὀπει, ὀπαι, ὀπυι, ὀπη, ὀπω (cf. Att. ὀπου beside ποῦ, in spite of αὐτοῦ, etc.). We accent ἔνδοι, ἔξοι, ἦχοι, etc., like οἴκοι, though ἐνδοῖ etc. (cf. ἐνταυθοῖ) may also be defended.

INFLECTION

NOUNS AND ADJECTIVES

Feminine ā-Stems

104. 1. Nom. Sg. -ᾱ, Att.-Ion. -η.

2. Gen. Sg. -ᾱς, Att.-Ion. -ης.—Arc. -ᾱυ after the masculine, as οἰκίαυ, ζαμίαυ, but only at Tegea, and here -ᾱς beside -ᾱυ in early inscriptions, and always τᾶς.

3. Dat. Sg. -ᾱι, Att.-Ion. -ηι, whence also -ᾱ, -η, -ει. See **38, 39.**—Boeot. -αι (-αε, -η, **26**), and this is to be assumed in the other dialects which have -οι (**106.**2)

4. Acc. Sg. -ᾱν, Att.-Ion. -ην.

5. Nom. Pl. -αι (Boeot. -αε, -η, **26**).

6. Gen. Pl. -άων, -έων, -ῶν, -ᾶν. See **41.**4.

7. Dat. Pl. In early Attic -ᾱσι(ν), -ησι(ν), sometimes -ᾱισι(ν), -ηισι(ν), after 420 B.C. -αις .—In Ionic usually -ησι(ν), rarely -ηις, -ησι(ν), also -αις.— -ᾱσι rarely elsewhere, as early Troez. Θέβᾱσσι, Cret. (Drerus) πύλᾱσι, ἀγέλᾱσι (BCH 70.590, 597).— -ᾱισι or -αισι in Lesbian (but ταῖς), Pamphylian also Corcyrean (ρhοϜαῖσι poet.), and rarely in Cretan (beside rare -ᾱσι and usual -αις). The majority of dialects have -αις from the earliest times.

8. Acc. Pl. -ανς, with the same development as has -ονς from o-stems, namely (see also **78**) :

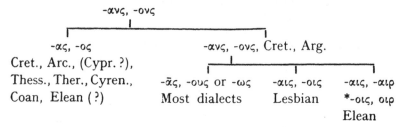

9. Nom.-Acc. Dual. Att. -ᾱ formed on the analogy of -ω in o-stems, but in pronouns usually τώ, etc., with o-stem form used

86

also for feminine. Examples in other dialects are rare, but Corinth. πύκτᾶ, and Boeot. δαρχμάω δύο, a blend of the two types.

10. GEN.-DAT. DUAL. Att. -αιν, examples in other dialects rare. Locr. τοῖν κόραιν (with ο-stem in the article, as in Attic), Arc. τοῖς Κράναιυν (with pl. ο-stem in article), and (AJA 1939, 196) Τυδαριδίαιυς. Cf. Arc. -οιυν, **106**.7.

11. The dual in general. The dual, which in Attic disappeared in the course of the fourth century B.C., and eventually everywhere, was lost at a still earlier period in some dialects. It is lacking in Ionic and Cretan inscriptions (cf. Cret. δύο στατε͂ρανς). But dual forms are quotable from several dialects, as Arc. -ω, -αιυν, -οιυν (no. 20), Boeot. Ϝαγάνω, δραχμάω, λέβε͂τε, all reinforced by δύο (no. 39), Locr. τοῖν κόραιν (no. 60), El. καταστατό, δυοίοις, αὐτοίοιρ (also dual verbal forms), Delph. δύο ὀδελώ, φρυκτώ (no. 53; but δύ' ὀδελός in the earlier no. 51), Lac. ἐπάκω, ἐπάκοε (nos. 72, 73), Corinth. πύκτᾶ, Arg. ἱλάρχω, Coan οἶε τέλεω.

Masculine ᾱ-Stems

105. 1. NOM. SG. -ᾱς (with secondary ς, after the analogy of -ος), Att.-Ion. -ης.

a. Forms without ς also occur, several in Boeotian, as Καλλία, Μογέα, etc., and a few from other parts of Northwest Greece, as Σϟόπα (Halae), Φιλοκλέδα (Dodona), etc. El. τελεστά is a form in -τᾱ like Hom. ἱππότα.

2. GEN. SG. -ᾱο (with ο, in place of ς, after that of ο-stems), whence Arc.-Cypr. -ᾱυ (**22**), elsewhere -ᾱ, Ion. -εω, -ω. See **41**.4. Att. -ου is not from -ᾱο, but the ο-stem form taken over as a whole.

a. There are a few Cypr. examples of -ᾱ, beside usual -ᾱυ, as 'Αμενίjα no. 23.19 vs. 'Ονασιγόραυ ll.1/2, 22.

b. -ᾱϜο, in ΤλασίαϜο, ΠασιάδαϜο, of two metrical inscriptions from Corcyra and Gela (nos. 93, 105), is a reminiscence of the epic -ᾱο (the spoken form was already -ᾱ, which appears in other equally early inscriptions, as 'Αρνιάδα no. 94, ΔϜενία no. 91) with the introduction of a non-etymological Ϝ, either representing a glide sound before the following ο (cf. ἀϜυτάν, no. 94; see **32**), or due to a false extension from forms with etymological Ϝ, as λᾱϜός = Hom. λᾱός (cf. Ion. 'ΑγασιλέϜο, no. 9).

c. Forms in -ᾱς, with the old ending unchanged and belonging with the nominatives in -ᾱ (above, 1a) occur in scattered examples in Megarian as Φάγας, etc. (no. 99) and from various parts of Northwest Greece, as Προκλείδας (no. 95).

d. Att.-Ion. proper names in -ης, from the fourth century on, frequently form the genitive after the analogy of σ-stems, e.g., Att. Καλλιάδους (after Δημοσθένους, etc.), Ion. Λεάδεος, 'Αριστείδευς. This type spreads to other dialects, e.g., Rhod. Μυωνίδευς.

o-Stems

106. 1. GEN. SG. -οιο (from *-οσιο, cf. Skt. -*asya*) as in Homer, whence, with apocope, Thess. (Pelasgiotis) -οι, as τοῖ, χρόνοι, etc. Elsewhere, with loss of ι and contraction, -ου or -ω (**25**).—In Cyprian -ōν beside -ō (at Idalium μισθōν, ἀργύρōν, Φιλοκύπρōν, etc., and so usually -ōν in nouns, whether vowel or consonant follows; but also ἀργύρō, ἄλϜō, before a consonant, and always τō).

a. -οιο is often employed in metrical inscriptions, in imitation of the epic, e.g., nos. 93, 94. But in Thessalian it also occurs in a few prose inscriptions, and the grammarians often refer to the Thessalian genitive in -οιο. This, together with the fact that apocope is more extensive in Thessalian than in any other dialect (see **95**), makes obvious the derivation of the usual Thess. -οι from -οιο, probably starting in the article, which was of course proclitic like the prepositions. For the added ν in Cyprian no explanation that has been offered is adequate.

2. DAT. SG. -ωι in most dialects, whence also -ω (**38**; Thess. ου, **23**).—οι in Arcadian (usually, but in no. 20 τῶι, τωινί, τῶινυ beside βουσοῖ, etc.), Elean, Boeotian (-οε, -υ, -ει, **30**), and in later inscriptions from various parts of Northern Greece (Delphi, Aetolia, Acarnania, Epirus, Cierium in Thessaly, Euboea).

a. In Euboea -οι replaces earlier -ωι and may be derived from it, like -ει from -ηι (see **39**). But in general -οι is rather the original locative (cf. οἴκοι) in use as the dative. In some dialects the history of the dative is obscure, owing to the lack of early material or the ambiguity of -OI in the pre-Ionic alphabets.

3. NOM. PL. -οι (Boeot. -οε, -υ, **30**).

4. DAT. PL. -οισι(ν), as in Homer, in early Attic, Ionic, where it lasts somewhat longer than in Attic (but some early examples of -οις, especially in West Ionic), Lesbian (but here always τοῖς), Pamphylian, and sometimes Cretan (but rare vs. -οις), Argive (only early), and Syracusan.—Elsewhere only -οις (Boeot. -υς, -εις, Elean -οιρ).

5. Acc. Pl. -ονς, with the same development as -ανς. See **78**, **104**.8.

6. Nom.-Acc. Dual. -ω. This is by far the most frequently attested dual form.

7. Gen.-Dat. Dual. -οιιν as in Homer, whence -οιν in most dialects in which the form occurs. But El. -οιοις, -οιοιρ. Arc. (no. 20) ἱμέσουν τοῖς Διδύμοιυν (cf. the preceding τὼ Διδύμω), like the -αιυν in ᾱ-stems (**104**.10).

a. The unique Arcadian forms seem to contain an inherited *u* connected with the *u*-diphthong to which the Sanskrit and Slavic dual forms point (Skt. *tayos*, ChSl. *toju*), but the detailed analysis is highly uncertain.

Consonant Stems in General

107. 1. Acc. Sg. -αν in place of the usual -α, with ν added after the analogy of vowel stems, occurs in Cypr. ἰjατε͂ραν, ἀ(ν)δριjά(ν)ταν, Thess. κίοναν, El. ἀγαλματοφῶραν (but possibly -φώρᾱν from nom. -φώρᾱς), and among late inscriptions of various dialects.

2. Nom. Pl. -εν for usual -ες occurs in late Cretan, having originated in pronominal forms. See **119**.2a.

3. Dat. Pl. -εσσι, as in Hom. πόδεσσι (either based on the -εσ-σι of σ stems or, as many prefer, formed to nom. pl. -ες after the analogy of -αισι, -οισι to -αι, -οι) is characteristic of the Aeolic dialects, Lesbian, Thessalian (but also χρέμασιν, ὑπάρχονσι), and Boeotian, also Pamphylian, Delphian, Locrian (no. 59 πα[μάτεσιν beside ἀνδράσιν, etc.; East Locr. χρημάτεσσι, etc.; but -οις in nos. 57, 58, 60), Elean (φυγάδεσσι no. 65; elsewhere -οις), with occasional forms in Cyrenaean (Εὐεσπερίδεσσι), and Corinthian colonies.—Heraclean has -ασσι in pres. pple. ἔντασσιν (a blend of ἐντ- with ἄσσι = Skt. *satsu*, see **163**.8), πρασσόντασσι, etc.— -οις, as πάντοις, etc., after the analogy of o-stems, is characteristic of Locrian (otherwise no. 59, see above), Elean, and the Northwest Greek κοινή, whence it finds its way into various dialects in later times. So in late inscriptions of Messenia, Laconia, Crete, and Tauromenium.

4. Acc. Pl. -ες in place of -ας, i.e., the nom. for the acc., perhaps first used in the numeral τέτορες owing to the influence

of the indeclinable πέντε, etc., is seen in Delph. δεκατέτορες, τέτορες, Δελφίδες (nos. 49, 51), and regularly in Elean ([τέτορ]ες, sixth century, πλείονερ, χάριτερ, no. 66, etc.) and Achaean (ἐλάσσονες, δαμοσιοφύλακες, etc.), also in the very late inscriptions of various dialects, even Attic.

Cret. -ανς beside -ας, e.g. θυγατέρανς, δρομέανς, κύνανς, after the analogy of -ανς, -ας from ᾱ-stems (104.8).

σ-Stems

108. 1. All dialects except Attic have the uncontracted forms. Gen. sg. in most dialects -εος, whence -ιος in Boeotian, Cretan, etc. (9), -ευς in later Ionic, Rhodian, etc. (42.5). Acc. sg. masc. and acc. pl. neut. -εα, or contracted η (42.1). Acc. pl. masc. fem. -εας in most dialects (Cyren. τριήρης, 42.1), Att. -εις (nom. used as acc.), also late in other dialects.

a. Proper names in -κλέης, -κλῆς. Cypr. -κλέϜὲς, whence -κλέης in Attic (beside -κλῆς), Boeotian (-κλέες, -κλές) till about 400 B.C., and regularly in Euboean (gen. -κλέω, 2), but in the other dialects regularly -κλῆς. Gen. sg. Cypr. -κλέϜεος, Boeot. -κλεῖος (= Hom. -κλῆος, cf. 16), Att. -κλέους, but in most dialects -κλέος.
For names in -κλέᾱς instead of -κλέης, see 166.1.

2. Proper names often have forms which are modeled after the analogy of the masc. ᾱ-stems, and this not only in Attic-Ionic (e.g., Att. Σωκράτην, Σωκράτου, Eretr. gen. Εὐκράτω, Τιμοκλέω), where the agreement in the nom. -ης was especially favorable to this, but also in other dialects. Thus acc. sg. in -ην (-ην : -ης = -ᾱν : -ᾱς), e.g., Boeot. Δαμοτέλειν, Arc. Ἐπιτέλην, and even in appellatives, e.g., Lesb. δαμοτέλην, Cypr. ἀτελέν.— Dat. sg. in -ηι, Lesb. Καλλίκληι, Cret. Δαμοκούδηι.—Gen. sg. in -η (like -ᾱ) in Lesb. Θεογένη, Thess. Φιλόκλει, Cret. Ἀλκιμένη, etc.; also, perhaps, -ης (like -ᾱς, 105.2b) in Thess. Ἱπποκράτεις, Φερεκράτες (no. 35; or Φερεκράτε(ο)ς?).—Voc. sg. in -η (like -ᾱ) in Arc. Ἀτέλη, etc., Delph. Πολυκράτη; in -ε (like -ᾰ in Δίκα) in Lesb. μελλιχόμειδε.

The numerous Boeotian hypocoristic names in -ει as Μέννει, Φίλλει, Θάλλει, Ξέννει, are also best understood as vocatives of this type used as nominatives. They correspond to names in -ης,

-ητος, in other dialects, but in Boeotian follow the analogy
of σ-stems (gen. sg. -ιος, acc. sg. -ειν).

ι-Stems

109. 1. In all dialects except Attic-Ionic, and, for the most
part, in Ionic too, the regular type of declension is that with
ι throughout, namely, -ις, -ιος, -ῑ, -ιν, -ιες, -ιων, -ισι, -ῑς (Arg.
Cret. -ινς) or -ιας (rare).

2. The type in -ις, -εως (from -ηος, as in Homer), -ει, pl. -εις,
etc., is almost exclusively Attic. In Ionic πόλεως occurs in
early inscriptions of Chios (no. 4) and Thasos, and Δυνάμει in
Teos (no. 3). But otherwise in Ionic, and always in other dialects,
forms of this type are late and to be attributed to Attic influence.
In general, the Attic datives, -ει and -εσι, are the first to be
adopted, next the nom.-acc. pl. -εις, and lastly the gen. sg. -εως.
Thus in the later inscriptions of many dialects it is common
to find gen. sg. -ιος, but dat. sg. -ει.

The nom. pl., originally -ειες whence Att. -εις, in other dialects
only in the numeral Cret. τρέες, Ther. τρῆς, etc.

A gen. sg. πόλεος is found in the κοινή and in later inscriptions
of various dialects.

3. Lesbian has a nom. pl. -ῑς (πόλις, no. 25), perhaps the accusative used as nominative.

4. Cyprian has such forms as gen. sg. ΤιμοχάριϜος, dat. sg.
πτόλιϜι. The Ϝ is certainly not original here, and is perhaps due
to the analogy of υ- and ηυ-stems (gen. -υϜος, -ēϜος).

5. A transfer to the type -ις, -ιδος, as frequently in Attic, is
characteristic of Euboean proper names in -ις, as Δημοχάριδος.

υ-Stems

110. Nearly all the inscriptional forms occurring are the usual
ones of the type -ῠς, -υος. Boeot. [Ϝ]άστιος (ι from ε, **9**) agrees
with the ἄστεος of non-Attic literature. For υἱύς see **112.2**.

Nouns in -ευς

111. The stem is ηυ, ηϜ throughout, nom. sg. -ευς (from -ηυς,
37.1), gen. sg. -ηϜος, etc.

1. The original forms in -ηϝος, -ηϝι, etc., are preserved, with or without the ϝ, in Cyprian (βασιλῆϝος, Ἐδαλιῆϝι, Ἐδαλιῆϝες), Lesbian (βασίληος, etc.), Boeotian (Πτōιῆϝι, γραμματεῖος, etc.), Thessalian (βασιλεῖος, etc.), and Elean (βασιλᾶες), as also in Homer.

2. Attic only are βασιλέως, βασιλέᾱ, with quantitative metathesis. But from the beginning of κοινή influence, βασιλέως is one of the Attic forms most widely adopted by other dialects.

3. Most dialects, namely, Ionic and the West Greek dialects except Elean, have βασιλέος, βασιλεῖ, etc., with shortening of the η. Generally these are the forms of even the earliest inscriptions (Cret. ϝοικέος, etc.), but we find Coan ἱερῆι, Πολιῆι, etc. (no. 108; later always ἱερεῖ, etc.), and once Rhod. Ἰδαμενῆος (cf. Ποντωρηίδος). Beside -εος sometimes -ευς (cf. 42.5), as Meg. ἱαρεῦς, but owing to the confusion with the nominative, this spelling is far less common than in the genitive of σ-stems.

Acc. Sg. -έα in Ionic, Locrian, Cretan. But in Delphian and most of the Doric dialects -ῆ is the regular form, e.g., Delph. ἱερῆ, βασιλῆ, Lac. βασιλῆ, Mess. ἱερῆ, Meg. ἱερῆ, Mycen. Περσῆ (no. 81, fifth century B.C.), Arg. βασιλῆ, Rhod. βασιλῆ, γραμματῆ, Coan βασιλῆ, etc. In these dialects -εα is of later occurrence, and due to κοινή influence.

Nom. Pl. -έες in Cretan (e.g., δρομέες) and elsewhere, but usually contracted to -εῖς. Also -ῆς (in part at least directly from -ῆες) in early Attic, Coan (τεταρτῆς), Laconian (Μεγαρῆς, etc., no. 69), and Arcadian (Μαντινῆς). At Cyrene occurs nom. and acc. pl. ἱαρές, and dat. pl. Μεγαρέσσι, etc. (cf. δρομέσι Callim.).

Acc. Pl. -έας in Ionic and Doric (Cret. δρομέανς, cf. 107.4), when not replaced by -εῖς of the κοινή.

4. Arcadian has nom. sg. in -ής, as ἱερής, γραφής, φονές (Cyprian also once ἰjερές, but usually -εύς), acc. sg. ἱιερέν (cf. 108.2), nom. pl. Μαντινῆς, gen. pl. Τορθυνήων, Μετιδριήων. Some proper names in -ής = -εύς are also found elsewhere.

5. In Miletus and colonies occurs nom. sg. ἱέρεως, gen. sg. ἱέρεω, likewise at Ephesus gen. sg. Φλέω belonging to Φλεύς.

a. The feminine OI-stems, most widely attested in proper names. Nom. sg. mostly -ω, but also -ωι, as Cyren. λεχώι, Corinth. Συϙόι, Φιλόι, etc. (OI regularly on old Corinthian vases; -ῳ beside -ω in grammarians).

Gen. sg. -οος, -ους, -ως (Cret. Λατῶς), but Cyren. λεχός (no. 115.109), Rhod. Φιλτός (IG XII.i.719), Delph. Λατός (so probably, not Λατὸς, Schwyzer 325.8). Dat. sg. Delph. λεχχοῖ, Cret. Λατοῖ, Λατῶι. Acc. sg. -οα, -ώ. Also inflection with ω throughout, parallel to ā-stems, as Boeot., Cret. -ώ, -ῶς, -ῶι, -ών.

Some Irregular Nouns

112. 1. Ζεύς. Ζεύς or Δεύς (84). Δι(F)ός, Δι(F)ί, Δί(F)α in most dialects. An old dative Διεί (cf. Oscan *Diúveí*) occurs alone, but rarely, and in Att. Διειτρέφης, Cypr. ΔιFείθεμις, ΔιFείφιλος (Hom. διΐφιλος). Also in various dialects (attested for East Ion., Coan, Ther., Cret., El.), as in Homer, Ζηνός, Ζηνί, Ζῆνα (Cret. Δῆνα, Τῆνα, etc., 84). See 37.1. There are some unexplained forms with α (or ā?), as Ion. Ζάς, gen. Ζανός.

2. υἱός, υἱύς. Aside from the o-stem forms, the inscriptional occurrences are as follows, mostly from a stem υἱυ-:

NOM. SG. υἱύς Cret., Lac., Att. (Att. also υύς, ὖς).
GEN. SG. υἱέος Cret., Att.; Thess. hυῖος (no. 35).
DAT. SG. υἱεῖ Argol., Phoc., Att.
ACC. SG. υἱύν Arc., Cret., Locr., etc.
NOM. PL. υἱέες Cret. (as in Hom.); Att. υἱεῖς.
DAT. PL. υἱάσι Cret. (as in Hom.), after analogy of πατράσι, etc.
ACC. PL. υἱύνς Arg., Cret.; Att. υἱεῖς.

3. μήν. Stem *μηνσ- (cf. Lat. *mēnsis*), whence (77.1) Lesb. μῆννος, Thess. μειννός, Att. etc. μηνός. The nom. *μήνς became *μένς (vowel-shortening before ν + cons., but later than the assimilation of medial νσ), whence regularly (78) Ion., Corcyr., Meg. μείς, Epid., Heracl. μής. In Attic, μείς was replaced by μήν formed after the analogy of original ν-stems in -ην, -ηνος. Elean μεύς is perhaps due to the analogy of Ζεύς, Ζηνός (above, 1).

4. λᾶς, Hom. λᾶας. Originally a neuter σ-stem τὸ λᾶας, becoming ὁ λᾶας, ὁ λᾶς, after the analogy of ὁ λίθος etc. Hence in genitive beside λᾶος also Att. λᾶου (Soph.), Cret. λᾶο̄.

5. Cret. Fῆμα nom.-acc. sg. = εἶμα, but gen. sg. τᾶς Fῆμᾶς from a stem in -μᾶ. So also Cret. *ἀμφίδημα 'ornament' (cf. διάδημα), but gen. sg. ἀμπιδήμᾶς.

6. χοῦς, which in Attic is declined as a consonant stem (gen. sg. χοός), is properly a contracted o-stem (from χόFο-) like πλοῦς,

and remains so in Ionic, e.g., acc. sg. χοῦν, gen. pl. χῶν.
7. χείρ, χήρ. See **25, 76**.

Comparison of Adjectives

113. 1. Beside μείζων and κρείττων, both with anomalous ει,
we find the normal μέζων (from *μέγιων) in Ionic and Arcadian,
and κρέσσων (from *κρέτιων) in Ionic. For Dor. κάρρων, Cret.
κάρτων (both from *κάρτιων) see **49.**2 with *a*, **80, 81**.

2. Beside πλέων, pl. πλέονες, σ-stem forms, like Hom. πλέες,
πλέας, occur in Lesbian (πλέας no. 25) and Cretan (e.g., Gortyn.
πλίες, πλίανς, πλία, beside πλίονος, πλίονα, πλίον. πλίασιν, Drerus,
is in origin a ν-stem form, cf. **77.**1*a*). Cf. also Arc. πλός (from
*πλέος, **42.**5g) adv. = πλέον.

Heracl. πόλιστος = πλεῖστος is formed directly from πολύς.

The rare μεῖστος, superlative of μείων and parallel to πλεῖστος,
is now confirmed by the Locr. adv. μεῖστον (no. 59.9).

3. El., Lac. άσιστα (άσσιστα also in Aesch.) = άγχιστα, is
formed from the compar. άσσον (this regularly from *άγχιον).

Cardinals and Ordinals

114.1-10. 1. Nom. sg. masc. Att., etc. εἷς, Heracl. ἧς (cf.
Lac. οὐδές), Cret. ἔνς (ἔνδ δ- = ἔνς δ-, Law-Code IX.50; see
97.4), from *ἔνς. Cf. **78**.—Fem. μία, but, of other origin, Lesb.,
Thess., Boeot. ἴα, as in Homer (so Lesb. μηδεία = μηδεμία).
Also ἰός in Hom. dat. sg. neut. ἰῶ and Mess. (probable reading)
τόν γ' ἰὸν ἐνιαυτόν 'the one (= same) year,' and in Cretan, but
here with pronominal force 'that one' = ἐκεῖνος.

Att.-Ion., Arc.-Cypr., Lesb. πρῶτος, Thess. προῦτος, West
Greek and Boeot. πρᾶτος. Cf. also Att.-Ion. πρώτιστος, Cret.,
Coan, Ther., Cyren. πράτιστος.

a. The still frequently stated derivation from a *πρόατος or *πρόϜατος
is untenable. Apart from the fact that such uncontracted forms do not
exist, the supposed contraction of o + α > Dor. ᾱ is contrary to the
other evidence (**44.**1). πρῶτος and πρᾶτος are parallel forms from πρω-
and πρᾱ-, the latter probably a weak grade, such as is seen in Skt. *pūrvas*
and Lith. *pirmas*. For such parallel forms, cf. Lat. *primus*, Pael. *prismu*
vs. Umbr. *promom*, from *prīs-* and *pro-* respectively.

2. δύο in most dialects, δύω beside δύο in Homer, etc. Chalcid. δύϝο (with glide, 53*b*). Boeot. δύο, δούο, and διού (24) attested before consonant as well as before vowel. Eretr., Aetol. δύϝε, Lac. δύε, with the third declension ending. Gen.-dat. Att.-Ion. δυοῖν, late Att. δυεῖν, El. δυοίοις. Plural forms in various dialects, as Ion. (Hdt. and Chios), Cret., Heracl. δυῶν, Thess. δύας, Cret. δυοῖς, late Att. δυσί(ν).

δεύτερος in all dialects so far as known, and quotable in many.

3. τρεῖς, Cret. τρέες, Ther. τρῆς (also Lesb., gram.), from *τρέιες. See 25, 45.5.—Acc. τρῖς, Cret. τρίινς (for τρίνς with ι introduced anew from τριῶν, etc.). Under the influence of the indeclinable numerals, the nominative or the accusative is used for both cases in some dialects, namely, nom. τρεῖς in Attic and elsewhere, and acc. τρῖς in Heraclean, Delphian, and Troezenian.

τρίτος, Lesb. τέρτος (18*a*).

4. Att. τέτταρες, Ion., Arc. τέσσερες (also τέσσαρες in Ionic and κοινή), Boeot. πέτταρες, Lesb. πέσσυρες (Hom. πίσυρες), Thess. πετροετηρίς = τετρο-, West Greek τέτορες. From *kʷetwer- (cf. Lat. *quattuor*, Skt. *catvāras*), the differences being due to inherited variations in the second syllable (*twer, twor, tur, twr̥*), and to the divergent development of *kʷ* (68) and *tw* (54*f*, 81)

τέταρτος, Hom. τέτρατος, Boeot. πέτρατος, Arc. τέτορτος (49.2*a*, 5).

5. πέντε, Lesb., Thess. πέμπε (68.3), Pamph. πέδε (66, 69.2). πέμπτος, Cret., Amorg. πέντος (86.2). Arc. πέμποτος after δέκοτος.

6. ἔξ, Cret., Delph., Heracl. ϝέξ. See 52*b*. Boeot. ἐσκηδέκατος, like ἐς from ἐξ (100).

ἔκτος, Cret. once ϝέκτος.

7. ἑπτά, Cret. once ἑττά (86.2).

Att.-Ion. ἕβδομος, West Greek ἕβδεμος (attested directly in Delph., Cyren., Aetol., by derivatives in Heracl., Epid.).

8. ὀκτώ, Lesb. ὄκτο, Boeot. ὀκτό (like δύο), Heracl. hοκτώ (58*c*), El. ὀπτό (with π from ἑπτά).

ὄγδοος, from ὄγδοϝος now attested in Aetol. [ὀγ]δόϝα (IG IX². i.152).

9. ἐννέα, Delph., Rhod., Coan, Cyren. ἐννῆ (42.1), Heracl. hεννέα (58c).

Att. ἔνατος, Ion. εἴνατος, Arg., Cret., Cyren. ἤνατος, from *ἐνϝατος (54), Delph., Ther. hένατος (58c), Lesb. ἔνοτος (6, 116a).

10. δέκα, Arc. δέκο. δέκατος, Arc., Lesb. δέκοτος (6, 116a).

115.11-19. ἔνδεκα, rarely δέκα εἷς (e.g., Heracl. δέκα hέν).— Att. and Hom. δώδεκα, but in most dialects δυώδεκα, rarely δυόδεκα (e.g., Boeot. δυοδέκατος), Delph., Heracl. δέκα δύο (also late Attic.)—τρεῖς καὶ δέκα, also indecl. τρεισκαίδεκα (Attic after 300 B.C.) and τρισκαίδεκα (Boeotian, etc.; cf. 114.3); also δέκα τρεῖς, especially when the substantive precedes (so Attic even in fifth century).—Similar variations for 14-19.

ἐνδέκατος, δωδέκατος, δυωδέκατος, δυοδέκατος (see above — 13th-19th, Att. τρίτος καὶ δέκατος, etc., but τρεισκαιδέκατος or τρισκαιδέκατος, etc., in East Ionic, Boeotian, and Lesbian (-δέκοτος).

116.20-90. εἴκοσι (from *ἐ-ϝίκοσι) in Attic, Ionic, Lesbian, Arcadian (no occurrence in Cyprian), but ϝίκατι, ἴκατι (cf. Ther. hικάδι, Thess. ἰκάδι) in West Greek, Boeotian, Thessalian and Pamphylian (φίκατι), with ι not ει, and τ retained (61.2). The ει of Heracl. ϝείκατι beside ϝίκατι is due to the influence of Att. εἴκοσι.—Att. etc. τριάκοντα, Ion. τριήκοντα.—τετταράκοντα, τεσσεράκοντα, τεσσαράκοντα, πετταράκοντα (see 114.4), Sicil. West Ion. τετράϙοντα (SEG 4.64), Dor., Delph. τετρώκοντα (so doubtless in all West Greek dialects previous to Attic influence). —πεντήκοντα, ἑξήκοντα (ϝεξήκοντα), etc., with η in all dialects (Ion. ὀγδώκοντα, 44.2).—Delph., Heracl. hεβδεμήκοντα, Heracl. hογδοήκοντα, hενενήκοντα. See 114.7-9.—Gen. τεσσ[ερ]ακόντων, πεντηκόντων, etc. in Chios, where the use of such inflected genitives (also δέκων) is one of the Aeolic features of the dialect (cf. πέμπων, δέκων in Alcaeus, also τριηκόντων in Hesiod).

Att., Ion. εἰκοστός etc., Boeot. ϝικαστός (-καστός doubtless in all West Greek dialects also; but Thess. ἰκοστός), Lesb. εἴκοιστος, τριάκοιστος, ἐξήκοιστος).

a. The earliest form of the ordinals is that in -καστος (from -k̥m̥t-to-, cf. Skt. triṅçat-tama-, etc.). Under the influence of the cardinals in -κοντα this became -κοστος in Attic, etc. Under the same influence also *-κονστος, the probable source of Lesb. -κοιστος, with the regular Lesbian development of secondary νσ (77.3, 78). For a different view of the Lesbian forms, see 20a. To the same analogy is due the ο of εἴκοσι, and of the hundreds in -κόσιοι (e.g., τριακόσιοι after τριάκοντα), instead of the more original α in Ϝίκατι (Skt. viṅçati-, Lat. vigintī), -κάτιοι, -κάσιοι (cf. ἑκατόν, Skt. çatam, Lat. centum). It is possible that a still further extension of this analogical ο is to be assumed in explanation of Arc. ἡεκοτόν, Arc., Lesb. δέκοτος, Arc. δέκο, Lesb. ἔνοτος.

117. 1. 100. Att. etc. ἑκατόν, Arc. ἡεκοτόν, See **6, 116a**.

2. 200-900. Att.-Ion., Lesb. -κόσιοι, West Greek, Boeot., Thess. -κάτιοι (Thess. ἐξεικάττιοι, SEG 2.264), Arc. -κάσιοι (with East Greek σ, but West Greek α). See **61.2, 116a**.

The ᾱ of τριᾱκόσιοι (Ion. τριηκόσιοι) is extended to διᾱκόσιοι (Ion. διηκόσιοι), and the α of τετρακόσιοι, ἑπτακόσιοι, ἐνακόσιοι to πεντακόσιοι, ἑξακόσιοι, ὀκτακόσιοι. But Thess. ἐξεικάττιοι with (ει=) η as in ἐξήκοντα. Lesb. ὀκτωκόσιοι.

3. 1000. Att. χίλιοι (**25e**), Ion. χείλιοι, Lac., Cyren. χήλιοι, Lesb., Thess. χέλλιοι, from *χέσλιοι. See **76.1**.

PRONOUNS

Personal Pronouns [1]

118. SINGULAR. 1. The stems, except in the nominative, begin with: 1. ἐμ- or μ-.—2. Original tw-, whence East Greek σ-, West Greek τ- (τέος, τίν, τέ). But enclitic τοι is from a form without w (cf. Skt. te), and occurs also in Ionic (Hom., Hdt., etc.). Hom. τεοῖο and τείν are from the possessive stem *tewo- (**120.2**).—3. Original sw-, whence Ϝ- in some dialects (Ϝέος, Ϝοι, Ϝίν), otherwise ʽ.

2. NOM. ἐγώ, ἐγών (Boeot. ἰώ, ἰών, **62.3**).—Att.-Ion., Lesb., Arc. σύ, Dor. τύ, Boeot. τού. See **61.5**.

3. GEN. a. -ειο (Hom. ἐμεῖο, etc., like τοῖο), whence -εο, later Ion. -ευ, Att. -ου.—b. -εος in West Greek, as lit. Dor. ἐμέος, τέος, Locr. Ϝέος.—c. -θεν in lit. Lesb. ἔμεθεν, σέθεν, Ϝέθεν, Hom. ἐμέθεν, σέθεν, ἔθεν, Epid. ἔθεν, Syrac. μεθέν (Sophron).

---

[1] As the personal pronouns, especially in the singular, are of comparatively rare occurrence in inscriptions, some forms are added which are quotable only from literary sources, but only a few out of the great variety, for which see Kühner-Blass I, pp. 580 ff.

4. Dat. *a.* -οι, as ἐμοί, μοι, σοί, σοι (lit. Dor. τοί, τοι, lit. Ion. τοι), οἵ, οἱ (Arg., Cret., Delph., Cypr., Lesb. Ϝοι).—*b.* -ιν in West Greek (where also -οι, but mostly in the enclitic forms, as μοι, never ἐμοί, Ϝοι, οἱ, and τοι, though also τοί), as Cret., Calymn., Rhod., Delph., and lit. Dor. ἐμίν, lit. Dor. τίν, Cret. Ϝίν.

5. Acc. 1. ἐμέ, με.—2. Att.-Ion., Lesb. σέ, lit. Dor. τέ (Cret. τϜέ, written τρέ, in Hesych.); also lit. Dor. and Epid. τύ (nom. used as acc.)—3. ἕ (Ϝέ); also lit. Dor. and Epid. νίν.

119. Plural. 1. The forms of the first and second persons contain, apart from the endings, ἀσμ- (cf. Skt. *asmān*, etc.) and ὑσμ- (cf. Skt. *yuṣmān*, etc.), whence Lesb., Thess. ἀμμ-, Lesb. ὑμμ-, elsewhere ἀμ- (Att.-Ion. ἡμ-) or ἄμ-, ὕμ-. See 76.1, and, for the spiritus asper or lenis in the first person, 57, 58*b*.

2. Nom. -ες in all dialects except Attic-Ionic, where it was replaced by -εις. Lesb. ἄμμες, ὕμμες, Dor. etc. ἀμές, ὑμές.

a. In late Cretan ἀμές was frequently replaced by ἀμέν under the influence of 1 pl. verbal forms in which Dor. -μες was often replaced by the κοινή -μεν. That is, ἀμέν for ἀμές after φέρομεν for φέρομες. From ἀμέν, -εν was extended to other pronouns and to participles, as ὑμέν, τινέν, ἀκούσαντεν, etc.

3. Gen. -ειων (Hom. ἡμείων), whence -εων, -ιων (9), -ῶν. Lesb. ἀμμέων, Thess. ἀμμέουν, El. ἀμέων, Dor. ἀμέων, ἀμίων (Cret.), later ἀμῶν.

4. Dat. -ι(ν), Lesb. ἄμμιν, ἄμμι, etc., Dor. ἀμίν, ὑμίν, Att.-Ion. ἡμῖν, ὑμῖν. So Dor. σφιν, σφι, Cret., Syrac. ψιν (87), but Att.-Ion. σφίσι, Arc. σφεις, the latter not satisfactorily explained.

5. Acc. -ε in all dialects except Attic-Ionic, where it was replaced by -έας, -ᾱς. Lesb. ἄμμε, ὕμμε, Thess. ἀμμέ, Dor., etc. ἀμέ, ὑμέ, Dor., etc. σφέ, Cret., Syrac. ψέ (87).

Possessives

120. 1. ἐμός.—Pl. Dor., etc., ἀμός (Lesb. ἄμμος) and ἀμέτερος (Lesb. ἀμμέτερος, Att.-Ion. ἡμέτερος).

2. *a. two-*, Att., etc., σός. *b. *tewo-*, Dor., Lesb. τεός, Boeot. τιός (all in literature only). Both forms in Homer.—Pl. ὑμός and ὑμέτερος.

3. *a. *swo-*, Att., etc., ὅς, Cret. Ϝός. *b. *sewo-*, Dor. (lit.), Thess. ἐός. Both forms in Homer.—Pl. σφός and σφέτερος.

Reflexive Pronouns

121. Aside from the reflexive use of the forms of the personal pronouns as given in **118, 119**, especially that of the third person, which is itself a reflexive in origin, various forms of expression are employed, as follows:

1. Combinations of the personal pronouns with αὐτός, each keeping its own inflection, as in Homer (σοὶ αὐτῷ, etc.). So Epid. αὐτοῦ ἔθεν, Cret. Ϝὶν αὐτοῖ, ψὲ αὐτόνς, πσὶν αὐτοῖς. Cf. also, with the possessive, Cret. τὰ Ϝὰ αὐτᾶς = τὰ ἑαυτῆς.

2. Compounds of the same elements, with only the second part declined. Att. ἐμαυτοῦ, σεαυτοῦ or σαυτοῦ, ἑαυτοῦ or αὐτοῦ (also late ἑατοῦ, ἀτῶν, with ᾱ from ᾱυ); Coan ηὐτῶν with η from εα; Thess. εὐτοῖ, εὐτοῦ, εὐτάς; Cret. Ϝιαυτō; Ion. (lit.) ἐμεωυτοῦ etc. The forms found in Ionic inscriptions are like the Attic.

3. αὐτός alone, as sometimes in Homer. Thus Delph. αὐτοῦ = ἐμαυτοῦ, El. αὐτᾶρ = ἑαυτῆς (no. 66.17), Lac. αὐτō = ἑαυτοῦ (no. 71.7, 16 ff.), Corinth. περὶ τᾶς αὐτοῦ γᾶς (no. 95), Thess. αὐτᾶ = ἑαυτῇ, Boeot. αὐτάν = ἑαυτήν.

4. αὐτὸς αὐτός, either with each declined separately, or, oftener merged into compounds of somewhat varying form.

This combination is comparatively late, replacing the earlier types mentioned under 1-3. It is most frequent in Delphian and Boeotian, but is found in several of the other West Greek dialects, and probably even in Attic (Kühner-Blass I, p. 600, anm. 5).

a. αὐτὸς αὐτός. Delph. αὐτοὶ ποτὶ αὐτούς, Boeot. κατ' αὐτὺ (= αὐτοὶ) αὐτῶν.

b. αὐτοσαυτός. Delph. αὐτοσαυτοῦ, etc., Boeot. ὑπὲρ αὐτοσαυτῶ, Heracl. μετ' αὐτοσαυτῶν, Cret. αὐτοσαυτοῖς, etc., Corcyr. αὐτοσαυτόν.

c. αὐσαυτός. Delph. αὐσαυτοῦ, etc., Cret., Argol. (Calauria) αὐσαυτᾶς, Arc. ὑπὲρ αὐσαυτόν.

d. ἀσαυτός. Boeot. ἀσαυτῦ.

e. αὐσωτός. Delph. αὐσωτᾶς, etc.

f. αὐταυτός. Heracl. αὐταυτᾶς (as in Sophron and Epicharmus), Aegin. αὐταυτόν.

g. Sicil. gen. sg. αὐτοῦτα (Segesta), gen. pl. αὐτῶντα (Thermae). Probably from αὐτατοῦ, αὐτατῶν (cf. late ἑατοῦ, above, 2), with transposition of the last two syllables.

Demonstrative Pronouns

122. The article. Nom. pl. τοί, ταί, as in Homer, in the West Greek dialects except Cretan, and in Boeotian. Att. etc. οἱ, αἱ, after the analogy of ὁ, ἡ. For ὁ, ἀ̄ in some dialects which in general have ', see **58a**. Thess. οἱ, but τοί at Pharsalus (Schwyzer 566). Forms with added ι, used like ὅδε, are found in Elean (το-ΐ, τα-ΐ) and Boeotian (ταν-ί; τοι-ΐ, τυ-ΐ).

For the relative use, see **126**.

a. Just as in Homer the use as article is less frequent than the demonstrative and the article is often lacking where it is obligatory or usual in later times, so (apart from certain categories in which the absence of the article is usual) in inscriptions of some dialects. So frequently in headings, like that of no. 67, Συνθήκα καὶ Συμμαχία (but El. ἀ Ϝράτρα nos. 61-63, etc.). With names of official bodies or officials, e.g., Cret. ἀδ' ἔϜαδε πόλι (no. 116), Arg. (no. 85) βōλὰ ἐπαγέτō, ἀ(Ϝρέτευε) βōλᾶς, ἀλιαίαι ἔδοξε, ἐπὶ κόσμος, Epid. ἔδοξε βουλᾶι καὶ δάμωι, κατάλογος βουλᾶς, Locr. (no. 59.10/11) ἐν πρείγαι ἐν πόλι ε̄ 'ν ἀποκλε̄σίαι. (In Att. fifth century inscriptions there are a few examples of βōλέ without article, but much more commonly with the article).

123. Thess. ὅ-νε, Arc. ὁ-νί, Arc.-Cypr. ὅ-νυ = ὅδε. Thess. τόνε, τάνε, and, with both parts inflected (cf. Hom. τοῖσδεσι), gen. sg. τοῖνεος, gen. pl. τοῦννεουν.—Arc. τωνί (gen. sg.), τωινί, ταιννί (dat. pl. fem.), ταννί, τανί (gen. sg., gen. pl., and acc. pl. fem.). Cf. also Boeot. προτηνί (**136**.1).—Cypr. ὄνυ, τόνυ, Arc. τάνυ (acc. pl. neut.), τῶννι (gen. pl.), τῶ̣ινυ (11 times in no. 20 vs. once τωινί), also by an alien engraver τάννυν, τόσυνυ. Cf. Hom., Boeot., Cypr. νυ.

From ὅδε, cf. also Arg. τōνδεōνέν, ταδέν with addition of emphatic -ην (ἥν, Lat. ēn).

124. οὗτος. Nom. pl. τοῦτοι, ταῦται, like τοί, ταί, in West Greek (examples from Cos, Delphi, Rhodes, Selinus). Att. etc. οὗτοι, αὗται, after οὗτος, etc. Boeotian, with τ replaced by ' throughout, οὗτον, οὗτων, etc.—Interchange of αυ and ου. Att. gen. pl. fem. τούτων after masc.-neut.; conversely El. neut. ταύτων, due to influence of ταῦτα. ου throughout is Boeotian (οὗτο, οὗτα) and Euboean (τοῦτα, τούτει, also ἐντοῦθα = ἐνταῦθα), also οὗτα = ταῦτα in Sophron. So also Delph. τοῦτα, τούτας (but also ταῦται). For the spelling with O instead of OV, see **34a**.

125. 1. ἐκεῖνος. Ion. κεῖνος, Lesb., Cret., Rhod., Coan κῆνος, both from *κε-ενος. Cf. **25.**—τῆνος, of different origin (cf. Hom. τῆ), in Delphian, Heraclean, Argolic (Aegina), Megarian, as well as in Sicilian Doric writers (Theocr., Sophron, Epicharmus). 2. αὐτός. Neut. αὐτόν in Cretan, as sometimes in Attic inscriptions.

Relative, Interrogative, and Indefinite Pronouns

126. The relative ὅς occurs in all dialects. But the relative use of forms of the article, frequent in Homer and Herodotus, is usual in Lesbian (so always in the earlier inscriptions and nearly always in Alcaeus and Sappho; ὅς in later inscriptions is due to κοινή influence, as shown by the spiritus asper, καθ᾽ ὅν, etc.), Thessalian (τά, καττάπερ; ἐν τοῦ 'in which', no. 33.27, but also ὅς in an early metrical inscription), and Arcado-Cyprian (Arc.ὅπερ, ταῖ, τοῖς, etc., Cypr. ὁ, τόν, etc., but also Arc. ἄν, Cypr. ὄι, οἴ). So also in Boeotian in a fourth-century inscription (no. 40), but later only ὅς (cf. Lesbian). It is also Heraclean (τόν, τά, etc.; so often in Epicharmus), and Cyrenaean (ὁ, τό, τά), but in most West Greek dialects it occurs, if at all, only in later inscriptions (so in late Delphian, Elean, and Cretan, never in the earlier period).

For the demonstrative use of ὅς, cf. Heracl. hᾶι μὲν... hᾶι δὲ (no. 79.82).

127. Cret. ὅτερος 'which of two' is the true relative correlative of πότερος (cf. Skt. yataras beside kataras), and so related to the usual ὁπότερος as οἷος to ὁποῖος, ὅτε to ὁπότε.

128. τίς, τις. Cypr. σις, Arc. σις, ὄζις, see **68**.3. Thess. κίς, κις, κινες, see **68**.4. The inflection with ν, gen. sg. τινός, etc., presumably based on the original acc. sg. *τίν, is widespread. But forms of the earlier type, without ν, like Hom. τεο, ὅττεο, τεω, ὀτέοισιν, Att. του, τω, ὅτοις, are seen also in Lesb. τίωι, τίοισι (9.2), Arc. ὀσέοι (68.3), gen. sg. Lesb. ὄττω, Boeot. ὄττω, Meg. σά (from *τϳα), Att.-Ion. ἄττα, ἄσσα (from *ἄτϳα), Cret. dat. sg. τῖμι in ὅτιμι, from *τι-σμι with the same pronominal sm as in Skt. kasmin, Umbr. pusme, etc.

129. The indefinite relative ὅστις, ὅτις.

1. ὅστις, with both parts declined, Att.-Ion., also in various dialects, e.g., Locr. hoίτινες, Cret. οἵτινες, Boeot. ὥστινας.

2. ὅτις, with only the second part declined, Att.-Ion., also in various dialects, e.g., Arc. ὅτις, ὅζις, ὀ̱έοι (68.3), Cret. ὅτιμι (128), Delph. ὅτινος, ὅτινι.—Further, with ττ spread from the neut. ὅττι (*ὅδ-τι), Lesb. ὅττις, ὅττινας, ὅττω, etc. (cf. also ὅππα, ὅππως, etc.), Boeot. ὅττω, Arg. ὅττινες.

a. Locr. Ϝότι (no. 58.6), at variance with all other evidence, is almost certainly an error for hότι (so nos. 57, 59, as in other dialects).

3. Neuter forms in -τι, with only the first part declined, in Cretan, e.g., ἄτι = ἄτινα, ὄ̰τι = οὖτινος.

130. Cret. ὀτεῖος = ὀποῖος, but used like adjectival ὅστις, as ὀτεῖος δέ κα κόσμος μὴ βέρδηι, γυνὰ ὀτεία κρέματα μὲ̰ ἔκει, ὀτείαι δὲ (sc. γυναικὶ) πρόθθ' ἔδōκε. Here also Boeot. dat. sg. fem. μηδοτίη (= μηδοτείαι). For the form (also Hesych. τεῖον ·· ποῖον, Κρῆτες), cf. Hom. τέο, τέῳ, etc., and Lesb. (lit.) τέουτος τοιοῦτος (with loss of ι 31).

131. Interrogative pronouns used as indefinite relatives. So regularly in Thessalian, e.g., κίς κε γινύειτει = ὅστις ἂν γίγνηται, διὲ κί (in form διὰ τί) = διότι, πὸκ κί (in form πρὸς τί) = ὅτι, φυλᾶς ποίας κε βέλλειτει = φυλῆς ὁποίας (ἥστινος) ἂν βούληται. Elsewhere the use of τίς = ὅστις is, with some rare exceptions in literature, found only in late Greek.

ADVERBS AND CONJUNCTIONS

Pronominal Adverbs and Conjunctions of Place, Time, and Manner

132. 1. -ου. Place 'where.' Att.-Ion. ποῦ, ὅπου, αὐτοῦ, ὁμοῦ, etc. These are of genitive origin, and are specifically Attic-Ionic.

2. -ει. Place 'where.' These are the usual equivalents of Att.-Ion. -ου, occurring in West Greek dialects and Boeotian, e.g., εῖ, πεῖ, πει (Cret. αἴ πει = Att. εἴ που), ὅπει, τεῖδε, τουτεῖ, τηνεῖ, αὐτεῖ (Boeot. αὐτῖ), ἀλλεῖ, ἀμεῖ, μηδαμεῖ. Here also Arg. hῖ, ῖ (25c) 'where' and 'when.' By analogy, Locr. παντεῖ 'everywhere,' Heracl., Arg. ποτεχεῖ = προσεχῶς, Delph. ἐπεχεῖ = ἐφεξῆς (beside Arg. ἐπεχές, Ach. ποτεχές, etc.), Cret., Heracl. διπλεῖ 'doubly.'

3. -οι. Place 'where' and (so usually in Attic) 'whither.' οῖ,

ποῖ, ὅποι in many dialects, and with -ς, Delph. οἷς. Cf. Lesb. αἴ
ποι = Att. εἴ που. By analogy Lesb. ὕψοι or ἴψοι (cf. ὑψί),
Orop. ἦχοι (from ἦχι, below, 6), also (**133**.3-5) ἔνδοι, ἔχθοι, ἔξοι.

4. -υι. Place 'where' and 'whither.' Cret. υἷ 'where' (Hierapytna, e.g., no. 119.16, 22), Cret. ὅπυι, Arg., Cyren. ὅπυι (Arg.
'for whatever purpose'); in -υις or -υς, Rhod. υἷς 'as far as' (no.
104.3), Arg. ὕς (IG IV.498.4 'whither', 'to whom'), Rhod. ὅπυς,
lit. Dor. (Syrac.) ὕς, πῦς. Cf. also Cret. πλίυι (to πλίες, **113**.2),
lit. Lesb. τυῖδε, ἄλλυι, πήλυι.

5. -ᾱι (Att.-Ion. -ηι). Place 'where' or (mostly Delph.) 'whither,'
and especially manner. Thus ἆι, ὅπαι in many West Greek dialects
and Boeotian (ὅπη). In Cretan used also as final, and (ἆι) temporal
conjunctions. Cret., Corcyr. ἀλλᾶι 'otherwise,' Heracl. πανταῖ 'in
all directions,' Lesb. πάνται. The indefinite παι (cf. Corcyr. ἀλλᾶι
παι 'in any other way') is used in Cyprian as a strengthening
particle (κάς παι 'and indeed,' ἰδέ παι 'then indeed,' no. 23.4, 12).

6. -ᾱ (Att.-Ion. -η). Uses as in the preceding. Delph., Cyren.
ἆδε, Cret. ἆδε (no. 116) 'in this way,' Lac. ταυτᾶ ἆτ' 'in such a
way as,' ἁμᾶ 'likewise,' Locr. ταὐτᾶ 'in the same way.' Locr.,
Cyren. ἆ κα 'in case that' (nos. 60.19; 115.93), lit. Dor. ἆχι = Hom.
ἦχι 'where.' Lesb. ὅππα 'where,' ἄλλα 'elsewhere' (no. 27.49 beside
dat. sg. -αι, and so better here than under 5, above).

7. -η. Place 'where,' time 'when,' etc. Cret. ἒ, Heracl., Cyren. ἦ
(this accent preferred here, vs. ἤ 'or, than' but practice varies),
'when' (so Heracl., Cyren., Cret.; Cret. also 'where', 'in case
that') Cret. ὅπε̄, Cyren. ὅπη 'where,' Lac. hόπε̄ 'in such a way as,'
Thess. ὅπει (ει=η) 'when' (no. 33.26; cf. ὀπειδεί, ibid. l. 12, in
form a blend of ὅπει and ἐπειδεί, in sense = ἐπειδή). Lac. πέποκα =
πώποτε. El., Meg., Ther., Eretr. τε̄δε 'here,' El. ταύτε̄ 'here.' Meg.
ἄ(λ)λε̄, Cyren. ἄλλη πη 'elsewhere,' Cret. Ϝεκατέρη 'in each place.'

8. -ω. Place 'whence.' Lit. Dor. ὤ, πῶ, ὅπω, Cret. ὄ, ὁπō̄, Locr.
hō̄, hόπō̄, Cret. τῶδε, Cret., Coan τουτῶ. Syrac. τηνῶ, τηνῶθε,
Meg. τηνῶθεν. Similarly Delph. Ϝοίκω 'from the house.'

a. These adverbs are not to be confounded with another class, mostly
from prepositions, meaning place 'where' or 'whither' and occurring in
Attic-Ionic also, as ἄνω, κάτω, ἔξω, etc. Here belong Delph. ἔνδω 'within,'
Coan ἑκατέρω 'on each side of.'

9. -θεν. Place 'whence.' Att.-Ion. ὅθεν, πόθεν, etc. This -θεν,

which though formally related must be distinguished from the -(σ)θεν, -(σ)θε of adverbs like ἄνωθε(ν), πρόσθε(ν) without the 'whence' sense (**133**.1), is mainly Attic-Ionic in pronominal adverbs (such forms in Doric, in place of the usual -ω, are rare). But in adverbs derived from place names it is also West Greek, as Ϙορινθόθεν, Κνωσόθεν, Μυκανέαθεν, Θήραθεν, Γορτύναθεν, Φλει-Ϝόντᾱθεν.

10. -ως. Manner. ὡς, πῶς, ὅπως, etc. in all dialects. ὡς also 'when' and in some dialects 'where.'

a. ὡς and ὅπως are also the most widespread final conjunctions. The final use of ἵνα, originally 'where,' developed in Attic-Ionic, but spread to other dialects (appearing mostly in late inscriptions; in the early Rhod. no. 100 clearly due to epic influence. Early Cretan had none of these, but only ὅπαι or ἇι in final sense (above, 5).

11. -τε, -τα, -χα. Temporal, ὅτε, τότε, πότε in Attic-Ionic and Arcado-Cyprian (Arc. τότε, ὁπότε, οὔποτε, Cypr. ὅτε μέποτε) but Att. εἶτα, ἔπειτα, Ion. εἶτεν, ἔπειτε, ἔπειτεν.—ὅτα, πότα, ἄλλοτα in Lesbian.—ὅκα, etc., in West Greek and Boeotian, as Boeot. πόκα, Cret. ὅκα, τόκα, ποκα, Cyren. ὅκα, τόκα, ὁπόκα, Rhod. ὅκα, Lac. πέποκα, El. τόκα, Delph. ὅκα, οὐδέποκα, μηδέποκα. The form ὅκκα (from ὅκα κα) occurs in Laconian, Megarian, Rhodian, Coan, and literary Doric.

12. Other temporal conjunctions. Besides ὅτε, etc. (above, 11), ἐπεί, and the occasional temporal use of forms in -ει, -αι, -η, -ως (above 2, 5, 6, 8), there are various words for 'so long as, while,' and 'until' (conjunction and preposition). ἕως, ἇς (**41**.4)—ἔστε, Boeot. ἔττε, Locr. ἔντε, Delph. ἧέντε (**135**.4) — μέχρι, ἄχρι — Cret., Cyren. μέστα (Cret. also μέττ' ἐς), Arc. [μέ]στε (probable, -τε as in ὅτε, etc.), μέστ', Thess. μέσποδι, Hom. μέσφα, all having in common μές now attested in Thess. preposition μές (no. **33**.6)— εἰς(ἐς) ὅ—Boeot. ἐν τάν (sc. ἁμέραν), **136**.1.

Prepositional and Other Adverbs

133. 1. -(σ)θεν, -(σ)θε, -(σ)θα. Att.-Ion. ἄνωθεν, ἄνωθε, ὕπερθεν, ὕπερθε, etc., Arc. μεσαχόθεν (65), Heracl. ἄνωθα. With -σθεν, etc. Att.-Ion. πρόσθεν, πρόσθε, Lesb. πρόσθε (so in inscriptions, in lyric also πρόσθεν), Thess. πρόστεν (**85**.1), Dor. πρόσθα (gram.), Heracl., Arg. ἔμπροσθα (but also Troez. ἔμπροσθε, ὄπισθε, and once Meg. πρόσθε), Cret. πρόθθα (85.3), Delph. πρόστα (85.1), Arc. προσθαγενές. Arc. θύσθεν 'outside of' from *θυρ-σθεν (cf. θύρδα, 2).

a. Also -θι, as in Hom., etc. So Arc. ὅθι, ὁπόθι, μηδεπόθι, ἰσόθι, αὖθι.

2. -δε (-ζε), -δα. Arc. -δα is seen in θύρδα·ἔξω = Hom. θύραζε.

3. For Delph., Locr., Arg. ἐχθός = ἐκτός, see 66. Hence, after the analogy of other adverbs in -ω (132.8) and -οι (132.3), Delph., Epid. ἔχθω, Epid. ἔχθοι.

4. From ἔνδον are formed—besides Att.-Ion. ἔνδοθεν, ἔνδοθι, Ion. ἐνδόσε (Ceos)—Cret., Delph., Meg., Syrac., ἐνδός (after ἐντός), Delph. ἔνδω, Lesb., Epid., Syrac., Cyren. ἔνδοι.

5. Beside ἔξω (132.8a) are formed, after the analogy of other adverbs, Lac. ἔξει, Thess., Cret., Syrac., Cyren. ἔξοι, Dor., Delph. ἔξος (after ἐκτός, etc., cf. ἐνδός).

6. -ις, -ιν, -ι. Forms with adverbial -ς or -ν sometimes interchange with each other and with forms without either -ς or -ν, as the numeral adverbs in -κις, -κιν, -κι. Thus in most dialects -κις, sometimes -κι, but -κιν in Lac. τετράκιν, ἑπτάκιν, ὀκτάκιν, Cret. ὀθθάκιν = ὁσάκις. Likewise -ιν in other adverbs of time (cf. Att. πάλιν), as Cret. αὖτιν, Rheg. αὖθιν = Ion., Arc. αὖτις, Att. αὖθις. Cret. αὐταμέριν = Att. αὐθημερόν, Lesb., Coan αὐταμερόν, Locr. αὐταμαρόν (accents uncertain), El. ὔσταριν = ὔστερον. Here also Thess. ἀίν, Arc. ἀί, Lesb. ἄι (also αἶιν Hdn.), Ion. αἰί (also ἀίδασμος 'under perpetual lease') = usual αἰές, αἰεί, αἰέν (all from *αἰϜί, *αἰϜίν, *αἰϜές, etc., cf. Cypr., Phoc. αἰϜεί), while a corresponding form in -ις is to be seen in Cypr. ὐϜαίς 'forever,' a combination like Att. εἰς ἀεί, containing ὐ = ἐπί and ἀίς from *αἰϜίς (omission of Ϝ peculiar, but cf. παῖς, 53).

Cf. also Epid. ἄνευν, El. ἄνευς = ἄνευ (Meg. ἄνις, also at Tauromeniun, and in late poets, is formed after χωρίς), Dor. ἔμπαν (Pindar) beside ἔμπᾱς = ἔμπης, Coan, Rhod., Ther. ἐξάν = ἐξῆς.

7. A combination of -ιν with -δην, -δᾱν (cf. -δα, -δον, etc.). Att. ἀριστίνδην, πλουτίνδην, ἀγχιστίνδην, Locr. ἀριστίνδαν, πλουτίνδαν, but ἀγχιστέδαν, formed from the stem ἀγχιστη- of ἀγχιστεύς.

134. 1. The conditional conjunction. εἰ in Attic-Ionic and Arcadian; αἰ in Lesbian, Thessalian, Boeotian (ἠ), and all the West Greek dialects; ἐ (ἠ) in Cyprian.

2. ἄν, κε, κα. ἄν is only Attic-Ionic and Arcadian. In all other

dialects the unrelated κε, κα is used—κε in Lesbian (also κεν), Thessalian, and Cyprian, κα in the West Greek dialects and Boeotian.

a. Arcadian once had κε, like Cyprian, and a relic of this is to be seen in the κ which appears, where there would otherwise be hiatus, between εἰ and a following ἄν, which had regularly replaced κε as a significant element (probably through prehistoric Ionic influence, cf. p. 4). Thus regularly εἰ κ' ἄν, or better εἰκ ἄν, since εἰκ has become a mere by-form of εἰ (like οὐκ beside οὐ), but εἰ δ' ἄν. Once, without ἄν, εἰκ ἐπὶ δῶμα πῦρ ἐποίσε, where some assume a significant κ', in place of usual ἄν, but best classed with the subjunctive clauses without ἄν (**174**).

b. In Attic-Ionic, εἰ combines with ἄν—in Attic to ἐάν or ἄν, in Ionic to ἤν.

c. The substitution of εἰ for αἰ belongs to the earliest stage of Attic (κοινή) influence in the West Greek dialects, but that of ἄν for κα only to the latest, being rarely found except where the dialect is almost wholly κοινή. Hence the hybrid combination εἰ κα is the rule in the later inscriptions of most West Greek dialects.

3. καί. Arc.-Cypr. κάς (also κά, for which see **97**.2), the relation of which to καί is obscure (antevocalic κα(ι) + ς ?). In Arcadian this occurs only in the early Mantinean inscription, no. 17, elsewhere καί. See **275**.

4. δέ. Thessalian uses μά, related to μέν, for δέ, e.g. τὸ μὰ ψάφισμα, τὰμ μὲν ἴαν ... τὰμ μὰ ἄλλαν (no. 32.22; τὰν δὲ ἄλλαν l. 45 is due to κοινή influence).

5. νυ, identical with -νυ in Arc.-Cypr. ὄνυ = ὅδε (**123**), and with Hom. νυν, νυ occurs as an independent particle in Cyprian and Boeotian, e.g., Cypr. δυϝάνοι νυ, δόκοι νυ, Boeot. ἄκουρύ νυ ἔνθω.

Cf. νι in Arc. τωνί, etc. (**123**), Boeot. προτηνί (**136**.1), Pamph. καί νι.

6. ἰδέ, in form = Hom. ἰδέ, occurs in Cyprian introducing the conclusion of a condition (ἰδέ παι 'then indeed,' ἰδέ 'then,' no. 23.12, 25), or a new sentence (ἰδέ 'and' no. 23.26).

7. ναί, νή. Arc. νεί (νεὶ τὸν Δία). Cf. εἰ, αἰ, ἠ, above, 1.

PREPOSITIONS

Peculiarities in Form

135. 1. For apocope of the final vowel, see **95**.

2. For assimilation of final consonants, see **96, 97, 99**.—ἐς =

ἐκ, **100.** For ὸν = ἀνά, see **6.**—ἰν = ἐν, **10.**—ἀπύ = ἀπό, **22.**—κατύ = κατά, **22.**

3. ὑπά, ὑπά = ὑπό, formed after the analogy of κατά, in Lesbian, Boeotian, and (quotable examples only compounds) Locrian (ὑπαπροσθιδίōν no. 59 vs. Ηυποκναμιδίōν no. 57) and Elean (ὑπαδυγίοις, ὑπαδυκιοίοις).

4. ἐν, εἰς. The inherited use of ἐν with the accusative (cf. the use of Lat. *in*) is retained in the Northwest Greek dialects (and in the Northwest Greek κοινή, **279**) together with Boeotian and Thessalian, and in Arcado-Cyprian (ἰν). Elsewhere this was replaced by an extended form ἐν-ς, whence εἰς, ἐς or (from *ἰν-ς) ἰς in Pamphylian and at Vaxus. See **78.**

Similarly ἔντε = ἔστε in Locrian, Delphian (hέντε, **58c**) and the Northwest Greek κοινή. But Boeotian, in spite of ἐν, has ἔττε = ἔστε.

5. μετά, πεδά. πεδά, unrelated to μετά in origin, is used in its place in Lesbian, Boeotian (probably in Thessalian too, though not yet quotable), Arcadian (πέ, **95**), Argolic, Cretan, and Theran. (Most of these dialects show also μετά, but at a time when κοινή influence is probable.) So also in compounds, as Lesb., Cret., Cyren. πεδέχω, Arg. πεδάγαγον, πεδάϝοικοι = μέτοικοι, Epid. πεδαφορᾶς, and proper names, as Boeot. Πεδάκων, Arg. Πεδάκριτος. The name of the month Πεδαγείτνυος or (by blend with μετα-) Πεταγείτνυος (or -ιος) = Att. Μεταγειτνιών occurs in Rhodes, Cos, Calymna, Megara, Sicily, and Magna Graecia, where πεδά alone is not attested.

a. The same blend of πεδα- and μετα- as in the month-name is also to be recognized in Del., Orop. πέτευρον 'notice-board, tablet' (so πετεύριον at Erythrae), elsewhere (with v.l. πέταυρον) 'roosting-perch, springboard,' etc., cpd. like Lesb. πεδάορος, Att. μετέωρος (ευ as in Thas. θευρός = θεωρός, **41.**4*a*).

6. πρός. There are two independent series of forms, one with and one without the ρ, each with variation between final -ς and -τι (**61.**4*a*)—1. προτί (= Skt. *prati*) in Homer (beside ποτί and usual πρός), quoted as Doric (Apoll. Dysc.), restored in Alcman, and almost certainly attested for Argive (πρὸτ' Schwyzer 84.3) Cret. πορτί (**70.**1), Pamph. περτ'—Att.-Ion., Lesb. πρός.

2. ποτί (= Avest. *pa'ti*) with πòτ, πò (95) in the West Greek dialects with Thessalian and Boeotian.— Arc.-Cypr. πός.

Still another form, ποί, occurring mostly, though not exclusively, before dentals (hence possibly to be explained as coming from ποτί by dissimilatory loss of τ) is frequent in Argive and Delphian, with scattered examples in Locrian (no. 58.14) and elsewhere. Numerous examples before dentals, as ποὶ τόν, etc. But also Arg. ποιγραψάνσθō, Epid. ποὶ ρόπτον, Delph. ποικεφάλαιον, ποὶ γᾶν, and a few others before non-dentals.

a. πός occurs also several times in inscriptions of Phrygia and Pamphylia, where it has been plausibly explained as introduced from Pamphylia (though a Pamph. πός is not actually attested) and so ultimately belonging with the Arc.-Cypr. πός.

7. σύν, ξύν. ξύν, as in Homer, in early Attic, elsewhere σύν. But Ion. ξῦνός from *ξυν-ι̯ός. Cypr. ὕγγεμος· συλλαβή (Hesych.).

8. Cypr. ὐ = ἐπί, e.g., ὐ τύχα = ἐπὶ τύχῃ, ὐχέρōν = ἐπιχείρου. Probably cognate with Skt. *ud*, Eng. *out* (cf. ὕσ-τερος = Skt. *uttaras*). There are traces of the same prefix in a few Rhodian and Boeotian proper names.

Peculiarities in Meaning and Construction

136. 1. Dative instead of the usual genitive construction in Arcado-Cyprian. (1) ἀπύ. Arc. ἀπὺ ταῖ (sc. ἀμέραι). Cypr. ἀπὺ ταῖ ζᾶι.—(2) ἐξ. Arc. ἐς τοῖ ἔργοι, Cypr. ἐξ ταῖ ζᾶι.—(3) περί. Arc. περὶ τοι-νί, Cypr. περὶ παιδί.—(4) ὑπέρ. Arc. ὑπέρ ταῖ τᾶς πόλιος ἐλευθερίαι.—(5) ὑπό. Arc. ὑπὸ πάντων τῶν γεγονότων ὑπὸ ταῖ πόλι.—(6) παρά. Arc. παρὰ ταῖ ἰδίαι πόλι 'from their own city.'—(7) πεδά. Arc. πὲ τοῖς Ϝοικιάται[ς].—(8) ἐπί. Arc. ἐπὶ ἱε[ρομνάμοσι το]ῖς.

ἐξ with dative occurs also in Pamph. ἐξ δὲ φυσελαι; πρό with dative in Boeot. προτηνί 'formerly,' i.e., πρὸ ται-νί (sc. ἀμέραι.) Cf. Thess. ὑππρὸ τᾶς (sc. ἀμέρας) 'just previously,' and Boeot. ἐν τάν (sc. ἀμέραν) 'until,' no. 43.49).

a. This growth, at the expense of the genitive, of the dative (locative) construction, which in the case of most of the above-mentioned prepositions was also an inherited one (cf. περί, ὑπό, etc., with dative), and its extension even to ἀπύ and ἐξ, was probably furthered by the influence of the most frequent locative construction, that with ἐν (ἰν).

2. παρά 'at, with,' with accusative instead of dative. Though

occasional even in Attic writers and elsewhere, this is especially common in the Northwest Greek dialects, including Thessalian and Boeotian, e.g., Thess. τοῖ παρ' ἀμμὲ πολιτεύματος (no. 32; corresponding to τοῦ παρ' ὑμῖν πολιτεύματος of Philip's letter in the κοινή), Boeot. ἀ σούγγραφος πὰρ Ϝιφιάδαν, Delph. παραμεινάτω δὲ Νικὼ παρὰ Μνασίξενον, El. πεπολιτευκὼρ παρ' ἀμέ.

a. Much later, and rarely seen in dialect inscriptions, is the more general confusion between the dative with verbs of rest and the accusative with verbs of motion, and the final supremacy of the accusative construction, as ἔμειναν εἰς τὸν οἶκον.

3. πρός 'by, in the sight of,' with accusative instead of genitive, in Elean πό (= ποτί). ὀμόσαντες πὸ τὸν θεὸν τὸν 'Ολύνπιον,—ὅτι δοκέοι καλιτέρōς ἔχēν πὸ τὸν θεόν,—Ϝέρēν αὐτὸν πὸ τὸν Δία 'he shall be judged guilty in the eyes of Zeus.' In a later Elean inscription (no. 65) the same idea is expressed by φευγέτω πὸτ τῶ Διόρ τὠλυμπίω αἴματορ where both the genitive construction and the use of φεύγω instead of the genuine Elean Ϝέρρω are concessions to Attic usage. This Elean use is only a step removed from that of πρός 'in relation to' with accusative.

4. El. ἄνευς = ἄνευ, with accusative instead of genitive, as ἄνευς βōλάν.

5. κατά 'according to' with genitive instead of accusative, in Locrian. καθ' ὧν = καθ' ἅ,—κὰ τῶνδε = κατὰ τάδε,—κὰ τᾶς συνβολᾶς, κατὰ ξενίας.

6. ἐπί with the dative of the deceased person, in epitaphs. This occurs in a few early epitaphs in Lesbian, Phocian, and Locrian, but is especially common in Boeotian, e.g., ἐπὶ Ϝhεκαδάμοε ἐμί, ἐπὶ 'Ὀκίβαε. In most dialects the name of the deceased appears in the nominative.

7. ἀμφί. In most dialects ἀμφί is obsolete. In the phrase ἀμφί τινα, which survives also in Attic prose, it occurs in Argive and Rhodian; in Argive also once in purely local force. In Cretan it is used freely in the meaning 'about, concerning' (as in Homer), with dative or accusative, e.g., αἰ δέ κ' ἀνπὶ δόλōι μōλίōντι 'if they contend about a slave.'—ἀνπὶ τὰν δαῖσιν 'about the division.'

8. ἀντί. The original local meaning 'in the face of, in front of, before' (cf. Lat. *ante*) is preserved in Cret. ἀντὶ μαιτύρōν 'before witnesses', Locr. ἀντὶ τō ἀρχō 'before the magistrate' (no. 59.19),

Att. ἀντὶ τοῦ Μινωταύρου, and a few other Att. examples. Hence the sense 'in return for' and the early and usual 'instead of.' This is sometimes weakened to denote mere equivalence ('in place of' = 'as, for'), e.g., Hom.ἀντὶ ... ἱκετάο 'as a suppliant'. From 'in return for' arose a freer distributive use seen in Arc. τρῖς ὀδελὸς ὀφλὲν ἀντὶ Ϝεκάσταυ 'shall pay a fine of three obols for each (wagon).' Further, Delph. ἀντὶ Ϝέτεος (no. 52 A 45), Arc. ἀντ' ἐνιαυτοῦ (IG V.ii.266), Boeot. ἀντ' ἐνιαυτῶ (cf. BCH 60.183), all meaning 'by the year, yearly,' and even Coan ἀντὶ νυκτός 'by night' (no. 108.42). Cf. Hesych. ἀντέτους· τοῦ αὐτοῦ ἔτους. Λάκωνες, ἀντὶ μῆνα· κατὰ μῆνα, and ἀνθ' ἡμέρας· δι' ὅλης τῆς ἡμέρας.

9. ἐξ. An extension of the regular use of ἐξ (or ἀπό) with the genitive to denote material and source, is seen in certain expressions of amount or value, e.g., Att. στεφάνωι ἀπὸ χιλίων δραχμῶν 'with a crown worth 1000 drachmas'.—Ion. στεφανῶσαι Μαύσσωλον μὲν ἐκ δαρεικῶν πεντήκοντα, Ἀρτεμισίην δὲ ἐκ τριήκοντα δαρεικῶν 'crown Maussolus with a crown worth fifty darics, Artemisia with one worth thirty.'—Att. κριθῶν...πραθεισῶν ἐκ τριῶν δραχμῶν τὸν μέδιμνον ἕκαστον 'barley purchased at three drachmas a medimnus,' and even more freely Ther. πυρῶν ἐγ μεδίμνου καὶ κριθῶν ἐγ δύο μεδίμνων 'a medimnus of wheat and two of barley.'

10. ὑπέρ 'in behalf of' with accusative instead of genitive, in late Locrian, Delphian, Epidaurian, Arcadian, Rhodian, e.g., Delph. ὑπὲρ τὰν πόλιν. Cf. above, 2 with a.

11. ὑπό instead of usual ἐπί with genitive in expressions of dating occurs with genitive in Elean (no. 66.2), and with accusative in Laconian (no. 71.66).

12. Noteworthy combinations are Thess. ὑππρό 'just before', and Arc. ἐπές from ἐπί and ἐς = ἐξ (cf. ὑπέκ, διέκ, παρέκ), meaning 'for and on occasion of, with reference to.'

VERBS

Augment and Reduplication

137. Most peculiarities are such as are due to divergence in the form of contraction where a consonant has been lost (εἶχον or ἦχον, cf. **25**), or in the treatment of consonant groups, as Att. εἴληφα, Phoc. εἰλάφει, from *σέσλᾱφα (**76**.2), but Ion., Epid., Arc. λελάβηκα after λέλοιπα, etc., with original initial λ, Arg. ϜεϜρεμένα, but Att.-Ion. εἴρηκα after forms like εἴληφα (**55***a*), Cret., El. ἔγραμμαι = γέγραμμαι, like Ion. ἔκτημαι = Att. κέκτημαι, ἔγνωκα in all dialects. Note also Cret. ἤγραμμαι, with which compare ἤθελον, ἠβουλόμην.

Active Personal Endings

138. 1. Second singular. The original primary ending -*si* (Skt. -*si*) is preserved in Hom., Syrac. ἐσσί, also in Epid. συντίθησι, and so perhaps regularly in West Greek dialects (inscriptional examples of the second singular are, naturally, very rare), the retention of intervocalic σ being due to the analogy of ἐσσί. But in the East Greek dialects, where 3 sg. τίθητι became τίθησι (**61**.1), τίθης, etc., with secondary ending, were employed.

Thematic primary -εις (with genuine ει) in nearly all dialects, but Cypr. ἔρπες, etc. (Hesych.), Dor. συρίσδες, etc. (Theocr.).

Also -σθα, starting from οἶσθα, ἦσθα, with the original perfect ending -θα, is widely used in literary Lesbian and Doric, as in Homer (τίθησθα, βάλοισθα, etc.).

a. Occasional examples of -ης (also -ηις) in literary Lesbian and Doric texts, beside the normal -εις, are almost certainly corruptions, due to the grammarians' false extension of η = secondary ει.

2. Third singular. The original primary ending -*ti* (Skt. -*ti*) is preserved in West Greek, Boeot. τίθητι, δίδωτι, etc., whence East Greek τίθησι, δίδωσι. See **61**.1. Thematic primary -ει (with genuine ει), secondary -ε in all dialects.

a. Herodian quotes as Aeolic τίθη, δίδω, ζεύγνυ, that is, with secondary ending as in ἐτίθη, etc. There is some confirmation of such forms, e.g., δείκνῡ in Hesiod, δάμνᾱ (correction of the impossible δάμνησι) in Alcaeus.

3. First plural. West Greek -μες (cf. Skt. -*mas*, Lat. -*mus* from -*mos*), originally the primary ending,—East Greek -μεν, originally the secondary ending. See **223***a*.

4. Third plural, primary. West Greek -ντι (Skt. -*nti*), East Greek -(ν)σι. Thus, in thematic verbs, West Greek φέροντι, Pamph. ἐξάγōδι (= ἐξάγωντι, see **66**), Arc. φέρονσι, Lesb. (and Chian) φέροισι, Att.-Ion. φέρουσι. See **61**.1, **77**.3.

So also in μι-verbs, West Greek ἐντί, φαντί, τίθεντι, δίδοντι, whence Att.-Ion. εἰσί, φᾱσί, Ion. (with the accent of contract forms, see 160) τιθεῖσι, διδοῦσι. But Att. τιθέᾱσι, διδόᾱσι, etc., represent a later formation, with -αντι (-ᾱσι) added to the final vowel of the stem, as also in Boeot. perf. δεδόανθι. Cf. Boeot. ἔθεαν, etc., below, 5.

In the perfect the earliest type is that in -ᾰτι (-n̥ti, Skt. -ati in redupl. pres. dadhati), whence also -ᾱσι. Thus Phoc. ἱερητεύκατι, Delph. καθεστάκατι, Aetol. γεγόνατι, Rhod. ἀνατεθήκατι, Hom. πεφύκασι, Arc. [Ϝο]φλέᾱσι, ἐσλελοίπασι. But this is commonly replaced by -αντι, as Dor. κεχάναντι (Sophron), Phoc. ἀνατεθέκαντι, Delph. ἐπιτετελέκαντι, Arg. ἐπιμεμηνάκαντι, Rhod. ἀπεστάλκαντι, etc., Att.-Ion. -ᾱσι. Late inscriptions of various dialects have also the secondary -αν, as Cret. ἔσταλκαν.

Boeotian and Thessalian have -νθι, as Boeot. οἴσονθι, ἴωνθι, δώωνθι, ἀποδεδόανθι, etc., Thess. ὑπάρχονθι, κατοικείουνθι (but also -ουντι at Phalanna). Similarly imv. -νθω in Boeot. ἔνθω, δαμιώνθω, etc., and θ in middle endings (139.2). Two different explanations have been suggested, (1) that the type started with a *ἐνθί derived from *ἐντί (163.2) by transposition of the aspiration, (2) that the θ started in the middle endings under the influence of -μεθα, -σθε.

5. Third plural, secondary. -ν (from -ντ) in ἔφερον, etc. So also in the μι-forms, as ἔθεν, ἔδον, which are retained in most dialects, as in Homer. Likewise pass. ἐλύθεν, ἐλέγεν (from -ηντ, with regular shortening), but also sometimes -ην (with η from the other persons), as Hom. μιάνθην, Cret., Epir. διελέγην, Corcyr. ἐστεφανώθην, Delph. ἀπελύθην.

But Attic-Ionic has ἔθεσαν, ἔδοσαν, ἐλύθησαν, etc., with -σαν taken over from the σ-aorist, as also ἦσαν, where most dialects have ἦν (163.3, 4). Similarly -ν is replaced by -αν (also, mainly after aorist forms like ἔλυσαν or ἤνικαν) in Boeot. ἀνέθεαν, ἀνέθειαν, ἀνέθιαν (9.4), παρεῖαν, Locr. ἀνέθεαν, Arc. συνέθεαν, Cypr. κατέθιjαν (9.6); and in Thessalian by -εν (an inherited ending seen in Hom. ἦεν, or perhaps from -αν, cf. 7, 27), as ἐδούκαεμ (ἔδωκαν), ὀνεθείκαεν (beside ὀνέθεικαν), and, with diphthongal αι from αε, ἐτάξαιν (similarly ἐδώκαιν, probably due to Thessalian influence, in a Delphian inscription), also once even in a thematic form, ἐνεφανίσσοεν = ἐνεφάνιζον.

a. In the κοινή the ending -σαν spread even to thematic forms and to the optative, and such forms occur in late inscriptions of various dialects, e.g., Delph. ἐλέγοσαν, ἔχοισαν, etc. Similar forms in LXX and NT.

6. Third dual, secondary. Att.-Ion. -την, elsewhere -τᾱν, e.g., Arc., Boeot., Epid. ἀνεθέταν, El. λεοίταν. Similarly 1 sg. mid. Att.-Ion. -μην, elsewhere -μᾱν.

Middle Personal Endings

139. 1. Third singular. Primary -ται, Boeot. -τη (**26**), Thess. -τει (**27**). Arcadian has -τοι (perhaps also Cyprian, but not quotable), due to the influence of the secondary -το (before its change to -τυ), e.g., γένητοι, δέατοι, βόλετοι. Cf. also 2 sg. κεῖοι = κεῖσαι, and 3 pl. διαδικάσωντοι.

Secondary -το, Arc.-Cypr. -τυ.

2. Third plural. Usually -νται, -ντο (Arc. -ντυ). But also -αται, -ατο, mostly in the perfect and pluperfect after a consonant (e.g., γεγράφαται), but also after a vowel in Boeotian (-αθη, see below); and so regularly in Ionic in the perfect (e.g., Hom. βεβλήαται, later εἰρέαται, contracted εἰρῆται), pluperfect, and optative, and even in unthematic presents and imperfects, e.g., τιθέαται and also δυνέαται, κιρνέαται, to δύνημι, κίρνημι (with suffix νᾱ, weak να), after the analogy of τιθέαται to τίθημι. Arg. γεγράβανται has -ανται for -αται like -αντι for -ατι (**138.**4).

Boeotian and Thessalian have θ in these, as in the active, endings. Boeot. ἀδικίωνθη (-νται), ἐστροτεύαθη, μεμισθώαθη (-αται), ἐποιείσανθο, ἀπεγράψανθο, etc. Thess. ἔλκονθαι, ἐπαγγέλουνθαι (subj.), ἐγένονθο, εἴλονθο, also ἐφάνγρενθειν = ἐφαιροῦνται, βέλλουνθειν = βούλωνται, with ει from αι (**27**) and an added ν (perhaps the active secondary ending; cf. the double pluralization in the imv. -ντων).

Imperative Active and Middle

140. In the third plural the dialects exhibit the following types.

1. The same form as the third singular. Rare, and only in the

middle. Corcyr. κρινέσθω, ἐκδανειζέσθω, Calymn. ἐπισαμαινέσθω, Coan αἱρείσθω, Thas. θέσθω, Rhod. ἐπιμελέσθω.

2. *a*. -των, formed from the third singular by the addition of the secondary ending -ν. ἔστων, as in Homer, in Ionic only. A corresponding thematic φερέτων is unknown.

b. -σθων, similarly formed from the third singular. φερέσθων, τιθέσθων, etc., the usual form in most dialects.

3. *a*. -ντω, formed after the analogy of 3 pl. indic. -ντι. φερόντω, τιθέντω, etc., in Arcadian, Boeotian (-νθω, **139**.2), Locrian, and the Doric dialects except Cretan, Theran, Cyrenaean.

Later Doric inscriptions often show the Att. -ντων beside -ντω. Conversely the later Delphian inscriptions often have the general Doric -ντω beside -ντων, which is the form of the earliest Delphian (likewise later Cret. -ντω vs. earlier -ντων.)

b. -νσθω, formed to act. -ντω and with the treatment of secondary νσ (**77**.2). Arg. ποιγραψάνσθō, χρόνσθō, Corcyr. ἐκλογιζούσθω, and so to be read with long vowel Epid. φερόσθō, Lac. ἀνελόσθō, Heracl. ἐπελάσθω (**159**) (-ᾱ-όνσθω). Similarly -ōσθōν in type 4*b*.

4. *a*. -ντων, with double pluralization, a combination of types 2 and 3. φερόντων, τιθέντων, as in Homer, in Attic-Ionic, Delphian, Cretan, Theran, Cyrenaean.

b. -(ν)σθων, formed to act. -ντων. Early Att. ἐπιμελόσθōν, χρόσθōν, etc., Locr. δαμευόσθōν, El. τιμόστōν.

c. The coexistence of act. -ντω, but mid. -σθων (where the pluralizing final ν was more essential) is found in several dialects (Arc., Locr., Aetol., Meg., Coan, Rhod.).

5. -ντον, -σθον. This is the regular type in Lesbian, e.g., φέροντον, κάλεντον, ἐπιμέλεσθον, and Pamphylian (e.g., ὄδυ = ὄντον), and also appears, probably through Pamphylian influence, in an inscription of Phaselis which is otherwise in the Rhodian dialect, and in a Rhodian decree at Seleucia in Cilicia.

6. -τωσαν, -σθωσαν, with -ν replaced by -σαν (cf. **138**.5). Att. ἔστωσαν, φερέτωσαν (more rarely φερόντωσαν), ἐπιμελέσθωσαν, etc., after abuot 300 B.C., hence in later inscriptions of various dialects.

Future and Aorist

141. "Doric future" in -σεω. Except for a few middle forms in Attic-Ionic (Hom. ἐσσεῖται, Att. πλευσοῦμαι, etc.), this type is confined to the West Greek dialects (examples in most of the Doric dialects and in Delphian; in Locrian and Elean no futures occur). Thus, from the very numerous examples, Delph. ταγευσέω, κλεψέω, Cret. σπευσίω (ι from ε, 9), πραξίομεν, βοαθησίοντι, τεισῆται, πραξῆται, Epid. βλαψεῖσθαι, Coan, Cnid. ποιησεῖται, Rhod. ἀποδωσεῦντι, Cyren. δησῆται, παισεῖται, ἐκτιμασέντι (42.5e). Ther. θησέοντι, πραξοῦντι (with Att. ου, as often in the Doric κοινή, see 278), Arg. ἐμφανιξόντας (cf. 42.5d).

a. The 3 sg. forms in -σει, though in themselves ambiguous, are rightly assumed to belong here and accented -σεῖ in dialects which show unambiguous forms of this type.

b. Heraclean shows the -σέω type unmistakably in ἐργαξῆται, καρπευσῆται, ἐσσῆται, etc., and so presumably the 3 sg. act. κοψεῖ, etc., is to be so accented. But the 3 pl. forms are act. κοψοντι, holσοντι, etc., mid. ἐργαξονται, ἐσσονται, etc. According to the current view, these belong to the -σω future and are accented κόψοντι, ἔσσονται, etc. But co-existence of the two types (barring the frequent intrusion of κοινή forms) with such a precise distribution is unknown elsewhere, and is difficult to credit. It now seems preferable to revert to the older view (Ahrens, Meister, IG XIV. 645) and assume that, despite the ιο for εο after liquids (ἀναγγελίοντι, etc.), we have here the same change of εο to ο before ντ that was formerly known only in parts of Crete but is now so well attested by Arg. κοινανόντι, etc., including the fut. pple. ἐμφανιξόντας (42.5d).

142. ξ in the future and aorist of verbs in -ζω. The extension of ξ, which is regular in the case of guttural stems, to other verbs in -ζω, which regularly have σσ, σ (δικάσω, ἐδίκασα), is seen in some isolated examples even in Homer (πολεμίξομεν, as, conversely, ἥρπασε beside ἥρπαξε) and Hesiod (φημίξωσι). But as a general phenomenon it is characteristic of the West Greek dialects, together with Thessalian and (in part) Boeotian, and Arcado-Cyprian. Thus, from the countless examples, Cret. δικάξει, Rhod. διωρίξαντο, Coan ἐργάξασθαι, Ther. δείπνιξεν, Meg. ἐτερμόνιξαν, Corcyr. ἀπολογίξασθαι, Heracl. ἐτέρμαξαν (ξ in forms of 12 verbs, but also κατεσσώισαμες, probably influenced by ἔσωσα from σώω), El. ποταρμόξαιτο, (Locr. ψάφιξξις, see below, *a*),

Delph. ἀγωνίξατο, Thess. ψαφίξασθειν, ἐργάξατο, Arc. παρετάξωνσι, ποινίξασθαι, Cypr. ἐξορύξε.

But in Argolic the ξ formation is avoided when a guttural preceded, e.g., Arg. ἐδίκασσαν, ἐργάσσαντο, Epid. ἐργάσασθαι, ἀνσχίσσαι, beside ἀγωνίξασθαι, προσεφάνιξε, ἐμφανιξόντας. Similarly Arc. ἐδικάσαμεν, δικάσασθαι, ἀναγκάσαι (but also ὥρισαν) beside παρετάξωνσι, etc.

Boeotian has, from different localities, both ξ and ττ (= Att. σ, 82), e.g., ἐκομιξάμεθα, ἐπεσκεύαξε, ἐμέριξε, ἰαρειάξασα, and κομιττάμενοι, κατασκευάττη, ἐψαφίττατο, ἀπολογίτταστη, καταδουλίτταστη.

a. A similar extension of guttural stems is sometimes seen in other forms, e.g., Heracl. ποτικλαίγω = προσκλείω, Argol., Mess. κλάιξ (as in Theocr.), κλαικτός, Lac. κέλεξ = κέλης, Dor. ὄρνιξ, gen. ὄρνιχος (lit. Dor., Coan, Cyren.) = ὄρνις, ὄρνιθος, Cret. ψάφιγμα (also ψάφιμμα) = ψήφισμα, Lesb. ψάφιγγι = ψηφῖδι, and especially the frequent abstracts in -ξις = -σις, as Aetol. ψάφιξις, Locr. ψάφιξξις (89.1), Corcyr. χείριξις, Cret. ἀπολάγαξις, χρημάτιξις.

143. σσ in the future and aorist of verb stems ending in a short vowel. The Homeric extension of σσ from ἐτέλεσ-σα to ἐκάλε-σσα is an Aeolic characteristic. Lesb. [καλε]σσάτωσαν, ὀμόσσαντες, Boeot. σουνκαλέσσαντες. Other dialects may have σσ from stems ending in σ or a dental, as ἐτέλεσσα or ἐδίκασσα (Boeot. ττ), ἐδασσάμην (Cret. ττ), later with one σ (82, 83), but always ἐκάλεσα, ὤμοσα.

144. Aorist in -α. εἶπα and ἤνεγκα, ἤνεικα, or ἤνικα in various dialects. Arc. pple. ἀπυδόας=ἀποδούς, Lesb. ἔχευα, elsewhere ἔχεα (e.g., Ion. συγχέαι, no. 2). In late times this type is extended to many other verbs, e.g., ἦλθα, γενάμενος.

a. ἤνεικα or ἤνικα, not ἤνεγκα, is the form of most dialects except Attic, e.g., Ion. ἤνεικα (Hom., Hdt.), ἐνεικάντων (Chios), also ἐξενιχθῆι (Ceos); Lesb., Delph., Argol., Calymn. ἤνικα, Boeot. ἐνενιχθείει (ι probably original, not = ει) and 3 pl. εἴνιξαν, the latter a blend with the σ-aorist.

b. Aorist in -ᾱ (beside the familiar ἔδρᾱν, etc.). Epid. ἐξερρύᾱ, Lac. ἀπεσσούᾱ, 3 sg. subj. Calymn. ἐγρυᾶι, Cyren. μιᾶι, ἴσᾱι.

c. Aorist of ἵζω. Corcyr. hίσατο, Arg. ἴσσατο, Cyren. ἴσσαντα, ἰσσάμενος vs. Hom. καθεῖσα, ἐφέσσαι, Arg. ἤσσαντο, ἐσσάμενος, from ἕζω.

d. σ-aorist forms with thematic vowel instead of the usual α by extension. Like Hom. ἐβήσετο, etc., are Pamph. ἐβόλάσετυ and 3 pl. imv. κατεϜερξόδυ.

145. Future passive with active endings. Rhod. ἐπιμελήθη-σεῦντι, ἀποσταλησεῖ, σταθησεῖ, Ther. συναχθησοῦντι, Cret., Carpath. ἀναγραφησ[εῖ], Astyp. ἐπιμελήθησεῖ, and φανησεῖν, δειχθη-σοῦντι in Archimedes. Although the inscriptional examples are, as yet, confined to the Doric islands, it is not improbable that this was a general Doric or West Greek characteristic. Forms with middle endings, like Ther. ἀνατεθησεῦνται, are from the κοινή with local coloring.

Perfect

146. 1. κ-perfect. This is usual for vowel stems in all dialects. But there are some few forms without κ, outside the indicative singular, like Hom. βεβάασι beside βέβηκας, κεκμηώς beside κέκμη-κας, etc., e.g., Boeot. ἀποδεδόανθι, καταβεβάων, δεδώωση = δεδω-κυῖαι, ϜεϜυκονομειόντων = ᾠκονομηκότων, πεπιτευόντεσσι, πεποι-όντεισσι, καταβεβλειώσας, ἀπειλθείοντες, Arc. [Ϝō]φλέασι (but pple. Ϝōφλε̄κόσι).

The gradual extension of the κ-type to other than original vowel stems is by no means confined to Attic (cf., e.g., Arc. ἐφθορκώς; Att. ἔφθαρκα but also ἔφθορα), and some verbs which usually have the strong perfect show dialect forms with a vowel stem and κ. So ἀνδάνω, λαμβάνω, with usual ἔᾱδα, εἴληφα (εἴλᾱφα), but Locr. ϜεϜαδε̄κότα, Ion. ἄδηκε (Hippon.), Arc., Ion., Epid. λελάβηκα, from the vowel stem which is present in many verbs in -άνω (cf. τετύχηκα, μεμάθηκα, etc.). Usual ἐλήλυθα, but ἤλθηκα in Boeot. διεσσείθεικε (pple. ἀπειλθείοντες without κ, see above), Arc. κατηνθηκότι. Similarly from a secondary ᾱ-stem, Lesb. ὑπαδεδρόμᾱκε (Sappho), Arg. ἐπιμεμηνάκαντι (η from aor.; cf. μεμενᾱκός Archim., Att. μεμένηκα). For secondary forms in -ωκα, see **162**.3.

2. Aspirated perfect. This is mainly an Attic-Ionic development. But there are some examples of aspirated forms of the κ-perfect, which even in Attic are only late (εἴρηχα, etc., in papyri), Syrac. ἐκρατερίχημες (Sophron), Arg. δέδωχε, Arc. ἱερίτευχε.

3. Dialectal variations in the grade of the root (**49**) are not infrequent, as Cret. ἀμπελελεύθεν, Cyren. κατεληλευθυῖα (vs.

Hom. εἰλήλουθα, εἰληλουθώς), Heracl. ἐρρηγεῖα = Att. ἐρρωγυῖα, Dor. ἔωκα = Att. εἶκα from ἵημι (cf. ἔρρωγα from ῥήγνυμι), also in the middle, Heracl. ἀνhεῶσθαι, Arc. ἀφεώσθω (so ἀνέωνται Hdt., ἀφέωνται NT).

4. For the reduplication, see 137; for the 3 pl. ending, see 138.4.

5. Heracl. γεγράψαται (no. 79.121) and subj. μεμισθωσῶνται (no. 79.106) have generally been taken as perfect forms, with difficult explanation. But they are rather future perfect forms, suitable to the context and much easier to explain. γεγράψαται has simply taken over the ending of the perfect γεγράφαται. μεμισθωσῶνται is precisely the form to be expected as subj. of 3 pl. indic. fut. perf. μεμισθωσόνται (on the accent, which would be the same as in the future, see 141b). To be sure, our grammars give an optative but no subjunctive for the future perfect, but both were given in the old τύπτω paradigm (cf. Uhlig, Dionysius Thrax, p. 125 ff., where the 3 pl. mid. fut. perf. subj. τετύψωνται is (apart our assumption of -σέω type and consequent accentuation) just what we assume for μεμισθωσῶνται.

147. Thematic forms in the perfect. Aside from the subjunctive, optative, and imperative, which regularly have thematic inflection, we find:

1. Indicative. Forms inflected like presents are often employed by the Sicilian Doric writers, e.g., Theocr. δεδοίκω, πεπόνθεις, πεφύκει, Epich. γεγάθει, Archim. τετμάκει, and occur in some inscriptions of Rhodes, Cnidus, and Carpathus, e.g., τετιμάκει, γεγόνει, ἑστάκει, and occasionally elsewhere, as Phoc. εἰλάφει.

2. Infinitive. Forms in -ειν (-εν, -ην) instead of -εναι (-εμεν, etc.) are found in Lesbian and in some West Greek dialects, e.g., Lesb. τεθνάκην, τεθεωρήκην, Delph. ἀποτετείκεν, Cret. ἀμπεληλεύθεν, Calymn., Nisyr. δεδώκεν, Rhod. γεγόνειν, Epid. λελαβήκειν. So Pindar κεχλάδειν, Theocr. δεδύκειν.

Cf. also Heracl. πεφυτευκῆμεν, etc., from -ε-εμεν instead of simply -εμεν.

3. Participle. The thematic inflection is regular in the Aeolic dialects, e.g., Lesb. κατεληλύθοντος, κατεστακόντων, Thess. πεφειράκοντες, ἐπεστάκοντα, Boeot. ϝεϝυκονομειόντων, δεδώωση (146.1). Cf. Hom. κεκλήγοντες.

a. There are some feminine forms in -ουσα in later Delphian (e.g., δεδωκούσας), and elsewhere, but these represent a more restricted phenomenon, quite independent of the preceding. Cf. also Ion. ἐστεῶσα, Att. ἐστῶσα.

148. The participle in its regular (unthematic) form usually has the feminine in -υῖα. But forms in -εῖα are found in late Attic and elsewhere, e.g., Heracl. ἐρρηγεῖα, Ther. ἐστακεῖα.

Subjunctive

149. The subjunctive of thematic forms. The mood sign is η/ω, to which the personal endings were added directly. So originally the second and third singular in -ης, -η, but replaced in the majority of dialects by -ηις, -ηι on the analogy of the indicative -εις, -ει. Thus 3 sg. -ηι from the earliest times in Attic-Ionic, Phocian (φάρει, ἄγηι, etc.), Locrian (ἀποθάνει, etc.), Cretan (πάθει, φέρHι, etc.) and so generally in the Doric dialects (or later -ει).

But the earlier type with 3 sg. -η prevails in Arcadian (Cyprian examples lacking) and is also attested elsewhere. Thus Arc. λέγε̄, νέμε̄, ἔχη, etc. (so uniformly), Thess. θέλε̄, Boeot. πίε̄ (and so later Thess., Boeot. -ει probably = η, **16**, though could also = ηι), El. ἐκπέμπᾱ (ā = η, **15**), Lac. ζόε̄ (no. 70, due to the Arcadian engraver? cf. ἀποθάνει in the same inscription and usual Lac. -ηι). Other scattered examples of -η, beside usual -ηι or -ει, may be merely graphic variants of the latter and are dubious representatives of the early type. Thus Lesb. ἐμμένη (no. 26, but -ηι in the earlier no. 25), Heracl. ἀμμισθωθῆ (once beside -ηι or usual -ει), Mess. ἐξάγη (beside χρήζηι in the same inscription), Corcyr. λίπη, Epid. πέτη, Coan λάθη, and many others.

Arc. 1 sg. ἀψευδήων (no. 21) is unique and variously explained. Probably -ω with addition of secondary ending, like Hom. subj. ἐθέλωμι, etc., with addition of the primary ending.

150. The subjunctive of the σ-aorist. As in the case of other unthematic formations (cf. Hom. ἴομεν to indic. ἴμεν), this was originally a short-vowel subjunctive in ε/ο, and only later came to follow the more common long-vowel type in η/ω. Besides Hom. βήσομεν (cf. βάσομεν Pindar), etc., the old short-vowel forms are widely attested for the σ-aorist and occur also in the α-aorist.

East Ion. ποιήσει, κατάξει, ἐκκόψει (no. 3, Teos), ἀποκρύψει, ἐξομόσει, ἐπάρει, κατείπει, κατακτείνōσιν (that is, -ουσιν, not -ωσιν), Chian πρήξοισιν (no. 4; with Lesb. οισ from ονσ, 77.3). Lesb. ἀποτείσει, κωλύσει, ἀποπεράσσει, χαλάσσομεν, and (with extension to the thematic aorist) τέκοισι. Cret. δείξσει, ἀδικήσει, etc. (hence the forms of the Law-Code are to be transcribed -ει, not -ēι), ἐξσαννήσεται, ὀμόσοντι, etc., Coan ὑποκύψει, Astyp. δόξει. Cyren. ἄρξεται, καταγγήλει, ἐνίχει.

a. Heracl. ἀρτύσει, πράξει, etc., do not belong here, but have -ει from -ηι as in the thematic forms ἀποθάνει, λάβει (with pres. subj. φέρει, νέμει, etc.). The long-vowel type is shown clearly in 3 pl. ἀρτύσωντι, etc.

b. The early Locr. forms ἀποτείσEι, διαφθείσEι, φυτεύσEται, though ambiguous, may well belong here, being much earlier than the Delph. forms, which show only the long-vowel type, ἀποτείσηι, κωλύσωντι, etc.

c. A still earlier type, with the ending added directly to the short vowel without the secondary ι of the usual forms (and so agreeing with the type Skt. -sas, -sat) is seen in Cyren. 2 sg. ποιῆσες and [ἐ]ρεῖσες (nos. 115.9, 119). In view of this positive evidence we should probably transcribe Aegin. στασEς (IG IV.177) as στάσες (for Argol. -ης would be anomalous). But Cypr. Ϝείσες (Schwyzer 685), is more probable than Ϝεῖσες (cf. meter, and Arc. -στάση, etc.). There is no similar evidence of a corresponding 3 sg. -σε (parallel to Skt. -sat). It is only a possibility that the Cypr. forms which are usually transcribed λύσē, ἐξορύξē, and the early Arc. forms with E, should be read with ε, in spite of the later Arc. -στάσης, -βλάψης, etc.

151. The subjunctive of unthematic vowel stems. There are two distinct types.

1. The endings are added directly to the long vowel of the stem. This type is found mostly in those forms of which the corresponding indicative has the short vowel. So especially in the middle, e.g., Cret. δύναμαι, νύναται, νύνανται, Lesb., Cyren. δύνανται beside indic. δύναμαι, Arc. ἐπισυνίστᾱται beside indic. ἴστᾱται, δέᾱτοι (cf. Hom. δέᾱτο). But also, when the indicative also has a long vowel, Cret. πέπᾱται, ἐστετέκνōται, Ther. πέπρᾱται. Further, in the active, Mess. τίθηντι beside indic. τίθεντι (hence also, beside ἐντί, Mess. ἤνται = ὦσι, Delph. ἦται = ᾖ), γράφηντι beside indic. ἔγραφεν, Cret. ἴσᾱντι, Cyren. ἴσᾱι, also (beside indic. ᾱ) Cyren. μιᾶι, Calymn. ἐγρυᾶι (cf. 144b).

After the relation of ἰστᾱται to ἰστᾱται there arose also an aor.

subj. σᾱ beside indic. σᾰ, e.g., Cret. παρθύσαται, Arc. βωλεύσᾶνται, likewise in Elean, with loss of σ (**59**.3), φυγαδεύᾱντι (no. 65), ποιήᾱται (no. 66).

2. The usual type is that in which the long vowel of the stem was followed by the short vowel subjunctive sign ε/o, this being generally replaced by the more usual η/ω (cf. **150**). Further change is due to the shortening, in the majority of dialects, of the long stem vowel before the following vowel (**43**). Hom. θήομεν (θείομεν), θήῃς, δώομεν, δώῃ, Boeot. καθιστᾱει, ἀποδώει, Delph. δώῃ, ἀντιπριάηται, Heracl. φᾶντι (from *φάωντι), Thess. δυνᾶεται, but with shortening Ion. θέωμεν, Att. θῶμεν, Cret. ἐνθίωμεν (ι from ε), etc. Similarly in the aorist passive, Hom. δαμήῃς, μιγήῃς, Boeot. κουρωθείει, ἐπιμελειθείει, κατασκευασθείει, ἐνενιχθείει, Arc. κακριθέε, but with shortening Ion. λυθέωμεν, Att. λυθῶμεν, Cret. πειθθίωντι (cf. ἐνθίωμεν), Heracl. ἐγϝηληθίωντι, Rhod. ἐργασθέωντι, etc.

3. Subjunctive of εἰμι. Att.-Ion. ἴω, etc., with weak grade of the root. But Cret. εἴει, ἐνσ-είει, Cyren. ἐπείηι, Syrac. εἴω (Sophron).

Optative

152. 1. Arc. 1 sg. ἐξελαύνοια represents a form long since assumed by comparative grammar (*-οi-m̥, whence -οια with ι retained under the influence of -οις, etc.), but generally replaced by -οιμι.

2. In the third plural *-οιαν (cf. 1) was replaced by -οιεν (after εἶεν, etc.), for which sometimes late -οιν, e.g., Delphian θέλοιν.

3. Unthematic type in contract verbs. See **157**b.

4. σ-aorist. Most dialects show the secondary type with αι (α spread from the indicative). But the old unthematic mood sign seen in present εἴην, etc., appears in Cret. 3 sg. κοσμησίε, δικακσίε, 3 pl. ϝέρχσιεν. The type -ειας, -ειε (perhaps starting in a 1 sg. -εια parallel to Arc. ἐξελαύνοια), more common than the αι-forms in Homer and early Attic writers, is also attested in Tean ἀ[ποχ]τένει[ε] (no. 3.10, probable reading), Lesb. [δ]ιαδέξειε (IG XII.ii.527.57), El. κατιαραύσειε, ἀδεαλτώhαιε. Arc. διακωλύσει (no. 19.6/7) and ὑνιερόσει (no. 16) would be variants of this type.

Infinitive

153. The infinitive of thematic forms.

1. -ειν or -ην, according as the dialect has ει or η from ε + ε (**25**). So Att.-Ion., Thess. (Thessaliotis), Locr., Corinth., Meg., Rhod. -ειν, but Lesb., El., Lac. -ην.

2. -εν. So in Arcadian (but -ην at Lycosura, Orchomenos) Cyprian (or -ēν?), Delphian, and many of the Doric dialects (Heracl., Argol., Cret., Ther., Cyren., Coan, etc.), also once in a late East Locr. inscription (IG IX.i.267).

3. Some of these dialects have -εν even from verbs in -εω, e.g., Ther. διοικέν, Cyren. πλέν, εὐτυχέν (cf. also mid. δωρέσθαι. ὠνέσθαι), Coan δειπνέν, Calymn. μαρτυρέν, Arg. πωλέν, Delph. ψαφοφορέν, ἐνοικέν (but usually -εῖν).

154. The infinitive of unthematic forms.

1. -ναι. So in Attic-Ionic and Arcado-Cyprian, e.g., Att.-Ion. εἶναι, δοῦναι, Cypr. δοϜέναι (-Ϝεναι, like -μεναι; or δοϜ-έναι going with δυϜάνω, **162.**5?), κυμερēναι, Arc. ἦναι.

2. -μεναι. So in Lesbian, as in Homer, e.g., ἔμμεναι, θέμεναι, δόμεναι. But see **155.**2, 3.

3. -μεν. εἶμεν, etc., in Thessalian, Boeotian, and most of the West Greek dialects.

4. -μην. Cret. ἤμην, etc.

5. -μειν. εἶμειν, etc. in Rhodes and vicinity (Carpathus, Telos) and the Rhodian colonies (Phaselis in Pamphylia; Gela and Agrigentum in Sicily; also at Tauromenium, Rhegium, Croton, and in Epicharmus).

a. Cret. -μην, Rhod. -μειν are probably formed from -μεν with the vowel influenced by the thematic type, Cret. *-ην (before it was replaced by -εν), Rhod. -ειν.

155. Interchange of thematic and unthematic types of infinitive.

1. -μεν is extended to thematic forms in Boeotian and Thessalian (Pelasgiotis), as sometimes in Homer (cf. εἰπέμεν, and εἰπέμεναι), e.g., Boeot. φερέμεν, Thess. ὑπαρχέμεν. Cf. also Cret. προϜειπέμεν in an early inscription of Lyttus.

2. The aorist passive infinitive, which is regularly unthematic (Att. γραφῆναι, Dor. γραφῆμεν), follows the thematic type in

Lesbian, e.g., ἐπιμελήθην, ὀντέθην, etc. This belongs with the following.

3. In Lesbian the present infinitive of unthematic vowel stems, as well as of the contract verbs, which otherwise follow the unthematic type (157), ends in -ν, not -μεναι, e.g., δίδων, κέρνᾶν, ὄμνῦν, κάλην, στεφάνων, κατείρων (καθιεροῦν). Once also aor. infin. πρόστᾶν (but usually -μεναι, as θέμεναι, δόμεναι).

4. For thematic forms of the perfect infinitive in various dialects see 147.2.

5. For Euboean τιθεῖν, etc., and even εἶν beside εἶναι, see 160.

156. The infinitives in -σαι and -σθαι. Thessalian (Larissa) has ὀνγράψειν, δεδόσθειν, ἔσσεσθειν, πεπεῖστειν, ἐλέστειν, etc., with -ει from -αι (27), and ν added after the analogy of other infinitives. Boeot. -σθη, -στη with η from αι (26), and στ = σθ (85.1).

Unthematic Inflection of Contract Verbs

157. The μι-inflection of contract verbs, sometimes known as the Aeolic inflection, is characteristic of Lesbian, Thessalian, and Arcado-Cyprian, e.g., Lesb. κάλημμι, φίλημμι, κάλεντον, κατάγρεντον, εὐεργετέντεσσι, [ὁ]μονόεντες, προσμέτρεις, στοίχεις (78), Thess. ἐφάνγρενθειν = ἐφαιροῦνται, εὐεργετές (78), στραταγέντος, Arc. ποίενσι, ποέντω, ἀδικέντα, κυένσαν, ἱεροθυτές (78), ζαμιόντω, καταφρονῆναι, Cypr. κυμερῆναι. μι-forms are also quoted as Boeotian by the grammarians, but the inscriptions show only the usual type (στραταγίοντος, etc.).

a. The stem ends in a long vowel, which is regularly shortened before ντ (though also, with analogical η, Lesb. κατοικήντων in contrast to usual εὐεργετέντεσσι, etc., and προνόηνται, διασάφηνται, δίννηντες, like Att. δίζηνται, in contrast to Thess. ἐφάνγρενθειν), but is otherwise retained throughout, e.g., Lesb. αἴτηται, κάλησθαι, ἐπιμελήσθω, ζαμιώσθω, ποιήμενος, προαγρημμένω, Thess. ἀπελευθεροῦσθειν, διεσαφείμενος, Arc. ἀδικήμενος, ζαμιώσθω. This type, then, follows the analogy of that seen in ἔβλην, βλῆτο, βλήμενος, δίζημαι, etc., rather than that of τίθημι, τίθεμεν, τιθέμενος, with vowel-gradation. But even the latter sometimes shows an extension of the long vowel from the singular active, e.g., Lesb. [προστί]θησ[θον], δίδωσθαι, like Hom. τιθήμεναι, τιθήμενος.

b. But also thematic forms. Thess. ἐρουτᾶι, hυλōρέοντος (no. 35), Lesb. ποτέονται, ὀγκαλέοντες, 2 sg. ὄπταις, χαύνοις, 3 sg. ἄγρει, τίμαι, βόαι (also γέλαι, νίκαι gram.).

c. The more limited extension of the μι-inflection to the optative of contract verbs, as in Att. φιλοίην, μισθοίην, etc., is occasionally found elsewhere. Ion. ἀνωθεοίη beside ποιοῖ, El. συλαίε, δαμοσιοία (= -οίη) beside δοκέοι, ποιέοι, ἐνπōι, Arg. οἰκείη. Cf. also the infinitives El. δαμοσιῶμεν, Cret. δαμιόμεν.

Middle Participle in -ειμενος

158. The middle participle in -ειμενος (or -ημενος) from verbs in -εω, as if from -ε-εμενος instead of -ε-ομενος, is characteristic of the Northwest Greek dialects and Boeotian, e.g., Locr. ἐνκαλείμενος, Delph. καλείμενος, ποιείμενος, χρείμενος, etc., Boeot. δείμενος (and so under Boeotian influence ἀφικνεμένων at Oropus), El. καδαλέμενος. But also Cret. χρήμενος, Cyren. χρείμενος (no 115.8; or here the Delph. form ᾽). This is due to the analogy of forms which regularly had ει (or η) from ε-ε, as the infinitive καλεῖσθαι. Cf. Phoc. ποιεῖνται = ποιοῦνται, formed after ποιεῖσθε, Delph. συντελείντω.

a. Lesb. καλήμενος, Arc. ἀδικήμενος, Thess. διεσαφείμενος probably do not belong here, but among the other μι-forms of these dialects. See 157*a*.

Type -ήω, -ώω, also -άω

159. Forms in -ηω, -ωω, with the long-vowel stem of the other tenses extended to the present, are found in various dialects. Lesb. ἀδικήει, ποθήω, Arc. ἀψευδήων, Thess. κατοικείουνθι (3 pl. subj.), Delph. στεφανωέτω, δουλώηι, ποιήουσα, Phoc. κλαρώειν, Boeot. δαμιωέμεν, δαμιώοντες, στεφανωέμεν (only in late inscriptions, and perhaps due to Aetolian influence).

A parallel type in -άω is to be recognized in certain forms with ᾱ from ᾱο or ᾱε (vs. Dor. ω or η from the -αω type). Syrac. ὀπτᾶντες (Epich.), ἐπεγγυᾶμενοι (Sophron), γελᾶντι, παρελᾶντα (Theocr.), and so to be read with ᾱ Epid. διεγέλᾱ, καταγελάμενος, and (ἐλάω vs. Hom. ἐλάω = ἐλαύνω) Coan ἐλᾶντι, ἐλάντω, Arg. ποτελᾱτō, Locr. ἀπελᾱōνται, Heracl. ἐπελᾶσθω. Here also τιμᾶντι (dat. sg. pple.) in an inscription of Dodona, and probably Thess. ἐρουτᾶι, Lesb. τίμαι, βόαι.

a. Further probable, though less certain, examples of the -ωω type are Coan καρπῶντι, ἱερώσθω, Calymn. ἐξορκώντω, ἀξιῶι, Astyp. στεφανῶι, στεφανῶν (στεφανῶι also at Gela and Thera), since in these dialects the contraction of ο + ο or ε usually appears as ου (cf., e.g., Coan ἀξιοῦντι, ζαμιούντω). Heracl. πριῶι (subj.) may belong here, but there is nothing against its derivation from -οει or -οηι (cf. ω from ο + ε in λωτήριον, **44**.4). The forms attributed above to γελάω, ἐλάω are taken by some as formed directly from unthematic stems γελα-, ἐλα-, in that case to be read with short α.

Transfer of μι-Verbs to the Type of Contract Verbs

160. The transfer of certain forms of μι-verbs to the inflection of contract verbs is found in various dialects, as Att. ἐτίθει, ἐδίδου, Delph. ἀποκαθιστάοντες, διδέουσα, but is most widespread in Ionic. With τιθεῖ, etc. in Homer and Herodotus, compare διδοῖ (Miletus) and the Euboean infinitives τιθεῖν, διδοῦν, καθιστᾶν, and even εἶν beside εἶναι. εἶν is also Chian. Cyren. καττιθέν, διδών, beside θέμεν, δόμεν.

Some Other Interchanges in the Present System

161. 1. Verbs in -ευω form their present in -ειω in Elean, as φυγαδείην = φυγαδεύειν, beside aor. φυγαδεύαντι, also (with α after ρ, **12**a) κατιαραίων = καθιερεύων, beside aor. κατιαραύσειε, and λατραι[όμενον], λατρειόμενον = λατρευόμενον. So also μαστείει = μαστεύει, in an inscription of Dodona. This represents the normal phonetic development from -εϝιω, the usual -ευω being due to the influence of the other tenses.

2. Verbs in -αω show forms in -εω in various dialects, but, with few exceptions, only where the ε is followed by an o-vowel, e.g., aside from literary examples (as Hom. μενοίνεον, Alcm. ὀρέων, Theocr. ὀρεῦσα), Delph. συλέοι, συλέοντες (but συλῆν, συλήτω), ἐπιτιμέοντες, θωεόντων (Att. θωᾶν, Locr. θōιέστō), Aetol. νικεόντοις, Rhod. τιμοῦντες and also τιμεῖν (Agrig.), Boeot. τιμίωσα, El. ἐνεβέοι, Cret. (with ι from ε, **9**.7) ἐβίōν, ἐπαριόμενον, μοικίōν (μοιχάω). Cyren. παρβεῶντας, ἐπαρεώμενοι (cf. **42**.5 b), σιγέν. According to many, this rests upon an actual phonetic change of αο to εο, the αο (ω) in Attic and elsewhere being a restoration due to leveling with the αε forms. But we may have to do simply with a trasfer to the -εω type, which was mainly favored where it offered uncontracted forms (in most dialects εο was uncontracted until late, but εε contracted; in all forms like Rhod. τιμοῦντες the ου is an Attic substitution for εο).

a. Conversely -αω = usual -εω. πονάω in Sappho, Pind., Theocr., πτοάω in Sappho, etc., φωνάω in Pind. Thess. δούρραντα from *δωράω =

δωρέω. Pamph. 3 sg. aor. ἐβōλάσετυ, from βōλάομαι, denominative of βωλά, but pres. pple. βōλέμενυς, like Cret. χρήμενος (158).

3. Spread of -οω type, especially in non-present forms. Boeot. ἐπίθωσε = ἔπεισε (Boeot. pres. not quotable; πίθω = πείθω, or πιθόω?), Heracl. 3 sg. subj. πριῶι, fut. πριωσεῖ (cf. πεπριωμένος Hippoc., πρίωμα Hesych.) vs. usual πρίω, El. τετίμōνται, τιμόστōν, Att. ἠτίμωσα, Ion. δοκιμῶσαι, Lesb. δοκίμωμι, δοκίμοι (= usual δοκιμάζω), Meg., Cret. ἐπεσκεύωσαν, Delph. κατεσκεύωται, Ther. κατεσκεύωκε, etc. (such forms, as if from σκευόω =σκευάζω, are widespread), Cyren. ἐφορευωκότων, ἰαριτευωκότων, from usual -ευω presents.

4. -ιζω = -οω, especially in West Greek. Boeot., Phoc. δουλίζω (Delph. δουλόω intrans. = Att. δουλεύω), Delph., Thess. ἀπελευθερίζω, Delph., Rhod., Mess., Cret. ὀρκίζω (but also Ionic and Attic sometimes), Dor. στεφανίζω (ἐστεφάνιξα Ar.). Cf. also -ιζω = usual -εύω in late Mess. γραμματίζω, Boeot. γραμματίδδω beside Ach., Boeot., Delph., Epir. γραμματιστάς (also -τής Hdt.) = usual γραμματεύς.

5. -αω = -οω. Lesb. ἀξιάω (ἀξιάσει), Thess., Dor. κοινάω, Heracl. ἀράω (ἀράσοντι) = ἀρόω. Cf. Cret. ἄρατρον = ἄροτρον.

162. Other more individual peculiarities in form or use (others in Glossary).

1. ἀγνέω = ἄγω in perfect forms. Aetol. ἀγνηκώς, ἀχνηκότας (66), Lac. ἄγνηκε (Hesych. emend.), διεξαγνηκέναι. Cf. also ἀγνεῖν· ἄγειν. Κρῆτες, Hesych.

2. Lesb., El. ἀγρέω, Thess. ἀνγρέω (58c) = αἱρέω. Cf. also Lesb. ἄγρεσις, Thess. ἄνγρεσις, Coan ἀγρεταί, Hom. ἄγρει, αὐτάγρετος, etc. Pamph. ἀνhαγλέσθō (blend with a form like Cret. αἰλέω?).

3. ἀνδάνω = δοκέω 'be approved, voted.' Cret. ἔϜαδε, Ion. ἔαδε, Locr. ϜεϜαδέκοτα. Cf. Ion. ἄδος 'decree,' and Hesych. ἅδμα, ἅδημα, ἅδισμα defined by ψήφισμα, δόγμα, also Ϝάδιξις (γάδιξις), Tarent. ἅδιξις. ὁμολογία (cf. ψάφιξις, 142a).

4. Boeot., Thess. γίνυμαι = γίνομαι.

5. Cypr. δυϜάνω (cf. Lat. duim) and δώκω (from ἔδωκα, cf. στήκω in NT) =δίδωμι.

6. ἕρπω 'go, come' (as sometimes in Att. poetry) in many dialects, Arc., Cypr. (Hesych.), Epid., Cret., etc.

7. El. Ϝάρρω, Ϝέρρω, Locr. Ϝέρρω (Att.-Ion. ἔρρω; cf. ἔρρε 'begone!') used as a legal term like Att. φεύγω. Cf. the similar use of Arg. τρέω (no. 85.5).

8. For Att. ζῶ, 3 sg. ζῇ (from *ζήει) most dialects have ζώω (Boeot., Cret. δώω), as in Homer.

9. Dor. ἴσᾱμι = οἶδα and formed from its 3 pl. ἴσαντι, Hom. ἴσᾱσι (this with σ from forms like ἴστε). Attested in Cret. Ϝισάμην, ἴσαντι (subj.), ἴθθαντες (**82b**), Cyren. ἴσαι (subj.), and in literary Doric (Pind., Epich., Theocr.).

10. Compounds of λεαίνω, λειαίνω, or λειόω 'make smooth' (from λεῖος 'smooth') used as financial terms. Boeot. ἀπο-, δια-, ἐσ-λιήνω, act. 'cancel,' mid. 'have cancelled,' Arc. ἀπυλιῶναι probably 'discharge, settle' (no. 22.20). Cf. ἀπολειόω 'erase'.

11. West Grk. λείω, λέω = θέλω. Cret. λείοι, λείοντι, etc., also λέοι, subj. λῆι, Cyren. λέων, subj. λῆι, El. 3 dual. opt. λεοίταν. Contracted forms λῶ, λῶμες, subj. λῆι, λῶντι, etc., attested in most Doric dialects and in Doric writers (Epich., Theocr., etc.).

12. πάομαι in sense = κτάομαι, aor. ἐπᾱσάμην, perf. πέπᾱμαι. Verb forms or derivatives in many West Greek dialects, also Arcadian, Lesbian, Boeotian, and probably common to all non-Att.-Ion. dialects (in Attic poetical, rarely in prose). Cret. perf. subj. πέπᾱται, aor. subj. πάσεται, πᾶμα = κτῆμα (also Arg., Boeot., Arc.), πᾶστας 'owner,' Heracl. πᾱμωχεῖ, Locr. ἐχεπᾱμῶν, πᾱματοφαγεῖσται 'be confiscated' (cpd. with the root of ἔφαγον, originally 'share in,' whence 'partake of, eat'), El. πεπᾱστō, Delph. πεπᾶσθαι, Arg. ἐνπιπάσκομαι 'acquire,' Lesb. (in Homer) πολυπάμων, Delph., Meg. ἔμπᾱσις, Arc. ἴμπᾱσις, Boeot. ἔππᾱσις. Root πᾱ- from ππᾱ- (this probably from an IE kwā- with ππ from kw as in ἵππος), seen in Boeot. τὰ ππάματα, Τυνό-ππαστος, Θιό-ππαστος, ἔππασις, from *ἔμ-ππᾱσις, ἀππᾱσάμενος (Corinna) from *ἀν-ππᾱσάμενος.

a. The ἔγκτησις which occurs in late inscriptions of Crete, Sparta, etc., is from the κοινή. Late Corcyr., Epir., Troez. ἔγκτασις, Thess. ἔντασις is probably to be read with ᾱ (not α as weak grade of η) and explained as a blend of ἔγκτησις with native ἔμπᾱσις.

13. χρηέομαι, forms of Chalced. χρηείσθω, El. χρέεσται, Boeot. χρειεῖσθη, Arc. χρέεσθαι, Att.-Ion., Heracl. χρῆσθαι, Cret. χρῆτθαι (**85**.3), Locr. χρέστō, χρέσται, Lac. χρῆσται, Arg. χρόνσθō (**140**.3b).

Ion. χρεώμενος, Att. χρώμενος, Dodon. χρεόμενος, Cret. χρήμενος, Delph., Cyren. χρείμενος (158).

14. χρηίζω, χρήιζω, χρήζω (37.2) often simply 'wish' = θέλω or βούλομαι, so even in Attic (ἴθ' ὅποι χρήζεις Ar., etc.) and in inscriptions of Delphi (no. 52 A 38), Argos (no. 86.24), Troezen, Rhodes, Cos, Cnidus, Nisyros, Thera, etc.

15. Το πεύθομαι, ὠνέομαι, ἐλεύσομαι Cretan has the active forms πεύθω 'inform,' ὠνέω (ὀνεν, ὀνίοι) 'sell,' ἐπελευσεῖ 'will bring' (cf. Hesych. ἐλευσίω·οἴσω), aor. ἐπελεῦσαι, etc.

The Verb εἰμί

163. 1. First singular present indicative. *ἐσμί, whence Lesb. ἔμμι, Thess. ἐμμί, elsewhere εἰμί or ἠμί. See 76.

2. Third plural present indicative. *ἐντί (cf. Skt. santi, Osc.-Umbr. sent), whence, with substitution of ἐ after the analogy of the other forms, West Greek ἐντί, Att.-Ion. εἰσί. See 61.1, 77.3.

3. Third singular imperfect. ἦς (from *ἦσ-τ, cf. Ved. Skt. ās) is attested for various West Greek dialects (Acarn., Corcyr., Delph., Epid., lit. Doric), Boeotian, Lesbian, Arcadian, and Cyprian, and is probably the form in all dialects (for Locr. ἔν, see no. 57.9, note) except Attic-Ionic, where it was replaced by ἦν (Hom. ἦεν), the old third plural (from *ἦσεν, cf. Skt. āsan).

4. Third plural imperfect. Most dialects had ἦν (see above, 3), examples of which are found in literary Doric, Delphian, and Locrian. For Boeot. παρεῖαν, Att.-Ion. ἦσαν, see 138.5.

5. Third singular imperative. ἔστω in most dialects. But late ἤτω, with ἠ of ἦν etc. after the analogy of, e.g., στήτω to ἔστην. El. ἤστω, also with analogical η but with retention of σ.

6. Third plural imperative. Arg. ἔντō, Boeot. ἔνθω (138.4), Cret. ἔντων, formed from 3 pl. indic. ἐντί. Also thematic ἐόντω, ἐόντων, e.g., in Delphian. Ion. ἔστων, Attic ὄντων, and late ἔστωσαν.

7. Present infinitive. The difference in the form of the ending (154) and also in the development of σ + nasal (76) explains the great variety of forms, Attic-Ionic εἶναι (also Eub. εἶν, 160), Arc. ἦναι, Lesb. ἔμμεναι, Thess. ἔμμεν, West Greek and Boeotian εἶμεν or ἦμεν (25), Rhod. ἤμειν, Cret. ἤμην.

8. Present participle. ἐών in most dialects, Att. ὤν. But also unthematic forms. Heracl. ἔντες, dat. pl. ἔντασσιν (blend with *ἄσσι = Skt. *satsu*), Arg., Lac. (Alcman) παρέντων, Thess. ἔνσα (*ἔντμα, **77.**3), all with ἐντ- for ἐντ- as in ἐντί (above, 2). Lesb., Epid., Troez. ἔσσα (also in some Doric writers; cf. ἐσσία = οὐσία Plato, Crat. 401 C), Arc., Mess. ἔασσα, Cret. ἴαττα, ἴαθθα, all from *ἄτμα = Skt. *satī*, with the substitution or prefixing of ε after the analogy of the other forms.

a. Other similar unthematic feminine forms are ἴεσσα (Hesych.), ἴασσα in 'Επίασσα, Cyren. κατίασσα = ἰοῦσα, and Cyren. ἔκασσα (beside ἐκοῖσα) = ἐκοῦσα, and in Hesych. ἀέκασσα, γέκαθα, the last presumably for a Cret. Ϝέκαθθα.

9. Middle forms, as imperf. ἤμην etc., are late. Cf. 3 sg. subj. ἦται at Delphi, 3 pl. subj. ἦνται at Andania, ἤμην in the κοινή, ἤμεθα in NT.

a. The middle inflection spread until, in Modern Greek, all the present and imperfect forms are of this type, except 3 sg., pl. pres. εἶναι, which is from ἔνι = ἔνεστι, with vowels after the other forms.

10. Confusion between third singular and third plural present (favored by expressions corresponding to Eng. *there are*, Fr. *il y a*). ἐντι as third singular in Rhodian (no. 103.10) and later Doric inscriptions and literature (frequent in Archimedes). ἐστι as third plural in late Lesbian, as ἕτοιμοί ἐστι, ἐψαφίσμενοί ἐστι (cf. also διαδεδίκασται αἱ δίκαι).

WORD-FORMATION

On the Form and Use of Certain Suffixes and Certain Peculiarities of Composition

164. 1. -ειος, -ηιος. The Att. adjectives in -εῖος, -ειος and the nouns in -εῖον, -ειον, and -εία are in many cases from earlier -ήιος (three syllables, also written -ηιος, but later sometimes -ηος; see 37.2), etc., these again in part from -ήϝιος, etc. (cf. Boeot. Καρυκεϝίō, Cypr. ἱερεϝίjαν). The earlier forms with η, besides the many in Homer, etc., are widely attested, e.g., ἱερήιον, ἱαρήιον in many dialects, Ion., Lesb., Cret. πρυτανήιον, Ion. βασιλήιος, φοινικήια, Delph. παιδήια, ἐντοφήια, Cret. οἰκήιος, ἀνδρήιον, ἀρχήία, πρειγήία, νυμφήιον, ἀγνήία, πολιτήία. Forms with ι lost, e.g., Ion. ἱερήον, Delph. ἀνδρῆος, Cyren. ἑταιρήα, Arg. μαντῆον, μαντήα, στρατήα, πρεσγέα, πρεσβήα.

2. Adjectives of the type χαρίεις are from -ϝεντ- (Skt. -vant-). The feminine was originally -ϝατια (like Skt. -vatī, from the weak stem -ṷṇt-; cf. ἔασσα 163.8), whence, with the substitution of ε for α from the analogy of the forms in -ϝεντ-, arose -ϝετια, this yielding -(ϝ)εσσα or -(ϝ)εττα (81). Cf. Boeot. χαρίϝετταν, Corcyr. στονόϝε(σ)σαν, Pamph. τιμάϝε(σ)σα (for ϝ cf. also Φλειϝόν-τᾱθεν). The genuine Attic forms have ττ, as μελιτοῦττα (Ar.), Μυρρινοῦττα (inscr.), those with σσ being poetical and in origin Ionic. Most adjectives of this type are poetical only, except in substantive use, especially the numerous place-names in -όεις, for which see also 44.4.

3. -τις, -σις. See 61.3. For -ξις see 142a. We find -σσις instead of usual -σις in Arg. ἀλιάσσιος, Epid. στεγάσσιος, Troez. ἑρμάσσιος, Boeot. ἀγόρασσιν. Probably *-ασ-τις, normal from dental stems (cf. πίστις), became -ασ-σις, with -σις after the analogy of the common type. Similarly Troez. ἱμασσία.

4. -σμος, -σμα. In most words σ has replaced, by analogy, an earlier dental, which is sometimes preserved, as in Hom. ὀδμή = Att. ὀσμή. So for Att. θεσμός, θέσμιος we find West Greek τεθμός,

Locr. also τετθμός, Lac., Epid., Thess. θεθμός, El. θεθτμός, Boeot. τέθμιον, Locr. θέθμιον (65). Locr., Sicil., Naxian δαιθμός (from δαίω) = usual δασμός (from δατέομαι). Other variations of -μα forms, partly unexplained, are Lesb. ὄππα (Sappho) = ὄμμα, γρόππα (Balbilla) = γράμμα. Also θμ in ὄθμα (Aeolic in Hesych.; also in Call. and Nic.) = ὄμμα, στέθμα (Hesych.) = στέμμα, Arg. γράθμα but also γράσσμα (after ψάφισμα) = γράμμα. For Cret. ψάφιγμα, ψάφιμμα = ψάφισμα see **86**.9, **142a**. Also from ν-stems usually -σμα, as ὕφασμα, μίασμα, πίασμα. But Att. also (inscriptions) ὕφαμμα, Cyren. ποτιπίαμμα. Analogical -σμος in Arc. ἀπυδοσμός = ἀπόδοσις.

5. -τηρ = -της(-τᾱς). As a productive suffix of nouns of agency the older -τηρ has been very largely displaced by -της (-τᾱς), but most fully in Attic prose. As forms with -τηρ = usual -της (-τᾱς) are not infrequent in poetry, e.g., Hom. ἐθελοντήρ, Hes. αὐλητήρ, so they occur also frequently in the dialects, e.g., Locr., Delph., Pamph. δικαστήρ, Argol. κριτήρ, τελεστήρ, ἐγδοτήρ, Lac. ἐγδοτήρ, Arc. ἐσδοτήρ, Locr., Delph., Aetol. βεβαιωτήρ, Corcyr. διορθωτήρ, Cyren. οἰκιστήρ, τιματήρ. Cf. also Cypr. ἰjατήρ like Hom. ἰητήρ = usual ἰατρός. But Cretan has -τᾱς from the earliest period, as δικαστάς, πάστας, τίτας, etc., the few examples of -τηρ (κοσμητήρ, νικατήρ) being late.

6. -ιος = -εος. In adjectives of material Lesbian and Thessalian have -ιος (phonetic change supported by parallel suffix; cf. **9**.2), as Lesb. χρύσιος, χάλκιος, ἀργύριος, Thess. λίθιος (cf. Hom. λίθεος, in most dialects λίθινος; conversely Boeot. λίνινος = λίνεος).

7. -ήν = -ων. Personal names in -ήν (short names, hypocoristic in origin) instead of usual -ων, e.g., 'Αρχήν, Τιμήν vs. usual "Αρχων, Τίμων, occur occasionally in Delphi, Megara, Epidaurus, Corinth, etc., but are conspicuously frequent in the Corinthian colonies of Apollonia and Epidamnus.

8. -ώνδας, -όνδας. Beside the usual (originally patronymic) personal names in -ίδης etc., forms in -ώνδας, or less commonly -όνδας, are most frequent in Boeotian, like the familiar 'Επαμεινώνδας, but occur also in Thessalian, Phocian, Megarian, and (-ώνδης) Euboean, rarely elsewhere.

9. The diminutive -ιχος, as in ὀρτάλιχος, ὅσσιχος and names

like Σίμμιχος, is to be recognized in Lac. παιδιχός beside usual παιδικός, δαριχίς, and μικκιχός implied by μικκιχιδδόμενος.

10. Individual cases of dialectal variation in suffix are of course frequent. So, for example, Thess. λίθιος = λίθινος (cf. above, 6), Ion. νόμαιος, Locr. νόμιος = νόμιμος, Thess. ὀνάλα (but also ὀνάλουμα) = ἀνάλωμα (cf. also Boeot. ἄλωμα), Boeot., Epir. ποθόδωμα (after ἀνάλωμα) = πρόσοδος, Delph., Mess. κεφάλωμα = κεφαλαῖον, Heracl. ἐπιζαμίωμα beside ἐπιζάμιον, Thess. συνκλείς (stem -κλη-τ-, cf. προβλής, etc.) = σύγκλητος ἐκκλησία, Cret. ἡμίνα (also Cypr. gloss) = τὸ ἥμισυ (also Sicil. ἡμίνα, used, like Epid. hēμίτεια, in the sense of ἡμίεκτον), Cret. θῖνος (from *θίινος formed from θιός after the analogy of ἀνθρώπ-ινος), ἔνθῖνος = θεῖος, ἔνθεος, Att. ἀδελφός but ἀδελφεός in other dialects, Delph. γάμελα (cf. γαμέτης) = γαμήλια. Arc. γνōσία, τιμασία, παναγορία = γνῶσις, etc.

11. Nouns in -ιος, -ιον appear frequently as -ις, -ιν in late inscriptions. See **45**.6.

165. 1. -τερος. Noteworthy examples of the use of this suffix to denote contrasted relations (not merely those of degree as in the comparatives), as in δεξιτερός, ἀριστερός, are Arc. ἀρρέντερος, El. ἐρσεναίτερος (for αι cf. γεραίτερος, παλαίτερος), θηλύτερος.

2. -ιδιος forming adjectives from adverbs or adverbial phrases, as ἀίδιος, ἐπιθαλασσίδιος. So El. προσθίδιος (προστιζίον), Locr. ὑπαπροσθίδιος, Cret. ἐνδοθίδιος (ἐνδοθιδίαν δōλαν 'household slave'), Epid. ἐνδοσθίδιος (ἐνδοσθίδια 'entrails'; so ἐντοσθίδια Arist., Hipp.), Cret. ἐξαρχίδιος = ἐξ ἀρχῆς γιγνόμενος.

3. -τρον. From words like λύτρον 'means of release,' hence 'ransom,' the suffix came to be used freely in words denoting reward or amount paid, as νίκαστρον 'reward of victory,' Epid. ἴατρα 'perquisites for healing,' Ion., Coan τέλεστρα 'expenses of inauguration' (of the priest. Cf. Coan τελέω 'inaugurate'), Cret. κόμιστρα 'gifts' (more specific?), and, even from a numeral, Cret. τρίτρα 'the threefold amount.'

4. -εων, -ων in nouns denoting place, as ἀνδρών (Ion. ἀνδρεών, Pamph. ἀ(ν)δριōν), ἀμπελών, νεκρών, ὀρνιθών. To this large class belong Heracl. τοφιών (**6**, **9**.9) = ταφεών 'burial place,' γαιών 'mound of earth' (cf. γχεών from Halaesa), βοών 'cow-shed,' Ion. στεφών 'ridge.'

This class is not to be confused with nouns of agency in Ion. -εών but Dor. etc., -άων, -άν, as Ion. ξυνεών, Dor. κοινάν. See **41**.4.

166. 1. Personal names in -κλέᾱς, instead of -κλέης, -κλῆς, as Ἱπποκλέας, are most common in Thessalian, but also occur in Boeotian, Locrian, Phocian, Aetolian, and Megarian (here in the form -κλίας). -κλέᾱς is a modification of -κλέης under the influence of hypocoristics in -έᾱς.

2. Διόζοτος (i.e., Διόσ-δοτος, cf. Διόσ-κουροι) and Θειόσδοτος Θεόσζοτος, Θεόζοτος, Θιόζοτος (formed after Διόσ-δοτος, cf. θεόσδοτος in Hesiod), instead of usual Διόδοτος, Θεόδοτος, are frequent in Boeotian, and Thessalian also has Θεόζοτος, Θιόζοτος, and Θεορδότειος (**60**.4). Elsewhere such forms are rare and doubtless imported.

167. The interchange of different vowel stems in the first member of a compound, or before a derivative suffix, is sometimes dialectal. Thus Τιμοκλῆς, Τιμοκράτης, etc., in most dialects, but Ion. Τιμηκλῆς, Τιμηκράτης, Cnid. Τιμᾱκλῆς, Rhod. Τιμᾱκράτης, Τιμάπολις, likewise Rhod. Τιμᾶναξ (*Τιμά-(Ϝ)αναξ) instead of usual Τιμῶναξ (*Τιμό-(Ϝ)αναξ). Thess. ὑλορός (hυλōρέοντος) from *ὑλο-Ϝορός and so related to Att. ὑλωρός (late poet. ὑληωρός) from ὑλᾱ-as ὑλοτόμος to ὑλᾱτόμος.

Arc., Locr., Thess. οἰκιάτας (or Ϝοικιάτας) from οἰκίᾱ, for usual οἰκέτης from οἶκος (Ϝοικεύς, fem. Ϝοικέα, are the forms used in Cretan). Ion. πολιήτης, Cret., Epid. πολιάτᾱς (also Pindar), Cret. πολιᾱτεύω, Arc. πολιᾱτις, for usual πολίτης, etc.; cf. Heracl. πολιᾱνόμος, Ion. πολιήοχος (Epic), Lac. πολιᾶχος (but Att. πολιοῦχος with -οῦχος from κληροῦχος etc.). Cret. ὀφέλōμα after ἀνάλωμα.

Late Att. ἱερᾱτεύω, Locr., Phoc. ἱερητεύω (also in some κοινή inscriptions), Lesb. ἱρητεύω, Cret., Cyren. ἱαριτεύω, Mess. ἱεριτεύω, Chalced. ἱερωτεύω, ἱερωτεία (cf. Att. ἱερωσύνη).

Carpath. δαμέτᾱς, like οἰκέτης, for usual δαμότᾱς, δημότης, as conversely οἰκότης in an Attic inscription. So Cret. βίετος (cf. Astyp. Βίεττος) = βίοτος, Arg. κωμέτᾱς, Rhod. κτοινέτᾱς, beside κτοινάτᾱς, after φυλέτᾱς. Dor. ἀνδρεφόνος (Hdn.), Locr. ἀνδρεφονικός for usual ἀνδρο-, Rhod. Ἱππέδαμος = Ἱππόδαμος, but Rhod. Ἀρχοκράτης = Ἀρχεκράτης, Cret. Μενοκράτης = Μενεκράτης.

After the analogy of names containing inherited ι-stems arose also forms like Ἀρχίλοχος, Ἀρχίδαμος, etc. (cf. ἀρχιτέκτων), in various dialects, Rhod. Μενίδαμος, El. Σαίκλαρος, Coan, Nisyr., Mel. Λαίστρατος, Nisyr. Λαισθένης.

Parallel forms *δᾱμιο-Fεργός and *δᾱμιο-Fοργός (attested by the verbal Arc. δαμιοFοργε̃, no. 16). From the former, Hom. δημιοεργός, and with contraction Att. δημιουργός (though of course this could equally well come from the second form), with elision δαμιεργός, occurring at Cyrene, Astypalaea, and Nisyros. The much more common δημιοργός (Ion.), δᾱμιοργός (Arc., El., Locr., Delph. and most Doric dialects), could come also from *δᾱμιοFεργός (cf. Locr. Ὀπόντιοι, Meg. Σελινόντιοι, from -ο-Fεντ, 44.4), but more easily with elision from *δᾱμιοFοργός.—Other compounds in this group, Boeot. γᾱFεργός (cf. 3 sg. fut. γαFεργείσι, no. 42.11), Lac. γαFεργόρ (Hesych.), frequently -εργός, rarely -οργός (ἀλοργός Sicil., Hesych., cf. Ion. ἀλοργής, ἀλοργίη), most commonly contracted -ουργός, also -ωργός; cf. Heracl. ἀμπελωργικός). Att. γεωργός from *γᾱ-(F)οργός (cf. Thess. γαοργεῖμεν) or γᾱο-F- (as in γεωγραφία, etc.)?

a. The well-known lengthening of the initial vowel of the second member of compounds, as in ἀνώνυμος, πανήγυρις, is seen in Ion. ἀνηρίθευτος = Att. ἀνερίθευτος, Att., Cret. εὐθυωρία, Heracl. εὐθυωρεία (vs. Arc. εὐθυορFία), Arc. δίωρος (like δι-ώβολος). To the analogy of forms like ἐπάκοος, ἐπήκοος, which are of the same kind, is due to the ἐπᾱ- of Cret., Boeot. ἐπᾱβολά 'share' (cf. Hesych. ἐπηβολή · μέρος) and Att.-Ion. ἐπήβολος. Cf. κατηβολή in Euripides.

168. Use of a patronymic adjective instead of the genitive singular of the father's name. Though occasionally found in literature, as in Hom. Τελαμώνιος Αἴας, this is the regular practice in prose only in the three Aeolic dialects. Thus Lesb. Μέλανχρος Πιθώνειος, Ἀρχίππα Ἀθανάεια, Thess. Σύχουν Ἀντιγόνειος, Νικόλαος Ἀγεισίαιος, Boeot. Θιόπομπος Ὀλυμπίχιος, Ἑρμάιος Νικιῆος. Examples in other dialects are rare.

a. When the father's name is itself a patronymic form in -δας or -ιος, the genitive is regularly employed in Boeotian; so also in early Thessalian, but later the adjective forms like Ἐπικρατίδαιος, Τιμουνίδαιος are usual.

b. Under κοινή influence the use of the adjective was given up in favor of the ordinary genitive construction. Thus in Boeotian the genitive is usual after about 250 B.C. and occasionally found earlier. There is some evidence that the Plataeans adopted the Attic usage at an early date. See no. 41, note.

c. There are also examples in Thessalian and Boeotian of adjectives in agreement with appellatives, in place of a genitive of possession. Thess. Πολυξεναία ἐμμί (sc. ἀ στάλλα), etc. See the following.

d. A genitive may be used in apposition to that implied by the adjective, as in Hom. Γοργείη κεφαλὴ δεινοῖο πελώρου. Boeot. Καλιαία ἐμὶ (sc. ἀ κύλιξ) τῶ Κέντρωνος, Γοργίνιός ἐμι ὁ κότυλος καλὸς κ[αλ]ῶ, Lesb. σ[τάλλ]α ᾽πὶ Σθενείαι ἔμμι τῶ Νικιαίοι (dat.) τῶ Γαυκίῶ (gen.) 'the son of Nicias, the son of Glaucus,' where Γαυκίῶ is also a patronymic adjective, but in apposition with the genitive implied in Νικιαίοι. Thess. ᾽Ανφιονεία στάλα τοὐφρόνετος (τοῦ Εὐφρόνητος).

SYNTAX

169. Although the syntax of the dialects deserves fuller investigation than it has received, yet syntactical differences between the dialects are much less striking than those of phonology and inflection. To a considerable extent they consist merely in the conservation in some dialects of early forms of expression which have become rare or obsolete in literary Greek, and in a less strict formalization of usage. Some peculiarities have already been mentioned in connection with the forms, e.g., in the use of certain pronouns (**121-31**), adverbs and conjunctions (**132-34**), and in the meaning and construction of prepositions (**136**). It is necessary to add here only a few comments on certain uses of the cases and the moods. Some other, more isolated, peculiarities are observed in the notes to the inscriptions.

CASES

The Genitive

170. Genitive of time. The genitive of the 'time within which' is especially frequent in the early Cretan inscriptions, although ἐν with the dative is already the more usual expression. Cf. Law Code, I.25 λαγάσαι τᾶν πέντ' ἀμερᾶν 'release within five days'; but I.6 ἐν ταῖς τρισὶ ἀμέραις, in another Gortyn inscription τὸ ἐνιαυτὸ 'within the year.' So also, but without the article, as in early Attic inscriptions, Cret. δέκα Ϝετίον (no. 116), Locr. τριὸν μενὸν beside ἐν τριάϙοντα ἀμάραις, Boeot. τριῶν ἀμεράων (no. 42.16).

Aside from the adverbial phrases νυκτός, etc., the use of the genitive of time is most persistent in dating, as μηνὸς ἑβδόμου, etc., the usual expression in most dialects. More noteworthy is the phrase καὶ πολέμου (-ω) καὶ εἰρήνης(-ας) which is common in the proxeny decrees of various dialects, though eventually replaced in many by ἐν πολέμωι κτλ.

136

The genitive of time is used distributively in various dialects, as also in Attic, e.g., τᾶς ἀμέρας or τᾶς ἀμέρας ϝεκάστας 'daily,' beside κατ' ἀμέραν. **171.** Genitive of the matter or person involved. Besides the familiar genitive of the charge or penalty, the genitive is also used more broadly to denote the matter or person involved, e.g., Cret. καταδικακσάτō τō ἐλευθέρō δέκα στατε̃ρανς, τō δόλō πέντε 'shall condemn him to a fine of ten staters in the case of a freeman, five staters in the case of a slave,' ἅι ϝεκάστō ἔγρατται 'as is prescribed for each case.' Such genitives may serve as headings, like Ἱκεσίων no. 115.110. In the long cult-inscription of Andania most of the headings are in the simple genitive, beside a few cases of περί with genitive.

The Dative

172. The adnominal dative is more common than in literary Greek, and is especially frequent in the introduction to inscriptions or their separate sections, e.g., El. ἁ ϝράτρα τοῖς ϝαλείοις, Locr. τὸ τέθμιον τοῖς Ηυποκναμιδίοις Λοϙροῖς, Phoc. ὁμολογία τᾶ πόλει Στειρίων καὶ τᾶ πόλει Μεδεωνίων, Boeot. διαγραφὰ Νικαρέτη, Att. ἀπαρχὲ τἀθε̄ναίαι, γραμματεὺς τῆι βουλῆι καὶ τῶι δάμωι.

For the dative instead of the genitive construction with various prepositions in Arcado-Cyprian, see **136.**1.

The Accusative

173. The accusative absolute of participles is common enough in literature (Hdt. +), but mostly in impersonal constructions. Examples of personal construction in the dialects are worth noting. Thus Arc. εἰ μὲ παρηεταξαμένος τὸς πεντέκοντα ἒ τὸς τριακοσίος 'unless the Fifty or the Three Hundred approve.' This is an extension from instances where the participle agrees with the accusative of a preceding clause, as Arc. μὲ νέμεν μέτε ξένον μέτε ϝαστόν, εἰ μὲ ἐπὶ θοίναν hίκοντα. Cf. also Arc. κατάπερ τὸς ἐπισυνισταμένος...γέγραπτοι 'as is prescribed in the case of those who conspire,' Coan αἱρεθέντας ἑκατέρων δέκα 'ten of each being chosen.' Such use is increasingly common in late Greek and led to the modern indeclinable participle in -οντα(ς).

The Moods

The Subjunctive

174. The subjunctive without ἄν or κα in conditional, relative, and temporal clauses, where the particle is regularly employed in Attic prose, though frequently omitted in Homer and sometimes elsewhere (Kühner-Gerth II, pp. 426, 449, 474), is attested for several dialects, though always as the less common construction. Locr. αἰ δείλετ᾽ ἀνχōρεῖν, αἴ τις ἀνχōρέει (no. 57.7, 26; ten examples with κα in the same inscription), Arc. εἰ δέ τις ἐπιθιγάνε̄, εἰκ ἐπὶ δō̂μα πῦρ ἐποίσε̄ (no. 18.21; other probable examples in no. 16) in contrast to usual εἰκ ἄν (see **134.**2a), Cypr. ὁ ἐξορύξε̄, οἱ . . . ἴōσι (no. 23.25, 31), Cret. θυγατρὶ ἒ διδō̂ι 'in case one gives it to the daughter' (Law-Code VI.1). Examples are not infrequent in later Locrian, Phocian, and Delphian inscriptions.

The Optative

175. In Elean the optative with κα is the usual form of prescriptions, e.g., συνμαχία κ᾽ ἔα ἑκατὸν Ϝέτεα 'let there be alliance for a hundred years,' ζέκα μναίς κα ἀποτίνοι Ϝέκαστος 'let each pay a fine of ten minae.' Similarly, but without the particle, Arc. ἐξόλοιτυ 'shall be put to death' (no. 16), Cypr. δόκοι νυ βασιλεύς 'the king shall give.'

The subjunctive without κα is used in the same sense in a late Elean inscription (66.32, 36).

176. 1. The optative in conditional clauses survives in several dialects, although, except in Elean, it is much less frequent than the subjunctive, and indeed is almost wholly eliminated in favor of the subjunctive in Attic-Ionic inscriptions, and in the majority of dialects. Where the optative survives, it is sometimes used with a still recognizable differentiation from the subjunctive, but oftener without such. In the Gortyn Law Code which offers the fullest material, there are in conditional clauses about 50 optatives to about 80 subjunctives. Some of these occur where the contingency is obviously one more remotely anticipated (e.g., VII.9 'but if there should not be any free persons,' as contemplated in the preceding subjunctive clauses; I.11 'but if one should deny'), others as mere variants of the subjunctive for parallel or even identical contingencies (e.g., opt. IX.18 = subj. VI.25). In Locrian nos. 57 and 58B have the subjunctive only, but nos. 58A and 59 the optative only. In Delphian, no. 52 has the subjunctive usually, but αἰ δ' ἐφιορκέοιμι A17, also αἰ δ' ἐφιορκέοι C6, in an oath, where Attic also would have the optative, and αἰ δέ τι τούτων παρβάλλοιτο C25, C50, D17; and in the numerous Phocian and Delphian manumission decrees the optative is of very frequent occurrence. The optative, beside the subjunctive, occurs also in Corcyraean, Achaean, and in the Northwest Greek κοινή (e.g., no. 67). In Argolic, the archaic nos. 83 and 85 have the optative only, and this occurs in some of the later inscriptions. In Arcadian, nos. 17 and 18 have the subjunctive only, but in no. 19 there are some examples of the optative. Even in the same clause the alternation of subjunctive and optative is not infrequent, e.g., Delph. εἰ δέ κα μὴ ποιῇ ἢ μὴ παραμένοι or εἰ δὲ μὴ ποιέοι ἢ μὴ παραμένη.

2. In relative and temporal clauses of future time, the predominance of the subjunctive is even more marked. Noteworthy is the Tean curse, no. 3, where ὅστις with the optative is used in the curse proper, ll. 1-34, while in the postscript warning against harming the stele on which the curse is inscribed, ll. 35-40, we find ὃς ἄν with the subjunctive. There are a few examples of the optative in Cretan (Law Code IV.14/15, and a few others), Locrian (Ϝότι συλάσαι no. 58.5, hόσστις δὲ δαιθμὸν ἐνφέροι no. 59.10 vs. hότι δέ κα φυτεύσεται l.6), Delphian, and elsewhere (see also **177**).

3. But in Elean the optative is regularly employed in conditional, relative, and temporal clauses. For examples in conditional and relative clauses, see nos 61-64. In the later no. 65 the subjunctive occurs once in a conditional clause with future perfect force, and in relative clauses.

4. In final clauses the optative occurs, e.g., Heracl. Tab. I.53 ff. ἐστάσαμες ... ἀνχωρίξαντες ..., hως μὴ καταλυμακωθὴς ἀδηλωθείη, Lesb. no. 26.13 ff. ἐπιμέλεσθαι ..., κατάγρεντον ..., ὥς κε ... ἐμμένοιεν. But it is very rare, and most dialects have only the subjunctive with or without ἄν (κα, κε), or sometimes the future indicative.

177. There are some examples of κα with the optative in conditional and other clauses as sometimes with κε or κα in Homer, Pindar, etc., e.g., Locr. αἴ κ᾽ ἀδίκō συλōι (no. 58.4), Cret. αἴ κα ... μὴ νυνατὸς εἴη, Epid. αἴ κα ὑγιῆ νιν ποιήσαι (no. 90.60), Delph. εἰ δέ [τίς] κα ἐφάπτοιτο, ἐπεί κά τι πάθοι, Corcyr. ἀφ᾽ οὖ κ᾽ ἀρχὰ γένοιτο, Ach. ἔστε κα ἀποδοῖεν, Arg. αἴ κα δικάσσαιεν.

The Imperative and the Infinitive

178. Both the imperative and the infinitive are freely used in prescriptions, often side by side in the same inscription. In general the infinitive is more frequent in early, the imperative in later, inscriptions. For the use of the optative with the same force, see **175**.

WORD ORDER

179. A peculiarity of word order which is worthy of mention is the position of τις before κα in the phrase αἴ τίς κα, αἰ δέ τίς κα. This is the regular order in the West Greek dialects, as contrasted not only with Att.-Ion. ἐάν τις, ἤν τις, but with Arc. εἰ δ᾽ ἄν τις, Cypr. ἔ κέ σις, Lesb. αἴ κέ τις, Thess. αἰ μά κέ κις, Boeot. ἤ δέ κα τις. Boeot. has also, though less frequently, the West Greek order ἤ τίς κα.

SUMMARIES OF THE CHARACTERISTICS OF THE SEVERAL GROUPS AND DIALECTS

180. The following summaries, while not exhaustive, are intended to call attention to the most important characteristics of each group and dialect. These are indicated in the briefest manner, sometimes by a mere example, sufficient to identify, but not always to define, the phenomenon in question, and these brief indications are always to be interpreted in the light of the sections to which reference is made in each case. Several features that are only occasional or late, though noted in the main texts, are ignored here.

To avoid needless repetition, many phenomena which are peculiar from the standpoint of Attic or Attic-Ionic, but are common to all or most of the other dialects, are usually omitted, e.g.:

1. Originial ᾱ unchanged. **8**
2. ᾱ from ᾱο, ᾱω. **41**.4
3. η from α + ε. **41**.1
4. σσ = Att., Cret., Boeot., Eub. ττ in φυλάττω, etc. **81**
5. σσ = Att. σ, Cret., Boeot. ττ in Att. ὅσος, μέσος, ἐδίκασα. **82**
6. σσ = original σσ, Att. σ. **83**
7. πόλις, πόλιος, etc. **109**.1
8. ἀμές, ὑμές, acc. ἀμέ, ὑμέ = ἡμεῖς, etc. **119**.2, 5
9. 3 pl. ἔθεν, ἔδον, etc. **138**.5
10. ἧς = ἦν. **163**.3
11. ἐών = ὤν **163**.8
12. αἰ = εἰ. **134**.1
13. ἅτερος = ἕτερος. **13**a
14. ἱστία = ἑστία. **11**
15. γίνομαι = γίγνομαι **86**.10
16. δέκομαι = δέχομαι. **66**
17. ὄνυμα = ὄνομα. **22**b
18. ἤνεικα, ἤνικα = ἤνεγκα. **144**a
19. πᾶμα = κτῆμα. **162**.12
20. ἵκω = ἥκω. Glossary

EAST GREEK

ATTIC-IONIC

181. Important characteristics of Attic-Ionic (1-7 specific Att.-Ion., 8-9 in common with Arc., 10 with Arc.-Cypr.):

141

1. η from ᾱ. **8**
2. Quantitative metathesis (λεώς, etc.). **41**.4, **43**
3. ν-movable. **102**
4. ἡμεῖς, acc. -έας, -ᾱς. **119**.2, 5
5. ποῦ, ὅπου, etc. **132**.1

6. ἔθεσαν, ἔδοσαν, etc. **138**.5
7. ἦν 3 sg. imperf. of εἰμί. **163**.3
8. Conjunction εἰ. **134**.1
9. Particle ἄν. **134**.2
10. Infin. -ναι. **154**.1
11. Very early loss of ϝ. **50**

Ionic

182. The chief characteristics of Ionic, as compared with Attic, are as follows. Some few of these are Ionic only (notably 1, also 8, 9, 14, 20, 22), but most are common to various other dialects, some indeed to all except Attic, being repeated here from **180** to bring out the contrast with Attic more fully. A few peculiarities which are not general Ionic, but are common to all branches except West Ionic, are included.

1. η from ᾱ even after ε, ι, ρ. **8**
2. εα, εο, εω, εοι usually uncontracted. **42**.1, 5, 6
3. ευ = εο, from fourth century on. **42**.5
4. Crasis of ο, ō (οι), ω, + α = ω, as τὠγῶνος. **94**.1
5. ω from οη. **44**.2
6. ξεῖνος, κούρη, etc. **54** with a
7. σσ = Att. ττ. **81**
8. ρσ = Att. ρρ. **80**
9. ἤν = Att. ἐάν, ἄν. **134**.1b
10. ᾱ-stems, gen. sg. m. -εω, -ω, gen. pl. -εων, -ῶν, dat. pl. -ηισι (ν). **41**.4, **104**.7
11. πόλις, πόλιος, etc. **109**.1, 2
12. βασιλεύς, -έος, etc. **111**.3
13. -κλῆς, -κλέος. **108**.1a
14. μι-verbs inflected like contracts, as τιθεῖ, τιθεῖν. **160**

15. 3 pl. τιθέαται, etc. **139**.2
16. ἐών = Att. ὤν. **163**.8
17. Suffix -ηιος = Att. -ειος. **164**.1
18. βόλομαι = βούλομαι. **75**b
19. ἱρός (ἰρός) beside ἱερός. **13**.1
20. μέζων = Att. μείζων. **113**.1
21. δέκνῡμι = Att. δείκνῡμι. **49**.1
22. κεῖνος = Att. ἐκεῖνος. **125**.1
23. ξυνός = Att. κοινός. **135**.7
24. καρτερός = Att. κρατερός, in meaning = κύριος. **49**. 2a, Glossary
25. δημιοργός = Att. -ουργός. **167**
26. ἱστία (ἰστία) = Att. ἑστία. **11**
27. ἤνεικα, ἤνικα = Att. ἤνεγκα. **144**a
28. ἰθύς = Att. εὐθύς. Glossary

183. East Ionic is further characterized by:
1. Psilosis. **57.** 2. αο, εο = αυ, ευ from fourth century B.C.
on. **33.** 3. Short-vowel subj. of σ aorist. **150.**

184. Chian. The dialect of Chios contains a few special characteristics, which are of Aeolic origin:
1. 3 pl. λάβωισιν, πρήξοισιν, etc., with ισ from νσ. **77.3.**
2. Inflected cardinals, δέκων, πεντηκόντων, etc. **116.**
Note also γεγωνέω 'call aloud,' as in Homer.

a. The Aeolic doubling of nasals (**73** ff.) is seen in the names of the mountain Πελινναῖον in Chios and the promontory Ἄργεννον opposite Chios, also in the personal name Φαννόθεμις in an inscription of Erythrae. Likewise Aeolic is the Phocaean Ζιονύ(σιος), **19.1.** All these features are relics of a time when the line between the Aeolic and the Ionic colonies was farther south than in the historical period.

185. Central Ionic differs from East Ionic in having the spiritus asper in early inscriptions. **57c.** Note also the restricted use of H as a vowel, i.e., only η from ᾱ, in the early inscriptions of some of the islands. **4.6.**

186. West Ionic, or Euboean, differs from the other divisions of Ionic as follows.

1. ττ as in Attic, not σσ. **81**
2. ρρ as in Attic, not ρσ. **80**
3. ξένος, etc. as in Attic, not ξεῖνος. **54**
4. -ει, -οι from -ηι, -ωι (in Eretria about 400 B.C.). **39a**
5. τοῦτα, τούτει, ἐντοῦθα=ταῦτα, ταύτηι, ἐνταῦθα. **124**
6. -κλέης, gen. -κλέω. **108.1a**
7. Proper names in -ις, gen. -ιδος, as often in Attic (East and Central Ion. -ιος). **109.5**
8. εἰν beside εἶναι. **160**

187. Eretrian. In addition to the other Euboean peculiarities, the dialect of Eretria, seen in inscriptions of Eretria and Oropus, is specifically characterized by the rhotacism of intervocalic σ, as ἔχουριν = ἔχουσιν, **60.3.** The use of ἄν (Oropus), ἐάν (Eretria) is due to Attic influence.

188. Attic influence. Ionic was the first of all dialects to yield to Attic influence, and after the fifth century B.C. there are few inscriptions that are wholly free from Attic forms. See **277.**

ARCADO-CYPRIAN [1]

189. Special characteristics of Arcado-Cyprian. [2]

1. ἰν = ἐν. **10**
2. Gen sg. -αυ. **22**
3. πός = πρός. **135**.6
4. κάς = καί (but Arc. usually καί). **134**.3

5. σις, ςις = τις. **68**.3
6. Mid. endings -τυ, -ντυ. **22**
7. ὄνυ = ὅδε. **123**
8. Dat. with ἀπό, ἐξ, etc. **136**.1
9. -χρέτης = -χράτης. **49**.2

190. Common to Arcado-Cyprian and various other dialects (1 Att.-Ion., 2 Ion., 3-6 Aeol., 7 N.W. Grk.).

1. Infin. in -ναι. **154**.1
2. βόλομαι = βούλομαι. **75**b
3. ἀπύ = ἀπό. **22**
4. ὀν (ὐν) = ἀνά. **6, 22**
5. ορ = αρ. **5**
6. μι -inflect. of contract vbs. **157**
7. ἐν (ἰν) = εἰς. **135**.4
8. η, ω = secondary ē, ō. **25**
9. ἐς = ἐξ before cons. (but Cypr. also ἐξ). **100**

10. Masc. σ-stems, acc. sg. -ην (Arc. also voc. sg. -η). **108**.2
11. ἱερής = ἱερεύς, etc. (but usual only in Arc.). **111** 4
12. Subj. -ης, -η. **149**
13. Article as relative. **126**
14. Opt. in prescriptions. **175**
15. πτόλις. **67**

191. Noteworthy is the considerable number of words or meanings which are otherwise known only, or with rare exceptions, as poetical, mainly Homeric. Some of the most striking examples are

1. In Arcadian and Cyprian, αἶσα 'share' (also Arg.), οἶ(F)ος 'alone,' εὐχωλά 'prayer' or 'imprecation.'

2. In Arcadian. δέαμαι, ἀπύω 'summon,' κέλευθος 'road,' δῶμα 'temple,' ἄμαρ (but see no. 17.22, note), λεύσσω 'behold.'

3. In Cyprian. Fάναξ, ἀνώγω, αὐτάρ, ἔλος 'meadow,' ἰjατήρ, κασίγνητος (also Lesb.; Thess. κατίγν[ειτος]), χραύομαι 'border on' (Hom. χραύω 'graze'), ἰδέ, νυ (also Boeot. **134**.5).

---

[1] Several of the characteristics cited below under the head of Arcadian or of Cyprian, for which corresponding forms are lacking or ambiguous in the other dialect, probably are also Arcado-Cyprian. See also **199**.
[2] In this and similar captions "special" is not to be taken too rigorously. Some few peculiarities of which occasional examples are found elsewhere are included, e.g., in this section, ἰν = ἐν, which is regularly found only in Arcado-Cyprian, but of which there are a few examples elsewhere.

Arcadian

192. Arcado-Cyprian characteristics. See **189/91.**

193. In common with various other dialects (1, 2 Att.-Ion., 3 Lesb., 5 Aeol., etc., 6, 16 West Greek).

1. Conjunction εἰ. **134.**1
2. Particle ἄν. **134.**2
3. δέκοτος = δέκατος. **6**
4. ἦνθον = ἦλθον. **72**
5. πεδά (πέ) = μετά. **135.**5
6. παρετάξωνσι, etc. **142**
7. ρρ = ρσ. **80**
8. πάνσα, etc. **77.**3
9. Acc. pl. -ος, nom. sg. pple. ἱεροθυτές. **78**
10. ἤμισσον. **81**
11. Dat. sg. -οι. **106.**2
12. Subj. δέᾱτοι, etc. **151.**1
13. Infin. -εν and -ην. **153.**2

14. 3 pl. imv. -ντω. **140.**3*a*; mid. -σθων **140.**2*b*
15. Adverbs in -θι place 'where,' as ὁπόθι, etc. **132.**9*a*
16. ὀδελός = ὀβολός. **49.**3
17. μέστ' 'until.' **132.**10
18. Peculiarities in the use of the spiritus asper. **58***d*
19. Ϝ in early inscr. initially and after cons., but lost between vowels; initially till about 300 B.C. **52, 53, 54**

194. Special Arcadian.

1. Gen. sg. fem. -ᾱυ (Tegea). **104.**2
2. 3 pl. -νσι. **77.**3
3. 3 sg. mid. -τοι = -ται. **139.**1
4. δέχο, ἑκοτόν = δέχα, ἑκατόν. **6**
5. Numerals in -κάσιοι = -κόσιοι. **117.**2
6. ι from ε before front vowels, and ῑ from ει. **9.**5

7. ὀνί = ὅδε. **123**
8. κατύ = κατά. **22, 95**
9. πλός = πλέον. **113.**2
10. εἰκ ἄν. **134.**2*a*
11. ἀπυδόας = ἀποδούς. **144**
12. τείω = τίνω. **162.**14
13. δέλλω = βάλλω. **68.**1
14. Ποσοιδᾶν = Ποσειδῶν. **49.**1, **61.**5
15. Dual forms in -αιυν, -οιυν. **106.**6

195. External influence in the dialect. The fact that κάς and σις, ὄζις, agreeing with Cyprian, are found only in the early inscriptions (nos. 16, 17), while all others have καί and τις, is probably due to external influence, though not specifically Attic. See **275.** The Tegean building inscription (no. 19) of the fourth century B.C. shows some few Attic κοινή forms, as πλέον instead

of πλός, once gen. sg. -ου, etc. From the latter part of the third
century on, when the chief Arcadian cities belonged to the Achaean League, or in some cases were controlled by the Aetolian
League, most of the inscriptions are in the Doric or the Northwest Greek κοινή, e.g., one from Stymphalus (IG V.ii.359) with
forms like χα, ὅκα, τετρώκοντα, πότ, τοῦ, τούς, δόντω and ἐν = εἰς.
But a decree of Megalopolis (Ditt. Syll. 559), of about 200 B.C.
in the time of a temporary revival of the Arcadian League, is
mainly in the native dialect (ἰν, acc. pl. -ος, ποίενσι, τοσνύν).
Curious is the occasional late occurrence of the Lac. σ = θ
(68), as Σιοῦ = Θεοῦ, Σίπομπος = Θεόπομπος, etc.

Cyprian

196. Arcado-Cyprian characteristics. See **189-91.**

197. In common with various other dialects.

1. ι from ε before vowels. **9.6**
2. Glide sound after ι expressed, as ἰjατῆραν. **56**
3. αἶλος = ἄλλος. **74**b
4. Psilosis. **57**
5. πείσει = τείσει. **68.**2a
6. F in all positions. **52-55**
7. Occasional omission of
   intervoc. and final σ.
   59.4

8. Dat. sg. -ō, -ᾱ beside -ōι, -ᾱι.
   38
9. Acc. sg. ἰjατῆραν, etc. **107.**1
10. βασιλεύς, -ēϜος. **111.**1
11. 3 pl. κατέθιjαν. **138.**5
12. χε = ἄν. **134.**2
13. ἔρπω 'go, come.' **162.**6
14. ἡμίνα. **164.**10
15. See also in Glossary, ἀκεύω,
    λιμήν, παῖς.

198. Special Cyprian.

1. Gen. sg. -ōν. **106.**1
2. πτόλιϜι, etc. **109.**4
3. Ϝρῆτα, Ϝρētάω. **55, 70.**3
4. ζᾶ = γᾶ, etc. **62.**4
5. ὐ = ἐπί. **135.**8
6. παι 'indeed.' **132.**5

7. ἔ = εἰ. **134.**1
8. δυϜάνω, δώκω = δίδωμι.
   162.5
9. See, in Glossary, ἄλϜον, ἰκ-
   μάμενος, ἰναλίνω, οἴρων, ὕγ-
   γεμος.

199. It is uncertain whether the infinitive should be transcribed with -εν or -ēν, the accusative with -ος, -ōς or -ο(ν)ς. In the
absence of any evidence to the contrary, we assume -εν and -ος
in agreement with Arcadian. But the dative singular is to be

transcribed -ōι, in spite of Arc. -οι, on account of the frequent omission of the final ι (**38**); and the third plural ending is transcribed with -σι, not -(ν)σι, in spite of Arc. -νσι, on account of φρονέōι (**59**.4).

Pamphylian

200. 1 (in part)-8 in common with Arcado-Cyprian, or Aeolic, 9-15 with West Greek or Cretan..

1. ἰν (written ἰ) = ἐν. ἰς from *ἰνς = εἰς. **10, 135**.4
2. υ from ο. **22**a
3. Dative with ἐξ. **136**.1
4. Particle νι. **134**.5
5. Spelling διά, etc. **56**
6. Omission of ν before consonants. **69**.2
7. Dat. pl. of cons. stems -εσσι. **107**.3
8. 3 pl. imv. -ντον (-δυ). **140**.5
9. ἱαρός. **13**.1
10. Retention of τι. **61**.1, 2. **138**.4
11. φίκατι = εἴκοσι. **51**b, **61**.2, **116**
12. ὄκα. **132**.9
13. τ for θ in ἄτρōπος, Πύτιος. **63**

14. 'Απέλλων Πύτιος. **49**.3, **63**
15. 'Αφορδίσιυς. **70**.1
16. ι from ε before vowels. **9**.6
17. Secondary ō, by lengthening ω, by contraction ου. **25**d
18. μhειάλαν, etc. **62**.3, **76**b
19. ὕπαρ = ὕπερ. **12**
20. Ϝ preserved, expressed by two different letters. **51**b
21. περτί = πρός. **61**.4, **70**.1, **135**.6
22. ἐβōλάσετυ, βολέμενυς. **22**a, **25**d, **142**c, **161**b
23. Change of ντ to νδ, with ν not written. **66, 69**.2
24. Final ν usually omitted. **89**.9

201. Aeolic characteristics, common to Lesbian, Thessalian, [3] and Boeotian (6 also Delph., etc., 7 also Arc.-Cypr., 8 also Arc.).

1. Labial instead of dental in πέμπε = πέντε, etc. **68**.2
2. Perf. act. pple. -ων, -οντος. **147**.3
3. Patron. adj. instead of gen. sg. of father's name. **168**
4. ἴα = μία. **114**.1
5. ρε = ρι. **18**
6. Dat. pl. πόδεσσι, etc. **107**.3
7. ρο = ρα, etc. **5**
8. Θερσ- = Θαρσ-. **49**.2

---
[3] In some cases only East Thessalian (Pelasgiotis). See **214**.

202. Aeolic characteristics, common to Lesbian and Thessalian (4-7 also Arc.-Cypr.).

1. Double liquids and nasals in ἐμμί, στάλλα, etc. **74-76, 77.**1, **79**

2. ἀγρέω (ἀνγρέω) = αἱρέω. **162.**2

3. ι̯ from ι before vowels. **19**

4. μι-inflection of contract verbs. **157**

5. ὀν = ἀνά. **6**

6. ἀπύ =· ἀπό. **22**

7. κε = ἄν. **134.**2

203. Characteristics common to Lesbian and Boeotian (2 also Arc., Cret., etc.).

1. ἐκάλε-σσα, etc. **143**

2. πεδά = μετά. **135.**5

204. Characteristics common to Thessalian and Boeotian only (of which, however, only 1, which is Homeric, belongs to the Aeolic elements of these dialects).

1. Infin. φερέμεν, etc. **155.**1

2. 3 pl. -νθι, etc. **139.**2

3. ει = η. **16**

4. γίνυμαι = γίγνομαι. **162.**4

5. Θεόζοτος. **166.**2

6. ἔλεξε = εἶπε in the official language of decrees (but also Argive).

7. ὑστερομει(ν)νία. Glossary.

Lesbian

205. Characteristics in common with one or both of the other Aeolic dialects. See **201-3**.

206. In common with various other dialects.

1. η, ω = secondary ε̄, ō. **25**

2. Final -ᾱ, -η, -ω = ᾱι, ηι, ωι, from end of fourth century on. **38**

3. Psilosis. **57**

4. Early loss of ϝ. **50**

5. δέκοτος = δέκατος. **6**

6. Dat. pl. -αισι, -οισι. **104.**7, **106.**4

7. βασίλευς, -ηος, etc. **111.**1

8. Masc. σ-stems, acc. sg. -ην, gen. sg. -η, etc. **108.**2

9. Article as relative. **126**

10. ὑπά = ὑπό. **135.**3

11. Infin. -ην. **153.**1

12. Perf. infin. -ην. **147.**2

13. Pass. infin. -ην. **155.**2

14. παῖς 'son.' Glossary

207. Special Lesbian (1 in part Elean and in part Cyrenaean).

1. ισ from νς, as παῖσα, etc.
(also Cyren.), acc. pl. ταίς,
τοίς (also El.), 3 pl. φέροισι.
77.3, 78

2. αἴμισυς = ἥμισυς, etc. **17**

3. αὔως, ναῦος, etc. **35**

4. ὅτα = ὅτε. **132.11**

5. ὅττι, ὅππως, etc. **129.2**

6. Infin. ἔμμεναι, etc. **154.2**

7. Infin. δίδων, κέρναν, etc. **155.3**

8. 3 pl. imv. -ντον, -σθον. **140.5**

9. Recessive accent. **103**

10. εἴκοιστος, etc. = Att. -κοστος. **116**

11. σπέλλω = στέλλω. **68.2a**

12. ἔταλον 'yearling.' **49.3**

13. ἀρνηάς 'ewe,' ἔπερος 'sheep', δικάσκοποι, official title. Glossary

14. πρότανις (rarely Attic) = πρύτανις. Glossary

208. External influence in the dialect. From the Macedonian period on—and very few of the inscriptions are earlier—there is usually some admixture of κοινή forms, as ἀνά beside ὀν, μετά beside πεδά, ὅτε beside ὅτα, etc. But in the main the dialect is employed in inscriptions till about the middle of the second century B.C. Its use in inscriptions of Roman imperial times (cf. no. 27) represents an artificial revival. See **280**.

Thessalian

209. Aeolic characteristics in common with one or both of the Aeolic dialects. See **201**, **202**.

210. West Greek and Northwest Greek characteristics (cf. **223**.1, 2, 3, 4, 6, and **226**.1, 4).

1. Retention of τ in 3 pl. -ντι -νθι **61**, **138.4**

2. ἴκατι = εἴκοσι. **116**

3. -κάτιοι (ἐξεικάττιοι). **117**

4. ψαφίξασθειν, etc. **142**

5. ἱαρός beside ἱερός. **13.1**

6. ἐν = εἰς. **135.4**

7. στ = σθ (rare). **85.1**

211. In common with various other dialects.

1. ι from ε before vowels (but oftener ε). **9.3**

2. ει, ου (but from η, ω) = secondary ē, ō. **25**

3. Final -ā, -ου (from ω), -ει (from η) = -āι, -ωι, -ηι. **38**

4. ἐς = ἐξ before cons. **100**

5. πάνσα, etc. **77.3**

6. Acc. pl. -ος. **78**

7. ττ = πτ. **86.2**

8. πτόλις beside πόλις. **67**

9. δδ = ζ. **84**

10. Doubling of ξ. **89**.1
11. Psilosis in article. **58***a*
12. Ϝ init. till about 400 B.C.
13. Gen. sg. -ᾱο, usually ᾱ. **41**.4
14. Gen. pl. -ᾰουν, usually -ᾶν. **41**.4
15. βασιλεύς, -εῖος, etc. **111**.1

16. Plural inflection of δύω, as δύας. **114**.2
17. Article as relative. **126**
18. παρά 'at, with,' with acc. **136**.2
19. Names in -κλέᾱς. **166**.1
20. Ϝοικιάτας = οἰκέτης. **167**

212. In common with Boeotian only. See **204**.

213. Special Thessalian.

1. ου = ω. **23**
2. Gen. sg. -οι (but see **214**). **106**.1
3. κίς = τίς (but see **214**). **68**.4
4. More extensive apocope than in any other dialect, namely in κάτ, πότ, πάρ, πέρ, ὀν, ἀπ, ἐπ, ὑπ. **95**
5. Consonant-doubling in πόλλιος, ἰδδίαν, κῦρρον = κύριον, etc. **19**.3
6. διέ = διά. **7**
7. βέλλομαι = βούλομαι. **75**
8. ὀστροφά = ἀναστροφή. **77**.2
9. ὄνε (τόνε, τοίνεος, etc.) = ὅδε. **123**
10. Relative use of κίς, ποῖος. **131**
11. ὄπει, ὀπειδεί = ἐπεί, ἐπειδή. **132**.7
12. μές, μέσποδι 'until.' **132**.12
13. μά = δέ. **134**.4
14. τᾶμον 'of the present time.' Glossary
15. 3 pl. ἐνεφανίσσοεν, ἐδούκαεμ, etc. **138**.5

16. 3 sg. mid. ἐψάφιστει, etc. (Larissa). **27**
17. 3 pl. mid. ἐφάνγρενθειν, etc. (Larissa). **27, 139**.2
18. Infin. δεδόσθειν, etc. (Larissa). **27, 156**
19. ἔνσα = οὖσα. **163**.8
20. πεστάντες = περιστάντες. **89**.7
21. Λασαῖος = Λαρισαῖος. **89***b*
22. Ἄπλουν = Ἀπόλλων. **49**.3
23. Πετθαλός = Θεσσαλός. **65, 68**.2
24. λίθιος = λίθινος. **164**.6, 9
25. δαύχνα = δάφνη. **68**.4*a*
26. ὀνάλα = ἀνάλωμα. **164**.9
27. λιμήν = ἀγορά 'market-place' (ἀγορά being = ἐν κλησία)
28. κίων often used in place of στάλλα (στήλη)
29. ταγός as title of a state or municipal official
30. σπόλος 'stake.' **68**.2*a*
31. συνκλείς. **164**.9
32. λειτορεύω. Glossary

214. Differences within Thessalian. The form of Thessalian which is best known is that of Pelasgiotis, represented mainly by inscriptions of Larisa, which show some special local peculiarities (**213**.8-10), Crannon, and Phalanna. [4] The dialect of Thessaliotis, represented mainly by inscriptions of Pharsalus and Cierium, differs from that of Pelasgiotis in two important respects, (1) gen. sg. of o-stems in -ō, -ου, not -οι, (2) pres. infin. of thematic verbs in -ἔν, -ειν, not -εμεν. The early inscription, no. 35, from Thetonium in the neighborhood of Cierium, shows, in addition to these two points of difference, τις not κις, dat. pl. of consonant stems in -σιν (χρέμασιν) not -εσσι (as at Pharsalus as well as in Pelasgiotis), hυλōρέοντος not -έντος, uncontracted gen. sg. in -αο, gen. sg. of father's name instead of patronymic adjective (? see no. 35.11, note). Late inscriptions of Cierium have dat. sg. -οι, -αι, though at Pharsalus we find -ου, -α, just as in Pelasgiotis, and in no. 35 ἐν ταγᾶ beside ἐν ἀταγίαι points to -ᾶι, -ōι. On δδ = ζ in ἐξξανακάδεν, no. 35, see **84**; on ττ beside σσ, see **81**c.

From Histiaeotis and Perrhaebia the material is very scanty. From Magnesia there are a few fragmentary archaic inscriptions, but most are late and in the Attic κοινή. An early inscription of Phthiotis (Μεθίστας Πιθούνειος Ἄπλουνι IG IX.ii.199) shows conclusively, what was only natural to expect, that its dialect was also Thessalian. But nearly all the inscriptions date from the period of Aetolian domination and are in the Northwest Greek κοινή (**279**.)

Many of the characteristics cited in the preceding sections are as yet attested only in the inscriptions of Pelasgiotis, but, except where there is evidence to the contrary as stated, it is to be assumed provisionally that they are general Thessalian. For the points of agreement are more pronounced than the differences.

215. External influence in the dialect. Occasional κοινή forms appear in the inscriptions of the third and second centuries B.C., especially ἀνά, ἀπό, περί, κατά, δέ, gen. sg. instead of patronymic adjective, η (not ει), γίνομαι (not γίνυμαι), etc. But the dialect as a whole is employed in inscriptions until about the end of the second century B.C. and occasionally later.

---

[4] Really in Perrhaebia, so far as this was recognized as a distinct division of Thessaly, but in the part near Pelasgiotis.

Boeotian

216. Aeolic characteristics in common with one or both of the other Aeolic dialects. See **201, 203.**

217. West Greek and Northwest Greek characteristics (cf. **223.**1-10, and **226.**1, 2, 4).

1. δίδωτι, etc., **61**
2. Fίκατι = εἴκοσι. **116**
3. πεντακάτιοι, etc. **116**a, **117**
4. ἐπεσκεύαξε, etc. (but oftener ττ). **142**
5. τοί, ταί = οἱ, αἱ. **122**
6. ἰαρός = ἱερός. **13.**1
7. Ἄρταμις = Ἄρτεμις. **13.**2

8. κα = κε, ἄν. **134.**2
9. πόκα. **132.**11
10. πρᾶτος = πρῶτος. **114.**1
11. αὐτῖ, i.e. αὐτεῖ = αὐτοῦ. **132.**2
12. ἐν = εἰς. **135.**4
13. δείμενος = δεόμενος. **158**
14. παρά 'at, with,' with acc. **136.**2

218. In common with various other dialects.

1. ει (from η), ω = secondary ē, ō. **25**
2. ι from ε before vowels. **9.**4
3. ττ in θάλαττα, εἴμιττον, etc. **81**
4. ττ in μέττος, ἐψαφίττατο, etc. **82**
5. δδ, initial δ = ζ. **84**
6. ἐς = ἐξ before cons. (see also **220.**1). **100**
7. πρισγεύς = πρεσβεύς. **68.**1, **86.**3
8. F initial and intervocalic frequently (but not consistently) until nearly 200 B.C. **50, 53**
9. Nom. sg. m. -ᾱ beside -ᾱς. **105.**1a
10. Gen. sg. m. and gen. pl. in -ᾱο, -ᾱων (but τᾶν). **41.**4

11. Dat. sg. -αι(-η), -οι (-υ), **104.**3, **106.**2
12. -ευς, -εῖος, -έFι. **111.**1
13. αὐτοσαυτός, αὐσαυτός, etc. **121.**4
14. ταν-ί, etc. **122**
15. ὑπά = ὑπό. **135.**3
16. ἀντί 'during.' **136.**8
17. Article as relative (rare). **126**
18. 3 pl. ἀνέθεαν, ἀνέθιαν, etc. **138.**5
19. 3 pl. imv. -ντω (-νθω). **140.** 3a
20. Perf. ἀποδεδόανθι, etc., without κ. **146.**1
21. ἔντω (ἔνθω) = ὄντων. **163.**6
22. Διοκλέας, etc. **166.**1
23. Consonant-doubling in hypocoristics. **89.**5
24. Names in -ώνδας. **164.**8
25. γραμματιστάς. **161.**4

26. ποθόδωμα. **164**.10

27. λάζομαι (λάδδουσθη) = λαμβάνω. Glossary

28. παῖς 'son.' Glossary

29. εἰλύτα 'a kind of cake' =
Ther. ἐλλύτα. **73***a*

219. In common with Thessalian only. See **204**.

220. Special Boeotian. Most of the peculiarities of the vowel system (**221**) also belong here.

1. ἐσς = ἐξ before vowels. **100**
2. ἔππασις = ἔμπασις. **69**.4
3. οὗτος, οὗτα, etc. **124**
4. εἴνιξαν = ἤνεγκαν. **144***a*
5. βείλομαι = βούλομαι. **75**
6. Hypocoristics in ει. **108**.2
7. ἄλωμα = ἀνάλωμα. **164**.10
8. γαεργός, 3 sg. fut. γαϜερ-
γείσι = γεωργός, etc. **167**
9. ἐπίθωσε = ἔπεισε. **161**.3

10. -λιηνω 'cancel.' **162**.10
11. Ϝίστωρ 'witness.' **52***d*
12. ἀφεδριατεύω. No. 41, note
13. προτηνί 'formerly.' **123**, **136**.1
14. πιτεύω 'irrigate.' Glossary
15. περίσαος 'left over, remaining.' Glossary
16. Several new words for utensils in no. 39

221. The Boeotian vowel-system. The most striking and obvious characteristic of Boeotian lies in its vowel-system. One peculiarity consists merely in the retention of the original sound, namely, that of υ as *u*. But even this led to a change in spelling to ου, while on the other hand the υ with its Attic value of *ü* as a basis was used to indicate approximately the sound, probably *ö*, which the diphthong οι had come to have. See **24**, **30**. The other peculiarities consist in changes of diphthongs to monophthongs and of more open to closer vowels, such as eventually prevailed everywhere and led to the Modern Greek pronunciation.

The chief orthographical peculiarities, with the approximate date of their introduction, are as follows:

ι = ε before vowels. **9**.4. Fifth century B.C. (in the epichoric alphabet ι, ε, ει, Ͱ)

ι = ει. **29**. Fifth century B.C. (in the epichoric alphabet ι, ει, Ͱ)

η = αι. **26**. Early fourth century B.C.

ει = η. **16**.

ου = υ. **24**. Early fourth century B.C., common after 300 B.C. (but great inconsistency is the spelling. υ = υ and οι = οι also frequent till near end of the third century), ιου = υ. **24.** About 300 B.C.

υ = οι. **30.** About 250 B.C.

ει = οι. **30.** Second century B.C. (rare)

222. External influence. Although Boeotia was for a short time in the Aetolian League, there are no Boeotian inscriptions in the Northwest Greek κοινή. But there are some scattered examples of the dative plural of consonant stems in -οις, as ἤγυς (αἴγοις), etc., and the appearance of στ = σθ (**85**.1) and δαμιωέμεν, δαμιώοντες (**159**) in some late inscriptions of Orchomenos is also probably due to Aetolian influence. The influence of the Attic κοινή becomes considerable toward the end of the third century B.C, and some inscriptions or portions of inscriptions are wholly in κοινή, e.g. the formal contract in the Nicareta inscription (no. 43.VI). But most of the inscriptions are substantially dialectal until the second half of the second century B.C.

WEST GREEK

223. General West Greek characteristics:

1. δίδωτι, etc. with retention of τ. **61.**
2. (Ϝ)ίκατι = εἴκοσι. **116** with a
3. -κάτιοι = -κόσιοι. **116a, 117.**2
4. ἐδίκαξα, etc. But restricted in Argolic. **142**
5. τοί, ταί = οἱ, αἱ. But Cret. οἱ, αἱ. **122**
6. ἱαρός (ἰαρός) = ἱερός. **13.**1
7. Ἄρταμις = Ἄρτεμις. But Cret. Ἄρτεμις. **13.**2
8. κα, τόκα, πόκα, ὄκα, γα. **132.**11, **134.**2
9. πρᾶτος = πρῶτος. **114.**1
10. ὄπει, etc. **132.**2
11. ὄπη, etc. **132.**7
12. ὄπω, etc. **132.**8
13. φέρομες, etc. **138.**3
14. Fut. -σέω. **141**
15. τέτορες = τέτταρες. **114.**4
16. τετρώκοντα = τετταράκοντα. **116**
17. ἔβδεμος = ἔβδομος. **114.**7
18. ἐμίν = ἐμοί, etc. **118.**4b
19. ἐμέος = ἐμοῦ, etc. **118.**3b
20. ὀδελός = ὀβολός. **49.**3
21. δήλομαι, δείλομαι. **68.**1, **75**
22. λείω, λέω = θέλω. **162.**11
23. Word-order αἴ τίς κα. **179**

a. Although only a part of these characteristics are actually quotable from every one of the West Greek dialects, some indeed from only a few, it is probable that, except for the divergence of Cretan in 5 and 7, they were common to all, and that the absence of examples in any dialect is accidental. Thus, forms like φέρομες are attested for Phocian and most of the Doric dialects, but there is no occurrence of a first plural form in Locrian and Elean, and in Rhodian only from the time when -μεν had been introduced from the κοινή, just as it was at Delphi before the end of the fourth century B.C. The early substitution of the κοινή forms of the numerals and the rare occurrence of the personal pronouns in inscriptions, account for the incomplete representation of 2, 3, 15-19.

b. The first ten of these characteristics are also Boeotian (**217**), several also Thessalian (**220**), and a few also Arcadian.

224. There are various other phenomena which are common to the West Greek dialects, but are not confined to them even in the widest application of the term. Several of those mentioned in **180** are often casually referred to as "Doric," e.g., αἰ = εἰ, ἦς = ἦν, ἁμές, ἔθεν, πᾶμα, ἵκω, but none of them has any claim to be regarded as specifically West Greek, with the possible exception of η from αε (**41**.1 with *a*).

a. Even of the peculiarities cited in **223** some consist merely in the retention of the original forms which must have been universal at one time; and that τοί, ταί or pron. datives like ἐμίν still existed in East Greek in the historical period is shown by their appearance in Homer. Some others also may prove to be of wider scope, e.g., ὅπει, since ὅπου is, so far as we know, only Attic-Ionic. But so far as the present evidence of inscriptions goes, the peculiarities given in **223** are distinctly characteristic of West Greek.

225. The declension of nouns in -εύς with gen. sg. -έος, acc. sg. -ῆ is common to Delphian and the majority, but not all, of the Doric dialects. See **111**.5. The 3 pl. imv. -ντω is common to all the Doric dialects except Cretan, Theran, Cyrenaean, but the distribution of -ντω and -ντων does not coincide at all with the East and West Greek divisions. See **140**.3, 4. There are various peculiarities which are West Greek in a limited sense, but demonstrably not general West Greek, e.g., τῆνος = ἐκεῖνος (**125**.1), αὐτοσαυτός (**121**.4), πρόσθα = πρόσθε (**133**.1), Ἀπέλλων (**49**.3), ντ, νθ = λτ, λθ (**72**).

NORTHWEST GREEK

226. The chief characteristics of Northwest Greek as distinguished from Doric, including however some which are not common to all the dialects of this group and some which are not strictly confined to them, are:

1. ἐν = εἰς. Also Thess., Boet., and Arc.-Cypr. (ἰν), **135**.4
2. καλείμενος, etc. (El. -ημε-νος). Also Boeot., etc. **158**
3. φάρω, etc. But rare in Delph. **12**
4. στ = σθ **85**.1
5. ἔντε, Delph. hέντε = ἔστε. No example in El. **135**.4

6. πάντοις, etc., dat. pl. But in Delph. only late and due to Aetolian influence, and in Locr. also other forms. **107**.3
7. τέτορες, etc., acc. pl. El., Ach., but not Locr., and rare in Delph. **107**.4

a. There are various other peculiarities the scope of which coincides even less definitely with the Northwest Greek dialects proper, but the spread of which in the northern part of Greece is noticeable, e.g., masc. ā-stems with nom. sg. -ᾱ, gen. sg. -ᾱς (**105**.1*a*, 2*e*), personal names in -ώνδας or -όνδας (**164**.8), and in -κλέας (**166**.1).

Phocian (Mostly Delphian)

227. West Greek characteristics. See **223-25**.

228. Northwest Greek characteristics. See **226**.

229. Aeolic elements: πάντεσσι, etc. in all the earlier inscriptions. **107**.3. Here also, perhaps, the words ταγός (also Thess., Cypr., and poetical), κεραίω (also Hom.) = κεράννυμι, δίδημι (also Boeot. and Hom.) = δέω 'bind'.

230. Characteristics mostly in common with various other dialects.

1. ει, ου = secondary ε̄, ο̄. **25**
2. F initial till about 400 B.C. Intervocalic only in a sixth century inscription.
3. Peculiarities in the use of the spiritus asper. **58***a*, *b*, *c*
4. ἐντοφήια. **6**
5. η from εα, in part. **42**.1
6. ἀποστράψαι. **49**.2
7. hε̄μιρρήνιον. **55***a*

8. φατρία (Stiris) = φρατρία. **70**.3
9. ἀμφιλλέγω. **76**
10. ρρ=ρσ in Θαρρίκων, etc. **80**
11. ἥμισσον. **81**
12. Crasis in κἤν, κηὔκλεια, κωὔ-τε, etc. **94**.6,7
13. Apocope in κάτ, πότ, πάρ, πέρ, and in compounds ἀν (ἀμμόνιον). **95** Elision in πέροδος. **91** *a*.

14. τῶλ Λαβυαδᾶν, τοὺν νόμους, etc. **96, 97**
15. αὐτός as reflexive. **121**.3
16. αὐτοσαυτός, αὐσαυτός.
121.4
17. τοῦτοι = οὗτοι, τοῦτα = ταῦτα. **124**
18. τῆνος (in τηνεῖ) = ἐκεῖνος.
125 I
19. ἄδε. **132.6**
20. Ϝοίκω = οἰκόθεν. **132.8**
21. ἐχθός, ἔχθω. **133.3**
22. ἐνδός, ἔνδω. **133.4**
23. ποί (beside πότ) = πρός.
135.6
24. 3 pl. perf. -ατι. **138.4**
25. 3 pl. imv. -ντων. **140.4**a
26. Infin. -εν. **153.2**
27. στεφανώω, etc. = -όω. **159**
28. συλέω = συλάω. **161.2**
29. ποιῶντι, ποιόντων, θεαρόντον. **42.5**d

30. ποεῖνται. **158**
31. ἦται (late). **163.**9
32. παρά 'at, with,' with acc.
136.2
33. ἀντί 'during.' **136.8**
34. ὑπέρ 'in behalf of' with acc.
136.10
35. χρήζω 'wish.' **162.14**
36. γραμματιστάς. **161.4**
37. κεφάλωμα = κεφαλαῖον.
164.10
38. πενταμαριτεύω. **12**, no. 52
D 16, note
39. ἀζετόω 'convict.' No. 55.17
note
40. δαράται and γάμελα. No.
52 A 24, note
41. πατρία 'gens.' No. 52 A 25,
note
42. See also, in Glossary, αἶνος,
ἀλία, ἀμμόνιον, ἀρέσμιον,
προτεράσιος, τέλειος.

231. External influence in the dialect. The temple accounts
of 353-325 B.C. show plain evidences of Attic influence. With the
Aetolian domination (278-178 B.C.) a new element is added, that
of the Northwest Greek κοινή (see **279**), resulting in the striking
mixture (e.g., dat. pl. πάντεσσι, πάντοις, πᾶσι) seen in the numerous
proxeny and manumission decrees, some of them as late as the
first and second centuries A.D. There are even some few traces
of Boeotian influence, as in ἰστάνθω, θέλωνθι, κλαρωσῖ (ῑ = εῖ)
from Stiris, near the Boeotian boundary, and the spellings κή
(= καί), ἄσουλον in a decree of the Phocians. The Amphictionic
decrees immediately following the Aetolian conquest are in the
pure Attic κοινή, but the dialect was gradually resumed, in the
mixed form which it shows in the other classes of inscriptions.

Locrian
232. West Greek characteristics. See **223-25**.

233. Northwest Greek characteristics. See **226**.

234. In common with various other dialects.

1. E, EI, O, OV, later ει, ου = secondary ē, ō. **25d**
2. κοθαρός (ΠερϞοθαριᾶν) = καθαρός. **6**
3. 'Οπόεντι, 'Οποντίους. **44**.4
4. Ϝ initial, rarely intervocalic. **52, 53**
5. Peculiarities in the use of the spiritus asper. **58a, d**
6. ἔμισον. **58d, 81, 89**.6
7. Doubling of ξ. **89**.1
8. τὸαροί = τοὶ ἱαροί. (Halae). **94**.9
9. Apocope, assimilation, and simplification in κὰ τᾶς, κὰ τόνδε, πὸ τούς. **89**.7, **95**
10. ἀμφιλλέγω. **76**
11. μεῖστον. **113**.2
12. ταὐτᾶ, ἄ. **132**.6

13. ἀριστίνδαν, πλουτίνδαν, ἀγχιστέδαν. **133**.7
14. ἐχθός = ἐκτός. **133**.3
15. ὑπα- = ὑπο-. **135**.3
16. ποί (once) = πρός. **135**.6b
17. 3 pl. imv. -ντō; mid. -ōσθōν. **140**.3a, 4b
18. ἐλᾶ- in ἀπελᾶōνται. **159**
19. Ϝέρρω = φεύγω. **162**.7
20. τεθμός, τετθμός, θέθμιον = θεσμός, and δαιθμός = δασμός. **164**.4
21. δικαστήρ. **164**.5
22. οἰκιάτας = οἰκέτης. **167**
23. τέλειος = κύριος 'valid.' Glossary
24. παῖς 'son,' κόρα 'daughter.' Glossary
25. πλέθα 'assembly.' Glossary

235. Special Locrian.

1. ἐ from ἐκ in ἐ δάμō, ἐ λιμένος, etc. **89**.7, **100**
2. αἴ τι συλōι, etc. = αἴ τις. **89**.7
3. ἁρέσται = ἑλέσθαι. **12**
4. φρίν = πρίν. **66**
5. ἀλάζω = ἀλλάσσω. **84a**
6. κατά 'according to' with gen. **136**.5
7. ἀνδρεφονικός. **167**

8. ἐχεπάμōν 'heir,' παματοφαγεῖσται 'be confiscated.' **162**.12
9. λιποτελέω. Glossary
10. πρείγα 'council.' **86**.3, no. 59.10
11. πεντάμεροι, title of officials. Glossary
12. ἀξιοδότας. No. 59b, note

236. The important inscriptions (nos. 57-59) are from the early fifth century B.C., and are from Western Locris. But one of these is presumably a copy of an original draft made at Opus. The other material, except for a few short inscriptions, is from a much later period and in mixed dialect. The view that East and West Locrian were materially different in the early period is without adequate foundation and must be given up.

Elean

237. West Greek characteristics. See **223-25.**
238. Northwest Greek characteristics. See **226.**
239. In common with various other dialects.

1. η, ω = secondary ε, ō. **25**
2. Psilosis. **57**
3. δδ (also ττ) = ζ. **84**
4. ρρ = ρσ. **80**
5. Rhotacism of final ς. **60**.1
6. Intervocalic σ > h or lost (late). **59**.3
7. Ϝ init. even before consonants, rarely intervoc.; late βοικίαρ = οἰκίας. **51,55**
8. αἰλότρια = ἀλλότρια .**74**b
9. Omission of ι in ἔα = εἴη, etc. **31**
10. γροφεύς = γραφεύς. **49**.2
11. Apocope in κά, πό, πάρ = παρά, and πάρ = περί. **95**
12. Nom. sg. τελεστά. **105**.1a
13. Dat. sg. -οι. **106**.2
14. Acc. pl. -αις, -αιρ, -οιρ. **78**
15. Dat. pl. φυγάδεσσι (but usually -οις). **107**.3
16. βασιλεύς, -ῆος. **111**.1
17. ἄσιστα = ἄγχιστα. **113**.3

18. αὐτός reflexive. **121**.3
19. τοί, ταί = τόδε, τάδε. **122**
20. ταύτον = τούτων. **124**
21. Article as relative (late). **126**
22. ὑπα- = ὑπο-. **135**.3
23. παρά 'at, with' with acc. **136**.2
24. ὑπό with gen. in dating. **136**.11
25. ἐγραμένος = γεγραμμένος. **137**
26. 3 pl. imv. -ντον; mid. -ōστον. **140**.4a, 4b
72. 3 sg. subj. -ā = -η. **149**
28. Aor. subj. in ā (φυγαδεύαντι, ποιήαται). **151**.1
29. 3 sg. aor. opt. -σειε, -hαιε. **152**.4
30. Infin. -ην. **153**.1
31. μι-forms συλαίε, δαμοσιοία, δαμοσιῶμεν. **157**c
32. Ϝάρρω, Ϝέρρω = φεύγω. **162**.7

240. Special Elean.

1. ā = η. **15**
2. α = ε, not only before ρ, but after ρ, before final ν, etc. **12** with a

3. πόλερ, βενέοι. **18**b
4. ζ = δ (only in earliest inscr.). **62**.2
5. πάσκω = πάσχω. **66**

6. σσ = σθ (late). **85**.2

7. Extreme elision in article. **94**.9

8. Gen.-dat. dual -οιοις, -οιοιρ. **106**.7

9. μεύς = μήν. **112**.3

10. ὀπτό = ὀκτώ. **114**.8

11. ὕσταριν = ὕστερον. **133**.6

12. ἄνευς = ἄνευ, and used with acc. **133**.6, **136**.4

13. Verbs in -ειω (-αιω) = -ευω. **161**.1

14. ἤστω = ἔστω. **163**.5

15. Opt. with κα in commands; also subj. (late). **175**

16. Opt. regularly in conditions etc. **176**.3

17. For peculiar words and meanings, see, in Glossary, γράφος, δίκαια, δίφυιος, Ϝράτρα, ἐπεμπάω, ἰαρόμαος, κατιαραίω, ἱμάσκω, θηλύτερος, ἐρσεναίτερος.

241. κοινή influence. In the amnesty decree (no. 65), from the second half of the fourth century B.C., αρ from ερ is, with one exception (ὕσταριν), given up, as in θηλυτέραν, ἐρσεναιτέραν (note also ἐρσ- vs. earlier ρρ. **80**), and περί (earlier πάρ, with apocope), though ρα from ρε is seen in κατιαραίων; πάσχω has its usual form (earlier πάσκω); the characteristic Elean words Ϝάρρω, Ϝέρρω = φεύγω in its technical sense, δίφυιον (ζίφυιον), and γράφος have given place to the usual φεύγω, διπλάσιον, and γράμμα. The Damocrates decree (no. 66), from the first half of the third century B.C., has ερ, never αρ, ὑπό not ὑπά, and shows considerable κοινή influence in the vocabulary, e.g., καθώρ (καθώς), ἔγκτησις.

On the other hand most of the characteristics of the dialect persist, and, in contrast to earlier inscriptions, the rhotacism of final ς is uniformly observed. Some of the differences between these two inscriptions and the earlier ones are due to chronological and local variation within the dialect, e.g., in both σσ, not στ, = σθ, loss of intervocalic σ; in no. 65 ττ, not δδ, = ζ, dat. pl. φυγάδεσσι (not -οις); in no. 66 subj. in prescriptions. Even in the earlier inscriptions there are some indications of local differences, but it is impossible with the present material to define their scope.

The definite substitution of the Attic κοινή in public inscriptions of Elis belongs to the end of the third century B.C.

Doric

Laconian

242. West Greek characteristics. See **223-25.**

243. Partly in common with various other dialects.

1. η, ω = secondary ε̄, ō. **25**
2. ι from ε before vowels. **9.8**
3. η from ε + α, in part. **42.**1
4. Intervocal σ > h or lost. **59.**1
5. Rhotacism of final ς (late). **60.**2
6. σ = θ (late in inscr.). **64**
7. Ποhοιδᾶν = Ποσειδῶν. **49.**1, **61.**4
8. 'Απέλλων = 'Απόλλων. **49.**3
9. F initial till about 400 B.C.; intervocalic in early inscriptions; later sometimes β. **50-53**
10. Apocope in κάτ, κά, πότ, πό, πάρ, πέρ. **95**

11. αὐτός reflex. **121.**3
12. τετράκιν, etc. **133.**6
13. ταυτᾶ, hᾶτ', πέποκα. **132.**6, 7, 11
14. ἄσιστα = ἄγχιστα. **113.**3
15. 3 pl. imv. -ντω; mid. -ōσθō. **140.**3a, 3b
16. Infin. -ην, -μεν. **153.**1, **154.**3
17. ἀγνέω = ἄγω. **162.**1
18. βοῦαι, βουαγόρ, πρατοπάμπαις, ἀτροπάμπαις, μικιχιδδόμενος, εἴρην, χελῦα, κασσηρατόριν. Nos. **75-78**, note.
19. See also, in Glossary, ἀπέλλα, βίδεοι, ὠβά.

244. κοινή influence. Inscriptions from the second century B.C. (from the fourth and the third there is very little material) and later are not even in the Doric κοινή (**278**), but substantially in the Attic κοινή, with but slight dialectal coloring. On the revival of the use of the dialect in some inscriptions of the second century A.D., probably representing crudely what still survived as a patois, see note to nos. 75-78.

Heraclean

245. West Greek characteristics. See **223-25.**

246. In common with various other dialects.

1. η, ω = secondary ε̄, ō. **25**
2. ἀνεπίγροφος. **49.**2
3. κοθαρός, τοφιών **6**

4. ι from ε before vowels. **9.**9
5. η from ε + α. **42.**1
6. εω (ιω) from εο. **42.**5b

7. τάμνω = τέμνω. **49**.4
8. F initial, with some irregularities. **50**b
9. Spiritus asper frequent, but
   with some irregularities.
   58d
10. ἐγϜηληθίωντι. **75, 151**.2
11. Apocope in ἄν, πάρ, κάτ,
    πότ. **95**
12. μής = μήν. **112**.3
13. hῆς = εἴς. **114**.1
14. τρῖς as nom. pl. **114**.3

15. αὐτοσαυτός, αὐταυτός. **121**.4
16. τῆνος = ἐκεῖνος. **125**.1
17. Article as relative. **126**
18. ποτεχεῖ. **132**.2
19. ἄνωθα, ἔμπροσθα. **133**.1
20. 3 pl. imv. -ντω, mid. -σθω.
    140.3a, 3b
21. ἀνhεῶσθαι. **146**.3
22. Infin. -εν, -μεν. **153**.2, **154**.3
23. ἐλᾱ- in ἐπελᾱσθω. **159**
24. πριῶι, πριωσεῖ. **161**.3
25. ἔντες = ὄντες. **163**.8

247. Special Heraclean.

1. προτερεία. **46**.2
2. ἐνδεδιωκότα. **68**.1
3. ἔντασσι, ποιόντασσι. **107**.3
4. πόλιστος = πλεῖστος. **113**.2
5. ποτικλαίγω. **142**a
6. γεγράψαται, μεμισθωσῶνται.
   146.5
7. πεφυτευκῆμεν. **147**.2

8. ἐρρηγεῖα = ἐρρωγυῖα. **146**.
   3, **148**
9. Special words or meanings,
   see, in Glossary, ἀμπώλημα
   ἄντομος, ἄρρηκτος, ἄφωνος,
   ἀρτύω, κάδδιξ, μασχάλα, μυχός, ὄρεγμα, πλάγος, ῥήτρα,
   ῥογός, σαρμεύω.

248. κοινή influence. κοινή forms appear now and then in the Heraclean Tables, especially in the numerals. Thus τρεῖς beside τρῖς — τέσσαρες, τεσσαράκοντα beside τέτορες, τετρώκοντα — -κόσιοι beside -κάτιοι — χίλιοι for χήλιοι — Ϝείκατι, with ει from εἴκοσι, beside Ϝίκατι — εἰ beside αἰ — hοι beside τοί.

Argolic

249. West Greek characteristics. See **223-25**. But δικάσσαι, not δικάξαι, **142**.

250. Mostly in common with various other dialects (but several special features included here, notably 59).

1. η, ω in part, but also ει, ῑ,
   and ου = secondary ε̄, ō.
   25c

2. ι from ε before vowels,
   sometimes. **9**.10
3. βῶν = βοῦν. **37**.1

4. η from ε + α. **42.**1
5. ο from εο before ντ. **42.**5*d*
6. γροφεύς, etc. **49.**2
7. φάρχμα, φάρξις. **49.**2*a*, **66**
8. καταλοβεύς = καταλαβεύς. **49.**3
9. τάμνω = τέμνω. **49.**4
10. F in all positions in earliest inscriptions; initial till *ca.* 400 B.C. **52-55**
11. hάλιιος, δαμιιοργοῖ, etc. **56**
12. Spiritus asper with some irregularities. **58***d*
13. Intervocalic σ>h or lost. **59.**2
14. ἐντάδε = ἐνθάδε. **65**
15. ῥόπτον, θύρωτον, φάτρα. **70.**3
16. Μίντων = Μίλτων. **72**
17. πάνσα, ἐνς, -ονς, etc. **77.**3, **78**
18. ἥμισσον. **81**
19. πεπεμμένος. **86.**8
20. ξύλλεσθαι = σκύλλεσθαι. **87**
21. βόλιμος, σπάδιον, φάλυρον. **88**
22. hεμίδιμμνον. **88***a*, **89.**2
23. γυμμνικός, πέττρινον. **89.**2
24. Apocope in ἄν, πάρ, πό, κάτ, κά. **95**
25. ἐς = ἐκ. **100***a*
26. Acc. pl. ανς, -ονς, -ινς (but also -ας, -ος, rarely -ως). **78, 104.**8
27. μής = μήν. **112.**3
28. ἔθεν, gen. sg. **118.**3
29. τύ, acc. sg., νίν acc. sg. **118.**5
30. αὐτοῦ ἔθεν, reflexive. **121.**1

31. αὐσαυτός, αὐταυτός. **121.** 4*c*, *f*
32. τῆνος = ἐκεῖνος. **125.**1
33. ποτεχεῖ, hῖ. **132.**2
34. ἔχθω, ἔχθοι, ἔνδοι, ἄνευν. **133.**3, 4, 6
35. πεδά = μετά. **135.**5
36. ποί = πρός. **135.**6
37. ὑπέρ 'in behalf of' with acc. **136.**10
38. 2 sg. συντίθησι. **138.**1
39. γεγράβανται. **66, 139.**2
40. 3 pl. imv. -ντω; mid. -νσθō. **140.**3*a*, 3*b*
41. κλάιξ, κλαικτός. **142***a*
42. ἔγεντο = ἐγένετο. No. 80, note
43. ἐξερρύᾱ, aor. **144***b*
44. λελάβηκα, ἐπιμεμηνάκαντι. **146.**1
45. στᾱσες, 2 sg. aor. subj. **150***c*
46. Infin. -εν, -μεν. **153.**2, **154.** 3
47. οἰκείη, opt. **157***c*
48. διεγέλᾱ, ποτελᾱτō. **159**
49. ἔρπω 'go,' ἐνιπᾱσκομαι 'acquire,' χρηίζω 'wish.' **162.**6, 12, 14
50. ἐντō = ὄντων, ἔντες = ὄντες, ἔσσα = οὖσα. **163.**6, 8
51. μαντήα, πρεσγήα. **164.**1
52. ἀλίασσις, etc. **164.**3
53. θεθμός (**65**), γράσσμα, γράθμα. **164.**4
54. hεμίτεια. **164.**10
55. ἐνδοσθίδια. **165.**2
56. ἴατρα. **165.**3
57. κωμέτας. **167**

58. Opt. with κα. **177**
59. ἀϝρέτευε, ἀρήτευε 'presided.' **55b**
60. ἔλεξε = εἶπε 'made the motion.' Glossary
61. Other special words or

meanings, see, in Glossary, ἀλιαία, ἀμβόλιμος, ἀνεπιβασία, ἀρτῦναι, δεμελεῖς, δενδρύω, δόκημα, Ϝhεδιέστας, ἐπιπῆν, καλαῖς, ὀπτίλλος, τέλειος, τέλλω, τρέω.

251. There are some differences between the dialect of Argos and vicinity and that which appears in the inscriptions of Epidaurus and other places in the Acte. So the absence in the latter region of the typical Arg. term ἀρήτευε, of the Argive change of intervocalic σ (see **59**.2 with *a*), the rarity of νσ (**77**.3, **78**; only early ποιϝέσανς Methana) which is usual in Argive inscriptions till within the second century B.C.; the infrequency of η, ω for secondary ē, ō (**25c**; only Epid. χηρός, χῆρα, ἀφήλετο, and gen. sg. -ω, acc. pl. -ως at Hermione). Some features are due to the fact that Attic influence was earlier and stronger in the East. Definite Attic forms are frequent in Epidaurian inscriptions of the early fourth century B.C. (see no. 90, note).

But more extensive early material from the Acte may alter the picture.

Corinthian

252. West Greek characteristics. See **223-25**.

253. In common with various other dialects.

1. ευ from εο. **42**.5
2. γροφεύς. **49**.2
3. Ἀπέλλων. **49**.3
4. ϝ early in all positions. **52-55**
5. ντ, νθ = λτ, λθ. **72**
6. ρh, Mh. **76a**
7. Apocope in ἄν, πάρ, πότ, πό (but more often full forms). **95**
8. ΦιλοκλέϜδα, nom. sg. **105**.1a
9. ΤλασίαϜο, gen. sg. **105**.2b
10. Προκλείδας, gen. sg. **105**.2c
11. Dat. pl. of consonant stems in -εσσι. **107**.3
12. Διεί, dat. sg. **112**.1
13. μείς = μήν. **112**.3
14. αὐτός, reflex. **121**.3
15. αὐτοσαυτός. **121**.4b
16. ποί = πρός. **135**.6
17. 3 pl. imv. -ντω; mid. -σθω. **140**.3a, b
18. hίσατο, aor. of ἵζω. **144c**
19. Infin. -ειν, -μεν. **153**.1, **154**.3
20. Personal names in -ήν frequent. **164**.7

254. Special Corinthian. Very early monophthongization of ει and ου and representation of both original ει and secondary ē by E or EI (vs. ʙ, Sicyon Ⴘ = ε or η) and of original ου and secondary ō by OV. **25d, 28, 34.**

255. After the early but brief inscriptions in the epichoric alphabet, there is but scanty material until the third and second centuries B.C., when the admixture of κοινή forms is considerable.

Megarian

256. West Greek characteristics. See **223-25**.
257. In common with various other dialects.

1. E, ει, O, ου = secondary ē, ō. **25**
2. E = original ει, rare. **28**
3. ευ = εο, late. **42.5**
4. τράφω = τρέφω. **49.2**
5. Ϝ init. in fifth century B.C., otherwise lost.
6. Φίντων = Φίλτων. **72**
7. Mh in Μηεγαρεύς. **76a**
8. ρρ = ρσ in Ὄρριππος. **80**
9. ἥμισσον. **81**
10. ἀμφιλλέγω. **76**
11. Apocope in ἄν, πάρ, κάτ, πότ. **95**
12. Gen. sg. masc. Φάγας, etc. **105.2c**
13. μείς = μήν. **112.3**
14. τοῦτοι = οὗτοι. **124**
15. τῆνος = ἐκεῖνος. **125**. τηνῶθεν. **132.8**
16. τέδε, ἄ(λ)λē. **132.7**
17. ὄκκα. **132.11**
18. ἐνδός. **133.4**
19. ἄνις. **133.6**
20. 3 pl. imv. -ντω; mid. -σθων. **140.3a, 2b**
21. Infin. -ειν, -μεν. **153.1, 154.3**
22. ἐπεσκεύωσαν. **161.3**
23. Names in -κλίας, as Εὐκλίας. **166.1**
24. λάζομαι = λαμβάνω. Glossary
25. τελαμών = στήλη. No. **82,** note

258. Special Megarian.

1. Θέδωρος, Θοκλείδας, etc. most frequent. **42.5f**
2. ἐνπίδες = ἐλπίδες. **72**
3. σά = τινα. **128**
4. αἰσιμνάτας, αἰσιμνάω = αἰσ-
υμνήτης, etc. **20.** Apart from the difference of vowel, the words are peculiar to Megarian and Ionic.

259. Except for the early inscriptions of Selinus and a few others, the material is from the end of the fourth century or later, and shows κοινή influence.

Rhodian

260. West Greek characteristics. See **223-25**.
261. In common with various other dialects.

1. η, ω and ει, ου = secondary ε̄, ō. **25**b
2. 'Αγλου- beside 'Αγλω- from 'Αγλαο-. **41**.2
3. η from ε + α. **42**.1
4. ευ = εο. **42**.5
5. ᾱ from ο + ᾱ in ὀγδᾶι, Βᾱδρόμιος. **44**.2
6. Early loss of ϝ. **50**
7. Ξην-, Ξειν-. **54**
8. ἱαρός, ἱερός with lenis. **58**b
9. τόζε = τόδε. **62**.2
10. Φιντίας = Φιλτίας **72**
11. Ζεὺ δέ = Ζεὺς δέ, etc. **97**.4
12. περιβολιβῶσαι. **88**
13. Πασιάδαϝο, gen. sg. **105**.2b
14. 'Ιδαμενῆος, gen. sg. **111**.3
15. ἐννῆ. **114**.9
16. τοῦτοι = οὗτοι. **124**
17. κῆνος. **125**.1

18. ὅπυς, υἷς. **132**.4
19. ὅκκα. **132**.11
20. ἐξάν. **133**.6
21. Πεδα- in month name. **135**.5
22. 3 pl. perf. ἀπεστάλκαντι, etc. **138**.4
23. 3 pl. imv. -ντω; mid. -σθων, -σθω. **140**.3a, 1, 2b
24. Fut. pass. with active endings. **145**
25. Perf. 3 sg. τετιμάκει, etc., infin. γεγόνειν. **147**.1, 2
26. τιμέω = τιμάω. **161**.2
27. χρήιζω 'wish.' **162**.14
28. ἐντί as 3 sg. **163**.10
29. Τιμᾱκράτης, 'Ιππέδαμος, 'Αρχοκράτης, κτοινέτας. **167**

262. Special Rhodian. Infinitive in -μειν. **154**.5. κτοίνα, denoting a territorial division like the Attic deme, is found only in Rhodes and Carpathos. The μαστροί are known as financial investigators at Delphi and Pallene, but as the chief local officers are peculiar to Rhodes (cf. no. 103), λέσχα in the sense of 'grave' (no. 101) is Rhodian only.

263. κοινή influence shows itself to a slight extent in the fourth century B.C. Most of the material is from the third century or later, and is in the Doric κοινή (**278**), though with frequent retention of the characteristic infinitive in -μειν. In this mixed form the dialect is one of the longest to survive, many peculiarities still appearing in inscriptions of the first and second centuries A.D.

Coan

264. West Greek characteristics. See **223-25**.

265. In common with various other dialects.

1. η, ω and ει, ου = secondary ε, ō. **25b**
2. η from ε + α, and special ηὐτῶν = ἑαυτῶν. **42.1**
3. ευ=εο, also from ε + secondary ō in κυεῦσα, etc. **42.5**
4. ᾱ from οᾱ in ὀγδᾶι, Βᾱδρόμιος. **44.2**
5. Δολφοί, ἔτελον. **49.3**
6. τάμνω = τέμνω. **49.4**
7. Early loss of Ϝ. **50**
8. στέπτω = στέφω. **66**
9. Palatalized λ, spelling λε, as ξύλεα = ξύλα. **71b**
10. Acc. pl. of o-stems -ος, also ἐς = εἰς. **78**
11. ἥμισσον. **81**
12. πρηγιστεύω. **86.3a**
13. πράτιστος. **114.1**
14. τοῦτοι = οὗτοι. **124**
15. τουτῶ, ἑκατέρω. **132.8** with a

16. ὅκκα. **132.11**
17. ἐξᾶν. **133.6**
18. 3 pl. imv. -ντω; mid. -σθω, -σθων. **140.3a, 1, 2b**
19. Short-vowel aor. subj. **150**
20. ἐγρυᾶι, aor. subj. (Calymn.) **144b, 151.1**
21. Infin. -εν, also in contract verbs; -μεν. **153.2, 3, 154.3**
22. ἐλάντω, etc.
23. καρπῶντι, ἱερώσθω, ἐξορκώντω, ἀξιῶι. **159a**
24. ἀγρεταί. **162.2**
25. ἕρπω 'go.' **162.6**
26. Other special words or meanings, see, in Glossary, αἱμάτιον, ἀμφεικάς, ἄποτος, γερεαφόρος, δίκρεας, ἔνδορα, ἐπίποκος, ἔτελον, θηκαῖον, καρπόω, ναῦσσον, προσπερμεία, σπυρός, τριχώλιος, χέλυος.

266. There are no very early inscriptions, and only a few even from the fourth century B.C. The most important of these, the sacrificial calendar (cf. no. 108), already shows some κοινή forms, as ἱερεύς beside ἱαρεύς, εἰκάς beside ἰκάς, acc. pl. τρεῖς, ἑστία beside ἱστία, etc., but preserves some forms which are never found later as ἱερῆι, τεταρτῆς (later always -ει, -εις, etc.). Ionic influence is shown in τέλεως, the hybrid ἱαρεωσύνα, and many women's names like Ἁλίη, Ἀρισταγόρη, etc. Most of the material is of the third and second centuries, and in the Doric κοινή as described in **278**.

Theran and Cyrenaean

267. West Greek characteristics. See **223-25**.
268. In common with various other dialects.

1. η, ω = secondary ē, ō, but also sometimes ει and (T.) ου. **25b**
2. αυ from ευ sometimes (T.). **33a**
3. η from ε + α. **42.1**
4. ευ from εο. **42.5**
5. εω (C.) from εο. **42.5b**
6. ὠδός (C.) = Att. ὁδός. **54**
7. ϝ lost in earliest times. **50**
8. ντ, νθ (C.) from λτ, λθ. **72**
9. Type παῖσα (C., traces in T.). **77.3**.
10. Final νς, loss of ν without change of preceding vowel. **78**
11. ρρ = ρσ (early T., later C. ρσ). **80**
12. Crasis of ο + α to ω. **94.1**
13. Assimilation of final ν to following initial λ (C.). **96.3**
14. Assimilation of final σ to following initial λ. **97.3**
15. Article as relative (C.). **126**
16. μέστα 'until.' **132.12**
17. Pron. advs. αὐτεῖ (C.), ὅπυι (C.), ἇδε (C.), ὅπη (C.), ὅκα (C.). **132.2, 4, 5, 6, 7, 11**
18. ἔνδοι, ἔξοι (C.), ἐξᾶν (T.). **133.4, 5, 6**
19. 3 pl. imv. -ντων. **140.4a**; mid. -σθων. **140.2b**

20. Aorist of ἵζω (vs. ἕζω) ἵσ-σαντα, ἱσσάμενος. **144c**
21. Aorist in -ᾱ, 3 sg. subj. μιᾶι, ἴσᾱι (Cyren.). **144b, 151.1**
22. Fut. pass. with act. endings (T.). **145**
23. Perfect forms as if from -ευόω, ἐφορευωκότων (C), κατεσκεύωκε (T)., **161.3**
24. Perf. act. pple. fem. -υῖα (C.) vs. -εῖα (T.). **148**
25. Short vowel subj. of σ- and α-aor. (C.) **150**
26. Long vowel subj. of unthematic vowel stems, δύ-νᾱνται, etc. (C.) **151.1**
27. Pres. subj. of εἶμι, ἐπείηι (C.). **151.3**
28. Infin. of thematic forms, -εν. **153.2, 3**
29. Mid, pple. χρείμενος (C.). **158**
30. Transfer of -αω to -εω type (C.). **161.2**
31. Pres. pple. fem. in unthematic form (C.) **163.8a**
32. ἴσᾱμι. **162.9**
33. -ηιο- = Att. -ειο- (C.). **164.1**
34. -τηρ in agent nouns = Att. -της. **164.5**
35. δαμιεργός (C.) vs. more common δαμιοργός. **167**

269. Special Cyrenaean.

1. ε from εο before ντ. **42.**5e
2. βάβαλος = βέβαλος. **46.**1
3. Nom. pl. and acc. pl. ἱαρές, dat. pl. Μεγαρέσσι, etc. **111.**3
4. λεχός gen. sg. of λεχώι (C.). **45, 111.**5a
5. ἐς νέω = εἰς νέωτα (C.)
6. Forms of μιαίνω, 3 sg. fut. μιανεῖ (trans.), μιασεῖ (pass.), aor. subj. μιᾶι (pass.)
7. παισεῖται = Att. πείσεται,

fut. mid. of πάσχω (with α apparently from that of πάσχω, ἔπαθον).
8. ποτιπίαμμα. **164.**4
9. Some other special words or meanings (C.) ἀδηίζων 'protecting,' δεκατός 'subject to a tithe,' ἴκνυς 'ashes' (?), οἰκισία 'settlement,' κοιτᾱτήριον = κοιμητήριον, ὄροφος 'house,' κολοσός 'plastic figure,' ἔκαμε 'died'

Cretan

270. West Greek characteristics. See **223-25.** But οἱ, αἱ, not τοί, ταί, and Ἄρτεμις not Ἄρταμις.

271. In common with various other dialects.

1. η, ω = secondary ē, ō. **25** with a
2. ι from ε before vowel. **9.**7
3. βῶς, βῶν = βοῦς, βοῦν. **37.**1
4. ο from εο before ντ (not Central Cretan). **42.**5d
5. τράπω, τράφω. **49.**2
6. κάρτος, στάρτος, etc. **49.**2a
7. Ἀπέλλων. **49.**3
8. ἀντίγροφον, ἔγγροφον. **48.**4
9. Ϝ initial till second century B.C.; sometimes β; intervocalic only in compounds or augmented forms. **50-54**
10. ξῆνος, ὦρος from ξένϝος, etc., but ϜίσϜος. **54** with d
11. Psilosis. **57** with b
12. μαίτυρες = μάρτυρες. **71a**
13. ἀμφιλλέγω. **76a**
14. πάνσα, ἐνς, -ονς, etc. (but also ἐς, -ος). **77.**3, **78**
15. ττ in ἴαττα ὁπόττος, μέττος, δάτταθθαι, etc. **81, 82**
16. δδ (sometimes ττ) = ζ. **84**
17. ττ = κτ and πτ. **86.**1, 2
18. γγ, γ = σγ. **86.**3
19. ττ = στ (rare). **86.**4
20. ψ = σφ. **87**
21. ἀλλόττριος. **89.**4
22. Apocope in ἄν, πάρ (rarely κα(τ), usually κατά). **95**
23. ἐς = ἐξ before consonants. **100**
24. Early loss of dual. **104.**11
25. υἱάσι. **112.**2
26. πλίες. **113.**2

27. Ϝὶν αὐτõι = ἑαυτῷ, etc.
121.1
28. αὐτοσαυτός. 121.4*b*
29. αὐτόν neut. = αὐτό 125.2
30. ὀτεῖος = ὁποῖος, in sense
adjectival ὅστις. 130
31. ὄπει, ὄπαι, ὄπē, ὄπυι. 132.2,
4, 5, 7
32. μέστα, μεττ' ἐς. 132.12
33. πρόθθα = πρόσθε. 133.1
34. ἐνδός, ἔξοι. 133.4, 5
35. αὖτιν, αὐταμέριν. 133.6
36. πεδά = μετά. 135.5
37. ποί = πρός (rare). 135.6*b*
38. ἀντί 'in presence of,' ἀμφί
'concerning.' 136.7, 8
39. ἔγρατται = γέγραπται. 137
40. 3 pl. perf. ἀπεστάλκαντι,
etc. 138.4
41. 3 pl. imv. -ντων; mid. -σθων.
140.4*a*, 1*b*

42. Fut. pass. with active endings. 145
43. Short-vowel aor. subj., 3
sg. δείκσει, etc. 150
44. Subj. νύνᾱται, πέπᾱται, etc.
151.1
45. Infin. -εν; also in contract
verbs. 153.2, 3
46. χρήμενος. 158
47. Verb-forms in -εω (-ιω) =
-άω. 161.2
48. -οω type in τρōόσει, ʹτρōό-
σάντων. 161.3
49. ἔρπω = εἶμι. 162.6
50. ἴσᾱμι. 162.9
51. ἔντων = ὄντων, ἴαττα = οὖσα. 163.6, 8
52. ἐπᾱβολά. 167*a*
53. πόλις = δῆμος. Glossary
54. καρτερός = κύριος 'valid.'
Glossary

272. Special Cretan.

1. ἀβλοπία = ἀβλαβία. 49.3, 66
2. τνατός, τετνακός = θνητός,
etc. 66
3. δέφυρα = γέφυρα. 68.2
4. θθ = σσ (late). 81*a*
5. θθ (also τθ) = σθ. 85.3
6. νν = ρν. 86.5
7. μμ = μν. 86.6
8. Ϝήρω = Ϝέρδω. 86.6
9. πρεῖγυς, πρείγων, etc. =
πρέσβυς, etc. 68.1, 86.3
10. Assimilation in external
combination more exten-
sive than elsewhere. 87.4,
5, 98

11. Acc. pl. of consonant stems
-ανς. 107.4
12. Ϝῆμα, gen. sg. Ϝήμᾱς. 112.5
13. Acc. pl. τρίινς. 114.3
14. νεότᾱς, gen. sg. νεότᾱς, acc.
sg. νεότα. 88*a*
15. ὄτερος = ὁπότερος. 127
16. ὄτις, gen. sg. ὄτι, dat. sg.
ὄτιμι acc. pl. ἄτι. 128, 129.3
17. ὄπαι as final conj. 132.5,
10*a*
18. πορτί = πρός. 135.6
19. 3 pl. opt. Ϝέρκσιεν. 152.4
20. Infin. -μην. 154.4
21. αἰλέω = αἱρέω. 12

22. ἄρατρον = ἄροτρον. **161**.5
23. ἐλευσέω, πεύθω, ὠνέω.
    162.15
24. ἀνδρήιον. **164**.1
25. ψάφιγμα, ψάφιμμα. **164**.4
26. ἐνδοθίδιος, ἐξαρχίδιος.
    165.2
27. κόμιστρα, τρίτρα. **165**.3
28. βίετος, Ϝοικεύς, fem. Ϝοικέα,
    ὀφέλōμα. **167**
29. ἐπᾱβολά. **167**a

30. Special words or meanings
    (not all Cretan only), see,
    in Glossary, ἀγέλα, ἄζωστος,
    ἀκεύω, ἀμφαίνομαι, ἄπατος,
    δρομεύς, ἔμμανις, ἔνδικος,
    ἔντιτος, ἐπιβάλλων, καρταῖ-
    πος, καρτερός, κόσμος, λα-
    γαίω, μωλέω, οὐρεῖον, πάσ-
    τας, πατρōιōχος, περαιόω,
    στέγα, συνεσσάδδω, τέλομαι,
    τίτας, φωνέω

273. Cretan, as commonly understood and as described above,
is the dialect of the inscriptions of Gortyn (which is by far the
most fully represented), Cnossus, Lyttus, Vaxus, and the other
cities of the great central portion of Crete. This is also known
more specifically as Central Cretan. Eastward, at Olus, Drerus,
Latus, etc., the dialect is much less uniform; and in the inscriptions of cities of the eastern extremity of the island, as Hierapytna, Praesus, and Itanus, and again in those from the cities
of the western extremity, as Aptera, Cydonia, etc., many of the
most striking Cretan characteristics are wholly lacking. Hence the
terms East Cretan, usually reckoned from Hierapytna eastward, and West Cretan, from Lappa westward, are sometimes
employed. But there is no sufficient ground for the belief that
the East, West, and Central Cretan are fundamental divisions
of the dialect, or that they reflect to any degree the various con-
stituent elements in the population. The East and West Cretan
inscriptions, the latter very meager, are comparatively late, and
show a large degree of obvious κοινή influence, partly Attic,
partly the Doric κοινή of the other islands. The absence of many
of the Central Cretan characteristics may well be, and probably
is, due to external influence, which was felt earlier and more
strongly than in Central Crete, where, especially at Gortyn,
most of the peculiarities persisted until Roman times. However,
an actual divergence of development, for which external causes
are not apparent, is to be recognized in the treatment of εο,
which, instead of becoming ιο, appears as ο or ω in East and West

Greek (**49***c, d*). There are also a few other local variations. But, if we had ample material from the early period, it is highly probable that we should find that in the main the characteristics of Central Cretan were also general Cretan.

SURVIVAL OF THE DIALECTS. GROWTH OF VARIOUS FORMS OF KOINH

274. Not only in early times, but also, in most parts of Greece, long after Attic had become the norm of literary prose, each state employed its own dialect, both in private and public monuments of internal concern, and in those of a more external or interstate character, such as decrees in honor of foreigners, decisions of interstate arbitration, treaties, and, in general, communications between different states. Thus, for example, an honorary decree of a Boeotian city is in the Boeotian dialect, no matter whether the recipient is a citizen of Athens, Delphi, Alexandria, or Tarentum. If the Eleans honor Damocrates of Tenedos, the decree is in the Elean of the time (no. 66). If Mytilene honors Erythrae, the decree is in Lesbian, and a copy in this form is set up at Erythrae. Such is the usual practice, examples of which could be cited by the hundred, and any departure from which is the exception.

A decision of the Argives in a dispute between Melos and Cimolos is in the Argive dialect (no. 87). A treaty between the Cretan cities of Cnossus and Tylissus (no. 86) is in Argive alphabet and dialect, not only the draft deposited at Argos, but also that at Tylissus. And so in general such decisions were regularly rendered in the dialect of the arbitrators, and inscribed in this form by the states involved in the dispute, usually at home, but sometimes also in one of the great religious centers as Delos or Olympia. The extant texts of treaties are, as a rule, in the dialect of that party in whose territory the text was found, and it is to be assumed that the version inscribed by the other party in its home was likewise in its dialect. Thus, for example, the monetary agreement between Mytilene and Phocaea in the Lesbian version found at Mytilene (no. 25), the treaty of alliance between Elis and Heraea (in Arcadia) in the Elean version found at Olympia (no. 62).

In communications between states using different dialects each party employs its own. For example, when Philip V of Macedon sends certain recommendations to the city of Larisa, he writes in the Attic κοινή, which had long been the language of the Macedonian court, but the decrees which the city passes in response are in the Thessalian dialect (no. 32). An inscription of Mytilene contains the text of a decree of the Aetolian league in favor of Mytilene, in its original Aetolian (Northwest Greek κοινή) form, a copy of which had been brought back by the Mytilenaean envoys, followed by a decree of Mytilene in Lesbian, quoting from the former decree and ordering the inscription of both. The regulations of the religious sanctuaries of Greece are drawn up in the dialect of the state which has direct charge of them, no less in the great Hellenic centers than in those of local fame. So, for example, an Amphictionic decree which is known to us only in the copy set up at Athens is in the Delphian dialect.

275. In the period before the rise of Attic as the language of literary prose, no one dialect was in a position even to influence other dialects except within narrow geographical limits. Yet it is probable that even then external influence was not wholly absent. There was no lack of intercourse to awaken consciousness of the peculiarities of one's own dialect as compared with those of others. Some of these peculiarities, especially such as were at variance with the practice of all or nearly all other dialects, might come to be regarded with disfavor as provincialisms, and be avoided in writing, and even in speech, or at least less consistently observed.

For example, the Laconians and the Argives, who were well aware that under certain conditions they omitted, or pronounced as a mere breathing, what was a σ in the speech of most other Greeks, may have felt that this, unlike some of their other peculiarities, was a sort of weakness, which did not deserve to be exploited in writing. This would explain the inconsistency in the treatment of intervocalic σ which is to be observed even in the early inscriptions of Laconia and Argolis, before any specific Attic influence is possible. See **59**.1, 2. The fact that Arcadian σις and κάς, agreeing with Cyprian σις and κάς, are found only in the earliest inscriptions (no. 17; ὄζις also no. 16), while all the later ones have τὶς and καί, may also be ascribed to the combined influence of the other dialects, just as in a later period, when specific Attic influence is more probable, πλός was replaced by the usual πλέον, in spite of the fact that other equally marked peculiarities like ἰν = ἐν were unaffected. The Eleans gave up even in the sixth century their use of ζ for the δ of other dialects, and if, as is likely, this was a concession in spelling only, it is none the less in point.

In fact it is increasingly evident that, more than is commonly recognized, we must reckon with external influence even in very early dialect inscriptions. Some of the disparities between inscriptions of the same dialect, some of those which are commonly attributed to local variation or even to prehistoric dialect mixture are due to nothing more than the elimination by the writer of one or another local peculiarity in favor of what is usual in the majority of dialects and especially in that literary form which was familiar to all, the Homeric.

276. Traces of Ionic influence are seen in the Doric islands, though the earliest evidence of this belongs rather to the history of the alphabet, namely the spread of the Ionic H = η (**4.6**). It is not accidental that ευ for εο, though occasionally found in continental Greece, is mainly found, outside of Ionic, in Rhodes, Cos, Thera, etc. In Cos occur many Ionic forms, as τέλεως etc. (see **266a**). Even in the fifth century the coins of the Rhodian Ialysus show ᾿Ιελυσίον beside ᾿Ιαλυσίον. Through the medium of the Doric κοινή of the other islands (**278**), some Ionic peculiarities have even spread to Crete, e.g., at Itanus ευ = εο, εο = ευ, and χρεώμεθα.

277. The Attic κοινή. The foundation of the ultimate supremacy of Attic is to be sought in the political conditions of the fifth century B.C. In this we refer to something more than the fact, important as it is, that in this period Athens became the intellectual center of Greece and Attic the recognized language of literary prose. It is within the sphere of influence represented by the confederacy of Delos and the Athenian empire that Attic made its first advance as an ordinary medium of communication. Of all dialects it is Ionic which shows the first signs of Attic influence and is the first to lose its identity as a distinct dialect. Some traces of this influence are seen even in the Ionic inscriptions of the fifth century, especially in the islands, and in the fourth century the majority of inscriptions show at least a mixture of Attic forms, and some, even from the early part of the century, are substantially Attic. After this, Ionic practically ceased to exist as a distinct dialect, though some Ionic peculiarities are occasionally found in much later times, mostly in proper names and certain conventional words or phrases. It is this Attic, already well-nigh established in Ionic territory, and in some respects modified by Ionic, that the Macedonians took up and spread, and which is henceforth termed the κοινή, or, more specifically, the Attic κοινή.

The Macedonian period, indeed, forms the principal landmark in the evolution of a standard language in Greece. For in it the Attic κοινή was spread over a vast territory and permanently established in places which were to become leading centers of Greek life. Yet this is only a stage, marking neither the beginning, as we have seen, nor, still less, the end. Excepting Ionic, and Cyprian, of which we have no later record, the other dialects, though showing more or less κοινή influence, remained in common use in inscriptions from one to upwards of three centuries later. But eventually the κοινή attained complete supremacy both as the written and the spoken language, and from it is descended Modern Greek. The only important exception is the present Tsakonian dialect, spoken in a small portion of Laconia, which is basically the offspring of the ancient Laconian.

278. The Doric κοινή. In most of the Doric dialects Attic influence shows itself, to some extent, even in the fourth century B.C., and there was gradually evolved a type of modified Doric which prevails in the inscriptions of the last three centuries B.C., and is conveniently known as the Doric κοινή. This is substantially Doric, retaining a majority of the general West Greek characteristics, but with a tendency to eliminate local peculiarities, and with a strong admixture of forms from the Attic κοινή. In spite of some variety in the degree of mixture, and the retention of some local peculiarities, e.g., the infinitive in -μειν at Rhodes, there is yet a very considerable unity, amply sufficient to justify us in speaking of a distinct type of κοινή.

That the mixture is not a haphazard one is shown, for example, in the fact that the substitution of ει for αι, side by side with the retention of κα, resulting in the hybrid εἴ κα, is very general, while the opposite, αἰ ἄν, is unknown. ἱαρός is replaced by ἱερός. The numerals show the forms of the Attic κοινή, e.g., acc. pl. τρεῖς for τρῖς, τέσσερες (or τέσσαρες, τέτταρες) not τέτορες, εἴκοσι for ἴκατι, τεσσεράκοντα (τεσσαράκοντα, τετταράκοντα) for τετρώκοντα, -κόσιοι for -κάτιοι, χίλιοι for χείλιοι or χήλιοι. In ι-stems we usually find πόλιος, πόλιες retained, but πόλει, πόλεσι, acc. pl. πόλεις. Nouns in -εύς follow the Attic type except in the accusative singular, e.g. βασιλέως, nom. acc. pl. βασιλεῖς, but acc. sg. βασιλῆ. So Att. βασιλέως is usual, but Att. πόλεως rare. The substitution of οἱ, αἱ for τοί, ταί is frequent, but there is great variation in this respect, τοί and οἱ occurring not infrequently even in the same inscription. Attic ου from εο is frequent, especially in verbs in -εω. In some places, as far apart as Rhodes and Corcyra, we find inscriptions which have the verb-forms uniformly in ου, but the genitive singular of σ-stems in -εος or -ευς, e.g., Rhod. ἐγκαλοῦντας, etc. but 'Ισοκράτευς, etc. (GDI 3758), Corc. ποιοῦντες, etc. but 'Αριστομένεος etc. (GDI 3206). Attic ω from εω is also more common in verbs than in nouns. In dialects which have ξῆνος or ξεῖνος etc. (54), such forms are often replaced by the Attic, especially in the case of πρόξενος. The first plural ending -μες is generally replaced by -μεν, though it persists in some places.

There are various other Attic forms which are not infrequent, but much less common than the dialect forms, e.g., ὤν beside ἐών, imperative ending -ντων beside -ντω, πρῶτος beside πρᾶτος, πρός beside ποτί, θεωρός beside θεαρός (conversely θεαρός occurs at Andros, no. 7, and Tenos!). Many of the dialectal peculiarities persist with scarcely any intrusion of the corresponding Attic forms, e.g., ᾱ = Att.-Ion. η, κα, verb forms like δίδωτι, φέροντι, Doric future, future and aorist in ξ (142), ἀμές, etc. Att. η, verb forms like δίδωσι, φέρουσι, infinitives in -ναι (also in large measure ἄν and ἅν, but see below, a) are almost unknown except in the very last stages when the Attic κοινή as a whole is practically established. ᾱ is sometimes found as late as the third century A.D., but only as a bit of local color, perhaps artificial, in what is otherwise the Attic κοινή.

a. An interesting example of mixture, though not in all respects typical, is furnished by the long cult inscription of Andania from the early first century B.C. The native Doric features (or in part general non-Attic) persist in ᾱ, ποτί, 3 pl. verb ending -ντι (3 sg. forms like δίδωτι happen to be lacking), 3 pl. imv. act. -ντω (but ἔστωσαν and mid. -σθωσαν), infin. -μεν, ξ in ὀρκιξάτω, etc., also κλάιξ, κλαικτός, ι-stem inflection gen. -ιος (παραδόσιος, παναγύριος, etc., but πόλεος 4 times), nom. pl. ἰδιῶτιες (but dat. sg. καταλύσει, παναγύρει, acc. pl. τρεῖς, δέρρεις), κα (beside ἄν, both frequent). Aetolian influence in dat. pl. of cons. stems in -οις (πλεόνοις, etc., 7 examples), and acc. pl. πάντες. Att. κοινή in ου from εο in verb forms (πωλοῦντες, etc.), ἱερός, ρρ in δέρρεις, οἱ, αἱ (never τοί, ταί), numerals εἴκοσι, τεσσαράκοντα, -κόσιοι, χίλιοι, ἔβδομος, some forms of ι-stems (see above), 3 pl. ἔστωσαν, mid. -σθωσαν, ἄν (beside κα) and ἄν (never εἴ κα), ὅταν, ἕως, ὄντων, mid. inflection in 3 pl. subj. ἤνται..

279. The Northwest Greek κοινή. This is very similar to the Doric κοινή, showing about the same mixture of Attic with West Greek forms. But it differs from it in that it retains two of the most characteristic features of the Northwest Greek dialects as compared with Doric, namely ἐν = εἰς, and the dative plural of consonant stems in -οις. The use of this type is closely connected with the political power of the Aetolian league. We find it employed, in the third century B.C. and later, in Aetolia and in all decrees of the Aetolian league, in Western Locris (Naupactus was incorporated in the league in 338 B.C., the rest of Western Locris somewhat later), Phocis (Delphi was in the hands of the Aetolians by at least 290 B.C.), the land of the Aenianes, Malis and Phthiotis, all of which became Aetolian in the course of the third century B.C. Without doubt it was also used in Doris, from which we have no material, and in Eastern Locris. In Boeotia, which was in the Aetolian league but a short time (245-234 B.C.), it was never employed, though there are some few traces of its influence (222). The only extant decrees of Cephallenia and Ithaca, of about 200 B.C., are in this same Northwest Greek κοινή, reminding us that Cephallenia, of which Ithaca was a dependency, was allied with the Aetolians (Polyb. 4.6). Parts of the Peloponnesus were also for a time under Aetolian domination, and the characteristic dative plural in -οις is found in Arcadia, Messenia (also ἐν = εἰς), and Laconia. There is one example even so far away as Crete (λιμένοις GDI 4942b; 159-138 B.C.), but clearly an importation. Aetolians had taken part in the internal wars of Crete, and Cretans had served in the armies of both the Aetolian and the Achaean leagues (Polyb. 4.53).

The inscriptions of this period from Acarnania, Epirus, and Achaea, including decrees of the Acarnanian, Epirotan, and Achaean leagues, are not in the Northwest Greek κοινή as defined above (they do not have ἐν = εἰς, or the dative plural of consonant stems in -οις), but in the Doric κοινή. At this time at least the speech of Acarnania and Epirus was not essentially different from that of Corcyra, nor that of Achaea from that of Corinth and Sicyon.

In the Arcadian inscriptions of this period the native Arcadian forms are wholly or in part replaced by West Greek forms, and this is probably due in large part to the influence of the Doric κοινή of the Achaean league. But the Aetolians also held parts of Arcadia for a time, and, as noted above, there are some examples of the dative plural in -οις and ἐν = εἰς from the Northwest Greek κοινή.

280. Some more detailed observations upon the time and extent of κοινή influence in the various dialects have been made in connection with the Summaries of Characteristics (**180-273**), and in the notes to some of the late inscriptions.

What has just been noted in the case of the Doric κοινή is true in all dialects, namely, that of the dialectal peculiarities some are given up much earlier than others. Furthermore it is nothing unusual to find hybrid forms, part dialectal, part κοινή, e.g., Doric future with Attic ου, as ποιησοῦντι etc. frequently,—Boeot. ἄως, a contamination of ἆς and ἕως,—Heracl. Ϝείκατι. a contamination of Ϝίκατι and εἴκοσι,—Boeot. ζώωνθι with dialectal present stem and personal ending, but Attic ζ (pure Boeot. δώωνθι), —Boeot. ἐκγόνως with dialectal case-ending, but Attic ἐκ- (pure Boeot. ἐσγόνως),—Thess. acc. pl. γινομένος with dialectal case-ending, but Attic stem (pure Thess. γινυμένος),—Epid. ἑώρη with Doric ending -η from -αε, but Attic stem ἑώρ- from *ἠόρ-.

Besides such hybrids, hyper-Doric or hyper-Aeolic forms are occasionally met with in late inscriptions, though less often than in our literary texts. Thus the Attic term ἔφηβος (with original η, cf. Dor. ἤβα), when adopted in other dialects, was sometimes given the pseudo-dialectal form ἔφαβος, e.g., in some late Doric and Lesbian inscriptions, in imitation of the frequent equivalence of dialectal ᾱ to Attic η. Conversely the Attic form was sometimes retained in opposition to what would be its true dialectal equivalent, as in Boeotian usually ἔφηβος, rarely ἔφειβος. Similarly the Doric Ἡρακλῆς and its derivatives keep η in Boeotian.

In Roman imperial times the antiquarian interest in local dialects is reflected in the revival of their use in parts of Greece where for some two centuries previously the Attic κοινή had been in general use, at least in inscriptions. So, for example, in the case of Lesbian (cf. no. 28), Laconian (cf. nos. 75-78) and to some extent in Elean, where examples of rhotacism reappear in the first and second centuries A.D. It is impossible to determine in every case whether this was a wholly artificial revival of a dialect which had long ceased to be spoken, or was an artificial elevation to written use of a dialect which had survived throughout the interval as a patois. The latter is true of Laconian (see **277**, end, and note to nos. 75-78). But for most dialects we have no adequate evidence as to the length of their survival in spoken form.

PART II
SELECTED INSCRIPTIONS

EXPLANATIONS

The brief introductory statement to each inscription gives its provenance and approximate date, with references to several of the most important collections. The extensive bibliographies in these collections make it unnecessary to cite the numerous special discussions in periodicals etc., except in the case of a few recently discovered inscriptions. For the abbreviations employed, see pp. 337 ff. References to the collections are by the numbers of the inscriptions unless otherwise stated, while those to periodicals are by pages.

It has seemed unnecessary to state in the case of every inscription whether the alphabet is the epichoric or the ordinary Ionic, since this is generally obvious from the date given, as well as from the transcription. It may be taken for granted, unless otherwise stated, that inscriptions of the fifth century B.C. or earlier are in the epichoric alphabet, those of the fourth century B.C. or later in the Ionic. Hence comments on the form of the alphabet employed are added only in special cases.

The transcription of texts in the older alphabet is such as to give the student some assistance, without confusing what is in the original and what is a matter of editing. The signs E and O, when representing long vowels, no matter whether the later spelling is η, ω or ει, ου, are transcribed simply ē, ō. The spiritus asper, when expressed in the original, is transcribed h, leaving the use of ' as a matter of editing. See p. 52, footnote. The use of the following signs is to be noted.

[ ] for restorations of letters no longer legible.
< > for letters inscribed by mistake, and to be ignored by the reader.
( ) for (1) expansion of abbreviations, (2) letters omitted by mistake, (3) corrected letters. Obvious corrections are given thus, without adding the original reading. Less certain corrections are sometimes commented on in the notes, with citation of the original reading, as are also obscure readings due to the mutilation of the letters. But often this is not done, it being thought unnecessary in a work of this kind to repeat the full critical apparatus of other collections.
- - - for a lacuna, where no restoration is attempted.
. . . . for a similar lacuna where it is desired to show, at least approximately, the number of missing letters, each dot standing for a letter. In general, these are employed only for short lacunae.
| for the beginning of each new line in the original.
|| for the beginning of every fifth line in the original.

183

× ||| for the division between sides or colums, where the text is printed continuously.

The occasional use of a dot under a letter indicates that it is mutilated. But this is commonly disregarded if the proper reading is reasonably certain.

Ionic

East Ionic

1. Sigeum. Early sixth century B.C. GDI 5531. Roberts 42 and pp. 334 ff. Ditt. Syll. 2. Schwyzer 731. Solmsen-Fraenkel 60. The second version (B) is in Attic.

A 5   Φανοδίκō | ἐμὶ τōρμοκ|ράτεος τō | Προκοννη||σίō· κρητῆρ|α δὲ
10   καὶ ὑποκ|ρητήριον κ|αὶ ἠθμὸν ἐς π|ρυτανήιον || ἔδωκεν Συκεεῦσιν.
B   Φανοδίκō εἰμὶ τō Η|ερμοκράτōς τō Προκο|νēσίō κἀγō· κρα-
5   τēρα | κἀπίστατον καὶ hēθ||μὸν ἐς πρυτανεῖον ἔ|δōκα μνēμα Σι-
γε(ι)|εῦσι, ἐὰν δέ τι πάσχ|ō, μελεδαίνēν με, ō | Σιγειēς. καί μ᾽
10   ἐπο||(ίε)σεν Ηαίσōπος καὶ hἀδελφοί.

Monument of Phanodicus of Proconnesus, recording his gift of a mixing bowl, a stand for it, and a wine-strainer, to the Sigean prytaneum. The pillar was prepared and furnished with its Ionic inscription at Proconnesus, which was a colony of Miletus. The Attic version was added at Sigeum, which was already at this time occupied by Athenians.

The divergence between A and the corresponding portion of B is partly due to the normal differences of dialect, e.g., Ion. κρητῆρα with η after ρ, πρυτανήιον = Att. πρυτανεῖον, and τōρμοκράτεος with psilosis and consequent crasis and uncontracted -εος in contrast to Att. τō Ηερμοκράτōς. So ὑποκρητήριον, in contrast to Att. ἐπίστατον, is an Ionic form found elsewhere. Other divergencies are due merely to the difference in alphabet or the early Attic practice of writing single for double consonants (Προκονēσίō)—or are accidental, as dat. pl. in -σιν or -σι. For the notably early but not unprecedented spelling εἰμί in B, see **25d**.

2. Halicarnassus. Before 454 B.C. GDI 5726. Ditt. Syll. 45. Roberts 145 and pp. 339 ff. Schwyzer 744. Solmsen-Fraenkel 62. Tod 25. For the character τ, see **4.4**. Letters which, though now lacking, are found in Lord Charlemont's copy, are printed without the marks of restoration.

Τάδε ὁ σύλλο[γ]ος ἐβōλεύσατο | ὁ Ἀλικαρνατέ[ω]ν καὶ Σαλμα-
κι|τέων καὶ Λύγδαμις ἐν τῆι ἱερῆ[ι] | ἀγορῆι, μηνὸς Ἑρμαιῶνος
5 πέμ||πτηι ἱσταμένō, ἐπὶ Λέοντος πρυ|ταν[εύον]τος τō Ὀατάτιος
κα|[ὶ] Σα[ρυτ]ώλλō τō Θεκυίλω νε|[ωπ]οί[ō. τ]ὸς μνήμονας μὴ
10 παρα|διδό[ναι] μήτε γῆν μήτε οἰκ[ί||α] τοῖς μνήμοσιν ἐπὶ Ἀπολ-
λω|νίδεω τō Λυγδάμιος μνημονε|ύοντος καὶ Παναμύω τō Κασβώ|λ-
15 λιος καὶ Σαλμακιτέων μνη|μονευόντων Μεγαβάτεω τō Ἀ||φυάσιος
καὶ Φορμίωνος τō Π[α]||νυάτιος. ἢν δέ τις θέληι δικάζε|σθαι περὶ
γῆς ἢ οἰκίων, ἐπικαλ[έ]||τω ἐν ὀκτωκαίδεκα μησὶν ἀπ᾽ ὅτ[εο] | ὁ
20 ἄδος ἐγένετο · νόμωι δὲ κατάπ[ε]||ρ νῦν ὀρκῶ‹ι›σ(α)ι τὸς δικαστάς ·
ὅτ[ι] | ἂν οἱ μνήμονες εἰδέωσιν, τοῦτο | καρτερὸν ἔναι. ἢν δέ τις
ὕστερον | ἐπικαλῆι τοῦτο τō χρόνō τῶν | ὀκτωκαίδεκα μηνῶν, ὅρκον
25 ἔναι τ||ῶι νεμομένωι τὴγ γῆν ἢ τὰ οἰκ|[ί]α, ὁρκōν δὲ τὸς δικαστὰς
ἡμί|[ε]κτον δεξαμένος · τὸν δὲ ὅρκον εἶ|[ν]αι παρεόντος τō ἐνεστη-
30 κότος · κ|αρτερὸς δ᾽ εἶναι γῆς καὶ οἰκίων οἵτινες || τότ᾽ εἶχον ὅτε
Ἀπολλωνίδης καὶ Πανα|μύης ἐμνημόνευον, εἰ μὴ ὕστερο|ν ἀπεπέ-
ρασαν. τὸν νόμον τοῦτον | ἢν τις θέληι συγχέαι ἢ προθῆτα||[ι]
35 ψῆφον ὥστε μὴ εἶναι τὸν νόμο||ν τοῦτον, τὰ ἐόντα αὐτō πεπρή-
σθω | καὶ τὠπόλλωνος εἶναι ἱερὰ καὶ α|ὐτὸν φεύγēν αἰεί · ἢν δὲ μὴ
ἦι αὐτ|ῶι ἄξια δέκα στατήρων, αὐτὸν [π]||επρῆσθαι ἐπ᾽ ἐξαγωγῆι
40 καὶ μη[δ]||αμὰ κάθοδον εἶναι ἐς Ἁλικαρν|ησσόν. Ἁλικαρνασσέων
δὲ τῶσ σ|υμπάντων τούτωι ἐλεύθερον ē|ναι, ὃς ἂν ταῦτα μὴ παρα-
45 βαίνηι, κατό|περ τὰ ὅρκια ἔταμον καὶ ὡς γέγραπτ||αι ἐν τῶι Ἀπολ-
λω[νί]ωι, ἐπικαλēν.

Decree of the council of Halicarnassians and Salmacitians
and Lygdamis regarding disputes over real estate. Lygdamis
is the tyrant who drove Herodotus into exile and whom a re-
volution eventually expelled from the city. It is probable that
this inscription dates from a period when the citizens had arisen
and restored the exiles, but had come to terms temporarily
with Lygdamis. The disputes would then be concerning the
property of the former exiles (cf. no. 22), although this is nowhere stated. Salmacis was a town partially merged with Halicarnassus, and represented with it by a common council, though
still retaining its own officials. Halicarnassus was originally Doric,
but had already become Ionic in speech. Many of the proper
names are of Carian origin.

8 ff. 'The recorders are not to transfer lands or houses to the incoming board consisting of Apollonides and his colleagues.' That is, apparently, property which had been in the hands of the recorders for settlement, or perhaps in sequestration, was now to be turned over to the presumptive owners instead of to the new board, in order to secure an immediate disposal of these matters, even though this might in many cases be only tentative and subject to further litigation. The phrase used in l. 30 'when A. and P. were recorders' has reference to future suits, and is not inconsistent with the view that these men constituted the incoming board at the time of the decree.—16 ff. 'Any one wishing to bring suit must prefer his claim within eighteen months of the time of the decree. The dicasts shall administer the oath (to the one bringing suit) in accordance with the present law. Whatever the recorders have knowledge of (e.g. through their records) shall be valid.'—22 ff. 'If one prefers a claim after the prescribed period, the one in possession of the property shall take the oath (that is, he shall have the preference in taking the oath; cf. the use of ὀρκιότερος in the Gortyn Law-Code). The dicasts shall administer the oath, receiving a twelfth of a stater as fee, and the oath shall be taken in the presence of the claimant. Those who held the property when Apollonides and Panamyes were recorders shall be the legal possessors, unless they have disposed of it later.'—**ἀπεπέρασαν**: ἀποπιπράσκω, a rare compound.—32 ff. 'If any one wishes to annul this law or proposes a vote to this effect, his property shall be sold and dedicated to Apollo, and he himself shall be an exile forever. If his property is not worth ten staters, he himself shall be sold for transportation and never be allowed to return.'—41 ff. 'Of all the Halicarnassians any one who does not transgress these things such as they have sworn to and as is recorded in the temple of Apollo, shall be at liberty to prefer claims.'—**τῶς συμπάντων**: τῶν συμπάντων. **96.**2.

3. **Teos.** About 475 B.C. GDI 5632. Roberts 142 and pp. 336 ff. Ditt. Syll. 37, 38. Schwyzer 710. Solmsen-Fraenkel 55. Tod 23.

A 〝Οστις φάρμακα δηλητή|ρια ποιοῖ ἐπὶ Τηίοισι|ν τὸ ξυνὸν ἢ
5 ἐπ' ἰδιώτηι, κ|ἔνον ἀπόλλυσθαι καὶ α||ὐτὸν καὶ γένος τὸ κένō. |
ὅστις ἐς γῆν τὴν Τηίην κ|ωλύοι σῖτον ἐσάγεσθαι | ἢ τέχνηι ἢ μη-

10 χανῆι ἢ κατ|ὰ θάλασσαν ἢ κατ' ἤπειρο||ν ἢ ἐσαχθέντα ἀνωθεοίη,
κ͞ε͞ν|ον ἀπόλλυσθαι καὶ αὐτ|ὸν καὶ γένος τὸ κ͞ε͞ν͞δ.

B   [1, 2 fragmentary] ὅστις Τηίων ε[ἰθ]ύνωι | ἢ αἰσυ[μ]νήτηι - - -
5 -ηι ἢ || ἐπανισταῖτο τ[ῶ]ι αἰ[συμ]|νήτηι, ἀπόλλυσθαι καὶ | αὐτὸν
καὶ γένος τὸ κείν|δ. ὅστις τ͞δ λοιπ͞δ αἰσυμ|νῶν ἐν Τέωι ἢ γῆι τῆι
10 Τη||ίηι [ἀδίκ](ω)ς ἄν(δρ)[α]ς ἀ[ποκ]τ|ένει[ε] ... αρον να [εἰδ]|-
ὡς προδο[ίη ...] τὴ[ν] πό|λ[ιν καὶ γῆν] τὴν Τηί|ων ἢ τ͞δ[ς] ἄνδρας
15 [ἐν ν]||ήσωι ἢ θα[λάσσηι] τὸ | μετέ[πειτ' ἢ τὸ] ἐν | Ἀρο[ί]ηι περι-
20 πό[λιον ἢ τ͞δ] | λοιπ͞δ προδο[ίη ἢ κιξα]|λλεύοι ἢ κιξάλλας ὑπο||δέ-
χοιτο ἢ ληίζοιτο ἢ λ|ηιστὰς ὑποδέχοιτο εἰ|δὼς ἐκ γῆς τῆς Τηίης
25 ἢ [θ]|αλάτης φέροντας ἢ [τι κ]|ακὸν βōλεύοι περὶ Τ[ηί]||ων τ͞δ
ξυν͞δ εἰδὼς ἢ π[ρὸς] | Ἕλληνας ἢ πρὸς βαρβάρο|υς, ἀπόλλυσθαι
30 καὶ αὐ|τὸν καὶ γένος τὸ κ͞ε͞ν͞δ. | οἵτινες τιμōχέοντες || τὴν ἐπαρὴν μὴ
ποιήσεα|ν ἐπὶ Δυνάμει καθημέν|͞δ τὠγῶνος Ἀνθεστηρίο|ισιν καὶ
35 Ἡρακλέοισιν | καὶ Δίοισιν, ἐν τὴπαρῆ||ι ἔχεσθαι. ὃς ἂν τὰ στήλ|ας,
ἐν ἧισιν ἠπαρὴ γέγρ|απται, ἢ κατάξει ἢ φοιν|ιχήια ἐκκόψει ἢ ἀφα-
40 νέ|ας ποιήσει, κ͞ε͞ν͞ον ἀπόλ||λυσθαι καὶ αὐτὸν καὶ γ|ένος [τὸ κ͞ε͞ν͞δ].

Imprecations against evil-doers.

A 1 ff. Against those who manufacture poisons.—τὸ ξυνόν:
adv. acc. 'as a community.'—6 ff. Against those who interfere
with the importation of grain, or '(push up =) raise' the price
of what has been imported.—ἀνωθεοίη: contrasted with ποιοῖ
l. 2. See 42.6, 157c.

B 3 ff. Against those who resist the authority of the magistrates. The εὔθυνος must have been a superior official to the
ordinary εὔθυνοι or auditors. The αἰσυμνήτης is often an extraordinary official like the Roman dictator, but possibly a regular
magistrate at Teos.—8 ff. Against unfaithful and treasonable
magistrates. The restoration of ll. 8-18 is uncertain.—29 ff.
Against magistrates who fail to pronounce the imprecations.—
The τιμοῦχοι are probably the regular annual magistrates, like
the archons elsewhere.—ποιήσεαν: ποιήσειαν. 31.—Δυνάμει:
109.2.—καθημένδ τὠγῶνος κτλ.: 'during the assembly at the
Anthesteria, etc.'—35 ff. Against those who damage the steles.—
τὰ στήλας: τὰς στήλας 89.7.—κατάξει, etc.: aor. subj. 150, 176.2.

4. Chios. Fifth century B.C. GDI 5653. Roberts 149 and pp.
343 ff. Schwyzer 688. Solmsen-Fraenkel 54.

A   -ος· ἀπὸ τούτō μέχρι [τῆς] | τριόδō, ἢ 'ς Ἑρμώνοσσαν [φ]|έρει,

5 τρῆ͞ς· ἀπὸ τῆς τριόδō ἄ[χ]|ρι Ἑρμωνόσσης ἐς τὴν τρίοδ||ον ἔξς·
    ἀπὸ τούτō μέχρι τō | Δηλίō τρῆ͞ς· σύνπαντες ὄρ|οι ἐβδομήκοντα

10 πέντε. | ὅση τῶν ὄρων τούτων ἔ|σω, πᾶσα Λοφῖτις. ἢν τίς τ||ινα
    τῶν ὄρων τούτων | ἢ ἐξέληι ἢ μεθέληι ἢ ἀ|φανέα ποιήσει ἐπ' ἀδι-

15 κί|ηι τῆς πόλεως, ἑκατὸν σ|τατῆρας ὀφειλέτω κάτι||μος ἔστω, πρη-
    ξάντων δ' ὁ|ροφύλακες· ἢν δὲ μὴ πρή|ξοισιν, αὐτοὶ ὀφειλόντω|ν,

20 πρηξάντων δ' οἱ πεντε|καίδεκα τὸς ὀροφύλακας· || ἢν δὲ μὴ πρήξοι-
    σιν, ἐν ἐπ|αρῆι ἔστων.

B1 [οἱ π||ε]ντεκα[ίδεκ]|α ἐς βōλὴ[ν ἐν]|εικάντων [ἐν] | πέντ' ἡμέ-

5 ρη[ι]||σιν· τὸς δὲ κή|ρυκας διαπέ|μψαντες ἐς τ|ὰς χώρας κη[ρ]||υσ-
10 σόντων κα||ὶ διὰ τῆς πόλ|εως ἀδηνέως | γεγωνέοντε|ς, ἀποδεκνύν|-
15 τες τὴν ἡμέρ||ην, ἢν ἂν λάβω|ισιν, καὶ τὸ π|ρῆχμα προσκ|ηρυσσόν-
20 των, | ὅτι ἀμ μέλλη||ι πρήξεσθαι· | κἀγδικασάν|των τριηκοσ|ίων
25 μὴ 'λάσσο|νες ἀνηρίθε|υτοι ἐόντες.

C   [ἢν δέ τι|ς τὸς πριαμένōς ἀποκλήι||ηι] ἢ δικά[ζηται, τὸς ἀπο-
    κλ|η]ιομένōς ἢ π[ό]λις δεξαμ[έ|ν]η δικαζέσθω κἂν ὄφληι, [ὺ]||περα-

5 ποδότω· τῶι δὲ πρια[μ]||ένωι πρῆχμα ἔστω μηδέν. [ὃ]|ς ἂν τὰς
    πρήσις ἀκρατέα[ς] | ποιῆι, ἐπαράσθω κατ' αὐτ[ō] | ὁ βασιλεός,
    ἐπὴν τὰς νομ[α]|ίας ἐπαρὰς ποιῆται. ||

10 τὰς γέας καὶ τὰς οἰκί<ε>α[ς] | ἐπρίαντο· τῶν Ἀννικῶ πα[ί]-|
    δων Ἱκέσιος Ἡγεπόλιος π|εντακισχειλίων τριηκ[ο]||σίων τεσ-

15 σ[ερ]ακόντων, Ἀθ[η]||ναγ[ό]ρ[η]ς Ἡ[ροδό]τō χειλί[ω]||ν ἑπτα-
    κοσίων· Θαργελέο[ς] | Φιλοκλῆς Ζηνοδότō τὰν [Ε]||ἰάδησιν δισ-

20 χειλίων ἐ[π]||τακοσίων, Θεόπροπος κο[ὶ]||νοπίδης τὰγ Καμινήηι
    χ[ε]||ιλίων καὶ ὀκτακοσίων [ἐπ]||τά· Κήφιος τὰ ἐμ Μελαίνη[ι] |

25 Ἀκτῆι τρισχελίων ἑπτακ|οσίων ἐνενηκόντων Βία[ς] || Ἀσιῶ.

D5 ..ιον ..... | [χ]ειλίων ἑνα|κοσίων· Λεύκ|ιππος Πυθῶ τ||ὴν
    οἰκίην τ[ὴ]||ν Ἀνδρέος π[ε]||ντακοσίων π|εντηκόντων | δυῶν· Ἄσ-

10 μιος || Θεόπομπος Ἀ|γυαίō τὰν Οἴ|ωι γειλίων τ|ριηκοσίων δ|έκων
15 δυῶν· Ἱ||κεσίō τō Φίλ|ωνος Στράτ[ι|ο]ς Λυσῶ τοίκ||[ό]πεδον
    διηκ||[ο]σίων ἑνός.

Decree fixing the boundaries of a district called Lophitis, followed by provisions for its sale and a list of the purchasers.

For the Lesbian elements in the Chian dialect, see **184**. For πρήξοισιν, short-vowel subj. like ποιήσει, see also **150**. For πόλεως, see **109**.2. βασιλεός (C 8) is the earliest example of εο = ευ (**33**).

B 'In the case of a lawsuit (πρῆχμα), the Fifteen are to bring it before the council within five days and make public announcement of it in the villages and in the city.'

C 1-8. 'If any one excludes the purchasers from possession or brings suit against them, the city, taking up the cause of those that are excluded, shall sustain the suit, and, if it loses, reimburse them. The purchaser shall be free from litigation. Whoever makes the sales invalid, him shall the βασιλεύς curse, when he makes the customary imprecations.'—10 ff. 'There purchased lands and houses: from the sons of Annices, Hicesius, son of Hegepolis, for 5340 (staters), and Athenagoras, son of Herodotus, for 1700; from Thargeleus, Philocles, son of Zenodotus, the property in Euadae for 2700'; etc.—20. κοινοπίδης: καὶ Οἰνοπίδης. 94.7.

5. Erythrae. About 357 B.C. GDI 5687. Ditt. Syll. 168. Schwyzer 703.

> Ἔδοξεν τῆι βουλ[ῆι, στρατηγῶν] | γνώμη· Μαύσσωλλο[ν
> Ἐ]κατ[όμνω] | Μυλασέα, ἐπεὶ ἀνὴρ ἀγαθὸς [ἐγέ]|νετο περὶ τὴν
> 5 πόλιν τὴν Ἐρυ||θραίων, εἶναι εὐεργέτην τῆς | πόλεως καὶ πρό-
> ξενον καὶ πολί|την· καὶ ἔσπλουν καὶ ἔκπλουν | καὶ πολέμō καὶ
> 10 εἰρήνης ἀσυλε[ὶ] | κα[ὶ] ἀσπονδεί, καὶ ἀτέλειαν κα[ὶ || πρ]οεδρίην·
> ταῦτα δὲ εἶναι αὐ[τῶ]ι καὶ ἐκγόνοις. στῆσαι δὲ α[ὐ|τō κ]αὶ εἰκόνα
> χαλκῆν ἐν τῆι ἀ|[γορῆ]ι καὶ Ἀρτεμισίης εἰκόνα | [λιθί]νην ἐν τῶι
> 15 Ἀθηναίωι, καὶ || [στεφ]ανῶσαι Μαύσσωλλον μὲν | [ἐκ δαρ]εικῶν
> πεντήκοντα, Ἀρτε|[μισίην] δὲ ἐκ τριήκοντα δαρε[ι]κῶν. γράψ]αι
> 20 ταῦτα ἐ(ς) στήλη[ν | καὶ στῆσα]ι ἐς τὸ Ἀθήναιον, || [ἐπιμελη-
> θ](ῆ)ναι [δὲ τοὺς ἐξεταστάς].

Decree in honor of Maussolus, the satrap of Caria, to whose memory the famous Mausoleum was erected by his widow Artemisia.—15 ff. See 136.9.

Central Ionic

6. Naxos. Found at Delos. Seventh or early sixth century B.C. IG XII.v.2 p. xxiv. GDI 5423. Roberts 25. Schwyzer 758. Solmsen-Fraenkel 63.

> Νικάνδρη μ' ἀνέθēκεν ἑκηβόλōι ἰοχεαίρηι,
> ϙόρη Δεινο|δίκηο τō Ναξσίō, ἔξοχος ἀλήōν,
> Δεινομένεος δὲ κασιγνέτη, | Φηράξσō δ' ἄλοχος ν[ῦν].

Inscribed on an archaic statue of Artemis at Delos. ᴎ is used as *h* and *he*, and for η from ᾱ, but not for original η. See 4.6, 8*a*. In Δεινοδίκηο and ἀλήōν the endings, as the meter shows, have the value of one syllable, like εω in Homer. See 41.4. The character which appears before σ in Ναᴎσίō, etc., is probably a special form of Ξ, the words to be read Ναξσίō, ἔξσοχος, Φηράξσō, parallel to Rhod. κύλιξς, etc. (89.1).

7. Andros, inscribed at Delphi. About 425 B.C. Daux, Hesperia 18.58 ff. The fragmentary first lines of A and B are omitted here.

A 6 τόσδε σῖτ[ο|ν μ]ὲ̄ τιθέναι μὲ̄δὲ φρ[υκ]|τός ·-ἀρχεθεάρō̄ς τρὲ̄ς,
10 μ|άντιν, ἄρχοντα, κέρυκα, || αὐλετήν, κυβερνήτεν, κ[ε]|λευστήν,
π[ρ]ōιρέτεν. Δέ[ρ]|μα δὲ φερέτō κῆρυξ, αὐλε|τής, κελευστὴς ἕκασ-
15 τος | τῶν δημοσίōν, ἱερέων σῖ||τον παρεχόντων τὲ̄ι πρό|τει, μᾶζαν,
κρέα, οἶνον ὁ|πόσ[ο]ν βόλονται καὶ τἄ[λ]λα ἁρμόδια. τὰς δὲ δύο
20 ἡμ|έρας, καίοντος τō̄ σίτō, τ||ιθέτω ἕκασ(τ)ος καὶ παῖς κ|αὶ ἀνὲρ
ὀβ[ο]λὸν Α(ἱ)γιναῖον | τῆς ἡμέρ[ε̄]ς ἑκάστης· οἱ δ|ὲ ἀρχεθέαροι
25 καθιερευ|όντōν ὑπὲρ ἔμισυ ἐνί. ὑπ||αρχέτō δὲ τὰ ἐξαίρετα π[ε|λ]α-
νὸ̀ς τέσσαρας, μεταξέ̄ν|[ι]α δύο, ἱερεῖ ἐξ ἀπὸ τῆς ἐ[κ|ατ]όμβης
30 ἑκάστ[η]ς. ὁ δὲ ἰδι|[ώτη]ς φερέτω τῶν δερμάτ||[ων ὦ]ν ἂν θύσει
τὸ τρίτομ μέ|[ρος, π]λὲν χρεστερίων καὶ κ|[αθαρσ]ίων, καὶ ὅσοι
σὺν τῶ|[ι βασι]λεῖ θεαρέō̄σιν - - -

B 5 Βō̄λὲ δὲ τōν || πλεόντōν ἐς Δελ|φō[ς] hελέσθō πέν|τ' ἄνδρας καὶ
10 ὁρκō̄|σάτō. σῖτον δὲ μὲ̄ φερόντō ταύτες ōν||εκα τὲ̄ς ἀρχῆς. οἱ δ|ὲ
κύριοι ἔστω ζε̄|μιο̄σαι τὸν ἀκοσμ|έοντα μέχρι πέν|τε δραχ[μέ]ōν
ἑκάσ|τε̄ς ἐμέρε̄ς· ὃν δ' ἀν|[ζ]ημιόσōσι ἀπογρ|αψάντōν ἐν βō̄λε̄ι.

Regulations on the duties of envoys sent to Delphi.

There is great fluctuation in the use of E and H and of O and Ω. H only once = *h* (hελέσθō, B 6) vs. 26 cases of omission. H and E about equally common for the η from ᾱ, but only E for the original η (μέ, μὲ̄δέ, ἀνέρ, ἔμισυ, etc.). O always for the secondary ō. Both O and Ω for original ω.

The 3 pl. imv. φερόντō (B 9) vs. the normal Ion. καθιερευόντōν, ἀπογραψάντōν, ἔστων, can hardly be attributed to the Delphian engraver, since even at Delphi at this time the form was -ντων (see 140.3*a*, 4*a*). Still more remarkable is θεᾱρός (in ἀρχεθέαροι three times, and verbal θεαρέō̄σιν) = Att.-Ion. θεωρός. Cf. also θεαροδοκίαν in a late inscription of Tenos (IG XII.v.837).

For the titles A 8 ff. see the editor's commentary.

A 7/8. φρυκτός 'beans' (originally 'roasted'), the religious value of which is widely attested for κύαμος. Cf. also ἐπὶ φρυκτώ no. 53.15/16 with reference to the 'two beans' in drawing lots. A 25 ff. Difficult passage. 'The parts remaining (after the preceding one over half?) shall constitute four pelanoi, two metaxenia (sense here?).' The πελανός is here not a sacrificial libation, but a monetary offering, as clearly in nos. 51, 53, 88, and at Amorgos (IG XII.vii.237.21 f., 241.11). Acc. construction with ὑπαρχέτο is strange.

8. Iulis in Ceos. Last quarter of fifth century B.C. IG XII.v.593. GDI 5398. Ditt. Syll. 1218. Schwyzer 766. Solmsen-Fraenkel 64.

Οἵδε νό[μ]οι περὶ τῶγ καταφθιμ[έ]νω[ν. κατὰ | τ]άδε θά[πτ]ἐν τὸν θανόντα · ἐν ἑματίο[ις τρ|ι]σὶ λευκοῖς, στρώματι καὶ ἐνδύματι
5 [καὶ | ἐ]πιβλέματι, ἐξἐναι δὲ καὶ ἐν ἐλάσ[σ]οσ[ι, μ||]ὲ πλέονος ἀξίοις τοῖς τρισὶ ἑκατὸν δρ[α|χ]μέων. ἐχφέρἐν δὲ ἐγ κλίνηι σφηνόπο[δ]ι [κ]|αὶ μὲ καλύπτἐν, τὰ δ' ὀλ[ο]σχερ[έ]α τοῖ[ς ἑματ]||ίοις. φέρἐν δὲ οἶνον ἐπὶ τὸ σῆμα [μ]ὲ [πλέον] | τριῶν χῶν καὶ ἔλαιον
10 μὲ πλέο[ν] ἑνό[ς, τὰ δὲ ¦¦ ἀ]γγεῖα ἀποφέρεσθαι. τὸν θανό[ν]τα [φέρἐν | κ]ατακεκαλυμμένον σιωπῆι μέχρι [ἐπὶ τὸ | σ]ῆμα. προσφαγίωι [χ]ρἐσθαι κατὰ τὰ π[άτρι|α. τ]ὴγ κλίνην ἀπὸ το[ῦ] σή-[μ]ατο[ς] καὶ τ[ὰ] σ[τρώ]||ματα ἐσφέρἐν ἐνδόσε. τῆι δὲ ὑστεραί[ηι
15 ἀ||π]οραίνἐν τὴν οἰκίην ἐλεύθερον θαλά[σση|ι] πρῶτον, ἔπειτα δ[ὲ] ὑσώπωι ο[ἰκ]έτη[ν ἐμβ]||άντα · ἐπὴν δὲ διαρανθῆι, καθαρὴν ἔναι τὴν οἰκίην καὶ θύη θύἐν ἐφί[στι|α.] τὰς γυναῖκας τὰς [ἰ]ούσ[α]ς [ἐ]πὶ
20 τὸ κῆδ[ος] | ἀπιέναι προτέρας τῶν <αν>ἀνδρῶν ἀπὸ [τοῦ] || σήματος. ἐπὶ τῶι θανόντι τριηκόστ[ια μὲ | π]οιἐν. μὲ ὑποτιθέναι κύλικα ὑπὸ τὴν [κλί|ν]ην μεδὲ τὸ ὕδωρ ἐχχἐν μεδὲ τὰ καλλύ[σμα]||τα φέρἐν ἐπὶ τὸ σῆμα. ὅπου ἂν θάνηι, ἐπὴ]ν ἐ]|ξενιχθἐι, μὲ ἰέναι γυναῖ-
25 κας π[ρὸ]ς τ[ὴν οἰ]||κίην ἄλλας ἒ τὰς μιαινομένας · μια[ίνεσθ]||αι δὲ μητέρα καὶ γυναῖκα καὶ ἀδε[λφεὰς κ|α]ὶ θυγατέρας · πρὸς δὲ ταύταις μὲ π[λέον π[έ]ντε γυναικῶν, παῖδας δὲ τ[ῶν θ]υγ[ατρῶν
30 κ|ἀ]νεψιῶν, ἄλλον δὲ μ[ὲ]δένα. τοὺς μια[ινομέ||νους] λουσαμένου[ς]
- - - - - - - - - - - - - - - - ¦ [ὕδατ]ος [χ]ύσι κα[θαρ]οὺς ἔναι εω
- - - - - - - .

Burial law directed against extravagance in the funeral rites, like those enacted at Athens under Solon, and at Sparta under Lycurgus.

With two exceptions (θάνηι, διαρανθῆι) H is used only for the η from ᾱ (or from εα, as ἐπήν, θύη). See **4.6, 8a.**

3. **στρώματι** κτλ.: 'a cloth underneath the corpse, one wrapped about it, and one over it.'—7. **μὲ καλύπτεν** κτλ.: they are not to use a special covering for the bier, but cover all, the bier and the corpse, with the cloths before mentioned.—9. **χῶν**: see **112.6.**—12. **προσφαγίωι** κτλ.: 'they are to perform the sacrifice according to the ancestral custom.' By the law of Solon the sacrifice of an ox was forbidden.—13 f. The bier and the coverings like the vessels (l. 10), are to be brought home, instead of being left at the tomb.—15 f. 'The house is to be purified first with sea-water by a free man, then with hyssop by a slave.' But the restoration ὁ[ιχ]έτη[ν ἐμβ]άντα is uncertain.—20. At Athens ceremonies in honor of the dead were performed on the third, ninth, and thirtieth days. The last are expressly forbidden here.—21. Directed against certain superstitious practices, the significance of which is not clear.

West Ionic (Euboean)

9. Seventh century B.C. GDI 5292. Rev. Arch. 1902.1.41 ff.

Πύ(ρ)ρος μ' ἐποίεσεν Ἀγασιλέϝō.

On a lecythus, now in the Boston Museum of Fine Arts, the provenance of which is not stated. Probably manufactured in Boeotia by a Chalcidian potter, or at least inscribed in the Chalcidian dialect. Note the retention of intervocalic ϝ in the proper name Ἀγασιλέϝō (or here secondary ϝ as in Τλασίαϝο **105.**2b?), though not in ἐποίεσεν.

10. Cumae in Italy. Sixth century B.C. IG XIV.865, GDI 5267. Roberts 173. Schwyzer 786.

Ταταίες ἐμὶ λ|έϝυθος· hὸς δ' ἄν με κλέφσ|ει, θυφλὸς ἔσται.

11. Cumae in Italy. Sixth century B.C. IG XIV.871. GDI 5269. Roberts 177a. Schwyzer 791.

hυπὺ τἔι χλίνἔι τούτἔι Λἔνος hύπυ.

'In this niche of the tomb rests Lenos.'—**τούτἔι: 124.**— **hύπυ**: ὕπεστι.

12. Amphipolis. 357 B.C. GDI 5282. Ditt. Syll. 194. Schwyzer 799. Solmsen-Fraenkel 66. Tod 150.

Ἔδοξεν τῶι δήμωι · Φί|λωνα καὶ Στρατοκλέ|α φεόγειν Ἀμφίπο-
5 λι|ν καὶ τὴγ γῆν τὴν Ἀμφ||ιπολιτέων ἀειφυγί|ην καὶ αὐτὸς καὶ τὸς
παῖδας, καὶ ἤμ πō ἁλί|σκωνται, πάσχειν αὐτὸς ὡς πολεμίōς καὶ ||
10 νηποινεὶ τεθνάναι, | τὰ δὲ χρήματ' αὐτῶν δ|ημόσια εἶναι, τὸ δ' ἐπ|ι-
15 δέκατον ἱρὸν τō Ἀ|πόλλωνος καὶ τō Στρ||υμόνος. τὸς δὲ προστ|ά-
τας ἀναγράψαι αὐτ|ὸς ἐστήλην λιθίνην. | ἢν δέ τις τὸ ψήφισμα | ἀνα-
20 ψηφίζει ἢ καταδ||έχηται τούτōς τέχν|ηι ἢ μηχανῆι ὀτεωιōν, τὰ χρή-
ματ' αὐτō δημ|όσια ἔστω καὶ αὐτὸς φεογέτω Ἀμφίπολιν | ἀειφυ-
γίην.

When Philip captured Amphipolis in 357 B.C., he caused the
banishment of his opponents. Cf. Diod. 16.8. Among this number
were the two men against whom this decree was enacted. Amphipolis was a colony of Athens, but the population was mixed.
Cf. Thuc. 4.102 ff. At this time evidently the Chalcidian element
predominated.

    3. **φεόγειν**: cf. φεογέτω, l. 24. **33.**—19. **ἀναψηφίζει**: 'proposes
to repeal.' ει for ηι, **39a.**

    13. Eretria. (A) End of fifth century B.C., (B) middle of
fourth century B.C. GDI 5308. Ditt. Syll. 105, 106. Schwyzer
804. Tod 82.

A   Θεοί. | Ἔδοξεν τεῖ βōλῆι Ἡγέλοχον | τὸν Ταραντῖνον πρόξενον
5 εἶ|ναι καὶ εὐεργέτην καὶ αὐτὸν || κ[α]ὶ παῖδας καὶ σίτηριν εἶνα|ι καὶ
αὐτῶι καὶ παιριν, ὅταν ἐ|[π]ιδημέωριν, καὶ ἀτελέην καὶ | προεδρίην
10 ἐς τὸς ἀγῶνας ὡς σ|υνελευθερώραντι τὴμ πόλιν || ἀπ' Ἀθηνάων.
B   Ἔδοξεν τεῖ βουλεῖ καὶ τοῖ δήμοι | Ἡράκλειτον τὸν Ταραντῖνον |.
πρόξενον εἶναι Ἐρετριέων αὐ|τὸν καὶ ἐκγόνους, εἶναι δὲ αὐτοῖ ||
προεδρίην καὶ σίτηριν καὶ αὐ|τοῖ καὶ παιριν, ὅσον ἂν χρόνον |
ἐπιδημέωριν, καὶ τὰ ἄλλα, καθ|άπερ τοῖς ἄλλοις προξένοις.

This and no. 14 are in the Eretrian variety of Euboean, for
which see **187.**

A. Ships of Tarentum formed part of the Peloponnesian fleet
which defeated the Athenians off Eretria in 411 B.C. and so led
to the Athenian loss of Eretria. Cf. Thuc. 8.91, 95. It is in gra-
titude for this that Hegelochus of Tarentum and his sons are
honored in this decree.

B. This decree is later than A, but was inscribed on the same stone, because both recipients of honor are from Tarentum, and possibly relatives.

14. Oropus. 411-402, or 386-377 B.C. IG VII.235. GDI 5339 Ditt. Syll. 1004. Schwyzer 811. Solmsen-Fraenkel 67.

Θεοί. | Τὸν ἱερέα τοῦ Ἀμφιαράου φοιτᾶν εἰς τὸ ἱερό|ν, ἐπειδὰν χειμὼν παρέλθει, μέχρι ἀρότου ὥρ|ης μὴ πλέον διαλείποντα ἢ τρεῖς
5 ἡμέρας καὶ || μένειν ἐν τοῖ ἱεροῖ μὴ ἔλαττον ἢ δέκα ἡμέρα|ς τοῦ μηνὸς ἐκ[ά]στō. καὶ ἐπαναγκάζειν τὸν ν|εωκόρον τοῦ τε ἱεροῦ ἐπιμελεῖσθαι κατὰ τὸ|ν νόμον καὶ τῶν ἀφικνēμένων εἰς τὸ ἱερόν.|
10 ἂν δέ τις ἀδικεῖ ἐν τοῖ ἱεροῖ ἢ ξένος ἢ δημότ||ης, ζημιούτω ὁ ἱερεὺς μέχρι πέντε δραχμέων | κυρίως καὶ ἐνέχυρα λαμβανέτω τοῦ ἐζημιωμ|ένου · ἂν δ᾽ ἐκτίνει τὸ ἀργύριον, παρεόντος τō | ἱερέος ἐμβαλέτω εἰς τὸν θησαυρόν. δικάζει|ν δὲ τὸν ἱερέα, ἄν τις ἰδίει ἀδικηθεῖ
15 ἢ τῶν ξέ||νων ἢ τῶν δημοτέων ἐν τοῖ ἱεροῖ, μέχρι τριῶν | δραχμέων, τὰ δὲ μέζονα, ἥχοι ἑκάστοις αἱ δίκ|αι ἐν τοῖς νόμοις εἰρῆται, ἐντōθα γινέσθων. | προσκαλεῖσθαι δὲ καὶ αὐθημερὸν περὶ τῶν ἐ|ν τοῖ ἱεροῖ
20 ἀδικίων · ἂν δὲ ὁ ἀντίδικος μὴ συνχ||ωρεῖ, εἰς τὴν ὑστέρην ἡ δίκη τελείσθω. ἐπαρ|χὴν δὲ διδοῦν τὸμ μέλλοντα θεραπεύεσθαι ὑ|πὸ τοῦ θεοῦ μὴ ἔλαττον ἐννέ᾽ ὀβολοὺς δοκίμου ἀργ|υρίου καὶ ἐμβάλλειν εἰς τὸν θησαυρὸν παρε|όντος τοῦ νεωκόρου - - - - - - - - - - - - - - ||
25 - - - - - κατεύχεσθαι δὲ τῶν ἱερῶν καὶ ἐπ|ὶ τὸν βωμὸν ἐπιτιθεῖν, ὅταν παρεῖ, τὸν ἱερέα, | ὅταν δὲ μὴ παρεῖ, τὸν θύοντα, καὶ τεῖ θυσίει α|ὐτὸν ἑαυτοῖ κατεύχεσθαι ἕκαστον, τῶν δὲ δη|μορίων τὸν ἱερέα.
30 τῶν δὲ θυομένων ἐν τοῖ ἱε||ροῖ πάντων τὸ δέρμα - - - - - - - -. θύειν δὲ ἐξ|εῖν ἅπαν ὅτι ἂν βόληται ἕκαστος · τῶν δὲ κρεῶ|ν μὴ εἶναι ἐκφορὴν ἔξω τοῦ τεμένεος. τοῖ δὲ | ἱερεῖ διδοῦν τōς θύοντας ἀπὸ τοῦ ἱερήου ἐκ|άστō τὸν ὦμον, πλὴν ὅταν ἡ ἑορτὴ εῖ · τότε δὲ
35 ἀπ||ὸ τῶν δημορίων λαμβανέτω ὦμον ἀφ᾽ ἑκάστου | τοῦ ἱερήου. ἐγκαθεύδειν δὲ τὸν δειόμενο|ν - | υαυ - - - - - - - - - - - - - - - - - πειθόμ|ενον τοῖς νόμοις.
40 τὸ ὄνομα τοῦ ἐγκαθεύδον||τος, ὅταν ἐμβάλλει τὸ ἀργύριον, γράφεσθαι τ|ὸν νεωκόρον καὶ αὐτοῦ καὶ τῆς πόλεος καὶ ἐκ|τιθεῖν ἐν τοῖ ἱεροῖ γράφοντα ἐν πετεύροι σ|κοπεῖν τοῖ βολομένοι. ἐν δὲ τοῖ κοι-
45 μητηρίο|ι καθεύδειν χωρὶς μὲν τὸς ἄνδρας, χωρὶς || δὲ τὰς γυναῖκας, τοὺς μὲν ἄνδρας ἐν τοῖ πρὸ ἠ|ōς τοῦ βωμοῦ, τὰς δὲ γυναῖκας ἐν τοῖ πρὸ ἑσπέ|[ρης] . . . . τὸ κοιμ]ητήριον τοὺς ἐν|[καθ-εύδοντας . . . .

Regulations of the temple of Amphiaraus at Oropus. Oropus seems to have been an Eretrian possession before it passed into the hands of the Thebans in the sixth century, and preserved the Eretrian dialect throughout the Boeotian and the subsequent Athenian domination. But from the end of the fourth century the inscriptions are in Attic, a few in Boeotian.

1 ff. The priest evidently passed the winters in the town, leaving the temple entirely in the charge of the custodian. But with the end of winter, when visitors became more frequent, he was expected to go to the temple regularly, never missing more than three days at a time and remaining there at least ten days each month. He was to see to it that the custodian took proper care of the temple and its visitors.—8. ἀφικνεμένων. 158.— 9 ff. 'If any one commits sacrilege in the temple, the priest shall have the right to impose a fine up to the sum of five drachmas and take pledges of the one penalized. If such a one offers the money, he must deposit it in the treasury in the presence of the priest. If any one suffers a private wrong in the temple, the priest shall decide matters of no more than three drachmas, but the more important cases shall be tried before the proper courts. The summons for wrongs done in the temple shall be made on the same day, but if the opponent does not agree, the case may go over till the next day.'—16. ἐκάστοις: 'for the several persons.'—17. εἴρηται: 43.—ἐντõθα: 34a, 124.—19. ἀδικίων: ἀδίκιον=ἀδίκημα.—21 ff. 'The one who is to be treated by the god shall pay a fee of not less than nine obols of current money (no bad coin was to be palmed off) and put it in the treasury in the presence of the custodian.'—ἐννέ' ὀβολούς is crowded into a space where a shorter word had been erased, presumably δραχμήν. Since the law was first inscribed, the amount of the fee had been raised, and at the same time another provision, which followed after νεωκόρου in l. 24, had been abrogated and erased.—25 ff. 'The priest shall make the prayers and place the victims on the altar, if he is present, but, if he is not present, the one who gives the offering. At the festival each shall make his own prayer, but the priest shall make the prayers for the sacrifices in behalf of the state, and he shall receive the skin of all the victims.'—30 ff. θύειν δὲ ἐξεῖν κτλ.: there was no

restriction as to the kind of victims to be offered, such as is often made in temple regulations, but in any case the flesh was not to be carried off.—31. **βόληται**: so, not βόληται (βούληται), for an Eretrian inscription of later date, which never has ο = ου, reads βόληται, βολόμενον.—32 ff. τοῖ δὲ ἱερεῖ κτλ.: 'the priest is to have the shoulder of each victim, except when there is a festival, and then only from the victims offered for the state.'— 33. **ἱερήου**: ἱερήιου. 37, 164.1.—36. **δειόμενον**: δεόμενον. 9.1.— 39 ff. 'The custodian is to inscribe the name of each one who consults the oracle, when he has paid his money, and place it on a tablet in the shrine so that any one who wishes may see it.'— **ἐγκαθεύδοντος**: as elsewhere, those wishing to consult the oracle went to sleep in a room of the temple assigned for this purpose (see following), and received the oracle in a dream.—**πέτευρον**: 135.5a.—43 ff. **ἐν δὲ τοῖ κοιμητηρίοι** κτλ.: 'the men and women are to lie in separate places, the men to the east of the altar, the women to the west.'—46. **ἦ͂ς**: 41.4b.—**hεσπέρης**: hε designated by h, as in no. 6, etc. 4.6.

Arcadian

15. Sixth or early fifth century B.C. IG V.ii.554. GDI 373. Ditt. Syll. 1034. Roberts 237a. Schwyzer 676.

Καμὸ ὐνέθυσε ταῖ Κόρϝαι.

Dedication inscribed on a bronze cymbal, which, according to the more probable of two varying reports, was found near the modern Dimitsana in Arcadia. Formerly read Κάμουν ἔθυσε κτλ. and ascribed to Thessalian, later as Καμὸ ὖν ἔθυσε. But the use of ὐνέθυσε = ἀνέθηκε is confirmed by a later dedication reading Φαυλέας ἀνέθυσε τοῖ Πανί, in which the earlier ὐν- (6, 22) is replaced by ἀνα-.

16. Cleitor or Lusoi? Sixth or early fifth century B.C. D. Robinson, CP 38.191 ff. Beattie, CQ 41.66 ff.

εἰ γυ]νὰ ϝέσε̄τοι ζτε̄ραῖον λο͂πος, | [ἱερὸ]ν ἔναι ταῖ Δάματρι Θεσμοφόροι. | [εἰ δὲ] μὲ̄ ὐνιερόσει, δῡμενὲς ἔασα ἐπὲ ϝέργο͂ |
5 [....]ς ζ' ἐξόλοιτυ, κὰ ὄζις τότε δαμιοϝοργε͂ || [ἀφάε]σται δαρχμὰς τριάκοντα. εἰ δὲ μὲ̄ ἀφάε̄τοι, | [ὀφλὲν] τὰν ἀσέβειαν. ἐχε͂ ὅδε χῦρος δέχο ϝέτεα. ἔνα[ι] | [......] τόδε.

Bronze tablet, probably the continuation (with the conclusion) of others, constituting a series of temple regulations. There are several serious difficulties, and the following translation is in part only tentative. 'If a woman wears a brightly colored robe, it shall be dedicated to Demeter Thesmophoros. If she does not dedicate it, being ill disposed in respect to the rite (?), let her perish, and whoever is demiurgus at the time shall pay thirty drachmas. If he does not pay, he shall be charged with the impiety. Let this (sc. νόμος) have validity for ten years. - - -'

1. The first (mutilated) letter is just above the second of l. 2, so that five letters may be missing or four with a slight inset,— hardly room for εἰκὰν γυ as read by Beattie.—Ϝέσετοι: 3 sg. aor. subj. without ἄν (150, 174).—ζτεραῖον: with freak spelling (cf. τζετραχάτιαι, no. 70) probably cognate with ζειρόν · ποικίλον and other glosses in Hesych. Cf. the forbidden λωπίον ποικίλον, Schwyzer 429.—3. ὑνιερόσει: probably 3 sg. aor. opt. (152.4).— δῦμενές = δυσμενής with normal development of σμ (76) instead of the usual restored δυσ-.—ἔασα: 163.8.—ΕΠΕϜΕΡΓΟ: perhaps to be read ἐπὲ Ϝέργō = ἐπὲς τοῖ ἔργοι, no. 19.54, with assimilation of the final ς and simplification of the double consonant, like Cypr. τᾶ Ϝανάσας = τᾶς Ϝανάσσας (97.2; cf. also Arc. τὰ Ϝάδω = τὰν Ϝάδω) and Ϝέργō with original genitive instead of the usual Arc. dative construction and archaic absence of the article (122a).—4. ζ': could be for τε with ζ as in ὄζις = ὅτις (68.3), but this, though the preceding word to be supplied is quite uncertain, seems to make no sense.—ἐξόλοιτυ: opt. in prescription, like Cypr. δώχοι (175).—δαμιοϜοργē̃: pres. subj. without ἄν (149, 174). Or read τότ' ἐδαμιοϜόργē̃, imperf. indic.? This is the first example of Ϝ attested in the various forms of this title, for which see 167.—5. ἀφάε]σται: probable restoration in view of the end of the line. στ = σθ though not previously attested in this dialect (85.1).—ἀφάετοι: pres. subj. mid. without ἄν (174) of an otherwise unknown ἀφάομαι, here meaning clearly 'pay', probably compound of ἄομαι 'satiate' (cf. ἄται · πληροῦται Hesych.), with development of 'fill' to 'fulfil' and 'pay,' as in πληρόω.—6. ἐχē̃: 3 sg. subj. in independent use as rarely in Elean (174).—At the end of the line probably ἔνα[ι], but the restoration of the first word in next line is wholly dubious.

17. Mantinea. Fifth century B.C. IG V.ii.262. Schwyzer 661. Solmsen-Fraenkel 5. Comparetti, Annuario 1.1 ff. Buck, CP 20.136 ff. For ν, which is transcribed σ, see 4.4, 68.3.

10 [Ϝō]φλέασι οἴδε ἰν Ἀλέαν· | [ll. 2-9 proper names] || Ἄδραν-
τος, | Ἀντιλαΐδας, | Βōθις, | Ἠσκλαρος, | Θέμανδρος. | ὀσέοι ἄν
15 χρεστέριον κακρίνē || ē γνōσίαι κακριθέē τōν χρεμάτōν, | πὲ τοῖς
Ϝοικιάται(ς) τᾶς θεō ἔναι, κὰ Ϝοικίας δάσασσθαι τὰς ἄν ōδ' ἐάσας. |
εἰ τοῖς Ϝōφλēκόσι ἐπὶ τοῖδ' ἐδικάσαμε[ν], | ἄ τε θεὸς κὰς οἰ δι-
20 κασσταὶ, ἀπυσεδομίν[ος] || τōν χρεμάτōν τὸ λάχος, ἀπεχομίνος |
κὰ τōρρέντερον γένος ἔναι | ἄματα πάντα ἀπὺ τοῖ ἱεροῖ, ἵλαον
ἔναι. | εἰ δ' ἄλλα σις ἔατοι κὰ τōνν[υ], ἰνμενφὲς ἔναι. | εὐχōλὰ
25 [δ'] ἄδε ἔ[σ]ετοι τοῖ ἀ[- - -]· || εἴ σις ἰν το(ῖ) ἱεροῖ τōν τότ[ε
ἀπυθανόντōν] | φονές ἐστι, εἴσ' αὐτός εἴσε [τōν ἐσγόνōν] |ˊ σις
κὰ τōρρέντερον, εἴσε τ[ōν ἀνδρōν] εἴσε τᾶς φαρθένō, ἰνμενφ[ὲς
30 ἔναι κὰ] | τὸ χρεστέριον· εἰ δὲ μὲ, ἵλαο[ν ἔναι]. || εἰ (Θ)έμανδρος
φονές ἐσστ[ι εἴσε] | τōν ἀνδρōν εἴσε τᾶς φαρθέν[ō] | τōν τότε
ἀπυθανόντōν ἰν [τοῖ ἱεροῖ] | κὰς μὲ προσσθαγενὲς τō Ϝέρ[γō] |
35 τō τότε ἔο[ν]τος, ἰνμονφον θε[οῖ ἔναι]. || εἰ δὲ προσσ(θ)αγενὲς
τō Ϝέργ[ō], | κὰς μὲ φονὲς, ἵλαον ἔναι.

Judgment against certain persons guilty of sacrilege toward Athena Alea, whose temple had been made the scene of a bloody fray. Most of the difficulties in the reading and interpretation have been cleared up, but some points are still uncertain.

1. 'The following have been condemned to pay a penalty to the temple of Alea.' Cf., with the aorist, ἡεκοτὸν δαρχμὰς ὀφλὲν ἰν δᾶμον, no. 18.4, and for the whole episode οἴδε ὦφλον Δηλίων ἀσεβείας - - - - - , τὸ τίμημα τὸ ἐπιγεγραμμένον καὶ ἀειφυγία, ὅτι ἐκ τοῦ ἱεροῦ τοῦ Ἀπόλλωνος τοῦ Δηλίου ἦγον τοὺς Ἀμφικτύονας καὶ ἔτυπτον, IG II².1635.134 ff.—14 ff. 'In the case of any one whom the oracle has condemned or who by judicial process has been condemned to forfeit his property, this together with the serfs shall belong to the goddess, and the houses which he may possess here (?) shall be distributed (i.e., confiscated and disposed of).'— 14. κακρίνē: κατακρίνη. 89.7, 95.—15. γνōσία: Att. γνῶσις in its legal sense.—17. τὰς ἄν ōδ' ἐάσας: ἄν with pple., Smyth 1846b, Kühner-Gerth I. 242. Some read ἄνōδ' 'above,' with various interpretations of its significance here.—18 ff. 'Inasmuch as we,

the goddess and the judges, have passed judgment upon the guilty parties as follows, namely that, having given up their inheritance, they shall forever be excluded from the temple, in the male line, it shall be well (propitious). But if any one permits anything else, contrary to these things, it shall be impious.'—22. κὰ τόρρέντερον: κατὰ τὸ ἀρρέντερον. 94.1, 165.1.—22. ἄματα πάντα: a formulaic expression, Hom. ἤματα πάντα, retained here in the imprecation, although ἀμέρα is the ordinary prose word for 'day' in Arcadian as elsewhere. Similarly νόμος ἱερὸς ἰν ἄματα πάντα in a Tegean inscription.—24 ff. 'The following shall be the imprecation upon the - -. If any one (present) in the temple is a murderer of those who perished at that time, either himself or any one of his descendants in the male line (that is, if any one of these present in the temple), (a murderer) of either the men or the maiden, it shall be impious in the eyes of the oracle; if not, it shall be propitious. If Themander is a murderer of either the men or the maiden who perished at that time in the temple, and not (merely, as he claims) present previously to (?) the deed of violence which took place then, he shall be held impious; but if (merely) present previously to (?) the deed, and not a murderer, it shall be propitious.' The reading and interpretation of the last few lines is much disputed.

18. Tegea. About 400 B.C. IG V.ii.3. Schwyzer 654. Solmsen-Fraenkel 1. Vollgraff, BCH 70.617 ff. Alphabet transitional; E = ε̄, O = ō, Ⴆ = h; Ion. Ⴈ = ξ, X = χ.

Τὸν ἱιερὲν πέντε καὶ εἴκοσι οἷς νέμεν καὶ ζεῦγο|ς καὶ αἶγα· εἰ δ' ἂν καταλλάσσε̄, ἰνφορβισμὸν ἔναι· τ|ὸν ἱιερομνάμονα ἰνφορβίεν· εἰ δ' ἂν λευτον μὲ̄ ἰνφ|ορβίε̄, ηεκοτὸν δαρχμὰς ὀφλὲν ἰν δᾶμον καὶ
5 κάταρ||Ϝον ἔναι.—τὸν ἱιεροθύταν νέμεν ἰν 'Αλέαι ὅτι ἂν ἀ|σκε̄θὲς ε̄̓· τὰ δ' ἀνασκε̄θέα ἰνφορβίεν· μὲ̄δ' ἐσπερᾶσα|ι πὰρ ἂν λέγε̄ ἱιερο-θυτές· εἰ δ' ἂν ἐσπεράσε̄, δυόδεκ|ο δαρχμὰς ὀφλὲν ἰν δᾶμον.—τᾶς τριπαναγόρσιος τ|ὰς ὑστέρας τρὶς ἀμέρας νέμεν ὅτι ηὰν βόλε̄τοι ὃς
10 με̄̓||ἰν τοῖ περιχόροι. εἰ δ' ἂν ἰν τοῖ περιχόροι, ἰνφο|ρβίεν.—ἰν 'Αλέαι μὲ̄ νέμεν μέτε ξένον μέτε Ϝαστὸν | εἰ μὲ̄ ἐπὶ θοίναν ηίκοντα· τοῖ δὲ ξένοι καταγομέν|οι ἐξε̄ναι ἀμέραν καὶ νύκτα νέμεν ἐπιζύγιον· 15 εἰ δ' | ἂν πὰρ τάνυ νέμε̄, τὸ μὲν μέζον πρόβατον δαρχμὰν ὀ||φλέν,

τὸ δὲ μεῖον ἰνφορβίεν.—τὰ hιερὰ πρόβατα μὲ | νέμεν ἰν 'Αλέαι
πλὸς ἀμέραυ καὶ νυκτός, εἰκ ἂν διε|λαυνόμενα τύχε̄· εἰ δ' ἂν νέμε̄,
δαρχμὰν ὀφλὲν τὸ πρό|βατον Ϝέκαστον τὸ μέζον, τὸν δὲ μειόνο̄ν
20 προβάτο̄|ν ὀδελὸν Ϝέκαστον, τᾶν συο̄ν δαρχμὰν Ϝεκάσταυ, ε[ἰ] || μὲ
παρhεταξαμένος τὸς πεντε̄κοντα ε̄ τὸς τριακα|σίος —εἰκ ἐπὶ δο̄μα
πῦρ ἐποίσε̄, δυόδεκο δαρχμὰς | ὀφλέν, τὸ μὲν ἔμισυ ταῖ θεοῖ, τὸ
δ' ἔμισυ τοῖς hιερο|μνάμονσι.—εἰκ ἂν παραμαξεύε̄ θύσθεν τᾶς
25 κελε[ύθ]|ο̄ τᾶς κακειμέναυ κὰτ 'Αλέαν, τρὶς ὀδελὸς ὀφλὲ[ν ἀν]||τὶ
Ϝεκάσταυ, τὸ μὲν hέμισυ ταῖ θεοῖ, τὸ δ' ἔμισ[υ τοῖ]|ς hιερομνάμον-
σι.—Ταῖ παναγόρσι τὸς hιερ[ομνάμ]|ονας ἀρτύεν τὰ ἰν ταῖς ἰνπο-
λαῖς πάντα τ[α .... —τ]ὸς δαμιοργὸς τὸν κόπρον τὸν ἀπυδόσμ[ιον
30 ἐξάγεν] ταῖ hεβδόμαι το̄ Λεσχανασίο̄ μενός· [εἰ δὲ μέ, δαρχ||μὰ]ν
ὀφλέν. τὸν Παναγόρσιον με̄να [31-35 only a few words left.]

Regulations of the temple of Athena Alea. The first five paragraphs, ll. 1-20, deal with the rights of pasturage in Alea, the
district in which the temple was situated and which was included
in the temple property. The temple officials mentioned are the
hieromnemon, the chief administrator of the affairs of the
temple (also, in the plural, the board of administrators), the
priest, and the hierothytes, a minor official charged with the
technical details of the sacrifice, though in some places this
title came to be one of high rank. The Fifty and the Three
Hundred were, doubtless, civic bodies.

The critical words are ἰνφορβίεν, ἰνφορβισμόν, plainly connected
with φέρβω 'feed,' φορβή 'fodder,' φορβεία 'halter.' The meaning
is not 'seize, seizure,' as the first editor, but 'impose a pasture
tax,' etc. Hesychius has ἐμφόρβιον· τελώνημα, which is parallel
to ἐνοίκιον 'house-rent,' ἐλλιμένιον 'harbor-dues,' etc. From this
would be derived ἰνφορβίεν 'impose a pasture tax,' and from this
again, as if from -ίζω, ἰνφορβισμός 'the imposition of a pasture
tax.' Cf. Solmsen, KZ 34.437 ff.

2. εἰ δ' ἂν καταλλάσσε̄: 'if he makes any change (substitution?).'—3. λευτον: meaning and etymology obscure.—5 ff. τὸν
hιεροθύταν κτλ.: 'the hierothytes may pasture in Alea animals
without blemish (and so suitable for the sacrifice), but for those
not unblemished (and so suitable only for personal use) one
shall impose a pasture tax. He shall not go beyond what he de-

clares in his function of hierothytes.' That is, his official statement as to the condition of the animals is final.—7. πὰρ ἄν: πὰρ ἀ ἄν. 58d.—ἱεροθυτές: ἱεροθυτέων. 78, 157.9. hάν: ἄν. 58d.—ὅς μέ: used like ὅσον μή.—20. 'Unless the Fifty or the Three Hundred approve.' Acc. abs. construction. 173.—21. δῶμα: 'temple.'— ἐποίσε: aor. subj. to fut. οἴσω, cf. Hom. οἰσέμεναι, Hdt. ἀνοῖσαι. For the absence of ἄν see 174.—23 ff. Meaning uncertain, but probably 'If one drives in a wagon outside of the high road leading through Alea, one shall pay a fine of three obols for each (wagon),' etc.—θύσθεν: adv. from *θύρ-σθεν=θύραζε, ἔξωθεν. 133.1.—κακειμέναυ: κατακειμένης. 89.7, 95.—26 ff. The officials are to make all arrangements for the market, which was held at ancient festivals as at our modern fairs. Cf. Ditt. Syll. 736.99 ff.—28. ἀπυδόσμ[ιον]: adjective derived from a now quotable ἀπυδοσμός 'payment' (no. 21.39) = ἀπόδοσις, but here probably meaning 'for sale.'

19. Tegea. Fourth century B.C. IG V.ii.6. GDI 1222. Schwyzer 656. Solmsen-Fraenkel 4. Kalén, Strena phil. Upsal. 1922, 187 ff. Many smooth breathings are debatable.

πε - - - - - - - - - - - - φι.λο. | εἰκ ἄν τι γίνητοι τοῖς ἐργώναις
τοῖς ἰν τοῖ αὐτοῖ | ἔργοι, ὅσα περὶ τὸ ἔργον· ἀπυέσθω δὲ ὁ ἀδική-
5 μενος | τὸν ἀδικέντα ἰν ἀμέραις τρισὶ ἀπὺ ταῖ ἄν τὸ ἀδί||κημα γένη-
τοι, ὕστερον δὲ μή· καὶ ὅτι ἀγ κρίνωνσι | οἱ ἐσδοτῆρες, κύριον ἔστω.
—εἰ δὲ πόλεμος δια|κωλύσει τι τῶν ἔργων τῶν ἐσδοθέντων ἢ τῶν |
ἠργασμένων τι φθέραι, οἱ τριακάσιοι διαγνόντω | τί δεῖ γίνεσθαι·
10 οἱ δὲ στραταγοὶ πόσοδομ ποέντω, || εἰκ ἄν δέατοί σφεις πόλεμος
ἦναι ὁ κωλύων ἢ ἐ|φθορκὼς τὰ ἔργα, λαφυροπωλίου ἐόντος κατὺ
τᾶς | πόλιος. εἰ δὲ τι(ς) ἐργωνήσας μὴ ἰγκεχηρήκοι τοῖς | ἔργοις, ὁ
δὲ πόλεμος διακωλύοι, ἀπυδόας [τ]ὸ ἀργύριον, | τὸ ἂν λελαβηκὼς
15 τυγχάνη, ἀφεώσθω τῶ ἔργω, || εἰκ ἂν κελεύωνσι οἱ ἐσδοτῆρες.—
εἰ δ' ἄ[ν] τις ἐπι|συνίστατοι ταῖς ἐσδόσεσι τῶν ἔργων ἢ λυμαίνη|τοι
κὰτ εἰ δέ τινα τρόπον φθήρων, ζαμιόντω | οἱ ἐσδοτῆρες, ὅσαι ἄν
δέατοί σφεις ζαμίαι, καὶ | ἀγκαρυσ[σόν]τω ἰν ἐπίκρισιν καὶ ἰνα-
20 γόντω || ἰν δικαστήριον τὸ γινόμενον τοῖ πλήθι τᾶς | ζαμίαυ.—
μὴ ἐξέστω δὲ μηδὲ κοινᾶνας γενέσθαι | πλέον ἢ δύο ἐπὶ μηδενὶ
τῶν ἔργων· εἰ δὲ μή, ὀφλέτω | ἕκαστος πεντήκοντα δαρχμάς,
ἐπελασάσθων | δὲ οἱ ἁλιασταί· ἰμφαῖνεν δὲ τὸμ βολόμενον ἐπὶ
25 τοῖ || ἡμίσσοι τᾶς ζαμίαυ. χὰ τὰ αὐτὰ δὲ καὶ εἰκ ἄν [τ]ις | πλέον

ἢ δύο ἔργα ἔχη τῶν ἱερῶν ἢ τῶν δαμ[ο]σίων | κὰτ εἰ δέ τινα τρό-
πον, ὅτινι ἂμ μὴ οἱ ἁλιαστα[ὶ] | παρετάξωνσι ὁμοθυμαδὸν πάντες,
ζαμιώ[σ]θω | καθ' ἕκαστον τῶν πλεόνων ἔργων κατὺ μῆνα || πεν- 30
τήκοντα δαρχμαῖς, μέστ' ἂν ἐπισ[χῆ πάντα] | τὰ ἔργα τὰ πλέονα.
—εἰ δ' ἄν τι[ς ἰνδ]ίκητοι τῶν | περὶ τὰ ἔργα συ[γγεγραμμένων]
κὰτ εἰ δέ τι, μη||[δὲν δεκέσθω τᾶς τιμα]ῦ· εἰ δὲ μή, μή οἱ ἔστω ἴν-
δικον μηδέποθι ἀλλ' ἢ ἰν Τεγέαι· εἰ δ' ἂν ἰνδικάζητοι, || ἀπυτει- 35
σάτω τὸ χρέος διπλάσιον τὸ ἂν δικάζητοι· | ἔστω δὲ καὶ τωνὶ τῶ
ἐπιζαμίω ὁ αὐτὸς ἴγγυος ὅπερ | καὶ τῶ ἔργω ἧς ἰν ἔστεισιν. —εἰ
δ' ἄν τις ἐργωνήσας | ἔργον τι ποσκατυβλάψη τι ἄλλυ τῶν ὑπαρ-
χόντων | ἔργων εἴτε ἱερὸν εἴτε δαμόσιον εἴτε ἴδιον || πὰρ τὰν 40
σύγγραφον τᾶς ἐσδοκαῦ, ἀπυκαθιστάτω | τὸ κατυβλαφθὲν τοῖς
ἰδίοις ἀναλώμασιν μὴ ἧσσον | ἢ ὑπάρχε ἰν τοῖ χρόνοι τᾶς ἐργωνίαυ·
εἰ δ' ἂμ μὴ | κατυστάση, τὰ ἐπιζάμια ἀπυτειέτω, κὰ τάπερ | ἐπὶ τοῖς
ἄλλοις ἔργοις τοῖς ὑπεραμέροις τέτακτοι. || — εἰ δ' ἄν τις τῶν 45
ἐργωνᾶν ἢ τῶν ἐργαζομένων | ἐπηρειάζεν δέατοι ἰν τὰ ἔργα ἢ ἀπει-
θῆναι τοῖς | ἐπιμελομένοις ἢ κατυφρονῆναι τῶν ἐπιζαμίων | τῶν
τεταγμένων, κύριοι ἐόντω οἱ ἐσδοτῆρες | τὸμ μὲν ἐργάταν ἐσδέλ-
λοντες ἐς τοῖ ἔργοι, || τὸν δὲ ἐργώνάν ζαμιόντες ἰν ἐπίκρισιγ κὰ τά- 50
περ | τὸς ἐπισυνισταμένος ταῖς ἐσδοκαῖς γέγραπ[τ]οι. | — ὅτι δ'
ἂν ἐσδοθῆ ἔργον εἴτε ἱερὸν εἴτε δαμόσι[ον], | ὑπάρχεν τὰγ κοινὰν
σύγγραφον ταν[ν]ὶ κυρί[αν] | πὸς ταῖ ἐπὲς τοῖ ἔργοι γεγραμμέν[αι
συ]γγράφ[οι].

Regulations governing building-contracts.

1 ff. 'if any trouble arises between the contractors on the
same work, as regards the work.'—4. **ἀπὺ ταῖ**: 'from the time
when,' relative use of the article, as in l. 14, etc. See **126**.—6 ff.
'If war should interrupt any of the works contracted for or
should destroy any of those completed.' For διακωλύσει see
152.4.—9 ff. 'The στραταγοί shall furnish revenue, if it seems
to them that it is war that is hindering or has destroyed the
works, the city having been subjected to a sale of booty.'—
12 ff. 'But if any one who has made a contract has not begun
on the works and war interrupts, he shall return whatever
money he may have received and be excused from the work,
if those giving out the contracts so order.'—15 ff. 'If any one
makes opposition to the allotments of the works or does an injury

in any way,' etc.—**κὰτ εἰ δέ τινα**: εἰ δέ τις, detached from verbal phrases, has come to be used independently in the sense of a simple indefinite, as is sometimes εἴ τις in Attic (e.g., Thuc. 7.21.5) Cf. κὰτ εἰ δέ τι l. 32.—18. **ὅσαι** κτλ.: 'with whatever penalty seems best to them.'—20. 'to the court which is constituted to suit the amount of the penalty.'—**πλήθι**:=πλήθει, like ἔτι = ἔτει, etc., on the reverse side of this same tablet. 9.5.—21 ff. 'No more than two partners for any one piece of work, and no contractor to have more than two pieces of work without the unanimous consent of the heliasts.'—24. **ἰμφαῖνεν** κτλ.: 'any one who wishes may be informer, receiving half the fine as a reward.'—30. 'until all the excess pieces of work cease.'—31 ff. Restorations uncertain, but perhaps 'If any one is a litigant concerning any of the terms of the contract, he shall receive no pay; otherwise he shall not have the right of trial elsewhere than at Tegea; and if suit is brought against him, he shall pay double the amount for which the suit is brought. And the same person who was (the surety) for the work, shall be surety for this fine, for its payment.' ἰν ἔστεισιν refers back to ἐπιζαμίω, not to ἔργω. ἴνδικος, like Cret. ἔνδικος, is used impersonally with the dative of the person involved in the suit. For ἰνδικάζητοι, cf. Aenian. τοῖς ἐνδικαζομένοις 'the litigants' GDI 1432a, and Delph. ἐνδικαζόμενοι 'subjected to suit' GDI 1795.—37 ff. 'If a contractor injures any of the existing works contrary to the terms of the contract, he must at his own expense put it in as good condition as it was at the time of the contract. Otherwise he must pay the same penalties that are fixed for other pieces of work overdue.'—43. **κὰ τάπερ**: Att. καθάπερ.—45 ff. 'If a contractor or workman seems to be abusing the works, or disobedient to those in charge, or disregardful of the established fines, the workman may be expelled from the work, and the contractor brought to trial and fined in the same way as is prescribed for those who make opposition to the allotments.'—46. **ἐπηρειάζεν**: this spelling with ει, found also in papyri, is the correct etymological one (cf. ἐπήρεια), while ἐπειρεάζω of our texts is like δωρεά for earlier δωρειά (31).—50. **ζαμιόντες ἰν ἐπίκρισιν**: condensed expression for ζαμιόντες καὶ ἀγκαρύσσοντες κτλ. Cf. ll. 17-19.—51. **τὸς ἐπισυνισταμένος**: acc. abs. 173.—**ἐσδοκαῖς**: ἐσδόσεσι in

l. 16. The 'giving out' of the 'contracts' and 'acceptance' of proposals is the same thing.—53 ff. 'This general contract shall be in force in addition to the special contract for the particular piece of work.'

20. Orchomenus. 369 B.C. Schwyzer 664. Solmsen-Fraenkel 2.

- - - - ος | - - - Κ]αλλείδας Τ|[. . . . .]ων Παρράσιος, ὥρισαν
5 δ|ὲ τὰνγ γᾶν· ἀπὺ τῶι ὁρίοι τῶι πὸς τ||ῶι Μελαμποδέοι τῶι τῶν
Ὀρχομ|ενίων καὶ τῶν Τορθυνήων καὶ Μετι|δριήων κοινοῖ ἐπὶ τὸ
Βουφαγέον μεσ|ακόθεν τοῖς κράναιυν· ἀπὺ τωινί | ἰν τὰν πορθιέαν
10 πρώταν· ἀπὺ τωιν||ὶ πὰρ μέσαν τὰν πορθιέαν ἰ νηάτ|αν· ἀπὺ
τῶινυ ἰν τὰν ἄλωνα νηάταν· ἀπὺ τ|ῶινυ ἰν τὸν λόφον τὸν ἰν τῶι
κρόμποι· ἀπὺ τῶι|νυ ἰν τὸν λόφον τὸν συμβολᾶν τὸν τραχύν· δύ|ο
15 ἀπὺ τῶινυ εὐθυορϜίαν πὸς δέρϜαν πὸς λόφο||ν· δύο ἀπὺ τῶινυ ἰν
τὰν δέρϜαν ἰν τᾶι βουσοῖ ὀπ|ὺ τὰ Ϝάδω· ἀπὺ τῶινυ ὁπὲρ τὰμ
Φυλάκω ἰν τῶι κ|ρόμποι· ἀπὺ τῶινυ ἱμέσος Πελειᾶν· ἀπὺ τῶινυ |
ἐπὶ δέρϜαν ἰν τᾶι βουσοῖ τᾶι ἐπὶ Παδόεσσαν· ἁ Παδ|όεσσα κοινὰ
20 ἀμφοτέροις· ἀπὺ Παδοέσσαι ἰν τὸν λ||όφον τὸν δίωρον· καὶ ἀπὺ
τῶινυ ἰν τὰν Τριάγκεια|ν· ἀπὺ τῶινυ ἰν τὸ στυμέον ὀπὺ τὸν ἄκρον·
δύο ἀ|πὺ τῶινυ ἰν τὰμ πέτραν ἰν Ἀρίαν· Ἀρία κοινὰ ἀ|μφοτέροις·
ἀπ' Ἀρίαι τᾶι βουσοῖ ἰν τὰν δρῦν ἰν τὰ|ν δέρϜαν τὰν ἰν τᾶι ἄλωνι·
25 ἀπὺ τῶινυ ὁπὲρ τὼ || Διδύμω· ἀπὺ τῶινυ ἰ μέσουν τοῖς Διδύ-
μοιυν· ἀ|πὺ τῶινυ ἰν τὸ συμβόλικτρον· ἀπὺ συμβολίκτροι || ἰν
ἄκραν Σμαρίαν ἰν τὸ οἱ Ἀρκάδες συνέθε|αν· ἀπὺ τῶινυ ἰγ κοίλαν
εὐθὺ ἰν τὸ Νικαγόρε(ο)ς ἄκρον τὸ οἱ Ἀρκάδες συνέθεαν. Ὀρχομεν-
30 || ίων θεαροὶ οἵδε· Μνασίας, Ἡραῖος, Κλεόδι|κος, Ἀτέκμαρτος,
Σαιθος· πολέμαρχοι οἵδ|ε· Νικέας, Κάμπος, Εὔδοξος, Φιλόδα-
μος, | Τιμοστρατίδας.

Boundaries between Orchomenus and Methydrium. Μεθύδριον is the usual form, but here Μετιδριήων. 4. τὰνγ γᾶν: merely a careless blend of the two spellings τὰν and τὰγ γᾶν.—4 ff. 'From the boundary (ὅριον, instead of usual ὅρος) near the shrine of Melampous that is common to the Orchomenians, etc., to the shrine of Bouphagus, (passing) between the two springs.' For the duals κράναιυν and ἰ μέσουν τοῖς Διδύμοιυν l. 25, see 105.10, 106.7.—9 ff. 'To the beginning of the πορθιέα ('passage, path'? Cf. πορεία, πορθμός),—along the middle of it to the end of it,—to the end of the plantation,—to the hill in the κρόμπος (meaning?),

—to the rocky hill at the confluence,—two (boundaries) from this point in a straight line to the ridge, to the hill,—two to the ridge in the cattle run below the land of Vadus,—hence above the land of Phylakus in the κρόμπος,—hence (the boundary line is) in the midst of the elms (or the Elms).' For ἰ νηάταν, ἰ μέσουν. ἰμέσος and τὰ Ϝάδω, see **89**.7.—νήατος: probably the earliest form = Hom. νείατος, νέατος, Att. νέατος. Cf. νήιστα Hesych.— 16. βουσός: **45**.—16. τὰ Ϝάδω: τὰν Ϝάδω. **89**.7, **96**.5.—21. στυμέον cf. στόμιον. 22b. Here 'cavern'?.—26. συμβόλικτρον: 'junction' of roads?—28. Νικαγόρε(ο)ς: **105**.2d.

21. Orchomenus. Middle of fourth century B.C. IG V.ii.343. Schwyzer 665. Solmsen-Fraenkel 3.

Θεός. τύχα ἀγαθ[ά]. συϜοικία Εὐαι|μνίοις Ἐρχομι|νίοις ἐπὶ
5 τοῖς Ϝί||σϜοις καὶ τοῖς ὑμ|οίοις. τὰ δὲ ἱερὰ | τὰ ἰν Εὐαίμονι ἀ|[t
10 κ]ὰ μην' αὖθι κὰ [τ|άπε]ρ ἔχει συντ||[ελῆσθαι - - - - a few lines
15 missing] || τὸς δὲ προτέρος [ἰ]|νϜοίκος τᾶς τομ|[ά]δος λαχῆν κὰ
20 τά|[π]ερ ἔδοξε ἀμφο[τ|έ]ροις · τῶν δὲ ἐπὶ || [Χ]αιριάδαι εἴτε [τ|ι]
χωρίον ἀμφίλλ|[ο]γον ἰν ταῖ τομά|[δ]ι, τὸς Ἡραέας δια|[δ]ικάσαι
25 καὶ τὰς δίκα[ς || τ]ὰς προδεδικασμί|νας πάνσας · πομπ[ὰ|ς] δ'
30 ἐπιγενέσθαι δ[ι]||ὰ τρία Ϝέτεα Ἀρ[κά|δω]ν ἐπὶ Ϝρήσι. κ[αὶ || τ]ὰ
χρῆα τὰ δαμόσι|[α] κοιναῖ φέρην ἀ|[μ]φοτέρος. γράφε|α γράψαν-
35 (τ)ας καθ[έ|σ]θ[αι] ὁπόθ' ἄν δεά[σ|η]τοι ἀμφοτέροις. [τ]|οῖς
ἐπὶ Χαιριάδαι, τ|ὰ χρῆα τὰ ὀφέλλον|σι ταῖ θεοῖ, περὶ τὸν ἀ|[π]υ-
40 δοσμὸν αὐτὸς δ[ι]||αβωλευσαμίνος χρό|νον τάξασθαι. καὶ περ[ὶ |
τὰ] μισθώματα τᾶς γᾶς | [τὰν] Μνασιτέλης ἐμί(σ)θ[ω]|σε, κὰ
45 ταῦτά. ὅτις ξέν[αν] || γεγάμηκε, τὸς παῖδας [κ|α]ὶ τὰς γυναῖκας
50 Ἐ[ρ]||χομινίας ἧναι. τὰ ὁρ|[κ]ια πάντα τὸ αὐτὸ [ἀ]|ἰ αὖτις. μὴ
ἐσκεθῆ|[ν] μηδ' ἀναγκάσαι μ|[η]δένα. τὰ δὲ δίκ[α|ς] ταν' οἱ
55 ξένοι ἔ[κ|ρ]ιvναν τάς τε ἰν Ε|[ὐ]αίμονι καὶ τὰς ἰ[ν || Ἐρχομιν]οῖ
60 [- - - - a few lines missing] || [Ϝε]κατέραι Ἰόλ[λα]ος. ὤμοσαν
οἱ Εὐα[ί]||μνιο(ι) τάδε · ἀψευ[δ]||ήων ἀ τὰν συϜοι[κί]αν τοῖς
65 Ἐρχομιν||[ί]οις πὸς τὰς συνθέ[σ|ι]ς, νεὶ τὸν Δία τὸν Ἄρ[η]||α,
νεὶ τὰν Ἀθάναν τ|ὰν Ἀρείαν. ναὶ τὸν ['Ι]||νυάλιον τὸν Ἄρηα · ||
70 [ο]ὐδ' ἄν ἀνισταίμα|ν ἀπὺ τοῖς Ἐρχομιν|(ί)οις οὔποτε, οὐ τὸν
75 | [Δ]ία τὸν Ἄρηα, οὐ τὰ|ν Ἀθάναν τὰν Ἀρε[ί]||αν, οὐ τὸν
Ἰνυάλιο|ν τὸν Ἄρηα · κεύορ|κέντι μὲν τἀγαθά, | [ἐ]πιορκέντι δὲ
80 ἐξο|[λέ]σθαι αὐτὸγ καὶ γ||ένος. ὤμοσαν Ἐρχ[ι|ο]μίνιοι τάδε ·

ἀψευ|δήων ἂν τὰν συϜο|[ι]κίαν τοῖς Εὐαιμν[ί]|οις πὸς τὰς συνθέ||-
85 [σ]ις, ναὶ τὸν Δία τὸν ῎Α[ρ]ηα, νεὶ τὰν ᾿Αθάναν | τὰν ᾿Αρήαν, νεὶ
90 τὸν ᾿Ιν|[υ]άλιον τὸν ῎Αρηα· οὐ|δ᾿ ἂν ἐξελαύνοια τ||ὸς Εὐαιμνίος
οὔπο|τε, οὐ τὸν Δία τὸν ῎Α|[ρ]|ηα, οὐ τὰν ᾿Αθάναν | [τ]ὰν ῎Αρηαν,
95 οὐ τὸν ᾿Ιν|υάλιον τὸν ῎Αρηα· || κεϜορ[κέντι] μὲν [τ]||ἀγαθά,
ἐπιορκέντ[ι] | δὲ ἐξολέσθαι κα(ὐ)|τὸν καὶ γένος. | ᾿Αριστάνωρ ||
100 ᾿Ονόμαντος | Λαέας | Σαοκλῆς | [- - - - a few lines missing]
108 | .ο ἢ ἀπεόν[τι ...] | | ὄνδικα ἦναι.

A joint-citizenship agreement (cf. no. 56) between Orchomenus
and Euaemon, with some matters left to the arbitration of
Heraea. Inscribed on three sides of a column, of which two
pieces were found separately, a small middle piece being missing.
For the purpose of continuous line numbering, the missing
portion is arbitrarily set at five lines.

1. συϜοικία: συνοικία. 89.7.—6 ff. 'The regular monthly sacred
rites at Euaemon shall be held there as is customary.'—15 ff.
'The former inhabitants shall share in the allotment in accordance with the vote of both parties. But as to those of the time
of Chaeriades, if any territory in the allotment is in dispute,
the Heraeans shall decide, and also all the cases in previous
litigation. Missions (of arbitration) shall be established over a
period of three years, upon declaration of the Arcadian league.'—
36 ff. 'For those of the time of Chaeriades, regarding the payment
of the debts which they owe to the goddess, they shall themselves
in consultation fix its time of payment.'—49. αὖτις: emphasizes
the preceding ἀί, as in Hom. ἐτ᾿ αὖτις, πάλιν αὖτις, etc.—ἐσκεθῆν:
for ἐσ-σκεθῆν= *ἐκ-σχεθεῖν (cf. 65). The meaning of the sentence
is 'one shall not keep out nor force in anyone,' that is in the matter
of citizenship, which is the subject of the preceding ll. 44-47.—
51. τὰ δὲ=τὰς δὲ.89.7, 97.4.—62-89. For the forms ἀψευδήων and
ἐξελαύνοια, see 149, 159, 152.1. The shift of mood is of interest
in connection with the observation (Smyth 1826a, 1833) that the
use of the optative with ἄν for strong assertions is especially
common after a negative. Here 'I will be faithful and I would
never revolt (expel).'

22. Decree of Tegea, found at Delphi. About 324 B.C. IG V.ii.p.
xxxvi. Plassart, BCH 38.101 ff. Ditt. Syll. 306. Schwyzer 657.
Tod 202. SEG 1.211.

·· - - - ση - - - [βασι|λεὺς 'Αλέξ]ανδρος τὸ διάγρ[α]μμα, γρα-
φῆναι κατὺ τὰ ἐ|[πανωρ]θώσατυ ἁ πόλις τὰ ἰν τοῖ διαγράμματι
5 ἀντιλ|εγόμενα. (I) τὸς φυγάδας τὸς κατενθόντας τὰ πατρῶια || κο-
μίζεσθαι ἐς τοῖς ἔφευγον, καὶ τὰ ματρῶια, ὅσαι ἀ|νέσδοτοι τὰ
πάματα κατῆχον καὶ οὐκ ἐτύγχανον ἀδ|ελφεὸς πεπαμέναι· εἰ δέ
τινι ἐσδοθένσαι συνέπεσ|ε τὸν ἀδελφεὸν καὶ αὐτὸν καὶ τὰν γενεὰν
ἀπολέσθα|ι, καὶ τανὶ ματρῶια ἦναι, ἀνώτερον δὲ μηκέτι ἦναι.
10 (II) ἐ||πὲς δὲ ταῖς οἰκίαις μίαν ἕκαστον ἔχεν κατὺ τὸ διά|γραμμα·
εἰ δέ τις ἔχει οἰκία κᾶπον πὸς αὐταῖ, ἄλλον μ|ὴ λαμβανέτω· εἰ δὲ
πὸς ταῖ οἰκίαι μὴ πόεστι κᾶπος, ἐ|ξαντίαι δ' ἔστι ἰσόθι πλέθρω,
λαμβανέτω τὸν κᾶπον· | εἰ δὲ πλέον ἀπέχων ὁ κᾶπός ἐστι πλέθρω,
15 τωνὶ τὸ ἥμι||σσον λαμβανέτω, ὥσπερ καὶ τῶν ἄλλων χωρίων
γέγρα|πται. τὰν δὲ οἰκιᾶν τιμὰν κομιζέσθω τῶ οἴκω ἑκάστ|ω δύο
μνᾶς, τὰν δὲ τιμασίαν ἦναι τᾶν οἰκιᾶν κὰ τάπε|ρ ἁ πόλις νομίζει·
τῶν δὲ κάπων διπλάσιον τὸ τίμαμ|α κομίζεσθαι ἢ ἐς τοῖ νόμοι. τὰ
20 δὲ χρήματα ἀφεῶσθα||ι τὰν πόλιν καὶ μὴ ἀπυλιῶναι μήτε τοῖς
φυγάσι μήτ|ε τοῖς πρότερον οἴκοι πολιτεύονσι. (III) ἐπὲς δὲ ταῖς
π|αναγορίαις ταῖς ἐσλελοίπασι οἱ φυγάδες, τὰν πόλ|ιν βωλεύσα-
σθαι, ὅτι δ' ἂν βωλεύσητοι ἁ πόλις, κύριο|ν ἔστω. (IV) τὸ δὲ δικα-
25 στήριον τὸ ξενικὸν δικάζεν ἐξήκ||οντα ἀμερᾶν· ὅσοι δ' ἂν ἰν ταῖς
ἐξήκοντα ἀμέραις μὴ | διαδικάσωνται, μὴ ἦναι αὐτοῖς δικάσασθαι
ἐπὲς τ|οῖς πάμασι ἰν τοῖ ξενικοῖ δικαστηρίοι, ἀλλ' ἰν τοῖ | πολιτικοῖ
ἀῖ· εἰ δ' ἄν τι ὕστερον ἐφευρίσκωνσι, ἰν ἀ|μέραις ἑξήκοντα ἀπὺ ταῖ
30 ἂν ἀμέραι τὸ δικαστήριο||ν καθιστᾶ. εἰ δ' ἂν μηδ' ἰν ταῖννυ διαδι-
κάσητοι, μηκέ|τι ἐξέστω αὐτῶι δικάσασθαι· εἰ δ' ἄν τινες
ὕστερον | κατένθωνσι, τῶ δικαστηρίω τῶ ξενικῶ [μ]ηκέτι ἐόντ|ος,
ἀπυγραφέσθω πὸς τὸς στραταγὸς τὰ πάματα ἰν ἀμ|έραις ἑξήκοντα,
35 καὶ εἰκ ἄν τι αὐτοῖς ἐ[π]απύλογον ἦ||ι, δικαστήριον ἦναι Μαντι-
νέαν· εἰ δ' [ἂν μὴ] διαδικάσ|ητοι ἰν ταιν(νὶ) ταῖς ἀμέραις, μηκέτ[ι]
ἦναι αὐτοῖ δι|κάσασθαι. (V) ἐπὲς δὲ τοῖς ἱεροῖς χρήμασιν .λωι..ν
τοῖς ὀφειλήμασι τὰ μὲμ πὸς τὰν θεὸν ἁ πόλις διωρθώ|σατυ, ὁ ἔχων
40 τὸ πᾶμα ἀπυδότω τῶι κατηνθηκότι τὸ ἥμ||ισσον κὰ τάπερ οἱ ἄλλοι·
ὅσοι δὲ αὐτοὶ ὤφηλον ταῖ θ|εοῖ συνινγύας ἢ ἄλλως, εἰ μὲν ἂν φαίνη-
τοι ὁ ἔχων τὸ | πᾶμα διωρθωμένος ταῖ θεοῖ τὸ χρέος, ἀπυδότω τὸ
ἥμ|ισσον τῶι κατιόντι, κὰ τάπερ οἱ ἄλλοι, μηδὲν παρέλ||[κ]ων· εἰ δ'
45 ἂν μὴ φαίνητοι ἀπυδεδωκὼς ταῖ θεοῖ, ἀπυδό||τω τοῖ κατιόντι τὸ
ἥμισσον τῶ πάματος, ἐς δὲ τοῖ ἡμ|ίσσοι αὐτὸς τὸ χρέος διαλυέτω·
εἰ δ' ἂν μὴ βόλητοι δ|ιαλῦσαι, ἀπυδότω τοῖ κατιόντι τὸ πᾶμα ὅλον,

ὁ δὲ κο|μισάμενος διαλυσάτω τὸ χρέος ταῖ θεοῖ πᾶν. (VI) ὅσαι δ|ὲ
50 γυναῖκες τῶν φυγάδων ἢ θυγατέρες οἴκοι μίνονσ||αι ἐγά[μ]αντυ,
ἢ φυγόνσαι ὕστερον ἐγάμαντυ [ἰ]ν Τεγέ|αν κα[ὶ] ἐπίλυσιν ὠνήσαν-
τυ οἴκοι μίνονσαι, ταννὶ μ|ήτ' ἀ[πυδοκ]ιμάζεσθαι τὰ πατρῶια μήτε
τὰ ματρῶια μ|ηδὲ τὸς ἐσγόνος, ὅσοι μὴ ὕστερον ἔφυγον δι' ἀνάγ-
55 κα|ς καί ἰν τοῖ νῦν ἐόντι καιροῖ καθέρπονσι ἢ αὐταὶ ἢ || παῖδες
ταννί, δοκιμάζεσθαι καὶ αὐτὰς καὶ τὸς ἐς τ|αιννὶ ἐσγόνος τὰ πα-
τρῶια καὶ τὰ ματρῶια κὰ τὸ διά|γραμμα. (VII) ὀμνύω Δία, 'Αθά-
ναν, 'Απόλλωνα, Ποσειδᾶνα εὐν|οήσω τοῖς κατηνθηκόσι τοῖς
ἔδοξε ταῖ πόλι κατυδ|έχεσθαι, καὶ οὐ μνασικακήσω τῶννυ οὐδεν[ὶ]
60 τ[ὰ] ἂν ἀμ||π[ε]ίϲῃ ἀπὺ ταῖ ἀμέραι ταῖ τὸν ὅρκον ὤμοσα, οὐδὲ
δια|κωλύσω τὰν τῶν κατηνθηκότων σωτηρίαν, οὔτε ἰν τα|ῖ
[ll. 62-66 fragmentary.].

Decree regarding the exiles returning under Alexander's edict
of 324 B.C. Cf. no. 26.

1 ff. The city had previously passed certain regulations, some
of which were objected to by Alexander in a special edict and
were now corrected.—4 ff. 'The returning exiles shall recover
the paternal property which they had at the time of their exile,
and likewise the women the maternal property, those who were
unmarried and in possession of the property and had no brothers.
If it happened to a married daughter that her brother and his
offspring died, then she too should share in the maternal property
(τανί = gen. sg. τασ-νί, 97.1), but it shall never be more' (than
the maternal property? or 'go beyond this' in line of inheritance?)
—13. ἐξαντίαι: 'over against, near by.' Cf. ἐκ τῆς ἀντίης (Hdt.).
The true Arcadian form would be ἐσαντίαι. There are some traces
of κοινή influence (cf. also πλέον, ει in ὀφείλημα, ει in Ποσειδᾶνα)
as in no. 19.—ἰσόθι πλέθρω: literally 'in equal place,' but here
clearly 'within the distance of a plethron.'—16 ff. τιμά is the
purchase price, while τιμασία (= Att. τίμησις) is the taxable
valuation, and τίμαμα the assessment. For the cultivated lots
(κᾶποι) the city is to receive double the normal tax.—19 ff. τὰ δὲ
χρήματα κτλ.: difficult passage, but perhaps meaning 'as
to monetary claims (as distinct from real estate) the city shall
be free of responsibility and shall not settle them in favor of
either party,' ἀφεῶσθαι being taken, not (with most editors) as

mid. = act. 'remit,' but (in spite of the crude condensed construction) as pass. as in ἀφεώσθω τῶ ἔργω 'be excused from the work' (no. 19.14) and ἀφεώσθω τᾶς μαρτυρίας 'be excused from testifying' (IG V.ii.357.12). For ἀπυλιῶναι, see **162.10**.— 23 ff. 'with reference to the festivals from which the exiles have been missing, the city shall take counsel,' etc. (probably as to the conditions under which the exiles may resume participation).

24 ff. The ξενικὸν δικαστήριον is a court constituted of judges from other cities, here perhaps Mantinea (cf. l. 35). 'The alien court is to serve for a period of sixty days. Those who do not have their cases settled within this time may not bring suit for property in this court, but only in the regular civic court. If they later discover any additional evidence (or claim), they may present it within sixty days of the time of the constitution of the court. But if any one does not have his case settled within this time, he may not bring action. If any return later, when the alien court is no longer serving, they shall file an inventory of the property with the στραταγοί within sixty days, and if there is anything in defense (against their claims) Mantinea shall serve as the court.—37 ff. Adjustment of debts to the goddess (that is, to the temple, which often served as a banking institution) which were secured by liens on the property.—49 ff. 'The wives of the exiles and the daughters who remained at home and married, or who from exile returned to Tegea and married and bought their release shall not be disqualified for their paternal or maternal inheritance, nor their descendants, except that those who were banished at a later time and are returning at the present time, either the women themselves or their children, they and their descendants shall be subject to investigation as to the paternal or maternal inheritance according to the edict.'—ταννί in l. 51 is acc. pl. (τασ-νί, **97.1**), but gen. pl. in l. 55.—57 ff. The citizens who remained at home take oath to show good will to the returning exiles and not to bear malice against any of them for what he may have plotted (?). **ἀμπείση**: aor. subj. of ἀναπείθω 'persuade,' used also in a bad sense 'mislead, corrupt, bribe', here perhaps 'plot,' referring to the exiles previous political intrigues.

Cyprian

The Cyprian Syllabary

Nearly all the Cyprian inscriptions are written in a special syllabary. This consists of signs for each of the five vowels— these being used where no consonant immediately precedes, that is initially and for the second element of diphthongs— and signs for each combination of consonant and following vowel, as *ma, me*, etc. But there is no distinction between long and short vowels, nor, in the case of stops, between voiceless. voiced, and aspirate. Hence the sign *te* (the transcription with *t* is a matter of convention) may stand for τε, τη, δε, δη, θε, or θη. Nasals before consonants are not written, e.g., *a ti* = ἀ(ν)τί. [1]

For a final consonant the sign containing the vowel *e* is used, e.g., *ka se* = κάς. For groups of consonants the first is indicated by the sign containing the vowel of the syllable to which this consonant belongs. That is, its vowel is determined by the following in the case of initial groups and consonant + liquid; by the preceding in the case of liquid + consonant, and also σ + consonant (cf. **89**.1). Thus *po to li ne* = πτόλιν, *pa ti ri* = πατρί, *e u ve re ta sa tu* = εὐϜρētάσατυ, *a ra ku ro* = ἀργύρō, *e se ta se* = ἔστασε. Examples of other groups are rare. [2]

Words are separated by a special sign, but this is commonly, though not uniformly, omitted after the article, and sometimes in other groups of words. In such groups a final consonant is often treated as medial, hence *ta po to li ne* = τὰ(ν) πτόλιν, etc.

23. Idalium. Probably second half of fifth century B.C. Schwyzer 679. Solmsen-Fraenkel 6. The first five lines only are given in the more exact syllabic transcription. In this | denotes the word separator, not the line division, which is indicated by numerals.

---

[1] In the Greek transcription the stops are distinguished and the nasal before consonants is supplied in parentheses. But ē and ā, not η, ω, are used, in accordance with the practice adopted for other inscriptions where the signs η and ω are not in use. For some uncertainties in regard to the proper transcription, see **199**.

[2] We find *me ma na me no i* = μεμναμένοι, *ka si ke ne to i se* = κασιγ-νέτοις but *i ki ma me no se* = ἰχμαμένος, *te re ki ni ja* = τέρχνιja, [ti pe te ra- = διφθερα-, *va na ko to se* = Ϝάνακτος.

1 o te | ta po to li ne e ta li o ne | ka te vo ro ko ne ma to
i | ka se ke ti e ve se | i to i | pi lo ku po ro ne ve te i to o na
sa ko 2 ra u | pa si le u se | sa ta si ku po ro se | ka se a po to
li se | e ta li e ve se | a no ko ne o na si lo ne | to no na si ku
po 3 ro ne to ni ja te ra ne | ka se | to se | ka si ke ne to se |
i ja sa ta i | to se | a to ro po se | to se | i ta | i | ma ka i | i ki
4 ma me no se | a ne u | mi si to ne | ka sa pa i | e u ve re ta
sa tu | pa si le u se | ka se | a po to li se | o na si 5 lo i | ka
se | to i se | ka si ke ne to i se | a ti to mi si to ne | ka a ti |
ta u ke ro ne | to ve na i | e xe to i | *etc.*

Ὅτε τὰ(ν) πτόλιν Ἐδάλιον κατέϜοργον Μᾶδοι κὰς ΚετιᾶϜες
2 ἰ(ν) τῶι Φιλοκύπρον Ϝέτει τῶ Ὀνασαγό|ραυ, βασιλεὺς Στασίκυπρος
κὰς ἁ πτόλις ἘδαλιᾶϜες ἄνōγον Ὀνάσιλον τὸν Ὀνασικύπ|ρōν
τὸν ἰϳατῆραν κὰς τὸς κασιγνέτος ἴϳασθαι τὸς ἀ(ν)θρόπος τὸς ἰ(ν)
4 τᾶι μάχαι ἰκ|ιαμένος ἄνευ μισθōν. κάς παι εὐϜρētάσατυ βασιλεὺς
κὰς ἁ πτόλις Ὀνασί|||λōι κὰς τοῖς κασιγνέτοις ἀ(ν)τὶ τō μισθōν κὰ
6 ἀ(ν)τὶ τᾶ ὑχέρōν δοϜέναι ἐξ τōι | Ϝοίκōι τōι βασιλēϜος κὰς ἐξ τᾶι
πτόλιϜι ἀργύρō τά(λαντον) α' τά(λαντον) · ᾶ δυϜάνοι νυ ἀ(ν)τὶ τō |
ἀργύρōν τōδε, τō ταλά(ν)τōν, βασιλεὺς κὰς ἁ πτόλις Ὀνασίλōι κὰς
8 τοῖς κασι|γνέτοις ἀπὺ τᾶι ζᾶι τᾶι βασιλēϜος τᾶ ἰ(ν) τōιρōνι τōι
Ἀλα(μ)πριϳάται τὸ(ν) χōρον | τὸν ἰ(ν) τōι ἔλει τὸ(ν) χραυόμενον
10 Ὄ(γ)κα(ν)τος ἄλϜō κὰς τὰ τέρχνιϳα τὰ ἐπιό(ν)τα || πά(ν)τα ἔχεν
πανόνιον ὐϜαὶς ζαν ἀτελέν. ᾶ κέ σις Ὀνάσιλον ᾶ τὸς | κασιγνέτος
ᾶ τὸς παῖδας τō(ν) παίδōν τōν Ὀνασικύπρōν ἐξ τōι χόρōι τōιδε | ἐξ-
ορύξē, ἰδέ παι ὁ ἐξορύξē πείσει Ὀνασίλōι κὰς τοῖς κασιγνέτοι|ς ᾶ
12 τοῖς παισὶ τὸν ἄργυρον τό(ν)δε, ἀργύρō τά(λαντον) α' τά(λαντον). |
14 κὰς Ὀνασίλōι οἰϜōι ἄνευ τō(ν) κασιγνέτōν τōν αἴλōν ἐϜρētάσατυ
βασιλεὺ||ς κὰς ἁ πτόλις δοϜέναι ἀ(ν)τὶ τᾶ ὑχέρōν τō μισθōν ἀργύρō
16 πε(λέχεϜα) δ' πε(λέχεϜα) | β' δι(μναῖα) Ἐ(δάλια) · ᾶ δόκοι νυ
βασιλεὺς κὰς ἁ πτόλις Ὀνασί|||λōι ἀ(ν)τὶ τō ἀργύρō τōδε ἀπὺ τᾶι
18 ζᾶι τᾶι βασιλēϜος τᾶ ἰ(ν) Μαλανίϳα|ι τᾶι πεδίϳαι τὸ(ν) χōρον τὸ(ν)
χραυζόμενον Ἀμενίϳα ἄλϜō κὰς τὰ τέρ|χνιϳα τὰ ἐπιό(ν)τα πά(ν)τα,
20 τὸ(ν) ποεχόμενον πὸς τὸ(ν) ῥόϜο(ν) τὸ(ν) Δρύμιον κὰς πὸ||ς τὰν
ἱερēϜίϳαν τᾶς Ἀθάνας, κὰς τὸ(ν) κᾶπον τὸν ἰ(ν) Σίμιδος ἀρούρα|ι,
τό(ν) ΔιϜείθεμις ὁ Ἀρμανεὺς ἔχε ἄλϜο(ν), τὸν ποεχόμενον πὸς
22 Πασαγόρα|ν τὸν Ὀνασαγόραυ κὰς τὰ τέρχνιϳα τὰ ἐπιό(ν)τα πά(ν)-
τα ἔχεν πανōνίος ὐ|Ϝαὶς ζαν ἀτελίϳα ἰό(ν)τα. ᾶ κέ σις Ὀνάσιλον ᾶ τὸς
24 παῖδας τὸς Ὀ|νασίλōν ἐξ τᾶι ζᾶι τᾶιδε ἰ ἐξ τōι κάπōι τōιδε ἐξορύξē

ἱ‖δὲ ὁ ἐξορύξε πείσει 'Ονασίλοι ε̄ τοῖς παισὶ τὸν ἄργυρον τό(ν)δε,
26 ἀργύρο̄|ν πε(λέχεϜα) δ' πε(λέχεϜα) β' δι(μναῖα) 'Ε(δάλια). ἰδὲ
τὰ(ν) δάλτον τά(ν)δε, τὰ Ϝέπιjα τάδε ἰναλαλισμένα, | βασιλεὺς κὰς
28 ἀ πτόλις κατέθιjαν ἰ(ν) τὰ(ν) θιὸν τὰν 'Αθάναν τά(ν)νε περ' 'Ε|δά-
λιον σὺν ὅρκοις μὲ̄ λῦσαι τὰς Ϝρέτας τάσδε ὐϜαὶς ζαν. | ὅπι σίς κε τὰς
30 Ϝρέτας τάσδε λύσε̄, ἀνοσίjα Ϝοι γένοιτυ. τάς γε ‖ ζᾶς τάσδε κὰς
τὸς κάπος τόσδε ο(ἰ) 'Ονασικύπρο̄ν παῖδες κὰς τὸ̄(ν) παίδο̄ν οἱ
πα|ῖδες ἕξο̄σι αἰϜεί, ο(ἰ) ἰ(ν) τὸιρο̄̃νι το̄ι 'Εδαλιε̄̃Ϝι ἴο̄σι.

Agreement of the king and city of Idalium with the physician Onasilus and his brothers for the care of the wounded without pay
(that is, for the individual cases) during the siege of the city by
the Persians and the inhabitants of the Phoenician city of Citium.

The king and the city promised to Onasilus and his brothers
instead of (special) pay the sum of a silver talent, or in place
of this a certain tract of land. And they promised to Onasilus
alone the sum of four 'axes' (each = 10 minae) and two double
minae, or another tract of land. Provision is made that, should
they be ousted from the land, the money should be paid.—1.
κατέϜοργον: 5.— 4, 14. εὐϜρε̄τάσατυ, ἐϜρετάσατυ: 55, 70.3.—
5. ἀ(ν)τὶ τὸ̄ μισθο̄̃ κτλ.: see 136.8.—τᾶ ὐχέρο̄ν: 59.4, 135.8.—8.
(ἰ)ν τὸιρο̄̃νι: 'in the district.' Cf. οἰρών 'boundary line' Hesych.
—9. 18, 21. ἄλϜο̄, ἄλϜον: cf. ἄλουα · κῆποι (Cypr.) Hesych., Hom.
ἀλωή, Att., Arc. ἄλων, Sicil. ἄλος, ἀ (GDI 5200 passim). In this
group the meaning is partly the broad 'tract of cultivated land,
plantation,' and partly more specific 'garden,' 'vineyard' or
'orchard.' Here, as shown by ll. 20, 21, the ἄλϜον is more specific
('vineyard'?) than the κᾶπος, which here has the broader sense,
as often elsewhere (e.g., no. 42.10, 22).—10. πανόνιον: 'with all
salable products,' agreeing with τὸ(ν) χο̄ρον, the intervening τὰ
τέρχνιjα being disregarded as subordinate.—ὐϜαὶς ζαν: ὐϜαίς
'forever' 133.6. ζαν: 'for life' (?). Cf. ζάει · πνεῖ, Κύπριοι. Hesych.
—12, 24. ἐξορύξε: 'expropriates,' from *ἐξορϜίζω = Att. ἐξορίζω
(cf. ὅρϜος, 54). For the ending here and in λύσε̄ l. 29 (-ε̄ or -ε?),
see 150c.—15. πε(λέχεϜα) so as neut. pl. in view of the gloss
τὸ γὰρ δεκάμνουν πέλεχυ παρὰ Παφίοις Hesych. s.v. ἡμιπέλεχχον.
πέλεχυς used elsewhere with other values.—29. 'whenever anyone (or whoever?) violates these agreements may impiety rest

upon him,' that is, he shall be guilty of an impious act. ὄπι is difficult, but possibly ὄπη (**132.**7). See **16a**.

Lesbian

24. Cebrene. Fifth century B.C. Roberts p. 324. Schwyzer 638. Solmsen-Fraenkel 7.

Σ[τάλλ]α 'πὶ Σθενείαι ἔμμι τῶ Νικιαῖδι τῶ Γαυκῖδ.

Monument to Stheneias, son of Nicias and grandson of Gaucus. See **168d**, and **38**.

25. Mytilene. First half of fourth century B.C. IG XII.ii.1 and XII Suppl. p. 2. Schwyzer 619. Solmsen-Fraenkel 8. Tod 112.

```
- - - - - - ˙ - ε - - - - - - - - - - - - - [ὄττι | δέ κε αἰ] πόλις
[ἀ]μφότ[εραι - - - - - - - - - - - | - - - - ] γράφωισι εἰς τὰν [στάλ-
5  λαν ἢ ἐκκ|ολάπ]τωισι, κύ[ρ]ιον ἔστω. τ[ὸν δὲ κέρναν||τα τὸ] χρύ-
    σιον ὑπόδικον ἔ[μμεναι ἀμφο|τέρ]αισι ταῖς πολίεσσι. δικ[άσταις
    δὲ | ἔμ]μεναι τῶι μὲν ἐμ Μυτιλήναι [κέρναν|τι] ταὶς ἄρχαις παίσαις
10 ταὶς ἐμ Μ[υτιλή]ναι πλέας τῶν αἰμισέων, ἐμ Φώκαι δὲ [τ]||αὶς
    ἄρχαις παίσαις ταὶς ἐμ Φώκαι πλ[έ]||ας τῶν αἰμισέω[ν]· τὰν δὲ
    δίκαν ἔμμεναι, | ἐπεί κε ὠνίαυτος ἐξέλθηι, ἐν ἒξ μήννεσι. αἰ δέ
    κε καταγ[ρ]έθηι τὸ χρύσιον κέρ|ναν ὑδαρέστε[ρ]ο[ν] θέλων, θανά-
15 τωι ζαμι||ώσθω· αἰ δέ κε ἀπυφ[ύ]γηι μ[ὴ] θέλων ἀμβρ[ό]||την,
    τιμάτω τ[ὸ] δικαστήριον ὄττι χρῆ α|ὖτ(ο)ν πάθην ἢ κατθέ[μ]εναι,
    ἀ δὲ πόλις ἀναί|τιος καὶ ἀζάμιος [ἔσ]τω. ἔλαχον Μυτιλή|ναοι πρό-
20 σθε κόπτην. ἄρχει πρότανις ὁ || πεδὰ Κόλωνον, ἐ[μ Φ]ώκαι δὲ ὁ
    πεδὰ Ἀρίσ[τ]||αρχον.
```

Monetary agreement between Mytilene and Phocaea. Coins of electrum, a compound of gold and silver, were issued by Mytilene and Phocaea, down to about 350 B.C., and it is to these that the inscription refers, though the term used of them is χρύσιον.

'Any one debasing the coinage is responsible to both cities. If at Mytilene, the magistrates of Mytilene are to constitute the majority of the judges. Similarly at Phocaea. The trial falls within six months of the expiration of the year. If one is convicted of intentional adulteration, he is to be punished with death. But if he is acquitted of intentional wrong-doing, the court shall decide the penalty or fine. The city is not liable. The

Mytilenians are to issue the coins first (the cities alternating each year.) The agreement goes into effect under the prytanis succeeding Colonus at Mytilene and Aristarchus at Phocaea.'

4-5. τ[ὸν δὲ κέρναντα]: κέρναμι, if correctly supplied here and in ll. 7-8, has the same meaning which is more forcibly expressed by κέρναν ὑδαρέστερον in ll. 13-14. The arrangements for trial immediately following show that the meaning required here is 'debase,' not 'make the alloy,' i.e., simply 'coin,' as often taken. Moreover, the electrum coinage of this time and place was based upon a natural, not an artificial, alloy.—9/10. **Φώκαι 31.**

26. Mytilene. Soon after 324 B.C. IG XII.ii.6 and XII Suppl. p. 3. Ditt. Orient. 2. Schwyzer 620. Solmsen-Fraenkel 9. Tod 201.

.... [καὶ οἰ β]ασί[ληες προστί]θησ[θον τῶι κατελη-
λύθον|τι ὡς τέχναν τεχνα]μέν[ω] τῶ ἐ[ν τᾶι] πόλι πρόσθε [ἔοντος.
αἰ δέ κέ τις | τῶν κατεληλυθόν]των μὴ ἐμμένη ἐν ταῖς διαλύσί[εσ]σι
ταύτ[αισι, | μη .... ἐφ]εζέσθω πὰρ τᾶς πόλιος κτήματος
5 μήδενος μη[δὲ στ||ειχέτω ἐπὶ μῆ]δεν τῶμ παρεχώρησαν αὔτωι οἱ
ἐν τᾶι πόλι πρό[σθε | ἔοντες, ἀλλὰ σ]τείχοντον ἐπὶ ταῦτα τὰ κτή-
ματα οἱ παρχωρήσαν[τ|ες αὔτωι ἐκ τῶν] ἐν τᾶι πόλι πρόσθε ἐόντων,
καὶ οἱ στρόταγοι εἰς | [αὖθις ἀποφέρον]τον ἐπὶ τὸν ἐν τᾶι πόλι
πρόσθε ἔοντα τὰ κτήματα | [ὡς μὴ συναλλαγ]μένω τῶ κατεληλύ-
10 θοντος· καὶ οἱ βασίληες προστί||[θησθον τῶι ἐν τ]ᾶι πόλι πρόσθε
ἔοντι ὡς τέχναν τεχναμένω τῶ κα|[τεληλύθοντος·] μηδ' αἴ κέ τις
δίκαν γράφηται περὶ τ[ο]ύτων, μὴ εἰσά|[γοντον οἱ περί]δρομοι καὶ
οἱ δικάσκοποι μηδὲ ἄ[λλ]α ἄρχα μηδεία. | [ἐπιμέλεσθαι δὲ] τοῖς
στροτάγοις καὶ τοῖς β[ασίλ]ηας καὶ τοῖς πε|[ριδρόμοις καὶ τ]οῖς
15 δικασκόποις καὶ ταῖς [ἄλλα]ις ἄρχαις αἴ κε || [μὴ γίνηται ἄπαν]τα
ὡς ἐν τῶι ψ[αφίσματι γέγραπτ]αι, κατάγρεντον | [δὲ τὸν ἀθέτεντά
τι τῶν ἐν τῶι ψαφίσματι γεγρα]μμένων, ὥς κε μῆδ|[εν διάφορον
εἴη τοῖς κατεληλυθόντεσσι π]ρὸς τοῖς ἐν τᾶι πόλι | [πρόσθε ἔον-
τας, ἀλλὰ διάγοιεν οἱ διαλε]λύμενοι πάντες πρὸς ἀλ|[λάλοις ἀνυ-
20 πόπτως καὶ ἀνεπιβουλεύ]τως καὶ ἐμμένοιεν ἐν τᾶι ἀ||[πυκρίσι τᾶι
τῶ βασίληος καὶ ἐν τᾶ]ι διαλύσι τᾶι ἐν τούτωι τῶι ψα|[φίσματι.
διαλλάκταις δ' ἔλεσθ]αι τὸν δᾶμον ἄνδρας εἴκοσι, δέκα | [μὲν ἐκ
τῶν κατελθόντων, δέκα] δὲ ἐκ τῶν ἐν τᾶι πόλι πρόσθε ἐόντων. |
[οὗτοι δὲ πρῶτον μὲν φυλάσσ]οντον καὶ ἐπιμέλεσθον ὡς μῆδεν
ἔσ|[σεται διάφορον τοῖς κατ]ελθόντεσσι καὶ τοῖς ἐν τᾶι πόλι πρό-

25 σ‖[θε ἐόντεσσι. πράξοισι δὲ] καὶ περὶ τῶν ἀμφισβατημένων κτημά-
των | [ὡς οἴ τε κατέλθοντες κ]αὶ πρὸς τοὶς ἐν τᾶι πόλι ἔοντας καὶ
πρὸς | [ἀλλάλοις μάλιστα μ]ὲν διαλυθήσονται, αἰ δὲ μή, ἔσσονται
ὡς διχ‖[αιότατοι, καὶ ἐν τα]ῖς διαλυσίεσσι, ταὶς ὁ βασίλευς ἐπέ-
κριννε, | [καὶ ἐν τᾶι συναλλάγ]αι ἐμμενέοισι πάντες καὶ οἰκήσοισι
30 τὰμ πό‖[λιν καὶ τὰγ χώραν ὁ]μονόεντες πρὸς ἀλλάλοις · καὶ περὶ
χρημάτων | [πεδὰ τὸ παραδέδεχ]θαι ταὶς διαλύσις ὡς πλεῖστα καὶ
περὶ ὄρκω | [τὸν κε ἀπομόσσωισι οἰ] | πόλιται, περὶ τούτων πάν-
των ὄσσα κε ὀμο‖[λογέωισι πρὸς ἀλλάλο]ις, οἰ ἀγρέθεντες ἄνδρες
φέροντον ἐπὶ τ‖[ὸν δᾶμον, ὁ δὲ δᾶμος ἀκο]ύσαις ἀι κε ἄγηται συμ-
35 φέρην βολλευέτω. ‖ [αἰ δέ κε ὁ δᾶμος ἄγηται τὰ] ὁμολογήμενα πρὸς
ἀλλάλοις συμφέρον‖[τα, ψαφίσασθαι καὶ τοῖς κα]τελθόντεσσι ἐπὶ
Σμιθίνα προτάνιος | [ὄσσα κε τοῖς λοίποισι ψαφ]ίσθη. αἰ δέ κέ τι
ἐνδεύη τῶ ψαφίσματος, | [περὶ τούτω ἀ κρίσις ἔστω ἐπ]ὶ τᾶι βόλ-
λαι. κυρώθεντος δὲ τῶ ψαφίσ‖[ματος ὑπὸ τῶ δάμω, σύμπαντα] τὸν
40 δᾶμον ἐν τᾶι εἰκοίσται τῶ μῆννος ‖ [πεδὰ τὰν θυσίαν εὔξασθαι] τοῖς
θέοισι ἐπὶ σωτηρίαι καὶ εὐδαι‖[μονίαι τῶμ πολίταν πάντων] γένε-
σθαι τὰν διάλυσιν τοῖς κατελ‖[θόντεσσι καὶ τοῖς πρόσθε] ἐν τᾶι πόλι
ἐόντεσσι · τοὶ[ς δ]ὲ ἴρηας τ|[οὶς δαμοσίοις ἄπαντας καὶ] ταὶς ἰρείαις
ὀείγην τ[οὶ]ς ναύοις καὶ | [τὸν δᾶμον πρὸς εὔχαν συνέλ]θην. τὰ δὲ
45 ἴρα τὰ ὁ δᾶμος [ε]ὔξατο, ὄτε ἐξ‖[έπεμψε τοὶς ἀγγέλοις πρὸς] τὸν
βασίληα, ἀπυδόμεναι τοῖς βασί|[ληος γενεθλίοισι κὰτ ἐνίαυ]τον ·
παρέμμεναι δὲ τᾶι θυσίαι καὶ [τ|οὶς εἴκοσι ἄνδρας καὶ τοὶς ἀ]γγέ-
λοις τοὶς πρὸς τὸν βασίληα πέ[μφ|θεντας τοὶς ἀπὺ τῶν πρόσθε] ἐν
τᾶι πόλι ἐόντων καὶ τοὶς ἀ[πὺ τῶν | κατελθόντων. τὸ δὲ ψάφισμα
τ]οῦτο ἀναγράψαντας τοὶς τ[αμίαις . . . .

Measures taken for the settlement of disputes arising between
the exiles who returned under Alexander's edict of 324 B.C. and
the remaining citizens of Mytilene.

Most of the restorations adopted are those preferred by Dittenberger l.c. But in many cases others are equally possible.

1 ff. 'The βασίληες shall favor the returned exile on the ground
that the one who remained in residence has been guilty of fraud.
But if any one of the returned exiles does not abide by these terms
of settlement, he shall not receive any property from the city,
nor shall he enter into possession of any of the property which
those who remained in the city have surrendered to him, but

rather those who surrendered it shall enter into possession of it, and the στρατηγοί shall return the property to the one who remained in residence, on the ground that the returned exile has not conformed to the agreement. And the βασίληες shall favor the one who remained in residence on the ground that the returned exile has been guilty of fraud. Nor, if any one brings suit, shall the clerks of the court and inspectors of justice, or any other magistrate, introduce it.'—13 ff. 'The officials are to intervene if all things prescribed in the decree are not carried out, and condemn any one who disregards them, so that there may be no disagreement between the two parties and they may live amicably and abide by the decision of the king and the settlement reached in this decree.'—21 ff. 'Twenty men are to be chosen as mediators, ten from each party. They are to see to it that no disagreement arises, and in the case of disputed property they are to bring it about that the parties shall be reconciled, or, if not, that they shall be as just as possible, and abide by the terms of settlement which the king decided upon and the agreement, and dwell in harmony.'—30-31 ff. 'Regarding questions of money, after the terms of settlement have been accepted as far as possible, and regarding the oath and other matters, the men selected shall report to the people, who shall take such measures as seem advantageous. If the people approve the matters agreed upon, they may decree the same privileges for the exiles returning in the prytany of Smithinas as for the others.'— 38/39 ff. 'When the decree has been confirmed, the people are to pray that the settlement may be for the general welfare. The priests and priestesses are to throw open the temples. The sacrifices which were promised when the messengers were sent to the king are to be made annually on the anniversary of the king's birthday in the presence of the twenty men and the messengers.'—39. For εἰκοίσται, now confirmed by six more occurrences of -κοιστος at Mytilene (IG XI.1064b and XII.ii.82), see 116a.

27. Nesos. Between 319 and 317 B.C. IG XII.ii.645. Ditt. Orient. 4. Schwyzer 634. Solmsen-Fraenkel 10. Only the text of side A is given here, the more fragmentary B being omitted.

.... κα]ὶ Ἀλέξανδρο[ς | .... χ]ώρας

τᾶι πόλι καὶ | [.............. ὅτα δὲ] Ἀλέξανδρος διάλ[λα|ξε τὸμ

5 πὰρ ἀνθρώ]πων βίον, Φίλιππος δὲ [ὁ || Φιλίππω καὶ] Ἀλέξανδρος

ὁ Ἀλεξάνδρω τ[ὰ|μ βασιλεί]αν παρέλαβον, Θέρσιππος ἔων | [τοῖς

βασ]ιλήεσσι φίλος καὶ τοῖς στροτ[ά|γοισι] καὶ τοῖς ἄλλοισι Μακε-

10 δόνεσσι μ[ε|γάλ]ων ἀγάθων αἴτιος γέγονε τᾶι πόλι. Ἀ[ν||τιπ]άτρω

γὰρ ἐπιτάξαντος χρήματα εἰς | τὸμ πόλεμον εἰσφέρην πάντων τῶν

ἄλλων |εἰσφερόντων Θέρσιππος παργενόμενος | πρὸς τοὶς βασίληας

καὶ Ἀντίπατρον ἐκ[ού]|φισσε τὰμ πόλιν, ἔπραξε δὲ καὶ πρὸς Κλε[ῖ-

15 ||τ]ον περὶ τᾶς εἰς Κύπρον στρατείας καὶ ἐ|[γ] μεγάλας δαπάνας εἰς

μῖκρον συνάγαγε. | [ἐγένετ]ο δὲ καὶ περὶ τὰν σιτοδείαν ἄνη[ρ | ἀγα-

θος] καὶ πὰρ τῶν σαδράπαν εἰσαγώγα[ν | σίτω κα]τεσκεύασσε,

20 ἔδωκε δὲ καὶ τᾶι πόλι || [χρήματ]α εἰς σωτηρίαν καὶ τόκοις ἐλάσ-

[σο|νας αἴτ]ησε τῶγ κατεστακόντων, ἐβαθόη | [δὲ χρη||μάτεσσι καὶ

τοῖς πολίταισι εἰς [σι|τωνία]ν. καὶ Πολυπέρχοντος εἰς τὰν Ἀσί[αν|

25 στάλε]ντος διώικησε φίλον αὖτον τᾶι πό||[λι ὑπά]ρχην, παρε-

σκεύασσε δὲ καὶ Ἀρράβαι|[ον καὶ] τοὶς ἄλλοις τοὶς ἐπί τινων τε-

τα||[γμένο]ις ὑπὸ τῶν βασιλήων φίλοις τᾶι π[ό|λι κα]ὶ τἆλλα

πράσσει μετ᾽ εὐνοίας πρὸς | [τὸν δ]ᾶμον πάντα · δέδοσθαι αὔτω

30 ἀτέλει[αν || πάντω]ν τὸμ πάντα χρόνον καὶ αὔτω καὶ [ἐκ|γόν]οισι,

στᾶσαι δὲ αὔτω καὶ εἴκονα χαλ[κί|αν], δέδοσθαι δὲ καὶ σίτησιν ἐμ

προτανη[ί|ω, κ]αὶ ὄτα κε ἀ πόλις ἱροποήται, μέρις δ[ι|δώ]σθω Θερσ-

35 ίππω καὶ τῶν ἐκγόνων ἄι τῶ γ[ε||ραι]τάτω, κάλησθαι δὲ καὶ εἰς

προεδρίαν · | [στε]φανώτω δὲ αὖτον ὁ χοροστάτας ἄι ὁ ἐν[έ|ων ἐ]ν

τῶ ἄγωνι καὶ ὀγκαρυσσέτω ἀνδραγ[α|θί]ας ἔνεκα καὶ εὐνοίας τᾶς

40 πρὸς τὸν δᾶ|[μον], ἴνα γινώσκωισι πάντες ὄτι ὁ δᾶμος ὁ || [Να]σιώ-

ταν τοὶς ἀγάθοις ἄνδρας [κ]αὶ εὐε[ρ|γέ]ταις τί[μαι] καὶ σώθεντος

αὔτω ἐστεφα|[να]φόρησεν ἀμέραις τρῖς καὶ εὐαγγέλια | καὶ σωτήρια

ἔ[θ]υσε καὶ παν[άγυρ]ιν συνά|γαγε δαμοτέ[λ]ην καὶ νῦν τίμαι

45 δικάως. ἀ||[νά]γραψαι δὲ τοῖς ταμίαις τοῖς μετ᾽ Ἡρα|κλείτω τὸ ψά-

φισμα εἰς στάλλαν λιθίναν | τῶ ἐκ Θέρμας λίθω καὶ στᾶσαι ὄππα

κε Θε[ρ]|σίππω συνα[ρ]έσκη μέχρι Πορνοπίας · ἐξέ[σ]|τω δὲ Θερσ-

50 ί[π]πω καὶ ἄλλα ὄππα κε θέλη τῶ[ν || ί]ρων στᾶσα[ι] τὸ ψά-

φισμα, καί κέ τι θέλη π[ρ]|οσγράφην, ἔμμεναι αὔτω, τῶγ κεν

εὐεργέ|τη τὰμ πόλιν.

Decree in honor of Thersippus for using his influence with
the Macedonians in behalf of the city. For the historical references

see Dittenberger, l.c. There are some κοινή forms, as μετά for πεδά, ἀνάγραψαι beside ὀγκαρυσσέτω.

47. ἐκ Θέρμας λίθω: 'of marble from Therma,' a place in Lesbos near Mytilene.—**μέχρι Πορνοπίας**: site of the temple of Apollo Parnopius, the epithet being derived from πάρνοψ, Lesb. Boeot. πόρνοψ **(5)**.—48 ff.: 'Thersippus may also have the decree set up elsewhere in any sanctuary that he chooses and add to it a statement of any of his other benefactions.'

28. Cyme. Between 2 B.C. and A.D. 19. Schwyzer 647.

- - - [δαμ]οσίαι[ς | - - - ταὶς ὑπαρκοί]σαις αὕτω κτή|[σιας ἐν τῶ
Ζμαραγήω] - - - - η τούτοισι τῶ δά[μω] | - - - - ονια πασσυδιά-
5 σαντος καὶ || [μεγαλο]πρεπεσ(τά)ταις τείμαις δογματίζοντος καὶ
ναύ|ω ἐν τῶ γυμ(ν)ασίω κατείρων προαγρημμένω, ἐν ὦ ταὶς τεί-|
μαις αὕτω κατιδρύσει, κτίσταν τε καὶ εὐεργέταν προσονυ|μάσθεσθαι,
εἰκονάς τε χρυσίαις ὀντέθην, καθὰ τοῖς τὰ μέ|γιστα τὸν δᾶμον εὐερ-
10 γετησάντεσσι νόμιμόν ἐστι, με||τά τε τὰν ἐξ ἀνθρώπων αὕτω μετά-
στασιν καὶ τὰν ἐν|τάφαν καὶ θέσιν τῶ σώματος ἐν τῶ γυμνασίω
γενήθην, | ἀποδεξάμενος ὑπερθύμως τὰν κρίσιν τᾶς πόλιος Λα|βέων,
στοίχεις τοῖς προυπαργμένοισι αὕτω καὶ προσμέ|τρεις τὰν ἑαύτω
15 τύχαν τοῖς ἐφίκτοισιν ἀνθρώπω, τὰν || μὲν ὑπερβάρεα καὶ θέοισι
καὶ τοῖς ἰσσοθέοισι ἀρμόζοι|σαν τᾶς τε τῶ ναύω κατειρώσιος τᾶς
τε τῶ κτίστα | προσονυμασίας τείμαν παρητήσατο, ἀρκέην νομί-|
ζων τὰν κρίσιν τῶ πλάθεος καὶ τὰν εὔνοαν ἐπιτεθε|ωρήκην, ταὶς δὲ
20 τοῖς ἀγάθοισι τῶν ἄνδρων πρεποί||σαις ἀσμενίζοισα χάρα συνεπέ-
νευσε τείμαις · ἐφ' οἷ|σιν πρεπωδέστατόν ἐστι τῶν ἐννόμων ἐόντων |
χρόνων τὰν παντέλεα τῶν εἰς ἀμοίβαν ἀνηκόντων | ἐπαίνων τε
καὶ τειμίων περὶ τᾶς καλοκἀγαθίας αὕτω | μαρτυρίαν ἀπυδέδοσθαι ·
25 δι' ἀ καὶ τύχα ἀγάθα δέδοχθαι || τᾶ βόλλα καὶ τῶ δάμω · ἐπαίνην Λα-
βέωνα παίσας ἔοντα τεί|μας ἄξιον καὶ διὰ τὰν λοίπαν μὲν περὶ τὸν
βίον σεμνότατα | καὶ διὰ τὰν φιλοδοξίαν δὲ καὶ τὰν μεγαλοδάπανον
εἰς | τὰν πόλιν διάθεσιν, καὶ ἔχην ἐν τᾶ καλλίστα διαλάμψει τε
καὶ | ἀπυδόχα, καὶ κάλην εἰς προεδρίαν, καὶ στεφάνων ἐν πάν-||
30 τεσσι τοῖς ἀγώνεσσιν, οἷς κεν ἁ πόλις συντελέη, ἐν τᾶ τᾶν | κατεύ-
χαν ἀμέρα ἐπὶ τὰν σπόνδαν κὰτ τάδε · ὁ δᾶμος στε|φάνοι Λεύκιον
Οὐάκκιον Λεύκίω υἷον Αἰμιλία Λαβέωνα, φι|λοκύμαιον εὐεργέταν,
στεφάνω χρυσίω ἀρέτας ἔνεκα | καὶ φιλαγαθίας τᾶς εἰς ἔαυτον · ὀν-
35 τέθην δὲ αὕτω καὶ εἴ||κονας, γράπταν τε ἐν ὅπλω ἐγχρύσω καὶ

χαλκίαν, κὰτ τὰ αὖ|τα δὲ καὶ μαρμαρίαν καὶ χρυσίαν ἐν τῷ γυμνα-
σίῳ, ἐφ' ἂν ἐπε|γράφην· ὁ δᾶμος ἐτείμασεν Λεύκιον Οὐάκκιον
Λευκίω | υἶον Αἰμιλία Λαβέωνα, φιλοκύμαιον εὐεργέταν, γυμνα-
40 σι|αρχήσαντα κάλως καὶ μεγαλοδόξως, ὄνθεντα δὲ || καὶ τὸ βαλά-
νηον τοῖς νέοισι καὶ πρὸς τὰν εἰς αὖτο κοραγί|αν ταῖς ὑπαρκοίσαις
αὖτω κτήσιας ἐν Ζμαραγήω, καὶ ἐ|πισκεάσαντα τὸ γυμνάσιον,
καὶ ἔκαστα ἐπιτελέσαντα | λάμπρως καὶ μεγαλοψύχως, ἀρέτας
ἔνεκα καὶ εὐνόας | τᾶς εἰς ἔαυτον. καὶ ἐπεί κε δὲ τελευτάσῃ, κατε-
45 νέχθεν||τα αὖτον ὑπὸ τῶν ἐφάβων καὶ τῶν νέων εἰς τὰν ἀγόραν |
στεφανώθην διὰ τῶ τᾶς πόλιος κάρυκος κὰτ τάδε· ὁ δᾶ|μος στεφά-
νοι Λεύκιον Οὐάκκιον Λευκίω υἶον Αἰμιλία Λα|βέωνα, φιλοκύμαιον
εὐεργέταν, στεφάνω χρυσίω ἀρέ|τας ἔνεκα καὶ εὐνόας τᾶς εἰς ἔαυ-
50 τον· εἰσενέχθην δὲ || αὖτον εἰς τὸ γυμνάσιον ὑπό τε τῶν ἐφάβων
καὶ τῶν | νέων, καὶ ἐντάφην ἐν ᾧ κ' ἂν εὔθετον ἔμμεναι φαίνηται
τό|πω. τὸ δὲ ψάφισμα τόδε ἀνάγραψαι εἰς στάλαν λίθω λεύ|κω καὶ
ὀνθέμεναι εἰς τὸ γυμνάσιον πὰρ ταῖς δεδο|γματισμέναις αὖτω τεί-
55 μαις. μῆνος Φρατρίω δεκάτα || ἀπίοντος ἐπὶ ἰερέως τᾶς Ῥώμας καὶ
Αὐτοκράτορος | Καίσαρος, θέω υἶω, θέω Σεβάστω, ἀρχιέρεος μεγί-
στω καὶ πά|τρος τᾶς πάτριδος Πολέμωνος τῶ Ζήνωνος Λαοδί|κεος,
πρυτάνιος δὲ Λευκίω Οὐακκίω Λευκίω υἶω Αἰμιλί|α Λαβέωνος, φι-
60 λοκυμαίω εὐεργέτα, στεφαναφόρω δὲ || Στράτωνος τῶ Ἡρακλείδα.

Decree in honor of L. Vaccius Labeo. This is a characteristic
example of the artificial revival of the dialect in Roman imperial
times (cf. **280**). With the genuine dialect forms are interspersed
κοινή forms as παρητήσατο, πρύτανις, ἀνα-, μετά, ἰερέως, καθά, ἐφ'
οἶσιν, etc.; hyper-Aeolic forms as ἐφάβων, πλάθεος (words with
original η, not ᾱ); and examples of late spelling as τείμαις, κατείρων
with ει = ι (**21**), ἐπισκεάσαντα (**36**), κοραγίαν, ὑπάρκοισαν with
κ = χ (**66a**). ἀρκέην (infin.), συντελέη beside the normal μι-forms
κάλην, στεφάνων, etc. (**155**.3) are probably artificial. ναύω (l. 5),
if correct, is a blend of ναῦον with Att. νεώ. ἐπεγράφην (l. 36-37)
is an aor. infin. pass., like ὀντέθην, with ε carried over from the
indicative (perhaps only by the engraver). With regard to psilosis,
we find κατείρων, κατιδρύσει, but ἐφίκτοισιν. The forms of the
relative, being borrowed from the κοινή (**126**), are transcribed
with ' throughout (cf. also ἐφ' οἶσιν etc.); and one might also
prefer ἰερέως and ἑαυτόν (instead of ἔαυτον with ' and Lesbian

accent). But it is impossible to determine whether in such cases the κοινή form was adopted as a whole or only in part (cf. **280**), and moreover by this time little, if anything, was left of the sound of the spiritus asper even in the κοινή. So the transcription chosen is of small consequence.

15 ff. 'He declined the excessive honor, suitable only to gods and demi-gods, of dedicating a temple and naming him founder, thinking it to be enough to have observed the judgment and good will of the people, but the honors suitable to good men he accepted with gratification.'—32. Αἰμιλία: name of the tribe, after the customary Latin abl. sg. (sc. *tribu*).—56 f. 'when Polemon was priest of Rome and Augustus.'

Thessalian

Pelasgiotis
(With Phalanna. See p. 151, footnote)

29. Larisa. Fifth century B.C. IG IX.ii.662-663. Roberts 240. Schwyzer 584.

a. Πολυξεναία ἐμμί.   *b.* Fεκέδαμος.

Πολυξεναία: sc. στάλλα. 168c.—**Fεκέδαμος:** 46, 52*b*.

30. Site of unknown identity, southeast of Larisa. Fifth century B.C. IG IX.ii.1027. Schwyzer 597.

Ἄπλōνι Λεσχα[ί]ō[ι] Ἀριστίōν ὀνέθēκε κοὶ συνδαυχναφόροι. Πρόνος ἐργάξατο.

'Aristion and his fellow δαφνηφόροι set up to Apollo of the Λέσχη.' **δαύχνα:** 68.4*a*.—Λεσχα[ί]ō[ι]: or Λεσχα[ί]ō (see **38**)? Λεσχηνόριος, an epithet of Apollo, occurs in Plutarch, and Λεσχανόριος is the name of a month in Thessalian and Cretan.

31. Phalanna. Fifth century B.C. IG IX.ii.1226. Schwyzer 608.

5 Νόμος. | αἴ κε τὸν | Fασστὸν | κις Fαλί||οσκēτα[ι] | κοινὰ χ[ρ]||έ-
10 ματα ἔ[χ]||ον καὶ μ[ὲ] | δυνάēτ[α]||ι ἀππε[ῖσ|αι] το - - - -

32. Larisa. About 214 B.C. IG IX.ii.517. Ditt. Syll. 543. Schwyzer 590. Solmsen-Fraenkel 12.

[Ταγ]ευόντουν Ἀναγκίπποι Πετθαλείοι, Ἀριστονόοι Εὐνομείοι,
2 Ἐπιγένεος Ἰασονείοι, Εὐδίκο[ι| Ἀδα]μαντείοι, Ἀλεξία Κλεαρχείοι,
γυμνασιαρχέντος Ἀλεύα Δαμοσθενείοι · Φιλίπποι τοῖ βασιλεῖος

ἐπιστολὰν ἀ|[π]υστέλλαντος πὸτ τὸς ταγὸς καὶ τὰν πόλιν τὰν
ὑπογεγραμμέναν ·
4 „Βασιλεὺς Φίλιππος Λαρισαί|ων τοῖς ταγοῖς καὶ τῇι πόλει
χαίρειν. Πετραῖος καὶ Ἀνάγκιππος καὶ Ἀριστόνους ὡς ἀπὸ τῆς
πρεσβείας ἐγένοντο. || ἐνεφάνιζόν μοι ὅτι καὶ ἡ ὑμετέρα πόλις διὰ
τοὺς πολέμους προσδεῖται πλεόνων οἰκητῶν · ἕως ἂν οὖν καὶ ἑτέ-|
6 ρους ἐπινοήσωμεν ἀξίους τοῦ παρ' ὑμῖν πολιτεύματος, ἐπὶ τοῦ παρ-
όντος κρίνω ψηφίσασθαι ὑμᾶς ὅπως τοῖς κατοι|κοῦσιν παρ' ὑμῖν
Θεσσαλῶν ἢ τῶν ἄλλων Ἑλλήνων δοθῇι πολιτεία. τούτου γὰρ
8 συντελεσθέντος καὶ συνμεινάν|των πάντων διὰ τὰ φιλάνθρωπα
πέπεισμαι ἕτερά τε πο[λ]λὰ τῶν χρησίμων ἔσεσθαι καὶ ἐμοὶ καὶ
τῇι πόλει καὶ τὴν | χώραν μᾶλλον ἐξεργασθήσεσθαι. ἔτους β'
Ὑπερβερεταίου κα'."
10 ψαφιξαμένας τᾶς πόλιος ψάφισμα || τὸ ὑπογεγραμμένον · „Πα-
νάμμοι τᾶ ἕκτα ἐπ ἰκάδι συνκλεῖτος γενομένας, ἀγορανομέντουν
τοῦν ταγοῦν πάν|τουν · Φιλίπποι τοῖ βασιλεῖος γράμματα πέμψαν-
τος πὸτ τὸς ταγὸς καὶ τὰν πόλιν διὲ κί Πετραῖος καὶ Ἀνάγκιπ-
12 πος καὶ | Ἀριστόνοος, οὓς ἀτ τᾶς πρεισβείας ἐγένονθο, ἐνεφανίσ-
σοεν αὐτοῦ, πὸκ κί καὶ ἀ ἀμμέουν πόλις διὲ τὸς πολέμος πο|τεδέετο
πλειόνουν τοῦν κατοικεισόντουν · μέσποδί κε οὖν καὶ ἕτερος ἐπι-
14 νοείσουμεν ἀξίος τοῖ πὰ[ρ] ἀμμὲ | πολιτεύματος, ἒτ τοῖ παρεόντος
κρεννέμεν ψαφίζασθειν ἀμμὲ ο(ὕ)ς κε τοῖς κατοικέντεσσι πὰρ ἀμμὲ
Πετθ[α]||λοῦν καὶ τοῦν ἄλλουν Ἑλλάνουν δοθεῖ ἀ πολιτεία · τοῖνεος
16 γὰρ συντελεσθέντος καὶ συμμεννάντουν πάν|τουν διὲ τὰ φιλάνθρουπα
πεπεῖστειν ἄλλα τε πολλὰ τοῦν χρεισίμουν ἔσσεσθειν καὶ εὑτοῦ καὶ
τᾶ πόλι καὶ | τὰν χούραν μᾶλλον ἐξεργασθείσεσθειν · ἐψάφιστει τᾶ
18 πολιτεία πρασσέμεν πὲρ τοῦννεουν κὰτ τὰ ὁ βα|σιλεὺς ἔγραψε, καὶ
τοῖς κατοικέντεσσι πὰρ ἀμμὲ Πετθαλοῦν καὶ τοῦν ἄλλουν Ἑλλά-
νουν δεδόσθειν τὰν πολι|τείαν καὶ αὐτοῖς καὶ ἐσγόνοις καὶ τὰ λοιπὰ
τίμια ὑπαρχέμεν αὐτοῖς πάντα ὅσσαπερ Λασαίοις, φυλᾶς ἑλομέ-||
20 νοις ἑκάστου ποίας κε βέλλειτει · τὸ μὰ ψάφισμα τόνε κῦρρον
ἔμμεν κὰπ παντὸς χρόνοι καὶ τὸς ταμίας ἐσδό|μεν ὀνγράψειν αὐτὸ
ἐν στάλλας λιθίας δύας καὶ τὰ ὀνόματα τοῦν πολιτογραφειθέντουν
22 καὶ κατθέμεν | τὰμ μὲν ἴαν ἐν τὸ ἱερὸν τοῖ Ἄπλουνος τοῖ Κερδοίοι,
τὰμ μὰ ἄλλαν ἐν τὰν ἀκρόπολιν, καὶ τὰν ὀνάλαν, κίς κε γι|νύειτει
ἐν τάνε, δόμεν ·" καὶ ὕστερον Φιλίπποι τοῖ βασιλεῖος ἐπιστολὰν
24 ἄλλαν ἀπυστέλλαντος πὸτ | τὸς ταγὸς καὶ τὰν πόλιν, ταγευόντουν
Ἀριστονόοι Εὐνομείοι, Εὐδίκοι Ἀδαμαντείοι, Ἀλεξίπποι Ἱππολο-

χείοι, ‖ Ἐπιγένεος Ἰασονείοι, Νυμεινίοι Μνασιαίοι, γυμνασιαρχέν-
τος Τιμουνίδα Τιμουνιδαίοι, τὰν ὑπογεγραμμέναν· |

26 „Βασιλεὺς Φίλιππος Λαρισαίων τοῖς ταγοῖς καὶ τῆι πόλει χαί-
ρειν. πυνθάνομαι τοὺς πολιτογραφηθέντας κατὰ | τὴν παρ' ἐμοῦ
ἐπιστολὴν καὶ τὸ ψήφισμα τὸ ὑμέτερον καὶ ἀναγραφέντας εἰς τὰς
28 στήλας ἐκκεκολάφθαι· εἴ|περ οὖν ἐγεγόνει τοῦτο, ἠστοχήκεισαν οἱ
συνβουλεύσαντες ὑμῖν καὶ τοῦ συμφέροντος τῆι πατρίδι | καὶ τῆς
ἐμῆς κρίσεως. ὅτι γὰρ πάντων κάλλιστόν ἐστιν ὡς πλείστων μετε-
30 χόντων τοῦ πολιτεύματος ‖ τήν τε πόλιν ἰσχύειν καὶ τὴν χώραν μὴ
ὥσπερ νῦν αἰσχρῶς χερσεύεσθαι, νομίζω μὲν οὐδ' ὑμῶν οὐθένα ἂν
ἀν|τειπεῖν, ἔξεστι δὲ καὶ τοὺς λοιποὺς τοὺς ταῖς ὁμοίαις πολιτο-
32 γραφίαις χρωμένους θεωρεῖν, ὧν καὶ οἱ Ῥωμαῖ|οί εἰσιν, οἳ καὶ τοὺς
οἰκέτας, ὅταν ἐλευθερώσωσιν, προσδεχόμενοι εἰς τὸ πολίτευμα καὶ
τῶν ἀρχαίων με|[ταδι]δόντες καὶ διὰ τοῦ τοιούτου τρόπου οὐ μόνον
34 τὴν ἰδίαν πατρίδα ἐπηυξήκασιν, ἀλλὰ καὶ ἀποικίας (σ)χεδὸν | [εἰς
ἐβ]δομήκοντα τόπους ἐκπεπόμφασιν. πλ[ὴ]ν ἔτι δὲ καὶ νῦν παρα-
καλῶ ὑμᾶς ἀφιλοτίμως προσελθεῖν ‖ [πρὸς τὸ] πρᾶγμα καὶ τοὺς
μὲν κεκριμένους ὑπὸ τῶν πολιτῶν ἀποκαταστῆσαι εἰς τὴν πολι-
36 τείαν, εἰ δέ | [τινες ἀ]νήκεστόν τι πεπράχασιν εἰς τὴν βασιλείαν
ἢ τὴν πόλιν ἢ δι' ἄλλην τινὰ αἰτίαν μὴ ἄξιοί εἰσιν | [μετέχ]ειν
τῆς στήλης ταύτης, περὶ τούτων τὴν ὑπέρθεσιν ποιήσασθαι, ἕως
38 ἂν ἐγὼ ἐπιστρέψας ἀπὸ τῆς | [στρα]τείας διακούσω· τοῖς μέντοι
κατηγορεῖν τούτων μέλλουσιν προείπατε ὅπως μὴ φανῶσιν διὰ
φ[ι|λο]τιμίαν τοῦτο ποιοῦντες. ἔτους ζ' Γορπιαίου ιγ'."

40 ψαφιξαμένας τᾶς πόλιος ψάφισμα τὸ ὑπογε‖[γ]ραμμένον· „Θε-
μιστίοι τᾶ ὑστερομειννία ἀγορανομέντος Ἀλεξίπποι πὲρ ἱεροῦν,
Ἀλεξίπποι λέξα[ν]|τος ἐψάφιστει τᾶ πολιτεία, ὅσσουν μὲν ἐφάν-
γρενθείν κινες τοῦν πεπολιτογραφειμένουν, τὸς ταγὸς ἐγγρά[ψαν]-|
42 τας ἐν λεύκουμα ἐσθέμεν αὐτὸς ἐν τὸν λιμένα, τοῦ[ν μ]ὰ λοιποῦν
τοῦν πεπολιτογραφειμένουν κὰτ τὰν ἐπιστ[ο]|λὰν τοῖ βασιλείος τὰ
ὀνύματα καὶ τὰς ἐπιστολὰς τοῖ βασιλείος καὶ τὰ ψαφίσματα τό
44 τε ὑππρὸ [τ]ᾶς γενόμενον | καὶ τὸ τᾶμον ὀγγράψαντας ἐν στάλλας
λιθίας δύας κατθέμεν τὰν μὲν ἴαν ἐν τὸν ναὸν τοῖ Ἀπλουνος τοῖ
Κερδοίοι, ‖ τὰν δὲ ἄλλαν ἐν τὰν ἀκρόπολιν ἐν τὸν ναὸν τᾶς Ἀθάνας,
46 καὶ τὰν ὀνάλαν τὰν ἐν τάνε γινυμέναν τὸς | ταμίας δόμεν ἀτ τᾶν
κοινᾶν ποθόδουν· τὸ μὰ ψάφισμα τόνε κῦρρον ἔμμεν κὰπ παντὸς
χρόνοι." οἱ πεπολιτογραφειμένοι κάτ τε τὰς ἐπιστολὰς τοῖ βα-
σιλείος καὶ κὰτ τὰ ψαφίσματα τᾶς πόλιος· |

48   Σαμόθρακες· Ἄρχιππος Καλλιφούντειος.
Κραννούνιοι· Ἀγεισίνοος Λυκίνειος, Φάλα|κρος Σιμίαιος, [κτλ. 49-78].
79   Γυρτούνιοι· Εὔθοινος Λεττίναιος, Φιλόδαμος Λεττίναιος, Βοΐ-
σκος Δαμμάτρειος, [κτλ. 79-92].

Decrees of Larisa made in accordance with recommendations of the Macedonian king Philip V, whose letters, dated 219 and 214 B.C. and written in the κοινή, are included. The Thessalians at this time were nominally independent, but actually subject to Macedonia. Cf. Polyb. 4.76.2.

10. **συνκλεῖτος**: συνκλείς (**164**.10) is used, like Att. σύγκλητος ἐκκλησία, of a specially summoned assembly.—16. **εὐτοῦ**: ἑαυτῷ. So also εὐτοῖ, εὐτῆς in two other inscriptions of Larisa.—19. **Λασαίοις**: Λαρισαίοις. **88b**.—19 f. **φυλᾶς** κτλ. : 'choosing each the tribe to which he wishes to belong.' ποίας gen. sg. with ἔμμεν understood, φυλᾶς gen. sg. by attraction to ποίας. Cf. Att. ἑλέσθαι δὲ αὐτοὺς φυλὴν καὶ δῆμον καὶ φρατρίαν, ἧς ἂν βούλωνται εἶναι. —28. **ἠστοχήκεισαν**: 3 pl. plpf. of ἀστοχέω 'miss the mark, fail.' Both word and ending are post-classical.—38. **μέντον**: μέντοι. This is now attested from some half dozen κοινή sources. It is probably due to the analogy of adverbs like πρῶτον, λοιπόν, etc.—40. **πὲρ ἱεροῦν**: apparently equivalent, in the language of adulation, to πὲρ βασιλικῶν.—41. **ὅσσουν** κτλ. : '(the names) of as many of the enrolled citizens as any accuse.' ἐφάνγρενθειν: **139**.2, **162**.2. In sense = κατηγοροῦσιν (cf. l. 38).—43. **καὶ τὰ ψαφίσματα** κτλ. : 'and the decrees, both the one just previously passed and the present one.' ὑππρὸ τᾶς, sc. ἁμέρας. Same phrase in another inscription of Larisa (IG IX.ii.512.30). **136**.1, 12.

33. Larisa. Second century B.C. Béquignon, BCH 59.55 ff. Lejeune, Rev. Ét. Gr. 54.77 ff.

Ταγευόντων Κρίτουνος Παυσανιαίοι, Κρατει|σίπποι Θερσαν-
δρείου, Θρασυμάχοι Ἀριστουνεί|οι, Φιλοφείροι Ἀσανδρείοι, Θερσ-
5 άνδροι Πολυξενε|[ί]οι, ταμιευόντουν Λυκίνοι Ἀλ[ε]ξανδρείοι
καὶ Μενε||κράτεος Εὔστρατ[ι]δαιοι, γυμνασιαρχέντουν | μὲς τᾶς
πέμπ[τ]ας [τ]οῖ Ὁμολουίοι Πλειστία Ἀσκα|λαπιαδαίοι καὶ Δου-
ριμαλαίοι Λαμείοι   , ἀτ τᾶ[ς] | μὰ πέμπτας Ἱπποδρομ[ίοι],
10 Αἰσκαναίοι καὶ Φερεκρ[ά]τεος Μενεκρατεί[οι] ||

Ἀπλουνίοι [ὑ]στέρα, ἀγορᾶς [ἔνσας, ἀ]γορανομέντος Κρίτουνος
Πα[υ]|σανιαίοι, Κρίτουν[ος Παυσα]νιαίοι λέξαντος· ὀπειδεὶ |
[Β]όμβος Ἀλφεί[οι] Α[ἰολεὺς ἀπ' Ἀλεξαν]δρείας, παρεπιδαμεί-|
15 [σ]ας ἐν τᾶ πόλι [ἐπὶ ἀμέρας πλείονα]ς, ἐπιδείξις ἐν τοῦ γ[υ||μ-]
νασί[ου ἐποιείσατο, εὐδοκίμεισε]ν τε τοῖς πεπραγματευμένοις |
αὐτ[οῦ καὶ ἐπεμνάσθει τοῦν γε]γ[ενει]μένουν ἐνδόξουν Λα|ρισαίοις
καὶ [εἰύξεισε τὰν εὐνο]ίαν καὶ φιλίαν ταῖς πολίεσσι π[ὸ]|θ' εὐτὰς,
ὀν[νεουσάμενος] καὶ τὰ φιλάνθρουπα τὰ ὑπάρχοντα | Αἰολείεσσι
20 πὸτ τὰν πόλιν τὰν Λαρισαίουν· ἐποιείσατο μὰ || καὶ τὰν ὀστροφὰν
[εὐσχαμόν]ους καὶ ὂν τρόπον ἐπέβαλλε ἀν|δρὶ καλοῦ καὶ ἀγαθοῦ·
ἔδοξε τοῦ δάμου τοῦ Λαρισαίουν· ἐπα[ι]|νείσειν τε Βόμ[βον] Ἀλ-
[φείοι] Αἰολέα ἀπ' Ἀλεξανδρείας ἔτ τε | τᾶ ὀστροφᾶ καὶ φ[ιλοτιμ]ία
πὲρ τὰν παιδείαν καὶ ἒτ τοῦ τὰ | κάλλιστα τοῦν ἐπιτα[δευ]μάτουν
25 ἐζαλουκέμεν, καὶ δοθέ||μεν αὐτοῦ καὶ ἐσγόνοις πολιτείαν καὶ ἔντασιν
καὶ τὰ λοι|πὰ τίμια ὑπαρχέμεν αὐτ[οῦ] ὅσσα καὶ Λαρισαίοις. καὶ
ὀπεί κε ὁ | [κ]αιρὸς κατενέχει ἐν τοῦ δεύει ἐς τοῦν νόμουν τὰ κὰτ
τᾶς πολ[ι]|τείας οἰκονομείσθειν, φροντίσειν τὸς τάγος οὔστε δοθεῖ
αὐτοῦ | ἀ πολιτεία. τὸ μὰ ψάφισμα τόνε κύριον ἔμμεν κὰ παντὸς
30 χρόνοι || καὶ τὸς ταμίας ἐσδόμεν ὀνγράψει[ν] αὐτὸ ἐν κίονα λιθίαν
καὶ κατα[θέ]||μεν ἐν τὸ ἱερὸν τοῖ Ἀπλουνος τοῖ Κερδοίοι καὶ τὰν
ὀνάλαν κίς κ[ε| γ]ίνειτει δόμεν.

Decree in honor of Bombus, an Aeolian from Alexandria. The
restorations, with some minor changes, are those of the editor.
6. **μές**: 'until.' **132**.12.—12. **ὀπειδεί** = ἐπειδή. **132**.7.—20.
ὀστροφά: from *ὀνστροφά (**6**,77.2) = ἀναστροφή, here 'behavior.'
For the whole phrase, cf. πεποίηνται τὰν ἀναστροφὰν καλὰν καὶ
εὐσχήμονα, Ditt. 740.—22 f. **καὶ ἒτ τοῦ**, κτλ.: 'and for his having
been zealous for the best practices.' Cf. τοῖς τῶν καλλίστων ἐπιταδευ-
μάτων προεστακόσι, Ditt. 721.40.—For ἒτ τοῦ (and ἔτ τε l. 22),
from ἔπ = ἐπί, see **95**, **99**.2.—26 ff. **καὶ ὀπεί κε**, κτλ.: 'and when
the time arrives in which it is necessary in accordance with the
laws for matters concerning citizenship to be regulated.'—**ὀπει**
'when': **132**.7.—**δεύει**: **35**.—ll. 32-45, omitted here, contain
another similar decree. The editor's reading Κρατεισίπποιο Ἐρ-
σανδρείοι (ll. 34 f., 39 f.) should be changed to Κρατεισίπποι Θε-
ρσανδρείοι, agreeing with l. 1/2.
34. Crannon. Second century B.C. IG IX.ii.461. Schwyzer 578.

[Στρατα]γέντος τοῦν Πε[τθαλοῦν | Λίοντος] Παυσανιαίοι Μα-
τροπολ[ίτα, | ταγευό]ντουν Σιλάνοι Ἀστο[μαχείοι, | Φίλ]ουνος
5 Ἀντιγενείοι, Γεν[νάοι Ἀσ||στον]οείοι, Γεννάοι Αἰσχυλ[είοι, - -]
- - Κ]αλλισθενείοι, ταμιε[υόντουν - - | - - Ἀ]ντιγονείοι, Φείδουνος
Εὐ[δοξείοι], | - - ος Ἀντιγενείοι λέξαντο[ς · ἐπει|δεὶ Λί]ουν Παυ-
10 σανίαιο[ς] Ματροπ[ολίτας || διετέ]λει εὐεργετὲς τὸ κοινὸν [τᾶς |
πόλι]ος ἔν τε τοῖς πρότερο[ν χρόνοις | καὶ ἐ]ν τᾶ ἀρχᾶ τᾶ ἐαυτοῖ
καὶ κ[οινᾶ τᾶ | πόλι κ]αὶ καθ' ἰδδίαν ἀὶν τοῦ χρείαν [ἔχο|ντι, ἔδο]ξε
15 τοῦ κοινοῦ τᾶς πόλιος [ἐπαι||νέσαι] Λίοντα ἐτ τᾶ προανγρέ[σι
τὰν | ἔχει καὶ π]ὸτ τὰν πόλιν καὶ πὸ[θ ἕκαστον | τοῦν] πολιτάουν
καὶ δεδόσ[θαι καὶ αὐ|τοῦ] κα(ὶ) τοῖς ἐσγόνοις ἀτ[έλειαν πάντουν |
20 καὶ] ἀουλίαν καὶ ἰσοτιμίαν καὶ [πάντα || τὰ λοι]πὰ αὐτοῦ ὑπαρχέ-
μεν τίμια [ὅσσα | καὶ] τοῖς λοιποῖς προξένοις, καὶ [φροντίσαι | τὸν]
ταμ[ί]αν Φείδουνα Εὐδόξει[ον οὕς κε | ἀτ τᾶς] τοῦν ταγοῦν γνού-
25 μας [τόνε τὸ | ψάφισμ]α ὀνγραφεῖ ἐν κίονα λιθίν[αν || καὶ τ]ε[θεῖ]
ακρουν ἐν τοῖς ἰαρουτοῖς, [τὸ | μὰ ὀ]νάλουμα τὸ γενόμενον [ἐν
τάνε | ἐγγραφέ]μεν ἐν τοῖς λόγοις τᾶ[ς πόλιος].

Decree in honor of Leon of Matropolis.—25. ακρουν: dubious.

Thessaliotis

35. Thetonium, not far from Cierium. Fifth century B.C.
IG IX.ii.257. Schwyzer 557. Ditt. Syll. 55. Solmsen-Fraenkel 13.

-ἐς ηυλōρέοντος Φιλονίκō ηυῖος. |

Θετόνιοι ἐδōκαν Σōταίρōι τōι Κ|ορινθίōι καὐτōι καὶ γένει καὶ
5 Ϝ|οικιάταις καὶ χρḗμασιν ἀσυλί||αν κάτέλειαν κεὐϜεργέταν ἐ|ποίε-
σαν κὲν ταγᾶ κὲν ἀταγ|ίαι. αἴ τις παρβαίνοι, τὸ|ν ταγὸν τὸν ἐπε-
10 στάχοντα ἐ|ξξανακάδ∈ν. τὰ χρυσία καὶ τὰ || ἀργύρια τ∈ς Βελφαίō
ἀπολ]όμενα ἔσōσε Ὀρέσταο Φερεκράτ-

Decree of the Thetonians in honor of Sotaerus the Corinthian,
who had recovered the gold and silver objects that had been
lost from the temple of Apollo. For similar "losses" cf. Ditt.
Syll. 405-6, 416-18.

1, 11. It is obvious that the text as it stands is incomplete
both at the beginning and the end, although the bronze tablet
on which it is inscribed is intact. A horizontal line was cut in the
bronze to indicate that l. 1 did not belong with the following.
It is probable that l.1 is the conclusion of the present decree,
and was added at the top when it was found that no space was

left at the bottom. In this case we read Ὀρέσταο Φερεκράτες (cf. **108**.2) or, with correction, Φερεκράτε(ο)ς hυλōρέοντος Φιλονίκō hυῖος 'when Orestes, son of Pherecrates of Philonicus, was ὑλωρός.' The use of the genitive instead of the patronymic adjective would be only another instance (see **214**) of divergence from the usual Thessalian. The addition of the grandfather's name is unusual, but not unprecedented (cf., e.g., no. 24), likewise the use of υἱός instead of the genitive alone (cf., e.g., GDI 1183, Arc.; Ditt. Syll. 121, Stratus; παῖς often so used in Lesbian and Cyprian). ὑλωρός occurs in Arist. Pol. 6.8.6 as the title of an official similar to the ἀγρονόμος,. but nowhere else than in this inscription as an eponymous officer. —5. κεὐϝεργέταν: 94.7.—6. κὲν ταγᾶ κὲν ἀταγίαι: 'in war and peace.' The phrase is plainly the equivalent of the usual καὶ πολέμου καὶ εἰρήνης (or ἐν πολέμωι κτλ.), and is explained by the fact that in early times, as also later in the time of Jason of Pherae, the ταγός was the military head of the united Thessalians, appointed only in time of war. Jason of Pherae, in boasting of the military strength of the Thessalians on a war footing, expresses this last by ὅταν ταγεύηται Θετταλία, ὅταν ταγὸς ἐνθάδε καταστῇ, ὅταν ταγεύηται τὰ κατὰ Θετταλίαν (Xen. Hell. 6.1.8. 9, 12). So ταγά (one would expect ταγία) and ἀταγία (cf. ἀκοσμία 'time when no κόσμος was in office') were times of war and peace respectively. But the use of the phrase does not necessarily show that the institution under which it originated was in vogue at the time of this inscription; and, in any case, the ταγός of l. 8 is the municipal official, like the ταγοί of no. 32.

36. Pharsalus. Third century B.C. IG IX.ii.234. Schwyzer 567.

Ἀ[γαθᾶ τύχα·] ἁ πόλις Φαρσαλίουν τοῖς καὶ οὓς ἐξ ἀρχᾶς συμπολιτευομένοις καὶ συμπο|λ[εμεισάντε]σσι πάνσα προθυμία ἔδουκε τὰν πολιτείαν καττάπερ Φαρσαλίοις τοῖς | ἐ[ξ ἀρχᾶς πο-λ]ιτευομένοις, ἐδούκαεμ μὰ ἐμ Μακουνίαις τᾶς ἐχομένας τοῦ Λου-έρχου | (γ)ᾶ[ς μόραν πλέ]θρα ἐξείκοντα ἑκάστου εἰβατᾶ ἔχειν
5 πατρουέαν τὸμ πάντα χρόνον. || τ[αγευόντου]ν Εὐμειλίδα Νικασι-αίου, Λύκου Δρουπακείου, Ὀιολύκου Μνασιππείου, Λύκου | Φερε-κρατείου, Ἀντιόχου Δυνατείου. (Four columns of names follow.)

Pharsalus grants citizenship to those who have assisted it, and gives land to each youth.

1 ff. **τοῖς καὶ οὕς** κτλ.: 'to those who have already from the beginning been politically associated (non-technical use of συμπολιτευομένοις, not 'those who have already enjoyed citizenship'), and to those who have zealously assisted in war, just as to those who have been citizens of Pharsalus from the beginning.'
—**καὶ οὕς**: 'even as it is, already.' Cf. GDI 2160 δουλεύων καθὼς καὶ ὡς 'serving just as at present,' GDI 1832.11 μετὰ τῶν καὶ ὡς συνηρημένων 'with those already chosen.'—3. **ἐμ Μακουνίαις**: 'in the district known as the Poppy (μήκων) Fields.'

Boeotian

37. Temple of Apollo Ptous, near Acraephia. Sixth century B.C. Bréal, MSL 7.448. Holleaux, ibid. 8.180. Buck, CP 4.76 ff., 437.

ΚαλϜὸν ἄγαλμα Ϝάνακτι Ϝ[εκαβόλοι 'Απόλōνι
- - -]ορίδας ποίϜēσε μ' 'Εχέστροτος. αὐτὰρ ἔπεμφσαν
[- - - - - - - - - - - - - - - - - - - -]ον ΠτōιēϜι.
τὸς τὺ Ϝάναχς, φεφύλαχσο, δίδοι δ' ἀρ(ε)τάν [τε καὶ ὄλβον.]

An epigram of four hexameter verses inscribed βουστροφηδόν on a small tile, broken at the bottom.

Vs. 1. **ἄγαλμα**: here used in its earlier and more general sense of 'pleasing gift, offering.'—Ϝ[**εκαβόλοι**]: or Ϝ[hεκαβόλοι], cf. Ϝhεκαδάμοε, no. 38.3.

Vs. 2. The first name, of which various restorations are possible, is in agreement with 'Εχέστροτος, and is either an epic patronymic or a designation of the gens or phratry to which 'Εχέστροτος (a Boeotian; note -στροτος 5) belonged.

Vs. 3. Here stood the subject of ἔπεμφσαν, the names of the donors. The form of which the final ον is preserved may be an adjective in agreement with, or a noun in apposition with, ἄγαλμα understood.

Vs. 4. **φεφύλαχσο**: Hom. πεφύλαξο, 65.—**δίδοι**: a rare imperative form which occurs in Pindar, and in another Boeotian and a Corinthian inscription, and is parallel to ἄγει, πίει. For the whole verse ending, compare those of Hom. Ar. 15 and 20.

38. Early vase inscriptions.

1. Probably from Tanagra. Sixth century B.C. 'Αρχ. 'Εφ. 1900.107.

Δεμοθέρες hιαρὸν 'Απόλōνος Καρυχ�̄Fίō.

2. Thebes. Sixth century B.C. 'Αρχ. 'Εφ. 1900.107.

Ηιαρὸν τō Πυθίō FισFόδιϘος ἀνέθēκε.

3, 4. Tanagra. Sixth century B.C. IG VII.593, 606.

'Επὶ Fhεκαδάμοε ἐμί. 'Επὶ 'Ōκίβαε.

5. Uncertain origin. Probably fifth century B.C. IG VII. 3467. Schwyzer 441.

Μογέα δίδōτι ταῖ γυναικὶ δōρον Εὐχάρι τēύτρētιφάντō κότυλον, ὅς χ' ἄδαν πίē.

1) Cf. Paus. 9.20.3 ἔστιν... ἐν Τανάγρᾳ, καὶ ὄρος Κηρύκιον, ἔνθα 'Ερμῆν τεχθῆναι λέγουσι. But here the epithet Καρύκειος is applied to Apollo. Δεμοθέρες is the same as Δαμοθέρσης found elsewhere, and, if the E is correctly read, the dedicator was an Athenian or Euboean.

3), 4) Examples of the early spelling οε and αε, **26**, **30**. For Fhεκα- see **52b**. For ἐπί with dat. see **136.6**.

5) Μογέα: masc. in -ā. **105**.1*a*.—τēύτρētιφάντō (see **94**.7): ταῖ Εὐ-, daughter of Εὐτρητίφαντος. The first part of the name is identical with that of the Boeotian town which appears in Homer as Εὕτρησις. Cf. Εὐτρειτιδεῖες in a later Boeotian inscription. See **61**.3.—ὅς: ὡς. **58a**.

39. Thespiae. Early fourth century B.C. Platon-Feyel, BCH 62.149 ff.

Θεός · τύχα. | hιερὰ χρέματα Θεσπιέω|ν Διοπείθεος ἄρχοντος ἐν |
5 Ηεραίωι λέβētες τριάκον||τα πέντε · ἐχῖνος · ὀβελίσσκω|ν δαρχμαὶ τριάκοντα πέν|τε · χάλκια πλατέα πέντε · σκόφοι δοώδεκα ·
10 ὑδρίαι hέν|δεκα · στάμνοι χάλκιωι τ||ρῖς · φιάλα · ἔπαρμα · κότος · χάλκια · ποδανιπτēρες hέξ · κρατēρες τρῖς χάλκιοι · Foι|νόχοια
15 χάλκια πέντε καὶ | δέκα · πελεκέες ὀκτό · ἄξιν||ος · hάμα · κόρτον χάλκιον · hέμ|ιττα χαλκία · θράγανα διπλ|όα · κρατευταὶ τριπλόαι · κρε|άγραι ὀκτό · τυροκνάσστιδες | τρῖς · Fαγάνω δύο · πούραυμα ||
20 φρυνοποπεῖον · λανπτερῶχ|οι σιδάριοι τρῖς · κλίναι πέν|τε · κλιν-

τέρες πεντέκον|τα · δύγαστρον · ὖκτας · ἔπαρ|μα χάλκιον · τρεπέδδαι
25 Ð Ð Ð · || μάχαιραι δέκα · Σίφαις λέβετες | τρῖς, ὀβελίσκων δαρχ-
μαὶ τρῖς · ἐν Κρείσυι λέβετε δύο, ὀβελίσκω|ν δαρχμάω δύο - - - -

Inventory of objects dedicated. Several of their names are
new and most of these of unknown meaning. So ἔπαρμα, ηάμα (=
ἄμμα?), κόρτον, θράγανον, Ϝάγανον, ὖκτας, φρυνοποπεῖον. Dual
forms occur, δαρχμάω, Ϝαγάνω, λέβετε, but always accompanied
by δύο.
The spelling is of the transition period. H ist still h, but also
stands for HE in ηένδεκα, ηέξ, and ηέμιττα (see 4.6). E still = ε
and the vowel η. But Ω is used, in some cases wrongly (χάλκιωι
nom. pl.). The υ is represented by V, also by O (σκόφοι, δοώδεκα,
perhaps also κόρτον and κότος), and once by OV (πούραυμα) so
common later.
40. Thebes. Middle of fourth century B.C. IG VII.2418.
Schwyzer 467. Ditt. Syll. 201. Tod 160.

[Τοὶ χρεί]ματα συνεβ[άλονθο ἐν τὸν πόλεμον | τὸν] ἐπο[λέμιον]
Βοιωτοὶ πε[ρὶ τῶ ἰαρῶ τῶ ἐμ Βελφοῖς | π]ὸτ τὼς ἀσεβίοντας τὸ
5 ἰαρὸ[ν τῶ Ἀπόλλωνος τῶ | Π]ουθίω. || Ἀριστίωνος ἄρχοντος ·
Ἀλυζῆοι - - - - - - - · | πρισγέες Χάροψ Δάδωνος, Ἀριστο - - - -
- - - - - · | Ἀνακτοριέες τριάκοντα μνᾶς · πρι[σγέες] - - - - - |
Φόρμω, Ἄρχος Τερέος. | Βυζάντιοι χρουσίω Λαμψακανῶ στ[α-
10 τεῖρας] || ὀγδοέκοντα πέτταρας, ἀργυρίω Ἀτ[τικῶ δρα]|χμὰς
δεκαέξ · σύνεδροι Βυζαντίων [εἴνιξαν] | τὸ χρυσίον Κερχῖνος
Εἰροτίμω, Ἀγ - - - - - - | Δηλοπτίχω, Διωνύσιος Εἰραίωνος.
15 | Ἀθανόδωρος Διωνυσίω Τενέ[διος], || πρόξενος Βοιωτῶν, χει-
[λ]ίας δ[ραχμάς]. | Νικολάω ἄρχοντος · Ἀλυζ[ῆοι] ἄλλας τριά-
κοντα μνᾶς εἴ[νιξαν] · | πρισγεῖες Ἀλυζαίων Θεο - - - - - | [Ἀ]λε-
20 ξάνδρου, Δίων Πολυ[- - -] || [Ἀ]γεισινίκω ἄρχοντος · Βυζάντιοι
[συνεβά|λ]ονθο ἄλλως πεντακατίως στατεῖρα[ς χρυ|σ]ίως Λαμ-
ψακανὼς ἐν τὸν πόλεμον τὸν ὑ[πὲρ τῶ] | ἰαρῶ τῶ ἐμ Βελφοῖς ἐπο-
25 λέμιον Βοιωτ[οί] · | σύνεδροι εἴνιξαν Σῶσις Καρα[ι]ίχω, || [Π]αρ-
μενίσκος Πυράμου.

List of contributions for the Sacred War 355 ff. B.C. Note the
retention of the older spelling E beside EI, as πρισγέες beside
πρισγεῖις, Att. αι in Ἀλυζαίων beside Ἀλυζῆοι, and Att. gen. sg.
in -ου beside -ω.

22. **τὸν ὑπέρ** κτλ.: relative use of the article, unknown in the later Boeotian inscriptions. See **126.**—24. **εἴνιξαν: 144***a*.

41. Temple of Apollo Ptous, near Acraephia. Between 312 and 304 B.C. IG VII.2723. Schwyzer 446. Solmsen-Fraenkel 16.

Βοιωτοὶ Ἀπόλλωνι Πτωΐοι ἀνέθιαν ἄρχοντος Βοιωτοῖς Φιλο-
κώμω Ἀ[ντ]ιγ[ενε]ίιω Θεισπιε[ῖος], | ἀφεδριάτευόντων Ἐμπεδο-
[κ]λεῖος Ἀθανοκριτίω Ταναγρήω, Πούθωνος Α[ὐ]τομειδε[ίί]ω
Ἐρχομενίω, | Ἱπποτίωνος Γαστυμειδοντίω Κορωνεῖος, Ἐπιϝά[λ-
τ]ιος Μαχωνίω Θειβήω, Νικίωνος Γ[ρ]υλ[ί]ωνος Πλαταεῖος, |
Ἀριστοκλεῖος Ἀγασιήω Ἀνθαδονίω, Σάωνος Θιο[τ]ιμίω Θεισπιεῖος, μαντευομένω Ὀνυμάστω Νικολαίω Θεισπιεῖος.

Dedication of a tripod to Apollo Ptous by the Boeotian league. This is one of a series of four belonging to the same period (IG VII.2723-2724*b*).

ἀφεδριατευόντων: 'those who serve as *ἀφεδριᾶται or official representatives at the dedication.' From ἑδριάω used like Att. ἱδρύω. Observe that in the case of the representative of Plataea the gen. sg. of the father's name is used, not the patron. adj. as in the case of the others. The same holds true in the other three dedications, and it is probable that this is not accidental, but that the Plataeans, so long associated politically with the Athenians, adopted the Attic usage at an early date.

42. Thespiae. About 230 B.C. Keramopoullos, Ἀρχ. Δελτ. 14.20 ff., πίναξ 2*a*. Feyel, BCH 60.181 ff., 405 ff. [ll. 1-9 fragmentary and omitted here].

10 ὁ μ[ι]σθωσάμενος πὰρ τᾶς ἀρχ[ᾶς τὸ]ν κᾶπον, ὃν ἀνέθεικε Σώ-
στρατος ἱαρὸν | τῆς Μώσης, γαϝεργείσι ϝέτε[α ϝίκατ]ι· ἄρχι τῶ
χρό[ν]ω ὅλας τᾶς μισθώσιος | ὅστις κα πεδὰ Νίκωνα ἄρχει· [τῶ
δ'] ἐπὶ Νίκωνος ἐνιαυτῶ καταβαλεῖ τὰν μίσθωσιν | δραχμάων
ΗΕΔΔ ▷ τὸ εἴμιτ[τον ΓΕ] ΔΤ τοῖ ταμίη. τῶν δὲ ϝίκατι ϝετέων
καταβαλῖ | τοῖ ταμίη τὰν Μωσάων τὰμ μίσθ[ωσι]ν ἑκάστω τῶ
15 ἐνιαυτῶ ἐν τοῖ Ἀλαλκομενείοι μεινὶ || πρὸ τᾶς πέμπτας ἀπίοντος.
ἐγγύως δὲ καταστάσι τῆ ἀρχῆ ἀξιοχρείας [vacat] | τῶ μὲν ψεύδεος
πάρχρειμα, ὅλας δὲ τᾶς μισθώσιος τριῶν ἀμεράων· κὴ ἐννέχυρον |
δώσι δύο ὀβολὼς ὑπέρ τε αὐτοσαυτῶ κὴ τῶν ἐγγύων ἑκάστω. ἠ δέ
κα μεὶ καθιστάει | τὼς ἐγγύως, ἐπαμμισθώσι ἁ ἀρχά. ἠ δέ κα μῖον
εὕρει ἐν τὰ ϝίκατι ϝέτεα, ἐν τὸ λεύκωμα | ἐσγραφείσετη ὑπὰ τᾶ[ς]

20 ἀρχᾶς αὐτὸς κὴ ὁ ἔγγυος τῶ ψεύδεος ἐπὶ τοῖ εἰμιολίοι. || ἡ δὲ κά
τις τῶν μισθωσαμένων μεὶ καταβάλλει τὰμ μίσθωσιν ἐν τοῖ γεγραμ-
μένοι | χρόνοι, ὁ ταμίας ὁ τᾶν Μ[ω]σάων ἐσγράψι αὐτὸν κὴ τὼς
ἐγγύως ἐπὶ τῇ μισθώσι τῇ ἀντὶ | ἐνιαυτῶ ἐπὶ τοῖ εἰμιολίοι, κὴ ἐπαμ-
μισθώσοντι τὸν κᾶπον ἐν τὰ περίσαα Ϝέτεα · | κὴ ἤ τί κα μῖον εὔ-
ρε[ι] ἐν τὸν λοιπὸν χρόνον, ἐν τὸ λεύκωμα ἐσγράψονθι αὐτὸν κὴ
τὼς | [ἐγ]γύως ἐφ' εἰμιολίοι τοῖ μιονώματι παντὶ τῶν περισάων
25 Ϝετέων · ἡ δέ || κά τι ἐπιϜοικίξ[ε]ιτη, ἐπί κα δ[ι]εσσέλθει ὁ χρόνος,
ἀ[π]ίσετη λαβὼν ὅ κα ἐπιϜοικο|δομ[εί]σει. εἰ δέ τι κα δείει τέλος
ἐμφερέμεν ἐν τὰν πόλιν εἰ ἐν τὸ κοινὸν | Βοιωτῶν, ὅσι ὁ γ[αϜ]-
εργός · καταλίψι δὲ περὶ τὸ ἰαρὸν τῶ Μειλιχίω ἑκατὸν πόδας |
ἐμβαδόν. [ll. 29-32 omitted here].

From a long series of regulations for leases of land.

1 ff. 'The one who has rented from the board of officials the
plantation (cultivated tract of land) which Sostratus dedicated
to the Muses shall cultivate it for twenty years. The whole lease
begins under the archon following Nikon. But for the year under
the archon Nikon one shall pay down the rental of drachmas—,
one half,—, to the treasurer.'—15 ff. 'He shall furnish trustworthy sureties to the board of officials,—in the case of a false
declaration (on the part of the lessee as to his ability to pay)
immediately, but for the whole lease within three days.'—17 ff.
'If he does not furnish sureties, the board of officials shall make
a new lease. If (under the new lease) one receives less for the
twenty years, the (original) lessee and the surety against false
declaration shall be entered on the tablet for half as much again
as the loss.' Similarly in l. 24, where the fuller εἰμιολίοι τοῖ μιονώ-
ματι.—ll. 22, 24. περίσαος: 'left over, remaining,' cpd. of -σαος =
σοος.—25 f. If the lessee has built anything, when the rental
period has elapsed, he may on leaving take with him whatever
he has built (that is, the materials).' Cf. Ditt. Syll. 1097 ὅταν δὲ
ὁ χρόνος ἐξίηι αὐτῶι τῆς δεκαετίας ἄπεισιν ἔχων τὰ ξύλα καὶ τὴν
κέραμον καὶ τὰ θυρώματα. —26 ff. If there is any failure to pay
the tax, the cultivator (the lessee) shall furnish it. (ὕσι =: οἴσει).
He shall leave free a space of a hundred feet around the shrine
of Meilichios.'

43. Orchomenus. Between 222 and 200 B.C. IG VII.3172.

Inscr. Jurid. I, pp. 276 ff., 509 f. Schwyzer 523. Solmsen-Fraenkel 20. The sections of the text are given in the order in which they were inscribed (cf. ll. 30 ff.), but the numbering of the original publication is added in parentheses.

I
(D) Τοὶ πολέμαρχοι τοὶ ἐπὶ Πολυχράτιος | ἄρχοντος Φιλόμειλος
Φίλωνος, | Καφισόδωρος Διωνυσίω, Ἀθανόδω|ρος Ἵππωνος ἀνέ-
5
(106) γραψαν καθὼς || ἐποείσανθο τὰν ἀπόδοσιν τῶν δα|νείων τῶν Νικα-
II ρέτας κὰτ τὸ ψά|φισμα τῶ δάμω.
(E) (Μει)ν(ὸ)ς Ἀλαλκομενίω | Ϝικαστῆ κὴ ἕκτη, ἐπεψάφιδδε | Φι-
10 λόμειλος Φίλωνος, Καφισόδωρος || Διωνουσίω ἔλεξε · προβεβωλευ-
(111) μένον | εἶμεν αὐτῦ ποτὶ δᾶμον, ἐπιδεὶ ἐπεψα|ψίττατο ὁ δᾶμος ἀπο-
δόμεν Νικαρέτη<ι> | Θίωνος τὸν ταμίαν τὸν προάρχοντα | τὰν τρί-
15 ταν πετράμεινον ἀπὸ [τ]ᾶν ὑπερ||αμεριάων τᾶν ἰωσάων κὰτ τᾶς
(116) πόλιος, ὃ ἐ|πίθωσε αὐτὰν ἁ πόλις, ἀργουρίω δραχμὰς | μουρίας
ὀκτακισχιλίας ὀκτακατίας τριά|κοντα τρῖς, κὴ τὼς πολεμάρχως
20 ἀνελέσ|θη τάν τε σύγραφον, ἂν ἔδωκαν οὑπὲρ || [ο]ὕτων τῶν χρει-
(121) μάτων κατ’ α[ὐ]τὺ αὐτῶ[ν] | κὴ ὁ ταμίας κὴ ὧν ποθείλετο Νικαρέ-
τα δέκ[α], | κὴ τὰς ὑπεραμερίας διαγράψασθη τὰς [κὰτ] | τᾶς πό-
λιος τὰς ἐπὶ Ξενοκρίτω ἄρχοντος | ἐν Θεισπιῆς, κὴ οὖτα ϜεϜυκονο-
25 μειόντων || τῶν πολεμάρχων κὴ τῶ ταμίαο ἀποδόν|τος τὰ χρείματα
(126) κὰτ τὸ ὁμόλογον τὸ πὰρ | Θιόφεστον Θιοδώρω Θεισπιεῖα τεθέν, |
δεδόχθη τῦ δάμυ · τὼς πολεμάρχως, | ἐπί κα τὸ ψάφισμα κούριον
30 γένειτη, ἀγγρά||ψη ἐν στάλαν λιθίναν τό τε ψάφισμα οὖτο (II) |
(131) κὴ τὸ οὑπὲρ τᾶς ἀποδόσιος (III), κἀ(τ) ταὐτὰ δὲ κὴ | τὰς ὑπερα-
μερίας τὰ(ς) κὰτ τᾶς πόλιος τὰς Νι|καρέτας (IV) κὴ τὸ ὄ[ν]ιουμα
τῶ γραμματεῖος τῶ δ[ι]||αγράψαντος αὐτὰς (V) κὴ τὰν σύγγραφον
35 τὰν || τεθεῖσαν πὰρ Ϝιφιάδαν (VI) κὴ τὸ ἀντίγραφον <κὴ | τὸ ἀντί-
(136) γραφον> τῶ ὁμολόγω τῶ τεθέντος πὰρ Θιό|φεστον (VII) κὴ τὰν
διαγραφὰν τῶν χρειμάτων ὧν ἔγραψαν αὐτῆ διὰ τρεπέδδας
40 (VIII), κὴ τὸ ἄλωμα | ἀπολογίτταστη ποτὶ κατόπ[τ]α[ς, π]όρον
(141) δ’ εἶμεν || ἀπὸ τῶν πολιτικῶν.
III Δαματρίω νιουμεινίη | πετράτη, ἐπεψάφιδδε Κ[α]φισόδωρος Δι-
(F) ω|νουσίω, Ἀθανόδωρος Ἵππωνος ἔλεξε · προβε||[β]ωλευμένον εἶ-
μεν αὐτῦ ποτὶ δᾶμον, ἐπιδεί, | παργενομένας Νικαρέτας Θίωνος
45 Θεισπικᾶς || [κ]ὴ πραττώσας τὸ δάνειον τὰν πόλιν κὰτ τὰς οὐ-
(146) πε[ρ]|αμερία[ς] τὰς ἰώσας αὐτῆ, [ἀνα]γκάσ[θε]ν τὺ πολέμαρ]χυ κὴ
ὁ ταμίας σουγχωρείσαντος τῶ δάμω δόμεν | [κ]ὰτ αὐ[τὺ] αὐ-

[τ]ῶν σούνγραφον πὸτ τῆ οὐπαρχώση οὔπε[ρ]|αμερίη, ἐ[ν τ]άν κα
50
(151) ἐνενιχθείει ἁ ἀνφορὰ ἐν οὗτο, κ[ὴ] || κομίττ[ειτη] τὰ συνχωρειθέν-
τα χρείματα, | δεδόχθη τῦ δάμυ · τὸν ταμίαν τὸν [π]ροάρχοντα |
[τὰν] τρίτα[ν] πετράμεινον ἀποδόμεν πεδὰ τῶν | πολεμάρχων Νι-
55 καρέτη ἀργ[υ]ρίω δραχμὰς μυρίας | [ὀκ]τακισχειλίας ὀκτακατία[ς]
(156) τριάκ[ο]ντα τρῖς Πολυ||κράτιος ἄρχοντος ἐν τῦ Δαματρίυ μεινὶ
κὴ τὰς ἐ[μ]πράξις τὰς ἰώσας Νικα[ρέτη κὰτ] τᾶς πόλιος Ξεν[ο]|-
κρίτω ἄρχοντος ἐν Θεισπιῆς πάσας διαλιάνασ[θη] | τὼς πολεμάρ-
χως, κὴ τὰν σουνγραφάν, ἂν ἔχι κὰτ τ[ῶν] | πολεμάρχων κὴ τῶ
60 ταμίαο, ἀνελέσθη, πόρον [δ' εἶ]||μεν ἐν οὗτο ἀπὸ τῶν τᾶς πόλιος
(161) ποθοδωμάτων πάντ[ων]. |
IV
(G)	Ξενοκρίτω, Ἀλαλκομενίω.—Νικαρέτα Θέωνος τᾶς π[ό]|λιος
Ἐρχομενίων κὴ τῶ ἐγγύω Θίωνος Συννόμω · τὰ π|πάματα μούριη
65 ὀγδοείκοντα πέντε διού[ο] ὀβολίω · | κὴ τῶ τεθμίω Ϝίστωρ Ἀρισ-
(166) τόνικος Πραξιτέλιος · || Λιουκίσκω, Θιουίω, τὸ σουνάλλαγμα.—
Νικαρέτα Θίω|νος τᾶς πόλιος Ἐρχομενίων κὴ τῶ ἐγγούω Θίωνος |
Σουννόμω · τὰ ππάματα δισχείλιη πεντακάτι[η] · | κὴ τῶ τεθμίω
Ϝίστωρ ὁ αὐτός · Λιουκίσκω, Ὁμολωίω, | [τ]ὸ σουνάλλαγμα.—
70 Νικαρέτα Θίωνος τᾶς πόλι[ος || Ἐ]ρχομενίων κὴ τῶ ἐγγούω Θίω-
(171) νος Σουννόμω · τὰ π|πάματα πετρακισχείλια · κὴ τῶ τεθμίω
Ϝίστωρ | ὁ αὐτός · χρόνος ὁ αὐτός.—Νικαρέτα Θίωνος τᾶς πόλιος |
75 [Ἐ]ρχομενίων κὴ τῶ ἐγγούω Θίωνος Σουννόμω · τὰ ππά|ματα
(176) χείλιη · κὴ τῶ τεθμίω Ϝίστωρ ὁ αὐτός · Λιουκίσκ[ω, || Θε]ιλου-
θίω, τὸ σουνάλλαγμα.
V
(H)	Διαγράψη τὰς οὔπερ[α|μ]ερίας τὰς Νικαρέτας ἐν Θεισπιῆς τὰς
κὰτ τᾶς | [π]όλιος · τῶν τεθμοφουλάκων γραμματεύς Σα.... |
VI
80 Ἐδάνεισεν Νικαρέτα Θέωνος | Θεσπική, παρόντος αὐτῆι κυ-||
(A 3) ρίου τοῦ ἀνδρὸς Δεξίππου Ε[ὐ]|νομίδου, Καφισοδώρωι Δι[ο]|νυ-
σίου, Φιλομήλωι Φίλωνος, | Ἀθανοδώρωι Ἵππωνος, Πο[λυ]||κρί-
85 τωι Θάροπος καὶ ἐγγύοις || εἰς ἔκτεισιν τοῦ δανείου | Μνάσων
(8) Μέχγαο, Τελεσίας | Μέχγαο, Λασίππωι Ξενοτί|μου, Εὐάρει Εὐ-
90 χώρου, Περι|λάωι Ἀναξίωνος, Διονυσο||δώρωι Καφισοδώρου,
(13) Κωμί|ναι Τελεσίππου, Ὀνασίμωι | Θεογείτονος, Καφισοδώρωι |
95 Δαματρίχου, Νικοκλεῖ Ἀθα|νοδώρου Ὀρχομενίοις ἀργυ||ρίου
(18) δραχμὰς μυρίας ὀκτα|κισχειλίας ὀκτακοσίας τρι|άκοντα τρεῖς ἄτο-
κον ἐχ Θεσ|πιῶν εἰς τὰ Παμβοιώτια τὰ ἐ|π' Ὀνασίμου ἄρχοντος
100 Βοιωτοῖ[ς]. || ἀποδότωσαν δὲ τὸ δάνειον | οἱ δανεισάμενοι ἢ οἱ ἔγ-
(23) γυ|οι Νικαρέται ἐν τοῖς Πανβοι|ωτίοις πρὸ τῆς θυσίας ἐν ἡμέ|ραις

105
(28) τρισίν. ἐὰν δὲ μὴ ἀποδῶσ[ι,] ‖ πραχθήσονται κατὰ τὸν νό|μον·
[ἡ] δὲ πρᾶξις ἔστω ἔκ τε | αὐτῶν τῶν δανεισαμένων | καὶ ἐκ τῶν

110
(33) ἐγγύων, καὶ ἐξ ἐνὸ[ς] | καὶ ἐκ πλειόνων καὶ ἐκ πάν‖των καὶ ἐκ τῶν
ὑπαρχόντων | αὐτοῖς, πραττούσηι ὃν ἂν τρό|πον βούληται. ἡ δὲ
συγγραφὴ | κυρία ἔστω, κἂν ἄλλος ἐπι|φέρηι ὑπὲρ Νικαρέτας.

115
(38) Μάρ‖τυρες Ἀριστογείτων Ἁρμο|ξένου, Ἰθιούδικος Ἀθανίαο, |
Φιφιάδας Τιμοκλεῖος, Φαρ|σάλιος Εὐδίκου, Καλλέας Λυ|σιφάν-

120
(43) του, Θεόφεστος Θεοδώ‖ρου, Εὐξενίδας Φιλώνδου | Θεσπιεῖς. ἁ

VII σούγγραφος | πὰρ Φιφιάδαν Τιμοκλεῖος. |

(B) Ὀνασίμω ἄρχοντος Βοιωτοῖ[ς,] | μεινὸς Πανάμω, ὁμολογὰ ‖

125
(48) Νικαρέτη Θίωνος Θεισπικῆ, | παριόντος Νικαρέτη Δεξίπ|πω Εὐ-
νομίδαο τῶ ἀνδρὸς Θε[ι]|σπιεῖος, κὴ τῆ πόλι Ἐρχομεν[ί]|ων·

130
(53) παρεῖαν οὑπὲρ τᾶς πόλ[ι]‖ος πολέμαρχοι Καφισόδω|ρος Διωνου-
σίω, Φιλόμειλος | Φίλωνος, Ἀθανόδωρος Ἵππω|νος· ἀποδόμεν

135
(58) τὰν πόλιν Ἐρ|χομενίων Νικαρέτη Θίωνος, ‖ ἃ ἐπίθωσαν οὑπὲρ
τᾶν οὑπε|ραμεριάων τᾶν ἐπὶ Ξενοκρί|τω ἄρχοντος ἐν Θεισπῆς,

140
(63) ἀρ|γουρίω δραχμὰς μουρίας ὀκτ[α]‖κισχειλίας ὀκτακατίας τρ[ιά-]‖|
χοντα τρῖς, ἔσχατον Ὀνασ[ί]‖μω ἄρχοντος ἐν τῦ Ἀλαλ[κο]‖μενίοι
μεινί· σούγγραφον δὲ | γράψασθη τῶ ἀργουρίω τὼς | <τὼς> πολεμ-

145
(68) άρχως Ἐρχομενίων ‖ κὴ ἐγγούως, ὥς κα δοκιμάδδ[ει] | Νικα-
ρέτα, κὴ θέσθη μεσέγγυ[υ]‖ον πὰρ Φιφιάδαν Τιμοκλεῖος | Θεισπι-

150
(73) εῖα. ἐπὶ δέ κα κομίττε[ι]‖τη Νικαρέτα τὸ ἀργούριον ‖ πὰρ τᾶς πό-
λιος, ἐσλιανάτω Νικαρέτα τὰς οὑπερ|αμερίας, ἃς ἔχι κὰτ τᾶς πό-
λιος, τὰς ἐπὶ Ξενοκρίτω | ἄρχοντος ἐν Θεισπῆς πάσας, κὴ τὰν
σούγγραφον ἀπο|δότω Φιφιάδας τοῖς πολεμάρχυς κὴ τοῖ ταμίη
κὴ το[ῖς] | ἐγγούοις. ἡ δέ κα μεὶ ἀποδώει ἁ πόλις Νικαρέτη τὸ

155
(78) ἀρ‖γούριον ἐν τῦ γεγραμμένυ χρόνυ, τὰς μουρίας κὴ ὀκτ[α]‖κισ-
χειλίας ὀκτακατίας τριάκοντα τρῖς, ἀποδότω | τὰν σούγγραφον
κὴ τὰς οὑπεραμερίας τὰς κὰτ τᾶς | πόλιος, ἅπαν τὸ ἀργούριον τὸ
ἐν τῦ ὁμολό[γ]υ γεγραμ|μένον· (ἡ δέ κα) ἐν τῦ χρόνυ τῦ γεγραμ-

160
(83) μένυ μεὶ ἐθέλει κ[ομ]ίδδ[ε]‖σθη Νικαρέ[τ]α τὸ ἀργούριον, ἀπο-
δότω Φιφιάδας τὰν | σούγγραφον τοῖς πολεμάρχοις κὴ τοῖ ταμίη
κὴ τοῖς | ἐγγούοις, κὴ ποταποπισάτω Νικαρέτα τῆ πόλι Ἐρχο-|
μενίων κὴ τοῖς πολεμάρχοις κὴ τοῖ ταμίη κὴ τοῖς ἐγ|γούοις ἀρ-

165
(88) γουρίω δραχμὰς πεντακισμουρίας, κὴ τὴ ‖ οὑπεραμερίη ἄκουρύ-
νυ ἔνθω. Ϝίστορες Ἀριστογί|των Ἁρμοξένα, Ἰθούδικος Ἀθα-
νίαο, Φιφιάδας Τιμο[κλεῖο]ς, Φαρσάλιος Εὐδίκω, Καλλέας
Λιουσιφάντω, Θιόφεις|τος Θιοδώρω, Εὐξενίδας Φιλώνδαο

Θεισπιεῖε‹ι›ς. τὸ ὁμό|λογον πὰρ Θιόφειστον Θιοδώρω Θει-
σπιεῖα.

170
(93)   Διαγραφὰ || Νικαρέτη διὰ τραπέδδας τᾶς Πιστοκλεῖος ἐν Θει-
σπι|ῆς · Ἐπιτέλιος ἄρχοντος ἐν Θεισπιῆς, μεινὸς Ἀλαλκομε|νίω
δευτέρω ἀμέρη ἐνακηδεκάτη, ἐπὶ τᾶς Πιστοκλεῖος | τραπέδδας
Νικαρέτη παρεγράφει πὰρ Πολιουκρίτω Θάρο|πος Ἐρχομενίω τα-
175
(98)   μίαο οὐπὲρ τᾶς πόλιος τὸ σουνχωρει||θὲν τᾶν οὐπεραμεριάων τᾶν
ἐπὶ Ξενοκρίτω ἄρχοντος, | παριόντος πολεμάρχω Ἀθανοδώρω
Ἵππωνος Ἐρχομενί[ω], | ἀργουρίω δραχμὴ μούριη ὀκτακισχείλιη
ὀκτακάτιη τριά|κοντα τρῖς.

Nicareta of Thespiae had lent various sums of money to the
city of Orchomenus, for which she held against it certain notes,
recorded in IV. When she appeared at Orchomenus to collect
these (ll. 44 ff.), the city was unable to meet them, and an agreement was entered into according to which the city was to pay
her the sum of 18,833 drachmas within a certain time and the
polemarchs were to give her a personal contract for the payment.
The text of the agreement (ὁμολογά) is given in VII, and of the
contract (σούγγραφος), written in the κοινή, in VI. The sum of
18,833 drachmas is more than the total of the notes recorded in
IV (17,585 dr., 2 obols), but probably less than they amounted
to with the normal penalties for delayed payment. For the phrase
ὃ ἐπίθωσε, ὃ ἐπίθωσαν (ll. 16, 135) 'which the city (they) persuaded
her to accept,' implies some concession on her part. Finally the
city passed a vote (III) to pay the amount and take up the notes
and the contract. When this had been accomplished it passed
a further vote (II) ordering all the documents to be inscribed in
a specified order. This was done as stated in I, which serves as
a heading to the whole inscription. Some of the typical financial
terms recur in an inscription from Thisbe, SEG 3.342.

10 ff. **προβεβωλευμένον** κτλ.: 'that he had a probouleuma
to present to the people, Whereas the people had voted that the
treasurer in charge for the third period of four months should
pay to Nicareta, in settlement of the notes of default which she
held against the city, the sum which the city persuaded her
(to accept), 18,833 drachmas, and that the polemarchs should
take up the contract they gave for the money against themselves,

they and the treasurer and the ten whom Nicareta selected, and cancel the notes against the city (maturing) in the archonship of Xenocritus, and since the polemarchs had arranged these matters and the treasurer had paid the money according to the agreement deposited with Theophestus, be it voted by the people,' etc.

40-41. νιουμεινίη πετράτη: τετάρτη ἱσταμένου. On νιου- from νεο-, see **42**.5a.—46 ff. 'The polemarchs and the treasurer were obliged, with the assent of the people, to give a contract against themselves in addition to the existing note of default, until the levy for this purpose should be made and the amount agreed upon provided.' This is the only satisfactory interpretation of the most troublesome passage in the inscription, though one difficulty remains, the use of the singular οὑπεραμερίη where we should expect the plural.—49. ἐ[ν τ]άν: 'until,' originating in ἐν τὰν ἁμέραν. Cf. **136**.1.—ἐν οὗτο: 'for this purpose.' Cf. πόρον ἐν οὗτο ll. 59. 60.—**ἐνενιχθείει**, not ἐνενιχθεῖ, is declared certain by Baunack, Philol. 48.413, and agrees with uncontracted forms found elsewhere, as κουρωθείει (**151**.2).—50. **κομίττ[ειτη]**, not κομίττ[η], also after Baunack l.c.—56. **διαλιάνασ[θη]**: cf. ἐσλιανάτω l. 150, and **162**.10.

61 ff. The first date, archonship of Xenocritus, month of Alalcomenius, applies to the following notes (cf. ll. 23, 56, 136, 151) and is probably the time at which they fell due, while the date given at the end of each is the time of the loan (τὸ σουνάλλαγμα). Cf. Thalheim, Berl. Phil. Woch. 1893.267. The expression throughout is condensed. Ξενοκρίτω (ἄρχοντος), (μεινὸς) Ἀλαλκομενίω, Νικαρέτα Θέωνος (κατὰ) τᾶς πόλιος.

78 ff. The text of the contract is in the κοινή, though dialect forms are retained in some of the proper names. The names of the first two sureties are given by mistake in the nominative, but with the third the error is rectified.—113-114. **ἐπιφέρηι** 'presents it.'

154 ff. 'If the city fails to pay Nicareta in the time specified, it will have to pay the amount stated in the contract and the sum of the notes of default besides. But if Nicareta refuses to accept the amount named in the contract (as she might do in order to secure the exorbitant penalty for delay),

she forfeits both contract and notes and pays a heavy penalty.'

169/170. **διαγραφὰ Νικαρέτη** κτλ.: 'memorandum of payment to Nicareta (adnom. dat. 172) through the bank of Pistocles.' διαγραφά 'cancellation' (cf. διαγράψασθη l. 22), and so 'payment.' So ll. 172 ff., 'at the bank of Pistocles there was paid over to Nicareta by Polycritus the treasurer in behalf of the city the sum agreed upon of the notes of default' (part. gen.; cf. ἀπὸ τᾶν ὑπεραμεριάων ll. 14-15).

44. Lebadea. Third century B.C. IG VII.3083. Schwyzer 509.

Θιὸς τούχα ἀγα|θά. | Γαστίαο ἄρχοντος | Βοιωτῦς, ἐν δὲ Λεβα-||
5 δείη Δόρκωνος, Δωίλος | ᾽Ιρανήω ἀντίθειτι τὸν | Fίδιον θεράποντα
10 ᾽Αν|δρικὸν τῦ Δὶ τῦ Βασιλεῖι | κὴ τῦ Τρεφωνίυ ἱαρὸν εἶ||μεν, παρ-
μείναντα πὰρ | τὰν ματέρα ᾽Αθανοδώ|ραν Fέτια δέκα, καθὼς ὁ |
πατεὶρ ποτέταξε· ἠ δέ κα | ἔτι δώει ᾽Αθανοδώρα, εἴσι [αὐτῆ] ||
15 ᾽Ανδρικὸς φόρον τὸν ἐν τῇ | θείκη γεγραμμένον· ἠ δέ τί | κα πάθει
᾽Αθανοδώρα, παρμ|ενῖ ᾽Ανδρικὸς· τὸν περιττὸν | χρόνον πὰρ Δωί-
20 λον· [ἔ]πιτα ἰα||ρὸς ἔστω με[ὶ] ποθ[ί]κων μει|θενὶ μειθέν· μεὶ
ἐσσεῖμε|ν δὲ καταδουλίττασθη | ᾽Ανδρικὸν μειθενί· ᾽Αν|δρικὸν δὲ
25 λειτωργῖμεν || ἐν τῆς θοσίης τῶν θιῶν | <ων> οὔτων.

45. Lebadea. Second century B.C. IG VII.3080. Schwyzer 512.

[Σάων - - - - - - ἀντίθειτι τὸ Fίδιον | πη]δάριον ᾽Αθάνωνα τῦ Δὶ
τεῖ Βασιλεῖ κὴ τεῖ Τρεφωνίει ἱαρὸν εἶμεν τὸν πάν[τα| χρό]νον ἀπὸ
τᾶσδε τᾶς ἁμέρας, μεὶ προθίκοντα μείτε αὐτεῖ Σάωνι μείτε ἄλλει |
[μ]ειθενὶ κατὰ μειθένα τρόπον. ἠ δέ κά τις ἀντιποιεῖτη ᾽Αθάνωνος
5 εἰ ἄλλο τι ἀδικῖ || [κ]αθ᾽ ὅντινα ὦν τρόπον, οὐπερδικιόνθω κὴ προϊ-
στάνθω τύ τε ἱαρεῖες κὴ τε[ὶ | ἱαρ]άρχη τὺ ἠὶ ἀντιτιουνχάνοντες
κὴ τῶν ἄλλων ὁ βειλόμενος. Fίστορε[ς] | .... λεις Σάωνος, Εὔβω-
λος Σωκράτιος, Νίκαργος κὴ Κράτων Εὐνοστίδ[αο].

46. Chaeronea. Second century B.C. IG VII.3303.

Καλλίκωνος ἀρχῶ μεινὸς Δαματρίω πεντεκηδεκάτη | Πούριππος
Προξένω ἀντίθειτι ἱαρὰν τὰν Fιδίαν θεράπη|[να]ν ᾽Αφροδιτίαν τῦ
Σαράπι, παραμείνασαν ἀσαυτῦ κὴ τῇ γου|[νη]κὶ αὐτῶ ἀγαθὴν ἄς
5 κα ζώωνθι, τὰν ἀνάθεσιν ποιόμε||[νος] διὰ τῶ σουνεδρίω κὰτ τὸν
νόμον· κὴ κατέβαλε τῦ ταμίη | [ἐ]πὶ τῶν ἱαρῶν τὸ γινιούμενον
δραχμὰς Fίκατι παραχρε[ῖ]μα.

47. Chaeronea: Second century B.C. IG VII.3352. Schwyzer 517.

Ἀρχείνω ἀρχῶ μεινὸς Θουίω | πεντεκηδεκάτη Διουκλεῖς κὴ Κω-|
τίλα ἀντίθεντι τὰν Ϝιδίαν θρε|πτάν, ἦ ὄνιουμα Ζωπουρίνα, ἱαρ[ὰν]||
5 τεῖ Σεράπει, παραμείνασαν αὐτε|ῖς ἅς κα ζῶνθι ἀνενκλείτως, τὰν |
ἀνάθεσιν ποιούμενει διὰ τῶ σ[ο]|υνεδρίω κατὰ τὸν νόμον.

44-47. Manumission decrees, of which there are over one
hundred examples from Chaeronea alone, all of about the same
period. Even from the same year some are in dialect, some in
the κοινή, and some in a mixture of both. In those given here
κοινή influence shows itself in ἀγαθήν no. 46, in the ζ of ζώωνθι,
ζῶνθι nos. 46, 47 (vs. δώει no. 44), κατὰ τὸν νόμον no. 47 (vs. κὰτ
τὸν νόμον no. 46), παραμείνασαν nos. 46, 47 (vs. παρμείναντα no.
44), in προθίκοντα no. 45 (vs. ποθίκων no. 44), in ποιούμενει no. 47
(vs. ποιόμενος no. 46 = ποιιόμενος). Note ει for usual υ from
οι (30) in εἶσι = οἶσει. For θοσίης no. 44, see 24.

As in similar decrees from other parts of Greece, the act of
manumission takes the form of a dedication or sale (ἀπέδοτο at
Delphi, e.g., no. 55) to the divinity of the local shrine, thus
securing religious sanction and protection of the rights of the
slave who has purchased his freedom. Often the manumission
does not go into immediate effect, but is subject to' various
conditions, such as remaining in service during the lifetime of
the master (nos. 46, 47) or for a term of years (no. 44), payment
of an annuity, etc. Cf. no. 55.

Phocian

Delphian

48. Delphi. Early sixth (or late seventh?) century B.C.
Schwyzer 317. Solmsen-Fraenkel 47. Tod 3. Homolle, Comptes
Rendus 1924, 149 ff. Daux, BCH 61.61 ff.

A [Κλέοβις καὶ Βί]τον τὰν ματάρα
   [illegible]
B ἐάγαγον τοὶ δυιοί
   [Πολυ]μέδες ἐποίϝεh' Ἀργεῖος.
Inscribed on the bases of the statues of Cleobis and Biton,

which, as Herodotus (1.31) tells us, the Argives made and set up at Delphi. Delphian dialect (cf. especially ματάρα) except the artist's signature, which is in Argive.

For the words following ματάρα Homolle's σταδίōς as a reading is declared impossible by Daux, and with it his enticing restoration, namely σταδίōς [τετρόϘοντα πέντ]ε, goes by the board. Further, it is most unlikely that the E, the first letter of B, goes with the preceding, and we must return to the old reading ἐάγαγον with syllabic augment. In the following the favorite reading τōι δυγōι must be rejected (Daux, l.c.). The letters ΤΟΙΔVΙΟΙ are best taken as τοὶ δυιοί = τοὶ δοιοί, with υ by influence of δύο. For the probable reading ἐποίϜēh' 'Αργεῖος see Buck, CP 20.139.

49. Delphi. Early fifth century B.C. GDI 1683 (with II, p. 722). Roberts 229. Schwyzer 320. Bourguet, BCH 49.25 ff.

Τοὶ πεντεκαίδεκα | τὸν Λαβυαδᾶν ΤΟΝ[. . ?] | Θρασύμαχον
5 καὶ Καμ|ιρέα ἐπὶ Τριχᾶ ἄρχον||το, κἀπέδειξαν μηᾶ|ς δεκατέτορες
καὶ | hēμιμναῖον κα|ὶ δραχμὰς πεντέ|κοντα καὶ Ϝέξ.

'The Fifteen of the Labyadae (cf. no. 52) - - - - held office and disbursed certain sums.' The construction and sense of the intervening clause are obscure.

50. Delphi. Fifth century B.C. Schwyzer 321. Solmsen-Fraenkel 48.

Τὸν Ϝοῖνον μὲ φάρεν ἐς τοῦ δρ|όμου · αἰ δέ κα φάρēι, hιλαξά-
στō | τὸν θεὸν hōι κα κεραίēται καὶ | μεταθυσάτō κἀποτεισάτō
5 πέν||τε δραχμάς · τούτου δὲ τōι κατα|γορέσαντι τὸ hέμισσον.

The inscription is on a wall connected with the stadium, where there were no doubt shrines of divinities. Prohibitions of the removal of the sacrificial meat are well known. Here we have a prohibition of the removal of the wine. 'If one does carry it off, one must propitiate the god for whom it is prepared (mixed), make an offering in its place,' etc.

51. Delphi. Late fifth century B.C. Schwyzer 322.

ἅδε Δελφοῖς Φασēλίτας τὸν | πέλανον διδόμεν, τὸ(ν) δαμόσ|ιον
ἑπτὰ δραχμὰς Δελφίδες δ|ύ' ὀδελός, τὸν δὲ Ϝίδιον τέτορε|ς ὀδελός.
Τιμοδίκō καὶ 'Ιστιαί|ō θεαρόντον, 'Ερύλō ἄρχοντος.

1. ἄδε certainly adv. 'in this way' (not for ἔαδε as taken by some), as clearly shown by Cret. ἆδ' ἔϝαδε (no. 116). See 132.6— 2 ff. For πελανός, see no. 7 A 25 ff., note.—τὸ(ν) δαμόσιον—, τὸν δὲ ϝίδιον 'the public'—'the private', agreeing with πέλανον. Cf. no. 53.

52. Delphi. About 400 B.C. GDI 2561. Schwyzer 323. Solmsen-Fraenkel 49. Ionic alphabet, but with F, and ᕮ = h (in contrast to H = η); lengthened o usually OY, but sometimes O.

A

[ὁ δὲ hόρκος] | ἔστω · "ταγε[υ]σέω δι[καίως κ]|ατὰ τοὺν νόμους
τᾶς [π]ό[λι]|ος καὶ τοὺς τῶν Λαβυαδ[ᾶν] | πὲρ τῶν ἀπελλαίων καὶ
5 τᾶ||ν δαρατᾶν · καὶ τὰ χρήματα | συμπραξέω κἀποδειξέω [δ|ι]καίως
τοῖς Λαβυάδαις [κ]|ωύτε κλεψέω οὔτε [β]λα[ψ]έω | οὔτε τέχναι
10 οὔτε μαχαν[ᾶ||ι] τῶν τῶλ Λαβυαδᾶν χρημ[ά]|των · καὶ τὸς ταγοὺ[ς
ἐπ]αξέ|ω τὸν hόρκον τοὺς [ἐν ν]έω[τ]|α κὰτ τὰ γεγραμμένα. hόρ-
15 κ|ος · hυπίσχομαι ποὶ τοῦ Δι||ὸς τοῦ πατρώιου · εὐορκέο|ντι μέμ μοι
ἀγαθὰ εἴη, αἰ δ' | ἐφιορκέοιμι [ϝε]κών, τὰ κα|κὰ ἀντὶ τῶν ἀγαθῶν."|
20 Ἔδοξε Λαβυάδαις Βουκατ||ίου μηνὸς δεκάται ἐπὶ Κ[ά]|μπου ἐν
τᾶι ἁλίαι σὺμ ψάφ|οις hεκατὸν ὀγδοήκοντα | δυοῖν · τοὺς ταγοὺς
25 μὴ δέκ|εσθαι μήτε δαρατᾶν γάμε||λα μήτε παιδῆια μήτ' ἀπελ|λαῖα,
αἱ μὴ τᾶς πατριᾶς ἐπ|αινεούσας καὶ πληθυόσα|ς ἅς κα ἦι. αἱ δέ
30 τί κα πὰρ νό|μον κελεύσωντι, τῶν κελε||υσάντων ὁ κίνδυνος ἔστω. |
τὰ δὲ ἀπελλαῖα ἄγεν Ἀπέλ|λαις καὶ μὴ ἄλλαι ἀμέραι | μήτε ἄγεν
35 τοὺς ἄγοντας μ|ήτε τοὺς ταγοὺς δέκεσθα||ι · αἱ δέ κα [δ]έξωνται
ἄλλαι | ἀμέραι ἢ Ἀπέλλαις, ἀποτει|σάτω ϝέκαστος δέκα δρα|χμάς ·
40 ὁ δὲ χρήζων καταγορ|εῖν τῶν δεξαμένων ἐπὶ τῶ||ν hυστέρων ταγῶν
καταγο|ρείτω ἐν τᾶι ἁλίαι τᾶι με|τὰ Βουκάτια, αἴ κ' ἀμφιλλέ|γωντι
45 τοὶ ταγοὶ τοὶ δεξά|μενοι. ἄγεν δὲ τἀπελλαῖα || ἀντὶ ϝέτεος καὶ τὰς
δαρά|τας φέρεν. hόστις δέ κα μὴ | ἄγηι τἀπελλαῖα ἢ τὰν δαρ|άταν
50 μὴ φέρηι, ἀμμόνιον κ|ατθέτω στατῆρα ἐπὶ ϝεκα||τέρωι, τῶι δὲ hυσ-
τέρωι ϝέ|τει ἀγέτω τἀπελλαῖα καὶ | τὰν δαράταν φερέτω · αἱ δέ | κα
55 μὴ ἄγηι, μηκέτι δεκέσθ|ων ἀμμόνια, ἀλλ' ἢ ἀγέτω ἀπ||ελλαῖα ἢ
ἀποτεισάτω ϝίκ|ατι δραχμὰς ἢ hυπογραφό|μενος τόκιομ φερέτω ·
60 καὶ | τὰν δαράταν τῶι hυστέρω|ι ϝέτει φερέτω ἢ ἀποτεισ||[άτω - - -.

B

5 [1-4 fragmentary. τ]||οἱ Λαβυάδα[ι Εὐκλείοι]|ς περὶ τᾶν δα[ρα-

τᾶν ἐπι]|κρινόντων καὶ ['Απέλλα]|ις περὶ τῶν ἀπελ[λαίων, | π]αρ-
10 εόντες μὴ μείδ[ς he||ν]ὸς καὶ hεκατόν · τὰ[ν δὲ] | ψᾶφον φερόντων
ἀνδ[εξ]|άμενοι ποὶ τ̄ 'Απόλλω[ν]|ος καὶ τοῦ Ποτειδᾶνος | τοῦ φρα-
15 τρίου καὶ τοῦ Δ||ιὸς πατρώιου δικαίως | οἰσεῖν κὰτ τὸν νόμους | τῶν
Δελφῶν · κήπευχέσθ|ω δικαίως τὰν ψᾶφον φέ|ροντι πόλλ' ἀγαθὰ
20 τοὺ[ς || θ]εοὺς διδόμεν, αἰ δὲ ἀ[δ]|ίκως, τὰ κακά. τοῦτα δὲ τ|οἱ τα-
25 γοὶ ἐπιτελεόντω|ν καὶ τῶι δεομένωι συν|αγόντων τοὺς Λαβυάδα||ς ·
αἰ δέ κα μὴ ποιῶντι κὰ|[τ] τὰ γεγραμμένα ἢ μὴ το|[ὺ]ς ταγοὺς τὸν
30 hόρκον ἐ|παγάγωντι, ἀποτεισάτ|[ω] ϝέκαστος ἐπὶ ϝεκατέ||[ρ]ωι
δέκα δραχμάς. hόστ|[ι]ς δέ κα μὴ ὀμόσηι, μὴ τα|[γ]ευέτω · αἰ δέ κ'
35 ἀνώμοτο|ς ταγεύηι, πεντήκοντα | δραχμὰς ἀποτεισάτω. || αἰ δέ κα
δέξωνται τοὶ [τ]|αγοὶ ἢ γάμελα ἢ παιδῆι|α πὰρ τὰ γράμματα, ἀπο-
40 τ|εισάτω πεντήκοντα δρ|αχμὰς ϝέκαστος τῶν δε||ξαμένων · αἰ δέ κα
μὴ ἀπο|τείσηι, ἄτιμος ἔστω ἐγ | Λαβυαδᾶν καὶ ἐπὶ τούτ|ωι καὶ ἐπὶ
45 ταῖς ἄλλαις | ζαμίαις, hέντε κ' ἀποτε||ίσηι. καὶ hῶ κα δέξωντα|ι ἢ
δαράταν ἢ ἀπελλαῖα | πὰρ τὰ γράμματα, μὴ ἔστ|ω Λαβυάδας
50 μηδὲ κοινα|νείτω τῶν κοινῶν χρημ||άτων μηδὲ τῶν θεμάτων. | αἰ
δέ τίς κα τῶν ταγῶν κ|αταγορῆι ποιῆσαί τι π|ὰρ τὰ γράμματα, ho
55 δὲ ἀν|τι[φ]ᾶι, τοὶ ταγοὶ ἐν τᾶι || - - - - - - - - - - -

C

[ὀμ|νύτω ποὶ τοῦ 'Απόλλωνος κ|αὶ Ποτειδᾶνος τοῦ φρ]ατ[ρ|ίου
καὶ Διός, καὶ δικ]άζο[ν|τι μὲν δικαίως ἐπ]ευχέσ[θ|ω πόλλ' ἀγαθὰ
5 τ]οὺς θεοὺς [δ||ιδόμεν, αἰ δ' ἐ]φιορκέοι, κα|[κά · αἰ δέ κα μ]ὴ δικά-
ζηι hαι|[ρεθείς, ἀπ]οτεισάτω πέντ|[ε δραχμάς], ἄλλον δ' ἀνθελό|[με
10 νοι τ]ὰν δίκαν τελεόντι||[ων. hόσ]τις δέ κα πὰρ νόμον | [τι] ποιέοντα
τᾶι δίκαι hέληι, τὸ hήμισσον ἐχέτω. το|ὶ δὲ ταγοὶ τῶι καταγορέ-
15 ον|τι τὰν δίκαν ἐπιτελεόν||των · αἰ δὲ μή, τὸ διπλο̄ν ϝέχ|αστος ἀπο-
τεισάτω. hόστι|[ς] δέ κα ζαμίαν ὀφείληι. ἄτ|[ι]μος ἔστω, hέντε
20 κ' ἀποτεί|σηι. — Hόδ' ὁ τεθμὸς πὲρ τῶ||ν ἐντοφήιων. μὴ πλέον
πέν|τε, καὶ τριάκοντα δραχμ[ᾶ]|ν ἐνθέμεν μήτε πριάμενο|[ν] μήτε
25 ϝοίκω · τὰν δὲ παχεῖ|[α]ν χλαῖναν φαωτὰν εἶμεν. || αἰ δέ τι τούτων
παρβάλλο|ιτο, ἀποτεισάτω πεντήκο|ντα δραχμάς, αἴ κα μὴ ἐξομ|ό-
30 σηι ἐπὶ τῶι σάματι μὴ πλ|έον ἐνθέμεν. στρῶμα δὲ hὲ||ν hυποβαλέ-
τω καὶ ποικεφ|άλαιον hὲν ποτθέτω · τὸν δ|ὲ νεκρὸν κεκαλυμμένον
35 φ|ερέτω σιγᾶι, κἠν ταῖς στρ|οφαῖς μὴ καττιθέντων μη||[δ]αμεῖ,
μηδ' ὀτοτυζόντων ἐ|[χ]θὸς τᾶς ϝοικίας, πρίγ κ' ἐ|πὶ τὸ σᾶμα hί-
κωντι, τηνεῖ | δ' ἔναγος ἔστω, hέντε κα hα | θιγάνα ποτθεθῆι. τῶν

40 δὲ π||ρόστα τεθνακότων ἐν τοῖς | σαμάτεσσι μὴ θρηνεῖν μη|δ' ὀτοτύ-
ζεν, ἀλλ' ἀπίμεν Fο|ίκαδε ἕκαστον ἔχθω ηομε|στίων καὶ πατραδελ-
45 φεῶν || καὶ πενθερῶν κῆσγόνων [κ]|αὶ γαμβρῶν. μηδὲ τᾶι ηυσ[τ]|ε-
ραία(ι) μηδ' ἐν ταῖς δεκάτ[α]|ις μηδ' ἐν τοῖς ἐνιαυτοῖ[ς | μ]ήτ' οἰ-
50 μώζεν μήτ' ὀτοτύ[ζε||ν]· αἰ δέ τι τούτων παρβ|άλλοιτο τῶν γε-
γραμ|μένων - - - - - - -

D

.........αχα...δ...|....... θοῖναι δὲ ταίδ|[ε νόμιμ]οι·
5 'Απέλλαι καὶ Β|[ουκά]τια, Ηηραῖα, Δαιδαφ||[όρια], Ποιτρόπια,
Βυσίου | [μην]ὸς τὰν ηεβδέμαν καὶ | [τ]ὰν ηενάταν, κηΰκλει[α
10 κ]|άρταμίτια καὶ Λάφρι[α κ]|αὶ Θεοξένια καὶ Τελχίν||ια καὶ Διοσ-
κουρῆια, Μεγ|αλάρτια καὶ Ηηράκλει[α], | καί κ' αὐτὸς θύηι ηια-
15 ρῆ[ι]|ον καί κα λεχχοῖ παρῆι [κ]|αί κα ξένοι Fοι παρέωντ||ι ηιαρῆια
θύοντες καί κ|α πενταμαριτεύων τύχη|ι· αἰ δέ τι τούτων παρβάλ-|
20 λοιτο τῶν γεγραμμένω|ν, | θωεόντων τοί τε δαμιορ||γοὶ καὶ τοὶ ἄλλοι
πάντε|ς Λαβυάδαι, πρασσόντων | δὲ τοὶ πεντεκαίδεκα. α[ἰ] | δέ κα
25 ἀμφιλλέγηι τᾶς θω|ιάσιος, ἐξομόσας τὸν νό||[μιμ]ον ηόρκον λελύ-
σθω. α|[ἰ δ' ἀ]λίαν ποιόντων ἄρχω|[ν ἀ]πείη, ἀποτεισάτω ὀδε|λόν,
30 καὶ συγχέοι, ἀποτει|σάτω ὀδελόν. τοιάδε κην || Φανατεῖ γέγραπται
ἐν [τ]|ᾶι πέτραι ἔνδω· "τάδε Φά[ν]|οτος ἐπέδωκε τᾶι θυγατ|ρὶ
35 Βουζύγαι, τὰ ηἐμιρρ[ή]||νια κῆκ τᾶς δυωδεκαῖδο||ς χίμαιραν καὶ
τῆμπροναίαν δάρματα|καὶ τὰ τῶι | Λυκείωι δάρματα καὶ τὰ|ν ἀγαί-
40 αν μόσχον." πάντων | καὶ Fιδίων καὶ δαμοσίω||ν τὸμ προθύοντα
καὶ προ|μαντευόμενον παρέχεν | τὰ γεγραμμέ·α Λαβυάδα|ις· τᾶι
45 δὲ θυσίαι Λαβυαδ|ᾶν τὠπελλαίου μηνὸς τῶ||ι Διονύσωι, Βουκατίοις|
τῶι Διὶ πατρωίωι καὶ τὠπ|όλλωνι τὰν ἀκρόθινα κα|ὶ συμπιπίσκεν
50 ηαμεῖ το|ὺς Λαβυάδας· τὰς δ' ἄλλας || θοίνας κὰ[τ] τὰν ηώραν
ἀπ|άγεσθαι.

Regulations of the phratry of the Labyadae.

A 3. τοὺν νόμους: τοὺς νόμους. So τὸν νόμους B 16, but usually
ς unassimilated. 97.1.—4. ἀπελλαίων: 'victims for the 'Απέλλαι.'
Cf. ll. 44-46 where ἄγεν is used with ἀπελλαῖα, in contrast to
φέρεν with δαράτας. 'Απέλλαι is the name of the Delphian festival
corresponding to the Attic 'Απατούρια, at which children were
introduced into the phratries and offerings for the occasion were
made by the parents.—5. δαρατᾶν: 'cakes.' Ath. 3.110d, 114b

cites a δάρατον meaning 'unleavened bread' and says the word
was used by the Thessalians. The δαράται at the Delphian
festival were of two kinds (cf. l. 25), the γάμελα or cakes offered
in behalf of the newly married wives that were introduced into
the phratry by their husbands, and the παιδῆια offered for the
children that were introduced into the phratry by their parents.
—6. **συμπραξέω κάποδειξέω**: 'I will collect and disburse.'
ἀποδείκνυμι, like Att. ἀποφαίνω, 'render account for, pay over.'
Cf. ἀπέδειξαν no. 49.—6/7 [x]ωῦτε, new corrected reading. BCH
61.69. See **94**.7.—10. **τῶλ Λαβυαδᾶν**: τῶν Λαβ-, elsewhere
unassimilated, as l. 3. **96**.3.—11. 'I will impose the oath upon
the ταγοί for the next year.' Cf. B 27.

23 ff. 'The ταγοί are to receive neither, in the case of the
cakes (lit. of the cakes), the γάμελα or the παιδῆια, nor the
ἀπελλαῖα, unless the gens to which one belongs approves in full
session.' The approval of the gens (πατριά, as in Elis; πάτρα in
most Doric dialects) was a prerequisite to the introduction
into the phratry, which was the larger body including several
gentes.—30. ὀ: without h, as also A 38, C 19, but ho (demonst.)
B 53, hόδε C 19. Cf. ἀς A 28 beside hō B 45, hόστις A 46, B 30,
C 19. See **58a**.—38 ff. 'Any one who wishes to accuse the ταγοί
of having received the offering at other than the stated times
shall bring the charge when their successors are in office.'—
45. **ἀντὶ Ϝέτεος**: 'by the year, annually.' **136**.8.—56 'Or let him
sign a note (for the twenty drachmas) and pay interest.'

B 11-12. **ἀνδεξάμενοι**: 'undertaking, promising.' They swear
by the gods of the city, phratry, and gens.—23/24. 'The ταγοι
shall carry out these prescriptions and in case of need (so τῶί
δεομένωι, Vollgraff) convene the Labyadae.'—50. **θεμάτων**:
probably 'established rites, institutions,' though this meaning
of θέμα is not quotable. Cf. τεθμός = θεσμός 'law, ordinance,'
C 19.

C 1 ff. Oath of the person appointed to act as judge. The
missing conclusion of B must have been the provision for such
an appointment.—6 ff. 'If the one chosen fails to serve as
judge, he shall pay five drachmas, and (the ταγοί) shall bring the
case to issue by appointing another in his place. Whoever convicts
one guilty of an unlawful action shall receive half the fine' (cf.

no. 19.24/25).—19 ff. Law concerning funeral rites. Like the law of Iulis in Ceos (no. 8), this is directed against extravagance. —20 ff. 'One shall not expend more than thirty-five drachmas, either by purchase or (in articles taken) from the home.'— 23/24. 'The shroud shall be thick and of a light gray color.' For φαωτός = *φαιωτός, see **31**, and, as used of mourning apparel, cf. φαιὰ ἱμάτια Polyb. 30.4, 5, and φαιὰ ἐσθής Ditt. Syll. 879.5— 25 ff. 'If one transgresses (παρβάλλω = παραβαίνω) any of these things, he shall pay fifty drachmas, unless he denies under oath at the tomb that he has spent more.'—29 ff. **στρῶμα δὲ** κτλ.: cf. no. 8.3/4.—31 ff. **τὸν δὲ νεκρὸν** κτλ.: cf. no. 8.10/11.—33 ff. **κὴν ταῖς στροφαῖς** κτλ.: 'they shall not set the corpse down anywhere at the turns of the road (but carry it straight on to the tomb without interruption), nor shall they make lamentations outside the house until they arrive at the tomb, but there there shall be a ceremony for the dead (? cf. ἐναγίζω) until the lid (?) is closed (cf. προστίθημι τὰς θύρας, etc.).' But the last part, from τηνεῖ on, is variously read and interpreted.—39 ff. 'There shall be no mourning for the former dead, but every one shall go home, except the members of the immediate family and the near relatives by blood or marriage.'—46 ff. 'There shall be no wailing or lamentation on the following days, nor on the tenth day, nor on the anniversaries.'—**ἐνιαυτοῖς**: See Glossary, and cf. τὰ ἐνιαύσια in the same sense at Ceos.

D 1 ff. Enumeration of the regular feasts. These are given in the order of their occurrence, as appears from the correspondence between many of them and the names of the months ('Απελλαῖος, Βουκάτιος, 'Ηραῖος, etc.).—5-7. 'Those which occur on the seventh and the ninth of the month Βύσιος.'—7/8. **κηΰκλεια κάρταμίτια**: καὶ Εὔκλεια καὶ 'Αρταμίτια.—12 ff. Feasts are also held 'if one sacrifices a victim for himself, if one assists (in the sacrifices for the purification of) a woman recently delivered of child, if there are strangers with him sacrificing victims, and if one is serving as πενταμαρίτας.' πενταμαρίτας is the name of some official appointed to serve five days (cf. Locr. πεντάμεροι, Halae), but nothing more is known about this office.—22. **τοὶ πεντεκαί-δεκα**: cf. no. 49.—26/27. 'If, when they hold an assembly, any official is absent.' ἄρχων nom. sg. ppl. 'one holding office.'—

29 ff. 'These things are written at Phanoteus on the inner side of the rock.' The ancient city of Phanoteus (Panopeus) was perhaps the original seat of the phratry of the Labyadae.—30. **Φανατεῖ**: cf. Φάνοτος ll. 30-31. Both Φανατεύς and Φανοτεύς occur in other inscriptions. See **46.**—35. **τῆμπροναίαν**: τὰ ἐμ Προναίαν. Cf. ἰαρήιον ἐμ Προναίαν of another inscription.— 38. **τὰν ἀγαίαν μόσχον**: the 'admirable' or 'holy' calf (cf. glosses in Hesych., Et. M. and especially in the late Favor. Cam. ἀγαῖος· κατὰ τοὺς παλαιοὺς σεμνός, καλός, λαμπρός, κόσμιος).— 38 ff. **πάντων** κτλ.: 'in the case of all undertakings, both private and public, for which one offers sacrifice or consults the oracle in advance, the one doing so shall furnish to the Labyadae the victims mentioned.' πάντων depends upon προθύοντα and προμαντευόμενον 'sacrificing etc. in advance of.'—47. **τὰν ἀκρόθινα** (ἀκρόθις = usual ἀκροθίνιον, as also in Pindar): sc. ταγοὺς παρέχεν 'the ταγοί shall furnish the first-fruits.'—48 f. **συμπιπίσκεν** κτλ.: 'invite the Labyadae to drink together.'—49 ff. **τὰς δ' ἄλλας** κτλ.: 'the other feasts one shall carry out in accordance with the season.'

53. Delphi. Second quarter (?) fourth century B.C. P. Amundry, BCH 63.183 ff. Ll. 19-36 are omitted here.

 Σ[κια]θίων |δά[μωι κα]ὶ ἀποίκοις · | τάδ[ε] ξύνθετα Δελ|φο[ῖς]
5 καὶ Σκιαθίο||ις · ἔ[δ]ωκαν προμαν|τεί[α]ν καὶ ἀτέλει|αν πά[ντ]ων
10 νόσφι π|ελαν[ō] · πελανὸν δ[ὲ] | τὸν μ[ὲν] δαμόσιον || στατῆ[ρ]α
αἰγιναῖ|ον, τὸν [δ]ὲ ἴδιον δύ|ο ὀδελώ· ἐς τὸ δέρμ|α τὸ δαμόσιον
15 δύο | ὀδελ[ώ], τὸ δὲ ἴδιον || ὀδελόν· αἴ κ' ἐπὶ φρ|υκτώ παρίηι, τὸ
μὲ|ν δαμόσιον στ[α]τῆ|[ρ]α αἰ[γιναῖον, τόδ|ε ἴδιον] - - -

For πελανός see no. 7 A 25 ff., note.—For τὸν δαμόσιον, etc., see no. 51.—15/16 f. **αἴ κ' ἐπὶ φρυκτώ παρίηι**: 'if anyone presents himself for the (drawing of lots by means of) two beans.' The use of beans in drawing lots is recorded in Plut. Mor. 492 A, B, where φρυκτός is also used, and indicated by various glosses.

54. Delphi. Between 240 and 200 B.C. GDI 2653. Schwyzer 332.

 Ἀγαθᾶι τύχαι. Δελφοὶ ἔδωκαν Νικάνδρωι | Ἀναξαγόρου Κολοφωνίωι, ἐπέων ποητᾶι, αὐ|τῶι καὶ ἐγγόνοις προξενίαν, προμαν-
5 τείαν, | ἀσυλίαν, προδικίαν, ἀτέλειαν πάντων, προε||δρίαν ἐν πάν-

τεσι τοῖς ἀγώνοις οἷς ἁ πόλις τί|θητι καὶ τἆλλα ὅσα καὶ τοῖς ἄλλοις προξένοις καὶ | εὐεργέταις τᾶς πόλιος τῶν Δελφῶν· ἄρχοντος | Νικοδάμου, βουλευόντων ᾿Αρίστωνος, Νικοδάμου, Πλεί|στωνος, Ξένωνος, ᾿Επιχαρίδα.

Proxeny decree in honor of the poet Nicander of Colophon, whose writings included a prose work on Aetolia. At this time the Aetolians were dominant in Delphi, and this shows itself in the language of the inscriptions. See **279**. Note in l. 5 the combination of Delph. πάντεσι with Aetol. ἀγώνοις.

55. Delphi. 186 B.C. GDI 2034. Schwyzer 335.

᾿Αρχοντος [Ν]ικοβούλου μηνὸς Βουκατίου, ἐπὶ τοῖσδε ἀπέδοτο Νεοπάτρα ᾿Ορθαίου | Δελφὶς τῶι ᾿Απόλλωνι τῶι Πυθίωι σώματα γυναικεῖα δύο αἷς ὀνόματα Ζωπύ|ρα, Σωσίχα, τιμᾶς ἀργυρίου μνᾶν ἕξ, καθὼς ἐπίστευσαν Ζωπύρα, Σωσίχα τῶι | θεῶι τὰν ὠνάν,
5 ἐφ᾿ ὧιτε ἐλευθέρας εἶμεν καὶ ἀνεφάπτους ἀπὸ πάντων τὸμ || πάντα βίον. βεβαιωτὴρ κατὰ τὸν νόμον· Δαμένης ᾿Ορέστα Δελφός. παραμε[ι]νάν|των δὲ Ζωπύρα, Σωσίχα παρὰ Νεοπάτραν ἄχρι κα ζώηι Νεοπάτρα ποέουσαι | τὸ ποτιτασσόμενον πᾶν τὸ δυνατὸν ἀνεγκλήτως· εἰ δέ τί κα μὴ ποιέωντι | Ζωπύρα ἢ Σωσίχα τῶν ποτιτασσομένων ὑπὸ Νεοπάτρας καθὼς | γέγραπται δυναταὶ οὖσαι, ἐξέστω
10 Νεοπάτραι κολάζειν καθώς || κα αὐτὰ δείληται καὶ ἄλλωι ὑπὲρ Νεοπάτραν ἀζαμίοις ὄντοις καὶ ἀνυ|ποδίκοις πάσας δίκας καὶ ζαμίας. εἰ δέ τί κα πάθηι Νεοπάτρα, ἐλεύθεραι | ἔστων Ζωπύρα καὶ Σωσίχα κυριεύουσαι αὐτοσαυτᾶν καὶ ποέουσαι ὅ κα θέλων|τι, καθὼς ἐπίστευσαν τῶι θεῶι τὰν ὠνάν. εἰ δέ τίς κα ἅπτηται Ζωπύρας | ἢ Σωσίχας ἐπεί κα τελευτάσηι Νεοπάτρα, βέβαιον παρε-
15 χέτω ὁ βεβαιωτὴρ τῶι || θεῶι τὰν ὠνὰν κατὰ τὸν νόμον. ὁμοίως δὲ καὶ οἱ παρατυγχάνοντες κύριοι ἐόν|των συλέοντες ὡς ἐλευθέρας οὔσας ἀζάμιοι ὄντες καὶ ἀνυπόδικοι | πάσας δίκας καὶ ζαμίας. εἰ δέ τί κα ἀζετωθέωντι περὶ Νεοπάτραν πεπο|νηρευμέναι ἢ τῶν Νεοπάτρας ὑπαρχόντων τι, κύριοι ἐόντω οἱ ἐπίνομοι κολά|ζοντες αὐτὰς
20 καθ᾿ ὅτι κα αὐτοῖς δοκῆι ἀζάμιοι ὄντες καὶ ἀνυπόδικοι || πάσας δίκας. μάρτυρες· τοὶ ἱερεῖς Ξένων, ᾿Αθαμβος, τῶν ἀρχόντων Εὐ|κλείδας, | ἰδιῶται ῾Ιεροκλῆς, Χαρίξενος, Βάχχιος.

A typical Delphian manumission decree, of which there are more than 1,600. See note to nos. 44-47. They show all varieties of mixture of Delphian, Northwest Greek κοινή, and Attic elements, e.g., in this inscription, 3 pl. imv. ἐόντω, ἐόντων, ἔστων. Nearly always at this time, the older αἰ, ἱαρός are replaced by εἰ, ἱερός, and τοί by οἱ, though τοί is frequently retained in the formal τοὶ ἱερεῖς beginning the list of witnesses.—17. ἀζετω-θέωντι κτλ.: 'are convicted of having done any wrong to Neo-patra or her possessions.' Cf. ἐξελεγχθείησαν in another of the manumission decrees, and Hesych. ἄζετον· ἄπιστον, Σικελοί.

Exclusive of Delphi

56. Stiris. About 180 B.C. IG IX.i.32. GDI 1539. Ditt. Syll. 647. Schwyzer 353. Solmsen-Fraenkel 50.

A

[Θ]εὸς τύχαν ἀγα|[θ]άν. στραταγέοντος | [τ]ῶν Φωκέων Ζευ-
5 ξίου, | [μ]ηνὸς ἑβδόμου, ὁμολο[γ||ί]α τᾶ πόλει Στειρίων καὶ | [τᾶ]
πόλει Μεδεωνίων· συ[ν|ε]πολίτευσαν Στείριοι κα[ὶ | Μ]εδεώνιοι
10 ἔχοντες ἱερά, πό|[λι]ν, χώραν, λιμένας, πάντα || [ἐ]λεύθερα, ἐπὶ
τοῖσδε. εἶμεν | [τ]οὺς Μεδεωνίους πάντας | [Σ]τιρίους ἴσους καὶ
ὁμοίους, | καὶ συνεκλησιάζειν καὶ συ|ναρχοστατεῖσθαι μετὰ τᾶς ||
15 [πό]λιος τᾶς Στιρίων, καὶ δικά|[ζ]ειν τὰς δίκας τὰς ἐπὶ πόλι|[ο]ς
πάσας τοὺς ἐνικομένους | [τ]αῖς ἁλικίαις. ἱστάνθω δὲ κα[ὶ | ἱ]εροτα-
20 μίαν ἐκ τῶν Μεδεω||[ν]ίων ἕνα τὸν θυσέοντα τὰς | θυσίας τὰς πα-
τρίους Μεδεων|[ί]οις, ὅσαι ἐντὶ ἐν τῶ πολιτικῶ νόμ[ω, | μ]ετὰ τῶν
25 ἀρχόντων τῶν στα|[θ]έντων ἐν Στίρι· λανβανέτω || [δ]ὲ ὁ ἱεροτα-
μίας ἀρέσμιον, ὃ τ[οὶ | ἄ]ρχοντες ἐλάμβανον, ἡμι|[μ]ναῖον καὶ
τῶν χοῶν τὸ ἐπ[ι|β]αλὸν τῶ ἱεροταμίαι. συνδι|[κ]αξεῖ δὲ ὁ ἱεροτα-
30 μίας μετὰ || [τ]ῶν ἀρχόντων τὰς δίκας, ἃς | [τ]οὶ ἄρχοντες δικά-
ζοντι, καὶ·[κ]λαρωσῖ τὰ δικαστήρια, ἅ κα | δέῃ κλαρώειν, μετὰ τῶν
35 ἀ[ρ]||χόντων. μὴ ἔστω δὲ ἐπάναγ||[κ]ες λειτουργεῖν τοὺς Μεδε-|
ωνίους ἐν Στίρι τὰς ἀρχάς, ὅσοι | γεγένηνται ἐν Μεδεῶνι ἄρ|χοντες,
40 ξενοδίκαι, πρακτῆρες, | δαμιουργοί, ἱερεῖς, ἱεράρχαι, καὶ || τὰν
γυναικῶν ὅσαι ἱερητεύ|κατι, εἰ μή τις ἑκὼν ὑπομένοι· | ἱστάνθων
δὲ ἐκ τῶν ἀλειτου|ργήτων τῶν Μεδεωνίων κ|αὶ ἐκ τῶν Στιρίων·
δαμιουρ||[γ]εόντων δὲ καὶ τὰ ἐν Μεδε|[ῶνι ἱ]ερὰ καθὼς ὁ πολιτι-
45 κὸς νό|μος κελεύει. καὶ τὰν χ[ώ|ραν] τὰν Μεδεωνίαν εἶμεν |[π]ᾶσαν
50 Στιρίαν καὶ τὰν Στι||ρίαν Μεδεωνίαν κοινὰν π[ᾶ|σα]ν. κοινω-
νεόντω δὲ οἱ Μεδε|[ώ]νιοι τᾶν θυσιᾶν τᾶν ἐν Στί|[ρι] πασᾶν καὶ τοὶ

55 ‹τοὶ› Στίριοι τᾶν ἐν Με|δεῶνι πασᾶν. μὴ ἐξέστω δ||ὲ ἀποπολιτεύ-
σασται τού[ς] | Μεδεωνίους ἀπὸ τῶν Στιρί|[ω]ν μηδὲ τοὺς Στι-
ρίους ἀπὸ | [τ]ῶν Μεδε[ωνί]ων. ὁπότεροι | [δ]έ κα μὴ ἐμμείνωντι
60 ἐν τοῖ||[ς] γεγραμμένοις, ἀποτει|σάντων τοῖς ἐμμεινά[ν]||τοις ἀρ-
γυρίου τάλαν|τα δέκα.

B

[. . . . . π]οιεόντων· | [γ]ραψάντων δὲ τὰν ὁμ[ο]||λογίαν ἐν
5 στάλαν καὶ ἀν[αθέ]|ντων ἐν τὸ ἱερὸν τᾶς 'Α[θάν]||ας, θέστων δὲ
τὰν ὁμο[λογί]|αν καὶ παρὰ ἰδιώταν ἐσ[φρα]|γισμέναν. ἁ ὁμολογία
10 π[αρὰ] | Θράσωνα Λιλαιέα. μάρ[τυ]||ρες Θράσων Δαματρίου 'Ε||λα-
τεύς, Εὐπαλίδας Θρά|σωνος Λιλαιεύς, Τιμο|κράτης 'Επινίκου Τι-
15 θορρε|ύς. δόντων δὲ τοὶ Στίριοι | τᾶ φατρία τῶν Μεδεωνί||ων ἐν
ἐτέοις τεττάροις | ἀργυρίου μνᾶς πέντε κα[ὶ | τ]όπον τὰν καλειμέ-
ναν | [Δ]α[μα]τρείαν.

Agreement establishing a συμπολιτεία or joint-citizenship between the Stirians and Medeonians.

10. ἐλεύθερα 'free, open to all' (of both towns).—11 ff. τούς κτλ.: 'all the Medeonians shall be Stirians with equal rights, and shall join with the city of the Stirians in the assembly and in appointing magistrates, and those who have arrived at proper age shall try all cases which come before the state.'—18. ἱστάνθω: Boeotian for ἱστάντω. So θέλωνθι in another Stirian inscription. Cf. also κλαρωσῖ l. 32 with Boeot. ι for ει. See 231.—34 ff. μὴ ἔστω κτλ.: 'those who have been officials in Medeon shall be exempt from compulsory office holding in Stiris.'—40-41. ἱερητεύκατι: 138.4.—55. ἀποπολιτεύσασται: στ = σθ as in θέστων B 5. 85.1.

B 13 ff. The phratry of the Medeonians, in distinction from the state, retained its own organization, and was to receive a subsidy of money and land from the Stirians.

Locrian

57. Oeanthea (Galaxidi). Early fifth century B.C. IG IX.i.334. GDI 1478. Roberts 231 and pp. 346 ff. Schwyzer 362. Ditt. Syll. 47. Solmsen-Fraenkel 44. Tod 24.

Ἐν Ναύπακτον κὰ τῶνδε hἀπιϜοικία. ΛοϘρὸν τὸν Ηυποκνα-
μίδιον, ἐπ|εί κα Ναυπάκτιος γένε̄ται, Ναυπάκτιον ἐόντα, hόπō
ξένον ὄσια λανχάν|ειν καὶ θύειν ἐξεῖμεν ἐπιτυχόντα, αἴ κα δείλε̄-
ται· αἴ κα δείλε̄ται, θύειν καὶ λ|ανχάνειν κὲ̄ δάμō κὲ̄ Ϙοινάνōν αὐ-
5 τὸν καὶ τὸ γένος καταιϜεί. τέλος το||ὺς ἐπιϜοίϘους ΛοϘρῶν τῶν
Ηυποκναμιδίōν μὲ̄ φάρειν ἐν ΛοϘροῖς τοῖ|ς Ηυποκναμιδίοις, φρίν
κ᾽ αὖ τις ΛοϘρὸς γένε̄ται τῶν Ηυποκναμιδίōν. αἰ | δείλε̄τ᾽ ἀνχō-
ρεῖν, καταλείποντα ἐν τᾶι ἱστίαι παῖδα hε̄βατὰν ἒ̄ ᾽δελφεὸν ἐξ|εῖ-
μεν ἄνευ ἐνετε̄ρίōν· αἴ κα hυπ᾽ ἀνάνκας ἀπελάōνται ἐ Ναυπάκτō
ΛοϘ|ροὶ τοὶ Ηυποκναμίδιοι, ἐξεῖμεν ἀνχōρεῖν, hόπō Ϝέκαστος ἒ̄ν,
10 ἄνευ ἐ||νετε̄ρίōν. τέλος μὲ̄ φάρειν με̄δὲν hότι μὲ̄ μετὰ ΛοϘρῶν τῶν
Ϝεσπαρί|ōν. — Α — Ἔνορϙον τοῖς ἐπιϜοίϙοις ἐν Ναύπακτον μὲ̄
᾽ποστᾶμεν ἀ(π᾽ ᾽Ο)ποντίōν | τέκναι καὶ μαχαναῖ με̄δεμιᾶι ϜεϘόντας.
τὸν hόρϙον ἐξεῖμεν, αἴ κα δεί|λōνται, ἐπάγειν μετὰ τριάϙοντα Ϝέτεα
ἀπὸ τō̄ hόρϙō̄ hεκατὸν ἄνδρας ᾽Ο|ποντίοις Ναυπακτίōν καὶ Ναυ-
15 πακτίοις ᾽Οποντίους. — Β — Ηόσστις κα λιποτελέε̄||ι ἐγ Ναυ-
πάκτō τῶν ἐπιϜοίϙō̄ν, ἀπὸ ΛοϘρῶν εἶμεν, ἔντε κ᾽ ἀποτείσει τὰ
νό|μια Ναυπακτίοις. — Γ — Αἴ κα μὲ̄ γένος ἐν τᾶι ἱστίαι ἒ̄ι ἒ̄
᾽χεπάμōν τὸν ἐπι|Ϝοίϙō̄ν ἒ̄ι ἐν Ναυπάκτōι, ΛοϘρῶν τῶν Ηυποκναμι-
δίōν τὸν ἐπάνχισ|τον κρατεῖν, ΛοϘρῶν hόπō κ᾽ ἒ̄ι, αὐτὸν ἰόντα, αἴ
κ᾽ ἀνὲρ ἒ̄ι ἒ̄ παῖς, τριῶν μ|ε̄νō̄ν· αἰ δὲ μέ, τοῖς Ναυπακτίοις νομίοις
20 χρε̄σται. — Δ — ᾽Ε Ναυπάκτō ἀνχōρέ||οντα ἐν ΛοϘρούς τοὺς
Ηυποκναμιδίους ἐν Ναυπάκτōι καρῦξαι ἐν τὰ|γορᾶι, κὲ̄ν ΛοϘροῖς
τοῖ(ς)· Ηυποκναμιδίοις ἐν τᾶι πόλι, hō̄ κ᾽ ἒ̄ι, καρῦξαι ἐν | τἀγορᾶι.
— Ε — ΠερϘοθαριᾶν καὶ Μυσαχέōν ἐπεί κα Ναυπάκτι(ός τι)ς
γένε̄τα|ι αὐτός, καὶ τὰ χρέματα τὲ̄ν Ναυπάκτōι τοῖς ἐν Ναυπάκτōι
χρε̄σται, | τὰ δ᾽ ἐν ΛοϘροῖς τοῖς Ηυποκναμιδίοις χρέματα τοῖς
25 Ηυποκναμιδί||οις ||| νομίοις χρε̄σται, hόπος ἀ πόλις Ϝεκάστōν νομί-
ζει ΛοϘρῶν τῶν Ηυποκν|αμιδίōν. αἴ τις hυπὸ τῶν νομίōν τῶν ἐπι-
Ϝοίϙō̄ν ἀνχōρέει ΠερϘοθαριᾶ|ν καὶ Μυσαχέōν, τοῖς αὐτῶν νομίοις
χρε̄σται κατὰ πόλιν Ϝεκάστους. | — Ϝ — Αἴ κ᾽ ἀδελφεοὶ ἔōντι τō̄
30 ᾽ν Ναύπακτον Ϝοικέοντος, hόπος καὶ ΛοϘρō̄||ν τῶν Ηυποκναμιδίōν
Ϝεκάστōν νόμος ἐστί, αἴ κ᾽ ἀποθάνει, τὸν χ|ρε̄μάτōν κρατεῖν τὸν
ἐπίϜοιϙον, τὸ κατιϙόμενον κρατεῖν. — Ζ — | Τοὺς ἐπιϜοίϙους ἐν
Ναύπακτον τὰν δίκαν πρόδιϙον hαρέσται πὸ τοὺς δ|ικαστε̄ρας,
hαρέσται καὶ δόμεν ἐν ᾽Οπόεντι κατὰ Ϝέος αὐταμαρόν. ΛοϘ|ρῶν τῶν
35 Ηυποκναμιδίōν προστάταν καταστᾶσαι τὸν ΛοϘρῶν τō̄πιϜ||οίϙōι
καὶ τὸν ἐπιϜοίϙōν τō̄ι ΛοϘρō̄ι, hοίτινες κα ᾽πιατὲς ἔντιμοι ‹ες›

(ἔοντι). — Η — Ηόσσ|τις κ' ἀπολίπει πατάρα καὶ τὸ μέρος τὸν χρεμάτον τõι πατρί, ἐπεί κ' | ἀπογένεται, ἐξεῖμεν ἀπολαχεῖν τὸν ἐπίϜοιϘον ἐν Ναύπακτον. | — Θ — Ηόσστις κα τὰ ϜεϜαδεϘότα διαφθείρει τέχναι καὶ μαχανᾶι κα|ὶ μιᾶι, ηότι κα μὲ ἀνφοτάροις
40 δοκέει, Ηοποντίον τε χιλίον πλέθ||αι καὶ ΝαϜπακτίον τὸν ἐπιϜοίϘον πλέθαι, ἄτιμον εἶμεν καὶ χρέ|ματα παματοφαγεῖσται. τὸνκαλει-μένōι τὰν δίκαν δόμεν τὸν ἀρ|χόν, ἐν τριάϘοντ' ἀμάραις δόμεν, αἴ κα τριάκοντ' ἀμάραι λείπōντ|αι τᾶς ἀρχᾶς · αἴ κα μὲ διδōι τõι ἐνκα-λειμένōι τὰν δίκαν, ἄτιμ|ον εἶμεν καὶ χρέματα παματοφαγεῖσται,
45 τὸ μέρος μετὰ Ϝο||ικιατᾶν. διομόσαι ηόρϘον τὸν νόμιον. ἐν ὑδρίαν τὰν ψάφιξ|ξιν εἶμεν. καὶ τὸ θέθμιον τοῖς Ηυποκναμιδίοις ΛοϘροῖς ταύ|τᾶ τέλεον εἶμεν Χαλειέοις τοῖς σὺν 'Αντιφάται Ϝοικέταις.

Law governing the relations between the Eastern Locrian colonists at Naupactus and the mother country. This does not refer to the founding of Naupactus, which was much earlier. Colonists are called ἄποικοι from the point of view of the mother country, but ἔποικοι as here (ἐπίϜοιϘοι) from the point of view of their new home. The Eastern Locrians are referred to ethnically as Hypocnemidians (of which Epicnemidians is an equivalent), politically as Opuntians, since Opus was the seat of government, the two terms standing in the same relation as Boeotian and Theban.

It is probable that one copy was set up at Opus, with another at Naupactus, and that the present tablet is still another copy, which with the addition of the last sentence, stating that similar relations are to subsist between colonists from Chaleion and the mother city, was set up at Chaleion, from which place it may easily have found its way to Galaxidi.

In both this and the following inscription double consonants (in part involving assimilation) are usually simplified in external combination (see 89.7). So ἐ δάμο, ἐ λιμένος, etc., with assimilation of ἐκ (100); similarly ἐ Ναυπάκτō (once ἐγ Ναυπάκτō), in contrast to which ἐν Ναύπακτον, ἐν Ναυπάκτōι with original ἐν are always written out. Simplification of σσ in (no. 58) αἴ τι συλōι, ἀνάτō συλέν,' ἀδίκō συλέν = αἴ τις, etc., in view of which ηόπō ξένον (no. 57.2) = ηόπōς ξένον, though not quite parallel, is probable. No other Greek inscription has so many examples of Ϙ as no. 57, where it is uniformly employed before o or ρο. In no. 58 it is no longer used. In no. 57 lengthened ε is expressed by EI, lengthened o by O in the genitive singular, OV in the accusative plural. But in no. 58 always E and O. See 25*d*. No. 57, beginning in l. 11, is divided into paragraphs by the letters A-Θ.

No. 57 exhibits many instances of repetition (see l. 3, note), and some of omission of what is essential to clearness (e.g., the subject of ἀποθάνει l. 30), and in general the style of both inscriptions is crude and obscure.

1. 'The colony to Naupactus on the following terms.'— **hἀπιϝοικία**: hα ἐπιϝοικία. **94.**5.—**χὰ τὸνδε**: **136.**5.—**Λοϙρὸν τὸν Ηυποκναμίδιον** κτλ.: 'A Hypocnemidian Locrian, when he becomes a Naupactian, being a Naupactian, may as a ξένος share in the social and religious privileges (i.e., in the mother country) when he happens to be present, if he wishes. If he wishes, he may share in these privileges, both those of the people and those of the members of the societies, himself and his descendants forever. The colonists of the H. Locrians are not to pay taxes among the H. Locrians, until one becomes a H. Locrian again.' In ὅσια λανχάνειν χαὶ θύειν there is probably the same contrast as in ἱερὰ χαὶ ὅσια or Cretan θεῖνα χαὶ ἀνθρώπινα.—3. **αἴ κα δείλεται**: for the repetition cf. also ἒι ll. 16 f., δόμεν ll. 41 f., χαρῦξαι ἐν τἀγορᾶι ll. 20 ff. —4. **χὲ δάμō χὲ ϙοινάνōν**: χαὶ ἐκ δήμου χαὶ ἐκ κοινωνῶν. **94.**6, **100.**—7 ff. 'If a colonist wishes to return, he may do so without taxes of admission (to citizenship), provided he leaves behind in his house an adult son or brother. If the H. Locrians are driven from Naupactus by force, they may return without admission taxes to the town from which they each came. They are to pay no taxes except in common with the Western Locrians,' i.e., they are not to be subject to any special taxes as colonists.—**αἰ δείλετ'**: for subj. without κα (also in l. 26), see **174.**—9. **hόπō ϝέχαστος ἔν**: a 3 sg. ἦν is otherwise known only in Attic-Ionic, other dialects retaining the original ἦς. See **163.**3. Hence this is the 3 pl. ἦν agreeing with the logical subject they (cf. the preceding). Cf. Hom. ἔβαν οἰχόνδε ἔχαστος, etc.—11 ff. 'The colonists to Naupactus must take oath not to forsake the alliance with the Opuntians willingly by any device. If they wish they may impose the oath thirty years after this

oath, one hundred Naupactians upon the Opuntians and the
Opuntians upon the Naupactians.'—11. **ἐνορϘον**: used impersonally with the dative, like ἔνδικον in Cretan etc.—14 ff.
'Whoever of the colonists departs from Naupactus with unpaid
taxes shall lose his rights as a Locrian until he pays the Naupactians his lawful dues.' **ἀποτείσει**: or -εῑ? See **150b**.—16 ff.
'If there is no family in the home, or heir to the property among
the colonists in Naupactus, the next of kin among the H.
Locrians shall inherit, from whatever place among the Locrians
he comes, and, if a man or boy, he shall go himself within three
months. Otherwise the laws of Naupactus shall be followed.'—
19 ff. 'If one returns from Naupactus to the H. Locrians, he
must have it announced in Naupactus in the market-place,
and among the H. Locrians in the city whence he comes.'—
22 ff. 'Whenever any of the ΠερϘοθαρίαι and the Μυσαχεῖς
(probably the names of two noble or priestly families, the first
obviously containing κοθαρός = καθαρός) becomes a Naupactian
himself, his property in Naupactus shall also be subject to the
laws in Naupactus, but his property among the H. Locrians
to the H. laws, as the law may be in the several cities of the
H. Locrians. If any of them, under the laws of the colonists,
return, they shall be subject to their own laws, each according
to the city of his origin.'—29 ff. 'If there are brothers of the one
who goes as a colonist to Naupactus, then, according to what
the law of the H. Locrians severally (i.e., in each city) is, if (one
of them) dies, the colonist shall inherit his share of the property,
shall inherit what belongs to him.' Note the double construction
with κρατεῖν according as the sense is partitive or not. But
many take TO as gen. sg. τȭ in relative sense, though this use is
not otherwise attested in Locrian, and understand ἐστί with
κατιϘόμενον, translating 'which it is proper for him to inherit.'—
32 f. 'The colonists may bring suit before the judges with right
of precedence, they may bring suit and submit to suits against
themselves in Opus on the same day.' This provision is intended
to secure for the colonists the greatest expedition in their
litigation at Opus. **hαρέσται** (i.e., ἑλέσθαι) **καὶ δόμεν** = λαβεῖν
καὶ δοῦναι (cf. Hdt. 5.83). δίκην λαβεῖν is usually 'to bring suit,'
as here, though sometimes the opposite, while δίκην δοῦναι is

usually 'to submit to suit' (e.g., Thuc. 1.28), as here, though sometimes used of a magistrate, 'to grant trial,' as below, ll. 41 f.— 34 f. 'Whoever are in office for the year shall appoint from among the H. Locrians a προστάτης, one of the Locrians for the colonist, one of the colonists for the Locrian.' τὸν Λοϙρὸν Ηυποκναμιδίον applies properly only to the appointment of the προστάτης for the colonist, this being the important provision in continuation of the preceding paragraph. Making the provision mutual was an afterthought.—καπιατες without correction is to be read κα 'πιατές, with hyphaeresis where we expect elision, from κα and ἐπιατές, and adv. cpd. of Ϝέτος for which we should expect ἐπιϜετές or ἐπιετές (intervocalic Ϝ is not always written, cf. 'Οπόεντι, δαμιουργούς). Some correct to 'πι(Ϝε)τές, but a by-form with (Ϝ)ατ is possible. ΕΣ after ἔντιμοι is due to dittography (cf. the ending of the preceding hοίτινες, 'πιατές). The omission of ἔοντι may be the engraver's error, or simply ellipsis, such as is not infrequent in a clause of this kind (Kühner-Gerth I, p. 41, n. 2c).—36 f. 'A colonist to Naupactus who has left behind a father and his portion of the property with the father, shall inherit his share when (the father) dies.'—38 ff. 'Whoever violates these statutes by any device in any point which is not agreed to by both parties, the assembly of the Thousand in Opus and the assembly of the colonists in Naupactus, shall be deprived of civil rights and shall have his property confiscated.' For the spelling ΝαϜπακτίον see **32**.—**παματοφαγείσται**: **162**.12.—41 ff. 'To the one who brings suit the magistrate shall grant trial within thirty days, if thirty days of his magistracy remain. If he does not grant trial to the one bringing suit he shall be deprived of civil rights and have his property confiscated, his real estate together with his servants. The customary oath shall be taken. The voting shall be by ballot.' For μέρος 'real estate', cf. the similar use of κλῆρος.—46 f. 'And this compact for the H. Locrians shall hold good in the same terms for the colonists from Chaleion under Antiphates.' See introductory note.

58. Oeanthea. Early fifth century B.C. IG IX.i.333. GDI 1479. Roberts 232 and pp. 354 ff. Schwyzer 363. Solmsen-Fraenkel 45. Tod. 34.

A. Τὸν ξένον μὲ̄ hἀγε̄ν ἐ τᾶς Χαλεῖδος τὸν Οἰανθέα, μ|ε̄δὲ τὸν
Χαλειέα ἐ τᾶς Οἰανθίδος, με̄δὲ χρέ̣ματα αἴ τι συ|λο̄ῖ· τὸν δὲ συ-
λο̄ντα ἀνάτο̄ συλε̄ν. τὰ ξενικὰ ἐ θαλάσας hἀγε̄ν | ἄσυλον πλὰν ἐ
5 λιμένος το̄ κατὰ πόλιν. αἴ κ' ἀδίκο̄ συλο̄ῖ, τέ|τορες δραχμαί· αἰ
δὲ πλέον δέκ' ἀμαρᾶν ἔχοι τὸ σῦλον, hε̄|μιόλιον ὀφλέτο̄ Ϝότι συ-
λάσαι. αἰ μεταϜοικέοι πλέον με̄νὸς ε̄̓ | ὁ Χαλειεὺς ἐν Οἰανθέαι ε̄̓
'Οἰανθεὺς ἐν Χαλείο̄ι, τᾶι ἐπιδαμίαι δίκαι χ|ρε̄στο̄. τὸν πρόξενον,
αἰ ψευδέα προξενέοι, διπλ|είο̄ι θο̄ιέστο̄.
10 B. Αἴ κ' ἀνδιχάζοντι τοὶ ξενοδίκαι, ἐπο̄μότας hελέσ|το̄ ὁ ξένος
ὀπάγο̄ν τὰν δίκαν ἐχθὸς προξένο̄ | καὶ Ϝιδίο̄ ξένο̄ ἀριστίνδαν, ἐπὶ
μὲν ταῖς μναιαίαις καὶ πλέον πεντεκαίδεκ' ἄνδρας, ἐπὶ ταῖς | μειό-
15 νοις ἐννέ' ἄνδρας. αἴ κ' ὁ Ϝασστὸς ποὶ τὸν Ϝ||αστὸν δικάζεται κὰ
τᾶς συνβολᾶς, δαμιοργὸς hελέσται το̄ς hορκο̄μότας ἀριστίνδαν τὰν
πε|ντορκίαν ὀμόσαντας. τὸς hορκο̄μότας τὸν αὐτὸ|ν hόρκον ὀμνύε̄ν,
πλε̄θὺν δὲ νικε̄ν.

The tablet consists of two documents inscribed by different
hands, as appears from forms of the letters and three vs. two dots
punctuation. The first, ending with χρέστο̄ l. 8, is a treaty between
Oeanthea and Chaleion of the kind known as σύμβολον or συμ-
βολά (the latter in l. 15). It is for the protection of foreigners,
that is citizens of other Greek states, visiting either city, from
reprisal at the hands of citizens of the other. Such reprisal or
seizure in enforcement of claims was freely employed, so far as
it was not specifically regulated by treaty. For graphic peculiarities see no. 57, introductory note.

1 ff. 'An Oeanthean shall not carry off a foreigner from Chaleian territory, nor a Chaleian from Oeanthean territory, nor his
property, in case one makes a seizure. But him who makes a
seizure himself one may seize with impunity. The property of a
foreigner one may carry off from the sea without being subject
to reprisal, except from the harbor of each city. If one makes
a seizure unlawfully, four drachmas (is the penalty); and if he
holds what has been seized for more than ten days, he shall owe
half as much again as the amount he seized. If a Chaleian sojourns
more than a month in Oeanthea or an Oeanthean in Chaleion,
he shall be subject to the local court.'

The second document consists of regulations of one of the two cities, presumably Oeanthea, regarding the legal rights of foreigners.

'The proxenus who is false to his duty one shall fine double (the amount involved in each particular case). If the ξενοδίκαι (the judges in cases involving the rights of foreigners) are divided in opinion, the foreigner who is plaintiff (ὁπάγōν = ὁ ἐπάγων) shall choose jurors from the best citizens, but exclusive of his proxenus and private host (who would be prejudiced in his favor), fifteen men in cases involving a mina or more, nine men in cases involving less. If citizen proceeds against citizen under the terms of the treaty, the magistrates shall choose the jurors from the best citizens, after having sworn the quintuple oath (i.e., oath by five gods). The jurors shall take the same oath, and the majority shall decide.'

59. Probably from the neighborhood of Polis, east of Amphissa. Early fifth century B.C. Papadakis, 'Αρχ. 'Εφ. 1924.119 ff. Wilamowitz, Ber. Preuss. Akad. 1927.7 f. Solmsen-Fraenkel 46. Pezopoulos, Πολέμων 1.97 ff. Chatzis, 'Αρχ. 'Εφ. 1927/8.181 ff.

A. Τεθμὸς ὅδε περὶ τᾶς γᾶς βέβαιος ἔστō κὰτ τὸν | ἀνδαιθμὸν πλακὸς 'Υλίας καὶ Λισκαρίας καὶ τōν ἀ|ποτόμōν καὶ τōν δαμοσίōν. ἐπινομία δ' ἔστō γο|νεῦσιν καὶ παιδί· αἱ δὲ μὲ παῖς εἴε, κόραι· αἱ
5 δὲ μὲ κόρα εἴε, || ἀδελφεōι· αἱ δὲ μὲ ἀδελφεὸς εἴε, ἀνχιστέδαν ἐπι-νεμέσθō κὰ τὸ | δίκαιον· αἱ δὲ μέ, τōι ἐπινόμōι (ὁμ)οίōν. hότι δέ κα φυτεύσεται |, ἄσυλος ἔστō. αἱ μὲ πολέμōι ἀνανκαζομένοις δόξ-ξαι ἀν|δράσιν hενὶ κέκατον ἀριστίνδαν τōι πλέθει ἄνδρας δια|κα-
10 τίōς μεῖστον ἀξξιομάχōς ἐπιϝοίκōς ἐφάγεσθαι, hόστ||ις δὲ δαιθμὸν ἐνφέροι ἒ ψᾶφον διαφέροι ἐν πρείγαι ἒ 'ν πόλι ἒ|'ν ἀποκλεσίαι, ἒ στά-σιν ποιέοι περὶ γαδαισίας, αὐτὸς μὲ|ν ϝερρέτō καὶ γενεὰ ἄματα πάν-τα, χρέματα δὲ δαμιευόσθōν | καὶ ϝοικία κατασκαπτέσθō κὰτ τὸν ἀνδρεφονικὸν τετθμόν. ὅδε τετθμὸς ἱαρὸς ἔστō τō 'Απόλλōνος τō
15 Πυθίō καὶ τōν συνν||άōν· ἔμεν τōι τα]ῦτα παρβαίνοντι ἐξξόλειαν αὐτōι καὶ γενεᾶι καὶ πα|μάτεσιν, τōι δ' εὐσεβέοντι hίλαος ἔσστō. ἁ δὲ γ[ᾶ τὸ μὲν ἔμισον] | (reverse side) τōν ὑπαπροσθι(δ)ίōν, τὸ δ' ἔμισον τōν ἐπιϝοίκōν ἔστō. | τὸς κοίλōς μόρōς διαδόντō. ἀλλαγὰ δὲ βέβαιο|ς ἔστō, ἀλαζέσθō δὲ ἀντὶ τō ἀρχō.

B. κομίζοιεν, ἀξιοδότας ἔστō τὰν αὐτō ōιτινι χρείζοι.

C. αἱ δὲ τοὶ] δαμιοργοὶ κερδαίνοιεν ἄλλο | τōν γεγραμμένōν,

ἱαρὸν τõ 'Απόλλō|νος ἐχέτõ ἄγαλμα δι' ἐννέα Fετ|έõν καὶ μὲ ποτι-
γράψαι κέρδος.

Like nos. 57, 58 this is a bronze tablet inscribed on both sides.
In contrast to no. 57 there is the boustrophedon writing, but
on the other hand no Ϙ, so that the relative date is problematical.
There is some difference in the forms, notably in the dat. pl. of
cons. stems, ἀνδράσιν, etc., vs. -οις of nos. 57, 58. The reverse
side contains three lines which are a continuation of the ob-
verse, but above these a line concluding another law (B), and
below them three lines, to be read by turning upside down,
concluding still another decree (C).

A 1 ff. 'This law concerning the land shall be in force for the
partition of the plain of Hyla and Liscara, both the separate
lots (?) and the public.' 'Υλίας: adj. formed from the name of
the town attested by St. Byz. "Υλη . . . ἔστι καὶ πόλις Λοκρῶν τῶν
'Οζολῶν, and indirectly by Thuc. 3.101, where 'Υαῖοι should be
read "Υλιοι. Similarly Λισκαρίας adj. based on an unknown name
*Λίσκαρος or *Λίσκαρα.—ἀποτόμōν variously interpreted, but
probably the parts cut off (from the public domain).—ἀνδαιθμόν:
with δαιθμόν l. 10, see 164.4.

3 ff. 'The right of pasturage shall belong to the heads of families and to the son; if there is no son, to the daughter; if there
is no daughter, to the brother, if there is not brother, one shall
make the assignment to the next of kin according to what is
right; if not (if there is no next of kin), to the assignee from
among those of like family but outside the strict line of kin-
ship(?).' The letters following ἐπινόμōι are said by Pezopoulos
to be definitely OIION, for which it is difficult to find any
acceptable interpretation. But it is quite possible that the engraver with his eye on the last letters of the preceding word
ἐπιNOMOI neglected to add another OM, and that we may read
(ὀμ)οιōν (for ' cf. ἱαρός l. 14), and understand 'like, similar'
persons as referring to collateral relatives, not within the limits
of technical kinship, the "ἔξω τῆς ἀγχιστείας" in the words of
Isaeus 11.7, etc. Cf. Pezopoulos, l.c., on such a possible use of
ὁμοῖος (but without the suggestion given above as to the reading).
—5. ἀνχιστέδαν: 133.7.—6. ἐπίνομος: here probably = κληρο-
νόμος, as in inscriptions of Delphi, etc.

6 ff. 'Whatever one plants, one shall be immune from its seizure. Except if under pressure of war the 101 men chosen from the best citizens, the majority, vote to introduce at least 200 colonists capable of bearing arms, whoever proposes partition or gives his vote for it in the council or in the assembly, or in the committee, or makes civil strife concerning partition of the land, he himself and his family shall be exiled for all time, his property confiscated, and his house destroyed just as under the law concerning murder.'—10. **πρείγα**: 'council' (of elders like the Spartan γερουσία). See **86**.3.—12. Ϝερρέτō: **162**.7.—**δαμιευόσθōν**: **140**.4*b*. —15/16. The letters at the beginning of l. 16 are obscure, but πα|μάτεσιν is more probable than πά|ντεσιν.—17. **ὑπαπροσ- θιδίōν**: The fourth letter from the end is A, but, although the conglutinate -ιαῖος is common enough, it is less likely in such a derivative as this, and the correction is probable.—18 f. 'The valley portions they shall distribute. Exchange shall be allowed, but one must make the exchange in the presence of the magistrate.'

B. Conclusion of another law. '(If/when) they receive (?), one shall be entitled to give his share to whomever he wishes.'— τάν (Wilamowitz τᾶν) acc. sg. after the verbal notion implicit in ἀξιοδότας. Cf. τὰ μετέωρα φροντιστής, Plato.

C. 'If the demiurgi gain anything other than the amounts prescribed, it shall be held sacred to Apollo as an offering for a period of nine years, and one shall not enter it in addition as profit.' Otherwise Wilamowitz, followed by Pezopoulos, reading Ἐχέτō as an epithet of Apollo.

60. Tolophon. About middle of third century B.C. Wilhelm, Oest. Jhrh. 14.163 ff. Leaf, ABS 21.148 ff. Nikitskij, "AIAN-TEIA" in Žurn. min. nar. pr. 1913. Schwyzer 366. The text given here is mainly that of Nikitskij, which Wilhelm later recognized as an advance on his own. The side B, containing only proper names is omitted here.

Ἀγαθᾶι τ[ύχαι. | ἐ]πὶ τοῖσδε Αἰάντειοι καὶ ἁ πόλις Ναρυκαίων Λοκροῖς ἀνεδέξαντο τὰς κόρα[ς πέμπειν ἐν Ἴλιον. εἶμεν Αἰαντείους ἀσύλους | κ]αὶ ἀρυσίους καὶ πολέμου καὶ εἰρήνας καὶ ἐφ' αἵματι μὴ ἐπικωλύειν καὶ προδικία[ν αὐτοῖς διδόμεν αἴ τί κα ἀδικέωνται] |

καὶ αὐτᾶι τᾶι πόλει. ξενίων μὴ ἀπελαθῆμεν κατὰ ξενίας ἐλθόντα
5 ἀπὸ δαμοσίο[υ Ναρυκαίων · αἰ δέ κα ἀπελαθῆι, δεκαπέν‖τ]ε
δραχμὰς τὸν ἄρχοντα ἀποτεῖσαι · αἰ δὲ δίκαι ἀλοίη, ὁ ἄρχων τριάκοντα δραχμὰ[ς ἀποτεισάτω · τῶν ἰδιωτᾶν τὸν συλλα]‖βόντα κατὰ
ξενίαν ἀζάμιον εἶμεν. αἰ τῶν Αἰαντείων ῥυσιάζοι καταειδώς, τριά-
κο[ντα στατῆρας ἀποτεισάτω καὶ τοὶ ἄρ|χ]οντες τὰ ῥυσιαχθέντα
ἀμπράξαντες ἀποδόντω αὐθαμερὸν ἦ τᾶι ὑστεραίαι · εἰ δ[ὲ μὴ ἀμ-
πράξαιεν ἦ μὴ ἀποδοῖεν, τὸ δι|π]λοῦν ἀποτεισάντω. αἰ δὲ τῶν
Αἰαντείων καταδῆσαι ἀδίκως ἦ ἔρξαι, ἑκατὸν στατῆρ[ας ἀποτει-
σάτω τᾶς ἀμέρας ἑκάστας] | καὶ τᾶς νυκτὸς ἄλλους ἑκάστας ἔντε
κα ἀφῆ. τροφεῖα τοῖς γονεῦσι τᾶν χορᾶν ἑκατέρ[ας μνᾶς ἐξ καθ᾽
10 ἔτος διδόμεν καὶ τοῖν] ‖ κόραιν ἑκατέραι πεντεκαίδεκα μνᾶς ἐν
κόσμον καὶ τροφὰν παρέχειν ἔντε κα [ἐπανέλθωντι · τῶν Αἰαντείων
μὴ ἐᾶν πρα]θῆμεν ἐν πολεμίους ἀλόντα. οἰκίας Θήμωνος κατα-
καείσας ὁποίας κα τᾶι πόλε[ι Ναρυκαίων δόξαι, ἀνοικοδομηθῆμεν ·]
| παντεῖ Λοκρῶν. Αἰαντείων εἴ τίς κα ἐλ Λοκροῖς οἰκεῖν δείληται,
ἀτέλειαν εἶμεν καθ[ὼς ἐν τᾶι πατρίδι · αἴ τις θύοι ἐν Ναρύκαι] |
θοίναν εἶμεν τοῖς Αἰαντείοις, εἶμεν πάντοις, καὶ τῶι ἱερεῖ τὰ δέρ-
ματα ἀποδιδόμεν καὶ τὰ [σκέλεα καὶ τἆλλα γέρεα · παναγυρίζειν] |
δὲ τοὺς Λοκροὺς πάντας τᾶι Λοκρίδι Αἰαντίαι ἐν Ναρύκαι · ἀγωνο-
θέτας δὲ εἶμεν Ναρυκα[ίους κατὰ τὰ πάτρια · ἐμ πολέμωι Αἰαντεί-] ‖
15 ους παῖδας ὁμήρους μὴ δόμεν ἄκοντας · ἐν τὰς χόρας | Ναρυκαίοις
ἀτέλειαν εἶμεν τᾶς ἐμ [πόλεμον ἱπποτροφίας καὶ εἰσφορᾶς ·] | εἰ δέ
τίς κα ἀνακκάζηι τρέφειν ἵππους ἦ ὁμήρους παῖδας διδόμεν, τοὺς
Λοκροὺς τὰς δαπάνα[ς Ναρυκαίοις δόμεν. ἀ δὲ πόλις Ναρυ]‖καίων
μὴ πεμψάτω ὅμηρα τῶν Αἰαντίων μηθένα. δίκαν τὸν ἄρχοντα
ἀμερᾶν τριῶ[ν τῶν Αἰαντείων τῶι ἐγκαλέσαντι] | καὶ ἐκπρᾶξαι
δέχ᾽ ἁμερᾶν τὸ κατὰ ξένον, μὴ ἀπογνῶμεν μάρτυρα παρεχόμεν[ον
ἀ]ξιόχρ[ειον · αἰ τίς κα ἀμφιλέγηι τᾶς δίκας τᾶς] | πρότερον, τὰν
δίκαν εἶμεν ἐν τοῖς αὐτοῖς δικασταῖς · ἃ κα ἁλῶι τὸ μαρτυρ[ηθέν,
20 ἀτελή]ς ἔστω ἁ δίκα καὶ ὁ μαρτυρήσας ἐν ταῖ ἐφι‖ορκίαι ἐχέστω
καὶ ἀποτεισάτω διπλόαν τὰν δίκαν · αἰ δέ κα μὴ πράξη ὁ ἄ[ρχων
- - - - - - - - προει]‖πάντω ὅντινα κα λάβη τῶν ἐκ τᾶς πόλιος ἐξ
ἇς κα τὸ ἔκκλημα ἦ ταῖ δί[και αἱρεῖσθαι πλουτίνδαν ἐκ τοῦ τέλεος
μὴ μεῖ]‖ον τριακοντοδράχμου ἔνδεκα ἄνδρας, ἐν δὲ Ναρύκαι ἐξ
ἀπάντων [- - - - αἰ δέ κα δέ]ηι δικάζειν, τοῖν κόραιν ἐπιδικῆσαι
τοῖν πρόσθ[ε]ν κὰτ τὸ δυ[νατόν - - - -, τοὺς ἄρχοντας Ναρυ]-|
καίων δίκαν δόμεν κὰτ ταὐτὰ καὶ ἐκπρᾶξαι. ὅρκος. ἐπὶ τ[ούτοις

ὑπισχόμεθα κατακολουθήσειν πάντοις τοῖς γεγραμμένοις ἐν τᾶι] ||
25 συνθήκαι καὶ ἐν τοῖς ὅρκοις· εὐορκεόντοις πολλ[ὰ ἀγαθὰ εἴη, ἐφι-
ορκεόντοις δὲ - - - -. ὀμόσαι ἄν]δρας πεντήκοντα πλουτίνδαν·
ὀμν[ύοντας ὅρκον τὸν νόμιμον - - - - - - περὶ τᾶν] χορᾶν τᾶν
πεμφθεισᾶν [- - - - -

Terms under which the Αἰάντειοι (the Ajax clan) and the town
of Naryca (the reputed birthplace of Ajax) undertook for the
Locrians the duty of sending the maidens to Troy—namely the
enjoyment of common rights among the Locrians, from which
apparently they had previously been excluded. Naryca was in
Eastern Locris, but this inscription comes from some Western
Locrian temple, either one at Tolophon or that of Athena Ilias
in the nearby Physcus. The stone is broken in an irregular line
on the right and bottom, so that many of the restorations are
highly problematical conjectures. The dialect is mixed (e.g.,
both αἰ and εἰ), much the same as the Northwest Greek κοινή,
but with a touch of more special Locrian (so at least κατὰ ξενίας
l. 4 vs. κατὰ ξενίαν l. 6; **136.**5).

2 ff. 'The Αἰάντειοι shall be immune from seizure and reprisal
both in war and peace, and one shall not interfere with them on
a charge of bloodshed (referring of course to Ajax's sacrilege),
and, if they are wronged in any way (?), priority of trial shall
be given to them and to the city. Anyone coming from the
public of Naryca shall not be excluded from the rights of hos-
pitality.'—3 f. [τῶν **ἰδιωτᾶν**, κτλ.: restoration and meaning very
uncertain.—6, 8. τῶν **Αἰαντείων**: partitive genitive as object
of the verb.—19. **ἀ κα ἀλῶι τὸ μαρτυρ[ηθέν**?] 'in case what
is testified is (lit. convicted =) proved false.'(?)—23. **ἐπιδικῆσαι**: probably 'render justice.'

Elean

61. Olympia. Before 580 b.c. GDI 1152. Inschr. v. Olympia 2.
Roberts 292 and pp. 364 ff. Schwyzer 409. Solmsen-Fraenkel 51.

Ἀ Ϝράτρα τοῖς Ϝαλείοις. πατριὰν θαρρῆν καὶ γενεὰν καὶ ταὐτό. |
αἰ ζέ τις κατιαραύσειε, Ϝάρρῆν ὂρ Ϝαλείō· αἰ ζὲ μὲ̄ 'πιθεῖαν τὰ ζί-|
καια ὂρ μέγιστον τέλος ἔχοι καὶ τοὶ βασιλᾶες, ζέκα μναίς κα | ἀπο-
5 τίνοι Ϝέκαστος τὸν μὲ̄ 'πιποεόντον καθυταὶς τοῖ Ζὶ 'Ολυν||πίοι.

ἐπενπōι ζέ κ' 'Ελλανοζίκας καὶ τᾶλλα ζίκαια ἐπενπ|έτō ἀ ζαμιορ-
γία· αἰ ζὲ μὲ 'νπōι, ζίφυιον ἀποτινέτō ἐν μαστρά|αι. αἰ ζέ
τις τὸν αἰτιαθέντα ζικαίōν ἰμάσκοι, ἐν ταῖ ζεκαμναίαι κ' ἐ|νέχο-
[ιτ]ο, αἰ Fειζὸς ἰμάσκοι. καὶ πατριᾶς ὁ γροφεὺς ταύ[τ]ά κα
πάσκοι, | [αἴ τ]ιν' [ἀζ]ικέο[ι]. ὁ π[ί]ναξ ἱαρὸς 'Ολυνπίαι.

'The law of the Eleans (adnom. dat., **172**). (An accused
man's) gens and family and his property shall be immune. If
any one brings a charge (against them), he shall be prosecuted
as in the case of (a charge against) a citizen of Elis. If he who
holds the highest office and the βασιλεῖς do not impose the fines,
let each of those who fail to impose them pay a penalty of ten
minae dedicated to Olympian Zeus. Let the Hellanodica enforce
this, and let the body of demiurgi enforce the other fines (which
they had neglected to impose). If he (the Hellanodica) does not
enforce this, let him pay double the penalty in his accounting.
If any one maltreats one who is accused in a matter involving
fines, let him be held to a fine of ten minae, if he does so wittingly.
And let the scribe of the gens suffer the same penalty if he
wrongs any one. This tablet sacred at Olympia.'

The numerous interpretations of this inscription have differed
fundamentally. According to that preferred here the object of
the decree is to do away with the liability which under primitive
conditions, such as survived longer in Elis than elsewhere, had
attached to the whole gens and family of an accused person,
also to prevent confiscation of his property and personal violence,
and to prescribe the manner in which penalties were to be
imposed.

1. **πατριάν**: like Delph. πατριά, Dor. πάτρα = γένος, while
γενεά is the immediate family.—**θαρρε̃ν**: 'be of good cheer,
without fear,' hence, as a technical term in Elean, 'be secure,
immune,' just as the Attic ἄδεια is in origin 'freedom from fear
(δέος).' It is used of persons and things. Cf. θ[άρρος] αὐτοῖ καὶ
χρε̄μάτοις in another inscription.—2. **κατιαραύσειε**: καθιερεύω,
but meaning first to 'utter an imprecation against some one' (cf.
κατεύχομαι), and then, since this was, or had been, the manner
of introducing a charge, simply κατηγορέω. Cf. κατιαραίων no. 65.5.
Like various other expressions in Elean, this reflects the essentially religious character of the legal procedure.—**Fάρρε̄ν** = Fέρε̄ν

(no. 63), cf. Locr. Ϝερρέτō (no. 59). **52, 162**.7.—**αἰ ζὲ μὲ κτλ.**:
cf. no. 52 C 13-16. For ἐπενπōι, μαστράαι, ἱμάσκω, etc., see the
Glossary.

62. Olympia. Sixth century B.C. GDI 1149. Inschr. v. Olympia
9. Roberts 291 and pp. 362 ff. Schwyzer 413. Ditt. Syll. 9.
Solmsen-Fraenkel 52. Tod. 5.

'Α Ϝράτρα τοῖρ Ϝαλείοις καὶ τοῖς 'Ερ|Ϝαδίοις. συνμαχία κ' ἔα
ἑκατὸν Ϝέτεα, | ἄρχοι δέ κα τοῖ. αἰ δέ τι δέοι αἴτε Ϝέπος αἴτε Ϝ|άρ-
5 γον, συνέαν κ' ἀλάλοις τά τ' ἄλ(α) καὶ πὰ||ρ πολέμō. αἰ δὲ μὰ
συνέαν, τάλαντόν κ' | ἀργύρō ἀποτίνοιαν τοῖ Δὶ 'Ολυνπίοι τοὶ
καδαλέμενοι λατρειόμενον. αἰ δέ τιρ τὰ γ|ράφεα ταὶ καδαλέοιτο
10 αἴτε Ϝέτας αἴτε τ|ελεστὰ αἴτε δᾶμος, ἐν τεπιάροι κ' ἐνέχ||οιτο τοῖ
'νταῦτ' ἐγραμένοι.

'The covenant of the Eleans and the Heraeans (of Arcadia).
There shall be an alliance for one hundred years, beginning with
the present year. If there shall be any need of word or deed, they
shall combine with one another both in other matters and in
war. If they do not combine, let those who violate (the agreement) pay a talent of silver consecrated to Olympian Zeus. If
any one violates these writings, whether private citizen, official,
or the state, let him be held in the penalty here written.'

63. Olympia. Sixth century B.C. GDI 1153. Inschr. v. Olympia
11. Roberts 294. Schwyzer 415.

'Α Ϝράτρα τοῖρ ΧαλαδρίΟρ καὶ Δευ|καλίōνι · Χαλάδριον ἔμɛν
5 αὐτὸν | καὶ γόνον Ϝισοπρόξενον, | Ϝισοδαμιοργόν · τὰν δὲ γᾶ[ν] ||
ἔχεν τὰν ἐν Πίσαι · αἰ δέ τις συλαίē, Ϝέρεν αὐτὸν | πὸ τὸν Δία, αἰ
μὲ̄ δάμοι δοκέοι.

1. ΧαλαδρίΟρ: confusion of acc. and dat. forms, as in another
inscription (Schwyzer 414).—5/6. Ϝέρεν κτλ.: **136**.3.

64. Olympia. Sixth century B.C. GDI 1156. Inschr. v. Olympia 7. Roberts 296 and pp. 369 ff. Ziehen, Leges Sacrae 61.
Schwyzer 412.

κα θεαρὸς εἴē. αἰ δὲ βενέοι ἐν τἰαροῖ, βοῖ κα θōάδοι καὶ κο-
θάρσι τελείαι, καὶ τὸν θεαρὸν ἐν τ|α(ὐ)ταῖ. αἰ δέ τις πὰρ τὸ γράφος
δικάδοι, ἀτελές κ' εἴē ἀ δίκα, ἀ δέ κα Ϝράτρα ἀ δαμοσία τελεία εἴ|ē
δικάδοσα · τōν δέ κα γραφέōν ὅτι δοκέοι καλιτέρōς ἔχεν πὸ τὸν θ(ε)όν,

ἐξαγρέōν καὶ ἐ|νποιον σὺν βōλαῖ (π)εντακατίōν ἀϜλανέōς καὶ
5 δάμοι πλēθύοντι δινάκοι· (δινά)κοι δέ κα (ἐ)ν τρίτ||ον, αἴ τι
ἐνποιοῖ αἴτ᾽ ἐξαγρέοι.

This is the conclusion of an inscription which was begun on
another tablet not preserved.

'If he (some one previously mentioned) commits fornication(?)
in the sacred precinct, one shall make him expiate it by the
sacrifice of an ox and by complete purification, and the θεαρός
in the same way. If anyone pronounces judgment contrary to the
regulation, this judgment shall be void, but the decree of the
people shall be final in deciding. One may make any change in
the regulations which seems desirable in the sight of the god
(136.3), withdrawing or adding with the approval of the whole
council of the Five Hundred and the people in full assembly.
One may make changes three times, adding and withdrawing.'—
The restoration and interpretation of the last sentence, (δινά)κοι
κτλ., is uncertain. In l. 4 the adverb ἀϜλανέōς (see 55) is used
loosely where we should expect an adjective in agreement with
βōλαῖ or πεντακατίōν.

65. Olympia. About middle of fourth century B.C. Schwyzer
424. Solmsen-Fraenkel 53.

Θεός· τύχα. ταίρ δὲ γενεαίρ μὰ φυγαδείημ μαδὲ κ|ὰτ ὁποῖον
τρόπον, μάτε ἐρσεναιτέραν μάτε θηλυτ|έραν, μάτε τὰ χρήματα
δαμοσιῶμεν· αἰ δέ τιρ φυγαδ|είοι αἴτε τὰ χρήματα δαμοσιοία, φευ-
5 γέτω πὸτ τῶ Δ||ιὸρ τώλυμπίω αἴματορ, καὶ κατιαραίων ὁ δηλομῆρ |
ἀνάατορ ἤστω. ἐξήστω δέ, καὶ κα φυγαδεύαντι, τοῖ δ|ηλομένοι νο-
στίττην καὶ ἀττάμιον ἦμεν, ὅσσα κα ὕ|σταριν γένωνται τῶν περὶ
Πύρρωνα δαμιοργῶν. το|ὶρ δὲ ἐπ᾽ ἄσιστα μὰ ἀποδόσσαι μάτε
10 ἐκπέμψαι τὰ χρ||ήματα τοῖρ φυγάδεσσι· αἰ δέ τι ταύτων πὰρ τὸ
γράμ|μα ποιέοι, ἀποτινέτω διπλ[ά]σιον τῶ κα ἐκπέμπα κα|ὶ τῶ κα
ἀποδῶται. αἰ δέ τιρ ἀδεαλτώhαιε τὰ στάλαν, | ὠρ ἀγαλματοφώραν
ἐόντα πάσχην.

'But one shall not exile the children (of an exile) either male
or female, under any circumstances, nor confiscate the property.
If any one exiles them or confiscates the property, he shall be
subject to trial before (in the name of) Olympian Zeus on a
capital charge, and any one who wishes may bring the charge

against him with impunity. And it shall be permitted, even in case they have exiled any, to any one who wishes to return and be free from punishment so far as concerns matters happening later than the time of the demiurgi under Pyrrhon. Those next of kin shall not sell or send off the property of the exiles, and if one does any of these things contrary to the regulation, he shall pay double the amount sent off and sold. If any one defaces the stele, he shall be punished like one guilty of sacrilege.' Several times during the fourth century B.C. the oligarchy and democracy alternated in power in Elis, with resulting banishment and recall of exiles. It is probable that this decree belongs to the Macedonian period and perhaps refers to the exiles of 336 B.C. who were recalled in 335 B.C. Cf. Arrian 1.10.1 Ἠλεῖοι δὲ τοὺς φυγάδας σφῶν κατεδέξαντο, ὅτι ἐπιτήδειοι Ἀλεξάνδρῳ ἦσαν. It is a supplementary decree to another on the same subject, as is shown by δέ in the first sentence after the introductory formula, and the use of γενεαίρ without modifier, which must be understood from the preceding. On the dialect as compared with that of the earlier inscriptions, see 241.

1. γενεαίρ: pl. of the collective γενεά 'offspring, family,' as in Mess. τὰν γυναῖκά τε καὶ τὰς γενεάς αὐτοῦ (GDI 4689.97).—4-5. φευγέτω πὸτ τῶ Διόρ κτλ.: see 136.3.—5. δηλομήρ: we expect δηλόμενορ. Probably an error, for which the existence of some such form as δηλοντήρ (cf. ἐθελοντήρ) may be responsible.— 6. φυγαδεύαντι: aor. subj. 151.1.—12-13. αἰ δέ τιρ ἀδεαλτώhαιε κτλ.: cf. ἢν δέ τις [τὴν στήλην] ἀφαν[ίζηι ἢ τὰ γράμματα], πασχέτω ὡς ἱερόσυλος in an inscription of Iasus, GDI 5517. ἀδελτόω = ἀδηλόω, ἀφανίζω, is probably from *δεαλος (cf. δέαμαι, δῆλος), whence—perhaps through the medium of a verb δεάλλω— *δεαλτός, *δεαλτόω. According to another view, from δέλτος 'tablet' (cf. Cypr. δάλτος), so that the meaning would be 'make the stele ἄδελτος,' i.e., remove the tablet from the stele. For τὰ στάλαν see 96.2.

66. Olympia. Late third or second century B.C. GDI 1172. Inschr. v. Olympia 39. Schwyzer 425.

Θεόρ · τύχα. | Ὑπὸ Ἑλλανοδικᾶν τῶν περὶ | Αἰσχύλον, Θυίω. |
5 ὅπωρ, ἐπεὶ Δαμοκράτηρ Ἀγήτορορ ‖ Τενέδιορ, πεπολιτευκὼρ

παρ' ἀμὲ | αὐτόρ τε καὶ ὁ πατάρ, καὶ ἐστεφανωμέ|νορ τόν τε τῶν
Ὀλυμπίων ἀγῶνα καὶ | ἄλλοιρ καὶ πλείονερ, ἐπανιτακὼρ ἐν τὰν |
10 ἰδίαν τάν τε τῶ πατρὸρ θεαροδοκίαν δια||δέδεκται καὶ ὑποδέχεται
τοὶρ θεαροίρ, | ὁμοίωρ δὲ καὶ τοῖρ λοιποῖρ τοῖρ παρ' ἀμέων | τὰν
πᾶσαν χρείαν ἐκτενέωρ καὶ ἀπρο|φασίστωρ παρέχεται, φανερὰν
15 ποιέων | τὰν ἔχει εὔνοιαν ποτὶ τὰν πόλιν, καθὼρ || πλείονερ ἀπε-
μαρτύρεον τῶμ πολιτᾶν · | ὅπωρ δὲ καὶ ἁ πόλερ καταξίαιρ φαίνα-
ται | χάριτερ ἀνταποδιδῶσσα τοῖρ αὐτᾶρ | εὐεργέταιρ, ὑπάρχην
20 Δαμοκράτη πρό|ξενον καὶ εὐεργέταν δ' ᾖ||μεν τᾶρ πόλιορ αὐτὸν καὶ
γένορ, καὶ τὰ | λοιπὰ τίμια ᾖμεν αὐτοῖ ὅσσα καὶ τοῖρ ἄλ|λοιρ προ-
ξένοιρ καὶ εὐεργέταιρ ὑπάρχει παρὰ | τᾶρ πόλιορ. ᾖμεν δὲ καὶ
ἀσφάλειαν καὶ πολέμω | καὶ εἰράναρ, καὶ γᾶρ καὶ βοικίαρ ἔγκτη-
25 σιν, καὶ || ἀτέλειαν, καὶ προεδρίαν ἐν τοῖρ Διονυσιακοῖρ | ἀγώνοιρ,
τᾶν τε θυσιᾶν καὶ τιμᾶν πασᾶν | μετέχην, καθὼρ καὶ τοὶ λοιποὶ
θεαροδόκοι | καὶ εὐεργέται μετέχοντι. δόμεν δὲ αὐτοῖ | καὶ Δαμο-
30 κράτη τὸν ταμίαν ξένια τὰ || μέγιστα ἐκ τῶν νόμων. τὸ δὲ ψάφι-
σμα | τὸ γεγονὸρ ἀπὸ τᾶρ βωλᾶρ γραφὲν ἐγ χάλκω|μα ἀνατεθᾶι
ἐν τὸ ἱαρὸν τῶ Διὸρ τῶ Ὀλυμπίω. | τὰν δὲ ἐπιμέλειαν τᾶρ ἀναθέ-
35 σιορ ποιήασσαι | Αἰσχίναν τὸν ἐπιμελητὰν τᾶν ἵππων. || περὶ δὲ
τῶ ἀποσταλᾶμεν τοῖρ Τενεδίοιρ | τὸ γεγονὸρ ψάφισμα ἐπιμέλειαν
ποιήαται | Νικόδρομορ ὁ βωλογράφορ, ὅπωρ δοθᾶι τοῖρ | θεαροῖρ
τοῖρ ἐμ Μίλητον ἀποστελλομέ|νοιρ ποτὶ τὰν θυσίαν καὶ τὸν
40 ἀγῶνα || τῶν Διδυμείων.

Proxeny decree in honor of Damocrates of Tenedos, who is
mentioned as one of the Olympian victors by Pausanias (6.17.1).
On the dialect as compared with that of the earlier inscriptions,
see **241**. With ὑπὸ Ἑλλανοδικᾶν l. 2 for usual ἐπί with gen.,
compare Lac. hυπό with acc. in no. 71.66.

Northwest Greek κοινή

67. Thermum. About 270 B.C. IG IX².i.3. Schwyzer 381.
Ditt. Syll. 421.

A

ΣΥΝΘΗΚΑ ΚΑΙ ΣΥΜΜΑΧΙΑ ΑΙΤΩΛΟΙΣ ΚΑΙ ΑΚΑΡΝΑΝΟΙΣ

Ἀγαθᾶι τύχαι. Συνθήκα Αἰτωλοῖς καὶ. Ἀκαρνάνοις ὁμόλογος.
εἰρήναν | εἶμεν καὶ φιλίαν ποτ' ἀλλάλους, φίλους ἐόντας καὶ συμ-
μάχους ἄμα|τα τὸμ πάντα χρόνον, ὅρια ἔχοντας τᾶς χώρας τὸν

Ἀχελῶιον ποταμ|ὸν ἄχρι εἰς θάλασσαν. τὰ μὲν ποτ' ἀῶ τοῦ Ἀχε-
5 λώιου ποταμοῦ Αἰτωλῶν εἶμεν, τὰ δὲ || ποθ' ἑσπέραν Ἀκαρνάνων
πλὰν τοῦ Πραντὸς καὶ τᾶς Δέμφιδος· ταύτας δὲ Ἀκαρνᾶν|ες
οὐκ ἀντιποιοῦνται. ὑπὲρ δὲ τῶν τερμόνων τοῦ Πραντός, εἰ μέγ κα
Στράτιοι καὶ Ἀγραῖ|οι συγχωρέωντι αὐτοὶ ποτ' αὐτούς, τοῦτο κύ-
ριον ἔστω, εἰ δὲ μή, Ἀκαρνᾶνες καὶ Αἰτωλοὶ | τερμαξάντω τὰμ
Πραντίδα χώραν, αἱρεθέντας ἑκατέρων δέκα πλὰν Στρατίων καὶ
Ἀγραί|ων· καθὼς δέ κα τερμάξωντι, τέλειον ἔστω. εἶμεν δὲ καὶ
10 ἐπιγαμίαν ποτ' ἀλλάλους καὶ γ||ᾶς ἔγκτησιν τῶι τε Αἰτωλῶι ἐν
Ἀκαρνανίαι καὶ τῶι Ἀκαρνᾶνι ἐν Αἰτωλίαι καὶ πολίταν εἶμε|ν τὸν
Αἰτωλὸν ἐν Ἀκαρνανίαι καὶ τὸν Ἀκαρνᾶνα ἐν Αἰτωλίαι ἴσογ καὶ
ὅμοιον. ἀναγραψάν|τω δὲ ταῦτα ἐν στάλαις χαλκέαις ἐπ' Ἀκτίωι
μὲν οἱ ἄρχοντες τῶν Ἀκαρνάνων, ἐν δὲ Θέρμ|ωι τοὶ ἄρχοντες τῶν
Αἰτωλῶν, ἐν Ὀλυμπίαι δὲ καὶ ἐν Δελφοῖς καὶ ἐν Δω(δ)ώναι κοι-
νᾶι ἑκάτ|εροι. ἐπὶ ἀρχόντων ἐμ μὲν Αἰτωλίαι στραταγέοντος Πολυ-
15 κρίτου Καλλιέος τὸ δεύτε||ρον, ἱππαρχέοντος Φίλωνος Πλευρωνίου,
γραμματεύοντος Νεοπτολέμου Ναυπακτίου, | ἐπιλεκταρχεόντων
Λαμέδωνος Καλυδωνίου, Ἀριστάρχου Ἐρταίου, Λέωνος Κα|φρέος,
Καλλία Καλλιέος, Τιμολόχου Ποτειδανιέος, Παμφαΐδα Φυσκέος,
Σίμου | Φυταιέος, ταμιευόντων Κυδρίωνος Λυσιμαχέος, Δωριμάχου
Τριχονίου, Ἀρίστ|ωνος Δαιᾶνος, Ἀριστέα Ἱστωρίου, Ἀγήσωνος
20 Δεξιέος, Τιμάνδρου Ἐριναῖος, || Ἀγρίου Σωσθενέος· ἐν δὲ Ἀκαρ-
νανίαι στραταγῶν Βυνθάρου Οἰνιάδα, Ἐπι[λ]|άου Δηριέος, Ἀγή-
σωνος Στρατίου, Ἀλκέτα Φοιτιᾶνος, Ἀλκίνου Θυρρείου, Θέων|ος
Ἀνακτοριέος, Πολυκλέος Λευκαδίου, ἱππαρχέοντος Ἱππολάου
Οἰνιάδα, | γραμματεύοντος Περικλέος Οἰνιάδα, ταμία Ἀγελάου
Στρατικοῦ. | — Συμμαχία Αἰτωλοῖς καὶ Ἀκαρνάνοις ἅματα τὸμ
25 πάντα χρόνον. || εἴ τίς κα ἐμβάλληι εἰς τὰν Αἰτωλίαν ἐπὶ πολέμωι,
βοαθοεῖν τοὺς | Ἀκαρνᾶνας πεζοῖς μὲν χιλίοις, ἱππεῦσι δὲ ἑκατόν,
οὕς κα τοὶ ἄρχοντε|ς πέμπωντι, ἐν ἁμέραις ἕξ. καὶ εἴ τις ἐν Ἀκαρ-
νανίαν ἐμβάλλοι ἐπὶ πολέμωι, | βοαθοεῖν Αἰτωλοὺς πεζοῖς μὲν χι-
λίοις, ἱππέοις δὲ ἑκατόν, ἐν ἁμέραις ἕξ, οὕς | κα τοὶ ἄρχοντες πέμ-
30 πωντι. εἰ δὲ πλειόνων χρείαν ἔχοιεν ἄτεροι πότεροι, || βοαθοούντω
τρισχιλίοις ἑκάτεροι ἑκατέροις, ἐν ἁμέραις δέκα. τᾶς δὲ βοαθοίας
τ|ᾶς ἀποστελλομένας ἔστω τὸ τρίτομ μέρος ὁπλῖται. πεμπόντω δὲ
τὰμ βοάθοιαν | ἐγ μὲν Ἀκαρνανίας οἱ στραταγοὶ τῶν Ἀκαρνάνων
καὶ οἱ σύνεδροι, ἐγ δὲ Αἰτωλίας | οἱ ἄρχοντες τῶν Αἰτωλῶν.
σιταρχούντω δὲ τοὺς ἀποστελλομένους στρατιώτ|ας ἑκάτεροι

τοὺς αὐτῶν ἀμερᾶν τριάκοντα· εἰ δὲ πλείονα χρόνον ἔχοιεν τᾶς
βοα||θοίας χρείαν οἱ μεταπεμψάμενοι τὰμ βοάθοιαν, διδόντω τὰς
35 σιταρχίας ἔστε κα | ἐν οἶκον ἀποστείλωντι τοὺς στρατιώτας. σι-
ταρχία δ' ἔστω τοῦ πλείονος χρόν|ου τῶ[ι μὲν ἱππεῖ στα]τὴρ Κορίν-
θιος τᾶς ἀμέρας ἑκάστας, τῶι [δὲ] τὰμ πανοπλίαν ἔχο||[ντι . . . . . .
. . . .], τῶι δὲ τὸ ἡμιθωράκιον ἐννέ' ὀβολοί, ψιλῶι ἕπτ' ὀβολοί.
ἀγείσθων | [39-42 fragmentary].

Treaty of alliance between the Aetolians and Acarnanians.
A fragment found at Olympia (Inschr. v. Olympia 40) has been
recognized as belonging to another copy deposited there. This
is an example of the mixed dialect current at this time in various
parts of Northwest Greece, which we call the Northwest Greek
κοινή. See **279**. Note, e.g., the retention of original ā, κα, ποτί,
infin. in -μεν, 3 pl. imv. in -ντω, ξ in aor. (τερμαξάντω), but Att.
εἰ for αἰ, ου beside εο (e.g., ἀντιποιοῦνται but στραταγέοντος), οἱ
beside τοί, εἰς beside ἐν with acc. (εἰς τὰν Αἰτωλίαν but ἐν 'Ακαρνα-
νίαν), ἱππεῦσι beside ἱππέοις.

2/3, 24. **ἄματα τὸμ πάντα χρόνον**, a blend of the old formulaic ἄματα πάντα with the current τὸμ πάντα χρόνον.—16.
ἐπιλεκταρχεόντων: this is the first reference to ἐπιλεκτάρχαι as
military officials in the Aetolian league. For the Achaean league,
cf. ἐπίλεκτοι, used of the citizen levies in contrast to the mercenaries, Polyb. 2.65, 5.91, 95, and ἐπιλεκτάρχης Plut. Arat. 32.

Laconian

68. Olympia. Sixth century B.C. IG V.i.1562. GDI 4405.
Inschr. v. Olympia 252. Roberts 261. Schwyzer 7.

[Δέξ]ο, Ϝάν[αξ] Κρονίδα [Ζ]εῦ 'Ολύνπιε, καλὸν ἄ[γ]αλμα
ℎιλέϜō[ι θυ]μō͂ι τοῖ Λακεδαιμονίο[ις].

· This is the inscription mentioned by Paus. 5.24.3, who repro-
duces it, eliminating the dialectal peculiarities, as follows:

Δέξο, ἄναξ Κρονίδα Ζεῦ 'Ολύμπιε, καλὸν ἄγαλμα
ἱλάῳ θυμῷ τοῖς Λακεδαιμονίοις.

τοῖ Λακ. = τοῖς Λακ. (**97**.3), 'from the Lacedaemonians.' Cf.
Hom. δέξατό οἱ σκῆπτρον and Mel. 'Εκπhάντōι δέκσαι κτλ. (no.
114).

69. Delphi. Soon after 479 B.C. GDI 4406. Ditt. Syll. 31. Roberts 259. Schwyzer 11. Solmsen-Fraenkel 21. Tod 19.

[Τ]ο[ίδε τὸν] | πόλεμον [ἐ]||πολ[έ]μεον · | Λακ[εδ]α[ι]μόν[ιοι], ||
5 'Αθ[α]ν[α]ῖ[ο]ι, | Κορίνθιοι, | Τεγεᾶτ[αι], | Σικυόνιοι, | Αἰγι-
10 νᾶται, || Μεγαρὲς, | 'Επιδαύριοι, | 'Ερχομένιοι, | Φλειάσιοι, |
15 Τροζάνιοι, || 'Ερμιονὲς, | Τιρύνθιοι, | Πλαταιὲς, | Θεσπιὲς, |
20 Μυκανὲς, || Κεῖοι, | Μάλιοι, | Τένιοι, | Νάξιοι, | 'Ερετριὲς, ||
25 Χαλκιδὲς, | Στυρὲς, | Γαλεῖοι, | Ποτειδιᾶται, | Λευκάδιοι, ||
30 Γανακτοριὲς, | Κύθνιοι, | Σίφνιοι, | 'Αμπρακιόται, | Λεπρεᾶται.

The famous bronze serpent-column which once supported the gold tripod set up at Delphi after the battle of Plataea. According to Thucydides (1.132.3) and others, the Lacedaemonians, after erasing the boastful epigram of Pausanias, inscribed simply the names of the cities which had taken part in the war and had set up the tripod. Note [ἐ]πολ[έ]μεον, for which the true Laconian form would be ἐπολέμιον.

70. Found at Tegea. Fifth century B.C. IG V.ii.159. GDI 4598. Ditt. Syll. 1213. Schwyzer 57. Solmsen-Fraenkel 35. Comparetti, Annuario 2.246 ff. Buck, CP 20.133 ff.

A　Ξουθίαι τōι Φιλαχαίō διακάτι|αι μναῖ. αἰ κ' αὐτὸς hίκε, ἀνελέσ-|
θō · αἰ δέ κ' ἀποθάνει, τōν τέκνōν | ἔμεν, ἐπεί κα πέντε Fέτεα ||
5 hεβōντι · αἰ δέ κα μὲ γενεὰ λ[ε]||ίπεται, τōν ἐπιδικατōν ἔμεν · | δια-
γνōμεν δὲ τὸς Τεγεάτα[ς] | κὰ τὸν θεθμόν.

B　Ξουθίαι παρκαθέκα τōι Φιλαχα|ίō τζετρακάτιαι μναῖ ἀργυρίō.
εἰ μ|έν κα ζόε, αὐτὸς ἀνελέσθō · αἰ δέ κ|α μὲ ζόε, τοὶ υἱοὶ ἀνελōσθō
5 τοὶ γνέ||σιοι, ἐπεί κα ἐβάσōντι πέντε Fέτε|α · εἰ δέ κα μὲ ζōντι,
ταὶ θυγατέρες | ἀνελōσθō ταὶ γνέσιαι · εἰ δέ κα μὲ | ζōντι, τοὶ
10 νόθοι ἀνελōσθō · εἰ δέ κα | μὲ νόθοι ζōντι, τοὶ 'ς ἄσιστα πόθικ||ες
ἀνελōσθō · εἰ δέ κ' ἀνφιλέγōντ|(ι, τ)οὶ Τεγεᾶται διαγνόντō κὰ
τὸν θεθμόν.

Statements of two deposits of money made by a certain Xuthias, son of Philachaeus, and the conditions for their future disbursement. The place of deposit was without doubt the temple of Athena Alea in Tegea, the Greek temples often being used for such purposes. But the dialect is not Arcadian, and must therefore represent that of a foreign depositor. The most natural assumption is that Xuthias was from the neighboring

Laconia, and we are expressly informed (cf. Ath. 6.233) that the Spartans used to deposit money with the Arcadians to evade the law against holding private property. It has been suggested, partly on account of the names (Xuthias, Philachaeus), but mainly because of the retention of intervocalic σ (γνέσιοι, ἐβάσōντι), that Xuthias was not a Spartan proper, but an Achaean perioecus. But there is no good evidence that the perioeci differed in speech from the Spartans at this time, and the retention of intervocalic σ and of antevocalic ε (Fέτεα) is sufficiently explained by the fact that the document was intended for use outside of Laconia. See **59**.1, **275**.

A. 'For Xuthias the son of Philachaeus (are deposited) two hundred minae. If he comes in person, let him take it, but if he dies, it shall belong to his children five years after they reach the age of puberty. If no offspring survives, it shall belong to those designated by law as heirs. The Tegeans shall decide according to the law.' 2. The letters following αὐτός are so mutilated that no reading is certain. But the sense required is clear.

B. This was inscribed later than A, which was thereupon canceled, as shown by its mutilation. The Tegean engraver is responsible for the use of εἰ instead of αἰ, the subj. ζόē (cf. **149**) in contrast to ἀποθάνēι of A, the omission of h in υἱοί, ἐβάσōντι (cf. **58**d); and his blunder in writing τζετρακάτιαι was perhaps due to the Arcadian pronunciation (cf. **68**.3). It is also possible that in ll. 10-11 we should read, without correction, ἀνφιλέγōντοι, with Arc. -τοι = -ται (**139**.1). But the passive with μναῖ understood as subject is less natural than the corrected reading usually adopted.

71. Sparta. Fifth century B.C. IG V.i.213. GDI 4416. Roberts 264. Schwyzer 12. Solmsen-Fraenkel 22.

> Δαμόνōν | ἀνέθēκε 'Αθαναία[ι] | Πολιάχōι
> 5   νικάhας | ταυτᾶ hᾶτ' οὐδὲς || πέποκα τōν νῦν. |
> Τάδε ἐνίκαhε Δαμ[όνōν] | τōι αὐτō̄ τεθρίππō[ι] | αὐτὸς ἀνιοχί-
> 10 ōν · | ἐν ΓαιαFόχō τετράκι[ν] || καὶ 'Αθάναια τετ[ράκιν] | κέλευhύ-
> νια τετ[ράκιν.] | καὶ Ποhοίδαια Δαμόνō[ν] | ἐνίκē Ηέλει, καὶ hο
> 15 κέλ[ēξ | hαμ]ᾶ, αὐτὸς ἀνιοχίōν || ἐνhēβόhαις hίπποις | hεπτάκιν ἐκ

τᾶν αὐτο͞ | hίππο͞ν κὲκ το͞ αὐ[τ]ο͞ [hίππο͞.] | καὶ Ποhοίδαια Δαμό-
20 νον | [ἐ]νίκε̄ Θευρίαι ὀκτά[κ]ι[ν] || αὐτὸς ἀνιοχίο͞ν ἐν|hε̄βόhαις
hίπποις | ἐκ τᾶν αὐτο͞ hίππο͞ν | κὲκ το͞ αὐτο͞ hίππο͞. | κὲν ᾿Αριοντίας
25 ἐνίκε̄ || Δαμόνο͞ν ὀκτάκιν | αὐτὸς ἀνιοχίο͞ν | ἐνhε̄βόhαις hίπποις |
30 ἐκ τᾶν αὐτο͞ hίππο͞ν | κὲκ το͞ αὐτο͞ hίππο͞, καὶ || ho κέλεξ ἐνίκε̄
h[αμᾶ]. | καὶ ᾿Ελευhύνια Δαμ[όνον] | ἐνίκε̄ αὐτὸς ἀνιοχίο͞ν | ἐνhε̄-
35 βόhαις hίπποις | τετράκιν. || τάδε ἐνίκαhε ᾿Ενυμα[κρατίδ|ας]
πρᾶτ[ος π]αίδο͞ν δόλ[ιχον | Λιθέ]hια καὶ κέλεξ μι[ᾶς | ἀμέρ]ας
40 hα[μᾶ] ἐν[ίκο͞ν. | - - - || - - - - | - - - -] | δόλιχο[ν καὶ ho κέλεξ
45 μιᾶς] | ἀμέρας hαμᾶ ἐνίκο͞ν. | καὶ Παρπαρόνια ἐνίκε̄ || ᾿Ενυμακρατί-
δας παῖδας | στάδιον καὶ δίαυλον | καὶ δόλιχον καὶ ho κέ[λεξ] | μιᾶς
50 ἀμέρας hαμᾶ | ἐνίκε̄. καὶ Δαμόνο͞ν || ἐνίκε̄ παῖς ἰὸν ἐν | ΓαιαϜόχο͞
στάδιον καὶ | [δί]αυλον. | [κ]αὶ Δαμόνο͞ν ἐνίκε̄ | παῖς ἰὸν Λιθέhια ||
55 στάδιον καὶ δίαυλον. | καὶ Δαμόνο͞ν ἐνίκε̄ | παῖς ἰὸν Μαλεάτεια |
60 στάδιον καὶ δίαυλον. | καὶ Δαμόνο͞ν ἐνίκε̄ || παῖς ἰὸν Λιθέhια | στά-
διον καὶ δίαυλον. | καὶ Δαμόνο͞ν ἐνίκε̄ | παῖς ἰὸν Παρπαρόνια |
65 στάδιον καὶ δίαυλον, || καὶ ᾿Αθάναια στάδιον. | hυπὸ δὲ ᾿Εχεμένε̄
ἔφορο[ν] | τάδε ἐνίκε̄ Δαμόνο͞ν, | ᾿Αθάναια ἐνhε̄βόhαις | hίπποις
70 αὐτὸς ἀνιοχίο͞ν || καὶ ho κέλεξ μιᾶς | ἀμέρας hαμᾶ ἐνίκε̄, καὶ | ho
hυιὸς στάδιον hαμᾶ | ἐνίκε̄. hυπὸ δὲ | Εὔιππον ἔφορον τάδε ||
75 ἐνίκε̄ Δαμόνο͞ν, ᾿Αθάναια | ἐνhε̄βόhαις hίπποις | αὐτὸς ἀνιοχίο͞ν
80 καὶ | ho κέλεξ μιᾶς ἀμέρας | hαμᾶ ἐνίκε̄, καὶ ho hυιὸς || στάδιον
hαμᾶ ἐνίκε̄. | hυπὸ δὲ ᾿Αριστε̄ ἔφορον | τάδε ἐνίκε̄ Δαμόνο͞ν, | ἐν
85 ΓαιαϜόχο͞ ἐνhε̄βόhαις | [h]ίπποις αὐτὸς ἀνιοχίο͞ν || [κ]αὶ ho κέλεξ
μιᾶς ἀμέρας | [h]αμᾶ ἐνίκε̄, καὶ ho hυιὸς | στάδιον καὶ δίαυλον καὶ |
90 δόλιχον μιᾶς ἀμέρας | ἐνίκο͞ν πάντες hαμᾶ. || hυπὸ δὲ ᾿Εχεμένε̄
ἔφορον | τάδε ἐνίκε̄ Δαμόνο͞ν, | ἐν ΓαιαϜόχο͞ ἐνhε̄βόhαις | hίπποις
αὐτὸς ἀνιοχίο͞ν, | [κ]αὶ ho hυιὸς στάδιον κ[αὶ - - -

Record of the victories of Damonon and his son.
3 ff. **νικάhας** κτλ.: 'Having won victories in such a manner as
never any one of those now living.'—7. 'With his own four-horse
chariot,' αὐτο͞ reflexive as in ll. 16, 17, etc. **121**.1-3.—9. 'In the
games of Poseidon,' with elliptical genitive as in εἰν ᾿Αίδαο, etc.
So ἐν ᾿Αριοντίας l. 24. **ΓαιάϜοχος** = Hom. γαιήοχος.—11, 31.
κελευhύνια: καὶ ᾿Ελευσίνια (**20**, **59**.1), games in honor of the
Eleusinian Demeter.—12, 18. **Ποhοίδαια**: Ποσειδώνια (**49**.1,
59.1, **61**.4) celebrated at Helos in Laconia and Thuria in Messe-

nia.—15 ff. 'Seven times with colts from his own mares and his own stallion.'—**ἐνhἐβόhαις hίπποις**: ἐνηβώσαις 'being in ἥβη, young mares.'—19. **Θευρίαι**: the usual form of the name is Θουρία.—24. **'Αριοντία**: the name of some goddess or heroine otherwise unknown.—35 ff. Victories won by 'Ενυμακρατίδας (cf. l. 45). The name (cf. also 'Ενυμαντιάδας IG V.i.97.20, 280) points to an ἔνυμα = ὄνυμα, ὄνομα, with an inherited e-grade in the first syllable, which is seen in some of the cognate forms of other languages, e.g. Old Prussian *emmens*, but was hitherto unknown in Greek.—44, 63. **Παρπαρόνια**: Πάρπαρος is the name of a mountain in Argolis where games were held.—49 ff. Victories won by Damonon as a boy.—54, 60. **Λιθέhια**: games in honor of Apollo Lithesius. —57. **Μαλεάτεια**: games in honor of Apollo Maleates. Cf. Paus. 3.12.8.—66 ff. Victories won by Damonon and his son at the same games.—66, 73, 81, 90. **hυπό** with acc.: **136.11**.

72. Taenarum. Fifth to fourth centuries B.C. IG V.i.1232. GDI 4591. Roberts 265c. Schwyzer 52.4). Transitional alphabet. н = h and once η.

5   'Ανέθεκε | τōι Ποhοιδᾶνι | Νίκōν | Νικαφορίδα || καὶ Λύhιππον | καὶ Νικαρχίδαν | καὶ ταύτᾶς πάντα. | ἔφορος | Εὐδαμίδας. || 10 ἐπάκοε | Μενεχαρίδας | 'Ανδρομέδης.

73. Taenarum. Fifth to fourth centuries B.C. IG V.i.1231. GDI 4592. Roberts 265d. Schwyzer 52,3). Transitional alphabet. н = h and η.

5   'Ανέθηκε | Αἰσχρίōν | 'Απειρότας | τōι Ποhοιδᾶ||νι 'Ηρακλήι-δαν | αὐτὸν καὶ | ταῦτō. ἔφορος | Ηαγηhίστρατος. | ἐπάκō Πρυαῖος,|| 10 'Επικύδη[ς].

Manumissions of slaves in the form of dedications to Poseidon. ἐπάκοε, ἐπάκō: dual forms of ἐπάκοος 'witness.' ἐπάκō is the contracted form, of which the uncontracted ἐπακόω occurs in another inscription of the same class. ἐπάκοε is due to the analogy of consonant stems, to which nouns in -οος are not infrequently subject, e.g., Att. χοῦς (**112**.6), late νοῦς gen. sg. νοός, nom. pl. νόες (after βοῦς, βοός, βόες).

74. Thalamae. Fourth century B.C. IG V.i.1317. GDI IV p. 691. Schwyzer 54. Ionic alphabet, but н = h as well as η.

Νικοσθενίδας τᾶι Παhιφᾶι | γεροντεύων ἀνέσηκε, | αὐτός τε καὶ
5 hο τῶ πατρὸς π|ατὴρ Νικοσθενίδας, προβειπ||άhας τᾶ σιῶ ποτ'
Ἀνδρίαν συ|νεφορεύοντα ἀνι[σ]τάμεν | Νικοσθενίδαν ἐ[ν] τῶι
ἱ[ε]ρῶι, h|ὸν καὶ σὺν καλῶι χρῆσται.

From the shrine of Pasiphae at Thalamae, an oracle often
consulted by the Spartan officials. The name of the goddess
was Πασιφάα (Att. Πασιφάη), whence the contracted Πασιφᾶ,
like Ἀθηνᾶ, and here, with Lac. h for intervocalic σ, Παhιφᾶ.
Since Nicosthenidas the dedicator was a member of the Council
of Elders, his grandfather of the same name could not have been
living at the time. He was carrying out an injunction previously
laid upon the grandfather by the goddess, which for some reason
had been unfulfilled.

4 ff. **προβειπάhας** κτλ.: 'since the goddess had declared that
Nicosthenidas should set up in the shrine a statue in honor of An-
dreas his fellow-ephor, and that he would then consult the oracle
with success.' The construction ποτ' Ἀνδρίαν . . . ἀνιστά μεν is unusual, but other possible interpretations are equally difficult in
this respect.—**hὸν** κτλ.: infin. clause depending on προβειπάhας
'who would' = 'and that he would.' For χρῆσται = χρῆσθαι see **85**.1.

75. Sparta. Second century A.D. IG V.i. 296. Artemis Orthia
p. 318.

5 Νεικάγορος | Σωσιδάμου Εὐ|δάμω κάσεν | νικάσας κελ||οῖαν
καὶ μῶα|ν καὶ καθηρα|τόρειν καὶ μ|ῶαν καὶ ἀπὸ μ|ικιχιζομένων ||
10 μέχρι μελλειρο|νείας τοὺ(ς) Γααό|χους καὶ Ἀσάνεα | τὴν τῶν παί-
δων | πάλην Ἀρτέ|μιτι Ὀρθεία.

76. Sparta. Second century A.D. IG V.i. 279. Artemis Orthia
p. 318.

Ὀνασικλείδας Φιλο|στράτου νεικάσας | κασσηρατόριν πρατο|παμ-
5 παίδων, ἀτρο||παμπαίδων, εἰρέ|νων δὲ κελοῖαν [Ἀρτέμιτι κτλ.].

77. Sparta. Second century A.D. IG V.i.307. Artemis Orthia
p. 329.

Κλέανδρορ | ὁ καὶ Μῆνιρ | Καλλιστράτω | βουαγὸρ ἐπὶ ||
5 πατρονόμω | Γοργίππω τῶ (Γοργίππω) | νικάαρ μῶαν Ἀρτέ-|
μιτι Βωρσέα ἀνέση|κε.

78. Sparta. Second century A.D. IG V.i.289. Artemis Orthia
p. 321.

Εὐδόκιμορ (Εὐδοκίμω) κε|λοία καὶ Εὐδόκι|μορ Δαμοκράτεορ |
5 ὁ καὶ 'Αριστείδαρ κασ||σηρατόριο(ν) νεικάαν|τερ ἐπὶ 'Αλκάστω
βουαγοὶ | μικιχιδδομένων Φωρθέα.

Nos. 75-78 belong to a series, now over 130 in number, of dedication to Artemis Orthia by the victors in certain juvenile contests.
The fullest edition is in Artemis Orthia (= JHS, Supplementary
Report V). The object dedicated, the prize itself, was an iron
sickle, which was let into a socket, with which each of the
stone slabs is provided, some with several, even (no. 75) four.
Of the contests, one is called κασσηρατόριν, κατθηρατόριν, καθθη-
ρατόριον, etc., i.e., καταθηρατόριον, not an actual chase of wild
beasts, but some athletic game call 'the hunt.' The μῶα, i.e.,
μοῦσα, was of course a musical contest. The word which is variously spelled κελοῖαν, κελῦαν, etc., probably from the root seen in
κέλαδος, κελαδέω, also denotes a musical contest. The βουαγόρ
was the 'leader of the βοῦαι (βοῦα· ἀγέλη παίδων Hesych.),' the
bands in which the Spartan boys were trained.—As was already
known from literary sources, an elaborate nomenclature applied
to the Spartan youth according to the successive years of their
training. The terms which occur in the inscriptions are as follows.
μικκιδδόμενος, μικκιχιδδόμενος, etc. (great variety of spellings),
derived from μικκός = μικρός (89.5a) or *μικκιχός with added
diminutive suffix (164.9), and probably denoting a ten-year-old
boy. πρατοπάμπαις 'in first year of full boyhood' (πάμπαιδος
occurs elsewhere). ἀτροπάμπαις 'in second year of full boyhood'
(ἀτρο- = ἀτερο-). μελλείρην (Plut., etc., but also implied by
μελλειρονεία no. 75) 'one about to be a εἴρην.' εἴρην 'ephebe.'
τριτίρην 'third-year ephebe.'—κάσεν, following a dative or genitive and meaning 'akin to,' belongs with κάσις 'brother' or
'sister,' κάσης· ἡλικιώτης, κάσιοι· οἱ ἐκ τῆς αὐτῆς ἀγέλης ἀδελφοί
τε καὶ ἀνεψιοί - - - Λάκωνες, Hesych., but the termination with
the invariable spelling -εν is unexplained.

A few of the dedications are in the κοινή, and a few show
Doric forms without specific Laconian coloring, e.g., νικάσας.
But most of them, like those given here, represent an artificial
revival of the local dialect, that is, artificial as regards its use
in inscriptions, but probably reflecting, though only crudely

and with great inconsistency in spelling (e.g., in the use of σ = θ), the form of speech which still survived as a patois among the Laconian peasants. Some of the peculiarities in spelling are not characteristic of Laconian especially, but of the late period, e.g., ει = ῑ in νεικάαντερ etc., ω for ο in Βωρθέα, final α for ᾱι in Βωρθέα etc.

Heraclean

79. The Heraclean Tables. End of fourth century B.C. IG XIV.645. GDI 4629. Schwyzer 62. Solmsen-Fraenkel 23. Ionic alphabet, but with Ϝ, and Ⱶ = h. Only Table I is given here.

I

Ἔφορος Ἀρίσταρχος Ἡρακλείδα · μὴς | Ἀπελλαῖος · ha πό-
λις καὶ τοὶ ὁρισταί, | Ϝε τρίπους Φιλώνυμος Ζωπυρίσκω, | πε καρυ-
5 κεῖον Ἀπολλώνιος Ἡρακλήτω, || αι πέλτα Δάζιμος Πύρρω, κυ
θρῖναξ | Φιλώτας Ἱστιείω, με ἐπιστύλιον | Ἡρακλείδας Ζω-
πύρω, Διονύσωι. |
Ἀνέγραψαν τοὶ ὁρισταὶ τοὶ haιρεθέντες ἐπὶ τὼς χώρως τὼς
hιαρὼς τὼς τῶ Διονύσω, | Φιλώνυμος Ζωπυρίσκω, Ἀπολλώνιος
10 Ἡρακλήτω, Δάζιμος Πύρρω, Φιλώτας Ἱστιείω, || Ἡρακλείδας
Ζωπύρω, καθὰ [ὥρ]ιξαν καὶ ἐτέρμαξαν καὶ συνεμέτρησαν καὶ
ἐμέρι|ξαν τῶν Ἡρακλείων διακνόντων ἐν κατακλήτωι ἀλίαι.
Συνεμετρήσαμες δὲ ἀρξάμε|νοι ἀπὸ τῶ ἀντόμω τῶ hυπὲρ Παν-
δοσίας ἄγοντος τῶ διατάμνοντος τώς τε hιαρὼς χώ|ρως καὶ τὰν Ϝι-
δίαν γᾶν ἐπὶ τὸν ἄντομον τὸν ὁρίζοντα τώς τε τῶ Διονύσω χώρως
καὶ | τὸν Κωνέας hο Δίωνος ἐπαμόχη. κατετάμομες δὲ μερίδας
15 τέτορας · || τὰν μὲν πράταν μερίδα ἀπὸ τῶ ἀντόμω τῶ πὰρ τὰ
Ηϝώιδεια ἄγοντος, | εὖρος ποτὶ τὰν τριακοντάπεδον τὰν διὰ τῶν
hιαρῶν χώρων ἄγωσαν, | μᾶκος δὲ ἄνωθα ἀπὸ τᾶν ἀποροᾶν ἄχρι ἐς
ποταμὸν τὸν Ἄκιριν, καὶ | ἐγένοντο μετριώμεναι ἐν ταύται τᾶι
μερείαι ἐρρηγείας μὲν δι|ακάτιαι μία σχοῖνοι, σκίρω δὲ καὶ ἀρρήκ-
20 τω καὶ δρυμῶ Ϝεξακάτιαι || τετρώκοντα Ϝὲξ σχοῖνοι ἡημίσχοι-
νον · τὰν δὲ δευτέραν μερίδα, εὖρος ἀπὸ | τᾶς τριακονταπέδω ἐπὶ
τὸν ἄντομον τὸν πρᾶτον, μᾶκος δὲ ἀπὸ τᾶν | ἀποροᾶν ἄχρι ἐς πο-
ταμόν, καὶ ἐγένοντο μετριώμεναι ἐν ταύται τᾶι με|ρείαι ἐρρηγείας
μὲν διακάτιαι ηεβδεμήκοντα τρῖς σχοῖνοι, σκίρω δὲ | καὶ ἀρρήκτω

25 καὶ δρυμῶ πεντακάτιαι σχοῖνοι · || τὰν δὲ τρίταν μερίδα, εὖρος ἀπὸ
τῶ ἀντόμω τῶ πράτω τῶ πὰρ τὰν τρι|ακοντάπεδον ἄγοντος ἐπὶ τὸν
ἄντομον τὸν δεύτερον ἀπὸ τᾶς τρια|κονταπέδω, μᾶκος ἀπὸ τᾶν
ἀποροᾶν ἄχρι ἐς ποταμόν, καὶ ἐγέ|νοντο μετριώμεναι ἐν ταύται
τᾶι μερείαι ἐρρηγείας μὲν τριακάτιαι | δέκα δύο σχοῖνοι ἡμί-
30 σχοινον, σκίρω δὲ καὶ ἀρρήκτω καὶ δρυμῶ πεντα||κάτιαι τριάκοντα
ηεπτὰ ἡμίσχοινον · τὰν δὲ τετάρταν μερίδα, εὖρος ἀπὸ | τῶ ἀντό-
μω τῶ δευτέρω ἀπὸ τᾶς τριακονταπέδω ἐπὶ τὸν ἄντομον τὸν |
ὁρίζοντα τάν τε ἱαρὰν καὶ τὰν Ϝιδίαν γᾶν, μᾶκος δὲ ἀπὸ τᾶν ἀπο-
ροᾶν | ἄχρι ἐς ποταμόν, καὶ ἐγένοντο μετριώμεναι ἐν ταύται τᾶι
μερείαι ἐρρη|γείας μὲν τριακάτιαι ηοκτὼ σχοῖνοι ηημίσχοινον,
35 σκίρω δὲ καὶ ἀρρήκτω || καὶ δρυμῶ πεντακάτιαι τετρώκοντα μία
ηημίσχοινον. |

Κεφαλὰ πάσας ἐρρηγείας χίλιαι ηενενήκοντα πέντε σχοῖνοι,
σκί|ρω δὲ καὶ ἀρρήκτω καὶ δρυμῶ δισχίλιαι διακάτιαι Ϝίκατι
πέντε · | τὰν δὲ νᾶσον τὰν ποτιγεγενημέναν ἐς τὰν ἄρρηκτον γᾶν
συνεμε|τρήσαμες. ἀπὸ ταύτας τᾶς γᾶς ἀπολώλη ἐρρηγείας μὲν
40 τριακάτιαι || τρῖς σχοῖνοι ηημίσχοινον, σκίρω δὲ καὶ ἀρρήκτω καὶ
δρυμῶ τετρα|κόσιαι τριάκοντα πέντε σχοῖνοι, ἐμ μὲν τᾶι πράται
μερείαι τᾶι | πὰρ τὰ Ηηρώιδεια ἐρρηγείας μὲν ηεβδεμήκοντα Ϝὲξ
σχοῖνοι, σκί|ρω δὲ καὶ ἀρρήκτω καὶ δρυμῶ ηεκατὸν ηογδοήκοντα
πέντε σχοῖ|νοι, ἐν δὲ τᾶι τετάρται μερείαι τᾶι πὰρ τὰ Φιντία ἐρρη-
45 γείας μὲν || διακάτιαι Ϝίκατι ηεππὰ σχοῖνοι ηημίσχοινον, σκίρω δὲ
καὶ ἀρρή|κτω καὶ δρυμῶ διακάτιαι πεντήκοντα σχοῖνοι. Κεφαλὰ
πά|σας γᾶς ηᾶς κατεσώισαμες τῶι Διονύσωι ηεπτακάτιαι τριά-|
κοντα ηοκτὼ σχοῖνοι ηημίσχοινον · ταύταν τὰν γᾶν κατεσώισα|μες
50 ἐγδικαξάμενοι δίκας τριακοσταίας τοῖς τὰν ηιαρὰν γᾶν Ϝι||δίαν
ποιόντασσιν. ηαύτα ἐμισθώθη [ηα γᾶ] κατὰ βίω | [ηόσσα]ν η[α]|-
μὲς κατεσώισαμες τριακατίων μεδίμνων τὸ Ϝέτος ηέκαστον, | ηα δὲ
πᾶσα γᾶ ηα τῶ Διονύσω τετρακατίων δέκα μεδίμνων κάδ|διχος
τὸ Ϝέτος ηέκαστον.

Ἐστάσαμες δὲ καὶ ηορως ἐπὶ μὲν τᾶς | πλευριάδος ἄνω, ηένα μὲν
55 ἐπὶ τῶ ἀντόμω τῶ πὰρ Πανδοσίαν || τῶ πὰρ τὰ Ηηρώιδεια τῶ ὁρί-
ζοντος τάν τε ηιαρὰν γᾶν καὶ τὰν Ϝιδίαν | ἀγχωρίξαντες ἀπὸ τᾶν
ἀποροᾶν ἐς τὰν Ϝιδίαν γᾶν, ηως μὴ καταλυ|μακωθῆς ἀδηλωθείη
καθὼς τοὶ ἔμπροσθα ηοροι, ἄλλον δὲ ἐπὶ τῶ ἀν|τόμω τῶ πὰρ τὰ
Φιντία ἄγοντος ἐστάσαμες πὰρ τὰν βυβλίαν καὶ | τὰν διώρυγα
60 ἀγχωρίξαντες ηωσαύτως ἐς τὰν Ϝιδίαν γᾶν ‹ταν›. ἄλ||λως δὲ ἀντό-

ρως τούτοις ἐστάσαμες ἐπὶ τᾶς ἀμαξιτῶ τᾶς διὰ τῶ χα|ράδεος ἀγώ-
σας τᾶς πὰρ τὸν δρυμόν, τὰς μὲν στάλας ἐς τὰν hιαρὰν | γᾶν, τὼς
δὲ ἀντόρως ἐς τὰν Ϝιδίαν γᾶν, καταλιπόντες Ϝικατίπεδον | ἄντομον.
ἐστάσαμες δὲ καὶ μεσσόρως, δύο μὲν ἐπὶ τᾶς hοδῶ τᾶς | ἀγώσας ἔκ
65 τε πόλιος καὶ ἐκ Πανδοσίας διὰ τῶν hιαρῶν χώρων, δύο || δὲ ἐν
ταῖς hακροσκιρίαις · τούτως πάντας ἂν εὐθυωρείαν hομολό|γως ἀλ-
λάλοις, τὼς μὲν ἐς τὸ hιαρὸν πλάγος τῶ ἀντόμω ἐπιγε|γραμμένως
"hιαρὼς Διονύσω χώρων," τὼς δὲ ἐν τᾶι Ϝιδίαι γᾶι ἐπι|γεγραμμέ-
νως "ἀντόρως." hωσαύτως δὲ καὶ ἐπὶ τῶ ἀντόμω τῶ | πὰρ τὰ
70 Φιντία ἄγοντος ἐστάσαμες μεσσόρως, δύο μὲν ἐπὶ || τᾶς hοδῶ τᾶς
ἐκ πόλιος καὶ ἐκ Πανδοσίας ἀγώσας διὰ τῶν | hιαρῶν χώρων, δύο
δὲ ἐπὶ τὰν hακροσκιριᾶν πὰρ τὰς τυρείας · | τούτως πάντας hομολό-
γως ἂν εὐθυωρείαν τοῖς ἐπὶ τᾶς hοδῶ | τᾶς διὰ τῶ χαράδεος ἀγώ-
σας πὰρ τὸν δρυμόν, τὼς μὲν ἐς τὸ hιαρὸν | πλάγος ἐπιγεγραμμέ-
75 νως "hιαρὼς Διονύσω χώρων," τὼς δὲ ἐς τὰν Ϝιδί||αν γᾶν ἐπιγε-
γραμμένως "ἀντόρως", ἀπέχοντας ἀπ' ἀλλάλων hως ἤ|μεν Ϝικα-
τίπεδον ἄντομον. ἐπὶ δὲ τᾶς τριακονταπέδω τᾶς διὰ τῶν hι|αρῶν
χώρων ἀγώσας ἐπὶ μὲν τᾶς πλευριάδος ἄνω δύο ἀπέχοντας ἀπ'
ἀλ|λάλων τριάκοντα πόδας, ἄλλως δὲ ἀντόρως τούτοις ἐπάξαμες
πὰρ | τὰν hοδὸν τὰν πὰρ τὸν δρυμὸν ἄγωσαν δύο ἀπέχοντας ἀπ'
80 ἀλλάλων || τριάκοντα πόδας · ἐν δὲ μέσσωι τῶι χώρωι ἐπὶ τᾶς τρια-
κονταπέδω τέ|τορας ἀπέχοντας ἀπ' ἀλλάλων hᾶι μὲν τριάκοντα
πόδας, hᾶι δὲ Ϝίκα|τι · ἐπὶ δὲ τῶ ἀντόμω τῶ πὰρ τὰν τριακοντά-
πεδον δύο ἀπέχοντας ἀπ' ἀλ|λάλων Ϝίκατι πόδας καὶ ἄλλως ἐπὶ τῶ
δευτέρω ἀντόμω ἀπέχοντας | ἀπ' ἀλλάλων Ϝίκατι πόδας · τούτως
85 πάντας ἀνεπιγρόφως ὁρίζοντας || τὰς μερείας τὰς ποτ' ἀλλάλως
τοῖς μεμισθωμένοις τὼς hιαρὼς χώ|ρως. τὼς δὲ πάντας χώρως
τὼς τῶ Διονύσω τερμάζοντι τοί τε ἄντομοι | hό τε πὰρ τὰ Ηηρώι-
δεια ἄγων καὶ hο πὰρ τὰ Φιντία ἀπὸ τᾶν ἀπορόαν ἄνω|θα ἄχρι ἐς
ποταμὸν τὸν Ἄκιριν. ἀριθμὸς ὅρων τῶν ἐστάσαμες τῶν μὲν | ἐπὶ
90 τῶ ἀντόμω τῶ πὰρ τὰ Ηηρώιδεια hεπτὰ σὺν τῶι ἐπὶ τᾶς πλευριά-
δος, || ἐπὶ δὲ τᾶς τριακονταπέδω hοκτὼ σὺν τῶι τετρώ‹ι›ρωι, ἐπὶ
δὲ τῶ ἀντόμω | τῶ τε πὰρ τὰν τριακοντάπεδον καὶ τῶ ἐχομένω δύο
ἐφ' ἑκατέρω, ἐπὶ δὲ τῶ | πὰρ τὰ Φιντία hεπτὰ σὺν τῶι πὰρ τὰν
βυβλίναν μασχάλαν καὶ πὰρ τὰν δι|ώρυγα. |
　　　　　Συνθήκα Διονύσω χώρων. ||
95 Ἐπὶ ἐφόρω Ἀριστίωνος, μηνὸς Ἀπελλαίω, hα πόλις καὶ τοὶ
πολιανόμοι, ᾱς βότρυς Τίμαρ|χος Νίκωνος, Ϝε ἄνθεμον Ἀπολλώ-

νιος Ἀπολλωνίω, καὶ τοὶ ὁρισταὶ F̄ε τρίπους Φιλώνυ|μος Ζωπυρί-
σκω, π̄ε καρυκεῖον Ἀπολλώνιος Ηρακλήτω, ᾱι πέλτα Δάζιμος
Πύρρω, | κ̄ν θρῖναξ Φιλώτας Ηιστιείω, μ̄ε ἐπιστύλιον Ηηρακλεί-
δας Ζωπύρω, μισθῶντι τὼς ηι|αρὼς χώρως τὼς τῶ Διονύσω ἔχον-
100 τας ηως ἔχοντι κατὰ βίω, καθὰ τοὶ Ηηρακλεῖοι διέ||γνον. τοὶ δὲ
μισθωσάμενοι καρπευσόνται τὸν ἀεὶ χρόνον, ηᾶς κα πρωγγύως πο-
τάγων|τι καὶ τὸ μίσθωμα ἀποδιδῶντι πὰρ Fέτος ἀεὶ Πανάμω μη-
νὸς προτερείαι· καί κ' ἔμπροσθα | ἀποδίνωντι, ἀπαξόντι ἐς τὸν δα-
μόσιον ῥογὸν καὶ παρμετρησόντι τοῖς σιταγέρταις τοῖς | ἐπὶ τῶν
Fετέων τῶι δαμοσίωι χοῖ μεστὼς τὼς χοῦς κριθᾶς κοθαρᾶς δοκί-
μας, ηοίας κα ηα γᾶ | φέρει· ποταξόντι δὲ πρωγγύως τοῖς πολια-
105 νόμοις τοῖς ἀεὶ ἐπὶ τῶν Fετέων ἔντασσιν πὰρ || πενταηετηρίδα, ηώς
κα ἐθέλοντες τοὶ πολιανόμοι δέχωνται. καὶ αἴ τινί κα ἄλλωι |
παρδῶντι τὰν γᾶν, ηάν κα αὐτοὶ μεμισθωσῶνται, ἢ ἀρτυσῶντι ἢ
ἀποδῶνται τὰν ἐ|πικαρπίαν, ἂν αὐτὰ τὰ παρηεξόνται πρωγγύως
ηοι παρλαβόντες ἢ ηοῖς κ' ἀρτύσει ἢ ηοι πρι|άμενοι τὰν ἐπικαρπίαν,
ἂν ηὰ καὶ ηο ἐξ ἀρχᾶς μεμισθωμένος. ηόστις δέ κα μὴ ποτάγει
πρωγγύ|ως ἢ μὴ τὸ μίσθωμα ἀποδιδῶι κὰτ τὰ γεγραμμένα, τό τε
110 μίσθωμα διπλεῖ ἀποτεισεῖ τὸ ἐπὶ τῶ Fέ||τεος καὶ τὸ ἀμπώλημα
τοῖς τε πολιανόμοις καὶ τοῖς σιταγέρταις τοῖς ἀεὶ ἐπὶ τῶ Fέτεος,
ηόσσωι κα | μείονος ἀμμισθωθῆ πὰρ πέντε Fέτη τὰ πρᾶτα, ηότι κα
τελέθει ψαφισθὲν ηάμα πᾶν τῶι πράτωι | μισθώματι, καὶ τὰ ἐν
τᾶι γᾶι πεφυτευμένα καὶ οἰκοδομημένα πάντα τᾶς πόλιος ἐσσόνται.
Ἐργαξόν|ται δὲ κὰτ τάδε· ηο μὲν τὸν πρᾶτον χῶρον μισθωσά-
μενος τὸν πὰρ τὸν ἄντομον τὸν ηυπὲρ Πανδοσί|ας ἄγοντα τὸν πὰρ
τὰ Ηηρώιδα ἄχρι τᾶς τριακονταπέδω ἀμπέλων μὲν φυτευσεῖ μὴ
115 μεῖον ἢ δέκα || σχοίνως, ἐλαιᾶν δὲ φυτὰ ἐμβαλεῖ ἐς τὰν σχοῖνον
ηεκάσταν μὴ μεῖον ἢ τέτορα ἐς τὰν | δυνατὰν γᾶν ἐλαίας ἔχεν· αἰ
δέ κα μὴ φᾶντι τοὶ μεμισθωμένοι δυνατὰν ημεν ἐλαίας ἔ|χεν, τοὶ
πολιανόμοι τοὶ ἀεὶ ἐπὶ τῶν Fετέων ἔντες καὶ αἴ τινάς κα ἄλλως
τοὶ πολιανόμοι ποθέ|λωνται ἀπὸ τῶ δάμω, ὀμόσαντες δοκιμαξόντι
καὶ ἀναγγελίοντι ἐν ἀλίαι θασάμενοι τὰν | γᾶν πὸτ τὰν τῶν ἐπι-
χωρίων. ἐπιμελησόνται δὲ καὶ τῶν ηυπαρχόντων δενδρέων· αἰ δέ
120 τινά κα || γήραι ἢ ἀνέμωι ἐκπέτωντι, αὐτοὶ ηεξόντι. ταῦτα δὲ πάντα
πεφυτευμένα παρηεξόντι καὶ ἐνδε|διωκότα, ηόσσα ἐν τᾶι συνθήκαι
γεγράψαται, ἐν τῶι πέμπτωι καὶ δεκάτωι Fέτει ἀπὸ τῶ ποτεχεῖ
Fέ|τεος ἢ Ἀριστίων ἐφορεύει· αἰ δέ κα μὴ πεφυτεύκωντι κὰτ τὰ
γεγραμμένα, κατεδικάσθεν πὰρ μὲν τὰν | ἐλαίαν δέκα νόμως ἀργυ-

ρίω πὰρ τὸ φυτὸν ἑκαστον, πὰρ δὲ τὰς ἀμπέλως δύο μνᾶς ἀρ-
γυρίω πὰρ τὰν | σχοῖνον ἑκάσταν. τὼς δὲ πολιανόμως τὼς ἐπὶ τῶ
Ϝέτεος ποθελομένως μετ' αὐτοσαυτῶν ἀπὸ τῶ || δάμω μὴ μεῖον ἢ
125 δέκα ἄνδρας ἀμφίστασθαι, ἤ κα πεφυτεύκωντι πάντα κὰτ τὰν συν-
θήκαν, | καὶ τὼς πεφυτευκότας ἀνγράψαι ἐς δόγμα · ἀνγράφεν δὲ
ἡόσσα κα πεφυτεύκωντι · ἂν αὐτὰ δὲ τὰ | καὶ εἴ τινές κα μὴ πεφυ-
τεύκωντι κὰτ τὰν συνθήκαν, ἀνγραψάντω καὶ ἐπελάσθω τὰ ἐπιζά-
μι|α τὰ γεγραμμένα πὸτ τῶι ἄλλωι μισθώματι. αἰ δέ τίς κα ἐπιβῆι
ἢ νέμει ἢ φέρει τι τῶν ἐν τᾶι ἱαρᾶι | γᾶι ἢ τῶν δενδρέων τι κόπτηι
ἢ θραύηι ἢ πριῶι ἢ ἄλλο τι σίνηται, ἡο μεμισθωμένος ἐγδικαξῆ||-
130 ται ἡως πολίστων καὶ ἡότι κα λάβει αὐτὸς ἑξεῖ.

Τὰς δὲ τράφως τὰς διὰ τῶν χώρων ῥεώσας καὶ | τὼς ῥόως οὐ
κατασκαψόντι οὐδὲ διασκαψόντι τῶι ἡύδατι οὐδὲ ἐφερξόντι τὸ ἡύ-
δωρ οὐδ' ἀφερξόν|τι · ἀνκοθαρίοντι δὲ ἡοσσάκις κα δέωνται τὰ πὰρ
τὰ αὐτῶν χωρία ῥέοντα · οὐδὲ τὰς ἡοδὼς τὰς ἀπο|δεδειγμένας ἀρα-
σόντι οὐδὲ συνhερξόντι οὐδὲ κωλυσόντι πορεύεσθαι · ἡότι δέ κα
τούτων τι ποι|ῶντι πὰρ τὰν συνθήκαν, τοὶ πολιανόμοι τοὶ ἀὲς ἐπὶ τῶ
135 Ϝέτεος ἐπικαταβα(λί)οντι καὶ ζαμιωσόντι, || ἄχρι ἡῶ κα ἀφομοιώ-
σωντι κὰτ τὰν συνθήκαν. οὐ κοψεῖ δὲ τῶν δενδρέων οὐδὲ θραυσεῖ
οὐδὲ πριωσεῖ | οὐδὲ ἡῆς οὐδὲ ἡὲν οὐδὲ ἄλλος τήνωι. οὐδὲ γαιῶνας
θησεῖ πὰρ τὼς ἡυπάρχοντας οὐδὲ σαρμευσεῖ, | αἰ μὴ ἡόσσα κα ἐν
αὐτᾶι τᾶι γᾶι ἡᾶι μεμίσθωται οἰκοδόμηται · οὐδὲ τοφιῶνας ἐν τᾶι
ἱαρᾶι γᾶι ποιησεῖ | οὐδὲ ἄλλον ἐασεῖ · αἰ δὲ μή, ἡυπόλογος ἐσσῆ-
ται ἡως τὰν ἱαρὰν γᾶν ἀδικίων. οἰκοδομησῆται δὲ καὶ οἰ|κίαν ἐν
τοῖς χώροις τούτοις, βοῶνα, μυχόν, ἀχύριον, τὸν μὲν βοῶνα τὸ μὲν
140 μᾶκος Ϝίκατι καὶ δυῶν πο||δῶν, τὸ δὲ εὖρος ἡοκτὼ καὶ δέκα ποδῶν,
τὸν δὲ ἀχύριον μὴ μεῖον τὸ μὲν μᾶκος ἡοκτὼ καὶ δέκα ποδῶν, | τὸ
δὲ εὖρος πέντε καὶ δέκα ποδῶν, τὸν δὲ μυχὸν πέντε καὶ δέκα πο-
δῶν πανταῖ. ταῦτα δὲ παρεξόντι οἰκο|δομημένα καὶ στεγόμενα καὶ
τεθυρωμένα ἐν τοῖς χρόνοις ἐν ἡοῖς καὶ τὰ δένδρεα δεῖ πεφυτευκῆ-
μεν · αἰ | δὲ μή, κατεδικάσθεν πὰρ μὲν τὸν βοῶνα Ϝὲξ μνᾶς ἀργυ-
ρίω, πὰρ δὲ τὸν ἀχύριον τέτορας μνᾶς ἀργυρίω, | πὰρ δὲ τὸν μυχὸν
τρὶς μνᾶς ἀργυρίω. τῶν δὲ ξύλων τῶν ἐν τοῖς δρυμοῖς οὐδὲ τῶν ἐν
145 τοῖς σκίροις οὐ πωλη||σόντι οὐδὲ κοψόντι οὐδὲ ἐμπρησόντι οὐδὲ
ἄλλον ἐασόντι · αἰ δὲ μή, ἡυπόλογοι ἐσσόντι κὰτ τὰς ῥήτρας | καὶ
κὰτ τὰν συνθήκαν. ἐς δὲ τὰ ἐποίκια χρησόνται ξύλοις ἐς τὰν οἰκο-
δομὰν ἡοῖς κα δήλωνται, καὶ ἐς τὰς | ἀμπέλως · τῶν δὲ ξηρῶν κο-
ψόντι ἡόσσα αὐτοῖς ποτ' οἰκίαν ἐς χρείαν · τοῖς δὲ σκίροις καὶ τοῖς

δρυμοῖς χρη|σόνται τοὶ μισθωσάμενοι ἀν τὰν αὐτῶ μερίδα ἕκασ-
τος. ὅσσαι δέ κα τᾶν ἀμπέλων ἢ τῶν δενδρέων ἀπο|γηράσωντι,
ἀποκαταοτασόντι τοὶ καρπιζόμενοι ἡως ἦμεν τὸν ἴσον ἀριθμὸν ἀεί.

150 Οὐχ ὑπογραψόνται || δὲ τὼς χώρως τούτως hοι μισθωσάμενοι
οὐδὲ τίμαμα hοισόντι οὔτε τῶν χώρων οὔτε τᾶς ἐπιοικοδο|μᾶς· αἰ
δὲ μή, hυπόλογος ἐσσῆται κὰτ τὰς ῥήτρας. αἰ δέ τίς κα τῶν καρ-
πιζομένων ἄτεκνος ἄφωνος ἀπο|θάνει, τᾶς πόλιος πᾶσαν τὰν ἐπι-
καρπίαν ἦμεν. αἰ δέ χ' ὑπὸ πολέμω ἐγϜηληθίωντι hώστε μὴ
ἐξῆμεν | τὼς μεμισθωμένως καρπεύεσθαι, ἀνheῶσθαι τὰν μίσθωσιν
κατθά κα τοὶ Ηηρακλεῖοι διαγνῶντι, καὶ μὴ | ἦμεν hυπολόγως μήτε
αὐτὼς μήτε τὼς πρωγγύως τῶν ἐν ταῖ συνθήκαι γεγραμμένων.

155 τὼς δὲ πρωγγύ||ως τὼς ἀεὶ γενομένως πεπρωγγευκῆμεν τῶν τε
μισθωμάτων καὶ τῶν ἐπιζαμιωμάτων καὶ τῶν ἀμ|πωλημάτων καὶ
τᾶν καταδικᾶν καὶ αὐτὼς καὶ τὰ χρήματα hά κα ἐπιμαρτυρήσωντι,
καὶ μὴ ἦμεν μήτε hάρ|νησιν μήτε παλινδικίαν μηδὲ κατ' ἄλλον μη-
δὲ hένα τρόπον ταῖ πόλι πράγματα παρέχεν μηδὲ τοῖς hυ|πὲρ τᾶς
πόλιος πρασσόντασσι· αἰ δὲ μή, ἀτελὲς ἦμεν.

Δεύτερος. Ηο δὲ τὸν δεύτερον μισθωσάμενος | καρπευσῆται
ἀπὸ τᾶς τριακονταπέδω τᾶς διὰ τῶν τετρώρων ἀγώσας ἐπὶ τὸν
160 ἄντομον τὸν πρᾶτον hόσ||σος κ' εἶ καὶ πραξεῖ πάντα κὰτ τὰν συν-
θήκαν καὶ hυπόλογος ἐσσῆται καὶ αὐτὸς καὶ τοὶ πρώγγυοι, hότι
κα | μὴ πράξει κὰτ τὰν συνθήκαν.

Τρίτος. Ηο δὲ τὸν τρίτον χῶρον μισθωσάμενος καρπευσῆται
ἀπὸ τῶ ἀν|τόμω τῶ ἀνώτερον τᾶς τριακονταπέδω πὸτ τὸν ἄντομον
τὸν δεύτερον ἀπὸ τᾶς τριακονταπέδω καὶ | πραξεῖ πάντα κὰτ τὰν
συνθήκαν καὶ hυπόλογος ἐσσῆται καὶ αὐτὸς καὶ τοὶ πρώγγυοι,
hότι κα μὴ πρά|ξει κὰτ τὰν συνθήκαν.

Τέταρτος. Ηο δὲ τὸν τέταρτον χῶρον μισθωσάμενος πάρ τε
165 τῶν πολιανό||μων τῶν ἐπὶ Ἀριστίωνος ἐφόρω καὶ τῶν ὀριστᾶν
καὶ πὰρ τῶν πολιανόμων τῶν ἐπὶ Ἀριστάρχω τῶ Ηηρα|κλείδα
ἐφόρω h̄α ἄνθεμα Φιλωνύμω τῶ Φιλωνύμω, h̄α ἔμβολος Ηηρα-
κλείδα τῶ Τιμοκράτιος καρπευ|σῆται ἀπὸ τῶ ἀντόμω τῶ τρίτω
ἀπὸ τᾶς τριακονταπέδω ἐπὶ τὸν ἄντομον τὸν ὀρίζοντα τώς τε τῶ
Διο|νύσω χώρως καὶ τὰ Φιντίας hο Κρατίνω παμωχεῖ. hο δὲ ἀν-
ηελόμενος ἐργαξῆται τὰ μὲν ἄλλα κὰτ τὰν | συνθήκαν, καθὼς κὰτ
τὼς λοιπὼς γέγραπται, τὰς δὲ ἀμπέλως τὰς hυπαρχώσας ἐργα-
170 ξῆται hως βέλτι||στα· ὅσσαι δέ κα τᾶν ἀμπέλων ἀπογηράσκωντι,
ποτιφυτευσεῖ hώστε ἀεὶ hυπάρχεν τὸν ἴσον ἀριθμὸν τᾶν | σχοίνων

τὸν νῦν hυπάρχοντα, Ϝίκατι τέτορας σχοίνως· αἱ δὲ μή, προκαδ-
δεδικάσθω δύο μνᾶς ἀργυρίω | πὰρ τὰν σχοῖνον hεκάσταν. τὰς δὲ
ἐλαίας καὶ τὰς συκίας καὶ τὰ ἄλλα δένδρεα τὰ hήμερα τὰ hυπάρ-
χον|τα πάντα ἐν τᾶι μερίδι ταύται περισκαψεῖ καὶ ποτισκαψεῖ καὶ
περικοψεῖ τὰ δεόμενα, καὶ αἴ τινά κα γήραι ἢ | ἀνέμωι ἐκπέτωντι,
ἀποκαταστασεῖ μὴ μείω τὸν ἀριθμὸν τῶν hυπαρχόντων· ποτιφυ-
175 τευσεῖ δὲ καὶ ἐλαίας || ἐν τᾶι ψιλᾶι hομολόγως ποιῶν τοῖς hυπαρ-
χόντασσι δενδρέοις καὶ τὸν ἀριθμὸν τὸν hίσον καθῶς καὶ ἐν τᾶι | ἄλ-
λαι συνθήκαι γέγραπται. hότι δέ κα μὴ πράξει hο ἀνhελόμενος
κὰτ τὰν συνθήκαν ἢ μὴ ἐν τοῖς χρό|νοις τοῖς γεγραμμένοις, hυπό-
λογος ἐσσῆται τοῖς πολιανόμοις καὶ τοῖς σιταγέρταις τοῖς ἐπὶ τῶ
Ϝέτεος | καθὼς καὶ ἐν τᾶι ἄλλαι συνθήκαι γέγραπται. αἱ δέ κα τοὶ
πολιανόμοι τοὶ ἀεὶ ἐπὶ τῶν Ϝετέων ἔντες μὴ πρά|ξωντι πάντα κὰτ
τὰν συνθήκαν, αὐτοὶ hυπόλογοι ἐσσόνται κὰτ τὰν συνθήκαν.
180 Ἐπὶ τούτοις ἐμισθώσαν||το τὰν μὲν πράταν μίσθωσιν ἀπὸ τῶν
τῶ Ηρώιδα μ̅ε̅ κιβώτιον Βορμίων Φιλώτα πεντήκοντα hεπτὰ
μεδί|μνων κάδδιχος· πρώγγυος τῶ σώματος μ̅ε̅ κιβώτιον Ἀρκὰς
Φιλώτα. τὰν δὲ δευτέραν μίσθωσιν h̅α̅ | ἔμβολος Δάμαρχος Φιλω-
νύμω τετρώκοντα μεδίμνων· πρώγγυος τῶ σώματος . . . . . Θεό-
δωρος Θε|οδώρω. τὰν δὲ τρίταν μίσθωσιν Ϝ̅ε̅ γυῖον Πεισίας Λεον-
τίσκω τριάκοντα πέντε μεδίμνων· πρώγγυος | τῶ σώματος κ̅ν̅
σφαιρωτῆρες Ἀριστόδαμος . . . . . . τὰν δὲ τετάρταν μίσθωσιν
185 α̅λ̅ λωτήριον || Φίλιππος Φιλίππω διακατίων hεβδεμήκοντα hοκτὼ
μεδίμνων· πρώγγυος τῶ σώματος π̅ε̅ καρυκεῖον | Ἀπολλώνιος
Ηρακλήτω.|
Γραμματεὺς Ϝ̅ε̅ γυῖον Ἀριστόδαμος Συμμάχω· γαμέτρας Χαι-
ρέας Δάμωνος Νεαπολίτας.

The lands which were the property of the temples of Dionysus
and Athena Polias having been encroached upon by private
parties, with a consequent diminution of their revenue, two
commissions were appointed to define and mark their boundaries,
survey them, and divide them into lots. Table I contains the
report of the commission dealing with the lands of Dionysus
(ll. 1-94), a statement of the regulations under which the lands
were offered for rental (ll. 95-179), and a list of those who took
leases, with their sureties and the amount of the rental (ll.
179-87). Table II contains a report of the commission on the
lands of Athena Polias.

On the 3 pl. fut. forms, as taken here, κοψόντι, καρπευσόνται, etc., see **141b**.

1-7. The groups of letters and names of objects which precede the name, as Ϝε τρίπους, etc. represent seals marking the tribe and family of the person.—11. **διακνόντων**: = διαγνόντων in table II.9.66.—17. **ἀποροᾶν**: 'watersheds' (?). Schwyzer, Rh.M. 77.225 ff.—18 ff. **ἐρρηγείας** κτλ.: '201 σχοῖνοι of arable land, 646½ of brushwood, barren, and wooded, land.'—38. **νᾶσον**: 'alluvial land' as once an 'island.' Schwyzer, Rh.M. 77.231 ff.— 39. **ἀπολώλη**: 'had been lost,' i.e., by private encroachment. This land the commissioners restored to Dionysus, bringing suits against those who had appropriated it to private use (ll. 47 ff.).—49. **δίκας τριακοσταίας**: 'suits which had to be tried within thirty days.' Cf. no. 57.42 and the Attic δίκαι ἔμμηνοι.—56. 'Setting it (the boundary) back from the springs onto the private land, so that it should not be covered over with stones (which were washed down by the current) and made invisible, like the former boundaries.'—81. **ἇι μὲν . . . ἇι δὲ**: demonst. use of ὅς.—102. **ἀποδίνωντι**: 'thresh.'—104. **φέρει**: for φέρηι. 39. So usually, but also ἐπιβῆι, κόπτηι, θραύηι ll. 138-39, and ἀμμισθωθῆ l. 111.—105 ff. **καὶ αἴ τινί κα ἄλλωι** κτλ.: 'if they assign to another the land which they shall have leased, or devise it by will, or sell the harvest rights, those who take it over or those to whom it has been willed, or those who purchase the harvest rights, shall furnish sureties in the same manner as the one who leased it in the beginning.' — **μεμισθωσῶνται**: fut. perf. subj. 146.5.—108 ff. **hόστις δέ κα μὴ ποτάγει** κτλ.: 'whoever fails to fulfill his obligations shall pay not only double the rental for the year, but also, all together with the first rental, whatever rebate, namely the decrease allowed in re-leasing for the first five years, is determined by decree.' To insure leasing the land again it was generally necessary to offer it at a rental less than that originally fixed. The ἀμπώλημα is the 're-bargaining,' hence concretely the amount involved in it, the 'rebate.' Cf. also ll. 115 ff. 'be surety for the rentals, fines, rebates, and judgments.' hάμα l. 111 seems from its position to go with πᾶν as well as with τῶι πράτωι μισθώματι. For the whole situation, cf. from a Delian inscription, BCH 14.432, ἀνεμισθώσαμεν δὲ καὶ τῆς Χαριτείας τὸ μέρος, ὃ ἐμίσθωτο Μνησίμαχος οὐ καθιστάντος τοὺς ἐγγύους Μνησιμάχου, - - -· τὸ δὲ λοιπόν, ὅσωι ἔλαττον ηὗρεν ἡ γῆ ἀναμισθωθεῖσα, ὀφείλει Μνησίμαχος κτλ.—120. **ἐκπέτωντι**: ἔπετον, aor. of πίπτω, occurs also in Pindar and Alcaeus and is probably the form of all dialects except Attic-Ionic, where ἔπεσον shows a change of τ to σ which does not fall under the usual conditions (**61**) and is not certainly explained.—121. **γεγράψαται** fut. perf. **146**.5.—122. **κατεδικάσθεν**: 'have been condemned,' i.e., are hereby condemned in advance. Cf. προκαδ-δεδικάσθω l. 171.—128. **ἐπιβῆι**: 'trespasses,' from ἐπιβάω == ἐπιβαίνω.—130 ff. **τὰς δὲ τράφως** κτλ.: 'the ditches and canals which run through the lands they shall not dig deeper nor make a breach in for the water, nor shall they dam in or dam off the water.'—ἐφερξόντι, ἀφερξόντι, συνhερξόντι: these belong with Ion. ἀπέργω (Hom. also ἀποέργω), συνέργω, etc. from Ϝέργω, while Att. ἀπείργω etc. are from *ἐϜέργω with prothetic ε. The spiritus asper is found mainly as here, with the forms in ξ, e.g., Att. καθεῖρξα beside κατείργω.—136. **γαιῶνας**: 'mounds of earth.' **165**.4.—**σαρμευσεῖ**: meaning of σαρμεύω uncertain, perhaps 'make pits (storage pits).' Cf. Hesych. σαρμός· σωρὸς γῆς, καὶ κάλλυσμα. ἄλλοι ψάμμον, ἄλλοι χόρτον, and Et.M. σάρμα· χάσμα.—137. οἰκοδόμηται: perf. subj. of the same type as Cret. πέπᾱται (**151**.1). For lack of reduplication, as also in οἰκοδομημένα ll. 112, 141, cf. οἴκημαι etc. in Ionic (Hdt.) and later Attic.—**τοφιῶνας** 'burial places' (so, not 'tufa quarries') 6, **165**.4.—146. **ἐς δὲ τὰ ἐποίκια** κτλ.: 'But they shall use what wood they wish for the construction of the farm buildings,' i.e., the βοών, μυχός, etc.—149 ff. **οὐχ ὑπογραψόνται**: 'the lessees shall not mortgage the lands or make a payment (perhaps 'pay a fine') out of either the lands or the buildings thereon.' Note that when a stop is changed to an aspirate by a following h the latter is not written. So also αἰ δέ χ' ὑπὸ l. 152.

Argolic

80. Mycenae. Sixth century B.C. IG IV.492. Schwyzer 97. Solmsen-Fraenkel 28. Vollgraff, Mnemos. 57.221 f.

Φραhιαρίδας Μυ|κανέαθεν παρ' 'Α|θαναίας ἐς πόλιος|ἱκέτας
5 ἔγεντο || ἐπ' 'Αντία καὶ Πυρ|Fία. εἶεν δὲ 'Αντί|ας καὶ Κίθιος
καἶσχρōν.

Very condensed and variously understood, but perhaps best
(with Vollgraff, l.c.) 'Phrasiaridas of Mycenae, (having been
sent as) a suppliant, arrived from Athena from the citadel in the
magistracy of Antias and Pyrrhias. (The reply?) Let Antias
and Cithius and Aeschron be - - -.' Since the nature of the
request is unknown, the meaning of the reply is obscure.—
ἔγεντο: unthem. form = ἐγένετο, occurring in poets and here
a formulaic expression.

81. Mycenae. Early fifth century B.C. IG IV.493. Schwyzer
98. Solmsen-Fraenkel 29.

Αἰ μὲ̄ δαμιοργία εἴε̄, τὸς ἱαρομνάμονας τὸς ἐς Περσε̄̃ το(ῖ)σι
γονεῦσι κριτε̄̃ρας ἔμεν κὰ τὰ FεFρεμένα.

'If there is no body of demiurgi, the temple administrators
to (the heroum of) Perseus shall judge between the parents
according to what has been decreed.' This is only the conclusion
of an inscription which must have been on the stone which once
rested upon the base containing this line. Pausanias reports a
heroum of Perseus on the road from Mycenae to Argos. It is
probable that boys were employed in the cult and that disputes
arose among the parents with regard to their appointment.

82. Argive Heraeum. Early fifth century B.C. IG IV.517.
Schwyzer 96. Solmsen-Fraenkel 26.

[Η]α στάλα καὶ hο τελαμō | [ἱ]αρὰ τᾶς Ηέρας τᾶς 'Αργε|[ί]ας.
5 ἱαρομνάμονες τοίδε · | ΠυρFαλίōν Δυμὰνς ἀFρέτευε, || 'Αλκαμένēς
Ηυλλεύς, | 'Αριστόδαμος Ηυρνάθιος, | 'Αμφίκριτος Πανφύλ|[λ]ας.

On the face of the stone, just below the inscription, is a rec-
tangular cutting, with dowel holes, evidently intended for the
reception of a tablet. This was the στάλα, while the τελαμō,
properly 'support, pedestal,' refers to the whole stone in which
the στάλα was set, and which would itself be called a στήλη in
Attic. In several inscriptions from the region of the Euxine
τελαμών is actually used as the equivalent of στήλη, e.g., ἀναγρά-
ψαντα τὸ ψάφισμα τοῦτο εἰς τελαμῶνα λευκοῦ λίθου ἀναθέμεν εἰς
τὸ ἱερὸν τοῦ 'Απόλλωνος (GDI 3078, Mesembria). This use is

doubtless of Megarian origin, and is closely allied to that seen here at Argos, though with complete loss of the original notion of 'support.'

The hieromnemones consist of a representative of each of four tribes, of which the Δυμᾶνες, whose representative presides, the Ὑλλεῖς, and the Πάμφυλοι, are the three tribes common to all Doric states, while the Ὑρνάθιοι are attested only for Argolis. Cf. Steph. Byz. s.v. Δυμᾶνες· φυλὴ Δωριέων. ἦσαν δέ τρεῖς, Ὑλλεῖς καὶ Πάμφυλοι καὶ Δυμᾶνες ἐξ Ἡρακλέους. καὶ προσετέθη ἡ Ὑρνηθία, ὡς Ἔφορος α'.

83. Argos. Sixth century B.C. Vollgraff, Mnemos. 57.206 ff. Boissevain, Mnemos. 58.13 ff. Schwyzer, Rh.M. 79.321 ff. Bourguet, Rev. Ét. Gr. 43.13 ff. SEG 11.314.

Ἐπὶ τōνδεōνὲν δαμιοργόντōν τὰ ἐ|[ν] Ἀθαναίας ἐπ[ο]ιϝέθε τα-
δέν· τὰ ποιϝέ|ματα καὶ τὰ χρέματά τε καὶ τὸν ...... | .....
ἀ[νέθεν] ταῖ Ἀθαναίαι ταῖ Πολιάδι. ||

5 Συλεύς τε   τοῖσι χρέμασι τοῖσι χρēστέρ-
   καὶ Ἐράτυιιος   ιίοισι τοῖσι τᾶς θιō μὲ̄ χρέ-
   καὶ Πολύϙτōρ   [σ]θō̄ ϝhεδιέστας [ἐ]χθὸς
   καὶ Ἐξάκεστο[ς]   τō̄ τεμένεος τō̄ τᾶς Ἀ[θαν-]
   καὶ Ηαγι..   [αίας] τᾶς Πολιάδος. δαμόσ-
10 καὶ Ἐρύϙο[ιρος]   ιον δὲ χ[ρ]ōνσθō̄ προ[τὶ τὰ
                          ιαρά]. αἰ δὲ σίναιτο, ἀφ[α]κεσ-
   άσθō̄, hοῖζ δὲ δαμιορ[γὸς ἐπ]α[να]νκασσάτō̄.
   hο δ' ἀμφίπολος μελεταινέτō̄ τούτōν.

'When the following (namely the six listed in ll. 5-10, left column) were demiurgi, these things were made in the temple of Athena. The works and the treasures and the—they dedicated to Athena Polias. Syleus, etc. The treasures that are utensils of the goddess a private citizen shall not use outside the shrine of Athena Polias. But the state may use them for the sacred rites. If anyone injures them he shall make good the damage,— with how much, the demiurgos shall impose. The sacristan shall attend to these matters.'

1, 2. τōνδεōνέν, ταδέν (the latter occurring in another early Arg. inscription): 123.—7. ϝhεδιέστας = ἰδιώτης, formed from *ϝhέδιος beside *ϝhίδιος in Arg. hίδιος, usual ϝίδιος, ἴδιος, after the analogy of τελέστας. Schwyzer, Rh.M. 79.323 ff.—10. **δαμόσιον**: Neut. sg. as collective with plural verb. So (Schwyzer) better than δαμοσίōν partitive gen. pl. (Vollgraff).—12. **hoῖζ δέ**: 97.4.

84. Argos. Sixth or early fifth century B.C. IG IV.554. Schwyzer 78. Solmsen-Fraenkel 24. Vollgraff, Mnemos. 58.29 ff.

[Θ]ε̄σαυρο̄ν [το̄ν] τᾶς 'Αθαναίας αἴ τις <τις> | [ε̃ τὰ]ν βο̄λὰν τ[ὰν] ἀνφ' 'Αρίστο̄να ε̃ τὸν(ς) συναρτύοντας | [ε̃ ἄ]λλον τινὰ ταμίαν εὐθύνοι τέλος ἔχο̄ν ε̃ δικάσ|[ζοι] ε̃ δικάσζοιτο το̄ν γρασσμά-
5 το̄ν hένεχα τᾶς κατα||θέσιος ε̃ τᾶς ἀλιάσσιος, τρέτο̄ καὶ δαμευέσσθο̄ ἐνς | 'Αθαναίαν. ha δὲ βο̄λὰ ποτελάτο̄ hὰντιτυχόνσα· αἰ | δέ κα μέ, αὐτοὶ ἐνόχοι ἔντο̄ ἐνς 'Αθαναίαν.

An act of indemnity for the management of the treasury of Athena, probably with reference to some specific irregularity which had occurred. Without such an act, persons who proposed or put to vote a proposition to use sacred funds for public purposes were liable to punishment. Cf. Thuc. 2.24, 8.15, Tod 51 B 11 ff.

'Concerning the treasures of Athena. If any magistrate calls to account the council under Ariston or his fellow ἀρτῦναι or any treasurer, or entertains or brings suit on account of the submission (to the assembly) of the proposals or on account of the action of the assembly, he shall be banished and his property be confiscated to treasury of Athena. The council which is in office shall enforce (the confiscation), otherwise they (the members of the council) shall themselves be liable to Athena.'

1. [θ]ε̄σαυρο̄ν, κτλ.: gen. of the matter involved. **171.**—Until the existence of a τιστις (cf. Lat. *quisquis*) is corroborated, it is better to assume simple dittography.—2. **συναρτύοντας**: the ἀρτῦναι as a body of Argive officials are mentioned by Thuc. 5.47.11.—3. **τέλος ἔχο̄ν**: cf. El. ὅρ μέγιστον τέλος ἔχοι, no. 61.—
4 ff. **το̄ν γρασσμάτο̄ν hένεχα καταθέσιος** κτλ.: 'on account of the deposition of written proposals (i.e., the formal introduction of a measure before the assembly) or the (consequent) act of the assembly.' This refers to some measure sanctioning the irregular use of the treasure. Those responsible for the introduction or passage of such a measure are to be immune from pro-

secution. For the order of words cf. Thuc. 1.57 τῆς Ποτιδαίας
ἕνεκα ἀποστάσεως. For γράσσμα = γράμμα, see **164**.4.

85. Argos. About 450 B.C. Ditt. Syll. 56. Schwyzer 83. Solmsen-
Fraenkel 27. Tod 33. SEG 11.316. Vollgraff, Verh. Kon. Ned.
Akad. Wet., Afd. Letterk., Nieuwe Reeks, Deel 51, no. 2.
[1, 2 fragmentary. τῶι Τυλισίοι ἐξε͂]μεν ξύλλεσθαι πλὰ[ν]
5 τ|[ὰ μέρε͂ τὰ Κνōσίōν συν]τέλλοντα ἐνς πόλιν. hότ[ι || δέ κα ἐκ
δυσμεν]έōν hέλōμες συνανφότεροι, δα[σ|μō͂ι τō͂ν κὰτ γ]ᾶν τὸ τρίτον
μέρος ἔχεν πάντōν, τ[ō͂|ν δὲ κὰτ] θάλασαν τὰ hέμισα ἔχεν πάντōν.
τὰν δὲ [δ|εκ]άταν τὸνς Κνōσίονς ἔχεν, hότι χ' ἕλōμες κοι[ν|ᾶ]ι.
10 τō͂ν δὲ φαλύρōν τὰ μὲν καλλ(ι)στεῖα Πυθō͂δε ἀπ[ά]||γεν κοινᾶι
ἀμφοτέρονς, τὰ δ' ἄλλα τō͂ι ῎Α[ρει Κνōσ|]ō͂ι ἀντιθέμεν κοινᾶι ἀμφο-
τέρονς. ἐξ[αγō͂γὰν δ' ε͂]|μεν Κνōσόθεν ἐνς Τυλισὸν κὲκ Τυλι[σō͂
Κνōσόνδ]|ε · α[ἰ] δὲ πέρανδε ἐξάγοι, τελίτō hόσσα[περ hοι Κν]|ό-
15 σιοι · τὰ δ' ἐκ Τυλισō͂ ἐξαγέσθω hόπυ[ι κα λε͂ι. τō͂]||ιΠοσειδᾶνι
τō͂ι ἐν 'Ιυτō͂ι τὸν Κνōσίō[ν ἰαρέα θύ]|εν. τᾶι Ἥραι ἐν 'Εραίōι θύεν
βō͂ν θέλει[αν ἀμφοτ]||έρον[ς κ]οινᾶι, θύεν δὲ πρὸ Ϝακινθ[ίōν - - - |
23 [lines 18-22 fragmentary or missing] χρέματα δὲ μὲ 'νπιπασ-
κέσθō ho Κνōσιο[ς] | ἐν Τυλισō͂ι, ho δὲ Τυλίσιος ἐν Κνōσō͂ι ho
25 χρεῖζ[ō]||ν. μεδὲ χόρας ἀποτάμνεσθαι μεδατέρονς μεδ' ἄ[π]||αν-
σαν ἀφαιρῖσθαι. ὅροι τᾶς γᾶς · Ηυō͂ν ὅρος καὶ Α|ιετοὶ κάρταμίτιον
καὶ τὸ τō͂ 'Αρχō͂ τέμενος κα[ὶ] | ho ποταμὸς κὲλ Λευκόπορον κά-
γάθοια, hᾶι hύδō͂|ρ ῥεῖ τō͂μβριον, καὶ Λᾶος. hῖ κα τō͂ι Μαχανεῖ
30 θύōμ||ες τὸνς Ϝεξέκοντα τελέονς ὄϜινς, καὶ τᾶι Ἥραι | τὸ σκέλος
Ϝεκάστō διδόμεν τō͂ Θύματος. αἰ δὲ συ|μπλέονες πόλιες ἐκ πολεμίōν
ἕλοιεν χρέματα, | hόπαι συγνοῖεν hοι Κνōσιοι καὶ τοὶ 'Αργεῖοι, |
35 hούτō ἔμεν. τō͂ι ῎Αρει καὶ τἀφροδίται τὸν Κνōσι||ον ἰαρέα θύεν,
φέρεν δὲ τὸ σκέλος Ϝεκάστō. τὸν 'Α|ρχὸν τὸ τέμενος ἔχεν τὸν
'Αχάρναι. τοῖς θύονσι | ξένια παρέχεν τὸνς Κνōσίονς, τὸνς δ' 'Αρ-
γείōνς τō͂ι χορō͂ι ἐν Τυλισō͂ι. αἴ κα καλε͂ι ho Κνōσιος πρ[ε]σγέαν,
40 hέπεσθαι hόπυι κα δέεται · καί χ' ὁ Τυλίσ||ιος τὸν Κνōσιον, κατὰ
ταὐτά. αἱ δὲ μὲ δοῖεν ξένι|α, βōλὰ ἐπαγέτō ῥύτιον δέκα στατέρōν
αὐτίκα ἐ|πὶ κόσμος, κὲν Τυλισō͂ι κατὰ ταὐτά ho Κνōσιος. hα στάλα
ἔσστα ἐπὶ Μελάντα βασιλέος. ἀϜρέτευ|ε Λυκοτάδας Ηυλλεύς. ἀλι-
45 αίαι ἔδοξε τᾶι τōν || ἰαρōν. ἀ(Ϝ)ρέτευε βōλᾶς 'Αρχίστρατος Λυκο-
φρονίδας. | τοὶ Τυλίσιοι ποὶ τὰν στάλαν ποιγραψάνσθō τάδε · | αἴ
τις ἀφικνοῖτο Τυλισίōν ἐνς ῎Αργος, κατὰ ταὐτά | σφιν ἔστō hαιπερ
Κνōσίοις.

Treaty between the Cretan cities of Cnossus and Tylissus arranged under the auspices of Argos, which was regarded as the mother state. It was no doubt Tylissus which had appealed to Argos for support in safeguarding its independence against its powerful neighbor, and it is in favor of the weaker party that certain articles are framed (cf. ll. 14, 22 ff.) and Argive support granted (cf. ll. 37-38).

This is the official Argive draft, in the Argive alphabet and in the main in the Argive dialect. Only the characteristic Argive *h* = intervocalic σ is eliminated, not only in the Cretan name Κνόσιος (but cf. Κνōhίαν in the draft at Tylissus), but in βασιλέος of the dating (l. 43). Cf. **59.**2, **275.** There is a trace of the influence of preliminary Cretan in l. 33 hοι Κνόσιοι καὶ τοὶ ᾿Αργεῖοι (Cret. οἱ, Arg. τοί, **122**).

A fragment found at Tylissus, containing another section of the same treaty (Schwyzer 84, revised text by Vollgraff, l.c.), is also in the Argive alphabet (⌐ = λ, ↳ = β, ⊟ = *h*, but once = η as in Cretan) and dialect, even having the Argive *h* = intervocalic σ, e.g., Κνōhίαν. The use of δυσμενέες for 'enemies,' which in literature is mainly poetical, is seen in both these inscriptions, and may be another Cretan element (cf. Law-Code VI.46), though not necessarily so. Likewise τέλλω =τελέω (l. 4, but τελῖτō l. 13), as in Law-Code X.42 etc.

3. **ξύλλεσθαι**: σκύλλεσθαι 'plunder.' **87.**—6 ff. Tylissus, being the party last named and the smaller of the two cities, is to be understood as the subject of ἔχεν. —9. **φαλύρōν**: λαφύρων. **88.**— 13. **τελῖτō**: τελείτω, cf. ἀφαιρῖσθαι l. 25, and **25c.**—17. **πρὸ Fαχινθίōν**: before the festival ῾Υακίνθια. **52c.**—23 ff. 'The citizen of Cnossus may not acquire property in Tylissus, but any citizen of Tylissus who wishes may do so in Cnossus. Neither partly shall detach any part of the other's land or take it all away.' Both provisions are obviously for the protection of Tylissus. —**ἐνπιπασκέσθō**: **162.**12.—28. **κἐλ Λ-**: καὶ ἐς Λ-, with crasis and assimilation (**97.**3).—28-29. 'where the rain-water flows, the torrent.'—29. **hī**: **25c.**—30. **Ηέραι**: written ⊟ΡΑΙ; cf. **4.**6.—36. **τὸν**: τὸ ἐν (**94.**2).—38 ff. 'If the Cnossian summon an embassy, (the Tylissian) shall conform for whatever purpose when it is required, and if the Tylissian (summons) the Cnossian,

he shall do likewise.'—39. καί χ' ὁ: καὶ αἴ κα ὁ.—41. 'The council shall impose upon the κόσμοι a pledge of ten staters.'— 44-45. The document originally closed in l. 44, with the official Argive dating. The rest, beginning ἀλιαίαι, is added in another hand, and with a later dating, and empowers the Tylissians to attach the provision of equal privileges with the Cnossians in visiting Argos. ποιγραψάνσθō: 140.3*b*.

86. Cimolos. Fourth century B.C. IG XII.iii.1259. GDI 3277. Schwyzer 85. Ditt. Syll. 261.

Θεός. | Ἔκρινε ὁ δᾶμος ὁ τῶν | Ἀργείων κατὰ τὸ δόκη|μα τοῦ
5 συνεδρίου τῶν || Ἑλλάνων, ὁμολογη|σάντων Μα[λ]ίων καὶ | Κιμωλίων ἐμμενὲν | ἆι κα δικάσσαιεν τοὶ | Ἀργεῖοι π[ε]ρὶ τᾶν ||
10 [ν]άσων, Κιμωλίων | ἦμεν Πολύαιγαν, Ἐτη|ρείαν, Λιβείαν. ἐδί-|κασσαν νικῆν Κιμωλί|[ο]υς. ἀρήτευε Λέων || [β]ωλᾶς σευτέρας,
15 Ποσίδα|ον γρο[φ]εὺς βωλᾶς, Πέριλ|λος Πεδίον.

Decision of the Argives in a dispute between Melos and Cimolos.—15. σευτέρας: δευτέρας. 97.4.—Ποσίδαον, Πεδίον: names of demes.

87. Argos. Third century B.C. Schwyzer 89.

Θεός. Πομάντιες ἀνέθεν | Ἀπόλλωνι Ἀρισ[τ]εὺς Σφυρή|δας,
5 Φιλοκράτης Νατελιά|δας, γροφέ[ες] Αἰσχύλος Ἀραχνά||δας, Τρύγης Αἰθωνίδας, καὶ κα|τεσκεύασσαν καὶ [ἤ]σσαντο [θείας] | ἐκ μαντήας γᾶς ὀμφαλὸν καὶ τ[ὰ]|ν περίσταιν καὶ τὸ φάργμα καὶ
10 τὸν | βωμὸν προ[άγαγ]ον ποτ' ἀ[F]ῶ καὶ πέτ||τρινον ῥόον καὶ τὰν ἀ....ραν | ὑπὲρ αὐτοῦ, καὶ θηαυρὸν ἐν τῶι μαν|τήωι κατεσκεύασσαν τοῖς πελα|νοῖς κλαικτόν, καὶ τὰν ὁδὸν ἠργάσ|σαντο ἅπανσαν
15 καὶ ὀφρύαν πεδ' ἱα||ρὸν καὶ τὰν ἐπιπολάν, καὶ τοὺς βω|μὸς ἐνς τάξιν πεδάγαγον καὶ τ[ὸν]|ς κολοσσόνς, καὶ τὰν ἐπιπολὰν ὠ[μά]-|λιξαν, καὶ τοῖχον [π]έτρινον πὰρ τὸ[ν] | - - - ἔθεν καὶ τὰνς θ[ύ-
20 ρα]νς τοῦ ναοῦ || ὠχύρωαν, [καὶ] λο[π]ίδας καὶ ἐπιχύ|[τ]αν ἀργυρέα ἔθεν καὶ θηαυρὸν ἐνς ἐ|[π]ο[ή]αντο [remainder fragmentary].

From the temple of the Pythian Apollo mentioned by Paus. 2.24.

2 ff. Σφυρήδας, Νατελιάδας, etc.: designations of the phratry or gens.—6 ff. 'Have had made and put in place, in accor-

dance with the divine oracle, the Omphalus of the Earth, the colonnade, the enclosing wall, have moved the altar to the east, have had made a stone conduit and the ... above it, and in the oracle chamber a treasury, which can be locked, for the monetary offerings; have constructed all the road, the ramp leading to the shrine, and the surface area; have rearranged the altars and the colossi, have leveled the surface, built a stone wall by the ..., strengthened the doors of the temple, and dedicated cups and a silver beaker.'—12/13. **πελανοῖς**: cf. no. 1 A 25 ff., note.—14. **ὀφρύαν**: here 'ramp.' Cf. the use of ὀφρύς for 'embarkment', etc.

88. Troezen. Early second century B.C. IG IV.752 and p. 381. Nikitskij, Hermes 38.406 ff. Schwyzer 104.

Εἰ δὲ δικάσαιτο, ἀποτεισάτω εἰ μὲν ἰδιώτας χιλίας δραχ[μάς],
5 εἰ δ[ὲ πόλις]‖ μυρίας, καὶ ἀ δίκα ἀτελὴς ἔστω. περὶ δὲ τῶν ἐρρυτι-
ασμένων ὑπὸ τᾶς πό|λιος ἢ ἀγμένων ἀπὸ τᾶς χώρας ἐν ταῖς ἀνε-
πιβασίαις· ἀπὸ τᾶγ κοινᾶ[ν] | πο[θ]όδων τᾶν ἐκ τῶν θυννείων
ἐπιλυθῆμεν τοὺς ἐρρυτιασμένους | στάσι ἀν' ὅ κα φέρηι ὁ λόγος
ὁ ταμία Φιλοκλέος, καὶ τοῖς σώμασιν τοῖς | ἀποπραχθεῖσιν ἀπὸ
10 τῶν πολεμάρχων, Ἀρτεμιδώρωι, Πύρρωι Θεο‖δότωι, ἑκάστωι
δραχμὰς διακοσίας ἂν Τροζάνιοι νομίζοντι, καὶ τὰ | χωρία καὶ τὰς
οἰκίας ὅσσα ἐστὶ ἐρρυτιασμένα ὑπὸ τᾶς πόλιος ἀποδό|μεν τοῖς ἐρρυ-
τιασμένοις, ἐπιλύσαντας ἀπὸ τᾶγ κοινᾶν ποθόδων τοῖς | πεπεμμένοις
τι τῶν ἐρρυτιασμένων ὑπὸ τᾶς πόλιος. τὰς δ' ἐπιγαμίας | καὶ τὰς
ἐγκτάσεις ὑπάρχειν ἑκατέροις ποτ' ἀλλάλους εἰς ἅπαντα τὸ[ν ‖
15 χρόνον. ὅπ]ως δὲ τὰ συμφωνηθέντα κύρια ἦι. ἀποσ[τ]ειλάντω
πρεσβείας [ἀμφότ]εροι εἰς Ἀθάνας καὶ ἀξιούντω δόμεν αὐτοῖς
ἄνδρας τρεῖς, οἵτι[ν]ες π[α|ραγ]ενόμεν[οι] τὰ γεγονότα αὐτοῖς
ὁμόλογα ἐπικρίναντες ἀνα[θη]σοῦντ[αι| ἐν σ]τ[άλ]αις εἰς τὰ ἱερὰ
τό τε ἐγ Κα[λα]υ[ρείαι τ]οῦ Ποσειδᾶνος [καὶ τὸ ἐν Ἐπι|δ]α[ύ]-
ρ[ω]ι το[ῦ] Ἀσκλαπίου καὶ τὸ ἐν [Ἀθάναις] ἐν [ἀκ]ρο[π]όλει
τ[ᾶ]ς [Ἀθάνα]ς.

Agreement by Troezen with another city, probably Hermione, in settlement of previous reprisals and certain other matters. A part of the copy ordered set up at Epidaurus (l. 19) has been found there (IG IV.²i.77). Influence of the κοινή appears in the numerals διακόσιοι, χίλιοι, acc. pl. τρεῖς, and the use of σῶμα

as 'person' (as in papyri).—6. ἀνεπιβασία 'prohibition of traffic.'
—ἀπὸ τᾶγ κοινᾶν κτλ.: 'from the common proceeds of the
tunny-fisheries those who have suffered by reprisal shall be
recompensed by payment according to the account of the treasurer;
and to those persons who were sold out by the polemarchs to
each shall be given 200 drachmas in the coinage of Troezen.'—
13. πεπεμμένοις: 'to those who have worked on,' that is 'cultivated' any of the lands seized, from πένομαι (86.8).

89. Epidaurus. End of fifth century B.C. IG IV.²i.40/41.
Ditt. Syll. 998. Schwyzer 108. Solmsen-Fraenkel 31. Alphabet
transitional (form of the letters mostly Ionic, but ꓐ = h, never η,
no Ω, gen. sg. O and OV).

[Τõι 'Απόλλōνι θύεν βõν ἔ|ρσενα καὶ hομονάοις βõ|ν ἔρσενα·
5 ἐπὶ τõ βōμοῦ τõ] | 'Απόλλō[νος] τα[ῦτα] θ[ύεν κ]||αὶ καλαῖδα τᾶι
Λατοῖ κα|ὶ τάρτάμιτι ἄλλαν, φερν|ὰν τõι θιõι κριθᾶν μέδι|μμνον,
10 σπυρõν hēμίδιμμ|νον, οἴνου hēμίτειαν κα||ὶ τὸ σσκέλος τοῦ βοὸς
το|ῦ πράτου, τὸ δ' ἄτερον σκέ|λος τοὶ ιαρομμνάμονες | φερόσθō·
15 τοῦ δευτέρου β|οὸς τοῖς ἀοιδοῖς δόντō || τὸ σκέλος, τὸ δ' ἄτερον
σκ|έλος τοῖς φρουροῖς δόν|τō καὶ τἐνδοσθίδια. |
20 Τõι 'Ασσκλαπιõι θύεν βõ|ν ἔρσενα καὶ hομονάοις || βõν ἔρσενα
καὶ hομονάα|ις βõν θέλειαν· ἐπὶ τοῦ β|õμοῦ τοῦ 'Ασκλαπιοῦ θύε|ν
25 ταῦτα καὶ καλαῖδα. ἀνθ|έντō τõι 'Ασκλαπιõι φερ||ὰν κριθᾶν μέ-
διμνον, σ|πυρõν hēμίδιμμνον, οἴν|ου hēμίτειαν· σκέλος τõ | πρά-
30 του βοὸς παρθέντō τ|[õι] θιõι, τὸ δ' ἄτερον τοὶ ι||[αρο]μνάμονες
φ[ε]ρόσθō· τ|[οῦ δε]υτέρō τοῖς ἀοιδοῖ|[ς δόντō,] τὸ δ' ἄτερον
το[ῖς | φρουροῖς δόντō καὶ τἐν|δοσθίδια.]

Regulations for sacrifices in the Asclepieum. For the frequent
doubling of consonants see 89.2, 101.2. For φερόσθō see 140.3b.—
καλαῖς: 'hen' (from καλαϝίς, cf. καλέω 'call,' like Eng. hen to
Lat. cano).—φερνά: here the gods' 'portion.'

90. Epidaurus. Late fourth century B.C. IG IV.²i.121. GDI
3339. Ditt. Syll. 1168. Herzog, Die Wunderheilungen von
Epidaurus (Philol. Supplementband 22).

Θεός. Τύχα [ἀγ]αθά. | ['Ιά]ματα τοῦ 'Απόλλωνος καὶ τοῦ
'Ασκλαπιοῦ. |
[Κλ]εὼ πένθ' ἔτη ἐκύησε. αὖτα πέντ' ἐνιαυτοὺς ἤδη κυοῦσα ποὶ
τὸν | [θε]ὸν ἱκέτις ἀφίκετο καὶ ἐνεκάθευδε ἐν τῶι ἀβάτωι. ὡς δὲ

5 τάχισ||[τα] ἐξῆλθε ἐξ αὑτοῦ καὶ ἐκ τοῦ ἱαροῦ ἐγένετο, κόρον ἔτεκε,
ὃς εὐ|[θ]ὺς γενόμενος αὐτὸς ἀπὸ τᾶς κράνας ἐλοῦτο καὶ ἅμα τᾶι
ματρὶ | [π]εριῆρπε. τυχοῦσα δὲ τούτων ἐπὶ τὸ ἄνθεμα [ἐ]πεγρά-
ψατο · "οὐ μέγε|[θο]ς πίνακος θαυμαστέον, ἀλλὰ τὸ θεῖον, πένθ'
ἔτη ὡς ἐκύησε ἐγ γασ|[τρ]ὶ Κλεὼ βάρος, ἔστε | ἐγκατεκοιμάθη, καί
10 μιν ἔθηκε ὑγιῆ."—Τριετὴς ||[φο]ρά. Ἰθμονίκα Πελλανὶς ἀφίκετο
εἰς τὸ ἱαρὸν ὑπὲρ γενεᾶς. ἐγ|[κοι]μαθεῖσα δὲ ὄψιν εἶδε · ἐδόκει αἰ-
τεῖσθαι τὸν θεὸν κυῆσαι κό|[ραν], τὸν δ' Ἀσκλαπιὸν φάμεν ἔγκυον
ἐσσεῖσθαι νιν καί, εἴ τι ἄλλο | α[ἰτ]οῖτο, καὶ τοῦτό οἱ ἐπιτελεῖν,
αὐτὰ δ' οὐθενὸς φάμεν ἔτι ποι|δ[εῖ]σθαι · ἔγκυος δὲ γενομένα ἐγ
15 γαστρὶ ἐφόρει τρία ἔτη, ἔστε πα||ρέβαλε ποὶ τὸν θεὸν ἱκέτις ὑπὲρ
τοῦ τόκου. ἐγκατακοιμαθεῖσα | δὲ ὄψ[ι]ν εἶδε · ἐδόκει ἐπερωτῆν νιν
τὸν θεόν, εἰ οὐ γένοιτο αὐτᾶι | πάντ[α] ὅσσα αἰτήσαιτο καὶ ἔγκυος
εἴη, ὑπὲρ δὲ τόκου ποιθέμεν | νιν οὐθέν, καὶ ταῦτα πυνθανομένου
αὐτοῦ, εἴ τινος καὶ ἄλλου δέ|οιτ[ο], λέγειν, ὡς ποιησοῦντος καὶ
20 τοῦτο · ἐπεὶ δὲ νῦν ὑπὲρ τούτου || παρείη ποτ' αὐτὸν ἱκέτις, καὶ τοῦ-
τό οἱ φάμεν ἐπιτελεῖν. μετὰ δὲ | τοῦτο σπουδᾶι ἐκ τοῦ ἀβάτου
ἐξελθοῦσα, ὡς ἔξω τοῦ ἱαροῦ ἦς, ἔτε|κε κό[ρ]αν.—Ἀνὴρ τοὺς τᾶς
·χηρὸς δακτύλους ἀκρατεῖς ἔχων πλὰν | ἑνὸς ἀ[φ]ίκετο ποὶ τὸν θεὸν
ἱκέτας. θεωρῶν δὲ τοὺς ἐν τῷ ἱαρῶι | [π]ίνακας ἀπίστει τοῖς ἰάμα-
25 σιν καὶ ὑποδιέσυρε τὰ ἐπιγράμμα||[τ]α. ἐγκαθεύδων δὲ ὄψιν εἶδε ·
ἐδόκει ὑπὸ τῶι ναῶι ἀστραγαλίζον|[τ]ος αὐτοῦ καὶ μέλλοντος βάλ-
λειν τῶι ἀστραγάλωι ἐπιφανέντα | [τ]ὸν θεὸν ἐφαλέσθαι ἐπὶ τὰν
χῆρα καὶ ἐκτεῖναί οὐ τοὺς δακτύλ|λους, ὡς δ' ἀποβαίη, δοκεῖν συγ-
κάμψας τὰν χῆρα καθ' ἕνα ἐκτείνειν | [τ]ῶν δακτύλων, ἐπεὶ δὲ
30 πάντας ἐξευθύναι, ἐπερωτῆν νιν τὸν θεὸν || [ε]ἰ ἔτι ἀπιστησοῖ τοῖς
ἐπιγράμμασι τοῖς ἐπὶ τῶμ πινάκων τῶν | [χ]ατὰ τὸ [ἱ]ερόν, αὐτὸς
δ' οὐ φάμεν · "ὅτι τοίνυν ἔμπροσθεν ἀπίστεις | [α]ὐτο[ῖ]ς ο[ὐκ]
ἐοῦσιν ἀπίστοις, τὸ λοιπὸν ἔστω τοι" φάμεν '"Ἄπιστος | ὄ[νομα]."
ἀμέρας δὲ γενομένας ὑγιὴς ἐξῆλθε.—Ἀμβροσία ἐξ Ἀθανᾶν | [ἀτε-
ρό]πτ[ι]λλος. αὕτα ἱκέτ[ις] ἦλθε ποὶ τὸν θεόν. περιέρπουσα δὲ ||
35 [κατὰ τ]ὸ [ἱα]ρὸν τῶν ἱαμάτων τινὰ διεγέλα ὡς ἀπίθανα καὶ ἀδύ-
να|[τα ἐόν]τα χωλοὺς καὶ τυφλοὺς ὑγιεῖς γίνεσθαι ἐνύπνιον ἰδόν-|
[τας μό]νον. ἐγκαθεύδουσα δὲ ὄψιν εἶδε · ἐδόκει οἱ ὁ θεὸς ἐπιστάς |
[εἰπεῖν] ὅτ[ι] ὑγιῆ μέν νιν ποιησοῖ, μισθὸμ μάντοι νιν δεησοῖ ἀν|-
40 [θέμεν ε]ἰς τὸ ἱαρὸν ὗν ἀργύρεον, ὑπόμναμα τᾶς ἀμαθίας · εἴπαν-||
[τα δὲ ταῦτα] ἀνσχίσσαι οὐ τὸν ὀπτίλλον τὸν νοσοῦντα καὶ φάρμ[α|
κόν τι ἐγχέ]αι. ἀμέρας δὲ γενομένας [ὑ]γιὴς ἐξῆλθε.—Παῖς ἄφω-

νος. | [οὗτος ἀφίκ]ετο εἰς τὸ ἱαρὸν ὑ[πὲ]ρ φωνᾶς. ὡς δὲ προεθύσα-
το καὶ | [ἐπόησε τὰ] νομιζόμενα, μετὰ τοῦτο ὁ παῖς ὁ τῶι θεῶι πυρ-
φορῶν | [ἐκέλετο, πο]ὶ τὸμ πατέρα τὸν τοῦ παιδὸς ποτιβλέψας,
45 ὑποδέκεσ||[σθαι αὐτὸν ἐ]νιαυτοῦ, τυχόντα ἐφ' ἃ πάρεστι, ἀποθυ-
σεῖν τὰ ἴατρα · | [ὁ δὲ παῖς ἐξ]απίνας "ὑποδέκομαι" ἔφα. ὁ δὲ πα-
τὴρ ἐκπλαγεὶς πάλιν | [ἐκέλετο αὐτ]ὸν εἰπεῖν. ὁ δ' ἔλεγε πάλιν καὶ
ἐκ τούτου ὑγιὴς ἐγέ||[νετο.—Πάνδαρ]ος Θεσσαλὸς στίγματα ἔχων
ἐν τῶι μετώπωι. οὗτος | [ἐγκαθεύδων ὄψ]ιν εἶδε · ἐδόκει αὐτοῦ
50 τ[αι]νίαι καταδῆσαι τὰ στί||[γματα ὁ θεὸς κα]ὶ κέλεσθαι νιν, ἐπεί
[κα ἔξω] γένηται τοῦ ἀβάτου, | [ἀφελόμενον τὰν] ταινίαν ἀνθέμ[εν
εἰς τ]ὸν ναόν. ἁμέρας δὲ γενο|[μένας, ἐξανέστα] καὶ ἀφήλετο τὰ[ν
ται]νίαν καὶ τὸ μὲν πρόσωπον | [ἐκεκάθαρτο τῶ]ν στιγμάτ[ων,
τ]ὰν δ[ὲ τ]αινίαν ἀνέθηκε εἰς τὸν να|[ὸν ἔχουσαν τὰ γρ]άμματ[α]
55 τὰ ἐκ τοῦ μετώπου.—Ἐχέδωρος τὰ Πανδά||[ρου στίγματα ἔλ]αβε
ποὶ τοῖς ὑπάρχουσιν. οὗτος λαβὼν πὰρ [Παν|δάρου χρήματα],
ὥστ' ἀνθέμεν τῶι θεῶι εἰς Ἐπίδαυρον ὑπὲρ αὐ[τοῦ, | οὐκ] ἀπεδίδου
ταῦτα. ἐγκαθεύδων δὲ ὄψιν εἶδε ·ἐδ όκει οἱ ὁ θε[ὸς] | ἐπιστὰς ἐπερω-
τῆν νιν, εἰ ἔχοι τινὰ χρήματα πὰρ Πανδάρου ἐ[ξ Ἀ]|θηνᾶν ἄνθεμα
60 εἰς τὸ ἱαρὸν, αὐτὸς δ' οὐ φάμεν λελαβήκειν οὐθὲ[ν] || τοιοῦτον πὰρ
αὐτοῦ, ἀλλ' αἴ κα ὑγιῆ νιν ποιήσαι, ἀνθησεῖν οἱ εἰκό|να γραψάμενος·
μετὰ δὲ τοῦτο τὸν θεὸν τὰν τοῦ Πανδάρου ταινί|αν περιδῆσαι περὶ
τὰ στίγματά οὗ καὶ κέλεσθαί νιν, ἐπεί κα ἐξ|έλθηι ἐκ τοῦ ἀβάτου,
ἀφελόμενον τὰν ταινίαν ἀπονίψασθαι τὸ | πρόσωπον ἀπὸ τᾶς κρά-
65 νας καὶ ἐγκατοπτρίξασθαι εἰς τὸ ὕδωρ. ἁ||μέρας δὲ γενομένας
ἐξελθὼν ἐκ τοῦ ἀβάτου τὰν ταινίαν ἀφήλετο | τὰ γράματα οὐκ
ἔχουσαν, ἐγκαθιδὼν δὲ εἰς τὸ ὕδωρ ἑώρη τὸ αὐτοῦ | πρόσωπον ποὶ
τοῖς ἰδίοις στίγμασιν καὶ τὰ τοῦ Πανδάρου γρά|ματα λελαβηκός.—
Εὐφάνης Ἐπιδαύριος παῖς. οὗτος λιθιῶν ἐνε[κά]|θευδε · ἔδοξε δὴ
70 αὐτῶι ὁ θεὸς ἐπιστὰς εἰπεῖν · "τί μοι δωσεῖς, αἴ τ[ύ]||κα ὑγιῆ
ποιήσω;" αὐτὸς δὲ φάμεν "δέκ' ἀστραγάλους", τὸν δὲ θεὸν γελά-|
σαντα φάμεν νιν παυσεῖν. ἁμέρας δὲ γενομένας ὑγιὴς ἐξῆλθε.— |
Ἀνὴρ ἀφίκετο ποὶ τὸν θεὸν ἱκέτας ἀτερόπτιλος οὕτως, ὥστε τὰ |
βλέφαρα μόνον ἔχειν, ἐνεῖμεν δ' ἐν αὐτοῖς μηθέν, ἀλλὰ κενεὰ εἶ|μεν
ὅλως. ἔλεγον δή τινες τῶν ἐν τῶι ἱαρῶι τὰν εὐηθίαν αὐτοῦ τὸ ||
75 νομίζειν βλεψεῖσθαι ὅλως μηδεμίαν ὑπαρχὰν ἔχοντος ὀπτίλ|λου, |
ἀλλ' ἢ χώραμ μόνον. ἐγκαθ[εύδον]τι οὖν αὐτῶι ὄψις ἐφάνη · ἐδό-
κει τὸν θεὸν ἑψῆσαί τι φά[ρμακον, ἔπε]ιτα διαγαγόντα τὰ βλέφα|ρα
ἐγχέαι εἰς αὐτά. ἁμέρ[ας δὲ γενομέν]ας β(λ)έπων ἀμφοῖν ἐξῆλθε.

—Κώθων. σκευοφόρος εἰ[ς τὸ] ἰαρ[ὸν ἀνιών], ἐπεὶ ἐγένετο περὶ
80 τὸ δε‖καστάδιον, κατέπ[ε]τε. [ὡς δ᾽ ἀ]νέστα, ἀνῶιξε τὸγ γυλιὸν
κα[ὶ ἐ]πεσκό|πει τὰ συντετριμμένα σ[κε]ύη. ὡς δ᾽ εἶδε τὸγ κώθω-
να κατε[αγ]ότα, | ἐξ οὗ ὁ δεσπότας εἴθιστ[ο π]ίνειν, ἐλυπεῖτο καὶ
συνετίθει [τὰ] ὄ|στρακα καθιζόμενος. ὁδοιπόρος οὖν τις ἰδὼν αὐ-
τόν, "τί, ὦ ἄθλι᾽," ἔ|φα, "συντίθησι τὸγ κώθωνα [μά]ταν; τοῦτον
85 γὰρ οὐδέ κα ὁ ἐν Ἐπιδαύ‖ρωι Ἀσκλαπιὸς ὑγιῆ ποιῆσαι δύναιτο."
ἀκούσας ταῦτα ὁ παῖς, συν|θεὶς τὰ ὄστρακα εἰς τὸγ γυλιόν, ἧρπε
εἰς τὸ ἱερόν. ἐπεὶ δ᾽ ἀφίκε|το, ἀνῶιξε τὸγ γυλιὸν καὶ ἐξᾶιρεν ὑγιῆ
τὸγ κώθωνα γεγενημέ|νον, καὶ τῶι δεσπόται ἡρμάνευσε τὰ πραχ-
θέντα καὶ λεχθέντα. ὡ|ς δὲ ἄκουσ᾽, ἀνέθηκε τῶι θεῶι τὸγ κώθωνα.
90 — ‖ Αἰσχίνας ἐγκεκοιμισμένων ἤδη τῶν ἱκετᾶν ἐπὶ δένδρεόν τι
ἀμ|βὰς ὑπερέκυπτε εἰς τὸ ἄβατον. καταπετῶν οὖν ἀπὸ τοῦ δέν-
δρεος | περὶ σκόλοπάς τινας τοὺς ὀπτίλλους ἀμφέπαισε. κακῶς δὲ
δια|κείμενος καὶ τυφλὸς γεγενημένος καθικετεύσας τὸν θεὸν ἐν-|
95 εκάθευδε· καὶ ὑγιὴς ἐγένετο. — ‖ Εὔιππος λόγχαν ἔτη ἐφόρησε
ἓξ ἐν τᾶι γνάθωι. ἐγκοιτασθέντος | δ᾽ αὐτοῦ ἐξελὼν τὰν λόγχαν ὁ
θεὸς εἰς τὰς χῆράς οἱ ἔδωκε. ἀμέρας | δὲ γενομένας ὑγιὴς ἐξῆρπε
τὰν λόγχαν ἐν ταῖς χερσὶν ἔχων. — | Ἀνὴρ Τορωναῖος δεμελέας.
οὗτος ἐγκαθεύδων ἐνύπνιον εἶδε· | ἐδοξέ οἱ τὸν θεὸν τὰ στέρνα
100 μαχαίραι ἀνσχίσσαντα τὰς δεμε‖λέας ἐξελεῖν καὶ δόμεν οἱ ἐς τὰς
χεῖρας | καὶ συνράψαι τὰ στή|θη. ἀμέρας δὲ γενομένας ἐξῆλθε τὰ
θηρία ἐν ταῖς χερσὶν ἔχων | καὶ ὑγιὴς ἐγένετο. κατέπιε δ᾽ αὐτὰ
δολωθεὶς ὑπὸ ματρυιᾶς ἐγ κυ|κᾶνι ἐμβεβλημένας ἐκπιών. — |
Ἀνὴρ ἐν αἰδοίωι λίθον. οὗτος ἐνύπνιον εἶδε· ἐδόκει παιδὶ καλῶι ‖
105 συγγίνεσθαι. ἐξονειρώσσων δὲ τὸλ λίθον ἐγβάλλει καὶ ἀνελόμε|νος
ἐξῆλθεν ταῖς χερσὶν ἔχων.— | Ἑρμόδικος Λαμψακηνὸς ἀκρατὴς τοῦ
σώματος. τοῦτον ἐγκαθεύ|δοντα ἰάσατο καὶ ἐκελήσατο ἐξελθόντα
λίθον ἐνεγκεῖν εἰς τὸ | ἰαρὸν ὁπόσσον δύναιτο μέγισ[τ]ον. ὁ δὲ τὸμ
110 πρὸ τοῦ ἀβάτου κείμε‖νον ἤνικε.— | Νικάνωρ χωλός. τούτου καθ-
ημένου παῖς [τ]ις ὕπαρ τὸν σκίπωνα ἁρ|πάξας ἔφευγε. ὁ δὲ ἀστὰς
ἐδίωκε καὶ ἐκ τούτου ὑγιὴς ἐγένετο.— | Ἀνὴρ δάκτυλον ἰάθη ὑπὸ
ὄφιος. οὗτος τὸν τοῦ ποδὸς δάκτυλον ὑ|πό του ἀγρίου ἕλκεος δει-
115 νῶς διακείμενος μεθάμερα ὑπὸ τῶν θε‖ραπόντων ἐξενειχθεὶς ἐπὶ
ἑδράματός τινος καθῖζε. ὕπνου δέ νιν | λαβόντος ἐν τούτωι δράκων
ἐκ τοῦ ἀβάτου ἐξελθὼν τὸν δάκτυλον | ἰάσατο τᾶι γλώσσαι καὶ
τοῦτο ποιήσας εἰς τὸ ἄβατον ἀνεχώρησε | πάλιν. ἐξεγερθεὶς δέ, ὡς
ἧς ὑγιής, ἔφα ὄψιν ἰδεῖν, δοκεῖν νεανίσ|κον εὐπρεπῆ τὰμ μορφὰν

120 ἐπὶ τὸν δάκτυλον ἐπιπῆν φάρμακον.— ||'Αλκέτας 'Αλικός. οὗτος
τυφλὸς ἐὼν ἐνύπνιον εἶδε · ἐδόκει ὁ θεὸς ποτελθὼν τοῖς δα|κτύλοις
διάγειν τὰ ὄμματα, καὶ ἰδεῖν τὰ δένδρη πρᾶτον τὰ ἐν τῶι ἱαρῶι.
ἀμέρας δὲ γε|νομένας ὑγιὴς ἐξῆλθε.—'Ηραιεὺς Μυτιληναῖος. οὗτος
οὐκ εἶχεν ἐν τᾶι κεφαλᾶι | τρίχας, ἐν δὲ τῶι γενείωι παμπόλλας.
αἰσχυνόμενος δὲ [ἅτε] καταγελάμενος ὑπ[ὸ] | τῶν ἄλλων ἐνεκάθ-
125 ευδε. τὸν δὲ ὁ θεὸς χρίσας φαρμάκωι τὰν κεφαλὰν ἐπόησε || τρί-
χας ἔχειν.—Θύσων 'Ερμιονεὺς παῖς ἀιδής, οὕ[τος] ὕπαρ ὑπὸ
κυνὸς τῶν | κατὰ τὸ ἱαρὸν θ[εραπ]ευόμενος τοὺς ὀπτίλλους ὑ[γιὴ]ς
ἀπῆλθε.

One of several stelae found in the Asclepieum recording the
cures effected. Cf. Paus. 2.27.3 στῆλαι δὲ εἰστήκεσαν ἐντὸς τοῦ
περιβόλου, τὸ μὲν ἀρχαῖον καὶ πλέονες, ἐπ' ἐμοῦ δὲ ἐξ λοιπαί. ταύταις
ἐγγεγραμμένα καὶ ἀνδρῶν καὶ γυναικῶν ἐστιν ὀνόματα ἀκεσθέντων
ὑπὸ τοῦ 'Ασκληπιοῦ, προσέτι δὲ καὶ νόσημα ὅ τι ἕκαστος ἐνόσησε καὶ
ὅπως ἰάθη· γέγραπται δὲ φωνῇ τῇ Δωρίδι.

The dialect shows considerable Attic influence, e.g., usually
εἰ rarely αἰ, contraction in ποιησοῦντος, etc., acc. pl. ἀκρατεῖς etc.
Secondary ō is always ου, and ē usually ει, but χηρός beside
χειρός, and ἀφήλετο (25c).—3. πενθ' ἔτη: 58c.—Cf. Paus. 2.27.1
οὐδὲ ἀποθνήσκουσιν οὐδὲ τίκτουσιν αἱ γυναῖκες σφίσιν ἐντὸς τοῦ
περιβόλου.—6. περιῆρπε: ἔρπω = εἶμι, 162.6.—7 ff. The words
on the votive offering form a rude epigram, hence the poetical
μιν, for which elsewhere νιν.—9/10. τριετὴς [φο]ρά: 'three year
gestation.'—43 ff. 'Then the boy who acted as torch-bearer for
the god, looking at the boy's father, bade him promise that he
(the boy), if he obtained what he was there for, would within
a year make the thank-offerings for his cure.'—66. ἐώρη: 280.—
74. ἔλεγον: probably error for ἐγέλαν; cf. διεγέλα l. 35.—75.
'When he had not even any rudiment of an eye, but only the
place for it,' i.e., the empty eye-socket.—98 f. δεμελέας: 'leeches.'
Cf. δεμβλεῖς· βδέλλαι Hesych.—102. αὐτά agrees in form with
θηρία, while with ἐμβεβλημένας we must understand δεμελέας.

Corinthian

91. Corinth. Early sixth century B.C. IG IV.358. GDI 3114.
Roberts 85. Schwyzer 124.

ΔϜΕνία τόδε [σᾶμα], τὸν ὄλεσε πόντος ἀναι[δές].

This and the following illustrate the Corinthian differentiation of ʙ = open ε or ē (η) and E= close ē corresponding to Attic spurious or genuine ει. See **28**. The epithaph forms a single hexameter. Cf. nos. 93-95.

92. Corinth. Early sixth century B.C. IG IV.210, 211, 219, 329. GDI 3119. Schwyzer 123.

- a. Σιμίōν μ' ἀνέθ(ē)κε ΠοτΕδαϜōν[ι Ϝάνακτι]. ΠοτΕδ[άν].
- b. Ϙυλōιδας μ' ἀνέθēκε Πο[τΕδάϜōνι Ϝάνακτι]. ΠοτΕδάν.
- c. -ōν μ' ἀνέθēκε ΠοτΕδᾶνι Ϝάν[ακτι]. ['Αμφι]τρίτα.
- d. ΠεραΕόθεν hίϙομες.

From a large collection of pottery fragments found near Corinth. They are mostly votive offerings to Poseidon, and contain the name in both uncontracted and contracted forms, as ΠοτΕδαϜōνι and ΠοτΕδᾶνι, but in the nominative only the contracted ΠοτΕδάν. See **41**.4. For ΠεραΕόθεν (d), cf. Πείραιον Xen. Hellen. 4.5.1 ff. Probably ʙ in the first syllable is an error.

93. Corcyra. Early sixth century B.C. IG IX.i.867. GDI 3188. Roberts 98. Schwyzer 133, 1. Solmsen-Fraenkel 34a.

Ηυιοῦ ΤλασίαϜο Μενεκράτεος τόδε σᾶμα,
Οἰανθέος γενεάν· τόδε δ' αὐτōι δᾶμος ἐποίει·
ἐς γὰρ πρόξενϜος δάμου φίλος· ἀλλ' ἐνὶ πόντōι
ὄλετο, δαμόσιον δὲ καϙὸν ῥό[θιον πόρε κῦμα]
5 Πραξιμένες δ' αὐτōι γ[αία]ς ἀπὸ πατρίδος ἐνθὸν
σὺν δάμ[ō]ι τόδε σᾶμα κασιγνέτοιο πονέθē.

Monument of Menecrates. This and the two following are examples of metrical inscriptions composed in the epic style and with retention of several epic words, i.e., ἐνί, κασιγνέτοιο, στονό-Ϝε(σ)σαν, ἀϜυτάν (**32**) = ἀυτήν, and inflectional forms, e.g., gen. sg. in -οιο and -ᾱϜο = -αο (**105**.2b), dat. pl. in -αισι, augmentless verb forms.

4. The restoration is that suggested by H. Frisk, Eranos 29.31 f.—6. **πονέθē**: transitive sense as in Homer.

94. Corcyra. Early sixth century B.C. IG IX.i.868. GDI 3189. Roberts 99. Tod 2. Schwyzer 133,2. Solmsen-Fraenkel 34b.

Σᾶμα τόδε 'Αρνιάδα · χαροπὸς τόνδ' ὄλε|σεν Ἄρες
βαρνάμενον παρὰ ναυσ|ὶν ἐπ' 'Αράθθοιο ῥhοϜαῖσι
πολλὸ|ν ἀριστεύ<τ>οντα κατὰ στονόϜεσαν ἀϜυτάν.

2. ῥhοϜαῖσι: cf. also Μhείξιος in another inscription of Corcyra.
See 76a.—3. ἀριστεύτοντα: error for ἀριστεύοντα or ἀριστεύϜοντα
(cf. 36).

95. Northern Acarnania (exact provenance unknown). Fifth
century B.C. IG IX.i.521. GDI 3175. Roberts 106. Schwyzer 140.

Προκλείδας τόδε σᾶμα κεκλ|έσεται ἐνγὺς ὁδοῖο,
    hὸς περὶ τᾶς αὐτοῦ γᾶς | θάνε βαρνάμενος.
Προκλείδας: gen. sg. masc. in -ας. 105.2c.

96. Sicyon. Fifth century B.C. Orlandos, Ἑλληνικά 10.5 ff.

Τούτον δὲ κοινὰ ἔστō τὸ ἐστιατόριον καὶ τὰ ὄρε καὶ hο χαλκιόν |
καὶ τᾶλα Ϝοικέουσίν γα καὶ τὰ τέλε φέρουσιν · πōλεν δὲ | μεδὲ συνα-
λάζεσθαι ἐξέστō. [There follows a list of 73 names].

The inscription has the characteristic Ⴟ = E, the san, but
the straight iota. The Ⴟ is used, like the Corinth. ᗺ for ε and η
(μεδέ and η from εα in ὄρε, τέλε). But E for secondary ē, as at
Corinth (25d) in ΠΟΓΕͶ to be read πōλεν rather than = Arg.
πωλέν. OV for secondary ō, as at Corinth (25d), in Ϝοικέουσιν,
φέρουσιν (for which see also 102).

97. Cleonae, found at Nemea. Sixth century B.C. Argive
alphabet, but Corinthian ᗺ = ē (but not ε). AJA 1927, 433.
'Αρχ. Ἐφ. 1931, 103. SEG 11.290.

'Αρίστις με ἀνέθ|ēκε Δὶ Ϙρονίōνι Ϝά|νακτι πανκράτιο|ν νιϙōν
τετράκις | ἐν Νεμέαι, Φείδō|νος Ϝhιὸς τō Κλεō|ναίō.

Dedication by Aristis, son of Pheidon of Cleonae. The Corinthian ᗺ is here used = η but not also = ε as at Corinth (cf.
ἀνΕθ ᗺκΕ vs. Corinth. ανᗺθзκᗺ no. 92b). Same practice in another archaic inscription of Cleonae (Schwyzer 129).—**Ϝhιός**:
52c.

Megarian

98. Selinus. Fifth century B.C. IG XIV.268. GDI 3046. Ditt.
Syll. 1122. Roberts 117. Schwyzer 166. Solmsen-Fraenkel 33.
Tod 37.

[Δι]ὰ τὸς θεὸς τό[σ]δε νικῶντι τοὶ Σελινόν[τιοι· | δι]ὰ τὸν Δία
νικῶμες καὶ διὰ τὸν Φόβον [καὶ] | δ[ιὰ] Ηερακλέα καὶ δι' Ἀπόλ-
λωνα καὶ διὰ Π[οτ]|ε[ιδᾶ]να καὶ διὰ Τυνδαρίδας καὶ δι' Ἀθ[α]-||
5 ν[ά]αν καὶ διὰ Μαλοφόρον καὶ διὰ Πασικ|ρά|τ]ειαν καὶ δι[ὰ] τὸς
ἄλλος θεός, [δ]ιὰ δ[ὲ] Δία | μάλιστ[α]. φιλί[ας] δὲ γενομένας ἐν
χρυσ|έō[ι] ἐλά[σα]ντα[ς, τὰ δ'] ὀνύματα ταῦτα κολ|άψαντ[ας ἐς] τὸ
10 Ἀ[π]ολ[λ]όνιον καθθέμε||ν, τὸ Διὸ[ς προ]γρά[ψα]ντες· τὸ δὲ χρυ-
σίον | ἐξέκ[οντα τ]αλάντōν ἔμεν.

The Selinuntians promise golden statues to the gods who
shall help them to victory. Instead of an express condition,
there is an enumeration of the gods who usually assist them,
the implication being that they will continue to do so.

1. 'Through the help of the following gods do the Selinuntians,
win victory. Through Zeus we conquer,' etc.—2. **Φόβον**: 'Ares'.
—5. **Μαλοφόρον**: 'Demeter.' Cf. Paus. 1.44.3 ἱερὸν Δήμητρος
Μαλοφόρου.—**Πασικράτεια**: 'Persephone.' Cf. Δέσποινα.—7 ff.
'(Resolved) when there is peace, making statues in gold and
engraving these names, to set them up in the temple of Apollo,
writing the name of Zeus first.'—**προγράψαντες**: nominative
carelessly written for accusative.

99. Decision of the Megarians. Epidaurus. Between 242 and
234 B.C. IG IV.926. GDI 3025. Ditt. Syll. 471. Schwyzer 157.

['Ε]πὶ στραταγ[οῦ τῶν 'Α]χαιῶν Αἰγιαλεῦς, ἐν δ' 'Επιδαύρωι
ἐπ' ἱαρεῦς | [το]ῦ 'Ασκλαπι[οῦ Δι]ονυσίου. κατὰ τάδε ἐκρίναν τοὶ
Μεγαρεῖς τοῖς | ['Επ]ιδαυρίοις καὶ Κορινθίοις περὶ τᾶς χώρας ἃς
ἀμφέλλεγον καὶ | [περ]ὶ τοῦ Σελλανύο[υ] καὶ τοῦ Σπιραίου, κατὰ
5 τὸν αἶνον τὸν τῶν 'Α||[χαι]ῶν δικαστήριον ἀποστείλαντες ἄνδρας
ἑκατὸν πεντήκοντα | [ἕνα]· καὶ ἐπελθόντων ἐπ' αὐτὰν τὰν χώραν
τῶν δικαστᾶν καὶ κρινάν|[των] 'Επιδαυρίων εἶμεν τὰν χώραν, ἀντι-
λεγόντων δὲ τῶν Κορινθί|[ων τῶ]ι τερμονισμῶι, πάλιν ἀπέστειλαν
τοὶ Μεγαρεῖς τοὺς τερμο|ν[ιξ]οῦ[ν]τας ἐκ τῶν αὐτῶν δικαστᾶν
10 ἄνδρας τριάκοντα καὶ ἕνα κα||[τὰ τ]ὸν αἶνον τὸν τῶν 'Αχαιῶν, οὗτοι
δὲ ἐπελθόντες ἐπὶ τὰν χώραν | ἐτερμόνιξαν κατὰ τάδε· ἀπὸ τᾶς
κορυφᾶς τοῦ Κορδυλείου ἐπὶ | [τ]ὰν κορυφὰν τοῦ 'Αλιείου· ἀπὸ τοῦ
'Αλιείου ἐπὶ τὰν κορυφὰν τοῦ | [Κ]εραυνίου· ἀπὸ τοῦ Κεραυνίου
ἐπὶ τὰν κορυφὰν τοῦ Κορνιάτα· | ἀπὸ τᾶς κορυφᾶς τοῦ Κορνιάτα
15 ἐπὶ τὰν ὁδὸν ἐπὶ τὸν ῥάχιν τὸν τοῦ || Κορνιάτα· ἀπὸ τοῦ ῥάχιος

τοῦ Κορνιάτα ἐπὶ τὸν ῥάχιν τὸν ἐπὶ ταῖ|ς 'Ανείαις ὑπὲρ τὰν Σκολ-
λείαν· ἀπὸ τοῦ ῥάχιος τοῦ ὑπὲρ τὰν Σκολ|λείαν ὑπὸ τᾶς 'Ανείας
ἐπὶ τὸν κορυφὸν τὸν ὑπὲρ τᾶς ὁδοῦ τᾶς ἀμα|ξιτοῦ [τᾶς κα]ταγού-
σας ἐπὶ τὸ Σπίαιον· ἀπὸ τοῦ κορυφοῦ τοῦ ὑπὲ|ρ τᾶς [ὁδοῦ] τᾶς
20　ἀμαξιτοῦ ἐπὶ τὸν κορυφὸν τὸν ἐπὶ τοῦ Φάγας· ἀπὸ || τοῦ κορυφοῦ
τοῦ ἐπὶ τοῦ Φάγας ἐπὶ τὸν κορυφὸν τὸν ἐπὶ τοῦ Αἰγι|πύρα[ς]· ἀπὸ
τοῦ κορυφοῦ τοῦ ἐπὶ τᾶς Αἰγιπύρας ἐπὶ τὸν κορυφὸν | τὸν τ[οῦ
'Αρα]ίας· ἀπὸ τοῦ 'Αραίας ἐπὶ τὸν κορυφὸν τὸν ὑπὸ τᾶι Πέτρ|αι·
ἀπ[ὸ το]ῦ ὑπὸ τᾶι Πέτραι ἐπὶ τὸν κορυφὸν τὸν ἐπὶ τοῦ Σχοινοῦν-|
τος· ἀ[πὸ τ]οῦ κορυφοῦ τοῦ ὑπὲρ τοῦ Σχοινοῦντος ἐπὶ τὸν κορυ-
25　φὸν || τὸν κ[ατὰ τ]ὰν Εὐόργαν· ἀπὸ τοῦ κορυφοῦ τοῦ ὑπὲρ τᾶς
Εὐόργας [ἐπὶ] | τὸν ῥάχιν τὸν ὑπὲρ τᾶς Συκουσίας· ἀπὸ τοῦ ῥά-
χιος τοῦ ὑπὲρ τᾶς | Συ[κουσί]ας ἐπὶ τὸν κορυφὸν τὸν ὑπὲρ τᾶς
Πελλερίτιος· ἀπὸ τοῦ | κορυφοῦ τοῦ ὑπὲρ τᾶς Πελλερίτιος ἐπὶ τὸν
κορυφὸν τὸν τοῦ Π[αν|ίου]· ἀπὸ τοῦ Πανίου ἐπὶ τὸν ῥάχιν τὸν ὑπὲρ
30　τοῦ 'Ολ[κοῦ]· ἀπὸ τοῦ ῥά||[χιο]ς τ[οῦ] ὑπὲρ τοῦ 'Ολκοῦ ἐπὶ τὸν
ῥάχιν τὸν (ὑπὲρ) τοῦ 'Απ[ολλ]ωνίου· ἀπὸ | τ[οῦ] ῥάχιος τοῦ ὑπὲρ
τοῦ 'Απολλωνίου ἐπὶ τὸ 'Απολλώνιον. δικασ|[ται τ]οὶ κρίναντες
τοίδε. [There follow, ll. 32—99, the names of the arbitrators
and of those appointed to lay out the boundaries for them.]

Decision of the Megarians, appionted by the Achaean league
to arbitrate in a territorial dispute between Epidaurus and
Corinth.

1. **Αἰγιαλεῦς, ἱαρεῦς**: gen. sg. in -εῦς from -έος. **111**.3.—
For the psilosis in ἐπ' ἱαρεῦς, see **58**_b_.—3. **ἀμφέλλεγον**: **76**.—
4. **Σπιραίου**: name of a harbor and promontory north of
Epidaurus, referred to by Thuc. 8.10.3 (with correction of
Πειραιόν to Σπίραιον) and Pliny, Nat. Hist. 4.18 (Spiraeum).—
αἶνον: αἶνος 'decree,' but distinct from a ψάφισμα. Cf. Delph.
μήτε κατὰ ψάφισμα μήτε κατ' αἶνον (GDI 2642.20).—19. **Φάγας**:
gen. sg. masc. in -ᾶς. **105**.2_c_. So 'Αραίας l. 22, but also the usual
form in Κορνιάτα ll. 13 ff. The confusion caused by the identity
with the feminine form is shown by τᾶς Αἰγιπύρας l. 21 beside
τοῦ Αἰγιπύρας l. 20.—32 ff. The list of names, arranged according
to the three Doric tribes, contains the characteristic forms
Θέδωρος, Θοκρίνης, etc. (**42**.5_f_).

Rhodian

100. Camirus. Sixth century B.C. IG XII.i.737. GDI 4140. Schwyzer 272.

Σᾶμα τόζ' Ἰδα|μενεὺς ποίη|σα hίνα κλέος | εἴη· ||
Ζεὺ δέ νιν ὅστις | πημαίνοι λειό|λη θείη.

τόζ': τόδε. **62.**2.—Ζεὺ δέ: Ζεὺς δέ. **97.**4.—λειόλη: 'accursed.'
Cf. Hesych. λεώλης· τελείως ἐξώλης, and, for the first part of
the compound, λείως = τελείως in Archilochus, Hesych., etc.

101. Camirus. Sixth century B.C. IG XII.i.709. GDI 4127.
Schwyzer 273.

Εὐθυ[τ]ίδα | ἠμὶ λέσχα | τō Πραξσιόδō | τōύφύλō ||τōύφυλίδα.

λέσχα: 'grave.' The original meaning of the word (from
*λεχσκᾱ, cf. λέχος) was 'resting place,' whence either 'grave'
or the usual 'place of recreation, club.'—The last words are to
be read, with resolution of the crasis, τō Εὐφύλō, τō Εὐφυλίδα.

102. Camirus. Fourth (or third) century B.C. IG XII.i.694.
GDI 4118. Ditt. Syll. 339. Schwyzer 281. Solmsen-Fraenkel 42.

Ἔδοξε Καμιρεῦσι τὰς κτοίνας τὰς Καμιρέων τὰς | ἐν τᾶι νάσωι
καὶ τὰς ἐν τᾶι ἀπείρωι ἀναγράψαι πάσας | καὶ ἐχθέμειν ἐς τὸ ἱερὸν
τᾶς Ἀθαναίας ἐ στάλαι | λιθίναι χωρὶς Χαλκῆς· ἐξήμειν δὲ καὶ
5 Χαλκήταις || ἀναγραφήμειν, αἴ κα χρήιζωντι. ἐλέσθαι δὲ ἄνδρας |
τρεῖς αὐτίκα μάλα, οἵτινες ἐπιμελεθησεῦντι ταύ|τας τᾶς πράξιος
ὡς τάχιστα καὶ ἀποδωσεῦνται | τῶι χρήιζοντι ἐλαχίστου παρα-
σχεῖν τὰν στάλαν | καὶ τὰς κτοίνας ἀναγράψαι καὶ ἐγκολάψαι ἐν
10 τᾶι στά||λαι καὶ στάσαι ἐν τῶι ἱερῶι τᾶς Ἀθάνας καὶ περιβολι-
βῶ|σαι ὡς ἔχηι ὡς ἰσχυρότατα καὶ κάλλιστα. τὰ δὲ τε|λεύμενα ἐς
ταῦτα πάντα τὸν ταμίαν παρέχειν. | ἐγ δὲ ταυτᾶν τᾶν κτοινᾶν ἀπο-
15 δεικνύειν τοὺς | κτοινάτας μαστρὸν ἐν τῶι ἱερῶι τῶι ἁγιωτάτωι || ἐν
τᾶι κτοίναι κατὰ τὸν νόμον τὸν τῶν Ῥοδίων · | τοῦτοι δὲ συνλεγέ-
σθων ἐν Καμίρωι εἰς τὸ | ἱερὸν τᾶς Ἀθαναίας, ὅκκα τοὶ ἱεροποιοὶ
παραγγ[έλ|λ]ωντι, καὶ ἀθρεόντω τὰ ἱερὰ τὰ Καμιρέων [τὰ δα|μο]-
τελῆ πάντα, αἴ τι - - - - - -

The names of the κτοῖναι or demes of Camirus are to be
inscribed, both those on the island and those on the mainland.
For the latter cf., from the Periplus of Scylax, Χώρα ἡ Ῥοδίων
ἡ ἐν τῇ ἠπείρῳ.—The neighboring island of Χαλκῆ (see **42.**2)

was under the control of Camirus at this time, yet evidently
sustained a relation to it different from that of the other demes.—
6. ἐπιμελnθησεῦντι: 145.—8 ff. ἀποδωσεῦνται κτλ.: 'shall give
out the contract to the one who is willing to furnish the stele at
the lowest figure.'
    103. Ialysus. Fourth (or third) century B.C. IG XII.i.677.
GDI 4110. Ditt. Syll. 338. Schwyzer 284.

Ἔδοξε τοῖς μαστροῖς καὶ Ἰαλυσίοις, | Στράτης Ἀλκιμέδοντος
εἶπε · | ὅπως τὸ ἱερὸν καὶ τὸ τέμενος | τᾶς Ἀλεκτρώνας εὐαγῆται
5 κα‖τὰ τὰ πάτρια, ἐπιμελnθήμειν | τοὺς ἱεροταμίας ὅπως στάλαι |
ἐργασθέωντι τρεῖς λίθου Λαρτ[ί]|ου καὶ ἀναγραφῆι ἐς τὰς στάλα|ς
10 τό τε ψάφισμα τόδε καὶ ἃ οὐχ ὅ‖σιόν ἐντι ἐκ τῶν νόμων ἐσφέ|ρειν
οὐδὲ ἐσοδοιπορεῖν ἐς τὸ τέ|μενος, καὶ τὰ ἐπιτίμια τῶ[ι] πράσ|σοντι
15 παρὰ τὸν νόμον · θέμειν δὲ | τὰς στάλας μίαμ μὲν ἐπὶ τᾶς ἐσό‖δου
τᾶς ἐκ πόλιος ποτιπορευομέ|νοις, μίαν δὲ ὑπὲρ τὸ ἱστιατόριον, |
ἄλλαν δὲ ἐπὶ τᾶς καταβάσιος τᾶ[ς] | ἐξ Ἀχαίας πόλιος. |
20 Νόμος ἃ οὐχ ὅσιον ἐσίμειν οὐδὲ ‖ ἐσφέρειν ἐς τὸ ἱερὸν καὶ τὸ
τέ|μενος τᾶς Ἀλεκτρώνας. μὴ ἐσί|τω ἵππος, ὄνος, ἡμίονος, γῖνος |
25 μηδὲ ἄλλο λόφουρον μηθέν, μη|δὲ ἐσαγέτω ἐς τὸ τέμενος μη‖θεὶς
τούτων μηθέν, μηδὲ ὑποδή|ματα ἐσφερέτω μηδὲ ὕειον μη|θέν · ὅτι
δέ κά τις παρὰ τὸν νόμον | ποιήσηι, τό τε ἱερὸν καὶ τὸ τέμενος | καθ-
αιρέτω καὶ ἐπιρεζέτω, ἢ ἔνο‖χος ἔστω τᾶι ἀσεβείαι · εἰ δέ κα |
πρόβατα ἐσβάληι, ἀποτεισάτω ὑ|πὲρ ἑκάστου προβάτου ὀβολὸν |
35 ὁ ἐσβαλών · ποταγγελλέτω δὲ | τὸν τούτων τι ποιεῦντα ὁ χρήι‖ζων
ἐς τοὺς μαστρούς.

4. Ἀλεκτρώνας: a daughter of Helios and the nymph Rhodos,
who was worshipped with divine honors by the Rhodians. Cf.
Diod. 5.56, where the name appears as Ἠλεκτρυώνη.—7. λίθου
Λαρτίου: also πέτρας Λαρτίας on another inscription, 'marble
from Lartus,' a place in the neighborhood of Lindus.—10. ἐντι:
pl. for sg. 163.10.—18. Ἀχαίας πόλιος: the name given to
the acropolis of Ialysus. Cf. Ath. 8.360 ἐν τῇ Ἰαλυσῷ πόλιν ἰσχυ-
ροτάτην τὴν Ἀχαίαν καλουμένην.

104. Rhodian (?) inscription from Abu-Symbel in Egypt.
Sixth century B.C. GDI 5261. Ditt. Syll. 1. Roberts 130. Schwyzer
301. Tod 4. The signatures added below (b-i) are omitted here.

a. Βασιλέος ἐλθόντος ἐς Ἐλεφαντίναν Ψα(μ)ματίχō | ταῦτα ἔγραψαν, τοὶ σὺν Ψαμματίχōι τōι Θεοκλōς | ἔπλεον. ἦλθον δὲ Κέρκιος κατύπερθε, υἷς ὁ ποταμὸς | ἀνίη. ἀλογλōσōς δ᾽ ἦχε Πο-
5 τασιμπτό, Αἰγυπτίōς δὲ Ἄμασις. || ἔγραφε δ᾽ ἀμὲ Ἀρχōν ἀμοιβίχō καὶ Πέλεϙος ōύδάμō.

Inscribed on the legs of one of the colossal statues at Abu-Symbel by Greek mercenaries who had taken part in an expedition up the Nile under Psammetichus II (594-589 B.C.). These mercenaries were from Asia Minor and the adjacent islands. Cf. Hdt. 2.154 and the names inscribed below, which include two Ionians, from Teos and Colophon, and one Rhodian. The main part of the inscription is clearly in Doric and may well have been written by one of the Rhodian mercenaries.

a.3. **υἷς ὁ ποταμὸς ἀνίη**: 'as far as the river let them go up.' For υἷς see **132**.4.—5. **ἀμοιβίχō ōύδάμō**: ὁ Ἀμοιβίχου, ὁ Εὐδάμου. **94**.1, 7.

106. Gela. Sixth century B.C. GDI 4247. Schwyzer 302.

Πασιάδαϝο τὸ | σᾶμα, Κράτες ἐ|ποίει.

Beginning of a hexameter. For Πασιάδαϝο see **105**.2*a*.

106. Agrigentum. Second half of third century B.C. (before 210). IG XIV.952. GDI 4254. Schwyzer 307.

Ἐπὶ ἱεροθύτα | Νυμφοδώρου τοῦ Φίλωνος | παραπροστά(τα)
5 τᾶς βουλᾶς, | προεδρευούσας τᾶς φυλᾶς || τῶν Ὑλλέων, προαγο-ροῦντος | Διοκλέος τοῦ Διοκλέος, | γραμματεύοντος Ἀδρανίωνος Ἀλεξάνδρου, | ἀλίασμα ἕκτας διμήνου, Καρνείου ἐξήκο[ντ]ος πανταῖ, | ὑπὲρ προξενίας Δημητρίωι Διοδότου Συρακοσίωι. ||
10 Ἔδοξε ταῖ ἀλίαι καθὰ καὶ ταῖ συ(ν)κλήτωι ρι´. ἐπειδὴ ἀνάγ|γελ-λον οἱ πρεσβέες οἱ ἐς Ῥώμαν πορευθέντες, Πασίων | Πασίωνος Κότητος καὶ Θεόδωρος Θεοδώρου Ξηνιάδα, | Δημήτριον Διοδότου Συρακόσιον πολλὰς καὶ μεγάλας χρείας | παρεισχῆσθαι τῶι ἀμῶι
15 δάμωι καὶ μεγάλων ἀγαθῶν παραίτιο(ν) || γεγόνειν, τοῖς δὲ Ἀκρα-γαντίνοις πάτριόν ἐστι καὶ ἐκ προγόνων | παραδεδομένον τιμεῖν τοὺς ἀγαθοὺς ἄνδρας καὶ προϊσταμέ|νους τοῦ ἀμοῦ δάμου ταῖς κα-ταξίοις τιμαῖς · | δεδόχθαι ἐπὶ ἀγαθαῖ τύχαι καὶ σωτηρίαι τοῦ δάμου τῶν Ἀκραγαντίνων · | εἴμειν πρόξενον καὶ εὐεργέταν Δημήτριον
20 Διοδότου Συρακόσι||ον, ὅπω(ς) πᾶσι φανερὸν ἦ ὅτι ὁ δᾶμος τῶν Ἀκραγαντίνων ἐπί|σταται χάριτας ἀπονέμειν καταξίας τοῖς εὐερ-

γετεῖν προαι|ρουμένοις αὐτόν. τὸ δὲ δόγμα τόδε κολάψαντας ἐς
χαλκώ|ματα δύο τὸ μὲν ἓν ἀναθέμειν εἰς τὸ βουλευτήριον, τὸ δὲ |
25 ἄλλο ἀποδόμειν Δημητρίωι Διοδότου Συρακοσίωι ὑπό||μναμα τᾶς
ποτὶ τὸν δᾶμον εὐνοίας· τοὺς δὲ ταμίας | ἐξοδιάξαι ἐς τὰ προγε-
γραμμένα ὅσον κα χρεία ᾖ, καὶ φέ|ρειν τὰν ἔξοδον διὰ τῶν ἀπολό-
γων. | ὁμογνώμονες τοῦ συνεδρίου πάντες.

Proxeny decree of Agrigentum in honor of Demetrius of
Syracuse. In view of l. 11 and of the fact that this inscription
was found at Rome, being evidently the copy given to Demetrius
(l. 24), it appears that he was resident in Rome, and his services
probably consisted in some dealings with the Roman senate in
behalf of Agrigentum.

8. ἀλίασμα κτλ.: 'decree in the sixth period of two months,
at the very end of the month Καρνεῖος.'—14. παρεισχῆσθαι:
εἴσχηκα, εἴσχημαι, for ἔσχηκα, ἔσχημαι, with ει after the analogy
of εἴληφα etc. (76), occur in several κοινή inscriptions.—15.
γεγόνειν: 147.2.

107. Rhegium. Second century B.C. IG XIV.612. GDI 4258.
Ditt. Syll. 715. Schwyzer 310.

ʼΕπὶ πρυτάνιος Νικάνδρου τοῦ Νικοδάμου, βουλᾶς προστατέον-
τος Σωσιπόλιος τοῦ Δαματρίου, Χίωι ʼΙππίου δυοδεκάται, ἔδοξε
τᾶι ἁλία | καθάπερ τᾶι ἐσκλήτωι καὶ τᾶι βουλᾶι· ἐπεὶ ὁ στρατα-
γὸς τῶν ʼΡωμαίων Γναῖος Αὐφίδιος Τίτου υἱὸς εὔνους ὑπάρχει τᾶι
ἁμᾶ πόλει, ἄξιος φαινόμενος | τᾶς αὐτοῦ καλοκἀγαθίας, δεδόχθαι
Γναῖον Αὐφίδιον Τίτου υἱὸν στραταγὸν ʼΡωμαίων στεφανῶσαι ἐν
τῶ ἀγῶνι τοῖς πρώτοις ʼΑθανίοις ἐλαίας στεφά|νω καὶ πρόξενον
καὶ εὐεργέταν ποιῆσαι τοῦ δάμ(ο)υ τῶν ʼΡηγίνων καὶ ἐγγόνους αὐ-
5 τοῦ, εὐνοίας ἕνεκεν ἃς ἔχων διατελεῖ εἰς τὸν δᾶμον τῶν ʼΡηγί||νων.
τὰν δὲ βουλὰν τὸ ἀλίασμα κολαψαμέναν εἰς χαλκώματα δισσὰ τὸ
μὲν ἀναθέμειν εἰς τὸ βουλευτήριον, τὸ δὲ ἀποστεῖλαι Γναίω Αὐφιδίω.

Rhegium was a Chalcidian colony, and in the few early inscriptions the Ionic element predominates. But after its destruc-
tion by Dionysius of Syracuse in 387 B.C. and its subsequent
restoration, there were continual changes in its population.
Some of its new inhabitants must have been furnished by Gela
or Agrigentum, if we may judge by the language of this inscription
which is not merely Doric, but contains the Rhodian infin. -μειν

and the word ἀλίασμα, otherwise known only from inscriptions
of Gela and Agrigentum.

1. **χίωι**: unexplained and probably an error of some kind.—
2. **ἐσκλήτωι**: refers to a small select body, probably mediating
between the council and the assembly. Cf. Hesych. ἔσκλητος·
ἡ τῶν ἐξόχων συνάθροισις ἐν Συρακούσαις. So also Corcyr. ἐπεί-
σκλητος.

Coan

108. Cos. Middle fourth century B.C. Paton-Hicks 37. GDI
3636. Schwyzer 251A. Solmsen-Fraenkel 43. Herzog, Abh.
Preuss. Akad. 1928. no. 6. pp. 6 ff. (revised text, followed here,
with omission of the dots marking mutilated letters).

[The fragmentary first three lines omitted here.] [ἐ]ς
5 [ἀ]πο[καρ]υσσόντω, ἱεροποιοὶ δὲ καὶ τοὶ κάρυκες ἰόντω κ[α||τ]ὰ
χ[ι]λ[ιασ]τύας, βοῦς δὲ ἐννῆ [ἐ]λᾶντι, βοῦν ἐξ ἐνάτας ἑκάστ[ας], |
[ἐ]ξ Α ... ἐων καὶ Πασθεμιαδᾶν πράτων καὶ Ν[οσ]τιδᾶν · ἐς δὲ |
[τ]ὰν ἀ[γο]ρὰν ἐλάντω Πάμφυλοι πρᾶτοι, ἐν ἀγορᾶι συμμίσ|[γ]ον-
ται · ὁ δὲ ἱερεὺς καθήσθω [παρὰ] τ[ὰ]ν τράπεζαν ἔχων τὰ[ν σ]||το-
λὰν τὰν ἱεράν, τοὶ δὲ ἱερ[οποιοὶ ἑκατ]έρω τᾶς τραπέζας · Π[άμ-||
10 φ]υλοι δὲ ἐπελάντω βοῦ[ς τρεῖς τοὺ]ς καλλίστους, αἱ [μέγ κα]
τούτων κριθῆι τις · αἱ δὲ [μή, Ὑλλεῖς τρ]εῖς ἐλάντω, αἱ μ[έγ κα
τ]ο]ύτων κριθῆι τις · αἱ δὲ μ[ή, Δυμᾶνες τρ]εῖς τοὺς λοιπούς, αἱ
[μέ]||γ κα τούτων κριθῆι τις · αἱ [δὲ μή, ἀτέρους] ἐλάντω ἐς τὰν
ἀ[γο|ρ]ὰν καὶ ἐπελάντω κατὰ τα[ὐτά, αἱ μ]έγ κα τούτων κριθῆι
15 τ[ις] · || αἱ δὲ μή, τρίτον ἐπελάντω κατὰ τα[ὐτ]ά · αἱ δέ κα τούτων
κρι[θῆι] | μηδείς, ἐπικρινόντω βοῦν ἐκ χι[λιασ]τύος ἑκάστας ·
ἐλά[σα]||ντες δὲ τούτους συμμίσγον[ται τοῖ]ς ἄλλοις καὶ εὐθὺ
κ[ρίν?] |οντι καὶ εὔχονται καὶ ἀποκαρύ[σσο]ντι · ἔπειτα ἐπελᾶντ[ι
αὖ]||τις κατὰ ταὐτά · θύεται δέ, αἱ μέγ κα ὑποκύψει, τᾶι Ἱστίαι ·
20 θύ[ει] || δὲ γερεαφόρος βασιλέων καὶ ἱερὰ παρέχει καὶ ἐπιθύει
ἱερὰ ἐξ [ἡ]||μιέκτου · γέρη δὲ λαμβάνει τὸ δέρμα καὶ τὸ σκέλος,
ἱεροποι[οὶ] | δὲ σκέλος, τὰ δὲ ἄλλα κρέα τᾶς πόλιος · τὸν δὲ
κριθέντα τ[ῶι] | Ζηνὶ κάρυκες ἄγοντι ἐς ἀγοράν · ἐπεὶ δέ κα ἐν τᾶι
ἀγορᾶι ἔω[ν]||τι, ἀγορεύει οὗ κα ἦι ὁ βοῦς ἢ ἄλλος ὑπὲρ κήνου ἐνδέ-
25 ξιο[ς] · || "[Κώ]ιοις παρέχω τὸμ βοῦν, Κῶιοι δὲ τιμὰν ἀποδόντω
<το> τᾶι Ἱστία[ι] ·" | τιμώντω δὲ προστάται ὀμόσαντες παραχρῆ-

μα· ἐπεὶ δέ κα τι[μα|θῆ]ι, ἀναγορευέτω ὁ κῆρυξ ὁπόσσου κα τιμα-
θῆι· τουτῶ δὲ ἐλᾶντ[ι πα|ρ]ὰ τὰν Ἱστίαν τὰν Ἑταιρείαν καὶ θύοντι
(?)· ὁ δὲ ἱερεὺς στέπτει καὶ [ἐπι]|σπένδει κύλικα οἴνου κεκραμένου
30 πρὸ τοῦ βοός. ἔπειτα ἄγοντι τὸ[μ β|ο]ῦν καὶ τὸγ καυτὸν καὶ φθοίας
ἑπτὰ καὶ μέλι καὶ στέμμα· ἐξάγο[ντ|ε]ς δὲ καρύσσοντι εὐφαμίαν·
χηνεῖ δὲ ἐκδήσαντες τὸμ βοῦν κα[τ]|άρχονται θαλλῶι καὶ δάφναι·
τοὶ δὲ [κάρυκες κ]αρπῶντι τὸμ μὲγ χοῖ|[ρο]γ καὶ τὰ σπλάγχνα ἐπὶ
τοῦ βωμοῦ ἐπισπένδοντες μελίκρατον, ἔ[ντ|ερ]α δὲ ἐσπλύναντες
35 παρὰ τὸ[μ βωμὸν καρ]πῶντι· ἐπεὶ δέ κα καρπω[θῆι] || ἄποτα,
ἐπισπενδέτω μελίκρατον· ὁ δὲ [κᾶρ]υξ καρυσσέτω ἑορτάζε[ν Ζη-
ν]|ὸς Πολιέως ἐνιαύτια ὡραῖα ἑορτάν· [ἱερεὺς] δὲ τοῖς ἐντέροις
ἐπιθυέ[τω |θ]ύη καὶ τοὺς φθοίας καὶ σπονδὰς [ἄκρατο]ν καὶ κε-
κραμέναν καὶ στέ[μ]|μα· τουτῶ δὲ ἰόντω πὰρ τοὺς ἱαροποιὸς ἐς τὸ
οἴκημα τὸ δαμόσιον ἱα[ρ]|εὺς καὶ κάρυκες, ἱαροποιοὶ δὲ ξενίζοντι
40 τ[ὸν] ἱερῆ καὶ τὸς κάρυκας τα[ύ]|ταν τὰν νύκτα· ἐπεὶ δέ κα σπον-
δὰς π[οιή]σ[ω]νται, αἱρέσθω ὁ ἱαρεὺς [σ|φ]αγῆ τῶν ἱαροποιῶν
βοὸς τοῦ θυομένου τῶι Ζηνὶ τῶι Πολιῆι καὶ προα[γο|ρ]ευέτω
ἀγνεύεσθαι γυναικὸς καὶ ἀνδ[ρὸ]ς ἀντὶ νυκτός· τοὶ δὲ κάρυ[κε|ς]
αἱρείσθω σφαγῆ τοῦ βοὸς ὅγ κα χρήιζωντι ἡύτῶν καὶ προαγορευ-
έ[τω | ὅς κα δή]ληται τῶι αἱρεθέντι κατὰ ταύτά. τᾶι αὐτᾶι ἀμέραι
45 Διονύσωι [Σκ]||υλλίται χοῖρος καὶ ἔριφος· τοῦ χοίρου οὐκ ἀπο-
φορά· θύει δὲ ἱερεὺς κ[αὶ ἱε|ρ]ὰ παρέχει· γέρη φέρει δέρμα, σκέλος.
Ἰκάδι· βοῦς ὁ κριθεὶς θύεται Ζηνὶ | [Πο]λιῆι· ἔνδορα ἐνδέρεται·
ἐφ' ἑστίαν θύεται ἀλφίτων ἡμίεκτον, ἄρτο[ι δ]ύο ἐξ ἡμιέκτου, ὁ
ἅτερος τυρώδης καὶ τὰ ἔνδορα· καὶ ἐπισπένδει ὁ ἱε[ρ]|εὺς τούτοις
οἴνου κρατῆρας τρεῖς· γέρη τοῦ βοὸς τῶι ἱερῆι δέρμα κ[αὶ σ|κέ]-
50 λος· ἱερὰ ἱερεὺς παρέχει· || καὶ χέλυος ἥμισυ καὶ κοιλίας ἥμ[ι|συ]·
θυαφόρωι δὲ τοῦ σκέλεος τοῦ τῶν ἱεροποιῶν δίδοται ἀκρίσχιον,
[κάρυ|ξι ν]ώτου δίκρεας, ὑπώμαια, αἱματίου ὀβελὸς τρικώλιος,
Νεστορίδαι[ς | δὲ] νώτου δίκρεας, ἰατροῖς κρέας, αὐλητᾶι κρέας,
χαλκέων καὶ κερα[μέ|ω]ν ἑκατέροις τὸ κεφάλαιο[ν· τὰ δὲ ἄλ]λα
55 κρέα τᾶς πόλιος· ταῦτα πάν[τα || οὐκ] ἀποφέρεται ἐκτὸς τᾶς π[ό-
λιος]. τᾶι αὐτᾶι ἀμέραι Ἀθαναίαι Πο[λι]|άδι ὄις κυεῦσα· θύει δὲ
ἱε[ρεὺς καὶ] ἱερὰ παρέχει· γέρη λαμβάνει δέ[ρ]|μα καὶ σκέλος.
ἐνάται με[τ' ἰκ]άδα Διονύσωι Σκυλλίται χοῖρος [καὶ] | ἔριφος·
τοῦ χοίρου οὐκ ἀποφορά· θύει ἱερεὺς καὶ ἱερὰ παρέχει· γέρη
[λ]|αμβάνει δέρμα καὶ σκέλος. ἑβδόμαι ἀνομένου ἐς Ἀλκηίδας
60 Δά[μ]||ατρι ὄις τέλεως καὶ τελέα κυεῦσα· τούτων οὐκ ἀποφορά·

κύλικες κ[αι|ν]αὶ δύο δίδονται· θύει ἱερεύς [καὶ ἱερ]ὰ παρέχει·
γέρη δὲ οὔατα. ἔχκτ[αι Δι|ο]νύσωι Σκυλλίτα[ι χοῖρος καὶ ἔριφος·]
τοῦ χοίρου [ο]ὐκ [ἀποφορά· κτλ.]

Portion of a sacrificial calendar, enumerating the rites appropriate to each day of the year.

The dialect is somewhat mixed, with fluctuation between
earlier and later forms (e.g., ἱερός, ἱερεύς, but also the earlier
ἱαροποιοί beside ἱεροποιοί) and with some Ionic influence (τέλεως,
ἱρεύς, ἱαρεωσύνα). Generally ει, ου for secondary ē, but κῆνος,
δῆλομαι, and old spelling E, O in αἱρέσθω (3 sg.) l. 40, vs. αἱρείσθω
(3 pl.) l. 43.

1-18. Selection of the ox for sacrifice to Zeus Polieus. After
the formal announcement and the arrival of the officials, they
(the tribes, each of them) drive in nine oxen, one from each
ninth (of the tribe). The Pamphyli first are to drive their oxen
to the agora and there they are united in a common herd (with
those of the other tribes, as they come in). When the priest
and the ἱεροποιοί have taken their place at the table, the Pamphyli are to drive up (ἐπελάντω 'drive up' for inspection) their
three finest oxen for selection. If none of these is chosen, the
Hylleis are to drive in three more, then the Dymanes, then,
if none has been chosen, (the same tribes in rotation) are to
drive up others, and again a third time. If still no choice has been
made (of the twenty-seven oxen driven up), they select an
additional ox from each χιλιαστύς (the third part of a tribe)
and unite these with the others. Then the choice is effected,
followed by vows and a proclamation of the choice.—ἐλᾶντι,
ἐλάντω, etc.: **159.**

18-22. The procedure is repeated and a sacrifice is made to
Histia. The main sacrifice, to which the preceding refers, is that
to Zeus Polieus as shown in l. 23.—19. ὑποκύψει: 'submits
tamely,' aor. subj. **150.**—20. γερεαφόρος: title occurring only
here and in an inscription from the neighboring small island of
Pserimos.—20/21. ἐξ ἡμιέκτου: cf. **136.9.**—24. οὖ κα, κτλ.:
the owner of the ox or another entitled to represent him (ἐνδέξιος
literally 'on the right').—30. καυτόν: 'burnt-offering,' in this
case a pig. Cf. χοῖρος προκατεύεται in another part of the calendar.

—35. ἄποτα: = ἄποινα 'without wine.' Cf. ἄποινος θυσία in schol. Hom.—42. ἀντὶ νυκτός: 'during the night.' 136.8.—43. ηὐτῶν: = ἑαυτῶν 121.2. —47. ἔνδορα ἐνδέρεται: the reference is to certain parts of the victim which are wrapped up in the skin and made a special offering. Cf. Hesych. ἔνδρατα· τὰ ἐνδερόμενα σὺν τῇ κεφαλῇ καὶ τοῖς ποσίν.—50. χέλυος (new reading): here 'breast, chest' as in Hippocr.

Theran, Melian

109. Thera. Eighth (?) century B.C. IG XII.iii.536. GDI 4787. Schwyzer 214. Solmsen-Fraenkel 36.

a. Πhειδιπίδας ὤιπhε. *b.* Τιμαγόρας καὶ 'Ενπhέρης καὶ ἐγὤιπh[ομες]. *c.* "Ενπυλος τάδε—πόρνος. *d.* 'Ενπεδοκλῆς ἐνεϘόπτετο τάδε. *e.* Ϙὼρκε̄το μὰ τὸν 'Απόλω.

No. 109 belongs to a series of inscriptions cut in the solid rock and mostly of obscene content. Like the epitaphs in no. 110 and the Mel. no. 114, it belongs to the oldest period of the alphabet, when there were no signs for φ and χ, which were indicated by πh and χh or Ϙh, in consequence of which even θ was sometimes indicated by θh. Even at this early time F was completely lost, cf. Κλεαγόρας, 'Ορθοκλῆς, Λεονίδας, ἐποίε̄. B = h (also hε, hε̄) and = original η, but ε for ε̄ by contraction Θ = ω.—In no. 109d, e apparently a pun was intended in ἐνεϘόπτετο, which may be used in an obscene sense, and perhaps in Ϙὼρκε̄το which some wish to read Ϙὼρκ(h)ε̄το from ὀρχέομαι 'dance.'

110. Thera. Seventh century B.C. IG XII.iii.762. GDI 4808. Roberts 2. Schwyzer 215, 1).

a. 'Ρε̄κσάνωρ ἀρχαγέτας, Προκλῆς, Κλεαγόρας, Περαιεύς.

b. "Αγλων, Περίλας, ΜάληϘος.

c. Λεοντίδας.

d. 'Ορθοκλῆς.

111. Thera. Sixth or early fifth century B.C. IG XII.iii. Suppl. 1324. Schwyzer 219. Solmsen-Fraenkel 37.

'Αγλōτέλης πράτισ|τος 'Αγοράν hικάδι |
Κα[ρ]νήια θεὸν δεί|πν[ι]ξεν hόνιπαντίδα ||
καὶ Λακαρτō̄ς.

'Agloteles, son of Enipantidas and Lacarto, was the first to honor with a Carnean banquet the god (Apollo Carneus) on the twentieth of the month in which the 'Αγοραί were celebrated' (cf. 'Αγορήιοις no. 113). But the words from πράτιστος to δείπνιξεν are variously interpreted. The inscription, up to the last two words, is metrical (two iambic trimeters), hence δείπνιξεν without augment and with the Att.-Ion. ν movable.

112. Thera. Fourth century B.C. IG XII.iii.436. GDI 4765. Ditt. Syll. 1032. Schwyzer 221. Solmsen-Fraenkel 38.

5 Οὗροι γᾶς | Θεῶν Ματρί. | Θεὸς ἀγαθᾶι τ|ύχαι ἀγαθοῦ δ||αίμονος
θυσία | 'Αρχίνου · τῶι ἔτ|ει τῶι πρατίστ|ωι θύσοντι βοῦ|ν καὶ πυ-
10 ρῶν ἐγ || μεδίμνου καὶ | κριθᾶν ἐγ δύο μ|εδίμνων καὶ οἴνο|υ μετρη-
15 τὰν καὶ ἄλλα | ἐπάργματα ὦν αἱ ὦρ||αι φέρουσιν, μηνὸς 'Αρτε|μι-
σίου πέμπται ἱσταμ|ένου καὶ μηνὸς 'Υακινθίο|υ πέμπται ἱσταμένου.

1 f. 'Boundaries of the land for the Mother of the Gods.' This was, doubtless, land dedicated to her service by Archinus, who also promises a sacrifice.—6 ff. 'In the very first year they shall offer an ox, a medimnus of wheat, etc.'—θύσοντι: instead of θυσέοντι (cf. no. 113), but with retention of the Doric ending, while φέρουσιν l. 15 is completely Attic, likewise 'Αρτεμισίου (cf. 'Αρταμιτίου no. 113).—ἐγ μεδίμνου, κτλ.: 136.9.

113. Thera. Fourth century B.C. IG XII.iii. 452. GDI 4772. Schwyzer 220.

'Αρταμιτίō τετάρται | πεδ' ἱκάδα θυσέοντι | ἱαρόν, 'Αγορήιοις δὲ | [δ]εῖπνογ καὶ ἱα[ρ]ὰ πρὸ τō̄ σαμηίō.

'On the twenty-fourth of the month Artemisius they shall offer a sacrifice, and at the Agoreia (name of a festival) a banquet, and sacrifices in front of the image.'

114. Melos. Early sixth century B.C. IG XII.iii.1075. GDI 4871. Roberts 7. Schwyzer 207.

Παῖ Διός, 'Εκπhάντōι δέξαι τόδ' ἀμενπhὲς ἄγαλμα
σοὶ γὰρ ἐπευχόμενον τοῦτ' ἐτέλεσσε γρόπhōν.

γρόπhōν(also γρόφōν in another inscription) = γράφων here 'carving.' 49.2. 'Εκπhάντōι: see no. 68, note.

Cyrenaean

115. Cyrene. Early fourth century B.C. Solmsen-Fraenkel 39.
SEG 9.1.no. 72 (with full bibliography of the extensive literature;
Oliverio, Documenti Antichi della Africa Italiana 2.14 ff., is the
latest full discussion, with the best photograph).

'Α]πόλλων ἔχρη[σε · | ἐς ἀ]εὶ καθαρμοῖς καὶ ἀγνηίαις κα[ὶ θε-|
ραπ]ηίαις χρειμένος τὰν Λεβύαν οἰκ[έν].

§ 1. [Αἴ] κα ἐπὶ τὰγ γᾶν ἢ ἐπὶ τὰμ πόλιν ἐπείηι νόσο[ς ἢ λι-||
5 μὸ]ς ἢ θάνατος, θύεν ἔμπροσθε τᾶμ πυλᾶν, [ἐναν|τίον] τῶ ἀποτρο-
παίω, τῶι 'Απόλλωνι τῶι ἀποτρό[π|ωι] χίμαρον ἐρυθρόν.

§ 2. [Κ]ᾶλον ἐν ἱαρῶι πεφυκός · αἴ κα τῶι θεῶι τὰν τιμὰ[ν |
10 ἐ]ρεῖσες, τῶι κάλωι χρησῆι καὶ ἐς ἱαρὰ καὶ ἐς βάβ[α||λα] καὶ ἐς
μιαρά.|

§ 3. 'Α[π]ὸ γυναικὸς ἀνὴρ τὰν νύκτα κοιμαθὲς θυσεῖ ὅ|[πυι κα]
δήληται · τὰν δὲ ἀμέραν κοιμαθὲς λωσάμεν[ος | θυσεῖ - - - - εἶτι,
ὅπυι κα δήλ[ητα]ι, πλὰν ἢ ἐς τ[ὸ | - - only a few letters legible
15 - - - - || - - -

§ 4. ['Α λ]εχώι ὄροφον μιανεῖ · τὸν μ[ὲν ὑπώροφον μιανεῖ, τὸν |
δ' ἐ]ξόροφον οὐ μιανεῖ, αἴ κα μὴ ὑπένθηι. ὁ δ' ἄ[νθρ|ω]πος, ὅ κα
ἔνδοι ἦι, αὐτὸς μὲν μιαρὸς τέντα[ι ἀμ|έρα]ς τρῖς, ἄλλον δὲ οὐ
20 μιανεῖ, οὐδὲ ὅπυι κα ἔνθ[ηι ο]||ὕτος ὁ ἄνθρωπος. |

§ 5. Ἅ κα μαντίων ὁσία παντὶ καὶ ἀγνῶι καὶ βαβάλω[ι] · |
πλὰν ἀπ' ἀνθρώπω Βάττω τῶ<τω> 'Αρχαγέτα καὶ | Τριτοπατέ-
ρων καὶ ἀπὸ 'Ονυμάστω τῶ Δελφῶι, | ἀπ' ἄλλω ὅπη ἄνθρωπος
25 ἔκαμε, οὐκ ὁσία ἀγνῶ[ι], || τῶν ἱαρῶν ὁσία παντί. |

§ 6. Αἴ κα ἐπὶ βωμῶι θύσηι ἱαρήιον ὅτι μὴ νόμος θύεν, τ[ὸ] |
ποτιπίαμμα ἀφελὲν ἀπὸ τῶ βωμῶ καὶ ἀποπλῦν|αι καὶ τὸ ἄλλο
λῦμα ἀνελὲν ἐκ τῶ ἱαρῶ, καὶ τὰν ἴκ|νυν ἀπὸ τῶ βωμῶ καὶ τὸ πῦρ
30 ἀφελέν ἐς καθαρόν · || καὶ τόκα δὴ ἀπονιψάμενος, καθάρας τὸ
ἱαρὸν καὶ | ζαμίαν θύσας βοτὸν τέλευν, τόκα δὴ θυέτω ὡς νομ|ο-
κώχιμος μέστα ἐς ἀδελφεῶν τέκνα. |

§ 7. Αἴ κα δεκατὸς ἦι ἄνθρωπος ἡβάτας, καθάρας α|[ὺ]τὸς
35 αὐτὸν αἵματι, καθαρεῖ τὸ ἱαρὸν καὶ πωλη||[θ]ὲς ἐν τᾶι ἀγοραῖ
ὁπόσσω κα πλείστω ἄξιος ἦ[ι], | προθυσεῖ πρὸ τᾶς δεκάτας ζαμίαν
βοτὸν τέλ|[ε]υν, οὐκ ἀπὸ τᾶς δεκάτας, καὶ τόκα δὴ θυσεῖ τὰν |
[δ]εκάταν καὶ ἀποισεῖ ἐς καθαρόν · αἰ δὲ μή, τῶν αὐ|[τ]ῶν δησῆ-
ται [σκ]οίκιον δὲ οἰσεῖ πᾶς ὁ θύων. ||

40　§ 8. [Ἄ]νηβος αἰ μή τί κα ἐκὼν μιᾶι, ἀποχρεῖ καθάρασ|[θ]αι
αὐτὸν καὶ ζαμίας οὐ δεῖ · αἰ δέκα ἐκὼμ μιᾶι, κα|[θ]αρεῖ τὸ ἱαρὸν
καὶ ζαμίαν προθυσεῖ βοτὸν τέλευν. |

§ 9. Αἴ κα χρήματα δεκατὰ ἦι, ἐκτιμάσας τὰ χρήματ|α, κα-
45 θαρεῖ τὸ ἱαρὸν καὶ τὰ χρήματα δίχα καὶ τόκα || [δ]ὴ προθυσεῖ
ζαμίαν βοτὸν τέλευν, οὐ τᾶς δεκάτ|[ας], καὶ τόκα δὴ θυσεῖ τὰν
δεκάταν καὶ ἀποισεῖ ἐς | [κα]θαρόν· αἰ δὲ μή, τῶν αὐτῶν δησεῖ.
τῶν δὲ χρημά|[τω]ν, ἅς κα δεκατὰ ἦι, ἐντόφιον οὐκ ἐνθησεῖ οὐδὲ
50 [ἧς ο]ὐδὲ ἕν, οὐδὲ χύτλα οἰσεῖ πρίν κα τῶι θεῶι ἀπο[δε||κατε]ύσει.
αἰ δέ κα χύτλα ἐνίκει ἢ ἐντόφια ἐνθῆι, κα|[θά]ρας τὸ Ἀπολλώνιον
ζαμίαν προθυσεῖ κατὰ τὰν | [ἅμα]ρτίαν βοτὸν τέλευν. |

§ 10. [Αἴ κ]α δεκατός ἐὼν ἄνθρωπος ἀποθάνηι, κατακομί-|
55 [ξα]ντες τὸν ἄνθρωπον, τᾶι μὲν πρατίσται ἀμέραι || [ἐπι]θησεῖ ὅ
τι κα δήληται ἐπὶ τὸ σᾶμα, δεύτερον δ|[ὲ ο]ὐδὲ ἕν, πρίγ κα ἀπο-
δεκατεύσει τῶι θεῶι, καὶ ο[ὐ]|δὲ θυ]σεῖ οὐδ' ἐπὶ τὸ σᾶμα εἶτι.
ἐκτιμασέντι δὲ οἵ[ω | κα πλ]είστω ἄξιος ἦς, κοινὸς ἐὼν τῶι θεῶι.
(κ)αθάρα[ς | δὲ τὸ] Ἀπολλώνιον καὶ τὰ χρήματα δίχα, προθύ-
60 [σα||ς αὐτὸ]ς ζαμίαν βοτὸν τέλευν, οὐκ ἀπὸ τᾶς δε(κ)ά[τ|ας, προ]-
βώμιον, θυσεῖ τὰν δεκάταν προβώμιον κ[α|ὶ ἀπο]ισεῖ ἐς καθαρόν.
αἰ δὲ μή, τῶν αὐτῶν δησεῖ. |

§ 11. [Αἴ κα ἀπ]οθάνηι δεκατὸς ἐὼν καὶ τὰ τέκνα καταλι-
65 [π|όμενα τ]ὰ μὲν ζῶι, τὰ δὲ ἀποθάνηι, ἐκτιμάσας τὰ [ἀ||πηλ-
λαγ]μένα, ὁπόσσω κα πλείστω ἄξια ἦι, καθάρα[ς τὸ | Ἀπολλώ]-
νιον καὶ τὰ χρήματα δίχα, προθυσεῖ ζαμ]ίαν | τὰν τῶ ἠ]βατᾶ προ-
βώμιον, καὶ τόκα δὴ θυσεῖ τὰν δε[κ|άταν προ]βώμιον. τὸν δὲ
ζοὸν καθάρας αὐτὸς αὐτ[ὸ|ν καθᾶρ]αι τὸ ἱαρὸν δίχα πωληθὲς ἐν
70 τᾶι ἀγοραῖ θ[υ||σεῖ τὰν τ[ῶ ἠβατᾶ ζαμίαν βοτὸν τέλευν καὶ
τόκ[α δὴ | θυσεῖ τὰ]ν δεκάταν καὶ | ἀποισεῖ ἐς καθαρόν· αἰ
[δὲ μ|ή, τῶν αὐτ]ῶν δησεῖ. |

§ 12. [Ἀρκτεῦε]ν ἐπεί κα ἄρξεται, θύεν κατὰ νόμον. [αἰ μέγ |
75 κα ἄρκος ἔν]θηι, τὸ λοιπὸν θυσεῖ ὁπόκα κα δήλη[ται· αἰ || δέ κα
μὴ ἔν]θηι, καθαρμὸς ἀποχρεῖ ὅπ[υι] τις τ[ὰν δεκέτ|ιν χαλάξει]·
καθᾶραι οὐ δεῖ, αἰ δέ κα δήλητ[αι, αἰ δέ κα μ|ή, κάθαρ]μα προ-
βώμιον οἰσεῖ ὅπυι τ[ις τὰν δεκέτιν χ|αλάξει· αἰ ἄ]νθρωπος δ'
80 ἐχάλαξε τ[ὰν παρθένον - - - | - - - -]ς μὲν ἐπ[ιθυσεῖ - - - || - - -
| - - - | - - - |

§ 13. [Νύμφ]αμ μ[ὲν αἴ κα ἔνθηι ἐς κοιτατή]ριον, ζ[αμίαν |
85 δεῖ] ἐς Ἄρτ[αμιν θύεν]· αὐτὰ δὲ οὐχ ὑπώροφ||[ος τῶι ἀνδρὶ

τένται οὐδὲ μιασεῖ, μέστα κα [ἐ|ς] Ἄρτεμιν ἔνθηι. ἃ δέ κα ταῦτα
μὴ ποιήσα[ι|σ]α μιᾶι ἔκασσα, καθάραισα τὸ Ἀρταμίτιον ἐπ[ι |
θ]υσεῖ ζαμίαν βοτὸν τέλευν, καὶ τόκα δὴ εἶτ|[ι] τὸ κοιτατήριον·
90 αἰ δέ κα μὴ ἐκοῖσα μιᾶι, κα||[θ]αρεῖ τὸ ἱαρόν. |

§ 14. [N]ύμφαν δὲ τὸ νυμφήιον ἐς Ἄρταμιν κατ[εν|θ]ὲν δεῖ,
ὁπόκα κα δήληται Ἀρτεμιτίοις, [ὥς κα | τ]άχιστα δὲ λώιον·
ἃ δέ κα μὴ κατένθηι, ἀ[ποθ|υ]σεῖ τᾶι Ἀρτάματι ἅ κ[α νομίζητ]αι
τοῖς [Ἀρταμιτίοις || ὡ]ς μὴ κατεληλευ[θυῖα, καὶ τόκα δὴ καθαρεῖ
τὸ ἱαρ|ὸ]ν καὶ ἐπιθυσεῖ ζ[αμίαν βοτὸν τέλευν] |

§ 15. [Νύμφα ἐπεί κα διακορηθῆι, κάτε]ιτι τὸ νυμφήι[ον] | ἐς
Ἄρταμιν [αὐτὰ] κ[αὶ τᾶι ἄρκωι δωσεῖ πόδας καὶ | τὰν κεφαλὰν
100 καὶ τὸ δέρμα· αἰ δέ κα μὴ κατ[έν]||θηι, πρὶν τεκὲν κάτειτι σὺμ
βοτῶι τελέωι· ἁ δ[ὲ] | κατίασσα ἀγνευσεῖ ἐβδέμαν καὶ ὀγδόαν |
καὶ ἠνάταν, καὶ ἁ μὴ κατεληλευθυῖα ἀγν|ευσεῖ ταύτας τὰς ἁμέρας·
αἰ δέ κα μιᾶι. καθα|ραμένα αὐτὰ καθαρεῖ τὸ ἱαρὸν καὶ ἐπιθυσ[εῖ] ||
105 ζαμίαν βοτὸν τέλευν. |

§ 16. Αἴ κα γυνὰ ἐγβάληι, αἰ μέγ κα διάδηλον ἦι, μ[ι]αίνονται
ὥσπερ ἀπὸ θανόντος, αἰ δέ κα μὴ | διάδηλον ἦι, μιαίνεται αὐτὰ ἁ
οἰκία καθάπε[ρ] | ἀπὸ λεχός. ||

110 § 17. Ἱκεσίων |
Ἱκέσιος ἐπακτός· αἴ κα ἐπιπεμφθῆι ἐπὶ τὰν | οἰκίαν, 'αἰ μέγ
κα ἴσαι ἀφ' ὅτινός οἱ ἐπῆνθε, ὀ|νυμαξεῖ αὐτὸν προειπὼν τρῖς ἁμέ-
115 ρας· αἰ δ[έ] | κα τεθνάκηι ἔγγαιος ἢ ἄλλη πη ἀπολώλη[ι], || αἰ
μέγ κα ἴσαι τὸ ὄνυμα, ὀνυμαστὶ προερεῖ, αἰ | δέ κα μὴ ἴσαι
"ὦ ἄνθρωπε, αἴτε ἀνὴρ αἴτε γυνὰ | ἐσσί", κολοσὸς ποιήσαντα
ἔρσενα καὶ θήλεια[ν] | ἢ καλίνος ἢ γαῖνος, ὑποδεξάμενον παρτιθ-
120 [έ]||μεν τὸ μέρος πάντων· ἐπεὶ δέ κα ποιῆσες τὰ || νομιζόμενα,
φέροντα ἐς ὕλαν ἀεργὸν ἐρε[ῖ]|σαι τὰς κολοσὸς καὶ τὰ μέρη· |

§ 18. Ἱκέσιος ἄτερος, τετελεσμένος ἢ ἀτελής. ἰσ|σάμενος ἐπὶ
δαμοσίωι ἱαρῶι, αἰ μέγ κα προ[φέ]|ρηται, ὁπόσσω κα προφέρηται,
125 οὕτως τελίσκ[ε]||σθαι· αἰ δέ κα μὴ προφέρηται, γᾶς καρπὸν θ[ύ]-|
εν καὶ σπονδὰν καθ' ἔτος ἀεί. αἰ δέ κα παρῆι ἐ[ς] | νέω, δὶς τόσσα.
αἰ δέ κα διαλίπηι τέκνον ἐπι[λα]|θόμενον καὶ οἱ προφέρηται, ὅ τι
κά οἱ μαντε[υ]|ομένωι ἀναιρεθῆι, τοῦτο ἀποτεισεῖ τῶι θεῶ<ι>
130 κ[αὶ] || θυσεῖ, αἰ μέγ κα ἴσαι, ἐπὶ τὸμ πατρῶιον, αἰ δὲ μή, [χρή]-
σασθαι. |

§ 19. Ἱκέσιος τρίτος, αὐτοφόνος· ἀφικετεύεν ἐς [τρι]|πολίαν
καὶ τριφυλίαν· ὡς δέ κα καταγγήλε[ι ἱκέ]|σθαι, ἴσσαντα ἐπὶ τῶι

135 ὡδῶι ἐπὶ νάκει λευκ[ῶι νί]||ζεν καὶ χρῖσαι καὶ ἐξίμεν ἐς τὰν δα-
μοσί[αν] | ὁδὸν καὶ σιγὲν πάντας, ἢ κα ἔξοι ἔωντι, [τὸ|ς] ὑποδεχο-
μένος τὸν προαγγελτ[ῆρα · ἐς τὸ ἱα|ρὸ]ν παρίμεν τὸν ἀφικτευ[ό]-
μενο[ν - - - - | - -] εων καὶ τὸς ἐπομένος [of the remaining lines
only a few letters are legible].

Ritual practices enjoined by the oracle of Apollo.

'Apollo proclaimed by oracle. Always practicing purifications
and holy acts and serv:ces they shall inhabit Libya.'—**χρείμενος**:
could be the Delphian form in this passage beginning Ἀπόλλων
ἔχρησε, but not necessarily so. See **158**.

§ 1. 'If disease or famine or death comes to the land or the
city, one shall sacrifice before the gates, facing the apotropaion,
a red goat to Apollo the averter of evil.'

§ 2. 'Timber grown in the sacred precinct. If you have deposited the price for the god, you may use the timber for things
sacred and profane and defiled.' —9. **ἐ]ρεῖσες** : probable reading.
Oliverio's π]οεῖσες = ποιῆοες 1. 119 is to be rejected, for ει =
original η is unknown. ἐρείδω 'prop up, support', also 'make
firm, fix,' and below 1. 120 probably 'deposit.' Here 'deposit'
or 'fix' = 'arrange for.'

§ 3. 'A man (purifying himself) from a woman, if he has
lain with her by night, he shall sacrifice wherever he wishes.
If he has lain (with her) by day, having washed himself, (he shall
sacrifice and) shall go wherever he wishes except into the - - - -.'
—13. The letters preceding ὅπυι κα δήληται are uncertain, but
εἶτι or κατεῖτι looks more probable than Oliverio's [μετ' ὀλίγ]ον τι.

§ 4. 'The woman in childbed will defile the house. The one
within the house she will defile, but the one outside the house
she will not defile, unless one comes inside. The person who is
inside shall himself be defiled for three days, but shall not defile
another, nor (any place) where this person comes.'—16. **ὄροφος**:
'roof' here = 'house', like Cret. στέγα. —18. **τένται**: = τέλεται =
ἔσεται. **72**.

§ 5 'As to oracles, sanction (to consult them) belongs to
everyone, both the holy and the profane—except that (for those)
from the person Battus the Founder and the Ancestors and
Onumastus the Delphian (and) from any other person who died

(lit. from anyone else where a person died) there is no sanction for the holy. As to the shrines, sanction belongs to everyone.'— This is the most difficult paragraph and there has been no agreement in the interpretation. ἄ κα 'in case that' (cf. l. 93) properly requires a verb, but probably is here an abbreviated form of ἄ κα ἦι.—μαντίων: not from μάντις 'seer,' but from a *μάντιον = μαντεῖον, like ἱαρῶν l. 25 and Ἱκεσίων l. 110., gen. of matters or persons involved (171).—The passage ll. 22 ff. plainly refers to oracles of the dead (cf. νεκυομαντεῖον Hdt. 5.92, Paus. 9.30.6).— 22. τῶ‹τω›: probably dittography. ἄνθρωπος points the contrast of oracles of deceased human beings to those of the gods.— 23. τῶ Δελφῶι: cf. 38a.—24. ἔκαμε: 'died.' Cf. Hom. βροτῶν εἴδωλα καμόντων.

§ 6. Regulations for one who has sacrificed a victim which it is not lawful to sacrifice.—27. ποτιπίαμμα: 'the fat that remains.' 164.4.—28/9 ἴκνυν. Cf. ἴκνυον· κονίαν, σμῆμα Hesych. Here 'ashes' ?—31, 32. ὡς νομοκώχιμος μέστα ἐς ἀδελφεῶν τέκνα: 'as bound by the law (which extends) up to the children of brothers.' νομοκώχιμος (or possibly νομωκώχιμος as Oliverio), parallel to κατοκώχιμος, is the probable reading. At the end of l. 31 there is no room after νομ for any more letters, so that the reading νόμ(ος) implies an abbreviation that is improbable.

§§ 7-11. Regulations for a δεκατός 'one subject to a tithe.'— 34/5 πωληθές κτλ.: 'having been offered for sale in the market-place for whatever he is worth.'—38, 46/7, 62, 72. ἀποισεῖ ἐς καθαρόν: 'shall restore (things) to a state of purity.'—39. [σκ]οίκιον, some kind of receptacle, quotable from papyri, is the probable reading. Oliverio reads ἐποίκιον 'supellex' but this is not the sense of the word in CIGI 1730 (= IG IX.i.47) to which he refers.—40, 41, 86, 89. μιᾶι: 3 sg. aor. subj. (144b, 151.1) in pass. sense 'be defiled,' as also 3 sg. fut. μιασεῖ l. 85 vs. trans. μιανεῖ ll. 16-19.—45. οὐ τᾶς δεκάτας: = οὐκ ἀπὸ τᾶς δεκάτας ll. 36, 60.—47. δησεῖ: so certainly here (where Oliverio assumes omission of ται), and from the photograph probable in l. 62 (Oliverio δησειτ[αι]) and l. 72 (Oliverio δησεῖται, but no visible traces after ΕΙ).—48/9. Read οὐδὲ [ἧς ο]ὐδὲ ἕν after Tab. Heracl. 1.136. Calhoun, CP 29. 345.—53 ff. 'If the one subject to a tithe has died, after they have buried him, on the first day (the heir) shall bring whatever he wishes to the grave, but afterwards nothing until he has paid off the tithe to the god, and he shall not make an offering or go to the grave. They shall evaluate (the deceased δεκατός) for the most that he was worth, he being a partner of the god (that is, in part indebted to him).'—57. ἐκτιμασέντι: **42.**5e.—65/6. **ἐκτιμάσας** κτλ.: '(the heir) having evaluated the deceased (children) for the most they are worth.'

§ 12. This paragraph is wholly obscure without extensive restorations. Those of Oliverio, repeated in SEG and with some minor changes in the text above, are only plausible conjectures, of which the critical ones are [ἄρκος] (the girl in the service of Artemis, mentioned in 1. 98), [ἀρκτεύε]ιν (should be rather [ἀρκτεῦε]ν), and [δεκέτιν]. Even so, the sense is none too clear.

§§ 13-15. Regulations regarding a bride.—The restorations in ll. 83/4 of the words before αὐτά and of διαχορηθῇ in l. 97 are of course uncertain.

§ 16. 'If a woman suffers a miscarriage or abortion, if it is plain (that is, if the fetus is fully formed), (persons) are defiled as from one dead, but if it is not plain the houshold itself is defiled as from one in childbirth.'

§§ 17-19, with the heading 'About Suppliants.' The view of Stukey, CP 32.32 ff., that the ἱκέσιοι were not suppliants but supernatural beings, is not convincing. Although the text is nearly perfect and the literal meaning generally clear, the interpretation of the real situation is in part uncertain.

§ 17. 'Suppliant from abroad. If he has been sent to the home, if (the master of the home) knows from whom he came to him, he shall name this person, giving notice for three days. If he (this person) has died within the land or has perished anywhere else, if he (the master) knows the name he shall give notice by name. But if he does not know, (then saying) "O person whether thou art man or woman," having made figures male and female of wood or clay, as host one shall place beside them the (proper) portion of all (that is, the customary food and drink). When you have done the things customary, bringing them to a virgin forest deposit the figures and the portions.'

§ 18. 'Second suppliant, initiated or uninitiated. Having been seated at the public shrine, if there is a declaration (by the priest), for whatever amount is declared so it shall be fulfilled. If there is no declaration, one shall sacrifice the fruit of the land and a libation annually forever. If he presents himself anew, then twice as much. If he leaves a child who has neglected it and a declaration is made to him (the child), whatever is ordained for him consulting the oracle this he shall pay to the god and shall sacrifice, if he knows (where it is) on the ancestral tomb,— if not, consult the oracle.'—126. **αἰ δέ κα παρῆι**: παρῆι is taken by most commentators as 'omit' and so from πάρειμι, cpd. of εἶμι in its use for 'pass by' (Hdt. 7.109, etc.). But from this one expects παρείηι like ἐπείηι l. 4. As it stands, παρῆι belongs to the cpd. of εἰμί. De Sanctis, Riv. fil. 55.206, so takes it.

19. 'Third suppliant, a homicide. One shall make intercession to the tribunal of the three cities and the three tribes. When one has announced that one is making supplication, having seated (the suppliant) on the threshold, on a white fleece, one shall wash and anoint him and go forth into the public road, and they shall all keep silent, so long as they are outside, following the announcer. The one for whom intercession is made shall procede to the shrine - - and those following - - -'

Cretan

116. Drerus. Sixth century B.C. P. Demargne et H. van Effenterre, BCH 61.333 ff., 62.194.

῾Αδ' ἔϝαδε πόλι· ἐπεί κα κοσμήσει δέκα ϝετίον τὸν ἀ|ϝτὸν μὴ κοσμέν· αἰ δὲ κοσμησίε, ὄπε δικασσίε, αὐτὸν ὀπῆλεν διπλεῖ κἀϝτόν, | θιὸς ὄλοι ὄν, ἄκρηστον ἤμεν, ἆς δόοι, κὄτι κοσμησίε μηδὲν ἤμην. | ὀμόται δὲ κόσμος κὄι δάμιοι κὄι ἴκατι οἱ τᾶς πόλ[ιος].

As in other early Cretan inscriptions, ᴇ = η, but here beside Ε which in some cases must also stand for η. Cf. ᴇ ᴎ Ε ᴎ beside ᴇ ᴎ ⊔ ᴎ. We therefore transcribe ἤμεν beside ἤμην, and so ὀπē, κοσμέν, κοσμησίē. ᴠ = λ in contrast to usual Cret. ᴧ.

'Voted by the city as follows. When one shall have been kosmos, the same one shall not be kosmos within ten years. If he has become kosmos (within ten years), in whatever case he pronounces judgment, he shall owe a double penalty and himself—god destroy him—be without function as long as he lives, and whatever he has done as kosmos shall be null and void. Jurors the kosmos and the damioi (those appointed from the people?) and the twenty of the city.'

1. ἄδ': 'in this manner, as follows' (132.6), confirming this interpretation of Delph. ἄδε in no. 51.—πόλι: for lack of article see 122a.—κοσμησίε, δικακσίε: 152.4.—The insertion between the first and second lines, just above κάϜτόν, is obviously an imprecation thrown in. The letters are clear except for the third from the end, and that, despite the peculiar form that appears in the photograph, is probably the crooked iota and so taken by the editor. Read θιὸς ὄλοι ὄν, with 2. aor. act. (otherwise only attested in mid.) of ὄλλυμι and demonstrative use of ὅς.—
3. ἄκρηστον: = ἄχρηστον 'useless', here 'without right to function.'—4. ἴκατι: the absence of Ϝ, in contrast to ἔϜαδε, Ϝετίον, is strange, but seen also in ἰκάδι of another archaic inscription of Drerus.

117. Gortyn. Fifth century B.C. GDI 4991. Inscr. Jurid. I, pp. 352 ff. Schwyzer 179. Solmsen-Fraenkel 40.

1   Θιοί. | Ὅς κ' ἐλευθέρōι ἒ δόλōι μέλλει ἀν|πιμōλἒν, πρὸ δίκας μὲ ἄγεν. αἰ δ|έ κ' ἄγει, καταδικακσάτō τō ἐλευθέρ|ō δέκα στατῆρανς,
5   τō δόλō πέν||τε, ὄτι ἄγει, καὶ δικακσάτō λαγάσαι | ἐν ταῖς τρισὶ ἀμέραις. αἰ [δέ] κα | μὲ [λαγ]άσει, καταδικαδδέτō τō μὲν | ἐλευθέρō στατῆρα, τō δόλō [δα]ρκν|ὰν τᾶς ἀμέρας Ϝεκάστας, πρίν κα
10   λα||γάσει· τō δὲ κρόνō τὸν δι[κ]αστ|ὰν ὀμνύντα κρίνεν. αἰ δ' ἀννί|οιτο | μὲ ἄγεν, τὸν δικαστὰν ὀμνύντ|α κρ[ί]νεν, αἰ μὲ ἀποπōνίοι
15   μαῖτυς. | αἰ δέ κα μōλἒι ὁ μὲν ἐλεύθε[ρ]ον, || ὁ δ[ὲ δ]ōλον, κάρτο- νανς ἔμἒν | [ὄτερο]ί κ' ἐλεύθερον ἀποπōνίōν|τι. αἰ δέ κ' ἀνπὶ δόλōι μōλίōντι | πōνίοντες Ϝὸν Ϝεκάτερος ἔμ|ἒν, αἰ μέν κα μαῖτυς ἀποπō-
20   νἒι, κ||ατὰ τὸν μαῖτυρα δικάδδεν, αἰ | δέ κ' ἒ ἀνποτέροις ἀποπōνί-ōντι | ἒ μēδατέρōι, τὸν δικαστὰν ὀ|μνύντα κρίνεν. ἒ δέ κα νικαθἒι
25   ὁ | ἐκōν, [τ]ὸμ μὲν ἐλεύθερον λαγ||άσαι τᾶν πέ[ν]τ' ἀμερᾶν, τὸν δὲ δō|λ[ον] ἐς κέρανς ἀποδόμēν. αἰ δέ | κα μὲ λαγάσει ἒ μὲ ἀποδōῖ, δικακ|σάτō νικἒν τō μὲν ἐλευθέρō | πεντέκοντα στατῆρανς καὶ
30   σ||τατῆρα τᾶς ἀμέρας Ϝεκάστ|ας, πρίν κα λαγάσει, τō δὲ δόλō | δέκα στατῆρανς καὶ δαρκνὰν | τᾶς ἀμέρας Ϝεκάστας, πρίν κ' ἀ|πο-
35   δōῖ ἐς κέρανς. ἒ δέ κα καταδι||κάκσει ὁ δικαστάς, ἐνιαυτōῖ π|ράδ-δεθθαι τὰ τρίτρα ἒ μεῖον, | πλίον δέ μἒ· τō δὲ κρόνō τὸν δι|κανστὰ

40 ὀμνύντα κρίνεν. αἰ δέ | κα ναεύει ὁ δῶλος ὅ κα νικαθῆ‖ι, καλίον ἀντὶ
μαιτύρον δυῶν δ|ρομέον ἐλευθέρον ἀποδεικσάτ|ο ἐπὶ τῶι ναῶι ὅπε
κα ναεύει ἒ α|ὐτὸς ἒ ἄ(λ)λος πρὸ τούτο · αἰ δέ | κα μὲ καλῆι ἒ μὲ
45 δείκσει, κατισ‖[τάτ]ο τὰ ἐ[γρα](μ)μένα. αἰ δέ κα μὲδ' | αὐτὸν
ἀποδῶι ἐν τῶι ἐνιαυτῶι, | τὰνς ἀπλόονς τ[ι]μὰνς ἐπικατ|αστασεῖ.
50 αἰ δέ κ' ἀποθάνει μ|ōλιομένας τᾶδ δί[κα]ς, τὰν ἀπλ‖όον τιμὰν κα-
τ(α)στασεῖ. αἰ δ|έ κα κοσ[μ]ίον ἄγει ἒ κοσμίοντο|ς ἄλλος, ἒ κ'
ἀποστᾶι, μōλέν, καί κ|α νικαθῆι, κατιστάμεν ἀπ' [ἄ]ς | [ἀμέρα]ς
55 ἄγαγε τὰ ἐγραμένα. ‖ [τὸ]ν δὲ νενικαμένο[ν] κα[ὶ τὸν κα]-‖|
II τακείμενον ἄγοντι ἄπατον | ἔμεν.

Αἴ κα τὸν ἐλεύθερον ἒ | τὰν ἐλευθέραν κάρτει οἴπει, ἐκα|τὸν
5 στατέρανς καταστασεῖ · α‖|ἰ δέ κ' ἀπεταίρō, δέκα · αἰ δέ κ' ὁ δῶλο|ς
τὸν ἐλεύθερον ἒ τὰν ἐλευθέρα|ν, διπλεῖ καταστασεῖ · αἰ δέ κ' ἐλε|ύ-
θερος Ϝοικέα ἒ Ϝοικέαν, πέντε | δαρκνάνς · αἰ δέ κα Ϝ[ο]ικεὺς Ϝοι-
10 κέα ‖ ἒ Ϝοικέαν, π[έν]τε στατέρανς. | ἐνδοθιδίαν δōλαν αἰ κάρτει
δαμ|άσαιτο, δύο στατέρανς κατασ|τασεῖ · αἰ δέ κα δεδαμν[α]μέ-
15 ναν πε|δ' ἀμέραν, [ὁ]δελόν, αἰ δέ κ' ἐν νυτ‖|τί, δύ' ὀδελόνς · ὀρκιō-
τέραν δ' ἔ|μεν τὰν δōλαν. αἴ κα τὰν ἐ|λευθέραν ἐπιπερεῖται οἴπεν
20 ἀκε|ύοντος καδεστᾶ, δέκα στατέ|ρανς καταστασεῖ, αἰ ἀποπōνίο‖|ι
μαῖτυς. αἰ κα τὰν ἐλευθέραν | μοικίον αἰλεθῆι ἐν πατρὸς ἒ ἐν ἀ|δελ-
πιō ἒ ἐν τō ἀνδρός, ἑκατὸν | στατέρανς καταστασεῖ · αἰ δέ κ' ἐ|ν
25 ἄ(λ)λō, πεντέκοντα · αἰ δέ κα τὰν ‖ τō ἀπεταίρō, δέκα · αἰ δέ κ' ὁ
δῶλος [τὰ]|ν ἐλευθέραν, διπλεῖ καταστασε|ῖ · αἰ δέ κα δῶλος δōλō,
30 πέν|τε. προϜειπάτō δὲ ἀντὶ μαιτ|ύρον τριῶν τοῖς καδεσταῖ‖|ς τō
ἐναιλεθέντος ἀλλύεθ|θαι ἐν ταῖς πέντ' ἀμέραις · | τō δὲ δōλō τōι
πάσται ἀντὶ | μαιτύρον δυōν. αἰ δέ κα μ|ὲ ἀλλύσεται, ἐπὶ τοῖς ἑλόν-‖|
35 σι ἔμεν κρέθθαι ὅπαι κα λε|ίōντι. αἰ δέ κα πονῆι δολō|σαθθαι, ὀμό-
40 σαι τὸν ἑλό|ντα τō πεντεκονταστατέ|ρō καὶ πλίονος πέντον αὐ‖|τὸν
Ϝὶν αὐτō̄ι Ϝέκαστον ἐπ|αριόμενον, τō δ' ἀπεταίρō | τρίτον αὐτόν,
τō δὲ Ϝοικέ|ος τὸν πάσταν ἄτερον αὐτ|ὸν μοικίοντ' ἑλέν, δολōσαθ-‖|
45 θαι δὲ μέ.

Αἴ κ' ἀνὲρ [κα]ὶ [γυ]νὰ διακρ[ί]νōν[τ]αι, τὰ Ϝὰ α|ὐτᾶς ἔκεν, ἄτι
ἔκονσ' ἔιε π|ὰρ τὸν ἄνδρα, καὶ τō καρπō̄ τ|ὰνν ἐμίναν, αἴ κ' ἔι ἐς
50 τōν Ϝō‖|ν αὐτᾶς κρεμάτōν, κὄτι | κ' ἐνυπάνει τὰν [ἐμίνα]ν ἄτι |
κ' ἔι, καὶ πέντε στατέρανς, αἴ κ' ὁ ἀ|νὲρ αἴτιος ἔι τᾶς κε[ρ]εύ-
55 σι|ος · α[ἰ] δὲ πōνίοι ὁ ἀνὲρ [αἴτι‖|ος μὲ ἔ]μεν, τὸν δικαστὰν ‖|
III ὀμνύντα κρίνεν. αἰ δέ τι ἄλλ|ο πέροι τō ἀνδρός, πέντε στ|ατέρανς

5 καταστασεῖ κ̄́τι | κα πέρ̄ει αὐτόν, κ̄́τι κα παρ‖έλ̄ει ἀποδότō
αὐτόν. ὅν δέ κ' | ἐκσαννέσεται δικάκσαι τ|ὰν γυναῖκ' ἀπομόσαι τὰν
Ἄρ|τεμιν πὰρ Ἀμυκλαῖον πὰρ τὰν | Τοχσίαν. ὅτι δέ τίς κ' ἀπομο-‖
10 σάνσαι παρέλ̄ει, πέντε στατ|έρανς καταστασεῖ καὶ τὸ κρ|έος αὐτόν.
αἰ δέ κ' ἀλλόττρι|ος συνεσάδδ̄ει, δέκα στ[ατ]έ̄|ρανς καταστασεῖ,
15 τō δὲ κρέ‖ιος διπλεῖ ὅτι κ' ὁ δικαστὰς | ὀμόσει συνεσσάκσαι. | αἰ
ἀνὲρ ἀποθάνοι τέκνα κατ|αλιπό̄ν, αἴ κα λ̄ει ἁ γυνά, τὰ Fὰ | αὐτᾶς
20 ἔκονσαν ὀπυίεθθα‖ι κάτι κ' ὁ ἀνὲδ δ̄οι κατὰ τὰ ἐγ|ραμμένα ἀντὶ
μαιτύρō̄ν τρ|ιō̄ν δρομέ̄ō̄ν ἐλευθέρō̄ν· αἰ |δέ τι τōν τέκνō̄ν πέροι, ἔν-
25 δι|κον ἔμ̄εν. αἰ δέ κα ἄτεκνον ‖ καταλίπει, τά τε Fὰ αὐτᾶς ἔκε|ν
κ̄́τι κ' ἐν[υ]πάνει [τ]ὰν ἐμ[ί]ν|αν κα[ὶ τ]ō καρπ[ō] τō ἐνδ[ο]θεν
π|εδὰ τōν ἐπιβαλλόντ[ō̄ν] μοῖρα|ν λακὲ[ν] καὶ τί κ' ὁ ἀνὲδ δ̄οι ἀι
30 ἔγ‖ραττται· αἰ δέ τι ἄλλο πέροι, ἔν|δικον ἔμ̄εν. αἰ δὲ γυνὰ ἄτεκ|νος
ἀποθάνοι, τά τε Fὰ | αὐτᾶς τοῖς ἐπιβάλλονσι ἀπ|οδόμ̄εν κ̄́τι ἐνύ-
35 πανε τὰν ἐ‖μίναν καὶ τō καρπō, αἴ κ' ἐ̄ι ἐς | τōν Fōν αὐτᾶς, τὰν
ἐμίνα|ν. κόμιστρα αἴ κα λ̄ει δόμ̄εν | ἀνὲρ ̄ε γυνά, ̄ε F̄εμα ̄ε δυōδεκ|α
40 στατ̄έρανς ̄ε δυōδεκα στατ‖έρō̄ν κρέος, πλίον δὲ μ̄έ. αἴ κ|α Fοικέος
Fοικέα κριθ̄ει δ̄ōō | ̄ε ἀποθανόντος, τὰ Fὰ αὐτᾶ|ς ἔκεν· ἄλλο δ' αἴ
τι πέροι, ἔνδ|ικον ἔμ̄εν.

45 Αἰ τέκοι γυνὰ κ‖ε̄[ρ]ε[ύο]νσα, ἐπελεῦσαι τōι ἀ|νδρὶ ἐπὶ στέγαν
ἀντὶ μαιτ|ύρō̄ν τριō̄ν. αἰ δὲ μὲ δέκσαι|το, ἐπὶ τᾶι ματρὶ ἔμεν τὸ
50 τέκ|νον ̄ε τράπεν ̄ε ἀποθέμεν· ὀρκ|ιō̄τέροδ δ' ἔμ̄εν τὸς καδεστ|ὰνς
καὶ τὸς μαίτυρανς, αἰ | ἐπέλευσαν. αἰ δὲ Fοικέα τέ|κοι κ̄ερεύονσα,
55 ἐπελεῦσαι | τōι πάσται τō ἀνδρός, ὅς ὄ‖πυιε, ἀντὶ μαιτύρō̄ν [δυ]-
IV ō̄ν. ‖‖ αἰ δέ κα μὲ δέκσεται, ἐπὶ τōι | πάσται ἔμ̄εν τὸ τέκνον τōι τ|ᾶς
5 Fοικέας. αἰ δὲ τōι αὐτōι αὖ|τιν ὀπυίοιτο πρὸ τō ἐνιαυτ‖ō̄, τὸ παι-
δίον ἐπὶ τōι πάσται | ἔμ̄εν τōι τō Fοικέος. κόρκιό|τερον ἔμ̄εν τὸν
ἐπελεύσαν|τα καὶ τὸς μαίτυρανς. γ|υνὰ κ̄ερεύονσ' αἰ ἀποβάλοι ‖
10 παιδίον πρὶν ἐπελεῦσαι κα[τ]|ὰ τὰ ἐγραμμένα, ἐλευθέρō μ|ὲν κα-
ταστασεῖ πεντέκοντα | στατ̄έρανς, δόλō πέντε καὶ Fί|κατι, αἴ κα
15 νικαθ̄ε̄ι. ὀ̄ι δέ κα μ' ‖εἴ[̄ε] τι(ς) στέγα ὅπυι ἐπελευσε|ῖ, ̄ε αὐτὸν μὲ
ὁρ̄ει, αἰ ⟨αι⟩ ἀποθ|είε τὸ παιδίον, ἄπατον ἔμ̄εν. | αἰ κύσαιτο καὶ
20 τέκοι Fοικ|έα μὲ ὀπυιομένα, ἐπὶ τōι τ[ō] ‖ πατρὸς πάσται ἔμ̄εν τὸ
τ|έκνον· αἰ δ' ὁ πατὲρ μὲ δ̄οι, ἐ|πὶ τοῖς τōν ἀδελπιōν πάσ|ταις
ἔμ̄εν.

25 Τὸν πατέρα τōν | τέκνō̄ν καὶ τōν κρ̄εμάτō̄ν κ‖αρτερὸν ἔμ̄εν τᾶδ

δαίσιος | καὶ τὰν ματέρα τὸν Ϝὸν αὐ|τᾶς κρε̄μάτōν. ἆς κα δόōντι, |

30 μὲ̄ ἐπάνανκον ἔμε̄ν δατε̄|θθαι · αἰ δέ τις ἀταθείε̄, ἀποδ||άττατθαι
τοῖ ἀταμένōι ἄ|ι ἔγρατται. ε̄̓ δέ κ᾿ ἀποθάνε̄ι τι(ς), | στέγανς μὲν
τὰνς ἐν πόλι κἄ|τι κ᾿ ἐν ταῖ(ς) στέγαις ἐνε̄ῖ, αἷ|ς κα μὲ̄ Ϝοικεὺς ἐν-
35 Ϝοικε̄ῖ ἐπ||ὶ κόραι Ϝοικίōν, καὶ τὰ πρόβατα κα|ὶ καρτα[ί]ποδα, ἅ
κα μὲ̄ Ϝοικέος ε̄̓, | ἐπὶ τοῖς υἱάσι ἔμε̄ν, τὰ δ᾿ ἄλ|λα κρέματα πάντα
40 δατε̄θθα|ι καλο̄ς, καὶ λανκάνεν τὸς μὲν || υἱὺνς ὁπόττοι κ᾿ ἴōντι δύ|ο
μοίρανς Ϝέκαστον, τὰδ δ|ὲ θυγατέρανς ὁπότται κ᾿ ἴōν|τι μίαν μοῖ-
45 ραν Ϝεκάσταν. δ|ατε̄θ[θ]αι δὲ καὶ τὰ ματρ[ο̄]ια, ε̄̓ || κ᾿ ἀποθα[νε̄]ι,
ἆιπε[ρ] τὰ [πατρōι᾿] | ἔ[γραττ]αι. αἰ δὲ κρέματα μὲ̄ εἴ|ε̄, στέγα δέ,
λακὲν τὰθ θ[υ]γατέ|ρας ἄι ἔγρατται. αἰ δέ κα λε̄̓|ι ὁ πατὲ̄ρ δōὸς ἰὸν
50 δόμε̄ν τᾶ||ι ὀπυιομέναι, δότō κατὰ τ|ὰ ἐγραμμένα, πλίονα δὲ μέ̄. |

V ὀτείαι δὲ πρόθθ᾿ ἔδōκε ε̄̓ ἐπέσ|πενσε, ταῦτ᾿ ἔκεν, ἄλλα δὲ μὲ̄ ||| ἀπο-
λαν[κά]νεν. γυνὰ ὁ[τ]είᾳ κ|ρέματα μὲ̄ ἔκει ε̄̓ [πα]τρὸδ δό|ντος ε̄̓
5 ἀ[δ]ελπιō ε̄̓ ἐπισπέν|σαντος ε̄̓ ἀπολα[κ]όνσα ἄ||ι ὀκ᾿ ὁ Αἰθ[α]λεὺ(ς)
σταρτὸς ἐκόσ|μιον οἱ σὺν Κύ[λ]λōι, ταύτ|ας μὲν ἀπολανκάνεν,
ταῖ|δ δὲ πρόθθα μὲ̄ ἔ[ν]δικον ἔμ|ε̄ν.

10 Ἔ κ᾿ ἀπ[ο]θάνε̄ι ἀνὲ̄ρ ε̄̓ γυν||ά, αἰ μέν κ᾿ ε̄̓ι τέκνα ε̄̓ ἐς τέ|κνōν
τέκνα ε̄̓ ἐς τούτōν τέ|κνα, τούτος ἔκε[ν] τὰ κρέμα|τα. αἰ δέ κα
15 μέτις ε̄̓ι τούτō|ν, ἀ‹α›δελπιοὶ δὲ τō ἀποθανόν||τος κέκς ἀδε[λ]πιο̄ν
τέκν|α ε̄̓ ἐς τούτōν τέκνα, τούτ|ος ἔκεν τὰ κρέματα. αἰ δέ κα |μέτις
20 ε̄̓ι τούτōν, ἀδευπιαὶ δ|ὲ τō ἀποθανόντος κὲς ταυτ||ᾶν τέκνα ε̄̓ ἐς τōν
τέκνōν τέ|κνα, τούτος ἔκεν τὰ κρέμα|τα. αἰ δέ κα μέτις ε̄̓ι τούτōν, |
25 οἷς κ᾿ ἐπιβάλλε̄ι ὀπō κ᾿ ε̄̓ι τὰ κρ|έματα, τούτος ἀναιλε̄̓θθα||ι. αἰ δὲ
μὲ̄ εἶεν ἐπιβάλλοντε|ς, τᾶς Ϝοικίας οἵτινές κ᾿ | ἴōντι ὁ κλᾶρος,
τούτονς ἔ|κεν τὰ κρέματα.

30 Αἰ δέ κ᾿ οἱ | ἐπιβάλλοντες οἱ μὲν λεί||ōντι δατε̄θθαι τὰ κρέματ|α,
οἱ δὲ μέ̄, δικάκσαι τὸν δι|καστὰν ἐπὶ τοῖλ λείοσι δ|ατε̄θθαι ἔμεν
35 τὰ κρέματα π|άντα, πρίν κα δάττονται. || αἰ δέ κα δικάκσαντος τō
δ|ικαστᾶ κάρτει ἐνσείε̄ι ε̄̓ ἄ|γε̄ι ε̄̓ πέρε̄ι, δέκα στατε̄̓ραν|ς καταστα-
40 σεῖ καὶ τō κρέ|ιος διπλεῖ. τνατο̄ν δὲ καὶ καρ||πō καὶ Ϝέμας κἀνπι-
δέμας κ|ἐπιπολαίōν κρεμάτōν, αἴ κα μ|ὲ̄ λείōντι δατε̄[θθαι - - - τὸν
45 δ|ικαστ]ὰν ὀμνύντα κρῖνα|ι πορτὶ τὰ μōλιόμενα. [α]ἴ [δ]||ί κα κρέ-
ματα δατιομένοι | μὲ̄ συνγιγνόσκōντι ἀν|πὶ τὰν δαῖσιν, ὀνε̄̓ν τὰ κρέ-
50 μ|ατα κὸς κα πλεῖστον διδ|ο̄ι ἀποδόμενοι τᾶν τιμᾶν || δια[λ]ακόν-
τōν τὰν ἐπαβο|λάν Ϝέκαστος. δατιομέ|νοιδ δὲ κρέματα μαίτυρα|νς

VI παρέμεν δρομέανς ἐλε|υθέρονς τρίινς ε̄̓ πλίανς. ||| θυγατρὶ ε̄̓ διδο̄ι,
κατὰ τὰ αὐ|τά.

VI Ἂς κ' ὁ πατὲδ δόἔι, τὸν τὸ π|ατρὸς κρεμάτον πὰρ υἱέος | μὲ

5 ὀνε̄θθαι μεδὲ καταθίθ||εθθαι · ἄτι δέ κ' αὐτὸς πάσετ|αι ε̃ ἀπολάκε̄ι
ἀποδιδόθθο̄, | αἴ κα λε̄ι. μεδὲ τὸν πατέρα τὰ το̄|ν τέκνον ἄτι κ' αὐ-
10 τοὶ πάσον|ται ε̃ ἀπολάκοντι. μεδὲ τὰ τ||ᾶς γυναικὸς τὸν ἄνδρα
ἀπο|δόθαι μεδ' ἐπισπένσαι, μεδ' | υἱὺν τὰ τᾶς ματρός. αἰ δ|έ τις
πρίαιτο ε̃ καταθεῖτο ε̃ ἐ|πισπένσαιτο, ἀλλᾶι δ' ἔγρατ||[τα]ι, ἆι τάδε
15 τὰ γράμματα ἔγ|[ρατται, τὰ] μ[ὲ]ν κρέματα ἐπὶ τᾶι ματρὶ ἔμ|εν
20 κἐπὶ τᾶι γυναικί, ὁ δ' ἀπο|δόμενος ε̃ καταθὲνς ε̃ ἐπι||σπένσανς το̄ι
πριαμένο̄ι | ε̃ καταθεμένο̄ι ε̃ ἐπισπεν|σαμένο̄ι διπλεῖ καταστα|σεῖ
25 καί τί κ' ἄλλ' ἄτας ε̃ι, τὸ ἀπ|λόον · τὸν δὲ πρόθθα μὲ ἐν||δικον ἔμεν.
αἰ δέ κ' ὁ ἀντίμ|ο̄λος ἀπομο̄λε̄ι ἀνπὶ τὸ κρ|έος ο̄ι κ' ἀνπιμο̄λίο̄ντι μ|ὲ
30 ἔμεν τᾶς ματ[ρ]ὸς ε̃ τᾶ|ς γυναικός, μο̄λὲν ὅπε̄ κ' ἐπ||ιβάλλε̄ι, πὰρ
το̄ι δικαστᾶι | ε̃ Ϝεκάστο̄ ἔγρατται. αἰ δέ κ' ἀ|ποθάνε̄ι μάτε̄ρ τέκνα
καταλιπό|νσα, τὸν πατέρα καρτερὸν ἔμεν | τὸν ματρο̄ίον, ἀποδόθαι
35 δὲ μὲ || μεδὲ καταθέμεν, αἴ κα μὲ τὰ τέκ|να ἐπαινέσει δρομέες ἰόν-
τες. | [α]ἰ δέ τις ἀλλᾶι πρίαιτο ε̃ κατα|θεῖτο, τὰ μὲν κρέματα ἐπὶ
40 τοῖ|ς τέκνοις ἔμεν, το̄ι δὲ πριαμ||ένο̄ι ε̃ καταθεμένο̄ι τὸν ἀποδ|όμενον
ε̃ τὸν καταθέντα τὰν | διπλείαν καταστάσαι τᾶς τ|ιμᾶς, καί τί
45 κ' ἄλλ' ἄτας ε̃ι, τὸ ἀ|πλόον. αἰ δέ κ' ἄλλαν ὀπυίε̄ι, τὰ τ||έκνα [το̄]ν
[μ]ατρο̄ίον καρτερὸν|ς ἔμεν.

Αἴ κ' ἐδ δυσ[μενίας] πε|ρα[θε̄ι κ]ὲ̄ς ἀλλοπολίας ὑπ' ἀν|άνκας
50 ἐκόμενος κελο[μ]ένο̄ τι|ς λύσεται, ἐπὶ το̄ι ἀλλυσαμέν||ο̄ι ἔμεν, πρίν
κ' ἀποδο̄ι τὸ ἐπιβά|λλον. αἰ δέ κα μὲ ὁμολογίο̄ντ|ι ἀμπὶ τὰν πλε̄-
θὺν ε̃ μὲ [κ]ελομέ|[ν]ο̄ αὐτο̄ [λ]ύσαθθαι, τὸν δικασ|τὰν ὀμνύντα
55 κρίνεν πορτὶ τὰ || μο̄λιόμενα. [τ]ο̄ ἐλευθέρο̄ τὸν | δε - - - -. [αἰ
VII κ' ὁ δο̄λος] |||| ἐπὶ τὰν ἐλευθέραν ἐλθὸν ὀπυίε̄ι, | ἐλεύθερ' ἔμεν τὰ
τέκνα. αἰ δέ κ' | ἀ ἐλευθέρα ἐπὶ τὸν δο̄λον, δο̄λ' ἔμ|εν τὰ τέκνα. αἰ
5 δέ κ' ἐς τᾶς αὐτ||ᾶς ματρὸς ἐλεύθερα καὶ δο̄λα | τέκνα γένε̄ται, ε̃
κ' ἀποθάνε̄ι ἀ | μάτε̄ρ, αἴ κ' ε̃ι κρέματα, τὸνς ἐλε|υθέρονς ἔκεν. αἰ
10 δ' ἐλεύθεροι | μὲ ἐκσεῖεν, τὸνς ἐπιβάλλον|τανς ἀναιλε̄θαι. α[ἰ]
κ' ἐκς ἀγ|ορᾶς πρ[ι]άμενος δο̄λον μὲ π|εραιόσει τᾶν Ϝεκσέκοντ'
15 ἀμ|ερᾶν, αἴ τινά κα πρόθ' ἀδικέ|κε̄ι ε̃ ὕστερον. το̄ι πεπαμέν||ο̄ι
ἔνδικον ἔμεν.

Τὰμ πα|[τ]ρο̄ι[ο̄]κον ὀπυίεθαι ἀδελπι|ο̄ι το̄ πατρὸς τὸν ἰόντον
το̄ι | πρειγ[ί]στο̄ι. αἰ δέ κα πλίες πατ|ρο̄ιο̄κοι ἴοντι κἀδελπι[ο]ὶ
20 το̄ πα||τρός, [τ]ο̄ι ἐπιπρειγίστο̄ι ὀπυί|εθαι. αἰ δέ κα μὲ ἴοντι
ἀδελπιο̄|ὶ το̄ πατρός, υἱέεδ δὲ ἐκς ἀδελ|πιο̄ν, ὀπυίεθαι ἰο̄ι το̄ι [ἐ]ς

25 τȏ π|ρειγίστȏ. αἰ δέ κα πλίες ἴοντ||ι πατρȏιȏκοι κυίες ἐκς ἀδε|λ-
πιȏν, ἄλλȏι ὀπυίεθαι τȏι ἐπ|ὶ τȏι ἐς [τ]ȏ̄ πρει[γί]στȏ. μίαν δ' |
ἔκεν πατρȏι[ȏ̄]κον τὸν ἐπιβάλ|λοντα, πλίαδ δὲ [μ]έ̣.
30 ῁Αδ δέ κ' ἄν||ȏ̄ρος ε̣ῖ ὁ ἐπιβάλλȏν ὀπυίεν ε̣̄ | ἁ πατρȏιȏ̄κος, [σ]τέ-
γαν μέν, αἴ | κ' ε̣ῖ, ἔκεν τὰν πατρȏιȏ̄κον, τᾱδ | δ' ἐπικαρπίας παν-
35 τὸς τὰν ἐμ|ίναν ἀπολανκάνεν τὸν ἐπιβ||άλλοντα ὀπυίεν. αἰ δέ
κ' ἀπό|δρομος ἰὸν ὁ ἐπιβάλλȏν ὀπυ|ίεν ἐβίȏν ἐβίονσαν μὲ λε̣ῖ
40 ὀπ|υίεν, ἐπὶ τᾶι πατρȏιόκȏι ἔμε̣|ν τὰ κρέματα πάντα καὶ τὸν κ||αρ-
πόν, πρείν κ' ὀπυίε̣ι. αἰ δέ κα | δρομεὺς ἰὸν ὁ ἐπιβάλλȏν ε̣|βίονσαν
λείονσαν ὀπυίε|θαι μὲ λε̣ῖ ὀπυίεν, μȏλε̣ν τὸς | καδεστὰνς τὸς τᾶς
45 πατρȏι||ȏ̄κȏ, ὁ δὲ [δ]ικα[σ]τ[ὰς] δικ[ακσά]|τȏ ὀπυίεν ἐν τοῖς δ[υ]οῖς
με̣|νσί. αἰ δέ κα μὲ ὀπυίε̣ι ἆι ἔγρα|ται, τὰ κρέματα πάντ' ἔκον-
50 σα|ν, αἴ κ' ε̣ῖ ἄλλος, τȏι ἐπιβάλλοντ||ι · αἰ δ' ἐπιβάλλȏν μὲ εἴε, τᾶς |
πυλᾶς τὸν αἰτιόντȏν ὅτιμ|ί κα λε̣ῖ ὀπυίεθαι. αἰ δέ κα τȏ|ι ἐπι-
55 βάλλοντι ἐβίονσα μὲ λε̣|ι ὀπυίεθαι ε̣̄ ἄνȏρος ε̣ῖ ὁ ἐπιβ||άλ[λ]ȏν
VIII[κα]ὶ μ[ὲ λ]ε̣[ι μέν]εν ||| ἁ πατρȏιȏ̄κος, στέγαμ μέν, | αἴ κ' ε̣ῖ ἐν
πόλι, τὰμ πατρȏιȏ̄κο|ν ἔκεν κάτι κ' ἐνε̣ῖ ἐν τᾶι στέγ|αι, τὸν δ' ἄλλȏν
5 τὰν ἐμίναν δ||ιαλακόνσαν ἄλλȏι ὀπυίεθαι τᾶς πυλᾶς τȏν αἰτιόν-
τȏν | ὅτιμί κα λε̣ῖ. ἀποδατε̣θαι δ|ὲ τὸν κρεμάτȏν ἰȏι. αἰ δὲ μὲ |
10 εἶεν ἐπιβάλλοντες τᾶι <παι> π||ατρȏιόκȏι ἄ[ι ἔ]γρατται, τὰ κρ|έ-
ματα πάντ' ἔκ[ον]σαν τᾶς πυ|λᾶς ὀπυίεθ[α]ι ὅτιμί κα λε̣ῖ. | αἰ δὲ
15 τᾶς πυλ[ᾶ]ς μέτις λε|ίοι ὁ[π]υίεν, τὸς καδεστὰνς || τὸς τᾶς πατρȏιό-
κȏ Fείπαι κ|ατὰ [τὰν πυλ]ὰν ὅτι οὐ λ[ε̣ῖ ὁ]πυ|ίεν τις; καὶ μέν τίς
[κ' ὁ]πυίε̣ι, ἐ|ν ταῖς τριάκοντα ε̣ κα Fείπον|τι · αἰ δὲ μ(ε̣), ἄλλȏι
20 ὀπυίεθαι ὅτι||μί κα νύναται. αἰ δέ κα πατρὸ|ς δόντος ε̣ ἀδελ-
πιȏ̄ πατρȏιȏκο|ς γένε̣ται, αἰ λείοντος ὀπ|υίεν ȏι ἔδȏκαν μὲ λείοι
25 ὀπυ|ίεθαι, αἴ κ' ἐστετέκνȏται, δια||λακόνσαν τȏν κρεμάτȏν ἆι
ἔ|γρατται [ἄλλ]ȏι ὀπυίεθ[αι τᾶ]ς [π]|υ[λ]ᾶ[ς]. αἰ δὲ τέκνα μὲ
εἴε, πάντ' | ἔκονσαν τȏι ἐπιβάλλον[τ]ι ὀπυ|ίεθαι, αἴ κ' ε̣ῖ, αἰ δὲ μέ,
30 ἆι ἔγραττ||αι. ἀνὲρ αἰ ἀποθάνοι πατρȏι|όκȏι τέκνα καταλιπόν, αἴ
κα [λ]ε̣ῖ, | ὀπυιέθȏ τᾶς πυλᾶς ὅτιμί κα ν|ύναται, ἀνάνκαι δὲ μέ.
35 αἰ δὲ τέ|κνα μὲ καταλίποι ὁ ἀποθανόν, || ὀπυίεθαι τȏι ἐπιβάλ-
λοντι ἆ|ι ἔγρατται. αἰ δ' ὁ ἐπιβάλλȏν τ|ὰν πατρȏιȏ̄κον ὀπυίεν μὲ
40 ἐπ|ίδαμος εἴε, ἁ δὲ πατρȏιȏκος | ὁρίμα εἴε, τȏι ἐπιβάλλοντι ὁ||πυί-
εθαι ἆι ἔγρατται.

Πατρȏιȏ̄|κον δ' ἔμεν, αἴ κα πατὲρ μὲ ε̣ῖ ε̣ ἀ|δελπιὸς ἐς τȏ αὐ[τȏ]
πατρός. τȏν | δὲ κρεμάτȏ[ν κα]ρτερὸνς ἔμεν τ|ᾶς Fεργα[σ]ία[ς τὸς
45 πάτρȏανς, || [τ]ᾶς [δ' ἐπικαρ]πίας δια[λ]α[νκά]ν|εν [τ]ὰν ἐμίναν,

ἇ; κ' ἄ[ν]ōρ[ο]ς ἔι. | αἰ δ' ἀν[ό]ρōι ἰάτται μὲ εἴε ἐπι|ιβάλλον, τὰν
50 πατρōιῶκον καρ|τερὰν ἔμεν τōν τε κρεμάτōν κι||αὶ τō καρπō̃, κἇς
κ' ἄν[ō̃]ρος ἔι, τ|ράπεθαι [π]ὰρ τᾶι ματρί· αἰ δὲ μ|άτερ μὲ εἴε,
πὰρ τοῖς [μ]άτρōσι | τράπεθθα[ι]. αἰ δέ ̇τις ὀπυίοι τὰ|ν πατρōιō̃-
55 κον, ἀλλᾶι δ' [ἔγ]ραττται, || πεύθεν [πορ]τὶ κόσμ[ο]ν ||| τὸνς ἐπι-
IX βά[λλοντανς.

'Ανὲρ αἴ | κ' ἀποθανὸν πα]τρōιῶκον κα|ταλίπει, ἒ αὐ[τὰν ἒ πρὸ
5 αὐτᾶς τ|ονς πάτρōανς ἒ τὸ]νς μάτρōαν||ς καταθέμεν [ἒ ἀποδόθαι
τōν | κρεμάτōν καὶ] δικαίαν ἔμεν τ|ὰν ὀνὰν καὶ τὰν κα[τάθεσιν. αἰ |
δ' ἀλλᾶι πρί]αιτό τις κρέματα ἒ | καταθεῖτο τōν τᾶς πα[τρōιόκō,
10 τ]||ὰ [μ]ὲν [κρ]έματα ἐπὶ τᾶι πατρōιόκ|ōι ἔμεν, ὁ δ' ἀποδόμενος ἒ
ᚲατ|αθὲνς τōι πριαμένōι ἒ καταθε|μένōι, αἴ κα νικαθει̃, διπλεῖ κα-|
15 ταστασεῖ καί τί κ' ἄλλ' ἄτας ἔι, τ||ὸ ἀπλόον ἐπικαταστασεῖ, ἄ|ι
[τά]δε τὰ γ[ράμμ]ατ[α ἔγραττται, τ]||ō̃[ν δ]ὲ πρόθα μ[ὲ] ἔνδικον
ἔμεν. | αἰ δ' ὁ ἀντίμōλος ἀπομ[ōλ]ίο|ι ἀ[νπ]ὶ τὸ κρέος ōι κ' ἀνπιμō-
20 λί||ōντι μὲ τᾶς πατρōιόκō [ἔμ]εν, | ὁ δ[ικ]ασστὰς ὀμνὺς κρινέτō· αἰ |
δὲ νικάσαι μὲ τᾶς πατρ[ōι]όκ|ō ἔμ[ε]ν, μōλεν ὀπε κ' ἐπιβάλλει, ἒ |
Ϝεκάστō ἔγραττται.

25 Αἰ ἀν[δ]εκσ||άμ[ε]νος ἒ νενικαμένο[ς ἒ ἐνκ]||οιōτὰνς ὀπέλōν ἒ δια-
βαλόμε|νος ἒ διαϜειπάμενος ἀπο[θ]ά|νοι ἒ τούτōι ἄλλος, ἐπιμōλ|εν̄ν
30 ἰō̃ πρὸ τō̃ ἐνιαυτō̃· ὁ δὲ δικα||σστὰς δικαδδέτō πορτὶ τὰ [ἀ]ποπ|ōνιό-
μενα· αἰ μέν κα νίκας ἐπι|μōλει, ὁ δικασστὰς κō̃ μνάμōν, | αἴ κα δόει
35 καὶ πολιατεύει, οἰ δὲ μ|αίτυρες οἰ ἐπιβάλλοντες, ἀνδοκ||ᾶδ (δ)ὲ κ̄εν-
κοιōτᾶν καὶ διαβολᾶς κ|αὶ διρέσιος μαίτυρες οἰ ἐπι|βάλλοντες ἀπο-
πōνιόντōν. ἒ δέ κ' ἀ|ποϜείποντι, δικαδδέτō ὀμόσ|αντα αὐτὸν καὶ
40 τὸνς μαίτυρ||ανς νικε̄ν τὸ ἀπλόον. υἰὺς α|ἴ κ' ἀνδέκσεται, ἇς κ' ὁ
πατὲ(δ) δόει, | αὐτὸν ἀτε̄θαι καὶ τὰ κρέματα | ἄτι κα πέπαται.
45 αἴ τίς κα πέρα|ι συναλ[λάκ]σει, ἒ ἐς πέρ[α]ν ἐπι||θέντι μὲ ἀποδιδōι,
αἰ ιιέν κ' ἀ|ποπōνίōντι μαίτυρες ἑβίοντ|ες τō̃ ἑκατονστατερō̃ καὶ
πλίο|νος τρέες, τō̃ μείονος μέττ' ἐ|ς τὸ δεκαστάτερον δύο, τō̃ μεί-||
50 ονος ἔνδ, δικαδδέτō πορ[τ]ὶ τὰ | ἀποπō[ν]ιόμενα. αἰ δὲ μαίτυρε|[ς]
μὲ ἀποπōνίοιεν, ἒ κ' ἔ[λ]θει ὁ συ|ναλλάκσανς, ὀτερόν κ[α] κέλē-
X [τ]αι ὁ | μενπόμενος, ἒ ἀπομόσαι ἒ συν ||| [ll. 1-9, and most of
15 10-14, lacking] ματρὶ || δ' υἰὺν [ἒ ἄνδρα γυναικὶ δόμεν ἐ]|κατὸν
στα[τ]ε̄ρα[νς] ἒ μεῖον, π|λίον δὲ μέ. αἰ δὲ πλία δοίε, αἴ | κα λείōντ'
20 οἰ ἐπιβάλλοντες, τ|ὸν ἄργυρον ἀποδόντες τὰ κρ||έματ' ἑκόντōν.
αἰ δέ τις ὀπέ|λōν ἄργυρον ἒ ἀταμένος ἒ μ|ōλιομένας δίκας δοίε, αἰ |

25 μὲ εἴε τὰ λοιπὰ ἄκσια τᾶς ἄ|τας, μεδὲν ἐς κρέος ἔμεν τὰν || δόσιν.
Ἄντρō[π]ον μὲ ὀνέθα[ι] κατακείμενον, πρίν κ' ἀλλύσ|εται ὁ
καταθένς, μεδ' ἀμπίμō|λον, μεδὲ δέκσαθαι μεδ' ἐπισ|πένσαθαι
30 μεδὲ καταθέθαι. αἰ || δέ τις τουτῶν τι Ϝέρκσαι, μεδ|ὲν ἐς κρέος
ἔμεν, αἰ ἀποπōνίο|ιεν δύο μαίτυρε(ς). |

Ἄνπανσιν ἔμεν ὅπō κά τιλ λ|ει. ἀμπαίνεθαι δὲ κατ' ἀγορὰν ||
35 καταϜελμένōν τōμ πολιατᾶ|ν ἀπὸ τō λάō ō̄ ἀπαγορεύοντι. | ὁ δ' ἀμ-
πανάμενος δότō τᾶ|ι ἑταιρείαι τᾶι Ϝᾶι αὐτō ἰαρέ|ιον καὶ πρόκοον
40 Ϝοίνō. καὶ || μέν κ' ἀνέλεται πάντα τὰ κρέ|ματα καὶ μὲ συννει γνέ-
σια τ|έκνα, τέλλεμ μὲν τὰ θῖνα καὶ | τὰ ἀντρόπινα τὰ τō ἀνπανα-
45 μέ|νō κἀναιλέθαι ἄιπερ τοῖς γ||νεσίοις ἔγρατται. αἰ [δ]έ κα μὲ |
λει τέλλεν ἄι ἔγρατται, τὰ κ[ρ]έ|ματα τὸνς ἐπιβάλλοντανς ἔχε|ν.
50 αἰ δέ κ' ει γνέσ[ι]α τέκνα τōι ἀν|παναμένōι, πεδὰ μὲν τὸν ἐρσ||ένōν
XI τὸν ἀμπαντόν, ἄιπερ αἰ θ|έ[λε]ιαι ἀπὸ τōν ἀδελπιōν λανκά|νοντι·
αἰ δέ κ' ἔρσενες μὲ ἴōν|τι, θέλειαι δέ, [Ϝ]ισϜόμοιρον ε||||[μεν] τὸν
ἀνπαντὸν καὶ μὲ ἐ|πάνανχον ἔμεν τέλλεν τ[ὰ τ|ō ἀν]παναμένō καὶ τὰ
5 κρέμα|τ' ἀναιλ(ε̄)θαι ἄτι κα κατα[λίπε]||ι ὁ ἀν]πανάμενος· πλίυι
δὲ τὸν | ἀνπαντὸμ μὲ ἐπικōρεν. [αἰ δ' | ἀπο]θάνοι ὁ ἀνπαντὸς γνέ-
10 σια | τέκνα μὲ καταλιπόν, πὰρ τὸ[νς τ|ō ἀν]παναμένō ἐπιβάλλον-
ταν||ς ἀνκōρὲν τὰ κρέματα. αἰ δ[έ κα | λει] ὁ ἀνπανάμενος, ἀπο-
Ϝειπ|άθθō κατ' ἀγορὰν ἀπὸ τō λά[ō ō̄ | ἀπα]γορεύοντι καταϜελ-
15 μέν|ōν τῶν πολιατᾶν· ἀνθέμε[ν δὲ || δέκ]α [σ]τατερανς ἐδ δικαστ|έ-
ριον, ὁ δὲ μνάμōν ὁ τō κσεν|ίō ἀποδότō τōι ἀπορρεθέντι. | γυνὰ δὲ
20 μὲ ἀμπαινέθθō μεδ' | ἄνεβος. κρέθαι δὲ τοῖδδε ἄ||ι τάδε τὰ γράμ-
ματ' ἔγραπσε, | τὸν δὲ πρόθα ὅπαι τις ἔχει ε̄ ἀ|μπαντύι ε̄ πὰρ ἀμ-
παντō μὲ ἔτ' ἐ|νδικον ἔμεν.

25 Ἄντρōπον ὅς κ' ἄγει πρὸ δίκας, || αἰεὶ ἐπιδέκεθαι. |

Τὸν δικαστάν, ὅτι μὲν κατὰ | μαίτυρανς ἔγρατται δικάδδ|εν ε̄
30 ἀπόμοτον, δικάδδεν ἄι ἐ|γρατται, τōν δ' ἀλλōν ὀμνύντ||α κρίνεν
πορτὶ τὰ μōλιόμεν|α.

Αἴ κ' ἀποθάνει ἄργυρον | ὀπέλōν ε̄ νενικαμένος, αἰ μέ|ν κα λεί-
35 ōντι, οἷς κ' ἐπιβάλλει | ἀναιλέθαι τὰ κρέματα, τὰν ἄ||ιταν ὑπερ-
κατιστάμεν καὶ τὸ | ἀργύριον οἷς κ' ὀπέλει, ἐκόντ|ōν τὰ κρέματα·
αἰ δέ κα μὲ λεί|ōντι, τὰ μὲν κρέματα ἐπὶ τοῖ|ς νικάσανσι ἔμεν ε̄ οἷς
40 κ' ὀ||πέλει τὸ ἀργύριον, ἄλλαν δὲ | μεδεμίαν ἄταν ἔμεν τοῖ|ς ἐπι-
βάλλονσι. ἀ[τ]έθαι δὲ ὑ|πὲρ μ[ὲ]ν τō [πα]τρὸς τὰ πατρō|ια, ὑπὲ(δ)
45 δὲ τᾶς ματρὸς τὰ μα||τρōια. |

Γυνὰ ἀνδρὸς ἅ κα κρίνεται, | ὁ δικαστὰς ὅρκον αἴ κα δικάκ|σει,
50 ἐν ταῖς Ϝίκατι ἀμέραις ἀ|πομοσάτō παριόντος τō δικα||στᾶ ὅτι
κ' ἐπικαλεῖ. ΠροϜ[ε]ιπάτ|ō δὲ ὁ ἄρκōν τᾶ δίκας τᾶι γυνα|ικὶ καὶ
XII τōι δικαστᾶι καὶ [τ]ōι | μ[νά]μονι προτέταρτον ἀντὶ μ||||[αιτύρōν
ll. 1-15 lacking] ματρὶ υἱὺ‹ι›ς ε̄̀ ἀ[ν]ὲ̄ρ γυναικὶ | κρε̄́ματα αἰ ἔδōκε,
ἆι ἔγρατ|το πρὸ τōνδε τōν γραμμάτōν, || μὲ̄ ἔνδικον ε̄̓́μεν· τὸ δ'
20 ὕστε|ρον διδόμεν ἆι ἔγρατται. |

Ταῖς πατρōιόκοις αἴ κα μὲ̄ | ἰōντι ὀρπανοδικασταί, ἄ|ς κ' ἀνόροι
25 ἰō\τι, κ‿ε̄͂θαι κατὰ | τὰ ἐγραμμένα. ὅπε̄ .. δέ κ' ἀ|| πατρ[ōι]ōκος
μὲ̄ ἰόντος ἐπι|βάλλοντος με̄͂δ' ὀρπανοδικ|αστᾶν πὰρ τᾶι ματρὶ τρά-
30 πε̄|ται, τὸ; πάτρōα καὶ τὸμ μάτ|ρōα τὸνς ἐγραμμένονς τ||ὰ κρε̄́-
ματα καὶ τὰν ἐπικαρπί|αν ἀρτύεν ὅπαι κα (νύ)ναται κά|λλιστα,
πρίν κ' ὀπυίεται. ὀπυί|εθαι δὲ δυōδεκαϜετία ε̄̓́ πρεί|γονα.

The famous Gortyn Law-Code. Although conveniently so
designated, it is not of course a complete code of laws, but a
series of regulations on various subjects, complete in itself,
as shown by the θιοί at the beginning and the unused space at
the end of the last column. The state of the alphabet (there are
no signs for φ and χ, which are not distinguished from π and κ.
See 4.1), the forms of the letters, and the direction of the writing
(βουστροφηδόν), are such as are usually characteristic of the sixth
century B.C., but the general style of the writing, precise and
regular, points to a later date. It is now generally believed that
the development of the alphabet was slower in Crete than elsewhere, and that the Code is of the fifth century B.C., probably
about the middle of it. There are also other inscriptions from
Gortyn containing regulations of a similar character but on
different subjects, one series of seven columns being known
sometimes as the Second Code (GDI 4998).

Although a sign for η is lacking in the Law-Code, the ⊟ had
already been used with this value in an earlier period and н is
regularly so used in the inscriptions of the "North Wall",
which are not much later than the Law-Code. The infinitives
of contract verbs in -EN and the infinitives in -MEN are here
transcribed -ε̄ν and -μεν. See 25a.

I.1-II.2. Disputes over the ownership of a slave or one alleged
to be a slave.

I.1 ff. 'Whoever is about to bring suit in relation to a free
man or a slave, shall not make seizure before the trial. If he
makes the seizure, (the judge) shall condemn him to a fine of
ten staters in the case of a free man, five in case of a slave,
because he seizes him, and shall decree that he release him within
three days. But if he does not release him, (the judge) shall
condemn him to a fine of a stater in the case of a free man, a
drachma in the case of a slave, for each day until he releases him;
and as to the time, the judge shall decide under oath.'—For the
use of the genitive in τῶ ἐλευθέρō, τῶ δōλō, see 171. Similarly
τῶ πεντēκονταστατέρō II.38. Observé the clear distinction in use,
here and elsewhere, between δικάδδεν and κρίνεν. The former is
used where the judge pronounces formal judgment according
to the law and the evidence, the latter where he acts directly
as arbiter. Cf. especially XI.26 ff.—11 ff. 'But if one denies
making a seizure, the judge shall decide under oath, unless a
witness testifies. If one party contends that a man is a free man,
the other that he is a slave, those who testify that he is a free
man shall be preferred. If they contend about a slave, each
declaring that he is his, if a witness testifies, (the judge) shall
declare judgment according to the witness, but if they testify
for both or for neither, the judge shall decide under oath. In
case the one in possession has been defeated, he shall release
the free man within five days, and he shall surrender the slave.
If he does not release (the free man) or surrender (the slave),
(the judge) shall decree that (the plaintiff) have judgment
(νικēν = Att. νικᾶν) against him, in the case of the free man
for fifty staters and a stater for each day until he releases him,
in the case of the slave ten staters and a drachma for each day
until he surrenders him. But at the end of a year after the judge
has pronounced judgment, one may exact three times the amount
(i.e., three times the original fines, instead of the accumulated
fines for delay) or less, but not more. As to the time the judge
shall decide under oath.'—The purpose of this last provision
seems to be to prevent the accumulation of fines out of all pro-
portion to the value of the slave.—τᾶν πέντ' ἀμερᾶν: gen. of
time. 170.—35. ἐνιαυτōι: not 'year,' but 'anniversary.' See
Glossary.—38 ff. 'If the slave on whose account one is defeated

takes refuge in a temple, (the defeated party), summoning (the successful party) in the presence of two witnesses of age and free, shall point out (the slave) at the temple where he takes refuge, either himself or another for him; but if he does not make the summons or point him out, he shall pay what is written. If he does not even (referring back to ll. 34 ff.) surrender him (the slave) at the end of a year, he shall pay the simple fines in addition (to what is stated in ll. 34 ff.). If (the slave) dies while the suit is being tried, he shall pay the simple fine (i.e. without any additional fines for delay). If a member of the κόσμος (see Glossary) makes a seizure, or another (seizes the slave) of a member of the κόσμος, the case shall be tried after he (the official) has gone out of office, and, if defeated he shall pay what is written from the time when he made the seizure. But there shall be no penalty for seizing one condemned for debt or one who has mortgaged his person.'—The penalties fixed in ll. 47-50 and their relation to the provision in l. 36 are variously understood. Many take τιμάνς and τιμάν as referring to the value of the slave.

II.2-45. Rape and adultery.

II.2 ff. 'If one commits rape upon a free man or woman, he shall pay one hundred staters; but if upon (the son or daughter) of an ἀπέταιρος, ten.' The ἀπέταιρος, one who was not a member of a ἑταιρεία or society made up of citizens, occupied a social position midway between the ἐλεύθερος and the Ϝοικεύς. Possibly the ξένοι are meant.—11 ff. 'If one violates a household slave by force, he shall pay two staters, but if one that has already been violated, by day one obol, but if in the night two obols; and the slave shall have the preference in the oath.'—16 ff. 'If one attempts to have intercourse with a free woman who is under the guardianship of a relative (that is, with a young maiden), he shall pay ten staters if a witness testifies.'—28 ff. 'One shall announce before three witnesses to the relatives of the one caught (literally 'caught in,' i.e., in the house of the father, etc.) that he must be ransomed within five days; but to the master of a slave before two witnesses. But if he is not ransomed, it shall be in the power of the captors to do with him as they wish.'— 36 ff. 'If one declares that he has been the victim of a plot, then the one who caught him shall swear, in a case involving a fine of fifty staters or more, with four others (literally 'himself as a fifth'), each calling down curses upon himself (if he testifies falsely), but in the case of an ἀπέταιρος with two others, in a case of a serf the master and one other, that he took him in adultery and did not lay a plot.'

II.45-III.44. Rights of the wife in the case of divorce or death of husband.

II.45 ff. 'If a man and wife are divorced, (the wife) shall have her own property with which she came to her husband, and half of the produce, if there is any from her own property, and half of whatever she has woven within (the house), whatever there is, and five staters, if the husband is the cause of the divorce. But if the husband declares he is not the cause, the judge shall decide under oath. But if she carries off anything else belonging to the husband, she shall pay five staters, and whatever she carries off and whatever she purloins this she shall return. But as regards matters which she denies, (the judge) shall decree that she take the oath of denial by Artemis, (proceeding) to the Amycleium to the archer-goddess. If any one takes anything away from her after she has taken the oath of denial, he shall pay five staters and the thing itself. If a stranger helps her carry things off, he shall pay ten staters and double the amount which the judge swears he helped carry off.'—49. τὰνν ἐμίναν: 101.1.—50. κὄτι: here and III.26, 34 = καὶ ὄτι, i.e., καὶ οὔτινος, gen. by attraction.—III.14-15. κρέιος: χρήιος from χρήεος, gen. sg. with διπλεῖ.—17 ff. 'If a man dies leaving children, if the wife wishes, she may marry again holding her own property and whatever her husband may have given her, according to what is written, in the presence of three witnesses of age and free. But if she takes anything belonging to the children, it shall be a matter for trial.'—27 ff. 'And of the produce in the house she shall share with the lawful heirs.,— τὸν ἐπιβαλλόντον: ὁ ἐπιβάλλον, 'the heir at law,' a short expression for ὅι ἐπιβάλλει (τὰ χρήματα); cf. V.21-22 οἷς κ' ἐπιβάλλει.—37 ff. 'If man or wife wishes to make gifts, (it is permitted), either clothing or twelve staters or something of the value of twelve staters, but not more.'—κόμιστρα: perhaps a technical term for certain kinds of gifts.

III.44-IV.23. Disposition of children born after divorce.

III.44 ff. 'If a divorced wife bears a child, she shall bring it to her husband at his house in the presence of three witnesses. If he does not receive it, the child shall be in the power of the mother either to bring up or to expose; and the relatives and witnesses shall have preference in the oath, as to whether they brought it.'—στέγαν: this is the regular word for 'house' in this inscription, Ϝοικία being 'household' (V.26) and Ϝοῖκος not occurring.— IV.14 ff. 'If the man has no house to which she shall bring (the child), or she does not see him, if she exposes the child, there shall be no penalty.'—ὅι δέ κα μ' εἴ[ε], κτλ.: this conforms to the reading of the stone, though the elision of the ε̄ of μέ is difficult (or read με̄'ί[ε] with aphaeresis?). For κα with the optative see 177.

IV.23-VI.2. Partition of property among children and heirs-at-law.

IV.23 ff. 'The father shall be in control of the children and the division of the property, and the mother of her own property. So long as they live there need be no division. But if any one should be condemned to pay a fine, the one fined shall have his portion taken out and given him as is written.'—33 ff. αἴς κα κτλ.: 'which are not occupied by a serf residing in the country.'— 44 ff. 'And the property of the mother shall be divided, when she dies, in the same way as is prescribed for the property of the father.'—V.1 ff. 'Whatever woman has no property either by gift of father or brother or by promise or by inheritance, since the time when Cyllus and his colleagues of the σταρτός (subdivision of the tribe) of the Aethalians composed the κόσμος, these women shall share in the inheritance, but those (whose claims are) of prior date shall have no recourse.'—22 ff. 'If there is none of these, those to whom it falls according to the source of the property shall receive it. But if there are no heirs-at-law, those of the household who compose the κλᾶρος (i.e., the body of κλαρῶται or serfs attached to the estate) shall have the money.'—28 ff. 'If some of the heirs-at-law wish to divide the property, and others not, the judge shall decree that all the property belong to those wishing to divide, until they divide it. If any one, after the decision of the judge, enters in by force or drives or carries off anything, he shall pay ten staters and double the value of the object. In the matter of live stock, produce, clothing, ornaments, and furniture, if they do not wish to make a division, the judge shall decide with reference to the pleadings. If, when dividing the property, they do not agree as to the division, they shall sell the property, and, disposing of it to whoever offers the most, they shall receive each his share of the price.'—34. δάττονται: aor. subj., cf. ἀποδάτταθθαι. 82, 151.1.—36. ἐνσείει: ἐνσ-είει (εἰμι). 151.3.—39.τνατὸν: θνητῶν = ζώων, as in Hdt. 2.68.—50. ἐπαβολά: also in a Boeot. inscr. (SEG 3.342, 15), ἐπη- Hesych.—VI.1. διδδι: subj. without κα. 174.

VI.2-46. Sale and mortgage of family property.

VI.2 ff. 'As long as the father lives, one shall not purchase any of the father's property from the son, nor take a mortgage on it. But whatever (the son) himself has acquired or inherited, he may dispose of, if he wishes.'—14 f. ἀλλᾶι δ' ἔγρατται: 'and it is written otherwise' = 'otherwise than is written.' Cf. l. 37 and VIII.54.—ἀι τάδε τὰ γράμματα ἔγρατται: 'since the inscription of this law,' contrasted with τὸν δὲ πρόθθα, l. 24, 'in matters of previous date.' So in IX.15 and XI.19.—25 ff. 'But if the opponent denies, with reference to the matter about which they are disputing, that it belongs to the mother or the wife, action shall be brought where it belongs, before the judge there where it is prescribed for each case.'

VI.46-VII.15. Repayment of ransom. Children of mixed marriages. Responsibility for the acts of a slave.

VI.46 ff. 'A ransomed person shall belong to the ransomer, until he pays what is proper.' The general sense is clear, but the restoration and precise interpretation are uncertain. Perhaps, with the reading of the text, 'if one is sold into hostile hands and some one, forced (to do so) upon his demanding it, ransoms him from his exile.'—51 ff. 'But if they do not agree about the amount, or on the ground that he did not demand to be ransomed.' etc.—55 ff. Something is certainly missing between the end of VI and the beginning of VII, either overlooked by the engraver in copying, or possibly added on the original substructure, which is not extant.—VII.1 ff. In the case of marriage between a male slave and a free woman, the status of the children depended on whether the slave went to live with the free woman, thus raising himself in a measure to her condition, or whether the woman went to live with the slave.—9. ἐκσεῖεν: εἶεν ἐξ αὐτᾶς.—10 ff. 'If one having purchased a slave from the market-place has not repudiated the purchase within sixty days, if the slave has wronged any one before or after, the one who has acquired him shall be liable.' The purchaser of a slave was allowed a certain time within which, upon discovering any faults, physical or otherwise, which had been concealed, he might repudiate the purchase. Not until the expiration of this period was the purchase binding, and the purchase liable for the acts of the slave. For the use of περαιόω, cf. also GDI 4998.vii αἴ κα μὴ περαιόσει ἦ κα πρίαται ἐν ταῖς τριάκοντ' ἀμέραις. But some take the meaning in both passages to be 'dispose of abroad.'

VII.15-IX.24. The heiress. Regulations for her marriage and the disposition of her property.

When, in default of sons, a daughter becomes the heiress (πατρōιō̄χος, cf. πατροῦχος παρθένος Hdt. 6.57, Att. ἐπίκληρος), the choice of a husband, who becomes the virtual head of the family, is determined by fixed rules. The person so determined, the groom-elect, is known as ὁ ἐπιβάλλōν ὀπυίεν (= ὅ̄ι ἐπιβάλλει ὀπυίεν 'the one to whom it falls to marry') or simply ὁ ἐπιβάλλōν.

VII.15 ff. 'The heiress shall marry her father's brother, the oldest of those living. If there are several heiresses and father's brothers, they shall marry the next oldest. If there are no father's brothers, but sons of the brothers, she shall marry that one (who is the son) of the oldest. If there are several heiresses and sons of brothers, they shall marry the second (in order) after the son of the eldest (and so on).'—35 ff. 'If the groom-elect, being a minor, does not wish to marry (the heiress), though both are of marriageable age, all the property and the income shall belong to the heiress until he marries her.'—47 ff. 'If he does not marry her, as is written, she with all the property shall marry the next in succession, if there is another. But if there is no groom-elect, she may marry any one of the tribe she wishes, of those who ask for her hand.'—VIII.7-8. 'But they shall give him (the rejected groom-elect) his proper share of the property',—20 ff. 'If one becomes an heiress after her father or brother has given her (in marriage), if she does not wish to remain married to the one to whom they gave her, although he is willing, then, if she has borne children, she may, dividing the property as is written, marry another of the tribe.' —24. ἐστετέκνōται: perf. subj. like πέπᾱται etc., **151**.1.

IX.24-X.32. Various subjects.

IX.24 ff. 'If one dies who has gone surety or has lost a suit or owes money given as security or has been involved in fraud (?) or has made a promise (?), or another (stands in such relations) to him, one shall bring suit against said person before the end of the year. The judge shall render his decision according to the testimony. If the suit is with reference to a judgment won, the judge and the recorder, if he is alive and a citizen, and the heirs as witnesses, (shall give testimony), but in the case of surety and pledges and fraud (?) and promise (?), the heirs as witnesses shall give testimony. After they have testified, (the judge) shall decree that (the plaintiff), when he has taken oath himself and likewise the witnesses, has judgment for the simple amount. If a son has gone surety, while his father is living, he and the property which he possesses shall be subject to fine.'—26-27. The precise technical meaning of διαβαλόμενος and διαϝειπάμενος with the corresponding nouns διαβολᾶς, διϝέσιος ll. 35-36 is uncertain.—28-29. The third letter in l. 29 is obscure, but the most probable reading is ἐπιμōλε̄ν ἰō̃, with νν as in τὰνν ἐμίναν II.48, and with ἰός used like ἐκεῖνος as in VIII.8.—43 ff. "If one has formed a partnership with another for a mercantile venture, in case he does not pay back the one who has contributed to a venture,' etc.—50. ἔνδ: for ἔνς (=εἰς) before following δ (97.4). —53. ὄτερόν κα κτλ.: 'whichever course the complainant demands, either to take oath of denial or —.' X 15.ff. 'Special legacies are not to exceed the value of 100 staters. If one makes a gift of greater value, the heirs, if they choose, may pay the 100 staters and keep the property.'—24. με̄δὲν ἐς κρέος: 'to no purpose, invalid.'

X.33-XI.23. Adoption.

X.33 ff. 'Adoption may be made from whatever source any one wishes. The adoption shall be announced in the place of assembly, when the citizens are assembled, from the stone whence they make proclamations.'—41. συνν-ε̃ι: **101**.1.—42 ff. 'He shall perform the religious and social obligations of the one who adopted him.'—XI.10 ff. 'If the adopter wishes, he may renounce (the adopted son) in the place of assembly,' etc.—16. ὁ δὲ μνά-μōν ὁ τō κσενίō: 'the recorder who looks after the interests of strangers.'— 19 ff. 'These regulations (τοῖδδε) shall be followed from the time of the inscription of this law, but as regards matters of a previous date, in whatever way one holds (property), whether by virtue of adoption (i.e., of being the adopted son) or from the adopted son, there shall be no liability.'

XI.24-XII.35. Various supplementary regulations.

XI.24 f. 'If one seizes a man before the trial, any one may receive him (i.e., may offer the man an asylum).'—26 ff. 'The judge shall decide as is written whatever it is written that he shall decide according to witnesses or by oath of denial, but other matters he shall decide under oath according to the plea-dings.' See note to I.11 ff.—31 ff. 'If one dies owing money or having lost a suit, those to whom it falls to receive the property, if they wish to pay the fine in his behalf and the money to those to whom he owes it, shall hold the property. But if not, the property shall belong to those who won the suit or those to whom he owes money, but the heirs shall not be subject to any further fine. The father's property shall pay the fine for the father, the mother's property for the mother.'—46 ff. 'When a woman is divorced from her husband, if the judge has decreed an oath, she shall take the oath of denial of whatever one charges within twenty days, in the presence of the judge.'—ὄτι: ōὗτινος as in II.50.—XII.21 ff. 'The heiresses, if there are no ὀρφανοδικα-σταί, so long as they are under marriageable age, shall be treated according to what is written. In case the heiress, in default of a groom-elect or ὀρφανοδικασταί, is brought up with her mother, the father's brother and the mother's brother, those designated (above), shall manage the property and the income as best they can until she marries. She shall be married when twelve years of age or older.'

118. Gortyn. Third century B.C. GDI 5011. Ditt. Syll. 525.

[Θιοί. | τάδ' ἔϝαδε τ]ᾶι [πόλι] ψαφίδδονσι τρια|[κατίων πα]ριόν-των· νομίσματι χρῆτ|θαι τῶι καυχῶι τῶι ἔθηκαν ἁ πόλις · τὸδ ||

5 δ' ὀδελὸνς μὴ δέκετθαι τὸνς ἀργυρίος. | αἰ δέ τις δέκοιτο ἢ τὸ νόμι-
σμα μὴ λείοι | δέκετθαι ἢ καρπῶ ὠνίοι, ἀποτεισεῖ ἀρ|γύρω πέντε
10 στατῆρανς. πεύθεν δὲ | πορτὶ τὰν νεότα, τᾶς δὲ νεότας ὀμν||ύντες
κρινόντων οἱ ἑπτὰ κατ' ἀγοράν, | οἱ κα λάχωντι κλαρώμενοι. νικῆν
δ' ὅτε|ρά κ' οἱ πλίες ὁμόσοντι, καὶ πράξαντες | τὸν νικαθέντα τὰν
μὲν ἡμίναν [τῶι νι|κάσ]αντι δόντων, τὰν δ' ἡμίναν [τᾶι πόλι].

Decree of Gortyn regarding the use of bronze coinage.

3 ff. 'One shall make use of the bronze coin which the state
has established, and not accept the silver obols. If one accepts
them, or is unwilling to accept the (bronze) coin, or sells for
produce (i.e., trades by barter), he shall pay a fine of five silver
staters. Report shall be made to the body of young men, and of
this body the seven who are chosen by lot as supervisors of the
market shall decide under oath.'—ὠνίοι, πεύθεν: 162.15.—
νεότα, νεότας: 88a.

119. Hierapytna. Third or second century B.C. GDI 5041.

.... [ἑρπό]ντων δὲ οἱ Ἱεραπύτνιοι τοῖς Λυττίοις ἐς τὰ - - | ....
[οἱ δὲ] Λύττιοι τοῖς Ἱεραπυτνίοις ἐς τὰν εὐάμερον τὰν [τῶν Θευ-
δαισίων. ὁ δὲ κόσμος τῶν | Ἱεραπυτνί]ων ἑρπέτω Λυττοῖ ἐς τὸ
ἀρχεῖον· κατὰ ταὐτὰ δὲ καὶ ὁ τῶ[ν Λυττίων κόσμος ἑρπέτω ἐν
Ἱεραπύτναι ἐς] | τὸ ἀρχ[εῖον.] αἱ δὲ οἱ κόσμοι ἐλλίποιεν τὰν θυ-
σίαν τὰν ἡγραμμέναν, αἴ κα μή τι πόλε[μος κωλύσηι, ἀποτεισάν]-||
5 των ὁ κόσμος ἕκαστος ἀργυρίω στατῆρας ἑκατόν, οἱ μὲν Ἱεραπύ-
τνιοι τοῖς Λυττίοις τᾶι πόλει, [οἱ δὲ Λύττιοι τοῖς] | Ἱεραπυτνίοις
τᾶι πόλει. ὅτι δέ κα δόξηι ταῖς πόλεσιν ἐξελὲν ἢ ἐνθέμεν, ὅτι μὲν ἐξέ-
λοιμεν·μήτε ἔνθινον μή|τε ἔνορκον ἦμεν, ὅτι δὲ ἐγγράψαιμεν ἔνθινόν
τε ἦμεν καὶ ἔνορκον. εἰ δέ τί κα θεῶν ἱλέων ὄντων λάβω|μεν ἀπὸ
τῶν πολεμίων, λαγχανόντων κατὰ τὸ τέλος ἑκάτεροι. μὴ ἐξέστω
δὲ ἰδίαι μήτε πόλεμον ἐ|χφέρεσθαι χωρὶς μήτε εἰρήναν τίθεσθαι, αἴ
10 κα μὴ ἀμφοτέροις δόξηι. αἱ δέ τινές κα ἰδίαι ἐξενέγκωνται, || αὐτοὶ
καὶ διαπολεμόντων, καὶ μὴ ἔνορκοι ἔστων οἱ μὴ συμπολεμόντες.
στασάντων δὲ τὰς στάλας ἑκά|τεροι ἐν τοῖς ἰδίοις ἱεροῖς, οἱ μὲν
Ἱεραπύτνιοι Ὠλεροῖ ἐν τῶι ἱερῶι, τὰν δὲ ἐν Ἀπόλλωνι, οἱ δὲ Λύτ-
τιοι ἐν τῶι [ἱ]|ερῶι τ[ῶ Ἀπό]λλωνος καὶ ἐμ πόλει ἐν Ἀθαναίαι.
στατάντων δὲ καὶ κοινὰν στάλαν ἐν Γόρτυνι ἐν | τῶι ἱερῶι τῶ
........ι. Ὅρκος Λυκτίων. "ὀμνύω τὰν Ἑστίαν καὶ Ζῆνα Ὁρά-
τριον καὶ τὰν Ἀθαναίαν Ὠλερίαν καὶ Ζῆνα | Μο[ννίτιον καὶ Ἥρ]αν

καὶ Ἀθαναίαν Πολιάδα καὶ Ἀπόλλωνα Πύτιον καὶ Λατὼ καὶ
15 Ἄρεα καὶ Ἀφροδίταν καὶ Κωρῆ||τας καὶ Νύμφας καὶ θεὸς πάντας
καὶ πάσας· ἦ μὰν ἐγὼ συμμαχησῶ τοῖς Ἱεραπυτνίοις τὸν πάντα
χρό|νον ἀπλ[όως] καὶ ἀδόλως, καὶ τὸν αὐτὸν φίλον καὶ ἐχθρὸν ἐξῶ,
καὶ πολεμησῶ ἀπὸ χώρας, υἷ κα καὶ ὁ Ἱεραπύτνιος, | καὶ τὸ δίκαιον
δωσῶ καὶ ἐμμενῶ ἐν τοῖς συνκειμένοις, ἐμμενόντων καὶ τῶν Ἱερα-
πυτνίων. ἐπιορκόντι μὲν | ἦμεν τὸς θεὸς ἐμμάνιας καὶ γίνεσθαι
πάντα τὰ ὑπεναντία, εὐορκῶσι δὲ τὸς θεὸς ἱλέος ἦμεν καὶ γίνεσθαι
πολ|λ<λ>ὰ κάγαθά." Ὅρκος Ἱεραπυτνίων. "ὀμνύω τὰν Ἑστίαν
20 καὶ Ζῆνα Ὀράτριον καὶ Ἀθαναίαν Ὠλερίαν κα||[ὶ] Ζῆνα Μοννί-
τιον καὶ Ἥραν καὶ Ἀθαναίαν Πολιάδα καὶ Ἀπόλλωνα Πύτιον
καὶ Λατὼ καὶ Ἄρεα καὶ Ἀφροδί|ταν καὶ Κωρῆτας καὶ Νύμφας
καὶ θεὸς πάντας καὶ πάσας· ἦ μὰν ἐγὼ συμμαχησῶ τοῖς Λυκτί-
οις τὸν | πάντα χρόνον ἀπλόως καὶ ἀδόλως, καὶ τὸν αὐτὸν φίλον
καὶ ἐχθρὸν ἐξῶ, καὶ πολεμησῶ ἀπὸ χώρας, υἷ | κα καὶ ὁ Λύττιος,
καὶ τὸ δίκαιον δωσῶ καὶ ἐμμενῶ ἐν τοῖς συνκειμένοις, ἐμμενόν-
των καὶ Λυκτίων. ἐ|[π]ιορ[κό]ντι τὸς θεὸς ἐμμάνιας ἦμεν καὶ
25 γίνεσθαι πάντα τὰ ὑπεναντία, εὐορκῶσι δὲ τὸς θε||[ὸ]ς ἱλέος ἦμεν
καὶ γίνεσθαι πολλὰ κάγαθά."

Treaty between Hierapytna and Lyttus. This illustrates the
mixed dialect sometimes known as East Cretan. See **273, 278**.

1. **Λυττίοις**: note the interchange of assimilated and unassimilated forms, e.g., **Λυκτίων** l. 13. See **86** with 1.—17.
ἐπιορκόντι: see **42.**5*d*.

120. Drerus. Late third or early second century B.C. GDI
4952. Ditt. Syll. 527. Schwyzer 193. Solmsen-Fraenkel 41.
Schwyzer, Rh. M. 77.237 ff. H. van Effenterre, BCH 61.327 ff.

Θεός τύχα. | ἀγαθᾶι τύχαι. | ἐπὶ τῶν Αἰθαλέ|ων κοσμιόν-
5 των || τῶν σὺγ Κυίαι καὶ | Κεφάλωι Πύρωι | Πίωι Βισίωνος, |
10 γραμματέος | δὲ Φιλίππου, || τάδε ὤμοσαν | ἀγελάοι παν|άζωστοι
15 ἑκα|τὸν ὀγδοή|κοντα· "'Ομνύω || τὰν Ἑστίαν τὰν | ἐμ πρυτα-
νείωι | καὶ τὸν Δῆνα τὸν | Ἀγοραῖον καὶ τὸν Δῆ|να τὸν Ταλλαῖον ||
20 καὶ τὸν Ἀπέλλωνα | τὸν Δελφίνιον καὶ | τὰν Ἀθαναίαν τὰν |
25 Πολιοῦχον καὶ τὸν | Ἀπέλλωνα τὸμ Ποίτιον || καὶ τὰν Λατοῦ ν
καὶ τὰν | Ἄρτεμιν καὶ τὸν Ἄρεα | καὶ τὰν Ἀφορδίταν καὶ | τὸ ν
30 Ἑρμᾶν καὶ τὸν Ἄλιον | καὶ τὰν Βριτόμαρτιν || καὶ τὸμ Φοίνικα
καὶ τὰν | Ἀμφι[ώ]ναν καὶ τὰγ Γᾶν | καὶ τὸν Οὐρανὸν καὶ | ἥρωας

35 καὶ ἡρωάσσας | καὶ κράνας καὶ ποτα||μοὺς καὶ θεοὺς πάντας | καὶ
πάσας · μὴ μὰν ἐγώ | ποκα τοῖς Λυττίοις | καλῶς φρονησεῖν | μήτε
40 τέχναι μήτε μα||χαναῖ μήτε ἐν νυκτὶ | μήτε πεδ' ἀμέραν. καὶ | σπευ-
σίω ὅτι κα δύναμαι | κακὸν τᾶι πόλει τᾶι τῶν Λυττίων. ||| δικᾶν
45 δὲ καὶ πρ[αξί]||ων μηθὲν ἔνορκον | ἤμην. καὶ τέλομαι | φιλοδρήριος
50 καὶ | φιλοκνώσιος | καὶ μήτε τὰμ πό||λιν προδωσεῖν | τὰν τῶν Δρη-
55 ρίων | μήτε οὔρεια τὰ | τῶν Δρηρίων | μηδὲ τὰ τῶγ Κν[ω]||σίων,
μηδὲ ἄν|δρας τοῖς πο|λεμίοις προδω|σεῖν μήτε Δρη|ρίους μήτε
60 Κνω||σίους, μηδὲ στά|σιος ἀρξεῖν καὶ | τῶι στασίζοντι | ἀντίος τέλο-
65 μαι, | μηδὲ συνωμοσί||ας συναξεῖν | μήτε ἐμ πόλει | μήτε ἔξοι τᾶς |
70 πόλεως μήτε | ἄλλωι συντέλε||σθαι · εἰ δέ τινάς | κα πύθωμαι συ-|
75 νομύοντας, | ἐξαγγελίω τοῦ | κόσμου τοῖς πλί||ασιν. εἰ δὲ τάδε |
μὴ κατέχοιμι, | τούς (τ)έ μοι θεούς, | τοὺς ὤμοσα, ἐμ|μάνιας
80 ἤμην<ι>ν || πάντας τε καὶ πά|σας, καὶ κακίστω(ι) | ὀλέθρωι ἐξόλ-
85 λυ|σθαι αὐτός τε | καὶ χρήια τάμά, || καὶ μήτε μοι γᾶν | καρπὸν
φέρειν ||| [μήτε γ]υναῖκας | [τίκτει]ν κατὰ φύ[σ]ιν μήτ]ε πάμα-
90 τα · || [εὐορκί]οντι δέ μοι | [τοὺς] θεούς, τοὺς | [ὤμοσα,] ἱλέους
95 ἤμεν || [καὶ πολ]λὰ κάγαθά | δι[δό]μ[ε]ν. ὀμνύω δὲ || τὸς αὐτὸς
θεούς · | ἦ μὰν ἐγὼ τὸγ κόσ|μον, αἴ κα μὴ ἐξορ|κίξοντι τὰν ἀγέ|λαν
100 τοὺς τόκα ἐ||γδυομένους τὸν | αὐτὸν ὅρκον, τόν|περ ἀμὲς ὀμωμό-|
105 καμες, ἐμβαλεῖν | ἐς τὰν βωλάν, ἆι || κα ἀποστᾶντι, | τοῦ μηνὸς
τοῦ Κο|μνοκαρίου ἢ τοῦ | 'Αλιαίου · ἁ δὲ β[ω]λὰ | πραξάντων
110 ἕκα||στον τὸν κοσμί|οντα στατῆρας | πεντακοσίους | ἀφ' ἇς κα
115 ἐμβάληι | ἀμέρας ἐν τριμήνωι · || αἰ δὲ λισσὸς εἴη<ι>, | ἀγγραψάν-
120 των | ἐς Δελφίνιον, | ὅσσα κα μὴ πρά|ξοντι χρήματα, || τοὔνομα
ἐπὶ πατρὸς | καὶ τὸ πλῆθος τοῦ ἀρ|γυρίου ἐξονομαίνον|τες · ὅτι δέ
125 κα πράξον|τι, ταῖς ἑταιρείαισιν || δασσάσθωσαν ταῖς | ἐμ πόλει
καὶ αἴ πεί | τινεν οὐρεύωντι Δρήριοι. ||| αἰ δὲ μὴ πρά[ξαι]|εν ἁ
130 βωλά, α[ὐτοὶ] || τὰ διπλόα ἀ[ποτει]|σάντων · πρα[ξάν]|των δὲ οἱ
135 ἐρευταὶ | οἱ τῶν ἀνθρωπίνων | καὶ δασσάσθωσαν || ταῖς ἑταιρείαι-
σιν | κατὰ ταὐτά." ||
140 Τάδε ὑπομνάμα|τα τᾶς Δρηρίας χώρας | τᾶς ἀρχαίας τοῖς || ἐπι-
γινομένοις ἀζώ|στοις · τόν τε ὅρ|κον ὀμνύμεν | καὶ κατέχειν. | καὶ
145 οἱ Μιλάτιοι || ἐπεβώλευσαν | ἐν τᾶι νέαι νε|μονηίαι τᾶι πόλει τᾶι
150 τῶν Δρηρίων ἕνεκα τᾶς | χώρας τᾶς ἁ||μᾶς, τᾶς ἀμφι|μαχόμεθα. |
155 Νικατὴρ | τᾶς ἀγέλας | . . . . || καὶ ἐλαίαν ἕ|καστον φυ-
160 τεύ|ειν καὶ τεθραμ|μέναν ἀποδεῖ|ξαι · ὃς δέ κα μὴ || [φ]υτεύσει,
ἀπ|[ο]τεισεῖ στα|τῆρας πεν|τήκοντα.

Oath taken by the Drerian epheḇi, promising loyalty to Drerus and the allied Cnossus, but enmity to Lyttus. The dialect shows a strong admixture of κοινή forms, but also retains many of the Cretan characteristics.

3 ff. The same magistrates appear in another inscription of Drerus, BCH 61.30, where the reading after Κεφάλωι is καὶ Πύρου [κ]αὶ Πίου καὶ Βισίωνος.—11. ἀγελάοι: for ἀγελαῖοι (see 31) 'ephebi' members of the ἀγέλαι or bands in which the Cretan youth were trained.—11/12. πανάζωστοι: cf. ἀζώστοις ll. 140/1, 'ungirded,' here an epithet of the ephebes.—45. δικᾶν δέ κτλ.: 'but nothing of lawsuits and executions shall be included in the oath.'—97 ff. αἴ κα μὴ ἐξορκίξοντι κτλ.: 'unless they impose the same oath upon the ἀγέλα, upon those who were then stripped' (that is, became ephebes).—103. ἐμβαλεῖν: εἰσαγγελεῖν 'impeach.' —104-5. ἅι κα ἀποστάντι: 'after they have gone out of office.'— 115. λισσός: metaphorical use, perhaps 'insolvent.'—127. τινεν: τινες. 119.2a.—132-33. ἐ[ρ]ευταὶ οἱ τῶν ἀνθρωπίνων: 'the collectors of public (in contrast to sacred) funds.' ἐρευταί = ζητηταί, πράκτορες. Cf. ἐρεύω = ἐρευνάω Hesych., Eustath.— 146-7. νεμονηίαι: for νεομηνίαι. 88.

APPENDIX

SELECTED BIBLIOGRAPHY OF WORKS OF REFERENCE
WITH THE ABBREVIATIONS EMPLOYED

PERIODICALS

Abh. Preuss. Akad. = Abhandlungen der preussischen Akademie der Wissenschaften.

ABS = Annual of the British School at Athens.

AJA = American Journal of Archaeology.

AJP = American Journal of Philology.

AM = Mitteilungen des deutschen archäologischen Instituts. Athenische Abteilung.

Annuario = Annuario della regia scuola archeologica di Atene.

'Αρχ. Δελτ. = 'Αρχαιολογικὸν Δελτίον.

'Αρχ. 'Εφ. = 'Αρχαιολογικὴ ἐφημερίς.

'Αθηνᾶ = 'Αθηνᾶ. Σύγγραμμα περιοδικὸν τῆς ἐν 'Αθήναις ἐπιστημονικῆς ἑταιρείας.

BCH = Bulletin de correspondance hellénique.

Ber. Preuss. Akad. = Sitzungsberichte der preussischen Akademie der Wissenschaften.

Ber. Sächs. Ges. = Berichte über die Verhandlungen der königlichen sächsischen Gesellschaft der Wissenschaften zu Leipzig. Philologisch-historische Classe.

Ber. Wien. Akad. = Sitzungsberichte der kaiserlichen Akademie der Wissenschaften in Wien. Philologisch-historische Classe.

(Berl.) Phil. Woch. = (Berliner) philologische Wochenschrift.

BzB = Bezzenberger's Beiträge zur Kunde der indogermanischen Sprachen.

CJ = Classical Journal.

Comptes Rendus = Comptes Rendus de l'Académie des inscriptions et belles-lettres.

CP = Classical Philology.

CQ = Classical Quarterly.

CR = Classical Review.

Diss. Argent. = Dissertationes philologicae Argentoratenses selectae.

Diss. Hall. = Dissertationes philologicae Halenses. Halle.

'Ελληνικά = 'Ελληνικά. 'Ιστορικὸν περιοδικόν.

Eranos = Eranos. Acta philologica Suecana.

Glotta = Glotta. Zeitschrift für griechische und lateinische Sprache.

Gött. Gel. Anz. = Göttingische gelehrte Anzeigen.

Gött. Nachr. = Nachrichten von der königlichen Gesellschaft der Wissenschaften zu Göttingen.

Hermes = Hermes. Zeitschrift für classische Philologie.

Hesperia.

IF = Indogermanische Forschungen.

IFAnz. = Anzeiger für indogermanische Sprach- und Altertumskunde.

JHS = Journal of Hellenic Studies.

Jb. arch. Inst. = Jahrb. des deutschen archäologischen Instituts.

Klio = Klio, Beiträge zur alten Geschichte.

KZ = Zeitschrift für vergleichende Sprachwissenschaft, begründet von
A. Kuhn.

Mnemos. = Mnemosyne. Bibliotheca philologica Batava.

Mon. Antichi = Monumenti antichi pubblicati per cura della reale ac-
cademia dei Lincei.

MSL = Mémoires de la Société de linguistique.

Mus. Ital. = Museo italiano di antichità classica.

Neue Jb. = Neue Jahrbücher für das klassische Altertum, Geschichte
und deutsche Literatur und für Pädagogik.

Oest. Jhrh. = Jahreshefte des oesterreichischen archäologischen Instituts
in Wien.

Philol. = Philologus. Zeitschrift für das klassische Altertum.

Rev. Arch. = Revue archéologique.

Rev. de Phil. = Revue de philologie.

Rev. Ét. Gr. = Revue des études grecques.

Rh. M. = Rheinisches Museum für Philologie.

Riv. Fil. = Rivista di filologia.

TAPA = Transactions of the American Philological Association.

Wiener Stud. = Wiener Studien. Zeitschrift für klassische Philologie.

Woch. f. klass. Phil. = Wochenschrift für klassische Philologie.

TEXTS AND COMMENTARIES

Ditt. Or. = W. Dittenberger, Orientis Graeci inscriptiones selectae.
Leipzig, 1903-5.

Ditt. Syll. = W. Dittenberger, Sylloge inscriptionum Graecarum. 3d ed.
Leipzig, 1915-24.

Greek Inscr. Brit. Mus. = The Collection of Ancient Greek Inscriptions
in the British Museum.

GDI = Collitz-Bechtel, Sammlung der griechischen Dialekt-Inschriften.
Göttingen, 1884-1915.

Hoffmann = O. Hoffmann, Die griechischen Dialekte in ihrem historischen Zusammenhange mit den wichtigsten ihrer Quellen dargestellt.
Göttingen.

    I. Der südachäische Dialekt [Arcadian and Cyprian]. 1891.

    II. Der nordachäische Dialekt [Thessalian and Lesbian]. 1893.

    III. Der ionische Dialekt, Quellen und Lautlehre. 1898.

IG = Inscriptiones Graecae consilio et auctoritate Academiae litterarum regiae Borussicae editae.

  IV. Inscriptiones Argolidis, ed. M. Fraenkel. 1902.
  IV.i². Inscriptiones Epidauri, ed. F. Hiller de Gaertringen. 1929.
  V.i. Inscriptiones Laconiae et Messeniae, ed. W. Kolbe. 1913.
  V.ii. Inscriptiones Arcadiae, ed. F. Hiller de Gaertringen. 1913.
  VII. Inscriptiones Megaridis et Boeotiae, ed. W. Dittenberger. 1892.
  IX.i. Inscriptiones Phocidis, Locridis, Aetoliae, Acarnaniae, insularum maris Ionii, ed. W. Dittenberger. 1897.
  IX.i². Inscriptiones Aetoliae, ed. Guentherus Klaffenbach. 1932.
  IX.ii. Inscriptiones Thessaliae, ed. O. Kern. 1908.
  XI.ii. Inscriptiones Deli liberae, ed. F. Dürbach. 1912.
  XI.iv. Inscriptiones Deli liberae, ed. P. Roussel. 1914.
  XII.i. Inscriptiones Rhodi Chalces Carpathi cum Saro Casi, ed. F. Hiller de Gaertringen. 1895.
  XII.ii. Inscriptiones Lesbi Nesi Tenedi, ed. W. Paton. 1899.
  XII.iii. Inscriptiones Symes Teutlussae Teli Nisyri Astypalaeae Anaphes Therae et Therasiae Pholegandri Meli Cimoli, ed. F. Hiller de Gaertringen. 1898.
  XII.iii. Supplementum, ed. F. Hiller de Gaertringen. 1894.
  XII.v. Inscriptiones Cycladum, ed. F. Hiller de Gaertringen. 1903, 1909.
  XII.vii. Inscriptiones Amorgi, ed. G. Delamarre. 1908.
  XII.viii. Inscriptiones insularum maris Thracici, ed. C. Friedrich. 1909.
  XII.ix. Inscriptiones Euboeae insulae, ed. E. Ziebarth. 1915.
  XII. Supplementum, ed. F. Hiller de Gaertringen. 1939.
  XIV. Inscriptiones Siciliae et Italiae, ed. G. Kaibel. 1890.
Inscr. Cret. = Inscriptiones Creticae, ed. N. Guarducci, I—IV. 1935+.
Inschr. v. Magnesia = O. Kern, Inschriften von Magnesia am Maeander. Berlin, 1900.
Inschr. v. Olympia = Dittenberger-Purgold, Inschriften von Olympia. Berlin, 1896.
Inschr. Jurid. = Dareste-Haussoullier-Reinach, Recueil des inscriptions juridiques grecques. Paris, 1895 ff.
Paton — Hicks = W. R. Paton and E. L. Hicks, The inscriptions of Cos. Oxford, 1891.
Roberts = E. S. Roberts, Introduction to Greek Epigraphy. Part I. Cambridge, 1887. Part II (with E. A. Gardner). Cambridge, 1905. All references are to Part I, unless II is added.
Schwyzer = E. Schwyzer, Dialectorum Graecarum exempla epigraphica potiora. Leipzig, 1923 (revised edition of Cauer's Delectus).
SEG = Supplementum Epigraphicum Graecum i—xii. Leyden, 1923+.
Solmsen-Fraenkel = F. Solmsen, Inscriptiones Graecae ad inlustrandas dialectos selectae. 4th ed. by E. Fraenkel. Leipzig, 1930.
Tod = Marcus Tod, A Selection of Greek Historical Inscriptions. 2d ed. Oxford, 1946, 1948.

Ziehen, Leges Sacrae = L. Ziehen, Leges Graecorum sacrae e titulis collectae. Leipzig 1906.

LEXICOGRAPHY

Bechtel, Personennamen = F. Bechtel, Die historischen Personennamen des Griechischen bis zur Kaiserzeit. Halle, 1917.
Fick-Bechtel = Die griechischen Personennamen nach ihrer Bildung erklärt und systematisch geordnet. 2d ed. by A. Fick and F. Bechtel. Göttingen, 1894.
Herwerden = H. van Herwerden, Lexicon Graecum suppletorium et dialecticum. 2d ed. Leyden, 1910.
LS = Liddell and Scott's Greek—English Lexicon. 9th ed. Oxford, 1940.
Pape = W. Pape, Wörterbuch der griechischen Eigennamen. 3d ed. Braunschweig, 1884.
Searles = Helen M. Searles, Lexicographical Study of the Greek Inscriptions. Chicago, 1898.

GREEK GRAMMARS

Kretschmer, Sprache (in Gercke und Norden, Einleitung in die Altertumswissenschaft). 3d ed. Leipzig, 1923.
Kühner-Blass = Kühner's Ausführliche Grammatik der griechischen Sprache. 3d ed. Part I, revised by Blass. 2 vols. Hannover, 1890-92.
Kühner-Gerth = Kühner's Ausführliche Grammatik der griechischen Sprache. 3d ed. Part II, revised by Gerth. 2 vols. Hannover, 1898-1904.
Lejeune, Traité de phonétique grecque. Paris 1947.
Meillet, Aperçu d'une histoire de la langue grecque. 3rd ed. Paris, 1930.
Schwyzer, Gr. Gram. = E. Schwyzer, Griechische Grammatik, 2 vols. München, 1939-50. (vol. 3, Index, by D.G. Georgacas, 1952).
Smyth = H. W. Smyth, Greek Grammar for Colleges. New York, 1920.

GREEK DIALECTS [1]

Ahrens = H. L. Ahrens, De Graecae linguae dialectis. 2 vols. Göttingen, 1839-43.
Bechtel = F. Bechtel, Die griechischen Dialekte. 3 vols. Berlin.
   I. Der lesbische, thessalische, böotische, arkadische und kyprische Dialekt. 1921.
   II. Die westgriechischen Dialekte. 1923.
   III. Der ionische Dialekt. 1924.

---

[1] A list of the numerous monographs on special dialects is omitted. The majority of these are now antiquated.

Hoffmann = Hoffmann, Die griechischen Dialekte. 3 vols. See above,
  p. 338.
Meister = R. Meister, Die griechischen Dialekte. 2 vols. Göttingen.
  I. Asiatisch-Äolisch, Böotisch, Thessalisch. 1882.
  II. Eleisch, Arkadisch, Kyprisch. 1889.
Thumb-Kieckers = A. Thumb, Handbuch der griechischen Dialekte. 2te
  Auflage von E. Kieckers. Heidelberg, 1932.

NOTES AND REFERENCES [1]

1. Interrelation of the dialects. Ahrens I, 1 ff. Collitz, Die Verwandt-schaftsverhältnisse der griechischen Dialekte mit besonderer Rücksicht auf die thessalische Mundart, 1885. Smyth, The Dialects of North Greece, AJP 7.421 ff., 1887. Hoffmann, De mixtis Graecae linguae dialectis, 1888. Hoffmann I, 1 ff., 1891. Solmsen, Thessaliotis und Pelasgiotis, Rh. M. 58.598 ff., 1903. Id., Eigennamen als Zeugen der Stammesmischung in Boeotien, Rh. M. 59.481 ff., 1904. Meister, Dorer und Achäer I, 1904. Thumb, Dialektforschung und Stammesgeschichte, Neue Jb. 1905, 385 ff. Buck, The Interrelations of the Greek Dialects, CP 2. 241 ff., 1907. Kretschmer, Zur Geschichte der griechischen Dialekte, Glotta 1.4 ff., 1907. Fick, Äoler und Achäer, KZ 44.1 ff., 1911. Debrunner, Die Besiede-lung des alten Griechenland, Neue Jb. 1918, 433 ff. Meillet, Aperçu 72 ff., 1930. Kretschmer, Sprache (Gercke und Norden, Einleitung³) 75 ff., 1927. Buck, CP 21.16 ff., 1926. Debrunner in Ebert, Reallexikon der Vorgeschichte IV, 510 ff. Kretschmer, Glotta 28.231 ff., 30.84 ff. Thumb-Kieckers 47 ff. Schwyzer, Gr. Gram. 1.75 ff. A. Tovar, Primitive geographical expansion of Ionic, Emerita 12 (1944) 245 ff.

3. Although, for reasons stated in the Note, a detailed treatment of the literary dialects is excluded from the plan of this book, the following summaries for those other than Homeric, later Ionic, or Attic, may be of service. They are arranged with references to the appropriate sections of the grammar.

ALCAEUS AND SAPPHO

Texts: Diehl, Anthologia Lyrica. Lobel, Sappho. Lobel, Alcaeus.

The language of Alcaeus and Sappho is substantially their native Lesbian, the characteristics of which, summarized in **201-3, 206-7**, are nearly all represented in the texts. Epic influence shows itself in the use of ν movable, a few cases of lack of augment, the occasional σ beside σσ (**82, 83**), -δειροι beside -δέραι, etc. (**54**), a few occurrences of gen. sg. -ᾱο, gen. sg. -οιο, ἄνερος, etc., as well as in various other matters of prosody and phraseology. The texts contain many cases of hyper-Aeolic αι, some of hyper-Aeolic ρρ, etc.; also the spelling σδ = ζ, which is late (**84**), and various other corruptions.

The papyrus fragments, and likewise the quotations in late authors,

---

[1] Except for the few following, those previously given (in the "In-troduction") are not repeated here. Any important corrections or additions have been incorporated in the main text, and the references, with others later, may be found in Schwyzer, Griechische Grammatik.

scholiasts, grammarians, so far as these latter have not been further corrupted in transmission, reflect the current Alexandrian text. This latter very probably goes back to a redaction by earlier grammarians from Aeolic Asia Minor (some such are known by name), who were familiar with the Aeolic of their time, say the late fourth or early third century B.C. This hypothesis receives support from the treatment of final ηι, ωι, ᾱι, which in some of the Oxyrhynchus texts, and likewise in the verses of Balbilla (a woman of Hadrian's time who imitated the Sappho of her copy), appear as η, ω, but αι, a differentiation which accords neither with contemporaneous practice nor with that of the poets' time, but agrees with that of some Lesbian inscriptions of the late fourth century (38). Cf. Kehrhahn, KZ 46.296 ff., Bechtel 1.45.

5. στρότος, βροχέως, ἄμβροτε, τρόπην, χόλαισι, ἐμμορμένον = εἱμαρμένον, ὄρπετον (cf. ἀρπετόν Hesych., from weak grade of ἕρπω) = ἐρπετόν, σπολέω (cf. σπόλεισα· σταλεῖσα Hesych.). So τετορταῖος in Theocritus.— 6. ὀν, ὀνία, ὀνίαρος, κόθαρος.—8. φάμα, etc., generally. But also hyper-Aeolic αι = ᾱ, due to the regular correspondence of αισ to ᾱς from ανς (see below, to 77.3, 78). So nom. sg. Αἰολίδαις, Κρονίδαις, βορίαις (similar forms in Balbilla and the grammarians), further ἐπέραισε, ἐπτόαισ' beside ἐπτόασεν (from πτοάω = πτοέω, 161.2a), μέμναισ', ὄμναισαι, φαισθ', 3 sg. φαῖσι (cf. regular 3 pl. φαῖσι), all these before σ, more doubtful μέμναιμ', μαχαίταν. (Some other cases in Diehl's text are without MS. authority and due to a wrong theory of αι = η; cf. CP 10. 215 ff.).—9.2. χρύσιον, πορφυρίαν, χάλκιαι, κυνίαισι, συκίαν, βορίαις, τίωι, but generally ε (θέοισιν, ἔων, etc.).—13.1. ῖρος.—13.3a. ἄτερος.—17. αἰμιόνοις, αἰμιθέων.—18a. κέρναις.—19.1. ζάβαις, ζάδηλος, ζακρυόεις, etc. = δια-.—19.2, 4. πέρροχος, περρέχοισ', περεθήκαο (cf. περρεθήκατο Hesych.), πὲρ ἀτιμίας (cf. πὲρρ ἀπάλω Theocr.), πορφύρον, πορφύρα, ἀργύρα; Περράμω, Περάμοιο.—22 with b. ἀπύ, ὔμοι, ὑπίσσω, ὔσδων.—25. η, ω, as κῆνος, ἦχεν, infin. -ην, gen. sg. -ω, ὤρανος (but also ὄρανος, the explanation of which is uncertain). —31. Ἄλκαος, Φωκάας, πόας, λαχόην, πόησαι, etc.—35 with a. αὔως, ναύω, ναύοις, δεύοντος, ἐπιδεύης, χεύάτω, αὐάταν, αὐάδην.—38. Regularly -ᾱι, but frequently (in some papyrus texts, always) -η, -ω. See above.— 41.2. φάος, σάος, μάομαι, περεθήκαο.—41.3. ἀελίω and ἀλίω.—41.4. gen. pl. -ᾱν, Ποσείδᾱν, but πεδάορον, Ἀίδαο.—42.1. εὐάνθεα etc., but ἦρος. κείσαι, but οἴχηι, πότηι.—42.3. ἦχεν, ἤλπετο, κῆνος, infin. -ην, but ὤκεες, ἔγχεε, καγχέεται.—42.4. φίλει, κατάγρει.—42.5, 6. ὀνκαλέοντες, ἔων, gen. sg. -εος, etc.—43. ἱππήων, βασίληες, etc.—44.3. gen. sg. -ω, gen. sg. αἴδως, αὔδως, acc. sg. νῶν beside νόον.—44.4. ἱμέροεν, νιφόεντος, etc. ο + ει, χαύνοις.—47. φᾶμι, not φαίμι. For 3 sg. φαῖσι, see above, to 8. For δοκίμοιμι the better reading is δοκίμωμι. Forms like γέλαιμι, ἵσταιμι, etc., quoted by the grammarians (cf. Hdn. 2.825), are not confirmed even for the Alexandrian text.—49.2. κρέτος, κρέτησαι.

52. Initial F before a vowel is so written or implied by the meter for the pronominal Fοῖσι, Fόν, Fέθεν, but generally ignored, as εἴπην, ἴδοισαν, ἴδμεν, ἔργον, etc., without preventing elision or causing position length.— 53. Intervocalic F lost, as κλέος, ῥόαι, etc., πάις (as in Homer), παῖδος. (But see above, to 35).—54. From νF etc., F lost without lengthening of the preceding vowel, μόνος, κάλος, κόρα, δέραι, περάτων, ἴσος. But also ποικιλόδειροι, περάτων, and ἴσος with first syllable long, probably due to epic influence, likewise ὔννεκα (also Theocr.) with hyper-Aeolic νν (cf. 54b) = Hom. εἴνεκα.—55. βρόδα, βροδοδάκτυλος, βραδίναν, βράκεα.—57. Psilosis.—67. πτόλις, probably epic.—68.2 with a. πέμπε, πήλυι, χασπολέω. —74. ἀέρρει, ἐγέρρην, ἱμέρρει, παρορίννει.—75. βόλλομαι, μελλιχόμειδε.— 76. ἄμμες, ὔμμες, ἔμμεναι, ἔμματα, σελάννα, φάεννος, ἐράνναν, ἱλλάεντι, χέρρας. But once with λ διsχελίοις.—77.1, 79. κτένναις, γέννατο, ἄγγελλαι, ἀέρρατε, συνέρραισα. But hyper-Aeolic ρρ in θόρρακες, better θώρακες.

—77.3. παῖσα, Μοῖσα, πλήθοισα, λίποισα, μειδιάσαισα, μίγεισα, etc., 3 pl. ἀπυκρύπτοισι, φαῖσι, ἵεισι, ἐπιρρόμβεισι, etc.—78. acc. pl. -αις, -οις, nom. sg. m. pple. οἴκεις, μέδεις (= μεδέων).—80. κόρσαι, χέρσω.—82, 83. Usually σσ, but also σ (epic influence), μέσσον, μέσοι, ὅσσος, ὅσα, ἔσσο, τέλεσσαι, τέλεσον, πόδεσσιν, γυναίκεσσιν, etc., ἄνδρεσι, ἄμμεσιν, στήθεσιν, etc.—84. ὕσδων, πέσδων, μέσδον, etc.—89.4. κάλημμι, etc., νόημμα, πεποιημ-μέναις, κλᾶμμα, ἀροτρώμμεν, δίννηντες, δινάεις. Cf. also below, to 101.1.— 89.8. ἔσλος, μάσλης.—94.1. ὤνηρ, τῶμον.—94.3. κώττι.—94.6. κἀπί, κάμματα, κάλέφαις, κἀν, etc. (α uniformly in pap. texts), but also κὴν, κὴκ.—94.7. κωὐκί, κωῦτε.—95-99. κὰτ τό, κὰμ μέν, κἀκ κεφάλας, κάββαλε, etc., πὰρ δὲ, πὲρ μὲν, πὲρ κεφάλας, περσκόπεισα, ἀπ πατέρων.—101.1. ὀννώρινε, ἀσύνετος, ἀσυννέτημμι.—102. ν movable frequent (epic influen-ce).—103. Recessive accent, attested by the grammarians, also shown in papyrus texts (so far as the accent is written at all), as κόθαρον, gen. pl. λύγραν, παίσαν, μερίμναν, etc., likewise Ζεῦς (for Ζεύς).

104. Voc. sg. Δίκᾰ, gen. pl. -ᾶν, dat. pl. -αισι(ν) but ταῖς, acc. pl. -αις. —105. Gen. sg. once -ᾱο (epic).—106. Gen. sg. -ω, rarely -οιο (epic), dat. pl. -οισι(ν) but τοῖς, acc. pl. -οις.—107.3. πόδεσσιν, etc.—108.2. Acc. sg. ἀβλάβην, ἐμφέρην, etc., dat. sg. Διννομένηι, voc. sg. μελλιχόμειδε (cf. -ᾰ in Δίκα).—109.2. πόλιος and πόληος (epic).—111. βασίληες, τοκήων, etc. (above, to 43). But Ἄρευς, gen. Ἄρευος, acc. Ἄρευα (Hom. Ἄρης, Ἄρηος) with ευ extended from nominative.—114. ἴα.—116. Gen. πέμπων, δέκων.—118.3c. Gen. ἔμεθεν, σέθεν, Ϝέθεν.—119. ἄμμες, ὔμμες, ἄμμι(ν), ὔμμι(ν), and ἄμμεσιν.—121.1. ἐμ' αὔται, ἐμ' αὔτωι.—125. κῆνος.—128. Dat. sg. τίωι, dat. pl. τίοισιν = Hom. τέω, etc.—129.2. ὄττινες, ὄττινας, gen. sg. ὄττω, dat. pl. ὄτοισι.—ὄππα, ὄππατα, ὄππασε.—130. τέουτος = τοιοῦτος.—132.4. πήλυι, ἄλλυι, τύιδε, ἔνδυς.—132.5. πάνται.—132.11. ὄτα, πότα, ὄππστα, ἄλλοτα.—133.6. ἀΐ.—134.1, 2. αἰ, κε, κεν.—135. ὀν, ἀπύ, ὑπά, εἰς, πεδά.

138.1. τίθησθα etc.—138.1a. -ης, -ηις ?—138.5. σύναχθεν, etc., but ἐστάθησαν (epic).—143. ἐκάλεσσα, χαλάσσομεν.—146.1. ὑπαδεδρόμακε.— 147.2. τεθνάκην.—147.3. λελάθων, ἐκγεγόνων, etc.—150. χαλάσσομεν.— 153. ἔχην etc.—154.2. ἔμμεναι.—155.2. μεθύσθην, τελέσθην.—157. κά-λημμι, φίλησθα, φόρημεθα, ἐπόημμεν, εὐωχήμενος, ἐπιρρόμβεισι, χόλαισι, ἐπαίνεντες, πολέμεντι, δίννηντες (cf. a), οἴκεις, μέδεις.—157b. βόα, ἄγρει. τίμαι, βόα(ι) ὄπταις, χαύνοις, ὀνκαλέοντες, ποτέουται.—159. ἀδικήει, ποθήω.— 161.2. ὄρημμι, ποτέονται beside ἀμφιπόταται, ἐκπεποταμένα.—161.2a. ἐξεπόνασαν, ἐπτόασεν (and ἐπτόαισ', above, to 8; cf. ἐπτοάθης Eur.).— 161.3. δοκίμωμι = δοκιμάζω.—162.2. ἄγρει.—162.8. ἐζώομεν.—163.3. ἦς.—163.8. ἔσσα and ἔοισα.—164.1. βασιλήιος, πεμπεβόηα.—164.2. ἰλλάεις = ἵλαος, like Hom. μεσήεις = μέσος.—164.4. ὄππα = ὄμμα.

ALCMAN

Text: Diehl, Anthologica Lyrica.

The language of Alcman agrees with Laconian in its general Doric features, and in several others that were not general Doric, as η, ω, not ει, ου (25), infin. -ην (153.2), acc. pl. -ως (106), ἐνθ- = ἐλθ- (72), κάρρων (80), etc. But some of the special Laconian peculiarities were ignored. So certainly the change of intervocalic σ (59.1), of which there is no trace. So probably the Lac. δδ = ζ (84), which occurs only in one MS of one passage (Diehl no. 100). Alcman probably wrote ζ, for which σδ, frequent in the texts, was a late spelling. The σ for θ (64) was much later than Alcman's time, but is frequent in the texts especially in certain words, as σιοί = θεοί. The ι for ε in this and some other forms represents a Laconian pronunciation (9.5), but one that is ignored in the spelling of the majority of forms (ὀρέων, αἰνέοντι, etc.), and very likely by Alcman himself. In the matter of spelling, σιοί may owe its ι as well as the σ to the redaction of grammarians.

The most conspicuous Lesbian feature in Alcman, as also in other lyric poetry, is the use of Lesbian participial forms like ἔχοισα, λιποῖσα, θεῖσα, etc. (77.3). Such forms are so frequent in Alcman as to indicate that his practice was uniform in this class and that exceptions in the text are to be suspected, not only καμοῦσιν with its Att.-Ion. ου, but also λαβῶσ' (Diehl no. 28), which, though good Laconian, rests on an emendation. It was only the Lesbian participial form that was adopted, not the general Lesbian treatment of vowel + νσ, which is not attested for other categories, not even the analogous Μοῖσα as in Pindar, but Μῶσα, and never in third plural forms. κλεννά (Diehl no. 1.44) is a Lesbian form (76), which may go back to the poet. Forms that are Lesbian, but also current in epic, as infin. -μεναι, dat. pl. παίδεσσι, etc., may be grouped with other examples of epic influence. Such are the frequent use of ν movable (102), σ beside σσ, as τόσσος, τόσος (82), γούνατα, δουρί (54), the latter wrongly emended to δωρί (Diehl no. 77; but Lac. δορϜί or δορί), πρότι (135.6), 3 pl. ἔχουσιν, εὔδουσιν.

8. ἀ, δᾶμος, ἀμέρα, etc.—**9**.5. σιοί, ἡμισίων, σιειδής, ἀργύριον, παγχρύσιος, but τέο, ἐπέων, αἰνέοντι, etc.—**13**.1. ἰαρός, also ἐπίασε (cf. Theocr. πιάξας), as in late Att. = ἐπίεσε.—**13**.3. ὄκα, etc., γα.—**25**. η, ω, as κῆνος, χηρός, ἦμεν, ὡρανόν, Μῶσα, gen. sg. -ω, acc. pl. -ως (but some cases of ει, ου left in text).—**41**.1. ὀρῆς, ποτήσθω.—**41**.2. φῶς, 3 sg. opt. νικῷ.—**41**.3. ἅλιον.— **41**.4. Ἀλκμάων, Ἀλκμάν, παιᾶνα, gen. pl. -ᾶν.—**42**.1. ἔπη, ἄνθη, ἦρ.— **42**.5. uncontracted εο, εω, or ιο, ιω.

52. Ϝάνακτι, Ϝέθεν, Ϝάδη, etc. (Ϝ written in some sources but mostly restored).—**53.** δάϜιον, αὐειρομέναι, but φῶς, ἅλιον, etc.—**61.** ἐντί, etc., τύ.—**64.** σιοί, παρσένος, σαλασσο-, σάλλει, etc.—**68.** βλῆρ = δέλεαρ. γλέπω, γλέφαρον = βλέπω, βλέφαρον.—**72.** ἐνθοῖσα, κέντο.—**76.** ἦμεν, ἀμές, χηρός, etc., but κλεννά (Lesb.).—**77**.3. Lesb. partic. forms ἔχοισα, φέροισα, λιποῖσα, ἐνθοῖσα, λυθεῖσα, etc.—**80.** κάρρων.—**82, 83.** τόσσος, τόσος, ἐδάσσατο, ἐσσαμέναι, παίδεσσι, etc.—**84.** Usually ζ or late σδ, as μάσδων, etc., once δδ, καθαρίδδην.—**94**.2, 6. κήν, κήπί, κώπώραν.—**95, 99.** κἀ(τ) τάν, καβαίνων.—**102.** ν movable frequent.

104. Gen. pl. -ᾶν, dat. pl. -αισι, -αις.—**106.** Gen. sg. -ω, acc. pl. -ως, dat. pl. -οισι(ν), -οις.—**107.** Nom. sg. μάκαρς, like Cret. μαίτυρς. Dat. pl. παίδεσσι, etc.—**118.** Gen. τέο, Ϝέθεν. Dat. μοι, τοι, τίν. Acc. ἐμέ, σέ, τέ, τύ, νίν.—**119.** ἀμές, ἀμέων, etc.—**120.** ἀμός, Ϝα, σφεά, σφοῖς, σφετέρως.— **122.** Nom. pl. ταί.—**125.** κῆνος.—**132**.2. αὐτεῖ.—**132**.8. ὦτ'.—**132**.11. ὄκα, ποκα, τόκα, also ὄκκα.—**134**.1. αἰ.—**134**.2. κα (ἀν in Diehl no. 81, but improbable).—**135.** ἐς, πεδά, προτί.—**138**.3. παρήσομες, ὑμνέωμες.— **138**.4. αἰνέοντι, ἐντί (εὔδουσιν, ἔχουσιν epic, if genuine).—**138**.5. ἐπέβαν.— **142.** ἀρμόξατο.—**142**a. ὀρνίχων.—**153**.1. φαίνην, etc. (mostly corrected from -εν or -ειν).—**154.** ἦμεν, etc., ἔδμεναι.—**163**.3. ἧς.—**163**.8. παρέντων. —Note also aor. ἔγεντο, as in Hesiod, Sappho, etc., likewise κέντο = κέλτο.

PINDAR AND BACCHYLIDES

Cf. Schöne, Leipziger Studien für klass. Phil. 19.181 ff. Texts: Pindar, Schroeder; Bacchylides, Blass-Suess.

The retention of original ᾱ = Att.-Ion. η, together with ᾱ from ᾱο ᾱω = Att.-Ion. εω, ω, is the most conspicuous characteristic of the choral lyric, and the only non-Att.-Ion. feature which prevails with any approach to consistency (even this not complete) and persists in the choruses of Attic tragedy. The weight of ᾱ-forms is further increased by the choice of Att.-Ion. ᾱ, not Dor. η, from αε (νικᾶν = Dor. νικῆν, etc.).

Of the general Doric characteristics (cf. **223**), which are common to the West Greek dialects and partly to Boeotian and Thessalian, only a few appear frequently, some occasionally, and others not at all. Thus Pindar, who uses much more Doric than Bacchylides (or Simonides), has usually 3d pl. -οντι, infin. -μεν = -ναι, frequently ξ in forms iike κατεφάμιξεν, τύ beside σύ, τίν beside σοι, rarely τόκα beside τότε (and only ὅτε, πότε), and never κα, πρᾶτος, (F)ίκατι, 3 sg. ἧς, 1 pl. -μες, but only the Att.-Ion. ἄν (or Aeol. κε(ν)), πρῶτος, εἴκοσι, ἦν, -μεν.

Aeolic features, occurring also in Homer, are κε(ν) = ἄν, the double nasals in ἄμμες, etc., κλεεννός (both P. and B.), perf. pple. with ντ (πεφρίχοντας etc.). Specific Lesbian, in Pindar regularly Μοῖσα, φέροισα, etc., frequently 3 pl. -οισι (in B. only Μοῖσα beside Μοῦσα).

Pindar has a few cases of ἐν with acc., sometimes attributed to his native Boeotian. But Delphian influence is perhaps more probable. There is no clear evidence that the poet's language was affected by his local dialect.

8. ᾱ most consistently in broad categories which could have only ᾱ in Doric, as the endings of ᾱ-nouns of the first declension, non-present tenses and derivatives of verbs in -αω, suffix -τᾱς, -τᾱτος, personal endings -μαν, -σθαν. In individual words Doric ᾱ usually retained, as μάτηρ, ἁδύς, φάμᾱ, but occasionally Att.-Ion. η (at least in our texts, and need not be rejected), as φήμᾱ (B.), which, though a hybrid form, is not stylistically offensive beside genuine Doric ἥβᾱ.

13. Non-Doric ἱερός (but σκιαρός), Ἄρτεμις, ὅτε, ποτε, τότε, rarely τόκα, never κα, γα.—25. ει, ου, not η, ω.—41.1. Att.-Ion. ᾱ, not Dor. η, as νικᾶν, νικᾶι, τιμᾶι, συλᾶται, ςtc.—41.2. τιμῶντες, etc.—φάος, σαόφρων (B.) and σώφρων.—41.3. ἀέλιος, ἅλιος.—41.4. Gen. sg. masc. -ᾱ, sometimes -ᾱο (P.), gen. pl. -ᾱν, ᾱς, Ποσειδᾱων, Ποσειδάν,. λᾱός (but Μενέλας, etc.), νᾱός, ᾱώς, ξυνᾱονος, ὀπᾱων, κοινᾱν, etc.—42.1. ἔτεα, βέλεα, etc., rarely -η. κέαρ, ἔαρ, ἦρος (P.).—42.3, 4. τρεῖς, φιλεῖ, etc.—42.5. εο or ευ, as gen. sg. -εος, -ευς, φιλέοντα, φιλεῦντας.—42.6. φιλέων, etc.—43. βασιλῆες, etc., also Ἀχιλλέος, etc.—49.2, 4. τράφω, τράχω, τάμνω.—52. Former F mostly ignored in prosody, but sometimes effective, especially in the case of reflexive οἱ.—53. Once ἀυάταν for ἀ(F)άταν.—54. μόνος, κόρα, ὅρος and less commonly μοῦνος, κούρα, οὖρος.—61. ἐφίητι, φέροντι, etc. (beside Lesb. or Ion. σ-forms, see below, to 138.4), τύ (beside σύ), but εἴκοσι, Ποσειδάν (once perhaps Ποτειδᾱνος).—68.2. φήρ.—76. Lesb. ἄμμες, etc., κλεεννός, κελεδεννός.—77.3. Lesb. Μοῖσα, in Pindar regularly φέροισα, etc., and frequently 3 pl. -οισι.—82, 83. ὅσσος, ὅσος, τόσσαι, τελέσαι, etc.—89.7. ἐσλός (P.).—88. γλέφαρον.—94. κῆν, κῆκ, χῶτι, etc.—95. ἄν frequent, rarely παρ, κατ, περ, as πὰρ ποδός, πὰρ χειρός, πάρφρων, κὰν νόμον, πέροδος, περ' αὐτᾶς.—102. ν movable frequent.

105-6. Gen. sg. masc. -ᾱ, sometimes -ᾱο, gen. pl. -ᾱν, dat. pl. -αις, -αισι.—106. Gen. sg. -ου, also frequently Hom. -οιο, dat. pl. -οις, -οισι.—107.3. πόδεσσι, etc. frequent.—109.1. -ις, -ιος, etc.—111. -ευς, -ῆος, and -έος.—114-5. πρῶτος, not Dor. πρᾶτος, εἴκοσι, not Dor. (F)ίκατι.—118. ἐγώ, ἐγών, τύ and σύ; gen. σέο, σέθεν; dat. ἐμοί, μοι, σοί, τοι, τίν, οἱ, ἱν (?); acc. ἐμέ, με, σε, ἕ, νιν.—120. τεός, ἑός, and σός, ὅς; ἁμός, ὑμός, σφός, and ἁμέτερος, etc.—122. ταί, τοί, and αἱ, οἱ.—126. Art. as rel. frequent.—132.11. ὅτε, ποτε, τότε, rarely τόκα.—134.1. εἰ, never αἰ.—134.2. ἄν and κε, κεν, never κα.—135.4. ἐς, εἰς, and rarely ἐν in Pindar.—135.5. πεδά beside usual μετά.—135.6. ποτί beside πρός.—136.7. ἀμφί frequent.—138.2. ἐφίητι, but τίθησι, δίδωσι.—138.3. -μεν, not -μες.—138.4. In Pindar ἐντί, φαντί, φέροντι, etc. usually, but also Lesb. -οισι(ν). In B. usually -ουσι(ν), rarely -οντι.—138.5. ἔβαν, τίθεν, φάνεν, etc.—142. κατεφάμιξεν, παιάνιξαν, etc. (beside forms with σσ, σ).—142a. ὄρνιχες.—147.2. γεγάκειν, κεχλάδειν.—147.3. πεφρίκοντας, κεχλάδοντας.—153.1. -ειν.—154. -μεν, also -μεναι, -ναι.—161.2a. πονάω.—162.7. ἴσᾱμι = οἶδα.—163. 3 pl. in

Pindar ἐντί, once εἰσίν, in B. εἰσί. 3 sg. imperf. ἦν, not ἦς.—164.4. τεθμός, τέθμιος.—162.12. πᾶμα, πέπαται.

THEOCRITUS

Cf. Magnien, Le syracusain littérair, et l'idylle XV de Théocrite, MSL 21.49 ff. A. S. F. Gow, Theocritus edited with introduction and commentary (1950) pp. LXXI ff.

The Sicilian literary Doric that appears in the scanty fragments of Epicharmus and Sophron and in the corrupt texts of other Sicilian and Italiot writers, but is best known from Theocritus, is based mainly on the Doric of Syracuse, though most of its characteristics are common to other Doric dialects. Its striking difference from the language of Pindar is due not so much to Sicilian peculiarities, though there are some, as to its much more thoroughgoing adherence to Doric.

Theocritus imitated various literary dialects, the epic (XII, XXII), the Lesbian lyric (XXVIII-XXX), the mild Doric of the choral lyric (XVI-XVIII, XXIV). But most of the poems are in the fuller Doric, based mainly on the Sicilian Doric of Epicharmus and Sophron and of his native Syracuse, but with many epic forms (ἄν, κε, εἰ, ν movable, gen. sg. -οιο, ἄμμες, ἐπέεσσι, etc.) and the Lesb. Μοῖσα, ἔχοισα, etc. It is to these poems that the following summary applies.

8. ᾱ regularly. Rarely Att.-Ion. η, as in Hom. phrase βίην καὶ κάρτος. Hyper-Doric ᾱ in ἄμισυς (but this in a Lesbian poem), other cases doubtful. —13. Epic ἱερός (ἱαρός in Epich., Sophron), but σκιαρός, κα, γα, ὅκα, etc.—25. η and ει, mostly ω but also ου, with great fluctuation in MSS.,e.g. ἦνθε, ἦμεν, εἰμές, gen. sg. -ω, κώρα, κούρα.—41.1 ὁρῆτε etc.—41.2. Normal Dor. ω in ὁρῶν, σιγῶντι, πειρώμενοι, etc. Hyper-Dor. ᾱ in 2 sg. aor. ἐπάξα, ἐκτάσα of some MSS.—41.4. ἄς, gen. sg. -ᾱ, also epic -ᾱο, gen. pl. -ᾶν, etc.—42.1. ἄνθεα, etc., but 2 sg. mid. -ηι from -εαι. —42.3, 4. εὐμενέες, φιλέει, etc., but usually contraction.—42.5. εο or ευ, gen. -εος, -ευς, ἐόντα, εὖντα, etc.— 42.6. ἐών, φιλέων, but fut. δοκῶ, ἀξῶ, etc.—43. βασιλῆος, etc. (also -εος).— 44.3. ἄθρως = ἄθροος, gen. sg. -ω.—52, 53. No F.—54. κώρα (κούρα), μώνα and κόρα, μόνα.—61. εἴκατι, τύ, πλατίον, τίθητι, ἐντί, etc.—72. ἦνθον, βέντιστος.—77.3. Lesb. Μοῖσα, ἔχοισα, etc. — 82, 83. ὅσσος, ὅσος, ἔσσεται, etc.—84. ζ and σδ.—89.5a. μικκός.—94. κην, κής, χώνήρ, etc.—95. ἄν, πάρ, πέρ, κάτ, πότ.—102. ν movable frequent.—104-5. Gen. sg. masc. -ᾱ (rarely epic -ᾱο), gen. pl. -ᾶν, dat. pl. -αις, -αισι(ν), acc. pl. -ᾱς frequent.— 106. Gen. sg. -ω (and epic -οιο), dat. pl. -οις, -οισι(ν), acc. pl. -ως, sometimes -ος.—107.3. πάντεσσι, etc., also epic ἔπεσσι(ν).—111. βασιλῆος, etc. (and -εος).—114, 116. πρᾶτος, τέτορες, εἴκατι (cf. Heracl. Fεἴκατι).—118. Nom. τύ; gen. ἐμεῦς, μευ, τεῦς, τευ, σέθεν; dat. ἐμίν, μοι, τίν, τοι, οἱ; acc. τύ, τέ, τίν, νιν.—119. Lesb. ἄμμες, ὕμμες, etc.—120. τεός, ἑός, ἁμός.— 122. τοί, ταί, and οἱ, αἱ.—125. τῆνος.—129.2 ὅττι.—132.2. τηνεῖ.—132.5. πᾶι, παντᾶι.—132.7. πῇ, ὅπῃ, τῇδε.—132.8. ὦ, τηνῶ, τηνῶθε.—132.11. ὅκα, πόκα, τόκα, ὅκκα.—133.4. ἔνδοι.—134.1. αἱ and εἱ.—134.2. κα, ἄν, and κε(ν).—135.6. ποτί, rarely πρός.
138. 2 sg. συρίσδες etc., beside usual -εις. 3 sg. τίθητι, προίητι. 1 pl. λέγομες, etc. 3 pl. ἐντί, φαντί, λέγοντι, etc.—141. ἐσσεῖται and ἔσσεται, οἰσεῦμες and οἴσεται, etc.—142. χαρίξηι, ἐργαξῆι, θεσπίξασα, etc.—142a. χλαίξ.—143. γελάσσαι.—147.1. δεδοίκω, πεποίθεις, πεφύκει, etc.—153. -ειν (or -ην) and -εν.—154. θέμεν, ἦμεν, etc.—157. Once ποθόρημι with Lesb. type.—159. πεινᾶντι, γελᾶντι, παρελᾶντι, (ὀπτᾶντες Epich.).—161.2. ποθορεῦσα, συλεύμενος.—161.2a. ἐξεπόνασεν.—162.6, 7. ἴσαμι = οἶδα. λέω = θέλω.—163. ἐντί, ἦς.

4. Kirchoff, Studien zur Geschichte des griechischen Alphabets, 4th ed. Roberts, Introduction to Greek Epigraphy, I. Rehm, Die Schrift des

griechischen Kreises, in Müller's Handbuch der Altertumswissenschaft VI.6.191 f. Hiller v. Gaertringen in Ebert, Reallexicon der Vorgeschichte II.357 ff. Falkner, Zur Frühgeschichte des griechischen Alphabets, in Brandenstein's Frühgeschichte und Sprachwissenschaft 110 ff.

Facsimiles of archaic inscriptions in Roberts, and Roehl, Imagines inscriptionum graecarum antiquissimarum. Photographs in Kern, Inscriptiones Graecae.

Kirchoff's map needs some revision in detail, e.g., Rhodes should be colored red. Cf. Wiedemann, Klio 8.523 ff., 9.364.

The Phoenician alphabet, now known from about 1000 B.C., was adopted and adapted to Greek speech. The significant innovation, one common to all the local alphabets, was the use of Phoenician consonant signs to express the five Greek vowels. The increase from 22 to 23 letters is due to the fact that the Phoenician wau is represented by two letters, (1) the F, based on a variant form, but with the original consonantal value and position in the alphabet, (2) the Y corresponding to the usual Phoenician form, but given vowel value and placed at the end of the alphabet. The four Phoenician signs for sibilants were taken over, but without stabilization in use (ϟ or Μ = σ, I and ‡ with varying values).

The origin of the supplementary letters, Φ, X, Ψ, has been widely discussed, without decisive results. But it is generally agreed that both X and Ψ have originally guttural value, and it is highly probable that the Ψ is based on a form of the Phoenician kaph (it agrees precisely with the kaph-form of the earliest Phoenician inscription), the source of K.

In view of the agreement in the use of the Phoenician consonant signs to express the vowels we can scarcely escape the conclusion that the adaptation was made at some particular time and place. For the time estimates have varied by several centuries, but the probability is that it should be placed sometime in the course of the ninth century B.C. The earliest records were very likely on perishable material, such as merchants' accounts on papyrus. Some interval must have elapsed between the original adaptation and the time of the earliest inscriptions on pottery or stone. The Dipylon vase, on which is inscribed the earliest known Attic inscription (with the only example of the reclining alpha, like the Phoenician aleph but already with the supplementary X) is now ascribed to the first half of the eighth century B.C., and somewhat later but still in that century the inscribed sherds from Hymettus and some from Corinth and elsewhere. The scrawls on the rocks at Thera, though un-dateable, are clearly among the oldest specimens of Greek writing. As to the place of origin, one can say no more than that one naturally thinks of some one of the islands most accessible to Phoenician commerce.

The belief that the Greek alphabet must have had its birth at a given time and place does not exclude the possibility that, under continued familiarity with the Phoenician alphabet in other places, some of the variant letter forms in local alphabets may be based on Phoenician variants.

Some of the striking variants in letter forms are the following:

A. ⊁ ("reclining alpha") Athens (Dipylon vase). ℕ ("four-barred alpha") usual in Boeotia, occasional elsewhere as in Locris (so no. 57), etc.

B. ꓶ Crete. Ƨ, ꓷ, ꓘ Thera. ᴝ Corinth. Ϝ, Ͱ Argos. ᴧ Selinus, Melos.

Γ. Γ, ⌐, Λ, <, C, / (this last in Ach. colonies).

E. Ε frequent in Boeotia. Ƀ Corinth, Corcyra, Acarnania, Cleonae, Megara. Ӿ Sicyon.

F. ꓛ, Ⴖ Crete. ᵕ Pamphylia and some Cretan towns (see **51***b*). ⊏ Chalcis, Corcyra, Thessaly, Boeotia, Ε frequent in Boeotia, sometimes elsewhere.

H. ⊟ early, ▢ Cnidus. ⊦ (source of ᴸ , ꞌ) Heraclea, rarely Cumae. Elis, Sicyon, Epidaurus.

Θ. ⊗, ⨁, ⊙ Rarely ⊖, ⊙, ⊟.

I. Ϟ, ᠈, ᠌ Athens (Dipylon vase), Crete, Thera, etc. Ϛ Corinth.

Λ. L Athens (but ᒋ Dipylon vase), Chalcis, Boeotia, East Locris (also Crete, no. 116). ᒋ Crete, Thera, Melos, Naxos, Corinth, Corcyra, West Locris, Elis, Thessaly.

M. Early ᶺᶺ. ꓳ Mantinea.

Ξ. Ⱶ Argos, Amorgos. ⊟ Etruscan abcdaria. ▢ Naxos (probably; see no. 6). Ⴟ Pamphylia.

O. Ω Delos, Paros Thasos Siphnos. ⊂ Melos, Cnidus.

Π. ᒋ, ᒍ Thera, Boeotia, etc. ⊂ Crete.

M (san) = σ. Crete, Thera, Melos, Sicinos, Corinth, Corcyra, Sicyon, Argolis (also Ϛ), Locris (once beside Ϛ in no. 59). ᶺ = σ Mantinea.

T = σσ Halicarnassus, Teos, Ephesus, Erythrae, Cyzicus, Naucratis, Selinus. Ψ = σσ Pamphylia.

Σ. Ϟ Athens, Euboea, Boeotia, Elis, etc. Ϟ Laconia, Abu-Symbol.

X. ⼂ Locris, Phocis, Thessaly, Boeotia, Arcadia, Selinus.

Ψ = ψ. Ⴟ Locris. Arcadia. Ⴟ Elis, Laconia. ψ = ξ Melos, Thera.

GLOSSARY AND INDEX

In the alphabetical arrangement the presence of F is ignored, in order to obviate the separation of the many forms which occur with and without it. Thus (F)ίκατι, i.e., Fίκατι or ίκατι, and να(F)ός in the position of ναός. Ϙ stands in the position of κ.

For inflectional forms the conventional captions (nom. sg., 1 sg. pres. indic.) are sometimes substituted, and in these the transcription which we have employed for forms occurring in the epichoric alphabets is frequently replaced by the more familiar spelling, e.g., ē, ō, h, by η, ω ', or Cret. π, κ, by φ, χ. But the precise form occurring is sometimes retained as a caption, or added, or given separately with a cross-reference. Brevity and convenience in each case have been preferred to consistency.

The references are: numbers in bold faced type, to the sections of the Grammar; otherwise to the numbers of the inscriptions.

ά = ἀ. 58a
ἀFάταται Lac. 53
ἀβέλιος Cret. = ἥλιος. 41.3, 54
ἀβλοπία Cret. = ἀβλαβία. 49.3, 66
ἀγαῖος Delph. No. 52 D 38, note
ἀγαλμα. No. 37, note
ἀγαλματοφώρ El. = ἱερόσυλος.107.1
Fάγανον Boeot., meaning? No. 39
ἀγαρρις West Ion. 'assembly.' 49.2, 80 with a
'ΑγασιλέϜō Eub. = 'Αγασίλεω. 41.4, 53
ἀγγροφά Epid. 49.2
ἀγέλαι Cret., 'bands' in which the Cretan youth were trained
ἀγελάοι Cret., 'ephebi.' 31, no. 120.11, note
ἀγερσις East Ion., 'assembly.' 49.2
'Αγλαο-, 'Αγλω-. 41.2
ἀγνέω = ἄγω. 162.1
ἀγορά Delph., Thess. = ἐκκλησία
ἀγορανομέω Thess., 'preside over the assembly,' like Att. ἐπιστατέω. See preceding. In other states the ἀγορανόμοι were officers in charge of the 'market' etc.
ἀγόρασσις Boeot. 164.3
ἀγρέω Lesb., El., ἀνγρέω Thess. (58c) = αἱρέω. 162.2
ἀγχιστέδαν Locr. 133.7

ἄδε, ἄδε 'in this way.' 132.6
ἀδεαλτώhαιε El., from ἀδεαλτόω = ἀδηλόω, ἀφανίζω. 59.3, 152.4, no. 65.12, note
ἀδελφεός = ἀδελφός. 164.9
ἀδευπιαί Cret. = ἀδελφαί. 71, 164.9
ἀδηλόω Heracl. 'make invisible'
ἀδηνέως 'without fraud, plainly.' Chian ἀδηνέως γεγωνέοντες 'calling out plainly,' no. 4 B. Cf. Hesych. ἀδηνέως · ἀδόλως, ἀπλῶς, χωρὶς βουλῆς
ἄδος, ὁ Ion. 'decree.' See ἀνδάνω
ἀέλιος = ἥλιος. 41.3
ἀζαθός Cypr. = ἀγαθός. 62.2
ἀζετόω Delph. 'convict.' No. 55.17, note
ἄζωστος Cret. 'ungirded,' epithet of the ephebes. No. 120.11/12, note
"Αθαββος Delph. = "Αθαμβος 69.3
αἰ West Greek, Aeol. = εἰ. 134.1, 2c
ἄι = ἦ adv. 132.5
ἀι Lesb., ἀί Arc., αἰι Ion., ἀίν Thess. = ἀεί. 133.6
ἀίδασμος Ion. 133.6
αἰϜεί Cypr., Phoc. = ἀεί. 53, 133.6
αἰλέω Cret. = αἱρέω. 12
αἱλος Cypr. = ἄλλος. 74 b
αἱλότρια El. = ἀλλότρια. 74 b

αἱμάτιον Coan, etc. 'coagulated blood and meat, sausage-meat.' Cf. Hesych. αἱμάτια· ἀλλάντια
αἰμίονος Lesb. = ἡμίονος. 17
αἰμισυς Lesb. = ἥμισυς. 17, 61.5
ἀίν Thess. = ἀεί. 133.6
αἶνος 'decree.' No. 99.4, note
αἱρεθές Ther. = αἱρεθείς. 78
αἶσα 'share.' 191
αἰσιμνάτας, αἰσιμνῶντες Meg. = αἰσυμνήτης, etc. 20, 258
ἀκεύω Cret. 'take care of, act as guardian.' Cf. ἀκεύει· τηρεῖ. Κύπριοι Hesych.
Ϝακίνθια Arg. = Ὑακίνθια. 52 c
ἀκκόρ late Lac. = ἀσκός. 86.3 b
ἀκρατής Ion. = ἄκυρος. Cf. καρτερός
ἀκρόθις Delph. = ἀκροθίνιον. No. 52 D 47, note
ἄκρος Corcyr. = ἄκρος. 58 c
haκροσκιρίαι Heracl. 'heights covered with brushwood.' 58 c
ἀϜλανέος El. 'wholly, in full.' 55, no. 64.4, note
ἀλία 'assembly.' (1) Delph. (no. 52), used of the meeting of the phratry; (2) Acarn., Corcyr., Heracl., Gela, Agrig., Rheg. = ἐκκλησία. 55
ἁλιαία 'assembly.' Arc., Arg., Mycen, Nemea
ἁλίασμα 'decree.' Gela, Agrig., Rheg.
ἁλίασσις Arg. 'act of the ἁλιαία.' 164.3
ἁλιασταί Arc., in form = Att. ἡλιασταί, but title of Tegean officials who enforced penalties etc. (no. 19.23)
ἅλινσις Epid. 'stuccoing.' 77.3 a
ἅλιος Dor., ἅλιος Lesb. = ἥλιος. 41.3
Ϝαλίσκομαι Thess. = ἁλίσκομαι. 52 c, 89.1
ἄλλα Lesb. 'elsewhere.' 132.6
ἀλλάζω Locr. = ἀλλάσσω. 84 a
ἀλλᾶι Cret., Corcyr. 'otherwise.' 132.5
ἀλλεῖ 132.2
ἄλλη 'elsewhere.' 132.7
ἀλλοπολία Cret. = ἀλλοδημία. Cf. Cret. πόλις = δῆμος
ἀλλότερρος Lesb. = ἀλλότριος. 19.2
ἀλλόττριος Cret. 89.2
ἄλλυ Arc. = ἄλλο. 22
ἄλλυι Lesb. 'elsewhere.' 132.4
ἀλλύω Cret. = ἀναλύω 'ransom'

ἀλϜόν Cypr. Sicil. ἅλος (ἁ), Arc. ἅλων (ἁ) 'plot of cultivated land, plantation.' Cf. Att. ἅλως, Hom. ἁλωή. No. 23.9, note
ἀλοργής Ion. 167
ἄλωμα Boeot. = ἀνάλωμα. 164.8
haμᾶ Lac. 132.6
hάμα Boeot. = ἅμμα (?). No. 39
ἁμάρα Locr., Delph. = ἡμέρα. 12, 58 b
'Αμάριος Ach. 12
ἀμβόλιμος 'adjourned.' Arg.
ἀμβρ[ό]την Lesb. = ἁμαρτεῖν. 5, 49.2a
ἀμεῖ Delph. = ὁμοῦ. 132.2
ἀμέν late Cret. = ἡμεῖς. 119.2a
ἀμέρα with lenis. 58b
ἀμές, ἀμές. 57, 58b, 76, 119
ἀμιθρέω Ion. = ἀριθμέω. 88
ἄμμες, ἄμμε Lesb., ἀμμέ Thess. = ἡμεῖς, ἡμέας. 76, 119
ἀμμόνιον Delph. 'penalty for delay.' From ἀναμένω. Cf. Hom. καμμονίη = καταμονή
ἀμοιϜά Corinth. = ἀμοιβή. 51a
ἀμπ- in early Cretan words, see under ἀμφ-
ἀμπείσῃ Arc., aor. subj. of ἀναπείθω. No. 22.60, note
ἀμπελωργικός Heracl. 167
ἀμπώλημα Heracl. 'rebate.' Heracl. Tab. I.108 ff., note
ἀμφαίνομαι Cret. (e.g. ἀμπαίνεθαι, ἀμπανάμενος, ἀνπανάμενος, ἄμπαντος, ἀνπαντος) 'adopt'
ἄμπανσις Cret. (ἄνπανσιν) 'adoption' (act of). 77.3a
ἀμφαντύς Cret. (ἀνπαντύι) 'adoption' (condition of, i.e., state of being an adopted son)
ἀμφεικάς 'day after the twentieth.' Coan, Ther.
ἀμφί. 136.7
ἀμφίδημα Cret. 'ornament,' gen. sg. ἀνπιδέμᾱς. 112.5
'Αμφικτίονες, -κτύονες. 20
ἀμφιλλέγω, ἀμφίλλογος. 76a
ἀμφιμωλέω, ἀμφίμωλος Cret., see μωλέω
ἀμφίσταμαι Heracl. 'investigate.' Cf. Hesych. ἀμφίστασθαι· ἐξετάζειν
ἀν = ἀνά. 95
ἄν Arc. = ἁ ἄν. 58d
hάν Arc. = ἄν. 58d
ἀνάατορ El., see ἄνατος
Ϝάναξ = ἄναξ. 52
ἀνασκηθής Arc., see ἀσκηθής

ἄνατος 'immune from punishment.' El. ἀνάατορ, Locr. adv. ἀνάτō(ς). **53**
ἀνδάνω = δοκέω 'be approved, voted.' **162**.3
ἀνδιχάζω Locr. 'be of divided opinion.' Cf. Hdt. 6.109 δίχα γίγνονται αἱ γνῶμαι
ἀνδρεφονικός Locr. = ἀνδρο-. **167**
ἀνδρήιος Cret.; ἀνδρήος Delph. **164**.1
ἀνέθεαν, ἀνέθιαν = ἀνέθεσαν. **9**.2, **138**.5
ἀνεκκλήτως Delph. = ἀνεγκλήτως. **69**.3
ἀνελόσθō Lac. = ἀνελέσθων. **140**.3b
ἀνεπίγροφος Heracl. = -γραφος. **49**.2
ἀνέσηκε Lac. = ἀνέθηκε, **64**
ἄνευν Epid. = ἄνευ. **133**.6
ἄνευς El. = ἄνευ. **133**.6, **136**.4
ἀνhεῶσθαι Heracl., from ἀνίημι. **146**.3
ἀνηρίθευτος Ion. = ἀνερίθευτος 'not venal.' **167**a
ἀνιοχίω Lac.= ἡνιοχέω. **9**.8
ἄνις Mess., etc. **133**.6
ἀννίομαι Cret. = ἀρνέομαι. **86**.5
ἀνοσίjα Cypr. 'impiety.' No. 23.29
ἀνπ- in early Cretan words, see under ἀμφ-
ἀνταποδιδῶσσα El. = -διδοῦσα. **89**.4
ἀντί. **136**.8
ἀντίγροφον Cret., Anaph. = ἀντίγραφον. **49**.2
ἀντίμολος Cret. 'opponent, defendant,' see μωλέω
ἀντιτυγχάνω Arg., Boeot., Delph., Lac. = παρατυγχάνω 'happen to be present,' or 'in office' (so nos. 45, 84)
ἄντομος Heracl. 'road, path'
ἄντορος Heracl. 'counter-boundary'
ἀντρῆιον Cret. = ἀνδρεῖον. **62**.2
ἄντρōπος Cret., Pamph. = ἄνθρωπος. **66**
ἀνφόταρος Locr. = ἀμφότερος. **12**
ἀνώγω Cypr. **191**
ἄνωθα Heracl. = ἄνωθεν. **133**.1
ἀνωθεοίη Ion. **157**c
ἄνōρος Cret., Thess. = ἄωρος
ἀξιάω Lesb. (ἀξιάσει) = ἀξιόω. **161**.5. ἀξιῶ̣ι Calym. **159**a
ἀξιοδότας Locr. No. 59b, note
αὐτός East Ion. = αὐτός. **33**
ᾱπ Thess. = ἀπό. **95**

ἀπαγορεύω Cret. 'proclaim'
ἄπατος Cret. = ἄνατος, used impersonally, e.g., ἄγοντι ἄπατον ἔμεν 'there shall be no fine for the one who seizes.' **53**
Ἀπείλōν Cypr. = Ἀπόλλων. **49**.3, **74**b
ἀπελάōνται Locr. **159**
ἀπελευθερίζω Delph., Thess. = ἀπελευθερόω. **161**.4. Thess. ἀπελευθερεσθένσα, **18**, **77**.3
ἀπέλλα. Lac. = ἐκκλησία. Cf. Ἀπελλαῖος, name of a month. Ἀπέλλαι Delph., name of a festival corresponding to the Attic Ἀπατούρια
ἀπελλαῖα Delph. 'victims for the Ἀπέλλαι'
ἀπέλλω Lesb. = ἀπειλέω. **75**
Ἀπέλλων = Ἀπόλλων. **49**.3
ἀπεσσούα Lac. **145**b
ἀπέταιρος Cret. 'one who is not a member of a ἑταιρεία.' **117**.II.5, note
ἀπεχομίνος Arc. = -μένους. **10**
Ἄπλουν Thess. = Ἀπόλλων. **49**.3
ἀποδεδόανθι Boeot. = -δεδώκασι. **138**.4, **146**.1
ἀποδείγνυσθαι Eretr. = -δείκνυσθαι. **66**
ἀποδόσσαι El. = ἀποδόσθαι. **85**.2
ἀπόδρομος Cret. 'a minor.' See δρομεύς
ἀποϝελέω El. = ἀπειλέω. **75**
ἀπολιήνω Boeot. **162**.10
ἀπολογίτταστη Boeot. = ἀπολογίσασθαι **82**, **85**.1, **142**
ἀπομωλέω Cret. 'contend in denial, deny.' See μωλέω
ἀποπιπράσκω 'sell,' Lesb., Ion., etc.
ἀποστράψαι Delph. = ἀποστρέψαι. **49**.2
ἀποτίνοιαν El. = ἀποτίνοιεν. **12**a
ἄποτος Coan = ἄοινος. No. 108.35, note
ἀποφορά Coan 'carrying off'
ἀποφωνέω Cret. (ἀποϝόνίοι, etc.) 'bear witness.' See φωνέω
ἀππασάμενος Boeot. = ἀνακτησάμενος. **69**.4, **162**.12
ἀππεισάτου Thess. = ἀποτεισάτω. **68**.2
ἀπύ Arc., Cypr., Lesb., Thess. = ἀπό. **22**
ἀπυδίει Arc. = ἀποδέει. **9**.5
ἀπυδόας Arc. = ἀποδούς **144**

ἀπυδόσμιος Arc. 'for sale.' No. 18.28, note

ἀπυδοσμός Arc. = ἀπόδοσις 'payment.' 164.4.

ἀπυλιῶναι Arc. 'smooth out, settle (?).' 162.10

ἀπυσεδομίν[ος] Arc. = ἀποδεδομένους. 10, 68.3a

ἀπυτείω Arc. See τίνω

ἀπύω Arc. 'summon' = poet. ἠπύω, 191

ἀπώμοτος Cret. 'under oath of denial'

ἄρατρον Cret. = ἄροτρον 161.5

ἀράω Heracl. (ἀράσοντι) = ἀρόω. 161.5

Ϝαργάναι Delph. = Ἐργάνη. 12

Ϝάργον El. = ἔργον. 12

ἀργύριος Lesb. = ἀργύρεος. 164.6. Lesb. ἄργυρα, 19.4, Thess. ἀργύρρος. 19.3

ἀρέσμιον Phoc. 'fee, perquisite.' From ἀρέσκω

ἡαρέσται Locr. = ἑλέσθαι. 12, 85.1

Ϝαρήν Cret. = ἀρήν (Att. inscr.), nom. of ἀρνός. 52

ἀϜϝέτευε, ἀρήτευε Arg. 55 with b

Ἀρίσταιχνος Coan. 69a

ἀριστίνδαν Locr. 133.7

ἀρνηάς 'ewe.' Lesb.

ἡάρνησις Heracl. = ἄρνησις. 58d

ἀρρέντερος Arc. = ἄρρην. 80, 165.1

ἄρρηκτος 'unplowed.' Heracl. Ϝάρρω El. 12, 162.7

ἄρσην. 49.2, 80

Ἄρταμις = Ἄρτεμις. 13.2

Ἀρταμίτιός = Ἀρτεμίσιος. 61.3

Ἀρτεμίρια Eretr. = Ἀρτεμίσια. 60.3

ἀρτύω Heracl. 'devise by will.' Cf. Hesych. ἄρτυμα· διαθήκη, and ἀρτῦναι· διαθεῖναι. In Cretan (no. 117.XII.32) 'manage.' In Arcadian 'arrange, prepare.' Cf. the official titles Arg. ἀρτῦναι (no. 85.2, note), Epid. ἀρτῦνοι, Ther. ἀρτυτήρ

ἀρχιδαυχναφορέω Thess., see δαύχνα

ἀρχιττολιαρχέω Thess. 'be the first ptoliarch.' See ττολίαρχοι

Ἀρχοκράτης Rhod. = Ἀρχεκράτης. 167

ἀρχός Boeot., Cret., Ion., Locr. = ἄρχων 'magistrate'

ἇς = ἕως. 41.4, 45.4, 132.12

ἀσαυτός reflex. pron. 121.4

ἄσιστα El., Lac. = ἄγχιστα. 113.3. Lac. τοὶ ἄσιστα πόθικες, El. τοὶρ ἐπ' ἄσιστα 'those next of kin.' Cf. Cret. οἱ ἐπ' ἄνχιστα πεπαμένοι 'the nearest owners,' Locr. ἐπάνχιστος 'next of kin'

Ἀσκαλαπιός Thess. = Ἀσκληπιός. 48

ἀσκηθής Arc., used of animals 'without blemish'

ἀστάς Epid. = ἀναστάς. Cf. 77.2

Ἀστο- Thess. = Ἀριστο-. 88b

Ϝαστός = ἀστός. 52

ἄτα Cret. 'penalty, fine.' 53

ἀταγία Thess. No. 35.6, note

ἀτάω Cret. (ἀταμένοι, ἀταθείε) 'fine. 53

ἄτε Lac. (hᾶτ'). 132.6

ἀτελέν Cypr. = ἀτελῆ. 108.2

ἀτερόπτιλος (and -ιλλος) Epic., see ὀπτίλος

ἄτερος = ἕτερος. 13.3

Ἀτθόνειτος Thess. = Ἀφθόνητος. 86.2

ἄτι Cret. = ἅτινα. 129.3

ἀτροπάμπαις Lac. Nos. 75-78, note

ἀττάμιος El. = ἀζήμιος. 84

ἀυάδης Lesb. = ἀηδής. 35

αὐάτα Lesb. = ἄτη. 35a, 53

αὖθι Arc. 133.1a

αὖθιν Rheg. = αὖθις. 133.6

Αὐχλίεια Arc. 9.5, 33a

αὔληρα Dor. 55a

αὔρηκτος Lesb. = ἄρρηκτος. 55a

αὐσαυτός, αὐσωτός Delph., reflex. pron. 121.4

αὖσος Cret. = ἄλσος. 71

αὐταμαρόν Locr. = αὐθημερόν. 12, 58b, 133.6

αὐταμέριν Cret. = αὐθημερόν. 133.6

αὐταμερόν = αὐθημερόν. 133.6

ἀϜυτάν Corcyr. = αὐτήν. 32

ἀϜυτάρ Att. = αὐτάρ. 32, 50

αὐταυτός reflex. pron. 121.4

αὐτεῖ, Boeot. αὐτῖ. 132.2

αὐτεῖς Boeot. = αὐτοῖς. 30

αὖτιν Cret.; αὖτις Arc., Ion. = αὖθις. 133.6

αὐτός 121.3, 4, 125.2

αὐτοσαυτός reflex. pron. 121.4

αὐτούτα, αὐτῶντα Sicil. = ἑαυτοῦ, ἑαυτῶν. 121.4

αὔφιτα Cret. = ἄλφιτα. 75

αὔως Lesb. = ἕως. 35

ἀφακεσάσθō Arg. 58c

ἀφεδριατεύω Boeot. 'serve as ἀφε-δριάτας or official dedicator.' No. 41, note

ἀφερξόντι Heracl. 'shut off' (water by damming). No. 79.130 ff.,note

ἀφεώσθω Arc., from ἀφίημι. 146.3

ἀφικνεμένων Orop. = ἀφικνουμένων. 158

'Αφορδίτα Cret. = 'Αφροδίτη. 70.1

ἀφφάνω Cret. = ἀμφάνω. 69.3

ἄφωνος Heracl. 'intestate'

ἆχι Dor. 'where.' 132.6

ἀχύριος Heracl. 'building to hold chaff.' Cf. Hesych. ἄχυρος· ὁ ἀχυρών. ἀχυροδόκη· ἀποθήκη τῶν ἀχύρων

ἀψευδήων Arc. 149, 159

ἀ(F)ώς Dor. etc. = ἕως. 35, 41.4

βάβᾶλος Cyren. = βέβηλος. 46.1

Βαδρόμιος Coan, Rhod. = Βοηδρομιών. 44.2

βαθοέω Lesb. = βοηθέω. 44.2

βανά Boeot. = γυνή. 68.1

βάρναμαι = μάρναμαι. 88

βασιλᾶες El. = βασιλῆες. 15

βασιλεύς official title in many states. In some the chief magistrate; in others restricted to religious functions, like the ἄρχων βασιλεύς at Athens, e.g., at Chios (no. 4 C) and Miletus; βασιλεῖς an official body, e.g., in Mytilene (no. 26) and Elis (no. 61)

βάω, βέω (cf. 161.2) Dor. = βαίνω. Heracl. ἐπιβῆι, Cyren. παρβεῶντα, also ἐκβῶντας Thuc. 5.77

βέβαιος Locr. = κύριος

βεβαιωτήρ Delph. = -τής. 164.5

βείλομαι Boeot. = βούλομαι. 49.3, 68.2, 75

βέλλομαι Thess. = βούλομαι. 49.3, 68.2, 75. 3 pl. subj. βέλλουνθειν, 27, 139.2

Βέλφαιον Thess. = *Δέλφαιον, Δελφίνιον. 68.2

Βελφοί Lesb., Boeot. = Δελφοί. 68.2

βενέω El. = βινέω. 18b

βέντιστος Dor. = βέλτιστος. 72

βεττόν Lac. = *Fεστόν. 86.4

βέφυρα Boeot. = γέφυρα. 68.2

βίδεοι, βίδυοι Lac., title of officials. 51

βίετος Cret. = βίοτος. 167

βλῆρ = δέλεαρ. 42.1, 68.1

βόα(ι) Lab. 41a 157b, 159

βοαθοέω, βοαθέω = βοηθέω. 44.2, 45

βοαθός, βοηθός = -θός. 45

βοιηθέω = βοηθέω. 31a

βοικίαρ El. = οἰκίας. 51

βόλιμος Delph., Epid. = μόλιβος. 88

βόλλα Lesb. = βουλή. 75

βολλεύω Lesb. = βουλεύω

Βολόεντα Cret. 44.4, 51

βόλομαι Arc., Cypr., Ion. = βούλομαι. 75b

Βόρθιος Cret. = 'Ορθιος. 51

βοῦα, βουαγόρ Lac. Nos. 75-78, note

βουσός Arc. 'cattle run.' 45

βοών Heracl. 'cow-shed.' 165.4

βροχύς Boeot., Thess., Arc. = βραχύς. 5

βυβλία Heracl. 'papyrus marsh.' τὰν βυβλίαν no. 79.I.58 = τὰν βυβλίναν μασχάλαν 92

βύβλινος Heracl., see preceding

βυβλίον = βιβλίον. 20

βωθέω Ion. = βοηθέω. 44.2, 45

βωλά Boeot., Cret., Arg., etc. = βουλή. 25, 75

Βωρθέα, Βωρσέα Lac. = 'Ορθία. 51, 64

βῶς Dor. = βοῦς. 37.1

γά W. Grk., Boeot. = γέ. 13.3

γαεργός Boeot.; γαFεργόρ Lac. = γεωργός. 167

ΓαιάFοχος Lac. = γαιήοχος. 53

γαιών Heracl. 'heap of earth, mound.' 165.4

γάμελα Delph. = γαμήλια 'wedding cakes.' 164.10

γεγράβανται Arg. = γεγράφαται. 66, 139.2

γεγράψαται Heracl. 146.5

γεγωνέω Chian 'call aloud.' 184

-γελᾶ, γελᾶντι 159

γενεά 'family, offspring,' also in plural 'descendants.' No. 61, 65

γερεαφόρος Coan, title of a priestly official. γερηφόρος occurs also in Pserimos near Calymna

γερουσία, Lac. γερωhία (59.1), title of the council at Sparta and some other places (as Ephesus, Andania, Dyme in Achaea)

γίνομαι = γίγνομαι, 86.10

γῖνος Rhod. = γίνος

γίνυμαι Boeot., Thess. = γίγνομαι. 86.10, 162.4

γινώσκω = γιγνώσκω. 86.10
γλάσσα Ion. = γλῶσσα. 49.5
γλέπω Dor. = βλέπω. 88
γλέφαρον Dor. = βλέφαρον. 88
γνῶμαν El. = γνῶμεν. 12a
γνώμη, γνῶμα 'opinion, declaration' of an official body, frequent in Ionic and Doric
γνῶσία Arc. = γνῶσις. 164.10
γράθμα Arg. = γράμμα. 164.4
γραμματίδδω Boeot. = γραμματεύω. 84, 161.4
γραμματιστάς = γραμματεύς 161.4
γράσσμα Arg. = γράμμα. 164.4
γραφής Arc. = γραφεύς. 111.4
γράφος El., Arc. = γράμμα. 241
γροφά, γροφεύς, etc. = γραφή etc. 49.2
γυμμνικός Arg. 89 2
γυμνάδδομαι Lac. 84
Γυνόππαστος Boeot. 69.4

δαιθμός = δασμός. 164.4
δαῖσις Cret. 'division'
δακκύλιος Boeot. = δακτύλιος. 87
δάλτος Cypr. = δέλτος. 49.3
Δαλφοῖς = Δελφοῖς. 12b
δαμέτας Carpath. = δημότης. 167
δαμιεργέντων Cyren. 42.5e
*δαμιοΓοργός, δαμιεργός, δαμιοργός, title of high officials, eponymous in many places. 167
δαμιόμεν Cret. 157c
δαμιοργόντον Arg. 42.5d
δαμιωέμεν, δαμιοῦντες Boeot. = ζημιοῦν, etc. 159
Δαμοκρέτω Lesb. = Δημοκρίτου. 18
δαμοσιολα El. = δημοσιοίη. 15, 157c
δαμοσιῶμεν El. = δημοσιοῦν. 157c
δαμοτέλην Lesb. = -τελῆ, 108.2
δαράτα Delph. 'a ceremonial cake.' No. 52 A 5, note
δαρκνά Cret., see δαρχνά
δάρμα Delph. = δέρμα. 12
δαρχμά = δραχμή. 49.2a. δαρχμάω, dual Boeot. 104.9
δαρχνά Cret. (δαρκνά) = δραχμή. 49.2a, 69a
δάτταθθαι, δάττονται Cret. = δάσασθαι, δάσωνται. 82
δαύχνα Thess., Cypr. = δάφνη. 68.4a
δέατοι Arc. = δοκῇ. 139.1, 151.1, 191
δείλομαι = βούλομαι. 49.3, 68.1, 75
δείμενος Boeot. = δεόμενος. 158

δέκετθαι Cret. = δέχεσθαι. 66, 85.3
δέκνυμι Ion. = δείκνυμι. 49.1
δέκο Arc. = δέκα. 6, 114.10, 116a
δέκομαι = δέχομαι. 66
δέκοτος Arc., Lesb. = δέκατος. 6, 114.10, 116a
δέκων Lesb., Chian, gen. pl. of δέκα. 116
δέλλω Arc. = βάλλω. 49.3, 68.1
δεμελεῖς Epid. 'leeches.' No. 90. 98, note
δενδρύω 'dive under water.' Epid.
ΔϜενίας Corinth. = Δεινίας. 28, 54d
δέρϜα Arc. = δέρη. 54
δέρεθρον Arc. = βάραθρον. 68.3
Δεύς Boeot., Lac., Rhod. = Ζεύς. 84
δεύω Lesb., Thess. = δέω 'want.' 35
δέφυρα Cret. = γέφυρα. 68.2
δήλομαι = βούλομαι. 49.3, 68.1, 75. El. δηλομήρ, no. 65.5, note
δημορίων Orop. = δημοσίων. 60.3
Δῆνα Cret. = Ζῆνα. 84. 112.1
διαχνόντων Heracl. = διαγνόντων. 66
διάλαμψις = διάληψις 'distinction,' in late Lesb., Cret., etc. Cf. And., Thess. λάμψομαι = λήψομαι, as also in Hdt. -λαμψις, like late -λημψις
διαλιήνω Boeot. 162.10
διατελόντι Arg. 42.5d
Διδύμοιυν Arc. = Διδύμοιν. 106.7
διέ Thess. = διά. 7
διεγέλα Epid. 159
διεσαφείμενος Thess. 158
Δι(Ϝ)ει- = Διί-. 112.2
διὲ κί Thess. = διότι. 68.4, 131
διηκόσιοι Ion. = διακόσιοι. 117.2
δικάδδω Cret., El. = δικάζω. 84
δίκαια El. 'legal penalties, fines.' ζίκαια, 62.2
δικάσζω Arg. = δικάζω. 89.1
δικάσκοποι officials at Mytilene 'inspectors of justice'
δικαστήρ Locr., Pamph. = -τής. 164.5
δικάως Lesb. = δικαίως. 31
δίκνυμι Cret. = δείκνυμι. 49.1
δίκρεας Cos, Chios 'double portion of flesh, a double cut'
δινάκω El. 'change, amend.' Cf. δίνω
δίννηντες Lesb. 89.4, 156a
Διόζοτος Boeot., Thess. = Διόδοτος. 166.2

Ϝεϟόντας Locr. = ἐκόντας. 52
ηεχοτόν Arc. = ἑκατόν. 6, 116a
117
ἐκπέτωντι Heracl. = ἐκπέσωσι. No.
79.120, note
ἔκτεισις, not ἔκτισις. 28a
ἐκτιμασέντι Cyren. 42.5e
ἐλάτω, ἐλάντω Coan 159
ἐλαύθερος late Delph. = ἐλεύθερος. 33a
ἔλεξε = εἶπε. So regularly in Boeotian and Thessalian decrees,
where Attic and most dialects
have εἶπε. Also Argive.
ηελέσται Locr. = ἑλέσθαι. 85.1
ἐλέστειν Thess. = ἑλέσθαι. 85.1,
156
Ἐλευθενναῖος Cret. = Ἐλευθε-
ρναῖος. 86.5
Ἐλευηύνια Lac. = Ἐλευσίνια. 20,
59.1
ἐλλευθερία Delph. 89.4
ἐλούθερος Cret. = ἐλεύθερος. 33a
ἐμέθεν Dor. = ἐμοῦ. 118.3
ἐμέος Dor. = ἐμοῦ. 118.3
ἐμετρίωμες Heracl. = ἐμετροῦμεν.
9.6, 42.5b
ἐμίν W. Grk. = ἐμοί. 118.4
ἔμμᾶνις 'wroth.' Cret.
ἔμμεν Thess. = εἶναι. 163.7
ἔμμεναι Lesb. = εἶναι. 154.2, 163.7
ἔμμι Lesb., ἐμμί Thess. = εἰμί. 76
ἔμπαν Dor. = ἔμπης. 133.6
ἔμπασις = ἔγκτησις. 162.12
ἔμπροσθα Heracl. 133.1
ἐμφανιξόντας Arg. 42.5d, 142
ἐμφανίσσω Thess. = ἐμφανίζω. 84a
ἐν = εἰς. 135.4
? ἔναγος Delph. 'ceremony for
the dead.' Cf. ἐναγίζω. No. 52 C
38, note
ηένατος Delph., Ther. = ἔνατος.
58c, 114.9
ἐνδεδιωκότα Heracl. = ἐμβεβιωκότα 'alive.' 68.1
ἐνδειγνύμενος Ther. = ἐνδεικνύμε-
νος. 66
ἐνδέρω, ἔνδορα Coan. No. 108.47,
note
ἐνδεύω Lesb. = ἐνδέω 'want.' 35
ἐνδικάζομαι, Arc. ἰνδικάζομαι (10),
'be subjected to suit.' No. 19.34,
note
ἔνδικος Cret., ἴνδικος Arc. (10),
used impersonally with dative of
the person who is 'liable to, or has
right to, trial.' No. 19.34, note

ἐνδοθίδιος Cret. 'belonging within.' 165.2
ἔνδοι 'within.' 133.4
ἔνδορα Coan. See ἐνδέρω
ἐνδόσε Ceos = εἴσω. 133.4
ἐνδοσθίδια Epid. 'entrails.' 165.2
ἔνδυς Delph. 'within.' 132.4, 133.4
ἔνδω Delph. 'within.' 132.8a, 133.4
ἐνενιχθείει Boeot. = εἰσενεγχθῆ.
144a, 151.2, no. 43.49, note
ἐνετέρια Locr. 'taxes of admission'
(to citizenship). From ἐνίημι, like
Att. εἰσιτήρια from εἴσειμι
ἐνεφανίσσοεν Thess. = ἐνεφάνιζον.
84a, 138.5
ἐνηεβόηαις Lac. from ἐνηβάω.
41.2, 59.1
ἐνθαῦθα Att. (inscr.) = ἐνταῦθα.
65
ἐνθαῦτα Ion. = ἐνταῦθα. 65
ἐνθεῖν = ἐλθεῖν. 72
ἔνθινος, from ἔνθα. Meg.
ἔνθῖνος Cret. = ἔνθεος. 164.10
ἔνθω Boeot = ἔστων. 138.4, 163.6
ἐνιαύτιος Coan, Delph. = ἐνιαύσιος. 61.3
ἐνιαυτός (1) 'end of the year,
anniversary,' (2) 'year.' For the
former and more original meaning, which the word sometimes
has in Homer, cf. Delph. no.
52 C 47, Cret. no. 117 I 35, IV 4
ἐνκοιοταί Cret., sc. δαρκναί 'money
given as security.' Cf. Hesych·
κοῖον· ἐνέχυρον, κοιάζει· ἐνεχυρά-
ζει. Deriv. of κεῖμαι
ηεννέα Heracl. = ἐννέα. 58c, 114.9
ἔννεκα Lesb. = ἔνεκα. 54b
ἐννῆ = ἐννέα. 42.1, 114.9
ἔνοτος Lesb. = ἔνατος. 6, 114.9,
116.9
ἐνπίδες Meg. = ἐλπίδες. 72
ἐνπιπάσκομαι 'acquire' Arg. 162.
12
ἔνς Cret. = εἰς, 114.1
ἔνσα Thess. = οὖσα. 77.3, 163.8
ἐντάδε Argol. = ἐνθάδε. 65
ἐν τάν Boeot. 'until.' 136.1, no.
43.49, note
ἔντασις Thess. = ἔγκτησις. 163.12
ἔντασσιν Heracl. = οὖσιν. 107.3,
163.8
ἐνταῦτα El. = ἐνταῦθα. 65
ἔντε Locr., ηέντε Delph. = ἔστε,
ἕως. 58c, 132.11, 135.4
ἔντες Heracl. = ὄντες. 163.8
ἐντί = εἰσί. 163.2

ἔντιμος Locr. 'in office.' Cf. Plat. Rep. 528 C

ἐντιτός 'liable to suit' Cret. Cf. ἐντιτόν· ἔνδικον Hesych.

ἐντοῦθα Cumae = ἐνταῦθα. 65, 124 ἔντόθα Orop. 34a

ἐντοφήια Delph. = ἐντάφια 'funeral rites.' Cyren. ἐντόφιον 'burial gift.' Cf. Hesych. ταφήια· ἐντάφια, εἰς ταφὴν ἐνθέντα ἱμάτια. 6, 164.1

ἔντω = ἔστων. 163.6

Ἐνυμακρατίδας Lac. = Ὀνυμα-. No. 71.35, note

ἐνυφαίνω Cret. (ἐνυπάνει), 'weave within' (the house)

Fέξ = ἔξ. 52b, 114.6

ἐξαγρέω El. = ἐξαιρέω. 162.2

ἐξάν = ἐξῆς. 133.6

ἐξαντίαι Arc. 'over against, near by.' No. 22.13, note

ἐξαρχίδιος Cret. 165.2

ἔξει Lac. = ἔξω. 133.5

ἐξεικάττιοι Thess. = ἐξακόσιοι. 19.3, 117.2

ἐξελαύνοια Arc. 152.1

ἐξερρύᾱ Epid. 144b

ἐξηκοιστος Lesb. = ἐξηκοστός. 116 with a

ἐξξαναχάδεν Thess. = ἐξαναγκά-ζειν. 69.3, 84, 89.1

ἔξοι = ἔξω. 133.5

ἐξόμεινννον Thess. = ἐξάμηνον. 6

ἐξορύξε͂ Cypr. 'expropriate.' No. 23.12, note

ἔξος = ἔξω. 133.5

ἐξ Ion. 101.2

Fέος Locr. = ἑαυτοῦ. 118.3

ἐπ Thess., Boeot. = ἐπί. 95

ἐπαβολά Cret., Boeot. 'share.' 167a

ἐπάκοε, ἐπάκο͂, ἐπακόω Lac., dual of ἐπάκοος. Nos. 72, 73, note

ἐπάναχκον = ἐπάναγχες. 69.3

ἐπανιτάω El. 'return.' Cf. ἰητέον = ἰτέον, and Hesych. εἰταχεῖν· ἐληλυθέναι

ἐπάνχιστος Locr. 'next of kin.' See ἄσιστα

ἐπαπύλογος Arc. 'in defense.' No. 22.34, note

ἔπαργμα Ther. = ἄπαργμα 'offering.' Cf. Att. (inscr.) ἐπαρχή beside ἀπαρχή

ἔπαρμα Boeot., meaning? No. 39

ἐπαρεώμενοι Cyren. 42.5b, 161.2

ἔπειτε, ἔπειτεν Ion. = Att. ἔπειτα. 132.11

ἐπελάω = ἐπελαύνω. 159. Coan ἐπελάντω 'drive up,' but Heracl. ἐπελάσθω and Arc. ἐπελασάσθων mean 'collect, enforce' (fines). Cf. also Arg. ποτελάτō 'enforce,' Ion. ἐνηλάσιον 'rental'

ἐπελευσεῖ (fut.), ἐπέλευσαν (aor.) Cret. 'bring.' 162.15

ἐπεμπάω El.(ἐπενπο͂ι, ἐπενπέτō) 'enforce'; also ἐμπάω (μὲ 'νπο͂ι). No. 61

ἔπερος 'sheep' (literally 'wooly') Lesb.

ἐπές Arc. 'with reference to.' 136.12

ἐπεστάκοντα Thess. = ἐφεστηκότα. 58b, 147.3

ἔπετον Dor., etc. = ἔπεσον, aor. of πίπτω. See no. 79.120, note

ἐπεχεῖ Delph., ἐπεχές Arg. = ἐφεξῆς. 132.2

ἐπηρειάζω = Att. ἐπηρεάζω. No. 19.46, note

ἐπί Boeot. = ἐπεί. 29

Fέπιja Cypr. = ἔπεα. 9.3

ἐπίαρον El. = *ἐφίερον 'sacred penalty'

ἐπιατές ('πιατές) Locr. 'for the year.' No. 57.35, note

ἐπιβάλλων Cret., short expression for ὡι ἐπιβάλλει. Sometimes = ὡι ἐπιβάλλει (τά χρήματα), i.e., 'heir-at-law'; sometimes ὡι ἐπιβάλλει (ὁπυίεν), i.e., 'groom-elect'

ἐπιβῆι Heracl., see βάω

ἐπιδεί Boeot. = ἐπειδή. 29

ἐπιδημέωριν Eretr. = ἐπιδημῶσιν. 60.3

ἐπιδικατοί Lac. = οἷς ἐπιδικάζεται 'those to whom property is adjudged by law, heirs-at-law.' No. 70. For -ατός cf. θαυματός beside θαυμαστός

ἐπιζημίωμα Heracl. = ἐπιζήμιον 'penalty.' 164.10

ἐπιζύγιον Arc. = ὑποζύγιον

ἐπιθεῖαν El. = ἐπιθεῖεν. 12a

ἐπιθιιάνε̄ Arc. = ἐπιθιγγάνη. 62.3

ἐπίθωσε Boeot. 161.3

ἐπικαταβάλλω Heracl. = ἐπιβάλ-λω 'impose upon'

ἐπίλεκτοι, ἐπιλεκτάρχαι. No. 67. 16, note

ἐπιμεμηνάκαντι Arg. 138.4, 146.1

ἐπιFοικία Locr. = ἐποικία

ἐπιοικοδομά Heracl., collective, used of the buildings belonging to the land. No. 79.150, note

ἐπίϜοικος Locr. = ἔποικος
ἐπιπῆν Epid. = καταπάσσειν. Cf. Hesych. πῆ καὶ πῆν ἐπὶ τοῦ κατάπασσε καὶ καταπάσσειν
ἐπιπηράω Cret. (ἐπιπέρε̄ται) = πειράω
ἐπίποκος 'unshorn' Coan. (also LXX)
ἐπιπόλαια χρήματα Cret. 'movable property.' Cf. Harpocration ἔπιπλα· τὴν οἷον ἐπιπόλαιον κτῆσιν καὶ μεταχομίζεσθαι δυναμένην
ἐπιπρείγιστος Cret. 'the next oldest.' See πρείγιστος
ἐπισκεάζω Corcyr. = ἐπισκευάζω 36
ἐπισπένδω Cret. 'solemnly promise.' Cf. Lat. spondeo. ἐπέσπενσε, 77.3
ἐπιτάδευμα Cret.
ἐπιχύτας Arg. = ἐπίχυσις 'beaker.' No. 87
ἐποίϜε̄hε Arg. 53, 59.2
ἐποίϜε̄σε Boeot. 53
ἐποίκια, τά Heracl. 'farm buildings'
ἐποίσε̄ Arc., aor. subj. to fut. οἴσω. No. 18.21, note
Ϝέπος = ἔπος. 52
ἔππασις Boeot. = ἔγκτησις. 69.4, 162.12
hεπτάκιν Lac. = ἑπτάκις. 133.6
ἐπώλον Arg. 42.5d
ἐπōμόται Locr. 'jurors'
ἐρανεσταί Ach. = -ισταί. 18b
Ϝέργον = ἔργον. 52
ἐρευταί Cret. = ζητηταί 'collectors.' No. 120.132, note
ϜεϜρεμένα Arg. = εἰρημένα. 55
ἐϜρετάσατυ Cypr., see Ϝρετάω
Ἑρμώνοσσα Chian = -ασσα. 46.1
ἐροτός Boeot., Thess. = ἐρατός. 5
ἐρουτᾶι Thes. 41.1a, 157b, 159
ἔρπω 'go, come.' 162.6
ἐρρηγεῖα Heracl. = ἐρρωγυῖα. 49.5, 146.3, 148
Ϝέρρω El., Locr. = ἔρρω = φεύγω. 52. 162.7
ἐρσεναίτερος El. = ἄρρην. 49.2, 80, 165.1
ἔρσην = ἄρρην. 49.2, 80
Ἐρχομενός Arc., Boeot. = Ὀρχομενός, 46.1
ἐς = ἐκ. 100 with a
ἔσγονος = ἔκγονος. 100
ἐσδέλλω Arc. = ἐκβάλλω. 49.3, 68.1, 100

ἐσδοκά 'contract' Arc., in form = ἐκδοχή (cf. 66, 100)
ἐσδοτήρ Arc., see ἐγδοτήρ
ἐσκεθῆν Arc., *ἐκσχεθεῖν 'keep out, exclude.' 65, no. 21.50, note
ἐσκηδεκάτη Boeot. = ἐκκαιδεκάτη. 114.6
ἔσκλητος Sicil., title of a select official body. 100a, no. 107.2, note
ἐσλιήνω Boeot. 162.10
ἐσλός, ἔσλος = ἐσθλός. 89.8
Ϝεσπάριος Locr. = ἑσπέριος. 21, 52d
ἐσπεράω Arc. = ἐκπεράω 'transgress' 100
ἐσπράτται Cret. = ἐκπράκται. 86.1
ἐσπρεμμίττω Cret. = ἐκπρεμνίζω. 84, 86.7
ἐος Boeot. = ἐξ. 100
ἔσσα = οὖσα. 163.8
ἐσσάμενος Arg. 144c
ἔσσομαι = ἔσομαι. 83
ἔστε 'until.' 132.12, 135.4
ἔστεισις Arc. = ἔκτεισις. 28a
ἔστελλα Lesb., Thess. = ἔστειλα. 79
ἑταιρήα Cyren. 164.1
ἔταλον Lesb., ἔτελον Coan 'yearling.' 49.3
ἑτάξαιν Thess. = ἔταξαν. 138.5
Ϝέτας El. = ἔτης 'private citizen'
Ϝέτος = ἔτος. 52. Cret. Ϝέτεθθι, 81b. Arc. dat. sg. ἔτι, 9.5
ἔτος = ἔτος. 58c
ἑττά Cret. = ἑπτά. 86.2
ἔττε Boeot. = ἔστε. 86.4
εὐάμερος, ἁ Cret. = ἑορτή
Εὐβάλκης Lac. 36
εὐεργετές Thess. = εὐεργετέων. 78, 157
εὐθυορϜία Arc. 54c
εὐῖδε Lesb. = εἶδε. 35a
ϜεϜυκονομειόντων Boeot. = ᾠκονομηκότων. 146.1, 147.3
Ϝευμένας Cret. = Ϝελμένας 'assembled.' 71, 75
εὔνοα = εὔνοια. 31
εὐϜρετάσατυ Cypr., see Ϝρετάω
εὐσαβέοι El. = εὐσεβέοι. 12a
εὐσχάμενος = εὐξάμενος. 87
εὑτοῦ Thess. = ἑαυτῷ. 121.2, no. 32.16, note
Εὔτρητις Boeot. = Εὔτρησις. 61.3
εὐχωλά Arc.-Cypr. 'prayer of imprecation.' 191
ἔφαβος pseudo-dial. = ἔφηβος. 280
ἐφακέομαι Delph. 'repair.' 58c

360 THE GREEK DIALECTS

ἐφάνγρενθειν Thess. = ἐφαιροῦνται, κατηγοροῦνται. 27, 58, 139.2,
157, 162.2, no. 32.41, note
ἐφερξόντι Heracl. 'shut in' (water
by damming). No. 79.130 ff., note
ἐφθορκώς Arc. = ἐφθαρκώς. 5
ἐφιορκέω = ἐπιορκέω. 58c
ἐφορευωκότων Cyren. 161.3
ἐχεπάμον Locr. 'heir.' 162.12
ἐχθός, ἔχθω, ἔχθοι = ἐκτός. 66,
133.3
ἐψαφίττατο Boeot. = ἐψηφίσατο.
82, 142
ἔωκα = εἶκα. 49.5, 146.3
Ϝέχω (cf. Lat. veho), Cypr.,
Pamph. 53

ζά Lesb. = διά. 19.1
ζᾶ Cypr. = γῆ. 62.4
ζαμιοργία El. 'the body of demiurgi.' 62.2, 167
ζαν Cypr., see no. 23.10, note
ζέλλω Arc. = βάλλω. 68.3
ζέρεθρον Arc. = βάραθρον. 68.3
Ζῆνα, Ζηνός, etc. 37.1, 112.1
ζίκαια El., see δίκαια
ζίφυιος El., see δίφυιος
Ζόννυσος Lesb. = Διόνυσος. 19.1
ζτεραῖον Arc. No. 16, note
ζώω, Boeot. δώω. 162.8

ἤ Boeot. = αἰ. 134.1
ἔ Cypr. = εἰ. 134.1
ἤ 'when, where,' etc. 132.7
ἤγραμμαι Cret. = γέγραμμαι. 137
Ϝῆμα Cret. = εἷμα. Gen. sg. Ϝήμᾶς.
112.5
ἤμεν, ἤμειν, ἤμην = εἶναι. 25, 76,
154.3-5, 163.7
ἤμην 1 sg. imperf. mid. of εἰμί.
163.9
ἠμί = εἰμί. 25, 76
ἡεμίδιμμνον Epid. = ἡμέδιμνον.
88a, 89.2
ἡμίνα Cret. 'the half.' 164.10
ἡεμιρρήνιον Delph., probably 'half-
grown sheep,' i.e. such as are
midway between lambs and full-
grown sheep. 55a
ἤμισσον, Boeot. εἴμιττον, ἡέμιττα.
81. ἤμισον. 89.6
ἡμίτεια Epid. 61.5, 164.10
ἡμιτυέκτο Cret. = ἡμιέκτου. 61.5
ἤμυσυ = ἤμισυ. 20
ἤν Ion. = ἐάν. 134.2b
ἤν = ἦσαν. 163.4
ἤναι Arc. = εἶναι. 154.1, 163.7

ἤνατος Cret., Arg. = ἔνατος. 54,
114.9
ἤνεικα, ἤνικα = ἤνεγκα. 49.1, 144a
ἤνται Mess. = ὦσι. 151.1, 163.9
Ϝηρόντων, Ϝέροντι Cret., fr. Ϝέρδω.
86.6
ἦς = ἦν. 163.3
ἦς Heracl. = εἷς. 114.1
ἤσσαντο Arg. 144c
ἤστω El. = ἔστω. 163.5
ἤται Delph. = ᾖ. 151.1, 163.9
ἤτω = ἔστω. 163.5
ἠύτῶν Coan = ἑαυτῶν. 121.2
ἤχοι Orop. = ὅπου. 132.3
ἠώς Ion. = ἕως. 41.4b

θάλαθθα Cret. = θάλαττα. 81a
θάλαττα. 81. θάλαττα. 89.4
θαρῆς Ther. 42.2, 80
θαρρέω El. = θαρσέω, θαρρέω, but
in technical sense of 'be secure,
immune.' So θάρρος 'security, im-
munity.' 80, no. 61.1, note
Θε- Meg., etc. = Θεο-. 42.5f
θεαρός, Arc. θεαορός = θεωρός.
41.4. θεαρόντον Delph. 42.5d
θέθμιον = θέσμιον. 65, 164.4
θεθμός = θεσμός. 65, 164.4
θεῖκα Boeot. = διαθήκη 'will'
Θεισπιεύς Boeot. 9.4a
Θεόζοτος Boeot., Thess. = Θεόδοτος. 166.2
θεομοιρία Coan = θεοῦ μοῖρα 'the
part consecrated to the god'
Θεόρδοτος Thess. = Θεόσδοτος. 60.4,
166.2
θεορός, θευρός = θεωρός. 41.4a
θέρσος = θάρσος. 49.2
θέστων Phoc. = θέσθων. 85.1
θηαυρός Arg. = θησαυρός. 59.2
θηκαῖον 'burial place' Coan (ὅρος
τῶν θηκαίων)
θηλύτερος El. = θῆλυς. 165.1
θιαωρία Boeot. = θεωρία. 41.4
θιγάνα Delph. 'lid, cover' (?). Cf.
Hesych. θίγωνος· κιβωτοῦ. See
no. 52 C 33 ff., note
θιθέμενος Cret. = τιθέμενος. 65
θῖνος Cret. = θεῖος. 164.10
Θιοκορμίδας Lac. 60.4
Θιόπαστος Boeot. 69.4
θιός = θεός. 9. θιιός Arg. 56
Θιόφειστος Boeot. 86.2
Θο- Meg., etc. = Θεο-. 42.5f
θοσία Boeot. = θυσία. 24
θράγανον Boeot., meaning? No. 39
θύρδα Arc. = θύραζε. 133.2

θύρωτον Epid. = *θύρωτρον. 70.3
θύσθεν Arc. 89.8, 133.1
θυφλός Cumae = τυφλός. 65
θύχα Cret. = τύχη. 65
θωάδδω El. (θōάδοι) 'impose a fine.' See following
θω(ι)άω 'impose a fine.' Locr. θōιέστō, Att. θōᾶν, Delph. θωεόντων. 161.2. Cf. Att. θω(ι)ά, Ion. θωιή (37.2), Delph. θωίασις

Ἰα Lesb., Thess., Boeot. = μία. 114.1
Ἰαθθα Cret. = οὖσα. 81a, 163.8
Ἰαρειάδδω Boeot. 'serve as priest.' 84
Ἰαρές Cyren. = ἱερεῖς. 111.3
Ἰαρήιον = ἱερεῖον. 164.1
Ἰαρόμαος, official title, El. Cf. Hesych. ἱερόμας· τῶν ἱερῶν ἐπιμελούμενος.
Ἰαρο(μ)μνάμονες, see ἱερομνήμων
Ἰαρός, ἱαρός = ἱερός. 13.1, 58b
Ἰασσα = ἰοῦσα. 163.8a
ἰjατήρ Cypr. = ἰατρός. 56, 164.5
ἰατρα, τά Epid. 'perquisites for healing.' 165.3
Ἰαττα Cret. = οὖσα. 81, 163.8
Ἰγγυος Arc. = ἔγγυος. 10
Ἰγκεχηρήκοι Arc., 3 sg. perf. opt. from verb = Att. ἐγχειρέω. 10, 25
Ἰδδιος Thess. = ἴδιος. 19.3, 58c
Ἰδέ Cypr. 'then, and.' 134.6
Ϝίδιος, Arg. hίδιος = ἴδιος. 52b, 58c
Ἰέρεως Mil. = ἱερεύς. 43, 111.5
Ἰέρηα = ἱέρεια. 28b
Ἰερηι(ι)ον = ἱερεῖον 37.2, 164.1
Ἰερής Arc.; ἰjερές Cypr. = ἱερεύς. 111.4. Arc. dat. sg. ἱερῖ 9.5
Ἰερητεύω = ἱερατεύω. 167. ἱερητεύχατι Phoc., 138.4
Ἰεριτεύω, ἰαριτεύω = ἱερατεύω. 167. ἰαριτευωκότων Cyren. 161.3
Ἰεροθυτέω Arc., Phoc., Rhod., etc., 'be ἱεροθύτης.' Arc. ἱεροθυτές, 78, 157
Ἰεροθύτης (-ας) official title. Sometimes applied to priestly attendants, sometimes to priestly officials of high rank, who were even, in some places, the eponymous officers
Ἰερομνήμων, -μνάμων title of certain superior officials, primarily in charge of religious matters, 'sacred commissioners, ministers of religion,' also delegated to the Amphictionic council. Arc. ἱιε-

ρομνάμονσι, 77.1a. Mycen., Epid. ἱαρο(μ)μνάμονες, 58b, 89.2
Ἰεροποιός title of officials in charge of religious matters, sometimes regular magistrates, sometimes extraordinary commissioners
Ἰερός, ἱερός. 58b
Ἰερωτεύω = ἱερατεύω. 167
Ἰθθάντες Cret. 82b, 162.9
Ἰθύς Ion., Boeot. (also lit. Dor.) = εὐθύς. As in lit. Ion., so also inscriptional ἰθύς (Ephesus), ἰθυνα (Chios), though εὔθυνος, εὐθύνω also occur. Proper names in 'Ἰθυ- are Ionic and Boeotian.
Ἰκάς = εἰκάς. 116. Ther. hικάδι, 58c
(Ϝ)ικαστός Boeot. = εἰκοστός. 116 with a
(Ϝ)ίκατι = εἴκοσι. 52, 61.2, 116
Ϝικατίδειος, ὁ Heracl., name of a particular (twenty-foot) road
Ϝικατίπεδος Heracl. 'twenty feet wide,' used with ἄντομος
Ἰκέτας Arg = ἱκέτης 58d
Ἰκμαμένος Cypr. 'stricken' (in battle), 'hit' Denom. from *ἰκμᾶ. Cf. ἴκταρ 'at one blow, at once,' Hesych. ἰκτέα· ἀκόντιον, Lat. icō
Ἰκοστός Thess. = εἰκοστός. 116
Ἰκω = Ath. ἥκω, in most, perhaps all, other dialects, e.g. (beside Homer and lit. Doric) Corinth. hίφομες, Delph. hίκωντι, Arc. hίκοντι
Ἰλαος, ἴλεος, ἴληος (Lac. hίλεϝος) = ἴλεως. 49.5, 53. Arc. ἴλαος 58d
hιλαξάστō Delph., from ἱλάσκομαι. 85.1
hίλεϝος Lac., see ἴλαος
Ἰμάσκω El., probably 'maltreat,' related to ἱμάς, ἱμάσσω
Ἰμάτιον Att. 25e
Ἰμπασις, ἴνπασις Arc. = ἔγκτησις. 10, 162.12
Ἰν Arc.-Cypr. = ἐν. 10, 135.4
Ϝίν = οἱ dat. 3 pers. pron. 118.4. Ϝίν αὐτōι Cret. = ἑαυτῷ. 121.1
Ἰνάγω Arc. = εἰσάγω. 10
Ἰναλίνω Cypr. 'write upon.' 10. Cf. Hesych. ἀλίνειν· ἀλείφειν, and ἀλειπτήριον· γραφεῖον. Κύπριοι
Ἰνδικάζομαι Arc., see ἐνδικάζομαι
Ἰνδικος Arc., see ἔνδικος
Ἰνμενϝφής, ἴνμονφος Arc. 'blameworthy, impious.' 10
Ἰνπολά Arc. = ἐμπολή. 10
Ἰνϝαίνω Arc. 'inform' in legal sense. Cf. εἰσφαίνω Ath. 75 A

ἰνφορβίω, ἰνφορβισμός Arc. No. 18, note
ἰός Cret. = ἐκεῖνος. 114.1
hϜιός = υἰός. 52c
ἰουιῶ Boeot. = υἰοῦ. 24
Ἱππέδαμος Rhod. = Ἱππόδαμος. 167
ἰππότας Boeot. (as in Hom., Hdt.) = ἰππεύς
ἰράνα, etc. = εἰρήνη. 8c, 58c
ἰρεια Lesb. = ἱέρεια 'priestess.' 13.1
ἰρευς Lesb. = ἱερεύς. 13.1
ἰρητεύω Lesb. = ἱερατεύω. 13.1, 167
ἰρος Lesb., ἱρός, ἱρός Ion. = ἱερός. 13.1
ἰσαμι Dor. = οἶδα. 162.9. Subj. Cret. ἰσᾱντι, Cyren. ἰσᾶι. 151.1
ἰσόθι Arc. 'within the distance of.' 133.1a, no. 22.13, note
Ϝίσος, Ϝίσϝος, ἴσος = ἴσος. 50b, 52, 54, 58c. Lesb. ἰσσοθέοισι, 54b
ἰσσατο, ἱίσατο, ἰσσάμενος, etc. 144c
ἰστία, ἰστία = ἐστία. 11
ἰστιατόριον Rhod. = ἐστιατόριον 'banquet-hall.' Cf. Hesych. ἰστια-τόρια· δειπνητήριον. 11
Ϝίστωρ Boeot. 'witness.' 52d
ἴττω Boeot. = ἴστω. 86.4
ἰών Boeot. = ἐγών. 62.3, 118.2

κα W. Grk., Boeot. = κε, ἄν. 134.2
κά = κατά. 89.7, 95
κά Arc.-Cypr. = κάς = καί. 97.2, 134.3
καδαλέομαι El. = καταδηλέομαι 'injure, violate.' καδαλέμενος, καζα-λέμενος. 89.7, 158
κάδδιξ, gen. κάδδιχος, Heracl., Mess., a measure. Cf. Hesych. κάδδιχον· ἡμίεκτον, and Lac. κάδδιχος 'urn' (Plut. Lyc. 12)
καθεστάκατι Delph. 138.4
κακριθέε Arc. = κατακριθῆ. 89.7, 151.2
καλαῖς Epid. 'hen.' No. 89, note
καλείμενος = καλούμενος. 158
καλλίτερος El. = καλλίων
καλλύ[σμα]τα Ceos 'sweepings.' Cf. Hesych. σάρματα· καλλύσματα
καλϜός Boeot. = καλός. 54
κάρζα Lesb. = καρδία. 19.1
καρπόω 'offer,' especially 'a burnt offering,' in Smyrna, Thera, Athens, as often in the Septua-

gint. Cf. Hesych. καρπωθέντα· τὰ ἐπὶ βωμοῦ καθαγισθέντα. = κάρπωμα· θυσία. Coan καρπῶντι, 159
κάρρων = κρείττων. 80, 113.1
καρταῖπος, pl. καρταίποδα, Cret. 'large cattle,' in contrast to πρό-βατα used of sheep and goats. Cf. καρταίπους 'bull' in Pindar.
καρτερός Ion., Cret. = κρατερός, in meaning often = κύριος 'valid.' Cf. also Ion. ἀκρατής 'invalid,' κρατεῖν 'be valid,' Cret. κάρτων q.v. 49.2a
κάρτος = κράτος. 49.2a
κάρτων Cret. = κρείττων, in mean-ịng = κυριώτερος, as κάρτονανς ἐμὲν 'shall prevail, be of greater authority.' Cf. καρτερός. 49.2a, 81, 113.1
ΚαρυκέϜ̄ο Boeot. = Κηρυκείου. 53, 164.1
κάς Arc.-Cypr. = καί. 134.3
κασίγνητος Lesb., Cypr.; Thess. κατίγν[ειτος] 191
-κάσιοι Arc. = -κόσιοι. 116a, 117.2
κασσηρατόριν, καθθηρατόριν, καθθη-ρατόριον Lac. 'the hunt,' name of an athletic game. 45.6, 64, Nos. 75-78, note
κάτ = κατά. 95
καταγελάμενος Epid. 159
καταγρέω Lesb. = καθαιρέω 'convict, condemn.' 162.2
καταδουλίτταστη Boeot. = -δου-λίσασθαι. Cf. 82, 85.1, 142
καταϜελμένον Cret. 'assembled.' 75
καταθένς Cret. = καταθείς. 78
καταιϜεί Locr. 53
κατακείμενος Cret. 'one whose person is mortgaged' passive of κατατίθημι 'mortgage,' mid. 'take a mortgage'
κατάκλητος Heracl. 'summoned.' κατάκλητος ἀλία = Att. σύγκλητος ἐκκλησία
καταλλάσσω Arc., intrans. 'act otherwise'
καταλοβεύς Cret., Epid. = *κατα-λαβεύς 'support.' 49.3
καταλυμακόω Heracl. 'cover over with stones.' Cf. Hesych. λύμακες· πέτραι. -λυμακωθής, 78
κατάπερ = καθάπερ. 57a. Also for κατταπερ. 126
κάταρϜος Arc. = κατάρατος. 54

κατατίθημι Cret., Mess. = ὑποτίθημι 'mortgage,' mid. 'take a mortgage'
κατέθιjαν Cypr. = κατέθεσαν. 138.5
κατείρων Lesb. = καθιερούν. 13.1, 155.3
κατενθόντας, κατηνθηκότι Arc. = κατελθόντας, κατεληλουθότι. 72, 146.1
κατέϜοργον Cypr., aor. of κατείργω. 5
κατιαραίω El. (κατιαραίον, κατιαραύσειε). 12a, 161.1, no. 61.2, note
κατίγν[ειτος] Thess., see κασίγνητος
-κάτιοι = -κόσιοι. 61.2, 116a, 117.2
κατιστάμεν Cret. 57a
κατοικείουνθι Thess. = κατοικῶσι. 138.4, 159
κατόπερ Ion. beside κατάπερ = καθάπερ
καττάπερ = καθάπερ. 126
κατύ Arc. = κατά. 22
καυχός Cret. = χαλκός. 65, 71
κε = ἄν. 134.2
κεῖνος = ἐκεῖνος. 125.1
κεκλεβώς Mess. 66
κέλευθος Arc. 'road.' 191
κέλεξ Lac. = κέλης 142a
κέντο Dor. = κέλτο. 72
κεραίω = κεράννυμι. 229
κέρναν Lesb. = κιρνάναι. 18a, 155.3
Κέτιον = Κίτιον. 10
κή Boeot. = καί. 26
κῆνος = ἐκεῖνος. 125.1
κέρευσις Cret. = χήρευσις 'divorce'
κεφάλωμα 164.9
Κιάριον Thess. = Κιέριον 12
κιξαλλεύω Ion. 'act as highwayman'
κιξάλλης Ion. 'highwayman.' Used with ληιστής in no. 3 B 19, as in Democr. fr. 260 ed. Diels. Probably of Carian or Lycian origin
κις Thess. = τίς. 68.4, 131
κίων, ἁ Thess., often used instead of στάλλα = στήλη
κλαικτός Argol., Mess. = κλειστός. 142a
κλάιξ Argol., Mess. = κλείς. 142a
κλᾶρος Cret. 'the body of κλαρῶται or serfs attached to the estate'
-κλέας, personal names in. 166.1

-κλέϜες, -κλέης, -κλῆς, personal names in. 108.1a
κλέϜος Phoc. 53
Κλευάς Thess. 35a
κλίνη Naples, Cumae 'niche in a tomb.' No. 11
Κνωσός. 89.4b
κοθαρός = καθαρός. 6
κόθαρσις El. = κάθαρσις. 6
κοινάν, κοινανέω = κοινών, κοινωνέω, 41.4. κοινανόντι Arg. 42.5d
κοινάω Thess., Dor. = κοινόω. 161.5
κόμιστρα, τά Cret. 'gifts.' 165.3
κομιττάμενοι Boeot. = κομισάμενοι. 142
κόρϜα = κόρη. 54
κορζία Cypr. = καρδία. 5, 19.1
κόρτον Boeot. = κύρτος (?) 24, no. 39
κοσμέω (-ίω) Cret. 'be a member of the κόσμος.' See following. κοσμόντες, 42.5d
κόσμος Cret. 'the body of chief magistrates' (collective; a single member was called κοσμίων, see preceding); also used of a single member of this body, with pl. κόσμοι
κότερος Ion. = πότερος. 68.4
κότος Boeot. = κύτος. 24, no. 39
κοτύλεα Coan = κοτύλη. 71b
κούρη = κόρη. 54
κραμάσαι Epid. = κρεμάσαι. 12c
κράνα = κρήνη. 8c
κράναιυν Arc. = κρήναιν. 104.10
κρατόντες Cret. = κρατοῦντες, 42.5d
κρέννω Thess. = κρίνω. 18. 74
κρέτος Cret. = κράτος. 49.2
κρίνω Lesb. = κρίνω. 74. Aor. ἔκρινα, 77.1
κριτήρ Argol. = κριτής. 164.5
κρόμπος Arc. No. 20.9 ff., note
κτέννω Lesb. = κτείνω. 74
κτοίνα Rhod., a territorial division similar to the Attic deme. Cf. κτίζω, κτίσις
κτοινάτας, κτοινέτας Rhod. 'member of the κτοίνα.' 167
κυεῦσα, κυεεῦσα Coan, 42.5
κυκάν Epid. = κυκεών. 41.4
ϙύϜνυς Chalcid. 22d, 24a
κυμερέναι Cypr. = κυβερνάν. 8,8
κυνία Lesb. 9.2
κῦρρον Thess. = κύριον. 19.3
κωμέτας Arg. 167

κώρα Cret. = κόρη. **25, 54**
κῶς Ion. = πῶς. **68.**4

Λᾶ- from Λᾶο-. **41.**4, **45.**3
λαββάνω Delph. = λαμβάνω. **69.**3
λάβωισιν Chian = λάβωσιν. **77.**3
λhαβών Aegin. = λαβών. **76**a
λαγαίω Cret. 'release;' aor. λαγάσαι. Cf. ἀπολάγαξις, **142**a
λάζομαι Meg., Boeot. (λάδδουσθη,
  ὑπολάδδουνθη), Ion. λάζυμαι =
  λαμβάνω
Λαππαίων Cret. **69.**3
Λάρισα. **89.**4b
λᾶς, Cret. gen. λᾶō. **112.**4
Λασαῖος Thess. = Λαρισαῖος. **88**b,
  no. 32.19, note
λατραι[όμενον], λατρειόμενον El. =
  λατρευόμενον 'consecrated.' **12**a,
  161.1
λαφυροπώλιον Arc. 'sale of booty.'
  No. 19.9 ff., note
λειτορεύω Thess. = ἱερατεύω. Cf.
  Hesych. λείτορες· ἱέρειαι, and
  λητῆρες· ἱεροὶ στεφανοφόροι. Ἀθα-
  μᾶνες. Related to Att. λειτουργέω
  (39)
λείω, see λέω
λειόλης Rhod. 'accursed.' No. 101,
  note
λεχχοῖ Delph., see λεχώι
λελάβηκα Arc., Ion., Epid. **137,
  146.**1
Λέντιχος Cyren. **42.**5e
λέσχα Rhod. 'grave.' No. 101,
  note
Λεσχαῖος Thess., epithet of Apollo.
  No. 30, note
Λεττίναιος Thess. = Λεπτίναιος. **86.**2
λεύσσω 'behold.' **191**
λευτον Arc., meaning? No. 18.3
λεχώι Cyren., gen. sg. λεχός Cyren.,
  dat. sg. λεχχοῖ Delph. **63, 111.**5a.
λέω, Cret. λείω = θέλω. **162.**12
-λιήνω (= -λεαίνω) Boeot. 'cancel.'
  162.10
λίθιος Thess. = λίθινος. **164.**6
λιμήν Thess. = ἀγορά 'market-
  place' (Thess. ἀγορά = ἐκκλησία).
  So also Cypr. (Hesych.) and Ion.
  (GDI 5545.25)
λίνινος Boeot. = λίνεος. **164.**6
λιποτελέω Locr., 'leave taxes unpaid.' Cf. λιποστρατία, etc.
λισσός Cret. 'insolvent' (?). No.
  120.115, note

λοπίς Arg., some kind of shallow
  vessel. Cf. λοπάς and λεπίς
Λόφριον Aetol. **5**
Λύττος Cret. = Λύκτος. **86.**1
λωτήριον Arg., Heracl. = λουτή-
  ριον. **44.**4

μά El. = μή. **15**
μά Thess. = δέ. **134.**4
μαίτυρες Cret., Epid. = μάρτυρες.
  71a
μάν El. = μέν. **12**a
μαντήα, μαντῆον Arg. **164.**1
μάντοι Epid. = μέντοι. **12**c
μάσλης Lesb. = μάσθλης. **89.**8
μαστράα El., μαστρεία Mess. 'accounting.' Cf. Hesych. μαστρίαι·
  αἱ τῶν ἀρχόντων εὔθυναι. **12**a, **31**
μαστρός title of an official at
  Delphi, Rhodes, Pelene. Cf.
  Delph. κατάμαστρος, Mess. ὑπό-
  μαστρος 'subject to fine'
ματάρα Delph. = μητέρα. **12**
μέδιμμνον Epid. **89.**2
μέζων Arc., Ion. = μείζων. **113.**1
μεθάμερα Epid. = μεθ' ἁμέραν.
  Adverb formed like ὑπερκέφαλα
  from ὑπὲρ κεφαλάν
μεί Boeot., Thess. = μή. **16**
μhειάλ[αν] Pamph. = μεγάλην.
  62.3, **76**a
μειννός, μεινός Thess. = μηνός.
  77.1, **112.**3
Μhείξιος Corcyr. **76**a
μείς = μήν. **112.**3
μείστον Locr. 'at least.' **113.**3
μεμισθωσῶνται Heracl. **146.**5
Μέννει Boeot. = Μένης. **89.**5,
  108.2
Μενοκράτης Cret. = Μενεκράτης.
  167
μέντον = μέντοι. No. 32.38, note
μερεία Heracl. = μερίς
μέρος Locr. 'real estate.' No. 57.44,
  note
μές Thess. 'until.' **132.**12
μεσακόθεν Arc. **65, 133.**1
μεσέγγουος Boeot., adj. 'with a
  third party.' Cf. μεσεγγυάω LS
μεσόμνη Att. = μεσόδμη. **87**
μέσποδι Thess. 'until.' **132.**12
μέσσορος Heracl. 'intermediate
  boundary'
μέστα Cret., Cyren. 'until.' Arc.
  μέστε. **132.**12
μεταϝοικέω Locr. = μετοικέω. **53**
μέτερρος Lesb. = μέτριος. **19.**2

μετριώμεναι Heracl. = μετρού-
μεναι. 42.5*b*
μέττ' ἐς Cret. 'until.' 86.4, 132.12
μέττος Boeot., Cret. = μέσος. 82
μεύς El. = μήν. 112.3
μηδαμεῖ Delph. = μηδαμοῦ. 132.2
μηδεῖα Lesb. = μηδεμία. 114.1
μηδεπόθι Arc. 133.1*a*
μηθείς = μηδείς. 66
μῆννος Lesb. = μηνός. 77.1, 112.3
μής Heracl. = μήν. 112.3
μιᾶι 3 sg. aor. subj., Cyren. 144*b*,
151.1, no. 115.40, note
μικκιχιδδόμενος Lac. 89.5*a*, nos.
75-78, note
μικκός. 89.5*a*
Μίντων Arg. = Μίλτων. 72
Μίργος Eretr. = Μίσγος. 60.4
μιστός Cret. = μισθός. 85.1
μναμμεῖον Thess. = μνημεῖον. 89.4
Μνασσᾶ Thess. = Μνασία. 19.3
μοῖσα Lesb. = μοῦσα. 77.3
μοιχέω Cret. (μοιχίον, etc.) = Dor.
μοιχάω = μοιχεύω. 161.2
μοῦνος Ion. = μόνος. 54
μυχός Heracl. 'storehouse, granary'
μῶα Lac. = μοῦσα. Cf. 59.1
μωλέω Cret. (μόλέν, μωλέν, etc.)
'contend' (in law). So also Cret.
ἀμφιμωλέω, ἀμφίμωλος, ἀντίμω-
λος, ἀπομωλέω, adv. ἀμωλεί. Cf.
Hesych. μωλήσεται· μαχήσεται.
Related to Hom. μῶλος 'contest.'
Cf. ἀγωνίζομαι as a law-term in
Attic
μῶσα = μοῦσα. 77.3

ναεύω Cret. 'take refuge in a temple'
νακόρος, see νεωκόρος
να(F)ός = νεώς. 41.4, 53, 54*d*
ναποῖαι, see νεωποίης
ναῦος Lesb. = νεώς. 35, 54*d*
ναῦσσον name of a tax, Coan, also
(spelled with T) at Cyzicus
νεί Arc. = νή, ναί. 134.7
νεμονηία Cret. = νεομηνία. 89
νεότας Cret. 'an official body of
young men,' gen. νεότας, acc.
νεότα. 88*a*
νεωκόρος Ion., Delph. ναοκόρος,
Delph., Epid., Coan νακόρος (41.4
45.3), custodian of the temple,
sacristan.' In some places the
office became one of considerable
rank and honor

νεωποίης Ion., Coan ναποῖαι. 31.
41.4. Cf. also Ion. νεωποιός,
Boeot. ναποιός. Title of officials
in general charge of the affairs
of the temple
νήατος Arc. = νέατος. No. 20.10 ff.,
note
νικάηας, νικάαρ Lac. = νικάσας.
59.1, 60.2
νίν = ἕ. 118.5
νιουμεινία, νιουμείνιος, νιυμείνιος Boeot.
= νουμηνία, νουμήνιος. 42.5*a*
νόμαιος Ion. = νόμιμος. 164.10
νόμιος Locr. = νόμιμος. 164.10
νόμος Heracl., a coin. Cf. Lat.
nummus
νοσσιά, etc. 42.5*f*
νοστίττω El. = *νοστίζω, νοστέω.
84
νυ Cypr., Boeot. 134.5
νύναμαι Cret. = δύναμαι. 88
νυττί Cret. = νυκτί. 86.1

ξεῖνος, ξῆνος, ξένF ος = ξένος. 54
ξέννος Lesb. = ξένος. 54*b*
ξενοδίκαι Locr., Phoc., title of
judges in cases involving the
rights of ξένοι. ξενοδίκης is used
by a late writer to translate the
Latin *praetor peregrinus*
ξύλεα Coan = ξύλα. 71*b*
ξύλλεσθαι Arg., in form = σκύλλεσθαι (87), but meaning 'pillage'
(cf. σκῦλον)
ξύν = σύν. 135.7
ξῦνός Ion. = κοινός. 135.7

ὁ = ὅ. 58*a*
Ὄαξος = Fάξος. 51*a*
ὀβελός Boeot., ὀβελλός Thess. =
ὀβολός. 49.3, 68.1, 89.4
ὀγδοίης, ὀγδοίήκοντα. 31*a*
ὄγδοος, ὄγδοF ος. 114.8
ὀγδῶι Ion. = ὀγδόη. 44.2
ὀγδώκοντα Ion. = ὀγδοήκοντα. 44.2
ὀδελός = ὀβολός. 49.3, 68.1
ὀδείγω Lesb. = οἴγω. 49.1
ὄζος Cret. = ὅσος. 82
ὀθθάκιν Cret. = ὀσάκις. 81*a*, 133.6
ὄθι Arc. 132.1*a*
ὄθμα Lesb. = ὄμμα. 164.4
Fοι = οἱ dat. 3 pers. pron. 118.4
Fοικιάτας = οἰκέτης. 167
οἰκείη Arg. 157*c*
Fοικεύς Cret. = οἰκέτης. 167
οἰκιστήρ = -τής. Cyren. 164.5
Fοῖκος = οἶκος. 52

Ϝοίκω Delph. = οἴκοθεν. **132**.8
Ϝοῖνος = οἶνος. **52**
οἶϜος Cypr. = οἶος 'alone.' **53, 191**
οἰρών Cypr. (ἰν τοἰρõνι) 'district.'
 Cf. οἰρών 'boundary line,' Hesych.
οἶς Delph. := οἶ. **132**.3
hοισόντι Heracl. = οἴσοντι. **58**d
οἴφω Cret. (οἴπεν, οἴπει), Ther.
 (οἴπhε, etc.), Lac. (Hesych.)
 'have sexual intercourse'
ὄκα, also ὄκκα = ὄτε. **132**.11
ὀκοῖος Ion. = ὀποῖος. **68**.4
hοκτακάτιοι Heracl. = ὀκτακόσιοι.
 58c, **117**.2
ὀκτάκιν Lac. = ὀκτάκις. **133**.6
ὀκτό Lesb. = ὀκτώ. **114**.8
ὀκττώ Ephes. **89**.1
hοκτώ Heracl. = ὀκτώ. **58**c, **114**.8
ὀκτωκόσιοι Lesb. = ὀκτακόσιοι,
 117.2
ὄλετρος Cret. = ὄλεθρος. **63**
ὀλίος = ὀλίγος. **62**.3
'Ολυππίχην = 'Ολυμπίχην. **69**.3
ὀμιώμεθα Lac. **42**.5b
ὀμολογά, ἀ, ὀμόλογον, τό Boeot. =
 ὀμολογία
ὀμονόεντες Lesb. = ὀμονοοῦντες.
 44.4, **157**
ὀν Lesb., Thess., Cypr. = ἀνά. **6**
ὀνάλα, ὀνάλουμα Thess. = ἀνάλωμα.
 164.10
ὀνγράψειν Thess. = ἀναγράψαι. **27,
 156**
ὄνδικος Arc. = ἀνάδικος. **6**
ὄνε Thess. = ὄδε. **123**
ὀνεθείκαεν Thess.=ἀνέθηκαν. **138**.5
ὀνί Arc. = ὄδε. **123**
ὄνιουμα Boeot. = ὄνομα. **22**c, **24**
ὄννα Lesb. = ὠνή. **25**f
ὄννιθα Cret. = ὄρνιθα. **86**.5
ὄνυ Arc.-Cypr. = ὄδε. **123**
ὄνυμα = ὄνομα. **22**c
ὄπαι. **132**.5
ὄπει. **132**.2
ὀπειδεί Thess. = ἐπειδή. **132**.7
ὀπέρ Boeot., Arc. = ὑπέρ. **24**
ὄπη. **132**.7
ὄπι Cypr. No. 23.29, note
ὀπιδδόμενος Lac. = ὀπιζόμενος. **84**
'Οπόεντι, 'Οποντίους, Ηοποντίον
 Locr. = 'Οποῦντι, 'Οπουντίους,
 etc. **44**.4, **58**d
ὀπόθι Arc. **133**.1a
ὀπόταρος El. = ὀπότερος. **12**
ὀπόττος Boeot., ὀπόττος Cret. =
 ὀπόσος. **82**

ὄππα Lesb. **129**.2, **132**.6
ὄππα Lesb. = ὄμμα. **164**.4
ὄππως Lesb. **129**.2
ὀπτίλος Dor. = ὀφθαλμός. Occurs
 in Epidaurian (-ίλος and -ίλλος,
 no. 90 passim), as Laconian in
 Plut. Lyc. 11, and in the writings
 of Archytas and Phintias. ὀπ-τ-
 ίλος (cf. ὀπ-τήρ etc.) like ναυ-τ-
 ίλος beside ναύ-της
ὀπτό El. = ὀκτώ. **114**.8
ὀπύ Arc. = ὑπό. **22, 24**
ὄπυι. **132**.4
ὄπυς Rhod. **132**.4
ὄπω Dor. (Cret. ὄπõ, Lac. hόπõ) =
 ὀπόθεν. **132**.8
ὄπωρ Eretr., ὄπωρ El. = ὄπως.
 60.1, 3, **97**a
ὄρβος Corcyr. = ὄρος. **51**
ὄρεγμα, measure of length, Heracl.
ὀρκίζω = ὀρκόω. **161**.4
ὀρκιότερος Cret. 'having preference
 in the oath'
hορκόμόται Locr., Arc. 'jurors'
ὄρνιξ = ὄρνις. **142**a
ὄρϜος Corcyr., ὄρος Heracl., ὧρος
 Arg. = ὄρος. **54, 58**c
ὄροφος 'house' Cyren. No. 115.16,
 note
ὀρτή Ion. = ἑορτή. **42**.5f
ὀρύξε͞ Cypr., see ἐξορύξε͞
ὀρφανοδικασταί Cret. (ὀρπανοδικα-
 σταί) 'officers appointed to look
 after the affairs of orphans or
 minors.' Cf. Att. ὀρφανοφύλακες
Ϝός Cret. = ὄς. **120**.3, **121**.1
ὀσέοι Arc. = ὄτεῳ. **68**.3, **128,
 129**.2
ὄσια Arc., Locr. = ὄσια. **58**e
ὀστροφά Thess. = ἀναστροφή. **77**.2,
 no. 33.20, note
ὄτα Lesb. = ὄτε. **13**.3, **132**.11
ὀτεῖος Cret. = ὀποῖος, ὄστις. **68**.1,
 130
ὄτερος Cret. = ὀπότερος. **127**
Ϝότι Locr., error for hότι. **129**.2a
ὄτιμι Cret. = ὄτινι. **128, 129**.2
ὄττις, etc. Lesb. = ὄτις, etc. **129**.2
ὄττος Cret. = ὄσος. **82**
οὐδές Lac. = οὐδείς. **114**.1
οὐθαμεῖ Epid. = οὐδαμοῦ. **132**.2
οὐθείς = οὐδείς. **66**
οὖλος Ion. = ὄλος. **54**
οὐρεῖον, ὠρεῖον Cret. 'guard-
 house.' From οὖρος 'watcher,'
 like Att. φρούριον from φρουρός
οὐρεύω Cret. 'watch'

πεπεμμένος Troez. 86.8, no. 88.13, note
πεποιόντεισσι Boeot. = πεποιηκόσι. 9.4a, 146.1
περ = περί. 91a
περαιόω Cret. 'set aside, repudiate' (the purchase of a slave). No. 117.VII.10, note
πέρανδε Arc. 'abroad'
περιβολιβόω Rhod. 'fasten round with lead.' 88
περίδρομοι, officials at Mytilene 'clerks of the court'
περίσαος 'left over, remaining.' No. 42.22
περιωρεσία Sicil. Dor. 18b
Περ϶οθαρίαι Locr. 6, 95
πέροδος Delph. = περίοδος. Cf. 95
Πέρραμος Lesb. = Πρίαμος. 19.2
περτ' Pamph. = πρός. 135.6
πέσσυρες Lesb. = τέτταρες. 68.2, 114.4
πεστάντες Thess. = περιστάντες. 89.8
Πεταγείτνιος = Μετα-. 135.5
πέτευρον Orop., Delos, πετεύριον Erythrae 'notice-board.' 135.5a
Πετθαλός Thess. = Θεσσαλός. 65, 68.2, 81c
πετράμεινον Boeot. = τετράμηνον. 68.2
πέτρατος Boeot. = τέταρτος. 49.2a, 68.2, 114.4
πετροετηρίς Thess. = τετρα-. 5, 68.2
πέτταρες, πετταράκοντα Boeot. = τέτταρες, τετταράκοκτα. 68.2, 114.4, 116
πέττρινος Arg. 89.2
πεύθω Cret. 162.15
πεφειράκοντες Thess. = τεθηρακότες. 68.2, 147.3
πεφυτευκῆμεν Heracl. 147.2
πήλυι Lesb. = τῆλε. 68.2, 132.4
πέποκα Lac. = πώποτε. 132.7, 11
πίσυρες Hom. = τέτταρες. 11, 68.2, 114.4
πιτεύω 'irrigate,' ἀπίτευτα 'un-irrigated.' Boeot.
πλάγος Heracl. 'side'
πλαθύοντα El. = πληθύοντα. 15
πλάν Dor., etc. = πλήν
πλέες Lesb. = πλέονες. 113.2
πλευριάς, -άδος Heracl. = πλευρά
πλέθα, ἁ Locr.; Boeot. πλείθα 'assembly'

πλῆθος (1) 'amount,' (2) 'majority.' (3) frequently 'people, assembly.' Arc. dat. sg. πλήθι 9.5
πληθύς = πλῆθος, as in Homer. Cret. 'the amount,' Locr. 'the majority'
πλίες Cret. = πλέες = πλέονες. 9.4, 42.7, 113.2
πλίυι Cret. = πλέον. 113.2, 132.4
πλός Arc. = πλέον. 42.5g, 113.2
πλουτίνδαν Locr. 133.7
ποεῖ, ποήσω, etc. = ποιεῖ, etc. 31
πόεστι Arc. = πρόσεστι. 59.4a
ποεχόμενον Cypr. = προσεχόμενον 'adjacent to.' Cf. προσεχής. 59.4
πόθικες Lac. = προσήκοντες. For stem πόθικ- to ποθίκω, cf. προίξ, προικός
ποθίκω Boeot. = προσήκω. Cf. ἵκω
πόθοδος = πρόσοδος. Cf. ποτί = πρός
ποθόδωμα Boeot., Epir. = πρόσοδος. 164.10
ποί = πρός. 135.6
ποιγραψάνσθο Arg. 77.2, 135.6, 140.3b
ποιεῖνται, ποιείμενος. 158
ποίενσι Arc. = ποιοῦσι. 77.3, 157
ποιϜέω = ποιέω. 53; Argol. ποιϜέσανς. 78.3
ποιήασσαι El. = ποιήσασθαι. 59.3, 85.2
ποιήαται El. = ποιήσηται. 59.3, 151.1
ποικεφάλαιον Delph. = προσκεφάλαιον. 135.6
ποιōν, ποιόντω, ποιόντων, etc. 42.5d
Ποίτιος Cret. = Πύθιος. 30a
πόκα = πότε. 132.11
πὸκ κί Thess. = ὅτι. 68.4, 131
πόλερ El. = πόλις. 18b
πολιανόμοι Heracl., title of municipal magistrates in charge of public buildings, streets, etc., like Roman aediles. Called ἀστυνόμοι at Athens, Rhodes, etc.
πολιάτας Dor. = πολίτης. 167
πολιάχος Arc. = πολιοῦχος. 167
πόλις = δῆμος. Especially frequent in decrees of Phocis, Locris, Thessaly, and other parts of Northwest Greece, and notably in Crete, where it is almost constant
πόλῖς Lesb. nom. pl. 109.3
πόλιστος Heracl. = πλεῖστος. 113.2, ἡως πολίστων = ὡς πλείστων

πτόλις Cypr., etc. = πόλις. 67
ΠύρϜος, ΠυρϜίας, ΠυρϜαλίōν 54e
πῦς Dor. = ποῖ. 132.4
Πύτιος = Πύθιος. 66
πῶ Dor., etc. 132.8

Ϝρῆσις Arc. 'declaration.' 55
ϸήτρα, El. Ϝρᾱτρα, Cypr. Ϝρέτα, originally 'saying'. (Cf. ῥήτρ, etc.)
  but in various dialects also used
  of a 'formal agreement, compact,
  decree, law.' Cf. Heracl. κὰτ τὰς
  ῥήτρας καὶ κὰτ τὰν συνθήκαν 'according to the laws and the
  compact,' Photius ῥῆτραι· Τα-
  ραντῖνοι δὲ νόμους καὶ οἷον ψη-
  φίσματα, and LS s.v. II. So El.
  Ϝρᾱτρα 'law, covenant' Cypr.
  Ϝρέτα 'compact,' Ϝρετάω 'promise.' 15, 55, 70.3
ῥηχμός Arg. = ῥηγμός. 66
phoϜαῖσι Corcyr. 53, 76a
ῥογός Heracl. 'granary.' Cf. Hesych. ῥογοί· σιροὶ σιτικοί, σιτοβο-
  λῶνες, and Pollux 9.45 σιτοβόλια·
  ταῦτα δὲ ῥογοὺς Σικελιῶται ὠνό-
  μαζον
ῥόϜος Cypr. 53
ῥόπτον Epid. = ῥόπτρον. 70.3
ῥύτιον, ῥυτιάζω Argol. = ῥύσιον,
  ῥυσιάζω. 61.3

σά Meg. = τίνα. 128
σαδράπας = σατράπης. Still other
  variations in the transcription
  of the Persian word (χšaϑªaᵖāvā)
  are seen in ἐξαιθραπεύοντος, ἐξ-
  σατραπεύοντος, ἐξατράπης
Σακρέτης, etc. 41.2
Σαλαμόνα El. = Σαλμώνη. 48
σαρμεύω Heracl. No. 79.136, note
Σαυγένεις, Σαυκράτεις Boeot. 41.2
σελάνα Dor. etc., σελάννα Lesb. =
  σελήνη. 76
Σελινόεντι, Σελινόντιοι. 44.4
σιός Lac. = θεός. 64 σίν = θεόν 42.5g
σις Cypr., σις Arc. = τις. 68.3, 128
σιταγέρται Heracl. 'receivers and
  inspectors of grain.' So ἀγέρται οἱ
  ἀπό σιτωνίας at Tauromenium,
  σιτοφύλακες at Athens, Tauromenium, etc., σιτῶναι at Athens,
  Delos, etc.
σίτηριν Eretr. = σίτησιν. 60.3
σκευάōν El. = σκευέων. 12a
-σκευω- Meg., Cret. ἐπεσκεύωσαν,
  etc. 161.3

σκόφος Boeot. = σκύφος. 24
σπάδιον Arg. = στάδιον. 88
σπέλλω Lesb., Thess. σπόλος. 68.2a
σποϜδδάν Cret. = σπουδήν. 32,
  89.4
σπυρός Coan, Epid., Syrac., Ther.,
  Cyren. = πυρός
στάλα Dor., etc.; στάλλα Lesb.,
  Thess. = στήλη. 75
σταρέστω Delph., fr. aor. of στέρομαι. 49.2
σταρτός Cret., a subdivision of the
  tribe. 49.2a
στέγα Cret. 'house.' No. 117.III.
  46, note
στέγασσις Epid. 164.3
στέππω Coan = στέφω. 66
στεφανίζω = -όω. 161.4
στεφάνοι Lesb. 157b
στεφανώι. 159a
στεφών Ion. 'ridge.' 165.4
στοίχεις Lesb. = στοιχέων. 78,
  157
στονόϜεσαν Corcyr. 164.2
στορπά, στορπάος Arc. = ἀστραπή.
  ἀστραπαῖος. 5, 31
στραταγός (Lesb. στρότ-), title of
  the chief magistrate of the
  Achaean and Aetolian Leagues,
  also at times of others, as the
  Arcadians, Thessalians, Phocians
  etc.; also of local magistrates in
  Mytilene (no. 26), Eresus, Tegea
  (no. 19), etc; under Macedonian
  rule = provincial 'governor', in
  Roman times 'prefect' (no.
  107).
στρατήα Arg. 164.1
στρότος, στρόταγος = στρατός, etc. 5
στροφά Delph. 'turn of the road.'
  No. 52 C 33 f.
στυμέον Arc. 22b
σύββολον Delph. = σύμβολον. 69.3
σύγγραφος, ἁ Arc., Boeot., Mess.,
  σύγγροφος (49.2) Delph., Argol.
  = συγγραφή 'contract'
συγχέαι Ion. 144
συκία Lesb. 9.2
συλαιε̄ El. 157c
συμβόλιχτρον ἁ Arc. No. 20.26,
  note
συμπιπίσκω Delph. 'invite to drink
  together'
συναρτύω Arg. 'belong to the body
  of ἀρτύναι.' No. 84.2, note
συναρχοστατέω Phoc. 'join in appointing magistrates'

συνδαυχναφόροι Thess. 'fellow δαφ-νηφόροι.' See δαύχνα
συνhερξόντι Heracl. 'enclose, cut off' (the roads). No. 79.130 ff., note
συνεσσάδδω Cret. = συν-εκ-σάττω 'assist in carrying off.' Cf. χρήματα ἐκσκευάζειν Strabo. 84a
συνκλείς, -εῖτος Thess. = σύγκλητος ἐκκλησία. 164.10
σφάδδω Boeot., σφάζω Ion. = σφάττω. 84a
σφεις Arc. = σφίσι. 119.4
σφηνόπους Ceos 'having wedge-shaped feet'
σφυχή = ψυχή. 87
σῶς, σω-, Σω-. 41.2

ταγά Thess. 'time when there is a ταγός,' hence 'time of war.' No. 35, note
ταγεύω Delph., Thess. 'hold the office of ταγός'
ταγός official title, Cypr., Delph., Thess. In Thessaly applied to (1) a military leader of the united Thessalians appointed only in time of war (cf. no. 35, note), (2) city officials like the ἄρχοντες of many places (nos. 32-34). At Delphi, officials of the phratry of the Labyadae (no. 52)
ταί = αί. 122
ταί El. = τάδε. 122
ταιννί, ταῖννυ Arc. = ταῖσδε. 97.1, 123
ταις Lesb., El. = τός. 78
τάμνω = τέμνω. 49.4
τᾶμον Thess. 'of the present time.' Cf. Hom. τῆμος 'then.'
τάνε Thess. = τάδε. 123
τανί Boeot. = τήνδε. 122
ταννί, τανί Arc. = τῆσδε, τῶνδε, τάσδε. 97.1, 123
τάνυ Arc. = τάδε. 123
ταōτα East Ion. = ταῦτα. 33
ταυτᾶ Lac. 132.6
ταυτᾶ Locr. 'likewise.' 132.6
ταῦται = αὗται. 124
ταύτε El. 132.7
ταύτων El. = τούτων. 124
τε̄δε. 132.7
τεθμός τετθμός, τέθμιος = θεσμός, θέσμιος. 164.4
τείδε. 132.2
τειμά, τειμή = τιμή. 21
τείω Arc., see τίνω

τέκνα Locr. = τέχνη. 66
τελαμό̄ Arg. 'support.' 89.9, no. 82, note
τέλειος, τέλεος (1) 'perfect, unblemished,' (2) frequently = κύριος 'valid' (examples in Arg., Delph., Locr., Aetol., El., Ach.), ἀγορά (ἀλιαία, etc.) τέλειος = Att. ἐκκλησία κυρία
τελεστά El. 'official.' Cf. τέλος 'office.' 105.1a
τελεστήρ Argol. 'priest.' 164.5
τέλεστρα, τά Ion., Coan 'expenses of inauguration.' 165.3
τελεσφορέντες Cyren. 42.5e
τέλεως Coan = τέλειος. 43, 276
τέλλω Arg., Cret. (as also in poetry) = τελέω
τέλομαι Cret. = ἔσομαι. No. 120. 46, 63, 69/70
τέντται Cyren. = τέλεται = ἔσεται. 72
τέος Dor. = σοῦ. 118.3
τεός Dor., Lesb., τιός Boeot. = σός. 120.2
τέουτος Lesb. = τοιοῦτος. 130
τέρτος Lesb. = τρίτος. 18a
τέρχνιĮα (or τρέχνιĮα) Cypr. 'shrubs, trees.' Cf. Hesych. τέρχνεα· φυτὰ νέα and τρέχνος· στέλεχος, κλάδος, φυτόν, βλάστημα
τέσσαρες, τέσσερες. 81, 114.4
τεσσερακόντων Chian, gen. pl. of τεσσεράκοντα. 116
τεταρτεύς Coan, a measure, like ἑκτεύς
τέταρτος, τέτρατος. 49.2a, 114.4
τετθμός, see τεθμός
τετιμῶνται El. 161.3
τέτορες W. Grk. = τέτταρες. 54e, 114.4. Acc. pl., 107.4
τέτορτος Arc. = τέταρτος. 5, 114.4
τετράκιν Lac. = τετράκις. 133.6
τετράϟοντα, τετρώκοντα = τεττα-ράκοντα. 116
τέτρωρον Heracl. 'group of four boundary stones.' 41.2
τε̄δε. 132.7
Τήιοι Ion. 37.2
Τῆνα, Ττῆνα Cret. = Ζῆνα. 84, 112.1
τηνεῖ 125.1, 132.2
τῆνος = ἐκεῖνος. 125.1
τίθηντι Mess. = τιθῶσι. 151.1
τίμαι Lesb. 41.1a, 157b, 159
Τιμαχλῆς, Τιμαχράτης, Τιμᾶναξ = Τιμοχλῆς, etc. 167

τιμασία Arc. = τίμησις. 164.10
τιματήρ Cyren. = -τής. 164.5
τιμόστόν El. 140.4b, 161.3
τίν Dor. = σοί. 118.4
τίνω, fut. τείσω, aor. ἔτεισα (not τίσω, ἔτῑσα), in Attic and elsewhere, 28a. πείσω, ἔπεισα, 68.1, 2. Arc. new present τείω in ἀπυτειέτω (no. 19.43)
τιούχα Boeot. = τύχη. 24
τιρ El. = τις. 60.1
τίτας 'magistrate who collects fines,' τᾶς τιτύϜος 'fine,' τιτουέσθō (33a) 'impose a fine.' Cret.
τίωι, etc. Lesb. 9.2
ΤλασίαϜο Corcyr. 105.2a
τνατός Cret. = θνητός. 66
τόζ' Rhod. = τόδε. 62.2
τοί = οἱ. 122
τοῖ El. = τόδε. 122
τοιί Boeot. = οἷδε. 122
τοῖνεος Thess. = τοῦδε. 123
τόκα = τότε. 132.11
τόκιος or τόκιον Delph. = τόκος 'interest'
τομάς Arc. = τόμος, τομή 'section of land'
τόνε Thess. = τόδε. 123
τῶτο = τοῦτο. 34a
τού Boeot. = σύ. 61.5
τοὔννεουν Thess. = τῶνδε. 123
τοῦτα, τούτας, τούτει = ταῦτα, etc. 124
τουτεῖ. 132.2
τοῦτοι = οὗτοι. 124
τουτώ. 132.8
τοφιών Heracl. = ταφεών 'burialplace.' 6, 165.4
τρακάδι Thess. = τριακάδι. 19.4
τράφη Amorg. = τάφρη. 70.2
τράφος Heracl. = τάφρος. 70.2
τρέες Cret. = τρεῖς. 42.3
τρέπεδδα Boeot. = τράπεζα. 18, 84
τρέω Arg. = φεύγω in legal sense. No. 84.5
τρῆς Ther. = τρεῖς. 25, 114.3
τριάκοιστος Lesb. = τριακοστός. 116 with a
τριακοντάπεδος (sc. ὁδός) Heracl. 'a road thirty feet wide'
τριηκόσιοι Ion. 117.2
τρίινς Cret. 114.3
τρικώλιος Coan = τρίχωλος. ὀβελὸς τρικώλιος 'three-pronged fork'
τριπανάγορσις Arc. See πανάγορσις
τρίς = τρεῖς. 114.3

τρίτρα, τά Cret. 'the threefold amount.' 165.3
ττολίαρχοι Thess. (Phalanna), for πτολίαρχοι. 67, 86.2. City officials. Cf. the πολιτάρχαι of Thessalonica (Acts 17.6) and other Macedonian towns (Ditt. Syll. 318)
Τροφώνιος Boeot. = Τρεφώνιος. 46.1
τύ Dor. = σύ, σέ. 61.5, 118.2,5
τύ, τῦς Boeot. = τοί, τοῖς. 30
τυί Boeot. = τοίδε. 122
τυῖδε Lesb. 132.4
τύμος Corcyr. = τύμβος
τυρεία Heracl. 'cheese-press'
τωινί, τῶινυ Arc. = τῷδε. 123
τωνί Arc. = τοῦδε. 123

ὁ Cypr. = ἐπί. 135.8
ὐϜαίς Cypr. 'forever.' 133.6
Ὑβρέστας Thess. = Ὑβρίστας. 18
ὐγγεμος Cypr. 135.7
ὐδαρέστερον Lesb. 'less pure.' Used with κέρναν of mixing water and wine, and so applied also to the debasement of coinage. No. 25, note
ὐδρία Locr. = ὑδρία. 58d
υἱ Cret.; υἱς Rhod. = οἱ. 132.4
Ϝυκία Boeot. = οἰκία. 30
ὑκτας Boeot., meaning? No. 39
hυλορέοντος Thess., from ὑλωρέω 'be ὑλωρός,' the official in charge of the public forests (cf. Arist. Pol. 6.8.6). 157b, 167
ὑμέν late Cret. = ὑμεῖς. 119.2a
ὑμές, ὑμέ = ὑμεῖς, ὑμέας. 119.2, 5
ὔμμες, etc. Lesb. = ὑμεῖς etc. 119
ὕμοιος, Arc., Lesb. = ὅμοιος. 22b
ὑνέθεκε Cypr. = ἀνέθηκε. 22
ὑνέθυσε Arc. = ἀνέθηκε. 22, no. 15, note
ὑνιερόσει Arc. 152.4
ὑός, ὑύς = υἱός, υἱύς. 31
ὑπ Thess. = ὑπό. 95
ὑπά or ὑπα = ὑπό. 135.3
ὑπαπροσθίδιος Locr. 'a previous citizen,' in contrast to a colonist. 135.3, 165.2
ὕπαρ Pamph. = ὕπερ. 12
ὑπεραμερία (also οὐ-, ὀ-) Boeot. 'note of default'
ὑποδεδρόμακε Lesb. 146.1
ὑπό El., Lac. = ἐπί with gen. in expressions of dating. 136.11
ὑποδιασύρω Epid. = διασύρω 'ridicule'

ὑππρὸ τᾶς Thess. 'just previously.' 136.1, 10. No. 32.43, note
hυπύ Cumae = ὑπό. 22d
ὕς Arg. = οἶ. 132.4
ὕσταριν El. = ὕστερον 12, 133.6
ὑστερομειννία Thess., οὑστερομεινία Boeot. = Att. ἔνη καὶ νέα 'the last day of the month.' Formed as a pendant to νεομηνία
ὕσωπος Ceos = ὕσσωπος. Semitic loan-word, hence variation in spelling
ὑχερὸν Cypr. = ἐπιχείρου. 135.8
ὕφαμμα = ὕφασμα. 86.8, 164.4

φάλυρον Arg. = λάφυρον. 88
Φανατεύς, Φανοτεύς Delph. 46.1
φάος. 41.2
φαρθένος Arc. = παρθένος. 65
φάρξις Epid. = φράξις. 49.2a
φάρχμα Epid. = φράγμα. 49.2a, 66
φάρω Locr., El., Delph. = φέρω. 12
φατρία, φάτρα = φρατρία. 70.3
φαωτός Delph. 'light-gray.' 31, no. 52 C 24, note
φερνά Epid. = φερνή, but meaning 'portion' (for the god)
φερόσθō Epid. 140.3b
Φετταλός Boeot. = Θεσσαλός. 68.2
φεῶν Dodona = θεῶν. 68.5
φήρ Lesb. = θήρ. 68.2
φθέραι Arc. = φθεῖραι 80, 89.7
φθέρρω Lesb. = φθείρω. 74
φθήρω Arc. = φθείρω. 25, 74
φίντατος Dor. = φίλτατος. 72
Φίντων, Φιντίας = Φίλτων, Φιλτίας. 72
φοινικήια Ion. = γράμματα. Cf. Hdt. 5.58. 164.1
φονές Arc. = φονεύς. 111.4
φράττω Boeot. = φράζω. 84a
φρήταρχος Naples = φρατρίαρχος. 70.3
φρίν Locr. = πρίν. 66
φρονέōι Cypr. = φρονέωσι. 59.4
φροντίδδω, φροντίττω Cret. = φροντίζω. 84
φρυκτός 'bean for drawing lots.' No. 53.15/16, note
φρυνοποπεῖον Boeot. meaning? No. 39
φυγαδείω El. = φυγαδεύω. 161.1. Aor. subj. φυγαδεύαντι, 151.1

φύοντες Dodona = θύοντες. 68.5
φωνέω Cret. (πōνίοι, etc.) 'declare, bear witness.' Cf. ἀποφωνέω (ἀποπōνίοι, etc.) in same sense

χάλκιος Lesb. ≐ χάλκεος. 9.2, 164.6
χάραδος Heracl. = χαράδρα 'ravine' Cf. Hom. χέραδος
χαρίϜετταν Boeot. = χαρίεσσαν. 53, 164.2
χείλιοι, χέλλιοι, χήλιοι 76, 117.3, Att. χίλιοι 25e
ΧελιδϜōν Aetol. 54f
χέλυος 'breast, chest' Coan. no. 108.50, note
χερρ- Lesb. = χειρ-. 76
χηρ- = χειρ-. 25, 76
χραι(δ)δω El. = χρήζω. 84
χραύζομαι Cypr. = following
χραύομαι Cypr. 'border on.' 191
χρῆα Arc. = χρέα. 43
χρηέομαι, forms of. 162.13
Χρήμενος, χρείμενος. 158
χρηίζω, χρῆζω 'wish.' 162.14
χρύσιος Lesb. = χρύσεος. 9.2. 164.6

ψάφιγμα, ψάφιμμα Cret. = ψήφισμα. 86.9, 142a
ψαφίδδω Boeot., Cret. = ψηφίζω. 84
ψάφιξις Aetol., ψάφιξξις Locr. = ψήφισις 'act of voting.' Locr. ἐν ὑδρίαν τὰν ψάφιξξιν εἶμεν (no. 57.45) ≐ Att. ψηφίζεσθαι ἐς ὑδρίαν. 89.1, 142a
ψήφιζμα = ψήφισμα. 60.4

ὦ Dor. etc. ≐ ὅθεν 132.8
ὠβά Lac., a division of the people. Cf. ὤας· τὰς κώμας and ὠγή· κώμη Hesych. (β and γ = Ϝ. 51 with a)
ὦν = οὖν. 25f
ὠνέω Cret. 162.15
ὠραῖα Coan 'festivals celebrated at a fixed date.' Cf. Hesych. ὠραῖα ... τάσσεται ... ἐπὶ τῶν καθ' ὥραν συντελουμένων ἱερῶν.—ὠραία ἡμέρα. ἡ ἑορτή
ὧρος Cret., Arg. = ὅρος. 54
ὅτι Cret. = οὕτινος. 129.3

CHARTS

Chart I exhibits, in a form which may be easily surveyed, the distribution of many important peculiarities common to several dialects.

The presence of a given peculiarity is indicated by a cross opposite the name of the dialect and beneath a caption which, is sufficient to identify the phenomenon, though not always to define it, and should always be interpreted in the light of the section of the Grammar to which reference is made. The cross is sometimes surrounded by a circle as an intimation of some reservation, the nature of which will be understood from the section referred to.

Chart II is condensation, showing the most striking isoglosses.

CHART 1

	8	41.4	119.2, 5	102	138.5	134.1	134.2	154.1	10	22	135.6	68.3	134.3	123	136.1	74-79	114.1	19	143	155.1	18	68.2	147.3	168	162.3	107.3	6	6	22	157	5	135.5	135.3
	η from ᾱ	λεώς	ἡμεῖς	ἔθηκεν	ἔθεσαν	εἰ	ἄν	Infin. in -ναι	ἰν = ἐν	gen. sg. -ᾱο	πός = πρός	σίς = τις	κάς = καί	ὄνυ = ὅδε	dat. w ἀπό, etc.	ἐμμί, στάλλα, etc.	ἴα = μία	antevoc. ι > ι	καλέσσαι	φερέμεν	ρε = ρι	πέμπε	perf. pple in -ων	patr. adj. = gen. sg.	ἀγρέω, ἀντρέω = αἱρέω	πόδεσσι	δέκοτος	ὀν (ὠν) = ἀνά	ἀπό = ἀπύ	φίλημι	op. ρο = αρ, ρα	πεδά	ὑπά, ὑπά = ὑπό
Attic	+	+	+	+	+	+	+	+																									
E.C.W. Ionic E.C.W.	+	+	+	+	+	+	+	+																									
Arcadian								+	+	+	+	+	+	⊙	⊙	+	+											+	+	+	+	+	+
Cyprian								+	+	+	+	+	+	+	+	+	+											+	+	+	+		
Lesbian																+	+	+	+		+	+	+	+	+	+	+	+	+	+	+	+	+
Thessalian																+	+	+		+	+	+	+	+	+			+	+	+	+		
Boeotian																+		+	⊙	+	+	+		+							+	+	+
Phocian																								+									
Locrian																								⊙									+
Elean																							+	⊙						⊙			+
Laconian																																	
Heraclean																																	
Megarian																																	⊙
Corinthian																								⊙									
Argolic																								⊙								⊙	+
Rhodian																																⊙	
Coan																											⊙					⊙	
Theran Cyrenaean																											⊙					⊙	+
Cretan									⊙																							⊙	+

Entry	Ref.
δίδωτι	61.1
(F)ίκατι	116
τριακάτιοι, -κάσιοι	61.2, 117.2
ξ in aor., etc.	142
τοί	122
ἱαρός	13.1
Ἄρταμις	13.2
κα, τόκα	13.3, 132.11
πρᾶτος	114.1
ὅπει	132.2
I pl. -μες	223a
fut. -σέω	141
τέτορες	114.4
τετρώκοντα	116
αἴ τίς κα	179
τῆνος	125
αὐτοσαυτός	121.4
fut. pass. w. act. end.	145
adv. in -ν = -ς	133.6
Ἀπέλλων	49.3
λέω, λείω = θέλω	162.11
masc. -ᾶ, gen. -ᾶς	105.1a, 2c
ἐν = εἰς	135.4
καλείμενος	158
φάρω	12
πάντοις	107.3
στ = σθ	85.1
dat. sg. -οι	106.2
acc. pl. -ες	107.4
Ἱπποκλέας	166.1
Φιλωνδας, -όνδας	164.8
ει = η	16
φέροντι	139.2
γίνυμαι	162.4
ἔλεξε = εἶπε	Glossary

CHART 11

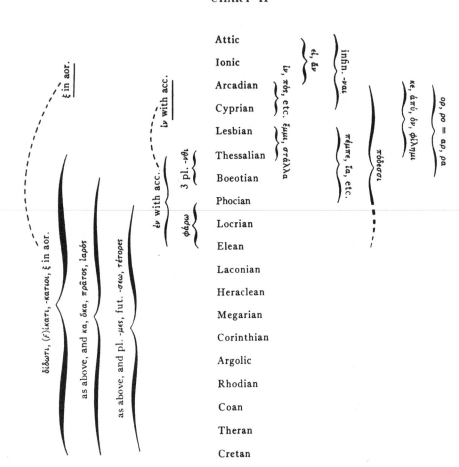

Attic

Ionic

Arcadian

Cyprian

Lesbian

Thessalian

Boeotian

Phocian

Locrian

Elean

Laconian

Heraclean

Megarian

Corinthian

Argolic

Rhodian

Coan

Theran

Cretan

Made in the USA
Monee, IL
07 November 2021

81562215R20216